AF677504

Law and Philosophy Library

Volume 114

Series editors
Francisco J. Laporta
Department of Law, Autonomous University of Madrid, Madrid, Spain

Frederick Schauer
School of Law, University of Virginia, Charlottesville, Virginia, U.S.A.

Torben Spaak
Department of Law, Stockholm University, Stockholm, Sweden

The Law and Philosophy Library, which has been in existence since 1985, aims to publish cutting edge works in the philosophy of law, and has a special history of publishing books that focus on legal reasoning and argumentation, including those that may involve somewhat formal methodologies. The series has published numerous important books on law and logic, law and artificial intelligence, law and language, and law and rhetoric. While continuing to stress these areas, the series has more recently expanded to include books on the intersection between law and the Continental philosophical tradition, consistent with the traditional openness of the series to books in the Continental jurisprudential tradition. The series is proud of the geographic diversity of its authors, and many have come from Latin America, Spain, Italy, the Netherlands, Germany, and Eastern Europe, as well, more obviously for an English-language series, from the United Kingdom, the United States, Australia, and Canada.

More information about this series at http://www.springer.com/series/6210

Humberto Ávila

Certainty in Law

Springer

Humberto Ávila
Department of Economic, Budgetary
and Tax Law
University of São Paulo – USP
São Paulo, São Paulo, Brazil

Translated by Jorge Todeschini
Revised by Kevin Mundy

ISSN 1572-4395 ISSN 2215-0315 (electronic)
Law and Philosophy Library
ISBN 978-3-319-33406-6 ISBN 978-3-319-33407-3 (eBook)
DOI 10.1007/978-3-319-33407-3

Library of Congress Control Number: 2016943191

© Springer International Publishing Switzerland 2016
This work is subject to copyright. All rights are reserved by the Publisher, whether the whole or part of the material is concerned, specifically the rights of translation, reprinting, reuse of illustrations, recitation, broadcasting, reproduction on microfilms or in any other physical way, and transmission or information storage and retrieval, electronic adaptation, computer software, or by similar or dissimilar methodology now known or hereafter developed.
The use of general descriptive names, registered names, trademarks, service marks, etc. in this publication does not imply, even in the absence of a specific statement, that such names are exempt from the relevant protective laws and regulations and therefore free for general use.
The publisher, the authors and the editors are safe to assume that the advice and information in this book are believed to be true and accurate at the date of publication. Neither the publisher nor the authors or the editors give a warranty, express or implied, with respect to the material contained herein or for any errors or omissions that may have been made.

Printed on acid-free paper

This Springer imprint is published by Springer Nature
The registered company is Springer International Publishing AG Switzerland

Preface

The literature on certainty in law occupies an entire library. A particularly important place is reserved for Humberto Ávila's book in this vast imaginary library.

While presenting itself as a work of jurisprudence on the Brazilian Constitution (and specifically on Brazilian tax law, a field in which the author is an acknowledged expert), this book undoubtedly has a far broader theoretical scope. Moreover, it is probably the most comprehensive and systematic study ever produced on this subject using the analytical method.

Professor Ávila deconstructs certainty in law, reducing it to its constituent elements and showing all its multiple dimensions, both conceptual and institutional.

1. The concept of legal certainty. In the prevailing legal doctrine and theoretical tradition, which dates from the Enlightenment and is rooted in legal positivism, law is certain if and only if everyone can accurately foresee the legal consequences of their own actions and know ex ante the limits of the state's coercive powers and how they are exercised. Ávila elaborates a far more articulate concept of legal certainty in a moderately "realist" theoretical context as far as interpretation is concerned.

   In his view, law can be considered "certain" provided it is (a) knowable and intelligible, (b) reliable, and (c) calculable.

   (a) Knowability in law involves two different problems: the knowability of normative texts and the knowability of their meaning. Normative texts are knowable, evidently, when they are published and accessible. Norms are knowable, in turn, not only when normative texts are intelligible because they are clearly written but also when their interpretation is guided by known and intersubjectively controlled methods of interpretation and strategies of argumentation. In these conditions, the law may be (relatively) knowable, despite its inevitable indeterminacy, about which more in a moment.
   (b) Reliability in law means norms do not have retroactive effects and respect res iudicata, acquired rights, and completed legal acts. However, law cannot be reliable unless it is also relatively stable. This means it must not change very frequently or suddenly, and any changes should always be accompanied by

intertemporal norms (which must also avoid affecting completed legal acts and acquired rights).

(c) Law is not a given, i.e., an object whose existence precedes its interpretation and application. Normative texts do not have a single unambiguous meaning. They often have gaps and express contradictory norms. In this sense, law is indeterminate. The indeterminacy of law means we cannot precisely predict the legal consequences of our actions. Nevertheless, the number of possible (and plausible) meanings of normative texts is finite, and their meanings are identifiable in light of the methods of interpretation and styles of argumentation in use. Law is calculable when it is knowable, intelligible, and reliable, and when citizens not only know the interpretation and argumentation practices in use but also have a significant capacity to anticipate the alternative interpretations available, so that they can predict, at least approximately, the possible decisions of the bodies that enforce the law, and especially of judges. Thus, rational control of interpretive arbitrariness is a key component of legal certainty.

Knowability, reliability, and calculability are evidently closely interrelated.

On the other hand, it is easy to infer that all the concepts involved are quantitative rather than classificatory. In sum, according to the theory propounded by Ávila, certainty is not a concept with two values but a matter of degree. "Absolute" certainty is unattainable.

2. The foundations of certainty. Many constitutions solemnly proclaim the value of "security" and "certainty," understood as the absence of (or protection against) threats to life, health, liberty, and property. The legal certainty principle, however, is rarely expressed in a constitution. The Spanish Constitution is an exception (as is the Brazilian, according to Ávila).

The principle in question, however, appears frequently in the arguments heard by constitutional courts, as a criterion for evaluating the "reasonableness" of laws. A good example of this is a decision by Italy's Constitutional Court which does not refer explicitly to legal certainty but rules partially unconstitutional the principle known as ignorantia juris non excusat (or nemo censetur ignorare jus) because it makes no provision for the impossibility of knowing and/or understanding the law (in this case criminal law) as a justification for ignorance.

Even when the legal certainty principle is not explicitly formulated, it can be "constructed" – obtained via argumentation – from a long list of constitutional provisions common to most liberal democratic legal orders. By this, I mean the kind of order typically referred to as the rule-of-law state, which is characterized by a combination of two symmetrical principles:

(i) The freedom principle – "citizens are (tacitly) allowed to do whatever is not (explicitly) prohibited" – which functions as the framing norm for the set of norms that discipline the conduct of private citizens.

(ii) The legality principle – "government is (tacitly) allowed to do whatever is not (explicitly) prohibited" – which functions as the framing norm for the set of norms that discipline the acts of state bodies.

Ávila shows that even when the legal certainty principle is not explicitly formulated in the Constitution, it is instrumental to the realization of the other principles that are expressed and has an evident connection with them, so that it is "implied" by them. Moreover, it is not uncommon to find in the constitutional jurisprudence of several countries the construction of an unexpressed principle based on the argument that it is a necessary condition for the efficacy of one or another explicit constitutional principle.

The explicitly expressed principles from which the unexpressed certainty principle can be inferred are mainly the principles of liberty, equality, and dignity. The latter is in fact an extremely elastic and obscure concept. Very sensibly, Ávila redefines it as the capacity to plan one's own future, so that the protection of dignity requires respect for individual autonomy, and legal certainty is necessary in this case as well.

On the other hand, even when the certainty principle is not expressly formulated, it provides an axiological justification for and is concretized in a long list of explicit principles and rules, some of which are constitutional while others are merely legislative. They include (it would be difficult to enumerate them all):

(a) The rules on publication of normative acts and vacatio legis
(b) The legality of jurisdiction principle (subjecting judges to the law and requiring that all judicial decisions be motivated)
(c) The legality of administration principle (and the related principle of the typicality of administrative acts)
(d) The strict legality and strict interpretation principle (prohibition of analogies) in criminal cases
(e) The tax legality principle
(f) The irretroactivity principle (although in some constitutions, this is circumscribed to criminal law)
(g) The inviolability of res iudicata, completed legal acts, and acquired rights
(h) The rigidity of the Constitution in its entirety, which contributes to legal certainty at the highest level of the source hierarchy

The legal certainty principle, therefore, is instrumental to the realization of higher principles that justify it. At the same time, it is the source and axiological foundation for the subordinate principles that concretize it.

3. The obstacles to certainty. Notwithstanding the above, the legal certainty principle is evidently overlooked or very imperfectly realized in all contemporary state orders. The many phenomena that yield legal uncertainty emerge clearly from Ávila's study.

   Leaving aside the direct causes of interpretive discretion (equivocal normative texts, vague norms, norms with an "open texture," general clauses, lacunae, antinomies, etc.), I enumerate below, in no particular order, some of the macroscopic obstacles to certainty.

(A) A first class of obstacles derives from the system of sources, or more precisely from the plurality of heterogeneous sources (central and local laws, government acts with legal force, etc.), not always clearly organized in hierarchical order. This is particularly true, of course, in the European Union, where EU norms interfere with national sources of law in member states.

(B) A second class of obstacles arises from the disorder of normative texts. For example:

(1) The insatiable appetite of the normative authorities, leading to an unending flux of normative provisions that are all in force at the same time
(2) Dispersion of valid provisions in a multiplicity of a normative documents (i.e., insufficient codification)
(3) The diachronic instability of normative texts, due to the fact that new provisions are introduced into the legal order every day while others are repealed, suppressed, or replaced

(C) A third class of obstacles derives from the (poor) drafting of normative texts. For example:

(i) The inclusion, in a normative text on any subject (x), of provisions that pertain to a completely different subject (y) totally unrelated to x, making the law in force on y very hard to identify.
(ii) The many normative texts that do not replace but partially modify a text previously in force, amending not an entire law but only one or two provisions, for example, so that the discipline on the matter in question is dispersed across several different legislative texts; or worse still, changing or striking out only a few words in an existing provision rather than the entire provision, so that to identify the provision in force it is necessary to join up one or more fragments of language dispersed in different normative texts.
(iii) Normative text A modifies normative text B, which previously modified normative text C, making knowability of the laws in force almost impossible.
(iv) Provisions that refer to other, preexisting, provisions without an autonomous meaning of their own, so that they cannot be understood except in combination with different provisions that are part of a completely different normative text; and on the other hand, provisions that refer to future provisions (i.e., provisions that do not exist) and hence lack normative content (unless they are accompanied by intertemporal norms).
(v) Total or partial repeal that fails to produce unambiguous effects unless it is explicit and refers to the repealed normative provisions with precision (by first and last name, as it were). On the other hand, when a normative authority dictates a new discipline for any given factual support without

expressly repealing the existing provisions (merely tacit revocation), the result is invariably doubtful and potentially controversial.

(D) Finally, a fourth class of obstacles derives from case law and judicial practice. Here I refer to such phenomena as:

α Nonuniform and unreasoned interpretation.
β Case-law revisions and departures from precedent (*revirements*), especially by last-instance jurisdictions.
γ The so-called "evolutionary" (or "dynamic") interpretation, which gives normative texts a different meaning than the commonly accepted one.
δ Application by analogy – while judges may redress lacunae (real or imaginary), as indeed they are required to do where non liquet is prohibited, arguments from analogy nevertheless produce decisions that are unpredictable ex ante because they are grounded in norms never hitherto expressed.

In his preface to a previous edition of this book, Jordi Ferrer asks a pertinent question: "Is there a golden thread running through such classic themes of legal theory as the justification of judicial decisions, the one-right-answer thesis, the defeasibility of norms, the dispute between cognitivism and interpretive skepticism, or the economic analysis of law?" And he answers in the affirmative: "Among other things, it is the central role performed in these debates by legal certainty." This is true.

Humberto Ávila's book shows that legal certainty is a kind of Aleph (in the sense used by Borges), which casts a bright light on many key problems of modern legal theory.

Genoa, Italy
November 22, 2013

Dr. Riccardo Guastini

Preface

1. Here is a request for a preface to a book that requires no introduction. The English word "preface" ultimately derives from the Latin *praefatio*, via the verb *praefari*, "to say beforehand," and literally means "fore-speaking." Speaking first or introducing might be taken as a suggestion that the illustrious author still experiences the insecurity of the young academic or, to his credit, will not dispense with an encomiastic foreword from fellow sojourners. Not so. Professor Humberto Ávila himself needs no introduction. His curriculum vitae is long and varied. His seminal works, from the celebrated *Theory of Legal Principles* to this noteworthy investigation of certainty in tax law, have passed the demanding test of critical intersubjectivity ever since their first editions. The enthusiasm with which they have been received is evidenced by the number of further editions and translations from Portuguese into several other languages.

   I hope the reader will therefore bear with me if I say there is little I can add to what has already been said about this book, and said far better. Let me simply highlight a few points, starting with its importance in today's public law environment. First, the title, even with the subtitle "Permanence, change and realization in tax law," does not do justice to the extraordinary richness of the content. This is a new treatise on the "theory of principles," a secure and informative introduction to the structuring principle of juridicity, a profound vision of the foundations of legal certainty and their reflection in the "constitutional superstructure," and, naturally, an irreplaceable investigation into permanence, change, and efficacy in tax law. Moreover, some of the most controversial aspects of method, methodology, and doctrine are discussed here with highly coherent and consistent argumentative rhetoric.
2. I am grateful to Professor Humberto Ávila for giving me this opportunity to point out the special political and legal sensibility of the theses he defends. For any citizen of Portugal, which for some time now has been a "house of horrors" thanks to three "memoranda of understanding" between the Portuguese government and a so-called Troika (the International Monetary Fund, the European Union, and the European Central Bank), Prof. Ávila's book provides an inestimable wealth of knowledge and wisdom. For the "austerity Taliban" anything goes: denying

the subjective right to a pension, decreeing heavy retroactive pay cuts, invoking principles that have nothing to do with tax justice (convergence between public- and private-sector salaries and pensions), or inventing a solidarity contribution and claiming it is not a tax because the revenue stream is earmarked to help pay for pensions.

But this is not all: we are forced to suffer the worst of both worlds in tax matters. The tax-imposing state massacres workers' incomes. The "fee-based state" (dubbed *Gebührenstaat* in Germany) piles up charges and other levies on top of taxes. If one asks whether this is constitutional, if most of these measures, besides being anti-egalitarian and unfair, do not annihilate completed legal acts, acquired rights and res iudicata, the reply fluctuates between the "duty of obedience to creditors" and the existence of a "state of financial exception." In other words, for the "austeritarians" the subjective and objective inviolability of individual situations have become no more than a figure of speech typical of the ideologues of the "prohibition of regression" and acquired rights. The underlying theological meaning of Prof. Àvila's exposition may well be this: Tell me what tax law you have and I will tell you whether there is law, justice, equity, or legal certainty in your juridical-constitutional system.

Coimbra, Portugal
February 25, 2014

Dr. José Joaquim Gomes Canotilho

Contents

Abbreviations

AC	Ação cautelar (injunctive suit)
ADCT	Ato das Disposições Constitucionais Transitórias (Constitutional Transitory Provisions Act)
ADI	Ação Direta de Inconstitucionalidade (direct unconstitutionality suit)
AG. REG	Agravo regimental (internal interlocutory appeal)
AI	Agravo de instrumento (interlocutory appeal)
AJDA	L'actualité juridique. Droit Administratif
AöR	Archives für Öffentliches Recht
AR	Agravo regimental (interlocutory appeal)
ARSP	Archiv für Rechts und Sozialphilosophie
BayVBl.	Bayerische Verwaltunsblätter
BB	Betriebs-Berater
BVerfG	Bundesverfassungsgericht
BVerfGE	Bundesverfassungsgerichtsentscheidung
CF/88	Constituição da República Federativa do Brasil de 1988 (Brazilian Constitution of 1988)
D	Recueil Dalloz Sirey
DB	Der Betrieb
DÖV	Die Öffentliche Verwaltung
DStJG	Veröffentlichungen der Deutschen Steuerjuristischen Gesellschaft
DStR	Deutsches Steuerrecht
DStZ	Deutsche Steuer Zeitung
DVBl.	Deutsches Verwaltungsblatt
ED	Embargo de declaração (motion for clarification)
FESDT	Fundação Escola Superior de Direito Tributário
FR	Finanz-Rundschau
FS	Festschrift
INF	Die Information über Steuer und Wirtschaft
IWB	Internationale Wirtschafts-Briefe
JA	Juristische Arbeitsblätter
JuS	Juristische Schulung

JöR	Jahrbuch des öffentliches Recht der Gegenwart
JZ	Juristen Zeitung
KÖSDI	Kölner Steuerdialog
MC	Medida cautelar (provisional remedy)
MS	Mandado de segurança (injunction, mandamus)
NJW	Neue Juristische Wochenschrift
NVwZ	Neue Zeitschrift für Verwaltungsrecht
ÖStZ	Österreichische Steuerzeitung
Orgs.	Organizadores (editors, eds.)
PGE	Procuradoria-Geral do Estado (State Attorney General)
QO	Questão de ordem (point of order)
RBDP	Revista Brasileira de Direito Público
RDA	Revista de Direito Administrativo
RDE	Revista de Direito do Estado
RDDT	Revista Dialética de Direito Tributário
RDP	Revue de Droit Public et de la Science Économique
RDT	Revista de Direito Tributário
RE	Recurso extraordinário (extraordinary appeal)
RePRO	Revista de Processo
RFDA	Revue Française de Droit Administratif
RT	Revista dos Tribunais (editora)
RTDP	Revista Trimestral de Direito Público
SJZ	Schweizerische Juristen-Zeitung
Stbg	Die Steuerberatung
StbJb	Steuerberater-Jahrbuch
SteuerStud	Steuer und Studium
StuR	Staat und Recht
StuW	Steuer und Wirtschaft
StVj	Steuerliche Vierteljahresschrift
ThürVBl.	Thüringisches Verwaltungsblatt
VRÜ	Verfassung und Recht in Übersee
vs.	versus
VVDStRL	Veröffentlichungen der Vereinigung der Deutschen Staatsrechtslehrer
WiVerw	Wirtschaft und Verwaltung
WM	Wertpapier Mitteilungen
ZaöRV	Zeitschrift für Ausländisches öffentliches Recht und Völkerrecht
ZG	Zeitschrift für Gesetzgebung
ZLR	Zeitschrift für das gesamte Lebensmittelrecht

Introduction

Certainty is, first and foremost, a radical human anthropological need, and "knowing what to hang on to" is a basic element of individual and social aspirations to certainty, the common root of its distinct manifestations in life, and the foundation of its raison d'être as a legal value. (Antonio Enrique Perez Luño, *La seguridad jurídica*, Barcelona, Ariel, 1991, p. 8)

Certainty thus becomes an issue when uncertainty and insecurity spread. And the more uncertain the circumstances in modern times, the more demanding men's expectations of certainty and security become. (Andrea Schrimm-Heins, "Gewissheit und Sicherheit: Geschichte und Bedeutungswandel der Begriffe 'certitudo' und 'securitas'" (*Teil* 2), in *Archiv für Begriffsgeschichte* 35, 204, 1992, Bonn, Bouvier)

Here is something my teachers never told me but life has taken upon itself to clarify: To enable anyone to know what he may want is a benefit that cannot be enjoyed unless the laws are few in number, but on the contrary they are many, a great many, and they follow one another in rapid succession, vertiginously, and in this multitude of laws men lose their way as in a labyrinth. (Francesco Carnellutti, "La certezza del Diritto", *Rivista de Diritto Civile*, n. 20, 1942, p. 81)

If all legal orders have two traditional elements, certainty and progress, the current concept of law deliberately sacrifices the former to the latter, thus prioritizing the political aspect of lawmaking, whereas the old concept was grounded in a more specifically juridical and conservative role of law. (Georges Burdeau, "Essai sur l'évolution de la notion de loi en Droit français", in *Archives de Philosophie du Droit*, 1939, p. 48)

1 Justification (or Why Legal (Un)certainty?)

1.1 Certainty as a Normative Principle

This book sets out to reconstruct legal certainty, in general and in the field of tax law, as a principle norm grounded in Brazil's Constitution, by means of a method capable of progressively reducing its indeterminacy while making it as functional as possible. Reasons abound for doing so.

© Springer International Publishing Switzerland 2016

H. Ávila, *Certainty in Law*, Law and Philosophy Library 114,
DOI 10.1007/978-3-319-33407-3_1

The primary justification is supplied by the constitutional order itself, which attributes foundational importance to legal certainty. Indeed, the Preamble refers to it. On one hand, the Preamble "institutes a Democratic State to assure [*assegurar*, i.e. make secure or certain]" both social and individual rights and values, including the value "security" or "certainty" itself (*segurança*).[1] On the other hand, the Preamble states that "liberty, [...] well-being, development, equality and justice" are this society's "supreme values" – and the list of those values includes *segurança*, which means both security and certainty. It also states that this society, besides being fraternal, pluralistic and free of prejudices, is to be founded on "social harmony" and committed, in the domestic and international "order", to the "peaceful" settlement of disputes. Considering that the expression "legal certainty" is associated with the ideals of determinacy, stability and predictability of law, among others, as we will see throughout this book, the Constitution clearly demonstrates a grave concern with legal certainty from the outset, as evidenced by terms such as "security" or "certainty," "assure," "harmony" and "order."

The Constitution proper also refers directly and indirectly to "certainty." Title I, "Fundamental Principles", states that Brazil is a democratic law-based state (art. 1), which is associated in legal doctrine with the idea of legal certainty, as I will demonstrate. Title II, "Fundamental Rights and Guarantees", not only includes the fundamental right to "security" or "certainty" (*segurança*, art. 5, head paragraph) but also establishes a number of "guarantees" or legally binding human rights instruments. In several normative areas it institutes numerous "guarantees" and "limitations" to the exercise of power, traditionally understood as partial elements of legal certainty, such as the legality principle (art. 5, II, and art. 150, I), the irretroactivity principle (art. 150, III, "a") and the anteriority principle (art. 150, III, "b").

This initial overview based only on constitutional provisions is enough to show that legal certainty – regardless of the far from trifling disputes about its meaning, foundations, elements, dimensions and efficacy, all of which this book will address in due time – is prioritized by the Constitution from a normative standpoint. In tax law the ideal of legal certainty is even more prominent in terms of legality, irretroactivity and anteriority, and as a consequence of the numerous competence rules. This is why Machado Derzi says "certainty is at maximum strength" in tax law.[2]

The Constitution also highlights other fundamental ideals, such as equality and solidarity, which could equally be the subject of a book like this one. With so many important topics to choose from, why focus on legal certainty? The first justification is the current state of uncertainty and insecurity. "Certainty is a value,

[1] José Souto Maior Borges, "O princípio da segurança jurídica na criação e aplicação do tributo", *RDDT*, n. 22, p. 25, São Paulo, 1997. Geraldo Ataliba, *República e Constituição*, 3rd ed., São Paulo, Malheiros Editores, 2011, p. 182.

[2] Misabel de Abreu Machado Derzi, *Modificações da jurisprudência no Direito Tributário*, São Paulo, Noeses, 2009, p. 159.

and it is therefore bipolar and relational, so that it logically implies its countervalue uncertainty, to which it is opposed," Maior Borges avers.[3] Thus the starting point for the analysis of certainty must be uncertainty.[4]

1.2 Certainty as an Old Goal

Of course, legal uncertainty is by no means a new topic. Nor is there anything novel about the concrete attempt to combat it and the goal of studying it scientifically. True, the study of legal certainty varies according to time and context.[5] Nevertheless, in the ancient and modern world alike many studies contain elements directly or indirectly linked to legal certainty or to one of its partial elements. The debate in Roman law about *ius certum*, or about *Pax Romana* and the implied concepts of *pax, securitas* and *libertas*, cannot be simply transplanted to the present day owing to the casuistic character of Roman law and the lack of state institutions that would not be consolidated until much later, yet it contains a distant embryo of the study of certainty in law;[6] in the sixteenth century the discussion of *certitudo iurisprudentiae* was an attempt to bring rationality into legal knowledge;[7] in the eighteenth and early nineteenth centuries, the codification debate was in part an endeavor to develop clear and determinate laws;[8] in the nineteenth and twentieth centuries, research into the protection of freedom and property by von Savigny (1814[9] and 1840[10]), Meyer (1851[11]), von Mohl (1855[12]) and Holleuffer (1864[13]) not

[3]José Souto Maior Borges, "Segurança jurídica: sobre a distinção entre competências fiscais para orientar e atuar o contribuinte", *RDT*, n. 100, pp. 19–26, São Paulo, s.d.

[4]Antonio Enrique Perez Luño, *La seguridad jurídica*, Barcelona, Ariel, 1991, p. 13.

[5]Herbert Wiedemann, "Rechtssicherheit – ein absoluter Wert? Gedanken zum Bestimmtheitserfordernis zivilrechtlicher Tatbestände", in Gotthard Paulus *et alii* (Orgs.), *FS für Karl Larenz*, München, Beck, 1973, p. 202.

[6]Winfried Brügger, "Gewährleistung von Freiheit und Sicherheit im Lichte unterschiedlicher Staats- und Verfassungsverständnisse", *VDStRL*, v. 63, p. 103, Berlin, 2004.

[7]Andreas Arnauld, *Rechtssicherheit*, Tübingen, Mohr Siebeck, 2006, p. 9. Italo Birochi, *Alla Ricerca dell'Ordine. Fonti e cultura giuridica nell'età moderna*, Torino, Giappichelli, 2002, pages. 159 and following.

[8]Bernd Mertens, *Gesetzgebungskunst im Zeitalter der Kodifikationen*, Tübingen, Mohr Siebeck, 2004, p. 354. Rémy Cabrillac, *Les codifications*, Paris, PUF, 2002, p. 137.

[9]Friedrich Carl von Savigny, *Vom Beruf unserer Zeit für Gesetzgebung und Rechtswissenschaft*, Heidelberg, Mohr und Zimmer, 1814, pp. 20, 161 (reprinted: Goldbach, Keip, 1997).

[10]Idem, *System des heutigen Römischen Rechts*, 2nd ed., v. 1, Berlin, Veit und Comp., 1840, p. 322 (reprinted: Aalen, Scientia, 1981).

[11]J. Meyer, *Conversations-Lexicon*, Zweite Abteilung, v. 8, entry on "Sicherheit".

[12]Robert von Mohl, "Die Geschichte und Literatur der Staatswissenschaften", in *Monographien dargestellt*, v. 1, Erlangen, 1855.

[13]Carl Eschwin Albert von Holleuffer, *Rechtssicherheit, unabhängige Justiz, ministerielle Cabinets-Justiz im Fürstenthum Schwarzburg-Sonderhausen*, Dessau, 1864, p. 101.

only assumed a degree of insecurity that existed at the time, but also set out to assure the security and certainty thus threatened through law and its uniform application; in the first half of the twentieth century, studies directly related to legal certainty reflect the environment of instability then prevailing and progressive construction of the elements of certainty in law, as exemplified by the exploratory work of Bendix (1914[14]), Rümelin (1924[15]), Germann (1935[16]) and Scholz (1955[17]), among many others.

Besides these older works, more recent studies have focused on legal certainty in general and more specifically on tax law certainty, or some of its aspects. The discussion is wide-ranging and includes representative works published in German,[18] French,[19] Italian,[20] Spanish,[21]

[14]Ludwig Bendix, "Das Problem der Rechtssicherheit", in Manfred Weiss (Org.), *Zur Psychologie der Urteilsfähigkeit des Berufsrichters und andere Schriften*, Neuwied und Berlin, 1968, p. 12.

[15]Max Rümelin, *Die Rechtssicherheit*, Tübingen, Mohr Siebeck, 1924.

[16]Oscar Adolf Germann, "Rechtssicherheit" (1935), *Methodische Grundfragen*, 6. Aufsätze, Basel, 1946, p. 59.

[17]Franz Scholz, *Die Rechtssicherheit*, Berlin, Walter de Gruyter, 1955.

[18]In German the most representative classics are: Max Rümelin, cherheit" (1935), *Methodische Grundfragen*, 6. Aufsätze, Basel, 1946; Franz Scholz, *Die Rechtssicherheit*, Berlin, Walter de Gruyter, 1955. More recently, on legal certainty, see: Andreas von Arnauld, *Rechtssicherheit*, Tübingen, Mohr Siebeck, 2006. On tax law certainty, see: Johanna Hey, *Steuerplanungssicherheit als Rechtsproblem*, Köln, Otto Schmidt, 2002; Anna Leisner, *Kontinuität als Verfassungsprinzip*, Tübingen, Mohr Siebeck, 2002; Heinz-Jürgen Pezzer (Org.), *Vertrauensschutz im Steuerrecht, Deutsche Steuerjuristische Gesellschaft*, t. 27, Köln, Otto Schmidt, 2004.

[19]In French the most representative classics are: Paul Roubier, *Théorie Générale du Droit*, 2nd ed. Paris, Sirey, 1951. Idem, *Le Droit transitoire: conflits des lois dans le temps*, Paris, Dalloz, 1929/1933 (1st ed., 2nd v.), 1960 (2nd ed., 1st v.), 2008 (2nd ed. reprinted). More recently, on legal certainty, see: Bernard Pacteau, "La sécurité juridique, un principe que nous manque?", *AJDA*, n. 20, p. 151, 1995; François Luchaire, "La sûreté, droit de l'homme ou sabre de M. Prudhomme?" *RDP*, p. 609, 1989; Louis Favoreu, "Une convention collective peut-elle comporter des dispositions à caractère rétroatif?", *D.* 1995–1, C. 82; Michel Fromont, "Le principe de sécurité juridique", *AJDA*, p. 178, 1996; Frank Moderne, "Actualité des principes généraux du droit", *RFDA*, p. 506, 1998; Anne-Laure Valembois, *La Constitutionnalisation de l'exigence de sécurité juridique en Droit français*, Paris, LGDJ, 2005. On tax law certainty, see: Frédéric Douet, *Contribution à l'étude de la sécurité juridique en Droit interne français*, Paris, LGDJ, 1997.

[20]In Italian the most representative classics are: Enrico Allorio, "La certezza del Diritto dell'Economia", *Rivista del Diritto dell'Economia*, pages 1198–1212, 1956; Massimo S. Giannini, "Certezza pubblica", *Enciclopedia del Diritto*, v. 6, Milano, Giuffrè, pages 769–792; Flavio Lopez de Oñate, *La certezza del Diritto*, Milano, Giuffrè, 1968; Massimo Corsale, *Certezza del Diritto e crisi di legittimità*, Milano, Giuffrè, 1979; Letizia Gianformaggio, "Certezza del Diritto", in *Studi sulla giustificazione giuridica*, Torino, Giuppichelli, 1986; Claudio Luzzati, *La vaghezza delle norme*, Milano, Giuffrè, 1990. More recently, on legal certainty, see: Enrico Diciotti, *Verità e certezza nell'interpretazione della legge*, Torino, Giappichelli, 1999; Gianmarco Gometz, *La certezza giuridica come prevedibilità*, Torino, Giappichelli, 2005. On tax law certainty, see: Eugenio Della Vale, *Affidamento e certezza del Diritto Tributario*, Milano, Giuffrè, 2001.

[21]In Spanish the most representative classics are: J. Mezquita de Cacho, *Seguridad jurídica y sistema cautelar:* (v. 1) *Teoría de la Seguridad Jurídica*; (v. 2) *Sistema Español de Derecho Cautelar*, Barcelona, Bosch, 1989; Gregorio Peces-Barba, "La seguridad jurídica desde la Filosofíadel

Portuguese[22] and English.[23] Brazilian legal scholars are no exception, having published studies on legal certainty in general as well as specific ones on tax law certainty.[24]

Derecho", *Anuario de Derechos Humanos*, n. 6, pages 215–229, 1990; Antonio Enrique Pérez Luño, *La seguridad jurídica*, Barcelona, Ariel, 1991. More recently, on legal certainty, see: Eduardo García de Enterría, *Justicia y seguridad jurídica en un mundo de leyes desbocadas*, Madrid, Civitas, 1999; Federico Arcos Ramírez, *La seguridad jurídica: una teoría formal*, Madrid, Dykinson, 2000; José Bermejo Vera, *El declive de la seguridad jurídica en el ordenamiento plural*, Madrid, Civitas, 2005. On tax law certainty, see: César García Novoa, *El principio da seguridad jurídica en materia tributaria*, Madrid, Marcial Pons, 2000.

[22]The fundamental texts by Portuguese scholars include: J. M. Sérvulo Correia, *Legalidade e autonomia contratual nos contratos administrativos*, Coimbra, Almedina, 1987; José Joaquim Gomes Canotilho, *Direito Constitucional e teoria da Constituição*, 7th ed., 6th reprint, Coimbra, Almedina, 2004, p. 257; Jorge Miranda, *Manual de Direito Constitucional*, v. 1, Coimbra, Almedina, 2003; Jorge Reis Novaes, *Os princípios constitucionais estruturantes da República Portuguesa*, Coimbra, Coimbra Editora, 2004, pages 261 and following. More recently, on tax law certainty, see: Ana Paula Dourado, *O princípio da legalidade fiscal – Tipicidade, conceitos jurídicos indeterminados e margem de livre apreciação*, Coimbra, Almedina, 2007.

[23]In Anglo-Saxon literature the most representative classics are: Jerome Frank, *Law and the Modern Mind*, New Brunswick, Transaction, 2009 (1st ed., New York, Brentano's Inc., 1930; 2nd ed. rev., New York, Coward-McCann, 1949); Lon Fuller, *The Morality of Law*, New Haven, Yale University Press, 1964; Joseph Raz, "The Rule of Law and its Virtue" (1977), *The Authority of Law. Essays on Law and Morality*, Oxford, Oxford Press, 1979, p. 221; Jeremy Waldron, "The Rule of Law in Contemporary Liberal Theory", *Ratio Juris*, v. 2, n. 1, pages 79–96, 1989. More recently, on legal certainty, see Juha Raitio, *The Principle of Legal Certainty in EC Law*, Dordrecht, Kluwer, 2003.

[24]In Brazil the most representative classics directly related to the theme are: Theophilo Cavalcanti Filho, *O problema da segurança no Direito*, São Paulo, Ed. RT, 1964; Miguel Reale, *Revogação e anulamento do ato administrativo*, 2nd ed., Rio de Janeiro, Forense, 1980. More recently, on legal certainty, see: Patrícia Ferreira Baptista, *Segurança jurídica e proteção da confiança legítima – Análise sistemática e critérios de aplicação no Direito Administrativo brasileiro*, PhD thesis, USP, 2006, unpublished. On tax law certainty, see: José Souto Maior Borges, "O princípio da segurança jurídica na criação e aplicação do tributo", *RDDT*, n. 22, pp. 24–29, São Paulo, 1997; Paulo de Barros Carvalho, "O princípio da segurança jurídica no campo tributário", *RDT*, n. 94, pp. 21–31, São Paulo; Misabel de Abreu Machado Derzi, "Mutações, complexidade, tipo e conceito, sob o signo da segurança e da proteção da confiança", in Heleno Torres (ed.), *Estudos em homenagem a Paulo de Barros Carvalho*, São Paulo, Saraiva, 2007, pp. 245–284; Tércio Sampaio Ferraz Júnior, "Segurança jurídica e normas gerais tributárias" *RDT*, 17–18, pp. 51–56, São Paulo, 1981; Luis Eduardo Schoueri, "Segurança jurídica e normas tributárias indutoras", in Maria de Fátima Ribeiro (ed.), *Direito Tributário e segurança jurídica*, São Paulo, MP, 2008, pp. 117–146; Ricardo Lobo Torres, "Segurança jurídica e as limitações ao poder de tributar", in Roberto Ferraz (ed.), *Princípios e limites da tributação*, São Paulo, Quartier Latin, 2007, pp. 429–445; idem, "Limitações ao poder impositivo e segurança jurídica", in Ives Gandra da Silva Martins (ed.), *Limitações ao poder impositivo e segurança jurídica*, São Paulo, Ed. RT e CEU, 2007, pages 61–77; idem, "Liberdade, segurança e Justiça", in Paulo de Barros Carvalho (Org.), *Justiça Tributária*, São Paulo, Max Limonad, 1998, pages 679–705; idem, *Tratado de Direito Constitucional, Financeiro e Tributário*, v. 2: *Valores e princípios constitucionais tributários*, Rio de Janeiro, Renovar, 2005, pages 167–180; Ricardo Lodi Ribeiro, *A segurança jurídica do contribuinte*, Rio de Janeiro, Lumen Juris, 2008.

Generally speaking these works take up the old theme of legal certainty again to explore some of its subelements more deeply, especially those relating to the protection of trust and the prohibition of retroactivity, and to examine some more recent subthemes, such as jurisprudential change.

I have nevertheless revisited the subject because I believe a deeper examination is still justified – by the current state of insecurity and uncertainty, on one hand; and by its unsatisfactory analysis in legal theory, on the other.

1.3 Social Causes of Legal Incertainty

Today legal uncertainty has reached unprecedented levels. The situation is evidenced by the widespread use of such terms as "complexity," "obscurity," "insecurity," "indeterminacy," "instability" and "discontinuity" of the legal order. There is even talk of a "flood of laws" (*Gesetzesflut*), "legislative hysteria" (*Gesetzgebungshysterie*) and "legislative chaos" (*Gesetzgebungschaos*).[25] We also hear complaints of a "normative hurricane",[26] "legislative incontinence",[27] an "avalanche of norms"[28] and an "orgy of lawmaking."[29] It has become almost commonplace to note the unstable, ephemeral and random character of the law.[30]

Why all this uncertainty? Solely as an initial *reference* to justify the research presented in this book, we can point to social and legal causes of the uncertainty prevailing today.

The social causes concern the characteristics of our society. We live in a plural society, also known as a risk society, global society or information society.[31] This kind of society is defined, first of all, by the existence of a massive amount of information. Suffice it to recall the quantity of statutes, supplementary laws, decrees, normative instructions, normative opinions and administrative rulings in each of the

[25] Dieter Grimm, "Normenflut – eindämmbar?", *Die Verfassung und die Politik. Einsprüche in Störfällen*, München, Beck, 2001, p. 151. Johanna Hey, *Steuerplanungssicherheit als Rechtsproblem*, Köln, Otto Schmidt, 2002, pages 1, 63, 73. Martin Stötzel, *Vertrauensschutz und Gesetzesrückwirkung*, Frankfurt am Main, Peter Lang, 2002, p. 25. Paulo de Barros Carvalho, "O princípio da segurança jurídica no campo tributário", *RDT*, n. 94, p. 22, São Paulo, s.d.

[26] José Luis Palma Fernández, *La seguridad jurídica ante la abundancia de normas*, Madrid, Centro de Estudios Políticos y Constitucionales, 1997, p. 14.

[27] Anne-Laure Valembois, *La Constitutionnalisation de l'exigence de sécurité juridique en Droit français*, Paris, LGDJ, 2005, p. 100.

[28] Antonio Enrique Pérez Luño, *La seguridad jurídica*, Barcelona, Ariel, 1991, p. 45.

[29] Federico Arcos Ramírez, *La seguridad jurídica: una teoría formal*, Madrid, Dykinson, 2000, p. 334.

[30] François Ost, *Le temps du Droit*, Paris, Odile Jacob, 1999, p. 281.

[31] Andreas von Arnauld, *Rechtssicherheit*, Tübingen, Mohr Siebeck, 2006, p. 218; Ulrich Beck, *Risikogesellschaft*, Frankfurt am Main, Suhrkamp, 1986, pages 7, 25. Christian Calliess, "Gewährleistung von Freiheit und Sicherheit im Lichte unterschiedlicher Staats- und Verfassungsverständisse", *DVBl*, n. 118, pages 1096–1105, 2003.

three branches of government and for each of the taxes established by the National Tax System. Now broaden this normative material to include international law, community law and comparative law. Reflect for a moment on the administrative and court decisions about each of these norms, as well as all the books and articles published about them. Almost intuitively it is clear that the mass of information is gigantic. Paradoxically this informative material both enables the world to be better understood and contributes to an increase in uncertainty. The more information there is, the more the future can be predicted but at the same time the more there is to be considered and assessed in order to do so. More knowledge therefore leads to a growing feeling of uncertainty: Citizens know more, but precisely because they know more, they also know what needs to be foreseen and what may not be confirmed in future. The future, which used to be in God's hands, has been placed by secularization in the hands of men, who must master it by planning and not by "divination."[32] Moreover, modern society and more complex relations due to technical and technological progress have augmented the future.[33] The pursuit of certainty has made us more uncertain – another paradox. After all, too much information causes misinformation.[34] In Brazil the problem is made worse by legislative inflation, in terms not just of statutes but also of provisional measures.[35]

This kind of society is also characterized by the existence of a huge diversity of interests. Each individual seeks protection for their personal interests in the legal norms, as do a plethora of groups: women, immigrants, ethnic minorities, environmentalists, consumers, liberals, conservatives, industrialists, workers, exporters, and so on ad infinitum. Hence the notions of groupism and moral disaggregation.[36] Each group lobbies for the enactment of norms that protect its interests. The number of norms therefore tends to multiply. In such a society, as Sendler ironically reminds us, one can no longer live with only ten commandments.[37] Worse still, the many groups' interests do not always coincide. On the contrary, they often collide, and the state has to try to coordinate them through the enactment of more norms. Thus the norms become not only more numerous but also quantitatively and qualitatively

---

[32] Andrea Schrimm-Heins, "Gewissheit und Sicherheit: Geschichte und Bedeutungswandel der Begriffe 'certitudo' und 'securitas'" (*Teil* 2), *Archiv für Begriffsgeschichte*, v. 35, pages 201, 208, 1992.

[33] Andreas von Arnauld, *Rechtssicherheit*, Tübingen, Mohr Siebeck, 2006, pp. 68, 73, 116. Martin Stötzel, *Vertrauensschutz und Gesetzesrückwirkung*, Frankfurt am Main, Peter Lang, 2002, p. 31. Theophilo Cavalcanti Filho, *O problema da segurança no Direito*, São Paulo, Ed. RT, 1964, p. 54.

[34] Anne-Laure Valembois, *La Constitutionnalisation de l'exigence de sécurité juridique en Droit français*, Paris, LGDJ, 2005, p. 8.

[35] Odete Medauar, "Segurança jurídica e confiança legítima", in Humberto Ávila (Org.), *Fundamentos do Estado de Direito*, São Paulo, Malheiros Editores, 2005, p. 118.

[36] Brian Z. Tamanaha, *Law as a Means to an End – Threat to the Rule of Law*, Cambridge, Cambridge University Press, 2006, pages 4, 223. Idem, *On the Rule of Law*, Cambridge, Cambridge University Press, 2004, p. 103.

[37] Horst Sendler, "Mehr Gesetze, weniger Rechtsgewährung?", *DVBl*, p. 979, 15.9.1995.

more complex: quantitatively because not only general and permanent norms are passed, but also exceptional norms (to govern marginal cases), transitory norms (to govern cases provisionally) and transitional norms (to govern the transition between and a previous normative system and a subsequent one);[38] qualitatively because such norms aim to solve technical and specific problems – from intricate tax problems to sophisticated environmental issues. Hence the references in the literature to so-called "value polytheism", i.e. the multiplicity of values that are present in the social environment and cannot be apprehended through absolute conceptual notions.[39]

The process described above justifies the state's assumption of responsibility for individual protection where social interests are asymmetrical, as in the case of relations between employees and employers, or sellers and consumers, as well as between state and citizens.[40] It also explains the state's assumption of responsibility for new tasks (by performing, coordinating or enforcing them), many of which are qualified as public policy, such as full employment, economic growth, education, health, fighting inflation and disaster relief, as well as occupations once assigned to a greater or smaller degree to individuals, such as environmental protection or assuring free market competition.[41] Besides these functions, the state also takes on the task of influencing or encouraging citizens to behave in accordance with public purposes.[42] Thus the Liberal State is superseded by the Welfare State (as provider of benefits), the Propulsive State (as maker of plans), the Reflexive State (as maker of programs), and finally the Conducive State (as producer of influences) under whose aegis bonds of coordination and cooperation are established.[43] State intervention, sometimes used to excess in pursuit of social purposes, and accelerating and multiplying social relations require steadily more laws, which become increasingly

[38]Luigi Ferrajoli, "The past and the future of the rule of law", in Pietro Costa, e Danilo Zolo (Orgs.), *The Rule of Law – History, Theory and Criticism*, Dordrecht, Springer, 2007, p. 337.

[39]Gianluigi Palombella, *Dopo la Certezza – Il Diritto in Equilibrio tra Giustizia e Democrazia*, Bari, Dedalo, 2006, p. 11.

[40]Dieter Grimm, "Normenflut – eindämmbar?", *Die Verfassung und die Politik. Einsprüche in Störfällen*, München, Beck, 2001, p. 152.

[41]Eduardo García de Enterría, *Justicia y seguridad jurídica en un mundo de leyes desbocadas*, Madrid, Civitas, 1999, p. 50. Federico Arcos Ramírez, *La seguridad jurídica: una teoría formal*, Madrid, Dykinson, 2000, p. 330. César García Novoa, *El principio de seguridad jurídica en materia tributaria*, Madrid, Marcial Pons, 2000, p. 32. Christian Calliess, "Gewährleistung von Freiheit und Sicherheit im Lichte unterschiedlicher Staats- und Verfassungsverständisse", *DVBl*, n. 118, pages 1096–1105, 2003.

[42]Luís Eduardo Schoueri, "Segurança na ordem tributária nacional e internacional: tributação do comércio exterior", in Aires Fernandino Barreto *et alii* (Orgs.), *Segurança jurídica na tributação e Estado de Direito*, São Paulo, Noeses, 2005, p. 376.

[43]Judith Martins-Costa, "Almiro do Couto e Silva e a ressignificação do princípio da segurança jurídica na relação entre Estado e cidadãos", in Humberto Ávila, (Org.), *Fundamentos do Estado de Direito – Estudos em homenagem a Almiro do Couto e Silva*, São Paulo, Malheiros Editores, 2005, p. 137.

filled with general and exceptional rules, and based on finalistic norms or goal-driven norms.[44]

This intervening action of the state also explains the increasing number of "omnibus laws" that introduce modifications to various broad sectors of the legal order with a single legislative instrument.[45] A good example in Brazil is Law 11,941, of May 27, 2009, which in a single act comprising more than 40 pages introduced modifications in a great many areas, from rules governing the payment of tax arrears by installment to the incidence rules for several federal taxes. This interventionism also makes intelligible the growth in administrative acts that create advantages for citizens in general and for taxpayers in particular. Instead of being merely restrictive, administrative acts also increasingly serve as an instrument for state action, which creates a variety of advantages for individuals.[46] Moreover, instead of placing itself vertically in a position to impose limits on individuals, the state seeks to establish horizontal connections of cooperation with them, justifying the movement that has been called a "flight to private law."[47] This new framework of state roles in turn drives the continuous creation of new branches of law, such as environmental law or telecommunications law, and even new sub-branches of traditional ones, such as tax law and its new sub-branches – environmental tax law or international tax law – to name only a few. Some are even more specialized, such as nuclear law (*Atomrecht*), pollution control law (*Immissionsschutzrecht*), genetic engineering law (*Gentechnikrecht*), data protection law (*Datenschutzrecht*), and so forth.[48] This constant division not only increases the complexity of law, but also

[44] Eros Roberto Grau, *Ensaio e discurso sobre a interpretação/aplicação do Direito*, 4th ed., São Paulo, Malheiros Editores, 2006, p. 45. Ricardo Lobo Torres, "Segurança jurídica e as limitações ao poder de tributar", in Roberto Ferraz (Org.), *Princípios e limites da tributação*, São Paulo, Quartier Latin, 2007, p. 440. Luis Eduardo Schoueri, "Segurança jurídica e normas tributárias indutoras", in Maria de Fátima Ribeiro (Org.), *Direito Tributário e segurança jurídica*, São Paulo, MP, 2008, p. 118. Almiro do Couto e Silva, "Princípios da legalidade da Administração Pública e da segurança jurídica no Estado de Direito contemporâneo", *Revista da Procuradoria-Geral do Estado do Rio Grande do Sul. Cadernos de Direito Público*, v. 27, n. 57, suplemento, p. 19, 2003. Anne-Laure Valembois, *La Constitutionnalisation de l'exigence de sécurité juridique en Droit français*, Paris, LGDJ, 2005, p. 113. Frédéric Douet, *Contribution à l'étude de la sécurité juridique en Droit interne français*, Paris, LGDJ, 1997, p. 28. Federico Arcos Ramírez, *La seguridad jurídica: una teoría formal*, Madrid, Dykinson, 2000, pages 334, 340.

[45] Eduardo García de Enterría, *Justicia y seguridad jurídica en un mundo de leyes desbocadas*, Madrid, Civitas, 1999, p. 77.

[46] Fritz Ossenbühl, *Die Rücknahme fehlerhafter begünstigender Verwaltungsakte*, 2nd ed., Berlin, Walter de Gruyter, 1965, p. 1. Almiro Couto e Silva, "Problemas jurídicos do planejamento", *RDA*, n. 170, p. 13, Rio de Janeiro, 1987.

[47] Almiro Couto e Silva, "Os indivíduos e o Estado na realização de tarefas públicas" *RDA*, n. 209, pp. 54–57, Rio de Janeiro, 1997. Fritz Ossenbühl, "Vertrauensschutz im sozialen Rechtsstaat", *DÖV*, n. 25, p. 26, 1972.

[48] Andreas von Arnauld, *Rechtssicherheit*, Tübingen, Mohr Siebeck, 2006, pp. 90, 271–317. Dieter Grimm, "Normenflut – eindämmbar?", *Die Verfassung und die Politik. Einsprüche in Störfällen*, München, Beck, 2001, p. 155. Klaus-Michael Groll, *In der Flut der Gesetze: Ursachen, Folgen, Perspectiven*, Düsseldorf, Droste, 1985, p. 45.

creates the phenomenon of superspecialization: Professionals initially know more and more about less and less, and eventually know less and less about less and less.[49]

The curious point is that this increased state involvement, albeit executed secondarily through administrative actions, primarily requires the enactment of new laws.[50] This creates two paradoxes. On one hand, as Gusy notes, in order to protect individuals and eliminate risks to their legal certainty, as well as their physical and social security, the state must know everything, be able to do everything (*alles können*) and be allowed to do everything (*alles dürfen*). But when that happens, it restricts freedom so much that it becomes another source of uncertainty, which it initially set out to banish.[51] As Bankowski argues, the aim is to obtain clarity and certainty, and to eliminate the danger of conflicts, but because of the excessive number of rules citizens end up acting heteronomously as if they were machines set in motion by the legal rules. As a result, individual autonomy paradoxically disappears.[52] On the other hand, the problem of a lack of law is solved with more law, but more law causes other problems, with their own complexity and uncertainty. In sum, solutions become problems. The paradox is that combating uncertainty contributes to uncertainty.

The phenomenon of increasing state intervention, however, is not linear. Once the state finds itself unable to perform all the activities it has taken upon itself, it begins to privatize, liberalize and deregulate in order to open up these activities to competition.[53] This does not decrease the complexity of the legal order: on one hand, because the state not only continues exercising essential activities but also takes on the task of overseeing the activities of citizens to further the public interest, entailing more rules to govern state regulation and more processes relating to it; on the other hand, because when citizens do not realize the public interest, the state reassumes its previous functions, and this in turn requires more rules. On this phenomenon Sendler is ironic: "Nowadays we first regulate. We then deregulate. When do we get to 'later'?"[54]

[49] José Luis Palma Fernández, *La seguridad jurídica ante la abundancia de normas*, Madrid, Centro de Estudios Políticos y Constitucionales, 1997, p. 86.

[50] Dieter Grimm, "Normenflut – eindämmbar?", *Die Verfassung und die Politik. Einsprüche in Störfällen*, München, Beck, 2001, p. 153.

[51] Christoph Gusy, "Gewährleistung von Freiheit und Sicherheit im Lichte unterschiedlicher Staats- und Verfassungsverständnisse", *VVDStRL*, Berlin, v. 63, p. 160, 2004.

[52] Zenon Bankowski, *Living Lawfully: Love in Law and Law in Love*, Dordrecht, Kluwer, 2001, p. 40.

[53] Almiro Couto e Silva, "Privatização no Brasil e o novo exercício de funções públicas por particulares. Serviço público 'à brasileira'?", *Revista da PGE – Cadernos de Direito Público*, n. 57, p. 202, Porto Alegre, 2004.

[54] Horst Sendler, "Mehr Gesetze, weniger Rechtsgewährung?", *DVBl*, p. 981, 15.9.1995.

To make matters worse, norms are not issued by a single authority.[55] They may come from various entities: in Brazil from the federal government, states or municipalities; or elsewhere from a specific country, a community or even an international organization. This creates the possibility of regional, national, supranational or international competition between different lawmaking bodies, so that coherence becomes impossible.[56] As if all this were not enough, authorities do not always issue norms with the purpose of solving problems; their goal is often to respond to public opinion, even if this entails issuing norms of whose inability to solve problems they are perfectly well aware. Such are the "propaganda laws" to which Ferrero Lapatza refers,[57] and which generate the phenomenon of Novoa's "decaffeinated laws".[58]

The state has to protect a large number of interests, so the legislative chooses to pass highly abstract norms capable of protecting everyone's interests equally. And because social processes are essentially dynamic in nature, any lawmaking entity tends to introduce norms with an open normative structure in order to avoid the need for continuous modification, such as principles or rules that establish indeterminate legal concepts or general clauses.[59] In sum, in order to further the largest possible number of interests and to do so equally and flexibly, the state issues general and abstract norms with a high degree of indeterminacy. The more abstract and general the norms, the easier they are to understand, but the less predictable their content owing to the lack of concrete elements concerning what is allowed, prohibited, or mandatory. Thus the attempt to regulate more broadly eventually increases vagueness and obscurity.[60] Moreover, any effort to introduce more concrete elements in order to enable the laws to provide more guidance requires the enactment of rules with more details and more exceptions. As a result,

[55]Christof Münch, "Rechtssicherheit als Standortfaktor. Gedanken aus Sicht der vorsorgenden Rechtspflege", in Albrecht Weber (Org.), *Währung und Wirtschaft. Das Geld im Recht. FS für Hugo J. Hahn*, Baden-Baden, Nomos, 1997, p. 680.

[56]Andreas von Arnauld, *Rechtssicherheit*, Tübingen, Mohr Siebeck, 2006, p. 218. Anne-Laure Valembois, *La Constitutionnalisation de l'exigence de sécurité juridique en Droit français*, Paris, LGDJ, 2005, p. 114.

[57]J. J. Ferrero Lapatza, "Reflexiones sobre Derecho Tributario y técnica jurídica", *REDF*, 85, 1995.

[58]César García Novoa, *El principio de seguridad jurídica en materia tributaria*, Madrid, Marcial Pons, 2000, p. 139.

[59]Bernd Mertens, *Gesetzgebungskunst im Zeitalter der Kodifikationen*, Tübingen, Mohr Siebeck, 2004, p. 375. Hinnerk Wissmann, *Generalklauseln – Verwaltungsbefugnisse zwischen Gesetzmäßigkeit und offenen Normen*, Tübingen, Mohr Siebeck, 2008, pages 297 and following, pages 306 and following. Klaus Meßerschmidt, *Gesetzgebungsermessen*, Baden-Baden, Nomos, 2000, pages 271 and following, pages 1007 and following. Anne-Laure Valembois, *La Constitutionnalisation de l'exigence de sécurité juridique en Droit français*, Paris, LGDJ, 2005, p. 109. Frédéric Douet, *Contribution à l'étude de la sécurité juridique en Droit interne français*, Paris, LGDJ, 1997, p. 87. Judith Martins-Costa, *A boa-fé no Direito Privado*, São Paulo, Ed. RT, 1999, pages 273 and following.

[60]Luigi Ferrajoli, "The past and the future of the rule of law", in Pietro Costa e Danilo Zolo (Orgs.), *The Rule of Law – History, Theory and Criticism*, Dordrecht, Springer, 2007, p. 337.

the laws become steadily less general and abstract and more specific and concrete.[61] Nevertheless, the more concrete and specific the norms, the harder they are to understand, even though their content is more predictable thanks to the introduction of concrete elements concerning what is allowed, prohibited or mandatory. This situation creates a dilemma and a paradox. The dilemma is that for law to be accessible it has to be simpler, but to be simpler it has to disregard many individual differences, so that protecting all interests is harder. For law to be more protective it must consider the largest possible number of interests, but doing so requires more complexity, which makes it harder to understand. Thus the dilemma is this: For law to be more certain because it is more accessible, it must guarantee less; to guarantee more by being more protective, it must be less accessible. Thus any gain in accessibility entails a loss of protectiveness, and any gain in protectiveness undermines accessibility. The paradox is that the more certainty is supposed to be guaranteed *through* law, the less certain law itself becomes. In short, the search for certainty leads to uncertainty. In this respect, law is a victim of itself.[62] And the lawyer cannot remain a mere interpreter but must become a sort of sleuth, given the difficulty of identifying the applicable norm.[63] Simply mastering the legislation becomes a science in its own right.[64] This is precisely why the problem of legal certainty always involves an attempt to react, through law, against the uncertainty created by law itself. The fight against legal uncertainty thus involves a fight of the legal system "against itself."[65] However, the battle must not be waged unchecked, lest it produce a paradoxical result: the establishment of rules that allow decisional alternatives but may lead to a reduction of the latter and in some extreme cases nullify them. Hence the conclusion, contradictory as it may seem, that freedom presupposes some degree of uncertainty. Otherwise, as Gusy reminds us, "the need for certainty devours the aspiration for freedom."[66]

The preference for vague(r) and (more) indeterminate norms, in turn, leads to more regulation because these norms more intensely require concretization through infralegal norms, which are quantitatively and qualitatively even more complex than

[61] Eduardo García de Enterría, *Justicia y seguridad jurídica en un mundo de leyes desbocadas*, Madrid, Civitas, 1999, p. 50.

[62] Anne-Laure Valembois, *La Constitutionnalisation de l'exigence de sécurité juridique en Droit français*, Paris, LGDJ, 2005, p. 8.

[63] José Luis Palma Fernández, *La seguridad jurídica ante la abundancia de normas*, Madrid, Centro de Estudios Políticos y Constitucionales, 1997, p. 14.

[64] Anne-Laure Valembois, *La Constitutionnalisation de l'exigence de sécurité juridique en Droit français*, Paris, LGDJ, 2005, p. 119.

[65] Nicolas Molfessis, "Combattre l'insécurité juridique ou la lutte du système juridique contre lui-même", in *Sécurité juridique et complexité du Droit*, Conseil d'État, *Rapport Public 2006, Études e documents* n. 57, Paris, Documentation française, 2006, p. 391.

[66] Christoph Gusy, "Gewährleistung von Freiheit und Sicherheit im Lichte unterschiedlicher Staats- und Verfassungsverständnisse", *VVDStRL*, v. 13, pages 165–180, Berlin, 2004.

legal norms. The legal order thus becomes supercomplex.[67] Regulation becomes super-regulation, causing what Jenetzky calls "the quagmire of tax administration."[68] Legislative activity earns the name of "legal productivism."[69] It is even said that rule by law has replaced rule of law.[70] Concerning the abundance of laws, Goethe quipped that if everyone had to study them they would have no time to break them.[71] It became commonplace to say that a legislator ought to think like a philosopher but write like a peasant. However, the opposite is the case today owing to the processes of social and normative specification mentioned above: Lawmakers think like disoriented peasants and write like neurotic philosophers. Among other reasons, this is because of the highly frequent practice of cross-referencing between laws or provisions, as well as generic repeals.[72] Hence the foundation for tax law becomes a "legally irrational system," an oxymoron if ever there was one.[73]

Aggravating the normative uncertainty portrayed so far, interests are not only different but also advocated by often powerful social and economic groups.[74] These groups demand quick and precise responses to protect their interests, causing a sort of "subjectivizing of law."[75] The greater the number of vested interests, the more norms have to be enacted, and the greater the juxtaposition of normative acts

---

[67]Eros Roberto Grau, *O Direito posto e o Direito pressuposto*, 7th ed., São Paulo, Malheiros Editores, 2008, p. 187. Federico Arcos Ramírez, *La seguridad jurídica: una teoría formal*, Madrid, Dykinson, 2000, p. 333. Eugenio Della Valle, *Affidamento e certezza del Diritto Tributario*, Milano, Giuffrè, 2001, p. 16. Jacques Chevallier, "Le Droit Économique: l'insécurité juridique ou nouvelle sécurité juridique?", in Laurence Boy, Jean-Baptiste Racine e Fabrice Siiriainen (Orgs.), *Sécurité juridique et Droit Économique*, Bruxelles, Larcier, 2008, p. 561. Jean-Pierre Bours, "Sécurité juridique et Droit Fiscal", in *Sécurité juridique et fiscalité* (Les Cahiers de l'Institut d'études sur la Justice, n. 4), Bruxelles, p. 31, 2003.

[68]Johannes Jenetzky, "Die Misere der Steuerverwaltung. Über die Wirklichkeit der Steuerrechtsanwendung durch die Steuerbehörden", *StuW*, p. 273, 1982. Eduardo García de Enterría, *Justicia y seguridad jurídica en un mundo de leyes desbocadas*, Madrid, Civitas, 1999, p. 47

[69]Frédéric Douet, *Contribution à l'étude de la sécurité juridique en Droit interne français*, Paris, LGDJ, 1997, p. 32.

[70]Jean Rivero, "État de Droit, état du Droit", in *L'État de Droit. Mélanges en l'honneur de Guy Braibant*, Paris, Dalloz, 1996, p. 610.

[71]Goethe *apud* Horst Sendler, "Mehr Gesetze, weniger Rechtsgewährung?", *DVBl*, p. 979, 15 Sep 1995.

[72]Federico Arcos Ramírez, *La seguridad jurídica: una teoría formal*, Madrid, Dykinson, 2000, p. 336.

[73]Rubén Asorey, "Seguridad jurídica y Derecho Tributario", *RDT*, São Paulo, n. 52, p. 40, 1990.

[74]Misabel Derzi, "Mutações, complexidade, tipo e conceito, sob o signo da segurança e da proteção da confiança", in Heleno Torres (Org.), *Estudos em homenagem a Paulo de Barros Carvalho*, São Paulo, Saraiva, 2007, p. 248. Idem, *Modificações da jurisprudência no Direito Tributário*, São Paulo, Noeses, 2009, p. 103. Horst Sendler, "Mehr Gesetze, weniger Rechtsgewährung?", *DVBl*, p. 981, 15 Sep 1995. Andreas von Arnauld, *Rechtssicherheit*, Tübingen, Mohr Siebeck, 2006, pp. 220, 225. José Luis Palma Fernández, *La seguridad jurídica ante la abundancia de normas*, Madrid, Centro de Estudios Políticos y Constitucionales, 1997, p. 28.

[75]Anne-Laure Valembois, *La Constitutionnalisation de l'exigence de sécurité juridique en Droit français*, Paris, LGDJ, 2005, p. 8.

adopted in terms of different perspectives, circumstances and motivations.[76] Law is required in all areas, for all interests: the result is "legal totalitarianism."[77] Politics therefore operates under time pressure (*Zeitdruck*).[78] And hurried legislation often takes on an experimental character.[79] The old maxim praising the "wise slowness" (*la sage lenteur*) of the legislative, which never deliberated without previous study and reflection, applies no more; instead, laws are ceaselessly cranked out in machine-gun fashion.[80] More often than not, these laws are so flawed that they must be immediately revised by the very same lawmaking body that enacts them. Hence the dictum that law, especially tax law, is in a state of permanent reform.[81] A fitting example is constitutional reform in Brazil: Since the Constitution was promulgated in 1988, six revising amendments and 67 modifying amendments have been passed, not to mention the permanent issues such as tax reform, which has been the focus for bills drafted since 1992 to reform the National Tax System. This is the "dictatorship of the moment," the "culture of urgency."[82]

This culture translates, on one hand, into a "high speed society" in which decisions are made as if society were in a perpetual "state of emergency", with implications for the legislative itself.[83] On the other hand, we have a "liquid society" in which change, flexibility and mobility are exalted, whereas the spatial dimensions of legal and social life become less and less important.[84] Here is another paradox: In order to protect the interests of citizens and guide their action, the legislators act quickly; however, precisely because they act in this way, they end up legislating incorrectly, so that new norms must be enacted to rectify the mistakes. The paradox is that if legislators act quickly, they act poorly and need to revise their acts, creating uncertainty; if they take time, they neither assure the rights demanded by the citizens nor guide them, again creating a state of uncertainty. In the pursuit of certainty, the

[76]Federico Arcos Ramírez, *La seguridad jurídica: una teoría formal*, Madrid, Dykinson, 2000, p. 323.

[77]Guy Carcassonne, "Société de Droit contre État de Droit", in *L'État de Droit. Mélanges en l'honneur de Guy Braibant*, Paris, Dalloz, 1996, p. 40.

[78]Andreas von Arnauld, *Rechtssicherheit*, Tübingen, Mohr Siebeck, 2006, p. 271.

[79]Johanna Hey, *Steuerplanungssicherheit als Rechtsproblem*, Köln, Otto Schmidt, 2002, p. 72. Hans-Detlef Horn, *Experimentelle Gesetzgebung unter dem Grundgesetz*, Berlin, Duncker und Humblot, 1989, pp. 20, 25. Martin Stötzel, *Vertrauensschutz und Gesetzesrückwirkung*, Frankfurt am Main, Peter Lang, 2002, p. 40.

[80]Eduardo García de Enterría, *Justicia y seguridad jurídica en un mundo de leyes desbocadas*, Madrid, Civitas, 1999, p. 48. Manoel Gonçalves Ferreira Filho, *Estado de Direito e Constituição*, 4ª ed., São Paulo, Saraiva, 2007, pages 49 and following.

[81]Johanna Hey, *Steuerplanungssicherheit als Rechtsproblem*, Köln, Otto Schmidt, 2002, pp. 1, 72, 74.

[82]François Ost, *Le temps du Droit*, Paris, Odile Jacob, 1999, p. 293.

[83]Hartmut Rosa e William Scheuermann, "Introduction", in Hartmut Rosa e William Scheuermann (Orgs.), *High-speed society: social acceleration, Power and modernity*, Pennsylvania, The Pennsylvania State University Press, 2009, pp. 14, 27.

[84]Anton Schütz, "How aufarbeiten 'Liquid Society'? Zygmunt Bauman's Wager", in Firi Pribán (Org.), *Liquid Society and Its Law*, Aldershot, Ashgate, 2007, pages 42–60.

legislators end up creating uncertainty. Alongside the phenomenon of particularized legislation, this leads to its rapid obsolescence, so that law loses its traditional characteristics, such as solemnity, generality and permanence.[85] This justifies the statement that more laws mean less law and fewer laws mean more law.[86]

In the era of the welfare state and the risk society, the state assumes tasks such as combating inequality and restoring a balance, so that many norms are specifically tailored to the needs of certain groups or sectors, also contributing to an increase in the number of laws and a decline in the basic characteristics of abstraction and generality of the laws.[87] In tax law this phenomenon is embodied in the growing numbers of tax benefits granted by means of agreements between government and taxpayers with the aim of correcting supposed regional or economic distortions. The essential point is that because of socio-economic complexity tax law as such must necessarily become supercomplex as well.[88]

Because the interpretation of norms involves value judgments and is subject to weighing, normative incomprehensibility and instability are also visible in the activities of the judiciary.[89] Different judicial bodies clearly interpret thc same laws differently, and interpretations even differ within the same body. An example of this is the Brazilian Supreme Court (STF), whose decisions in many cases display jurisprudential change.

This is particularly common in tax cases. In a 2003 decision concerning the transfer of assets in lieu of monetary payment to settle tax debts, the STF ruled that state governments were not competent to create new forms of extinction for tax arrears.[90] In 2007, however, it ruled that states do indeed have the competence to do so.[91] Concerning the requirement to deposit 30 % of the disputed amount for the filing of an administrative appeal, in 1995 the STF ruled it compatible with due process of law.[92] In 2007, however, the STF ruled it incompatible with due process, with the right to petition, and with the duty of proportionality.[93] Concerning the right to value-added tax credits in operations that benefit from a reduced taxable base, in

[85] Anne-Laure Valembois, *La Constitutionnalisation de l'exigence de sécurité juridique en Droit français*, Paris, LGDJ, 2005, pages 105, 128. Frédéric Douet, *Contribution à l'étude de la sécurité juridique en Droit interne français*, Paris, LGDJ, 1997, p. 31.

[86] Horst Sendler, "Mehr Gesetze, weniger Rechtsgewährung?", *DVBl*, p. 978, 15 Sep 1995.

[87] Federico Arcos Ramírez, *La seguridad jurídica: una teoría formal*, Madrid, Dykinson, 2000, p. 337. Fritz Ossenbühl, "Vertrauensschutz im sozialen Rechtsstaat", *DÖV*, n. 25, p. 26, 1972. Klaus-Michael Groll, *In der Flut der Gesetze: Ursachen, Folgen, Perspektiven*, Düsseldorf, Droste, 1985, p. 41.

[88] Misabel de Abreu Machado Derzi, *Modificações da jurisprudência no Direito Tributário*, São Paulo, Noeses, 2009, p. 103.

[89] Anne-Laure Valembois, *La Constitutionnalisation de l'exigence de sécurité juridique en Droit français*, Paris, LGDJ, 2005, p. 94.

[90] ADI n. 1917 MC, Tribunal Pleno, Rel. Min. Marco Aurélio, *DJ* 19 Sep 2003.

[91] ADI n. 2.405 MC, Tribunal Pleno, Rel. Min. Carlos Britto, *DJ* 17 Feb 2006.

[92] ADI n. 1.049 MC, Tribunal Pleno, Rel. Min. Carlos Velloso, *DJ* 25 Aug 1995.

[93] ADI n. 1.976, Tribunal Pleno, Rel. Min. Joaquim Barbosa, *DJ* 18 May 2007.

1997 the STF declared the unconstitutionality of a norm that prohibited offsetting of the amount paid in the previous operation, ruling that it conflicted with the non-accumulation principle.[94] In 2005 the STF ruled the same norm constitutional based on the view that a reduced taxable base is a partial exemption.[95] Concerning application of the anteriority rule to cases of exemption, in 1993 the STF decided that the rule did not apply to the revocation of exemptions.[96] In 2006, based on an interpretation in accordance with the Constitution, it decided that anteriority must be observed in such cases.[97]

Examples of changing Supreme Court case law can also be found in other areas. A few examples will suffice to demonstrate this. Concerning progression of custody levels for prisoners convicted of heinous crimes, in 1993 the STF ruled that denial of parole was constitutional in such cases, based on the understanding that the principle of sentence individualization was not violated since a judge could still apply it, especially with regard to intensity.[98] In 2006 the STF ruled denial unconstitutional, precisely because it violated the sentence individualization principle.[99] Concerning the requirement of public examinations for induction into a quasi-state company, in 1993 the Court decided that such examinations were not mandatory.[100] In that same year, however, it decided that quasi-autonomous government agencies, state-owned enterprises and mixed-capital companies were subject to the rule that access to the civil service must be via competitive public examination.[101] Concerning party loyalty, in 1994 the STF ruled that elected candidates did not lose their mandates if they left the party or alliance through which they had been elected.[102] In 2008 the STF decided they did.[103] Concerning the detention of a debtor deemed to be an unfaithful depository, in 2005 the STF ruled that the civil imprisonment of a trustor in default was constitutionally legitimate and did not violate the protection system established by the American Convention on Human Rights (the Pact of San José).[104] In 2008 the STF ruled the ACHR supralegal, so that no one may be imprisoned for debt.[105] Concerning the right of a convicted defendant to release from custody pending appeal, in 2002 the STF decided that

[94] RE n. 161.031, Tribunal Pleno, Rel. Min. Marco Aurélio, *DJ* 6 Jun 1997.

[95] RE n. 174.478, Tribunal Pleno, Rel. Min. Marco Aurélio, Redator para Acórdão Min. Cezar Peluso, *DJ* 30 Sep 2005.

[96] RE n. 99.431, 2ª Turma, Rel. Min. Djaci Falcão, *DJ* 6. 5.83, Súmula n. 615.

[97] ADI n. 2.325 MC, Tribunal Pleno, Rel. Min. Marco Aurélio, *DJ* 6 Oct 2006.

[98] HC n. 69.657, Tribunal Pleno, Rel. Min. Marco Aurélio, *DJ* 18 Jun 1993.

[99] HC n. 82.959, Tribunal Pleno, Rel. Min. Marco Aurélio, *DJ* 1 Sep 2006.

[100] Acórdão 056/93, publicado no *DOU* de 13 Dec 1993.

[101] MS n. 21.322, Tribunal Pleno, Rel. Min. Paulo Brossard, *DJ* 23 Apr 1993.

[102] MS n. 20.927, Tribunal Pleno, Rel. Min. Moreira Alves, *DJ* 15 Apr 1994.

[103] MS n. 26.604, Tribunal Pleno, Rela. Ministra Cármen Lúcia, *DJ* 2. Oct 2008.

[104] HC n. 81.319, Tribunal Pleno, Rel. Min. Celso de Mello, *DJ* 19 Aug 2005.

[105] HC n. 92.566, Tribunal Pleno, Rel. Min. Marco Aurélio, *DJe* 104, 4 Jun 2009, *Ement.* 2.363-03, p. 451.

extraordinary appeals do not have suspensive effect and hence the issuance of an arrest warrant did not violate the presumption of innocence.[106] In 2009 the STF ruled that the presumption of innocence guarantees a convicted defendant's right to remain undetained until the last-instance appeal.[107] In sum, all these cases show that the judiciary's understanding may vary considerably over time.

The modification of precedents is not only more and more frequent, but also increasingly intense, giving rise to talk of "zigzag" case law ("*Zick-Zack-Rechtsprechung*"),[108] or "gaseous law" since it disappears before its addressees can understand it.[109] Voluntary admission of tax arrears with a request for payment in scheduled installments can be used as an example. Following divergent rulings on the issue by various panels of the Superior Court of Justice (STJ), Brazil's highest non-constitutional appellate court, in 2001 its First Section finally decided that if a taxpayer formally and voluntarily recognizes a tax debt and undertakes to pay off the arrears in installments, no late penalty is enforceable in light of article 138 of the National Tax Code.[110] However, this supposedly uniformizing decision was not followed by all the panels, so the First Section revisited the case in 2004 and decided that when a tax debt is scheduled for payment in installments, the benefit of voluntary recognition of an infringement ought not to be granted since scheduling is not the same as paying and it cannot be assumed that all installments will be paid, pursuant to article 158, I, of the Code.[111]

This jurisprudential instability can be observed to an even greater extent in another case. First, in a judgment entered on February 21, 2002, the First Panel of the STJ ruled that the definition of a "hospital service" referred to its nature, which ought to be directly related to healthcare and not whether the service was provided inside or outside a hospital.[112] The Second Panel took the same view,[113] case law did not change until another decision of the First Panel, which on August 17, 2006, ruled that the reduced taxable base granted to "hospital services" was in fact a partial exemption and as such embodied an exception that must be interpreted restrictively, thus excluding services that lacked "hospital structure" while providing "complete patient care."[114] Given the disagreement between the First and Second Panels, the First Section was required to uniformize the court's understanding.

[106] HC n. 81.685, 2ª Turma, Rel. Min. Néri da Silveira, *DJ* 17 May 2002.

[107] HC n. 84.078, Tribunal Pleno, Rel. Min. Eros Grau, *DJ* 5 Feb 2009.

[108] Johanna Hey, *Steuerplanungssicherheit als Rechtsproblem*, Köln, Otto Schmidt, 2002, p. 87. Guido Alpa, *La certezza del Diritto nell'età dell'incertezza*, Napoli, Scientifica, 2006, p. 23.

[109] José Luis Palma Fernández, *La seguridad jurídica ante la abundancia de normas*, Madrid, Centro de Estudios Políticos y Constitucionales, 1997, p. 41.

[110] EREsp n. 180.700-SC, Rel. Min. Francisco Falcão, Primeira Seção, decided 27 Sep 2000, *DJ* 25 Jun 2001, p. 99.

[111] REsp n. 378.795-GO, Rel. Min. Franciulli Netto, Primeira Seção, *DJ* 21 Mar 2005, p. 209.

[112] REsp n. 380.584-RS, Rel. Min. Garcia Vieira, 1ª Turma, *DJ* 25 Mar 2002.

[113] REsp n. 380.087-RS, Rel. Min. João Otávio de Noronha, 2ª Turma, *DJ* 7 Jun 2004.

[114] REsp n. 837.778-SC, Rel. Min. Teori Albino Zavascki, 1ª Turma, *DJ* 31 Aug 2006.

This it did on October 11, 2006, accepting the First Panel's view that a "hospital service" is defined by "the existence of physical facilities and staffing structured to receive inpatients."[115] The Second Panel was initially reluctant to accept this new interpretation in some cases,[116] but soon fell in line.[117] The STJ applied the restrictive interpretation until May 15, 2007, when the Second Panel once again decided to espouse the understanding that the matter ought to be analyzed according to the services rendered and not the venue or structure.[118] Nevertheless, the Second Panel's rulings were occasionally inconsistent with this interpretation owing to the views of Justice Eliana Calmon.[119] The First Panel maintained its position unchanged despite renewed disagreements with the Second Panel on a few occasions.[120] On April 22, 2009, the First Section again issued an opinion with the aim of unifying the STJ's case law on the matter. Surprisingly, it reverted to its initial understanding, stating that the legislator "did not take into account the cost to the taxpayer, but rather the nature of the service, which is essential to the population to guarantee the fundamental right to health," and excluding medical consults performed by professionals not involved in any other outpatient procedures.[121] In sum, the court changed its view several times, eventually returning to its initial interpretation, perhaps.

At this point it is worth recalling that all three branches of government are under constant time pressure. Financial pressure is equally intense. The state's new tasks in several spheres require new sources of funding. This in turn requires new laws to create new taxes or raise the existing ones. It also entails new legal decisions to negate possible unconstitutionalities in tax laws or maintain past effects even when they frontally oppose the Constitution. Compared to its previous role, the social or welfare state has more tasks to perform and a larger apparatus, requiring growth in expenditure and revenue.[122] Revenue growth is not only achieved through norms that apply to future events. The state also targets past events, creating the "drama of retroactive laws."[123] Some even say retroactivity is not only a necessary remedy for abundant and imprecise laws but actually the only solution.[124] In sum, problems

---

[115]REsp n. 786.569-RS, Rel. Min. Teori Albino Zavascki, 1ª Seção, *DJ* 30 Oct 2006; e REsp n. 832.906-SC, Rel. Min. José Delgado, 1ª Seção, *DJ* 27 Nov 2006.

[116]REsp n. 807.312-RS, Rel.a Ministra Eliana Calmon, 2ª Turma, *DJ* 27 Nov 2006.

[117]REsp n. 873.944-RS, Rel. Min. Castro Meira, 2ª Turma, *DJ* 14 Dec 2006.

[118]REsp n. 807.128-RS, Rela. Ministra Eliana Calmon, 2ª Turma, *DJ* 28 May 2007; e REsp n. 836.783/SC, Rela. Ministra Eliana Calmon, 2ª Turma, 15 May 2007.

[119]REsp n. 889.960-RS, Rel. Min. Castro Meira, 2ª Turma, *DJ* 1 Jun 2007.

[120]REsp n. 958.421-PR, Rel. Min. José Delgado, 1ª Turma, *DJ* 6 Sep 2009.

[121]REsp n. 951.251-PR, Rel. Min. Castro Meira, 1ª Seção, *DJ* 3 Jun 2009.

[122]Martin Stötzel, *Vertrauensschutz und Gesetzesrückwirkung*, Frankfurt am Main, Peter Lang, 2002, p. 33.

[123]Idem, p. 55.

[124]Amélie Lièvre-Gravereaux, *La rétroactivité de la loi fiscale: une nécessité en matière de procédures*, Paris, Harmattan, 2007, pages 383–384. See also: Antonio Enrique Perez Luño, *La seguridad jurídica*, Barcelona, Ariel, 1991, p. 96.

are solved by creating new problems. Even so-called "self-medication" by means of simplification laws that are supposed to make the legal order more intelligible fails to do so because of its paradoxical complexity and actually exacerbates the problem, prompting the question whether "the remedy is worse than the disease" and a request that "we stop 'simplifying' like this!"[125]

In sum, citizens in general and taxpayers in particular are governed on one hand by laws that are often inaccessible, but not understandable or stable even when they are accessible; and on the other hand by decisions that suffer from instability even when they are relatively intelligible. Chevallier uses the expression "transitory law."[126] Ost mercilessly says law is "in transit."[127] This is the age of speed.[128]

Regardless of this situation, however, taxpayers need to do their jobs and run their businesses. They may even mitigate financial risk by taking out insurance, staying away from certain markets, opting for a conservative pricing strategy and transferring risk to third parties, among other measures; what they cannot do is avoid depending on legal norms.[129] Their plans and actions have to be based precisely on the norms: primary normative acts, usually statutes in the strict sense of the term; secondary normative acts, embodied in regulations that interpret the laws (*norminterpretierende Verwaltungsvorschriften*), clarify facts (*Verwaltungsvorschriften der Sachverhaltermittlung*), typify facts (*Typisierungsvorschriften*) and guide the administration's discretionary appreciation (*ermessenslenkende Verwaltungsvorschriften*); administrative acts, such as tax assessments and rulings in response to queries, for instance; and judicial acts, such as decisions directly addressed to a taxpayer or other taxpayers, with normative force (judicial review decisions in concentrated control of constitutionality, or in diffuse control of constitutionality but embodied in a binding precedent or suspension of a law by the Senate), or without normative force (judicial review decisions in diffuse control of constitutionality or control of legality but that create an expectation of equal treatment in similar future cases). The essential point is that the effect of such acts is to "stimulate initiatives" (*dispositionsinitiierende Wirkung*), "modify initiatives" (*dispositionsmodifizierende Wirkung*) or "inhibit initiatives" (*dispositionsinhibierende Wirkung*) on the part of taxpayers, who act

[125]Nicolas Molfessis, "Combattre l'insécurité juridique ou la lutte du système juridique contre lui-même", in *Sécurité juridique et complexité du Droit*, Conseil d'État, *Rapport Public 2006*, Études e documents n. 57, Paris, Documentation française, 2006, pages 394–396.

[126]Jacques Chevallier, *L'État de Droit*, 2nd ed., Paris, Montchrestien, 1994, p. 106.

[127]François Ost, *Le temps du Droit*, Paris, Odile Jacob, 1999, p. 282.

[128]Luís Roberto Barroso, "Em algum lugar do passado: segurança jurídica, Direito Intertemporal e o novo Código Civil", in Cármen Lúcia Antunes Rocha (Org.), *Constituição e segurança jurídica: direito adquirido, ato jurídico perfeito e coisa julgada, Estudos em homenagem a José Paulo Sepúlveda Pertence*, Belo Horizonte, Fórum, 2004, p. 141.

[129]Alain Couret, "La sécurité financière", in Laurence Boy, Jean-Baptiste Racine e Fabrice Siiriainen (Orgs.), *Sécurité juridique et Droit Économique*, Bruxelles, Larcier, 2008, p. 363.

and plan based on the acts concerned.[130] And while taxpayers should rely on the possibility of future change, the fact is that such normative acts create expectations on the part of taxpayers, who not only trust their permanence and bindingness, but may even be encouraged by them to behave in certain ways. The key point, it bears repeating, is that the predictability of state action, whatever the act or manifestation on which it is based, is fundamental to the freedom of individual and corporate action.[131]

1.4 Legal Causes of Legal Incertainty

Besides these social causes, referred to here only to justify the subject of this study, legal uncertainty also has legal causes. On one hand, legal doctrine does not always offer controllable criteria to eliminate or decrease legal uncertainty. Theoretical studies increasingly use excessively abstract language or leave normative determinacy entirely to individual decisions. Moreover, instead of defining interpretative criteria that help understand and apply law, many studies confine themselves to using and coining highly imprecise definitions, such as the idea that legal certainty involves the capacity to predict the results assignable by law to conduct, without specifying the meaning of "capacity," "predict," "results" and "law." This is why it has been said that the merely rhetorical dimension of legal doctrine has reached a spectacular level.[132] However, this kind of analysis produces the opposite to the desired outcome in the case of legal certainty. If it is discussed in vague language and without minimally clear criteria to determine meanings, the attempt to decrease uncertainty paradoxically creates more uncertainty. The high degree of abstraction neither eliminates nor decreases the problem of unpredictability in the legal order, but actually aggravates it. This phenomenon explains why Racine & Siiriainen say "legal certainty that seems to be an integral part of the legal system has never been defined with precision, which is the height of absurdity for a notion that stresses the requirement of certainty!"[133]

On the other hand, new theories developed by jurisprudence and case law, synthetically described here, paradoxically increase the complexity of the legal order.[134] The essentiality theory (*Wesentlichkeitstheorie*) holds that the more impor-

[130] Johanna Hey, *Steuerplanungssicherheit als Rechtsproblem*, Köln, Otto Schmidt, 2002, pages 21, 28, 48.

[131] Geraldo Ataliba, *República e Constituição*, 2nd ed., São Paulo, Malheiros Editores, 1998, p. 174.

[132] Andreas von Arnauld, *Rechtssicherheit*, Tübingen, Mohr Siebeck, 2006, pages 60, 263.

[133] Jean-Baptiste Racine e Fabrice Siiriainen, "Sécurité juridique et Droit Économique. Propos introductifs", in Laurence Boy, Jean-Baptiste Racine e Fabrice Siiriainen (Orgs.), *Sécurité juridique et Droit Économique*, Bruxelles, Larcier, 2008, p. 13.

[134] Andreas von Arnauld, *Rechtssicherheit*, Tübingen, Mohr Siebeck, 2006, pages 221, 248.

tant the norm, the more detailed the rules enacted by the legislative must be.[135] The prohibition of insufficiency (*Untermaßverbot*) requires the state not to fall short of a minimum level in protecting fundamental rights (*grundrechtliche Schutzpflicht*) and enacting rules that assure their minimum efficacy.[136] Equality theory proposes that what is essentially different must be treated differently by legal norms.[137] And social state theory advocates that the state is the main guarantor of the social order.[138] Regardless of their correctness and complete apprehension of their extensive meanings, all these theories have two specific consequences: They increase the number of norms and make the norms more complex.[139] Indeed, the more detailed the rules, the less understandable they become; the more the state assumes the task of protecting fundamental rights, the more norms there will be; and the more norms there are, the less intelligible the legal order will be; the more specific rules there are, the less accessible they become. Thus law and legal theory create legal uncertainty.

1.5 Problems Derived from Legal Uncertainty

For present purposes, the key point is that the scenario briefly outlined above gives rise to certain problems for citizens in general and for taxpayers in particular.[140]

The first problem is lack of intelligibility of the legal order (*Unerkennbarkeit der Rechtsordnung*). Citizens do not know exactly which rules are valid, or if they do, they are in doubt as to what the rules require, prohibit or permit. The rules are not accessible, comprehensive, comprehensible or sufficiently determinate. In sum, they are not user-friendly, omitting the information citizens need in order to know how to behave. As a result, law cannot perform its guiding function. To put it boldly, in these circumstances law is no longer *serious*. Citizens are governed by laws they do

[135] Walter Krebs, "Rechtliche und reale Freiheit", in Hans-Jürgen Papier e Detlef Merten (Orgs.), *Handbuch der Grundrechte*, v. 2, Heidelberg, C. F. Müller, 2006, pages 316 and following.

[136] Mathias Mayer, *Untermaß, Übermaß und Wesensgehaltsgarantie*, Baden-Baden, Nomos, 2005, p. 48. Manfred Stelzer, *Das Wesensgehaltsargument und der Grundsatz der Verhältnismäßigkeit*, Wien, Springer, 1991, p. 100. Johannes Dietlein, *Die Lehre von den grundrechtlichen Schutzpflichten*, 2nd ed., Berlin, Duncker und Humblot, 2005, p. 128. Peter Szczekalla, *Die sogenannten grundrechtlichen Schutzpflichten im deutschen und europäischen Recht*, Berlin, Duncker und Humblot, 2002, p. 223.

[137] Letizia Gianformaggio, *Eguaglianza, donne e Diritto*, Bologna, Il Mulino, 2005, pages 33 and following. Rolf Eckhoff, *Rechtsanwendungsgleichheit im Steuerrecht*, Köln, Otto Schmidt, 1999, pages 67 and following.

[138] Hans Michael Heinig, *Der Sozialstaat im Dienst der Freiheit*, Tübingen, Siebeck, 2008, p. 291.

[139] José Luis Palma Fernández, *La seguridad jurídica ante la abundancia de normas*, Madrid, Centro de Estudios Políticos y Constitucionales, 1997, p. 27. Klaus-Michael Groll, *In der Flut der Gesetze: Ursachen, Folgen, Perspektiven*, Düsseldorf, Droste, 1985, p. 103.

[140] Andreas von Arnauld, *Rechtssicherheit*, Tübingen, Mohr Siebeck, 2006, pages 167, 271, 391.

not know, making a mockery of the principle that ignorance of the law is no excuse for breaking it.[141]

The second point concerns the legal order's unreliability (*Unzuverlässigkeit der Rechtsordnung*). Citizens do not know whether a valid rule will remain valid, or if they do they are not sure whether valid rules will actually be applied to their case. Thus rules and decisions are erratic. Law is not serious – and can *no longer be taken seriously*.

The third bottleneck is the legal order's incalculability (*Unberechenbarkeit der Rechtsordnung*). In other words, citizens are not sure which norms will be enforced. They have very little chance of obtaining information about future decisions. Law is therefore neither predictable nor calculable. Citizens do not know whether law, which is already neither serious nor taken seriously in the present, *will be taken seriously in future*.

Absence or weakness of the ideals of knowability, reliability and calculability of law foster uncertainty, distrust and indecision in the social environment, fueling doubt about even traditional principles such as legal certainty, contributive capacity, equality and legality.[142]

These difficulties are magnified in tax law. First because of the particularities of this normative field. The legality rule correlates tax law very closely with the statutes, which are the main basis of trust for taxpayers, given the impact on their freedom and property. However, statutes aim not only to achieve fiscal goals but also to guide taxpayer behavior and to pursue a number of economic, social, cultural, scientific and public health purposes, among others. To an even greater extent, these statutes are the basis for taxpayer reliance. Tax statutes, whether fiscal or extrafiscal, affect the economic activities of taxpayers differently. Some affect income, others property, yet others consumption. Trust protection in tax law must therefore be the result of several factors. Moreover, in contrast with other fields of law, the incidence hypotheses stipulated by tax laws affect certain activities that take place over time, often starting while one statute is in force and ending under the aegis of another.[143] All these factors heighten the concern with legal certainty in tax law because of the uncertainty they cause.

Second, these obstacles are intensified because of the need for planning to maintain an economic activity. Any business or occupation requires planning that includes forecasting of future legal consequences and assessment of economic alternatives from the perspective of their tax impact. The difficulties faced when

[141]Eduardo García de Enterría, *Justicia y seguridad jurídica en un mundo de leyes desbocadas*, Madrid, Civitas, 1999, p. 49. Eros Roberto Grau, *O Direito posto e o Direito pressuposto,* 7th ed., São Paulo, Malheiros Editores, 2008, p. 185.

[142]Misabel de Abreu Machado Derzi, "Mutações, complexidade, tipo e conceito, sob o signo da segurança e da proteção da confiança", in Heleno Torres (Org.), *Estudos em homenagem a Paulo de Barros Carvalho*, São Paulo, Saraiva, 2007, p. 247.

[143]Rudolf Mellinghoff, "Vertrauen in das Steuergesetz", in Heinz-Jürgen Pezzer (Org.), *Vertrauensschutz im Steuerrecht*, Deutsche Steuerjuristische Gesellschaft, v. 27, Köln, Otto Schmidt, 2004, pages 32–33.

making this assessment may include uncertainty as to both the existing normative basis and its effects (static uncertainty), and the permanence of this basis over time (dynamic uncertainty). Both kinds of uncertainty may restrict or annihilate planning capacity, in which case the adverse effect on the continuity of the taxpayer's economic activities will be severe.[144] Certainty for taxpayers can exist only if they are able to plan ahead and anticipate to a large extent the tax consequences of their actions. For this to be possible, they need to know the applicable normative sources, their effects, and their duration. In sum, they need knowability and calculability of law. However, for a long time this has not been the case with the desirable intensity. Surprising as it may seem, Rümelin said this as far back as 1924: "For private enterprise the possibility of forecasting the tax burden has simply vanished, and lack of clarity about the legal situation acts as a constraint above all on scrupulous citizens who are loyal to the state, whereas unlimited possibilities remain open for fraudsters."[145]

In this context, it can be said that not only the future but also the past ends up creating uncertainty. Given the lack of intelligibility of the legal order, citizens do not know what is valid today (uncertainty about current law); given the lack of predictability of the legal order, they do not know what will be valid or binding tomorrow (uncertainty about future law); given the lack of stability of the legal order, paradoxically they do not know whether what was valid yesterday will remain valid today (uncertainty about past law). Law is not certain. And law that is not certain is not law, as Carnelutti recalls.[146]

1.6 The Urgence of Analyzing Legal Certainty

But it is precisely because we realize the full significance of a good only when we lose it, and precisely because certainty only acquires significance as a legal value in contrast with its opposite, uncertainty, that the investigation of legal certainty regains all its vitality. Legal certainty thus appears to be a sort of paradise in contrast with the current state of deep uncertainty.[147] The paradise of certainty arises from the hell of uncertainty. Certainty becomes a "raft of salvation" (*un'ancora di salvezza*), as Alpa puts it.[148] Or, as Schrimm-Heins reminds us, as already quoted in the epigraph, certainty "thus becomes an issue when uncertainty and insecurity spread. And the

[144] Joachim Voß, *Ungewißheit im Steuerrecht*, Wiesbaden, Gabler, 1992, p. 1.

[145] Max Rümelin, *Die Rechtssicherheit*, Tübingen, Mohr Siebeck, 1924, p. 38.

[146] Francesco Carnelutti, "Certezza, autonomia, libertà, Diritto", in *Il Diritto della Economia*, n. 2, p. 1.190, 1956.

[147] Andreas von Arnauld, *Rechtssicherheit*, Tübingen, Mohr Siebeck, 2006, pages 15, 68, 90.

[148] Guido Alpa, *La certezza del Diritto nell'età dell'incertezza,* Napoli, Scientifica, 2006, p. 43.

more uncertain the circumstances in modern times, the more demanding men's expectations of certainty and security become."[149]

It must be emphasized that the search for this ideal state is justified by the negative effects legal uncertainty causes. Legal uncertainty can harm or prevent the maintenance of personal, professional and economic activities, given the lack of minimum requirements for all to live and freely carry on their lawful activities, in Carazza's precise formulation.[150] Planning and acting are possible only when there is certainty to plan and to act. Thus certainty is a means to realize individual freedoms, a sort of functional principle concerning them.[151] After all, anyone who cannot trust the legal conditions when acting will refrain from major undertakings, since freedom means being able to shape life according to one's own projects. Hence Grau's acute insight that without calculability a market economy cannot prevail.[152] Legal certainty is therefore instrumental with regard to freedom: the more certainty there is, the more freedom for individuals to plan their future according to their ideals. Paradoxically, however, the more freedom, the greater the possibility that individuals will do something different, and the less other individuals can foresee what others will do. As Gusy notes, "certainty is absence of risks; freedom, on the contrary, causes and increases risks."[153] This is the dilemma: More certainty means more freedom; more freedom permits the existence and protection of more interests through legal norms, which in turn increases the complexity of the legal order. The interesting paradox is that certainty creates uncertainty.[154]

[149] Andrea Schrimm-Heins, "Gewissheit und Sicherheit: Geschichte und Bedeutungswandel der Begriffe 'certitudo' und 'securitas'" (*Teil* 2), *Archiv für Begriffsgeschichte,* v. 35, p. 204, 1992.

[150] Roque Antonio Carrazza, *Curso de Direito Constitucional Tributário*, 27ª ed., São Paulo, Malheiros Editores, 2011, p. 426.

[151] Arnauld von Andreas, *Rechtssicherheit*, Tübingen, Mohr Siebeck, 2006, p. 663. Gianmarco Gometz, *La certezza giuridica come prevedibilità*, Torino, Giappichelli, 2005, p. 3.

[152] Eros Roberto Grau, *A ordem econômica na Constituição de 1988*, 12th ed., São Paulo, Malheiros Editores, 2007, p. 32. Idem, *O Direito posto e o Direito pressuposto*, 7th ed., São Paulo, Malheiros Editores, 2008, p. 102. About the legal conditions of a market capitalist Economy, see: Stefan Uecker, *Die Rationalisierung des Rechts,* Berlin, Wissenschaftler Verlag, 2005, pages 70 and following; Christof Münch, "Rechtssicherheit als Standortfaktor. Gedanken aus Sicht der vorsorgenden Rechtspflege", in Albrecht Weber (Org.), *Währung und Wirtschaft. Das Geld im Recht. FS für Hugo J. Hahn*, Baden-Baden, Nomos, 1997, p. 673; Max Weber, *Wirtschaft und Gesellschaft*, Frankfurt am Main, Zweitausendeins, 2008, pp. 49 e ss., 233 e ss., 599 e ss.; Franz Neumann, "Über die Voraussetzungen und den Rechtsbegriff einer Wirtschaftsverfassung", in *Wirtschaft, Staat, Demokratie*, Frankfurt am Main, Suhrkamp, 1978, pages 76 and following. Idem, "Der Funktionswandel des Gesetzes im Recht der bürgerlichen Gesellschaft", in *Demokratischer und autoritärer Staat – Studien zur politischen Theorie*, Frankfurt am Main, Europäische Verlagsanstalt, 1967, pages 31 and following.

[153] Christoph Gusy, "Gewährleistung von Freiheit und Sicherheit im Lichte unterschiedlicher Staats- und Verfassungsverständnisse", *VVDStRL*, Berlin, v. 63, p. 155, 2004.

[154] Andreas von Arnauld, *Rechtssicherheit*, Tübingen, Mohr Siebeck, 2006, pages 71, 692.

Legal certainty is also an objective element of the legal order. It is a means to attain the general interest.[155] When there is a high degree of uncertainty, individuals avoid actions that foster integration, so that social cooperation is repressed.

Legal certainty is also a means to assure human dignity. Respect for dignity includes treating people as capable of planning their future. Human beings are future-oriented, seeking to stabilize the future through their actions.[156] Thus guaranteeing dignity includes respecting individual self-determination.[157]

Finally, legal uncertainty harms the lives of citizens. It has a negative impact on institutions and on investment, domestic and foreign, because it impairs long-term decision making owing to the absolute impossibility of anticipating future norms and relying on past decisions.[158] Frequent changes in legislation frighten away investment and prevent the medium- and long-term actions needed in a market economy.[159]

Uncertainty is a problem of law but it is especially intense in tax law. First because the state's new tasks lead to an increase in extrafiscal purposes: Besides maintaining or increasing revenue, the state adopts specific goals to be attained through taxation, such as protecting the environment or assuring free competition. The new tasks both make the laws more complex and change the elements to be considered because the trust in the state that encourages taxpayers to follow its guidance must be protected even more intensely. Second because the pressure of time and money affects tax law most of all: The state sets out to finance its new activities through taxation, and it is in this field that pressure to uphold or change legal norms is strongest, owing to the onerousness and conduciveness of tax norms.[160]

This emphasis on the importance of the reliability of the legal order, especially through its stability and bindingness, is not intended to deny the importance of normative variability, and hence of flexibility and innovation.[161] Law is always

---

[155]Andreas von Arnauld, *Rechtssicherheit*, Tübingen, Mohr Siebeck, 2006, p. 153.

[156]Franz-Xaver Kaufmann, *Sicherheit als soziologisches und sozialpolitisches Problem*, 2nd ed., Stuttgart, 1973, p. 11.

[157]Joseph Raz, "The Rule of Law and its Virtue" (1977), *The Authority of Law. Essays on Law and Morality*, Oxford, Oxford, 1979, p. 221. John Rawls, *Theory of Justice*, Cambridge, Belknap, 1971, p. 407.

[158]Andreas von Arnauld, *Rechtssicherheit*, Tübingen, Mohr Siebeck, 2006, pages 111, 113; Johanna Hey, *Steuerplanungssicherheit als Rechtsproblem*, Köln, Otto Schmidt, 2002, p. 99.

[159]Jean-Baptiste Racine, Fabrice Siiriainen, "Sécurité juridique et Droit Économique. Propos introductifs", in Laurence Boy, Jean-Baptiste Racine, Fabrice Siiriainen (Orgs.), *Sécurité juridique et Droit Économique*, Bruxelles, Larcier, 2008, pp. 16, 18. Jacques Chevallier, "Le Droit Économique: l'insécurité juridique ou nouvelle sécurité juridique?", in Laurence Boy, Jean-Baptiste Racine, Fabrice Siiriainen, (Orgs.), *Sécurité juridique et Droit Économique*, Bruxelles, Larcier, 2008, p. 572.

[160]Andreas von Arnauld, *Rechtssicherheit*, Tübingen, Mohr Siebeck, 2006, p. 90.

[161]Eberhard Schmidt-Aßmann, "Flexibilität und Innovationsoffenheit als Entwicklungsperspektiven des Verwaltunsrechts", in Wolfgang Hoffmann-Riem, Eberhard Schmidt-Aßmann (Orgs.), *Innovation und Flexibilität des Verwaltungshandelns*, Baden-Baden, Nomos, 1994,

situated between tradition and innovation, permanence and adaptability.[162] By establishing formal requirements that hinder constitutional change, and by forbidding constitutional amendments on certain subjects, the Brazilian Constitution protects the stability of the legal order. On the other hand, however, it assumes that the legal order is variable and changeable, otherwise changes would not have to be restricted.[163] The democratic principle empowers the legislative to protect society's interests continuously by enacting laws, and to configure and define premises.[164] The competence rules contained in that same Constitution empower the judiciary to interpret and apply the norms enacted by the legislative, continually seeking the best interpretation and hence revising previous decisions or issuing new decisions that take into consideration previously overlooked or incorrectly assessed circumstances. All these fundamentals not only assume but also permit the changeability of the legal order. My argument in this book will not be that no changes should ever be made to the legal order, however much I stress the importance of stability as an integral part of the state of reliability that is such a key part of legal certainty. What I do advocate is that changes, presupposed and permitted as they are, should be made in a stable and calculable manner.[165] Total immobility would make law ineffective: Interests and values change, and laws that do not minimally reflect social interests and values lack effectiveness because ultimately they are not even enforced. As Valembois says, too much law eventually kills law itself; analogously we can agree that "too much certainty would kill certainty."[166] Sendler follows the same path in stating that "too much law is not law" (*Zuviel Recht ist Unrecht*).[167] Reale had already pondered that

pages 407–423. Friedrich Schoch, "Der Verwaltunsakt zwischen Stabilität und Flexibilität", in Wolfgang Hoffmann-Riem, Eberhard Schmidt-Aßmann (Orgs.), *Innovation und Flexibilität des Verwaltungshandelns*, Baden-Baden, Nomos, 1994, pages 199–244. Reiner Schmidt, "Flexibilität und Innovationsoffenheit im Bereich der Verwaltungsmaßstäbe", in Wolfgang Hoffmann-Riem, Eberhard Schmidt-Aßmann (Orgs.), *Innovation und Flexibilität des Verwaltungshandelns*, Baden-Baden, Nomos, 1994, pages 67–110. Hartmut Bauer, "Anpassungsflexibilität im öffentlich-rechtlichen Vertrag", in Wolfgang Hoffmann-Riem, Eberhard Schmidt-Aßmann (Orgs.), *Innovation und Flexibilität des Verwaltungshandelns*, Baden-Baden, Nomos, 1994, pages 245–288. Wolfgang Hoffmann-Riem, "Ermöglichung von Flexibilität und Innovationsoffenheit im Verwaltungsrecht: einleitende Problemskizze", in Wolfgang Hoffmann-Riem, Eberhard Schmidt-Aßmann (Orgs.), *Innovation und Flexibilität des Verwaltungshandelns*, Baden-Baden, Nomos, 1994, pp. 9–66. Niklas Luhmann, *Ausdifferenzierung des Rechts. Beiträge zur Rechtssoziologie und Rechtstheorie*, Frankfurt am Main, Suhrkamp, 1999, p. 95.

[162] Paul Kirchhof, "Rückwirkung von Steuergesetzen", *StuW*, p. 222, 2000.

[163] Werner Krawietz, "Rechtstheorie und Rechtsstaatlichkeit", in Werner Krawietz, Mihály Samu, Péter Szilágyi (Orgs.), *Rechtstheorie, Sonderhaft – Verfassungsstaat, Stabilität und Variabilität des Rechts im modernen Rechtssystem*, v. 26, t. 3, Berlin, Duncker und Humblot, 1995, p. 435.

[164] Rudolf Mellinghoff, "Vertrauen in das Steuergesetz", in Heinz-Jürgen Pezzer (Org.), *Vertrauensschutz im Steuerrecht, Deutsche Steuerjuristische Gesellschaft*, v. 27, Köln, Otto Schmidt, 2004, p. 27. Paul Kirchhof, "Rückwirkung von Steuergesetzen", *StuW*, p. 221, 2000.

[165] Anna Leisner, *Kontinuität als Verfassungsprinzip*, Tübingen, Mohr Siebeck, 2002, p. 5.

[166] Anne-Laure Valembois, *La Constitutionnalisation de l'exigence de sécurité juridique en Droit français*, Paris, LGDJ, 2005, p. 21.

[167] Horst Sendler, "Mehr Gesetze, weniger Rechtsgewährung?", *DVBl*, p. 979, 15 Sep 1995.

"absolutely guaranteed certainty is a reason for uncertainty".[168] In sum, too much law makes us "sick from a surfeit of law" (*maladie du trop-de-droit*).[169] Excessive predictability ultimately eliminates the efficacy of law.[170] The key is to reconcile the demands of stability and change that are indispensable not only to law but to the human life law should serve, as correctly noted by Cavalcanti Filho.[171]

The first reason for choosing legal certainty as the subject of this study is thus the current state of high uncertainty. In addition to this justification, which may be termed causalistic, the doctrinal justification is that although there are excellent studies on the subject, the way it is presented and addressed justifies new and different research.

On one hand, the study of legal certainty is presented with a high degree of *skepticism*.[172] First, it is alleged that legal certainty has little to offer as a principle.[173] Given its high degree of abstraction and different functions depending on the context, as well as the possibility of collision with other principles, the argument runs, studying it does not and cannot lead to practical results capable of eliminating or decreasing the legal uncertainty that currently exists.

Second, it is said that legal doctrine cannot define legal certainty as an abstract solution to concrete future interpretative problems. Because the content of a decision can only be verified a posteriori, legal certainty as the possibility of prior knowledge of decisions is simply indefensible. Moreover, it is said that the pursuit of a single foundation for the comprehension of law (hence the derogatory term "foundationalism") runs up against the inability of a single doctrine or interpretative model to provide a simple solution to innumerable concrete problems, which are necessarily complex, uncertain and inconsistent.[174]

Third, it is said that the search for legal certainty as an ideal of absolute determinacy of the content of legal norms is bound to fail since language is always indeterminate to some extent. Determinacy in law does not and cannot exist. And to borrow an expression from Kozinski, writing about it is like "a scholarly essay about snakes in Ireland. There are none."[175]

---

[168] Miguel Reale, "Prefácio", in Theophilo Cavalcanti Filho, *O problema da segurança no Direito*, São Paulo, Ed, RT, 1964, p. V.

[169] Alessandro Pizzorusso, Paolo Passaglia, "Constitution et sécurité juridique – Italie", *Annuaire International de Justice Constitutionnelle 1999*, Paris, Economica, 2000, pp. 199–225.

[170] Fabien Lafay, *La Modulation du Droit par le Juge*, t. 2, Aix-en-Provence, PUAM, 2006, p. 576.

[171] Theophilo Cavalcanti Filho, *O problema da segurança no Direito*, São Paulo, Ed. RT, 1964, p. 172.

[172] Gianmarco Gometz, *La certezza giuridica come prevedibilità*, Torino, Giappichelli, 2005, p. 2.

[173] Manfred Stelzer, "Was leistet das Prinzip Rechtssicherheit? Bemerkungen zur Rücknahme rechtswidriger Verwaltunsakte nach §48 VwVfG", *Verwaltung*, n. 30, pages 139–160, 1997.

[174] Daniel Farber, Suzanna Sherry, *Desperately seeking certainty: the misguided quest for constitutional foundations*, London, The University of Chicago, 2002, pages 5, 140.

[175] Alex Kozinski, "What I Ate for Breakfast and Other Mysteries of Judicial Decision Making", in David M. O'Brien (Org.), *Judges on Judging*, New Jersey, Chatham, 1997, p. 71.

Last, it is said that society today is necessarily and ineluctably characterized by complexity, that predictability in such a society is unattainable given the complexity of the social, economic and legal processes discussed above, and that the study of legal certainty is therefore a waste of time because it will never produce minimally satisfactory practical results. This means legal uncertainty is an insoluble problem.[176] And legal certainty is therefore an illusion. Because legal certainty is unattainable and it is a waste of time to study it, the only alternative is fatalism and resignation.[177]

On the other hand, when scholars do stoop to study legal certainty, they do so with a high degree of *partiality* and *vagueness*. *Partiality*, or excessive specialty, because, as this study will demonstrate, the examination of legal certainty typically focuses on one of its manifestations or is excessively skewed towards one of its aspects.[178] Sometimes it is presented with an emphasis on trust protection;[179] at other times as the duty of determining the concept of incidence hypotheses;[180] or as the ideal of predictability;[181] or again as the sum of some of its parts, such as the guarantees of legality, irretroactivity and anteriority.[182] Legal certainty is not considered as a totality but identified with one of its parts or studied only in terms of one part.

Vagueness, or excessive generality, because the study of legal certainty is too broad, even when it focuses on one manifestation, with no indication of functionally appropriate criteria to make it effective in practice.[183] Here the study of legal certainty offers no certainty for its application. Its content is presented as too obvious

[176]Hans Kelsen, *Reine Rechtslehre*, 1st ed., Leipzig und Wien, Franz Deuticke, 1934, p. 99 (Hans Kelsen, Reine Rechtslehre. Studienausgabe der 1, Auflage 1934, Matthias Jestaedt (Org.), Tübingen, Mohr Siebeck, 2008, p. 109).

[177]Gianmarco Gometz, *La certezza giuridica come prevedibilità*, Torino, Giappichelli, 2005, p. 33.

[178]Federico Arcos Ramírez, *La seguridad jurídica: una teoría formal*, Madrid, Dykinson, 2000, p. 1. Andreas von Arnauld, *Rechtssicherheit*, Tübingen, Mohr Siebeck, 2006, pages 102, 153.

[179]Hermann-Josef Blanke, *Vertrauensschutz im deutschen und europäischen Verwaltungsrecht*, Tübingen, Mohr Siebeck, 2000. Kyrill-A. Schwarz, *Vertrauensschutz als Verfassungsprinzip*, Baden-Baden, Nomos, 2002. Sylvia Calmes, *Du principe de protection de la confiance légitime en Droits allemand, communautaire et français*, Paris, Dalloz, 2001. Soren Schonberg, *Legitimate Expectations in Administrative Law*, Oxford, OUP, 2007. Almiro do Couto e Silva, "O princípio da segurança jurídica (proteção à confiança) no Direito Público brasileiro e o direito da Administração Pública de anular os seus próprios atos: o prazo decadencial do art. 54 da Lei do Processo Administrativo da União (Lei n. 9.784/99)", *RBDP*, v. 6, Porto Alegre, Jul/Sep 2004, pages 7–59.

[180]Alberto Xavier, *Tipicidade da tributação, simulação e norma antielisiva*, São Paulo, Dialética, 2001.

[181]Gianmarco Gometz, *La certezza giuridica come prevedibilità*, Torino, Giappichelli, 2005, p. 22.

[182]Leandro Paulsen, *Segurança jurídica, certeza do Direito e tributação*, Porto Alegre, Livraria do Advogado, 2006.

[183]Federico Arcos Ramírez, *La seguridad jurídica: una teoría formal*, Madrid, Dykinson, 2000, p. 1.

to require clarification.[184] As Gometz ironically reminds us, none of the concepts considered by legal philosophy is as "uncertain" as "certainty of law."[185] In other words, the characteristics of legal certainty mean that its study is not sufficient to solve the current problem of uncertainty.

It must be noted that previous works dealing solely with legal certainty in toto (like the present work), albeit extremely important, and hence repeatedly quoted herein, focus solely on a specific perspective. This can be seen in some of the recent works already quoted. For example, although von Arnauld claims to examine the entire archetype of the legal certainty principle, he does not adopt an analytical perspective and hence fails to specify the principle's several aspects, elements and dimensions or to construct its foundations; Valembois also analyzes legal certainty very broadly but sets out to answer a specific question, which is whether legal certainty can be considered a constitutional principle in the French legal order; Arcos Ramírez offers a general concept of legal certainty but lacks a more analytical investigation of its dimensions, aspects and foundations, or an attempt to address more specific philosophical questions, such as the relationship between legal certainty and the idea of law, and the value of legal certainty; Gometz is the only one who investigates legal certainty analytically but does so from a single perspective (from the present to the future, i.e. as a requirement of predictability), omits all other perspectives (atemporal, as a requirement of knowability, and from past to present, as a duty of reliability), and fails to justify it according to constitutional principles. In sum, while these works and many others like them examine the legal certainty principle specifically, they do not do so in the way intended here, i.e. as a principle norm grounded in constitutional norms, using a methodology that progressively reduces its indeterminacy and shows how it operates in practice by indicating the behavior whose adoption contributes to the realization of the states legal certainty requires.

The point is that the approach used to present and deal with the issue of legal certainty by no means weakens but greatly strengthens the importance of reexamining it. Indeed, it is precisely because the legal certainty principle is highly abstract, may perform different functions depending on the context and may collide with other principles depending on how it is defined that it is necessary to reduce its abstractness, identify its different functions, and weigh it against other principles. It is precisely because of the doctrinal focus on legal certainty as an abstract solution to future problems of concrete interpretation that the pursuit of "certainty of meaning" (*Bedeutungssicherheit*) must be replaced by the pursuit of "certainty of criteria" (*Kriteriensicherheit*), i.e. the pursuit of abstract parameters with which to solve subsequent concrete problems of interpretation. It is precisely because legal certainty is pursued as an ideal of absolute determinacy of the content of legal norms

---

184 Franz-Xaver Kaufmann, *Sicherheit als soziologisches und sozialpolitisches Problem*, 2nd ed., Stuttgart, 1973, p. 5. Federico Arcos Ramírez, *La seguridad jurídica: una teoría formal*, Madrid, Dykinson, 2000, p. 7.

185 Gianmarco Gometz, *La certezza giuridica come prevedibilità*, Torino, Giappichelli, 2005, p. 22.

that the main axis must be the pursuit of relative predictability for citizens in general and taxpayers in particular. Lastly, it is because society today is characterized by complexity that it is necessary to restore the ordering function of law through a broader and less vague investigation of legal certainty.

In sum, the challenges inherent in the study of legal certainty ought not to be a reason for resignation on the part of scholars concerning the role of law; on the contrary, we should feel stimulated to overcome such challenges.

1.7 The Present Task

Far be it from me to suggest some sort of desperate search for "absolute certainty." All I advocate is the pursuit of "relative certainty". This is an appropriate task. Thus I have taken care in this book not to commit the straw man fallacy by misrepresenting another's arguments in order more easily to refute them. To avoid examining legal certainty, legal science treats it as a "fantasy", an "illusion".[186] As advised by von Arnauld, the science of law cannot resign itself to law's inefficacy, but must function on the contrary as a counterweight to modernity by restoring one of law's traditional functions, that of assuring expectations.[187] This is not to deny that law really is uncertain. In the words of Machado Derzi, the question is how the legal system can offer stability in an unstable world, making longer time horizons more bearable by creating a predictability that decreases to tolerable levels the high level of uncertainty intrinsic to differentiated societies.[188] Indeed, certainty is continuously desired in an uncertain environment, as she points out.[189] If this quest is not undertaken, according to Gometz, what will prevail is "uncertainty about certainty", potentially generating total disillusionment regarding legal certainty, which is already so often treated as a "dinosaur" or "chimera" of legal philosophy.[190]

Here it is worth pointing out that the statement "there is no certainty" enunciates a description of reality as it is, not as it should be. It is an assertion in the realm of being rather than becoming.[191] The claim that legal certainty cannot exist because

[186] Anne-Laure Valembois, *La Constitutionnalisation de l'exigence de sécurité juridique en Droit français*, Paris, LGDJ, 2005, p. 8.

[187] Andreas von Arnauld, *Rechtssicherheit*, Tübingen, Mohr Siebeck, 2006, p. 98.

[188] Misabel de Abreu Machado Derzi, "Mutações, complexidade, tipo e conceito, sob o signo da segurança e da proteção da confiança", in Heleno Torres (Org.), *Estudos em homenagem a Paulo de Barros Carvalho*, São Paulo, Saraiva, 2007, p. 279. Idem, *Modificações da jurisprudência no Direito Tributário*, São Paulo, Noeses, 2009, p. 213. Likewise: Martin Stötzel, *Vertrauensschutz und Gesetzesrückwirkung*, Frankfurt am Main, Peter Lang, 2002, p. 147.

[189] Misabel de Abreu Machado Derzi, "Princípio da segurança jurídica", *RDT*, n. 64, p. 186, s.d.

[190] Gianmarco Gometz, *La certezza giuridica come prevedibilità*, Torino, Giappichelli, 2005, p. 160.

[191] Federico Arcos Ramírez, *La seguridad jurídica: una teoría formal*, Madrid, Dykinson, 2000, p. 4.

certainty is impossible is based on the assumption that legal certainty means total a priori certainty about the content of legal norms. Of course, if certainty is a *specific point* of absolute normative predetermination, the only certainty is that there is no certainty. To quote Cavalcanti Filho: "Invariability and total uniformity are impossible in human affairs because they negate that which is specific to man. Thus a concern with absolute constancy and stability entails an utterly implausible assumption."[192]

However – and here we come to one of the aims of this study – if certainty is the synthesis of the ideal states of normative knowability, reliability and calculability, realized by means of instruments that assure the accessibility, comprehensiveness, intelligibility, stability, continuity, anteriority and bindingness of the legal order; and if this synthesis is not a point but a *broad spectrum* to be gradually attained in reality by defining clear criteria, parameters and procedures; then the ontological barriers to the search for legal certainty disappear, and the justification of its study reappears intact before the investigator. Thus the problem lies not exactly with legal certainty, but with a specific manner of understanding it: If instead of a dualistic concept (all or nothing), we accept a gradually verifiable concept, then its examination shifts to a new level.[193] In this way we can circumvent Bours's melancholic claim that an autopsy of Belgian law in search of the legal certainty principle, about which there is endless discussion but which is no longer respected, leads to despair.[194]

These considerations serve only to illustrate the scope of this study. My aim is to break with the traditional approach to the analysis of legal certainty (skeptical, partial, vague), and instead to present legal certainty in all its architecture – its signification, its foundations, its structural elements, its dimensions, and its efficacy in the field of public law, especially tax law. I will endeavor to delimit *general criteria* for the restoration of legal certainty as a principle, in the belief that a knowable, reliable and calculable legal order is a precondition both for the realization of fundamental rights and for the realization of state purposes. Here we have yet another paradox: In order to combat uncertainty in law, we must use legal instruments.[195] Thus the uncertainty existing in society is not a reason for resignation but the very best reason to seek an ideal of certainty. In the words of Machado Derzi, "the legal system plays an irreplaceable role, particularly in highly complex contemporary societies."[196]

---

[192]Theophilo Cavalcanti Filho, *O problema da segurança no Direito*, São Paulo, Ed. RT, 1964, p. 159.

[193]Gianmarco Gometz, *La certezza giuridica come prevedibilità*, Torino, Giappichelli, 2005, p. 33. Anne-Laure Valembois, *La Constitutionnalisation de l'exigence de sécurité juridique en Droit français*, Paris, LGDJ, 2005, p. 252.

[194]Jean-Pierre Bours, "Sécurité juridique et Droit Fiscal", in *Les Cahiers de l'Institut d'Études sur la Justice*, n. 4, *Sécurité juridique et fiscalité*, Bruxelles, Bruyant, 2003, p. 63.

[195]Anne-Laure Valembois, *La Constitutionnalisation de l'exigence de sécurité juridique en Droit français*, Paris, LGDJ, 2005, p. 9.

[196]Misabel de Abreu Machado Derzi, *Modificações da jurisprudência no Direito Tributário*, São Paulo, Noeses, 2009, p. 218.

In sum, the justification for this work lies first in the topical relevance and difficulty of the subject, and second in the need to revisit it in order to make fundamental rights and the legal order more effective as a whole.

2 Object (or in What Sense Will Legal Certainty Be Examined?)

The analysis of legal certainty requires a process of progressive semantic delimitation, owing especially to the many meanings of the expression "legal certainty".[197] The first step is to distinguish between legal certainty and other kinds of certainty. Not all certainty is *legal* certainty. There is certainty in the sense of security, physical or external safety, understood as the pursuit of protection against external threats to life, physical or mental integrity, property, and social peace. The state is duty-bound to guarantee "internal security" and "external security" against the threat of violence and terrorism, and performs this duty through preventive and repressive strategies delimited by administrative law and criminal law.[198] There is certainty in the sense of internal or psychological security, understood as a mental state of serenity toward reality.[199] There is certainty or security in a strictly behavioral sense, as a state of mutual trust between two individuals, both in strictly personal relationships and in collective relationships.[200] Although they may relate to it, "legal" certainty differs from all these denotations. Besides denoting a social value protected by the legal order, legal certainty concerns a specific configuration of reality by means of legal institutions. Rather than involving a match between a rule and reality itself, as in the case of the constitutional principles that protect freedom, for example, the legal certainty principle involves a contrast between a constitutional norm and a legal

---

[197]Federico Arcos Ramírez, *La seguridad jurídica: una teoría formal*, Madrid, Dykinson, 2000, p. 7.

[198]Matthias Kötter, *Pfade des Sicherheitsrechts. Begriff von Sicherheit und Autonomie im Spiegel der sicherheitsrechtlichen Debatte der Bundesrepublik Deutschland*, Baden-Baden, Nomos, 2008, pp. 85, 157, 223. Maria José Bernuz Beneitez e Ana Isabel Pérez Cepeda (Orgs.), *La tensión entre libertad y seguridad – Una aproximación sociojurídica*, Rioja, Universidad de La Rioja, 2006. Walter Rudolf, "Sicherheit und Grundrechte", in Michael Brener *et alii* (Orgs.), *Der Staat des Grundgesetzes – Kontinuität und Wandel. FS für Peter Badura zum siebzigsten Geburtstag*, Tübingen, Mohr Siebeck, 2004, p. 464. Ignácio Muñagorri, Juan Pegoraro, (Orgs.), *La relación seguridad-inseguridad en centros urbanos de Europa y América Latina*, Madrid, Dykinson, 2004. Thomas Feltes, "Akteure der Inneren Sicherheit: Vom Öffentlichen zum Privaten", in Hans-Jürgen Lange, H. Peter Ohly, Jo Reichertz (Orgs.), *Auf der Suche nach neuer Sicherheit. Fakten, Theorien und Folgen*, Wiesbaden, VS, 2008, pages 105 and following.

[199]José Luis Palma Fernández, *La seguridad jurídica ante la abundancia de normas*, Madrid, Centro de Estudios Políticos y Constitucionales, 1997, p. 37.

[200]Franz-Xaver Kaufmann, *Sicherheit als soziologisches und sozialpolitisches Problem*, 2ª ed., Stuttgart, 1973, p. 65. Hermann Jahrreiß, *Berechenbarkeit und Recht*, Leipzig, Theodor Weicher, 1927, pages 5, 8.

reality, so that its object is not directly the configuration of reality, but configuration of the law or of a right as an instrument to configure reality, as discussed in detail below.[201]

Even so, legal certainty can still mean many things: certainty "of law"; certainty "through law"; certainty "before the law" or "against the law"; certainty "of rights"; certainty "under the law"; certainty "for a right"; certainty "as a right"; and "certainty in law." To these can be added other meanings which also reflect the ambiguity of the phrase "legal certainty" and the internal dialectics of the "legal certainty principle" itself.

Besides showing the semantic plurality of the phrase "legal certainty", the point of these considerations is to demarcate the object of this study, which is legal certainty in its entirety: certainty of law, through law, before law, of rights, under law, for a right, as a right and in law. The aim is not only to reveal its full extent as a constitutional principle, but also to demonstrate that legal certainty can exist only when *all* these aspects are minimally efficacious, and that a decision can be justified on grounds of legal certainty when *all* its subelements *as a whole* are promoted more than restricted. In other words, it is impossible to attain a minimum of reliability and calculability of the legal order on the basis of its knowability unless legal certainty exists in all its dimensions. If the content of a norm is minimally determinate but its application is arbitrary, there is no legal certainty. Nor can legal certainty exist if norms are determinate and uniformly applied but unjustifiably and permanently altered – and so on. That is to say, legal certainty is either entire or it is not certain.

Although this book sets out to develop a more comprehensive understanding of legal certainty, some aspects are emphasized more than others. However, the more emphasized aspects are not those usually prioritized, such as the duty of determining incidence hypotheses or the protection of trust and legitimate expectations with regard to legislative acts. The elements privileged here, traditionally left in the background or ignored altogether, mostly relate to the analytical decomposition of the legal certainty principle itself, to its normative foundations, to its dimensions, and to its efficacy. In this long list, the highlights are the treatment of normative change by all three branches of government, the effects of judicial decisions in the field of tax law, and the protection of trust or legitimate expectations in the case of invalid state manifestations.

3 Method (or from What Perspective Will Legal Certainty Be Analyzed?)

Having defined the object of this study as legal certainty as a constitutional principle, we still need to determine the method of analysis in the field of tax law, since this analysis could be carried out from several angles. The analysis of

[201] César García Novoa, *El principio de seguridad jurídica en materia tributaria*, Madrid, Marcial Pons, 2000, pages 43, 45.

legal certainty from a *historical* angle involves investigating its development over time, focusing mostly on the following question: How and when did the concept arise and how did legal certainty itself develop? To answer this question, it is necessary to investigate legal doctrine and law over time and in its evolutionary coherence.[202] The analysis of legal certainty from a *sociological* perspective entails investigating its role in social and political systems and institutions, above all in order to answer the following question: Does legal certainty characterize law or set it apart from other systems and institutions? To answer this question, it is necessary to appraise other value systems, such as ethics and economics, and compare their key elements, as well as the evolution of societies, particularly industrial society.[203] In the same perspective, legal certainty can also be investigated in terms of behavioral regularity, i.e. observing whether people's behavior is repetitive and causal, so that whenever 'x' happens, 'y' occurs. This descriptive examination of factual situations in terms of behavioral regularity sets out to anticipate future behavior by analyzing past behavior.[204] The analysis of legal certainty from a *philosophical* standpoint mainly involves an axiological assessment geared to the following questions: Is there a connection between law and legal certainty? What is the (moral) value of legal certainty? To answer these questions successfully, it is indispensable to investigate the concept of law, the meaning of morality, and the relationship between legal certainty and other values.[205] The analysis of legal certainty from a *political* perspective focuses on this question: Is legal certainty a requirement for power to be held legitimately? The answer requires an investigation of the meaning of power and legitimacy, as well as the relationship between the two.[206] The analysis of certainty, including legal certainty, from a *sociopsychological* viewpoint is behavioral and sets out to answer the following questions: What feelings are connected with insecurity and certainty, including legal (un)certainty? Are citizens influenced by legal norms in their decision making? The answers require investigation of people's feelings in response to insecurity and uncertainty, such as fear, panic, serenity, disquiet

---

[202]On this perspective, representing all sources, see Andrea Schrimm-Heins, "Gewissheit und Sicherheit: Geschichte und Bedeutungswandel der Begriffe 'certitudo' und 'securitas'", *Archiv für Begriffsgeschichte*, v. 34, pages 123–213, 1991 (*Teil 1*); v. 35, pages 115–213, 1992 (*Teil 2*).

[203]On this viewpoint, see especially: Franz-Xaver Kaufmann, *Sicherheit als soziologisches und sozialpolitisches Problem,* 2ª ed., Stuttgart, 1973, pages 75 and following; Niklas Luhmann, "Vertrautheit, Zuversicht, Vertrauen. Probleme und Alternativen", in *Vertrauen: Die Grundlage des sozialen Zusammenhalts*, Frankfurt, Campus, 2001, pages 143–160.

[204]Hermann Jahrreiß, *Berechenbarkeit und Recht*, Leipzig, Theodor Weicher, 1927, pages 5, 8. Theophilo Cavalcanti Filho, *O problema da segurança no Direito*, São Paulo, Ed. RT, 1964, p. 24.

[205]On this perspective, see among others: Ricardo García Manrique, *El valor de la seguridad jurídica*, México, Fontanamara, 2007; Federico Arcos Ramírez, *La seguridad jurídica: una teoría formal*, Madrid, Dykinson, 2000, pages 110 and following.

[206]On this perspective, see among others: Federico Arcos Ramírez, *La seguridad jurídica: una teoría formal*, Madrid, Dykinson, 2000, pages 89 and following; Ricardo García Manrique, *El valor de la seguridad jurídica*, México, Fontanamara, 2007, pages 31–80.

or concern, and their reactions to norms, such as obedience or disobedience.[207] The analysis of legal certainty from the perspective of *legal doctrine* focuses on a given legal order and aims to answer this question: What is legal certainty and what requirements arise from it? To do so, it is necessary to examine the elements that comprise the principle in a given legal order, and their relationships with one another. Other perspectives besides these can be adopted, depending on the investigator's interests.

The perspective favored here is the last: the approach based on legal doctrine. This approach can also take several forms, however. One is to analyze legal certainty as a legal norm but focus on the justification of its importance. This perspective may be required by history, if there is no explicit constitutional provision to guarantee legal certainty, or if it is continually violated. Examples in which juridical and political legitimacy are emphasized include, each in his own manner and for his own time, Lopez de Oñate in the suggestive year of 1942, and Corsale in 1970.[208] However, neither produced a detailed investigation of how legal certainty acquires functionality or what types of behavior are indirectly prescribed to make it effective.

Another approach is to examine legal certainty as a norm. In this case the norm is established by the Brazilian Constitution and the investigation revolve around two poles: the search for the meaning and foundations of legal certainty within the constitutional order itself; and an analysis of the functions and significations of the legal certainty principle as a norm according to the Brazilian constitutional order and as realized by the legislative, executive and judiciary. More than seeking to know "why" legal certainty ought to be protected, I set out to determine "how" it must be realized, not least in light of the controversy not about "whether" certainty should be protected, but about "when" and "how" it should be guaranteed.[209] This does not mean the other viewpoints listed above are not also covered. Because the legal certainty principle arose within a given normative context, it reveals a given value and protects specific juridical goods without which it cannot be configured as a minimally effective legal norm. Indeed, in order to know the meaning of legal certainty and the requirements to which it gives rise, in this study it will sometimes be necessary to resort to historical, philosophical and sociological analysis, while maintaining the focus on legal doctrine and theory.

---

[207] On this perspective, see among others: Adalbert Evers, Helga Nowotny, *Über den Umgang mit Unsicherheit. Die Entdeckung der Gestaltbarkeit von Gesellschaft*, Frankfurt am Main, Suhrkamp, 1987; Jerome Frank, *Law and the Modern Mind*, New Brunswick, Transaction, 2009 (1st ed., New York, Brentano's Inc., 1930; 2nd ed., rev., New York, Coward-McCann, 1949).

[208] Flavio Lopez de Oñate, *La certezza del Diritto*, 2nd ed., Milano, Giuffrè, 1968 (1ª ed., 1942). Massimo Corsale, *Certezza del Diritto e crisi di legittimità*, 2nd ed., Milano, Giuffrè, 1979 (1st ed., 1970).

[209] Johanna Hey, *Steuerplanungssicherheit als Rechtsproblem*, Köln, Otto Schmidt, 2002, pages 109, 131.

What is most important is that in this study, convinced as I am that the greatest obstacle to the effectiveness of the legal certainty principle is lack of precision in its analysis, I have set out to reduce the *vagueness* of the phrase "legal certainty" by creating a model capable of enhancing the principle's *realization* and *control*. This avoids justifying Boissart's dictum that "the notion of legal certainty is so general that we can make it say whatever we want."[210] In doing so I decompose the words "legal" and "certainty" semantically and functionally to explore their various aspects, elements and dimensions. This analytical perspective provides a clearer view of the semantic and syntactic problems that are found in theoretical writings on the subject of legal certainty.

The first problem presented by a close reading of the literature is a failure to explore in depth the *semantic extent or breadth* of the phrase "legal certainty." The absence of an accurate definition of the *set of objects designated* by legal certainty has generated interesting but merely apparent doctrinal conflicts. For instance, while Frank treats legal certainty as something unattainable (an "illusion" or "myth"),[211] Bobbio refers to it as something necessary (an intrinsic element) to the existence of law.[212] But how can something be possible and impossible at the same time? The reason is simply that these scholars are not actually discussing the same object. Whereas Frank means by legal certainty the capacity accurately to predict a future judicial decision, Bobbio means calculability of the legal phenomenon in all its complexity. The former analysis is in the plane of being, where legal certainty is a fact, whereas the latter is in the plane of what-ought-to-be, examining legal certainty as a norm.[213] The doctrinal conflict is merely apparent, since the notions of legal certainty at stake do not have the same length, breadth or depth. This is enough to demonstrate that an in-depth analysis of the semantic length and breadth of the expression "legal certainty" is absolutely necessary to a reliable investigation of the legal certainty principle.

The second problem is a failure to explore the *intensity* or *semantic depth* of the terms "legal certainty." The lack of an accurate definition of the *set of properties of the object* referred to as "legal certainty" has generated a high degree of indeterminacy in its doctrinal treatment.

---

[210] "[...] la notion de sécurité juridique est un concept si général que l'on peut lui faire dire ce que l'on veut". S. Boissard, "Comment garantir la stabilité des situations juridiques sans priver l'autorité administrative de tous moyens d'action et sans transiger sur le respect du principe de légalité? Le difficile dilemme du juge administrative", *Les Cahiers du Conseil Constitutionnel*, n. 11, p. 70, 2001.

[211] Jerome Frank, *Law and the Modern Mind*, New Brunswick, Transaction, 2009, p. 13 (1st ed., New York, Brentano's Inc., 1930; 2nd ed., rev., New York, Coward-McCann, 1949).

[212] Norberto Bobbio, "La certezza del Diritto é un mito?" *Rivista Internazionale di Filosofia del Diritto*, n. 28, p. 150, 1951.

[213] Letizia Gianformaggio, "Certezza del Diritto", in Enrico Diciotti, Vito Velluzzi (Orgs.), *Filosofia del Diritto e ragionamento giuridico,* Torino, Giappichelli, 2008, p. 84.

This doctrinal indeterminacy may be the result, on one hand, of a failure to specify the aspect of legal certainty that is being examined. For example, while Calmes treats legal certainty as a "principle",[214] Sobota treats it as a "right."[215] But how can something be a "principle" and a "right" at the same time? This happens because the expression "legal certainty" can be used to mean both an objective norm designed to guarantee the stability of the legal order as a whole to the benefit of the community, and the reflexive application of that very same norm to a specific situation, benefiting one individual. Although both writers examine the same object, one analyzes its objective aspect while the other analyzes its subjective or reflexive aspect.

Doctrinal indeterminacy may be the result, on the other hand, of a failure to specify the angle from which a given aspect of legal certainty is analyzed. Three examples will suffice to clarify the importance of the angle of analysis to the examination of the elements of legal certainty. First, whereas irretroactivity is part of the ideal of predictability of the legal order for Calmes,[216] for von Arnauld it is part of the ideal of stability of the legal order.[217] It is legitimate to ask who is right. In fact, while both refer to the same aspect (finalistic) of the same object (legal certainty), they are not examining this aspect from the same angle. The former analyzes irretroactivity prospectively (from present to future), i.e. as a requirement for maintaining present norms in the future. The latter analyzes irretroactivity retrospectively (from present to past), i.e. as a requirement for maintaining past accomplishments in the present. In other words, irretroactivity can mean both the requirement of present stabilization of effects produced in the past and the duty of future stabilization of effects produced in the present. Second, while Novoa treats the same irretroactivity as part of normative certainty of orientation and hence of the ideal of knowability,[218] Perez Luño includes it in the structural dimension of certainty rather than the functional dimension,[219] and von Arnauld treats it as an integral part of the ideal of reliability.[220] Again, it is a matter of perspective: The former examines irretroactivity from a present perspective to show that citizens can be guided only by a norm in force at the time of their action, whereas von Arnauld investigates irretroactivity from a past perspective with the aim of proving that it

[214]Sylvia Calmes, *Du principe de protection de la confiance légitime en Droits allemand, communautaire et français*, Paris, Dalloz, 2001, p. 163.

[215]Katharina Sobota, *Das Prinzip Rechtsstaat*, Tübingen, Mohr Siebeck, 1997, p. 507.

[216]Sylvia Calmes, *Du principe de protection de la confiance légitime en Droits allemand, communautaire et français*, Paris, Dalloz, 2001, p. 159.

[217]Andreas von Arnauld, *Rechtssicherheit*, Tübingen, Mohr Siebeck, 2006, p. 324.

[218]César García Novoa, *El principio de seguridad jurídica en materia tributaria*, Madrid, Marcial Pons, 2000, p. 76.

[219]Antonio Enrique Perez Luño, *La seguridad jurídica*, Barcelona, Ariel, 1991, p. 24.

[220]Andreas von Arnauld, *Rechtssicherheit*, Tübingen, Mohr Siebeck, 2006, p. 324.

is wrong to surprise citizens by retroactively applying a new norm if they comply with the norm in force at the time of their action. Third, protection of acquired rights depends on objective elements for Valembois[221] but is a form of subjective inviolability for Arcos Ramírez.[222] Who is right? Strictly speaking, although both refer to the same element (acquired rights), they do so from different angles, the former from the angle of the subjective situations presupposed by its application, the latter from the angle of the objective factors required by the legal order for its application. In other words, acquired rights can be analyzed both in terms of the subjective situations they are supposed to protect and from the angle of the objective requirements for such protection. In short, acquired rights are an instrument for the protection of subjective situations whose application depends on the observance of objective requirements.

Doctrinal indeterminacy with regard to the object of the analysis and the angle from which it is analyzed occurs because authors address legal certainty with differing degrees of intensity, depth and understanding, but fail to point out or discuss this diversity. Hence the imperative need for an in-depth analysis of the intensity or semantic profundity of the expression "legal certainty" if the legal certainty principle is to be examined with security and reliability.

The point of the above considerations is merely to justify the analytical method used below. Either the object of the analysis, the aspect investigated and the perspective adopted are properly defined, or legal certainty will prove a "giant with feet of clay" (*un colosse aux pieds d'argile*), to quote Valembois.[223] The analysis developed in this book therefore starts from the presupposition that the more precisely *certainty* is defined, the more intersubjectively certain and secure the results of the investigation will be.[224] And the more certain the results, the more certain the efficacy of the legal certainty principle. What is absolutely unacceptable, as stressed by Arcos Ramírez, is not to define legal certainty because it is considered so obvious that no definition is necessary.[225]

[221] Anne-Laure Valembois, *La Constitutionnalisation de l'exigence de sécurité juridique en Droit français*, Paris, LGDJ, 2005, p. 202.

[222] Federico Arcos Ramírez, *La seguridad jurídica: una teoría formal*, Madrid, Dykinson, 2000, p. 3.

[223] Anne-Laure Valembois, *La Constitutionnalisation de l'exigence de sécurité juridique en Droit français*, Paris, LGDJ, 2005, p. 65.

[224] Gianmarco Gometz, *La certezza giuridica come prevedibilità*, Torino, Giappichelli, 2005, p. 161.

[225] Federico Arcos Ramírez, *La seguridad jurídica: una teoría formal*, Madrid, Dykinson, 2000, p. 9.

4 Plan (or How Will the Analysis of Legal Certainty Be Structured?)

The decision to investigate legal certainty as a norm of the Brazilian Constitution from a doctrinal perspective based primarily on the analytical and functional method entails the following work plan.

Since the foundations and elements of something can be analyzed only when it is known what they are foundations and elements of, the first part of the study examines the meaning of legal certainty. This part examines the various denotations of legal certainty so as to delimit legal certainty compared to other types of certainty and to understand the several meanings that the expression "legal certainty" may have.

The second part addresses the foundations of or justifications for legal certainty. Not only those expressed by the Constitution, but also all the foundations and justifications that directly or indirectly relate to the pursuit of the ideals of reliability and calculability of the legal order based on its knowability. Only then is a normative concept of legal certainty and tax law certainty proposed.

Once legal certainty has been defined and its foundations established, the analysis proceeds to its elements: knowability, reliability, and calculability. This third part is the core of the study and analyzes the requirements for legal certainty to be effective. As stated earlier, while the aim is to examine all elements of the legal certainty principle, this does not mean some are not more thoroughly investigated than others. Thus topical issues in case law and jurisprudential change, as well as the effects of unconstitutionality rulings, are investigated in greater depth. The focus is therefore on the dynamic dimension of legal certainty, which is more elucidatory with regard to transition in tax law.

The fourth part examines the efficacy of the legal certainty principle, encompassing an analysis of its effects and of its weight, especially against other principles, also known as "sibling principles" (*Geschwisterprinzipien*), such as the principles of justice and solidarity.

This plan is not without its problems of circularity, which are unavoidable since before the meaning of an object can be analyzed, it is necessary to investigate its foundations but before analyzing the foundations it is necessary to verify exactly what they are the foundations of. In other words, meaning depends on foundations, and foundations depend on meaning. The circularity does not end there: Before defining the elements of an object, it is necessary to analyze its foundations because they are the basis from which arises the object whose elements are to be explained, but before analyzing the foundations it is necessary to investigate the elements of the object for which they are a basis. In other words, the elements depend on the foundations, and the foundations on the elements. And so forth, from the beginning to the end of this study.

This circularity is not only in the work plan. It is also identifiable in the construction of the elements of the legal certainty principle itself. The ideals of knowability, reliability and calculability are shown here to be parts of the ideal states that together make up the legal certainty principle. They are distinct but interpenetrate to some extent.[226] One example suffices to illustrate the point: Trust and reliance on law requires knowledge of the laws; knowledge of law is therefore a presupposition for it to be stable; however, laws that change often and are unstable are hard to know; thus stability of law is a condition of its knowability. In other words, knowledge of law is a presupposition of its stability, but stability is also a condition for knowledge of law. This interpenetration applies to all the elements of legal certainty. On one hand, it explains the differences between theoretical definitions of legal certainty, which are mostly apparent: For example, von Arnauld argues that certainty of law is a precondition of certainty through law,[227] whereas for Novoa, on the contrary, certainty through law is a presupposition for certainty of law.[228] On the other hand, it clarifies the internal relationships between the states of affairs that are treated here as elements of legal certainty, since they mutually require and condition one another. Not surprisingly, certainty is often called "protean" because it changes shape so frequently.[229]

The work plan for this study acknowledges these pitfalls and attempts to avoid them by building and developing parts separately and in a progressive and related manner. The definition of certainty presented in the first chapter is both preliminary, built on the etymology of the word, and based on jurisprudence directly relating to the theme; the foundations are analyzed on the basis of this preliminary definition presented in chapter "Non-legal Certainty", whereby this definition is progressively reworked and perfected; the elements are analyzed in terms of the foundations but going further to include the realization of the foundations in statutory legislation, administrative law and case law. Circularities are circumvented whenever possible through these precautions, while retaining clarity.

In sum, this study sets out to perform a hard task: the analysis of the meaning, dimensions, elements, foundations and efficacy of legal and tax law certainty as a principle of the Brazilian constitutional order. Throughout the study attempts are made to answer the most important questions concerning legal certainty: Certainty based on what – on its own protection, on the anticipation of behavior or on the establishment of ideals? Which certainty – non-legal certainty or legal certainty and, if the latter, legal certainty as certainty of law, through law, before the law, under law, of rights, of a right, as a right, or in law? Certainty of whom – citizens or the state? Certainty by whom –citizens or the state and, if the latter, by the legislative, executive or judiciary? Certainty for whom – citizens, the state or society as a whole? Certainty how – by means of predictable rules, the application of rules,

[226] Anne-Laure Valembois, *La Constitutionnalisation de l'exigence de sécurité juridique en Droit français*, Paris, LGDJ, 2005, p. 251.

[227] Andreas von Arnauld, *Rechtssicherheit*, Tübingen, Mohr Siebeck, 2006, p. 392.

[228] César García Novoa, *El principio de seguridad jurídica en materia tributaria*, Madrid, Marcial Pons, 2000, p. 72.

[229] Frédéric Douet, *Contribution à l'étude de la sécurité juridique en Droit interne français*, Paris, LGDJ, 1997, p. 4.

the establishment of procedures or guarantees for rights? And so on. This conceptual separation of the aspects, elements and dimensions of legal certainty by no means ignores the difficulty of doing so in many cases or forgets that they are often applied simultaneously. As well noted by Zanella Di Pietro, the various principles that make up the legal order are intertwined and it is often hard to tell them apart.[230]

The normative basis for this study is the Brazilian legal order. This material research field does not prevent but rather calls for the examination of foreign jurisprudence, notably German, Italian, French, Spanish, Anglo-American and Portuguese. However, the point is not to glean conclusions about foreign legal orders, in the sense that if a given position is favored abroad it should also be adopted in Brazil. On the contrary, the point of investigating foreign jurisprudence and law is to observe the arguments scholars use to interpret and apply rules and principles positivated in a similar manner as in Brazil. In addition, the painstaking examination of foreign jurisprudence regarding several aspects of the legal certainty principle both reveals the deficiencies of foreign legal doctrine and case law and pinpoints, by comparison, the unique features of the Brazilian legal order. An example of the deficiencies of foreign models is the case law of Germany's Federal Constitutional Court concerning modulation of the effects of concentrated judicial review decisions. While this technique is copied in Brazil by legislators as well as judges as if it were the quintessence of theoretical development, it is vigorously criticized by a great many German legal scholars, who go so far as to state that "the Constitutional Court's decision-making model is not worthy of imitation (*nachahmenswert*)",[231] or, referring to the upholding of unconstitutional acts, that "this concept should be abandoned".[232] An example of the unique features of the Brazilian legal order can be found in the normative foundations of the legal certainty principle. Because the Constitution of Brazil, unlike those of other countries, contains express provisions concerning the partial ideals that make up the legal certainty principle, not only is its concept different but also some of its subelements must be applied more rigidly than in other orders. This is true for the rules protecting acquired rights, completed legal acts, *res iudicata* and taxable events, which cannot be overruled on public interest grounds, as they can exceptionally in Germany, Spain, France and Italy. In sum, I refer to foreign legal doctrine carefully and only to reveal the peculiarities of the Brazilian legal system. These unique features are especially evident in tax law, as the Brazilian Constitution is rigid and detailed

[230]Maria Sylvia Zanella Di Pietro, "Os princípios da proteção à confiança, da segurança jurídica e da boa-fé na anulação do ato administrativo", in Fabrício Motta (Org.), *Direito Público Atual: estudos em homenagem ao Professor Nélson Figueiredo*, Instituto de Direito Administrativo de Goiás (IDAG), Belo Horizonte, Fórum, 2008, p. 298.

[231]Roman Seer, Jörg Peter Müller, "Begrenzung der Wirkungen seiner Richtersprüche durch den EuGH", *IWB*, n. 5, Gruppe 2, Fach 11, p. 262, 2008.

[232]Christoph Moes, "Die Anordnung der befristeten Fortgeltung verfassungswidriger Steuergesetze durch das Bundesverfassungsgericht", *StuW*, n. 1, p. 36, 2008.

in tax matters.[233] My considerations regarding comparative law at all times obey Legrand's requirement as to its main purpose: the perception of differences.[234]

In contrast, this book presents a different concept of legal certainty in the field of tax law.

The concept of legal certainty developed below is different in form, construction methodology and verification method.

The difference in form resides in the use of a non-classificatory concept of legal certainty. Instead of a bivalent concept of legal certainty based on the duality "certainty/uncertainty", I propose a gradual multi-layered concept grounded in the range of gradations between states of "greater or lesser certainty." This concept of legal certainty in turn reflects a semantic-argumentative concept of law: Instead of understanding law as something entirely given a priori, to be merely described by the judge through discourse (the objectivist concept of law), or as a mere argumentative activity not subject to any prior constraints in terms of limits to the decision-making process (the argumentative concept of law), the framework developed here envisages law in an intermediate position between these two conceptions, i.e. as a reconstructive practice in which minimum meanings are realized on the basis of juridico-rational structures of legitimation, determination, argumentation and justification. The definition of legal certainty in turn reflects this concept of law.

The differentiating factor with regard to the construction methodology is the analytical process used to reduce conceptual vagueness. Instead of investigating the legal certainty principle by means of an analysis that focuses on a description of its evolution in history and legal doctrine, and/or presenting a mere eulogy, I have chosen to pursue an investigation based on decomposition of the concept into the various aspects that must be distinguished in order for it to be understood properly. This entails developing a model capable of explaining and operationalizing control of the legal certainty principle.

The difference in conceptual verification method lies in the introduction of a legal concept of legal certainty: Instead of a direct empirical concept of legal certainty verified by means of effective and factually observable prediction, this study deploys a normative concept that identifies properties whose controllability depends on observing certain theoretical conditions capable of pointing to the potential to promote certain states of affairs. This concept is also normative in the sense that instead of being presented merely as something desirable legal certainty is described as a prescription for behavior that increases the degree to which certain states of affairs are made possible.

As for the elements of the concept of legal certainty, this book proposes a different and more complex concept: Instead of analyzing legal certainty partially, i.e. as a norm that aims to preserve only one ideal (such as predictability or

---

[233] Geraldo Ataliba, *Sistema constitucional tributário brasileiro*, São Paulo, Ed. RT, 1968, p. 39.

[234] P. Legrand, "Comparer", in *Le Droit Comparé: aujourd'hui et demain*, Paris, Société de Législation Comparée, 1995, p. 37.

stability), one dimension (as objective principle or fundamental right) or one aspect (certainty of law, through law, before the law, under law, of rights, of a right, for a right, or as a right), for example, the study seeks to present and explain the legal certainty principle as a norm made up of a multiplicity of ideals, dimensions and aspects to be considered together, depending on the normative context in which it is applied. Even with regard to each of these elements, moreover, the study proposes to change not only the nomenclature but also the content of the ideal states whose promotion is determined by the legal certainty principle: instead of determinacy, knowability; instead of immutability, reliability; instead of predictability, calculability. Underlying this conception is an understanding of law not precisely as a given object or as an object to be entirely constructed, but as an argumentative activity involving the reconstruction of normative meanings based on hermeneutical and applicative postulates.

The legal certainty principle determines a search for the ideals of knowability, reliability and calculability in law. These ideals, however, can be compared to the tip of an iceberg, in the sense that they correspond only to that portion of legal certainty that can be seen above sea level, as it were, while most of its mass is submerged at greater depths. Given that the legal certainty principle delimits all that is fundamental for citizens to shape the present and freely and autonomously plan the future in accordance with law and without deceit or unjustified surprise, an inquiry into legal certainty entails investigating on one hand the rights of freedom, equality, and dignity, and on the other the principles relating to state action. Moreover, the ideals in question indirectly reveal the kind of society desired via the type of state and citizenry that result from their configuration. The requirement of knowability enables citizens to "know" what they "may or may not do" according to law. In a state of reliability and calculability this requirement enables citizens to act or refrain from acting with autonomy and freedom, so that they are able to "be or not to be" what they wish and have the potential to be. In other words, legal certainty is an instrument whereby citizens know, in advance and seriously, what they can do so that they can better become what they are capable of being and what they want to be. As stressed by Ataliba, citizens are certain and secure when they are sure that law is objectively monolithic and that the behavior of the state and other citizens will not deviate from it.[235] In sum, legal certainty is the instrument with which to achieve freedom, and freedom is the means to dignity.

In light of the above, it should be added that parallel to the gradations between the poles of legal certainty and uncertainty there is a scale between types of citizen at either extreme: active and passive, outgoing and reticent, noncommittal and surefooted, confident and diffident, innovative and repetitive, investor and saver, punctilious taxpayer and tax evader. There are also different kinds of state: acting openly or in secrecy, loyal or disloyal, candid or deceitful, respectful or

[235] Geraldo Ataliba, *República e Constituição*, 3rd ed., São Paulo, Malheiros Editores, 2011, p. 184.

disrespectful, careful or careless. Relations between the state and citizens may be close or distant, adversarial or associative, collaborative or separatist. The values that flourish in society range from certainty or uncertainty to belief or disbelief, strictness or permissiveness, order or chaos, stability or instability. As all these consequences of (un)certainty show, depending on the degree to which legal certainty is realized, law – or taxes and the activities involved in enforcing and collecting them – can be either a "wall" or a "bridge" for human realization under the rule of law. It can therefore be said that investigating legal certainty is to discover what kind of state, citizens, society and values to construct. This book is indeed about legal certainty, but more importantly it is about freedom, equality and dignity, and therefore about moderation or temperance, about civility, and about decency in exercising the power to tax.

The title of this book (*Certainty in Law*) was not chosen by chance. It could have been "Tax Law Certainty", but this would emphasize tax law instead of certainty, as if the latter were only an appendage of the former. As will be explained in due course, the expression "legal certainty" can have several meanings: certainty "of law," "through law," "as a right," "before the law," "under law," "of a right (or rights)" or "in law." However, the expression that best represents the concept of legal certainty advocated in this book is "certainty in law", because it illustrates most clearly the understanding that legal certainty is not an intrinsic quality of law or legal norms, linked to their prior determination, but a product whose existence to a greater or lesser extent depends on a combination of criteria and argumentative structures to be verified within the very process of applying the law. This justifies the emphasis on legal certainty in general and on its realization "in" law.

The subtitle focuses on permanence, change, and realization. The emphasis is thus placed on transition. In this sense, the title of this book could also be "Transitional Tax Law". However, the overarching idea, the golden thread running through legal certainty, is the understanding of taxation as it relates to time, connecting past, present and future, and as it relates to application, connecting the abstract and concrete planes. Thus the ideal of knowability delimits the conditions for the present exercise of freedom and property rights; the ideal of reliability represents the retrospective perspective in terms of the change from past to present, showing what from the past should remain in the present; the ideal of calculability prospectively illustrates the passage from present to future, showing what in the present should be kept in the transition to the future; and the transparency of semantic-argumentative control reveals the need for discoursive objectivity in the transition from provision to norm, and from norm to decision. In other words, the subject of this book is transition in tax law based on the legal certainty principle and from the angle of the fundamental rights of freedom, property, equality, and dignity. Hence the preference for the more general title *Certainty in Law*. Because transition is founded on the legal certainty principle, which serves as the criterion for deciding what can change and what ought to remain, this study differs from other more common studies. "Transitory law" is the term traditionally used to refer to the set of norms that regulate conflicts between laws over time, typically based on the notion of legal status and solved by conflict rules.[236] The question underlying this analysis is whether events were completed while a changed law was in force, in which case validity is one of the main criteria. The expression "transitional provisions" in turn typically refers to a set of temporary and secondary provisions that govern the application of others, using various techniques such as deferred efficacy. These aim to increase clarity, temporarily disregard traditional rules relating to conflicts between laws, decrease complexity, or even defer the enforcement of a new law.[237] However, this book adopts a different perspective: It does not examine conflicts of law from the perspective of completed acts or facts, nor does it analyze secondary temporary provisions designed to assure the immediate or deferred application of new laws. What it does do is investigate the limits of transition in the legal order, and in tax law, from the angle of legal certainty, which in turn is grounded in fundamental rights, within the scope of the executive and judiciary as well as the legislative, even when properly speaking there is no conflict between laws or acquired rights, but simply rights that must be respected because they were exercised in a certain manner and with a certain intensity in the past. Thus the object of this study is not circumscribed to the succession of norms over time, but extends to the very realization of law, be it from a temporal or applicative perspective. This new and broader analysis, based on equally innovative criteria, indeed deserves to be called transitional law.[238]

Transitional law in the sense defined here is not the same as intertemporal or transitory law. They differ in object, purpose, criteria, foundations and scope. The central object of intertemporal law is conflicts between laws in time, whereas transitional law deals with any normative changes originating in the legislative, executive or judiciary, seeking to differentiate them according to the role of each branch. Intertemporal law aims basically to permit change by eliminating conflicts among norms, thereby preserving the power to legislate and furthering the public interest, whereas transitional law aims to harmonize change with permanence, mainly in order to assure respect for the fundamental rights of freedom, property, equality and dignity. Intertemporal law employs criteria found primarily at the abstract normative level to verify the occurrence of acts or facts from the perspective of the modified norm, whereas transitional law seeks a solution based above all on the concrete facts by verifying the extent to which acts of disposal have been performed from the angle of fundamental rights, regardless of the validity of the previous norm and the occurrence of acts or facts according to its provisions. Intertemporal law is grounded primarily in competence rules, whereas transitional law combines these

---

[236]Paul Roubier, *Le Droit transitoire: conflits des lois dans le temps*, Paris, Dalloz, 1929/1933 (1st ed., 2. vs.), 1960 (2nd ed., 1 v.), 2008 (reprint of 2nd ed.), pages 3 and 146 and following. Michael Koch, *Die Grundsätze des intertemporalen Rechts im Verwaltungsprozess – Vertrauensschutz im verwaltungsgerichtlichen Verfahren*, Berlin, Duncker und Humblot, 2009, p. 40.

[237]Gweltz Éveillard, *Les dispositions transitoires en Droit Public français*, Paris, Dalloz, 2007, pages 6, 8, 49, 117, 193 and following.

[238]Ake Frändberg, "Retroactivity, Simulactivity, Infraactivity", in Jes Bjarup, Mogens Blegvad (Orgs.), *Time, Law and Society*, Stuttgart, Franz Steiner, 1995, p. 55.

with fundamental rights. Intertemporal law concerns the relationship between two norms by virtue of a fact, or metaphorically and in brief between two norms and a point, whereas transitional law involves the relationship between two norms and the exercise of fundamental rights by one or more individuals, or between two norms and a line. Thus transitional law is grounded in the legal certainty principle, and this principle in turn is grounded in a combination of principles with fundamental rights. Transitional law, constructed by delimiting the definition, content and efficacy of the legal certainty principle in the field of tax law, may be called "transitional tax law", grounded in tax law certainty, or the realization of law from a foundational viewpoint applied to tax law. It is "tax law in movement", including in the semantic field of the word "movement" the semantic-argumentative activity necessary to its concretization. In sum, it is "tax law in action."

Given the importance and complexity of the subject, the fundamental questions regarding legal certainty listed above are raised throughout this book in order to determine intersubjective criteria that lead to the discovery and control of the concrete behavior whose effects contribute to the promotion of the goals of reliability and calculability of the legal order based on its knowability. Without this meticulous construction, the normative ideal of legal certainty, like other ideals such as equality or freedom, cannot be completely realized. As Molfessis recalls, the ends of legal certainty "are not obtained by proclamation."[239] Without painstaking reduction of indeterminacy in all respects, legal certainty will be no more than a propagandistic slogan (*propagandistisches Schlagwort*) or a "legal and political sedative."[240]

The arguments set out in this book are also intended to be knowable, reliable and calculable (at least minimally so, given the limitations of its author). Thus it is an attempt to study certainty with certainty and through certainty. The challenges of the subject are far from negligible. There are indeed subjects so complex that they cannot be dealt with exhaustively in a single work, but at the same time so fundamental that they need to be examined in a single work. The legal certainty principle is one such subject – complex but fundamental. This conclusion justifies Ferraz Júnior's statement that "legal certainty is at the same time one of the simplest and most complex aspects of law."[241]

Because the subject is broad and multifaceted, and the analysis is full of paradoxes and circularities, the task of examining certainty must begin with the progressive elimination of the spiritual uncertainty that so daunting a task inspires in the mind of one who humbly dares take it on.

[239] Nicolas Molfessis, "Combattre l'insécurité juridique ou la lutte du système juridique contre lui-même", in *Sécurité juridique et complexité du Droit*, Conseil d'État, *Rapport Public 2006, Études et documents* n. 57, Paris, Documentation française, 2006, p. 391.

[240] Andreas von Arnauld, *Rechtssicherheit*, Tübingen, Mohr Siebeck, 2006, pages 48, 116.

[241] Tércio Sampaio Ferraz Júnior, "Segurança jurídica e normas gerais tributárias", *RDT*, issues 17–18, p. 51, São Paulo, 1981.

Part I
Meaning of Legal Certainty

Legal certainty requires positivity of law: when it is impossible to say what is just, then it is necessary to define what ought to be legal, so that what the law determines can be enforced. (Gustav Radbruch, *Rechtsphilosophie. Studienausgabe*, 2nd ed., Heidelberg, C. F. Müller, 2003 (1932), p. 73)

The law may be unjust or flawed, but it must never be uncertain, for lack of certainty negates the very essence of law. (L. Recaséns Siches, *Filosofía del Derecho*, México, Porrúa, 1959, p. 224)

The Meaning of Legal Certainty (or What Can Legal Certainty Mean?)

Although great care should be taken when making generalizations about mental states interpreted from a specifically cultural point of view – which seems imperative for the current stage of our subject –, one can hardly deny the fundamental anthropological notion that man is an imperfect being, a frightened being, an active being who orients his behavior toward the future and seeks to create and stabilize the conditions of his own future existence. (Franz-Xaver Kaufmann, *Sicherheit als soziologisches und sozialpolitisches Problem*, 2nd ed., Stuttgart, 1973, p. 11)

Without security, it is impossible for man either to develop his powers or to enjoy the fruits of his exertion; for without security there can be no freedom. (Wilhelm von Humboldt, *Über die Grenzen der Wirksamkeit des Staates (1792)*, 2nd ed., Heidelberg, Carl Winter, 1954, p. 66)

Trust is the foundation of human relations and also of the law. Anyone who wishes to learn from another, undertake something with him or follow his example must trust him. This is why the reliability of the legal order is a fundamental condition of a libertarian constitution. People trust the law only if it is familiar to them. (Paul Kirchhof, "Vertrauensschutz im Steuerrecht", in Heinz-Jürgen Pezzer (Org.), *Vertrauensschutz im Steuerrecht*, "Deutsche Steuerjuristische Gesellschaft", v. 27, Köln, Otto Schmidt, 2004, p. 1)

> Only trust in the continuity of state institutions and binding rules can lay the foundations for the development of human freedom. (Dieter Birk, "Kontinuitätsgewähr und Vertrauensschutz", in Heinz-Jürgen Pezzer (Org.), *Vertrauensschutz im Steuerrecht*, "Deutsche Steuerjuristische Gesellschaft", v. 27, Köln, Otto Schmidt, 2004, p. 11)

Scholars have long used the expression "legal certainty" with various meanings.[1] The most evident reason derives from the several meanings of "certainty" and of "legal certainty" itself.[2] The former can denote a psychological state of absence of fear or distance from danger. Possible connotations of the latter depend on how "certainty" and "legal" are defined.

Thus the meaning of "certainty" must first be defined. The next step is to explain the concept of "legal certainty" and compare it to other types of certainty.[3] This is not enough, however. It is also necessary to define the connotations of "legal certainty" in order to proceed to a precise analysis of the expression "tax law certainty." Otherwise the discussion of legal certainty would become a "pathetic shipwreck in the semantic ocean," to quote Mezquita del Cacho's warning.[4] This is the focus of the rest of parts "Meaning of Legal Certainty", "Justification of Legal Certainty", and "Definition of Legal Certainty".

[1] Max Rümelin, *Die Rechtssicherheit*, Tübingen, Mohr Siebeck, 1924, p. 2.

[2] Andreas von Arnauld, *Rechtssicherheit*, Tübingen, Mohr Siebeck, 2006, pp. 39, 64 e 103; Bertrand Mathieu, "La sécurité juridique: un principe constitutionnel clandestin mais efficient", in Patrick Fraisseix (Org.), *Mélanges Patrice Gélard – Droit Constitutionnel*, Paris, Montchrestien, 1999, p. 301.

[3] Gianmarco Gometz, *La certezza giuridica come prevedibilità*, Torino, Giappichelli, 2005, p. 9.

[4] José L. Mezquita del Cacho, *Seguridad jurídica y sistema cautelar*, v. 1, "Teoría de la seguridad jurídica", Barcelona, Bosch, 1989, p. 48.

Non-legal Certainty

Abstract The various non-legal meanings of the concept of certainty are discussed, starting with the meaning of the word "certainty" as often used to refer to a sense of external, physical, or objective security. Next is certainty in the sense of trust (in psychology, economics, philosophy, and political science), and protection of individual or collective goods. These definitions are used to differentiate simple certainty from legal certainty properly speaking. The goal is to demonstrate that legal certainty takes on importance only when it transcends the individual psychological dimension and enters the socio-axiological (but not merely behavioral) dimension: thus legal certainty represents certainty as an intersubjective value event associated with the law of a given society, either as a norm or as a value, and with the legal universe as its object or instrument.

The word "certainty" is often used to refer to a sense of external, physical or objective security, i.e. the feeling of being safe and protected against external threats such as violence, crime, or pain.[1] This meaning can be illustrated by the expression "at home man is safe from cold" (certain to be warm) and "in a bunker the citizen is safe from airstrikes" (certain to be protected). In this definition, "being safe" means being protected from or against something that represents an external threat. Instead of the absence of doubt, certainty or safety is the absence of fear.[2] Indeed, French has both *sécurité*, meaning safety, and *sûreté*, meaning security.[3] The former may also denote certainty or assurance.[4] English also has two different words: *certainty*, meaning something objective, and *safety*, meaning mostly something subjective.

---

[1]Andrea Schrimm-Heins, "Gewissheit und Sicherheit: Geschichte und Bedeutungswandel der Begriffe 'certitudo' und 'securitas'" (Teil 1), *Archiv für Begriffsgeschichte* 34, p. 133, 1991; Federico Arcos Ramírez, *La seguridad jurídica: una teoría formal*, Madrid, Dykinson, 2000, p. 15; Andreas von Arnauld, *Rechtssicherheit*, Tübingen, Mohr Siebeck, 2006, p. 97.

[2]José L. Mezquita del Cacho, *Seguridad jurídica y sistema cautelar*, v. 1, "Teoría de la seguridad jurídica", Barcelona, Bosch, 1989, p. 213.

[3]Frédéric Douet, *Contribution à l'étude de la sécurité juridique en Droit Interne Français*, Paris, LGDJ, 1997, p. 2.

[4]Bertrand Mathieu, "La sécurité juridique: un principe constitutionnel clandestin mais efficient", in Patrick Fraisseix (Org.), *Mélanges Patrice Gélard – Droit Constitutionnel*, Paris, Montchrestien, 1999, p. 303.

© Springer International Publishing Switzerland 2016
H. Ávila, *Certainty in Law*, Law and Philosophy Library 114,
DOI 10.1007/978-3-319-33407-3_2

That's whay certainty may also be used in an internal, psychological or subjective sense to refer to freedom from fear and anxiety, or peace of mind.[5] In English this feeling is called safety, but in other languages the word certainty also embodies this meaning. In these cases it expresses an individual psychological dimension and is thus part of the subject matter of *Psychology*, which analyzes the mental or emotional causes of fear and the elements of trust, as in Freud,[6] and of *Anthropology*, which seeks the ideal of certainty in the very nature of man, as in Evers & Nowotny.[7] In sum, certainty as a psychological state reflects what the ancients called *animi tranquillitas*, which as an absence of worries underlies the origins of *segurança* in Portuguese in the Latin "*sine + cura*" (without a care).[8] The distinction is acutely noted by Reale:

> One ought to distinguish between a 'feeling of certainty' – i.e. the state of mind of individuals and groups with the intent of enjoying a set of guarantees – and the guarantees in themselves as a set of instrumental measures sufficient to generate and protect such a state of peace and harmony.[9]

The same differentiation is identified within the scope of tax law by Villegas, who distinguishes between subjective certainty – a "feeling of trust" – and objective certainty expressed in the guarantees assured to people, assets or rights by society.[10]

Certainty in the sense of trust can be further analyzed from several angles: that of *Psychology*, focusing on features of relations of trust such as uncertainty and risk, and its effects, such as motivation, as in Petermann[11]; *Economics*, investigating trust as a principle for organization and exchange in order to learn how relations between economic agents are formed and enhanced, as in Ripperger and Schweer & Thies;[12] *Sociology*, observing trust as a social value that predicts behaviors and is fundamental to intensify social relations, control the future and decrease

---

[5]Franz-Xaver Kaufmann, *Sicherheit als soziologisches und sozialpolitisches Problem*, 2nd ed., Stuttgart, 1973, p. 10; Andrea Schrimm-Heins, "Gewissheit und Sicherheit: Geschichte und Bedeutungswandel der Begriffe 'certitudo' und 'securitas'" (Teil 1), *Archiv für Begriffsgeschichte* 34, p. 137, 1991.

[6]Sigmund Freud, *Abriß der Psychoanalyse*, Frankfurt am Main, 1960; Franz Petermann, *Psychologie des Vertrauens*, 3rd ed., Göttingen, Hogrefe, 1996.

[7]Adalbert Evers e Helga Nowotny, *Über den Umgang mit Unsicherheit. Die Entdeckung der Gestaltbarkeit von Gesellschaft*, Frankfurt am Main, Suhrkamp, 1987.

[8]Andrea Schrimm-Heins, "Gewissheit und Sicherheit: Geschichte und Bedeutungswandel der Begriffe 'certitudo' und 'securitas'" (*Teil* 1), *Archiv für Begriffsgeschichte* 34, p. 134, 1991; José Roberto Vieira, "Medidas provisórias tributárias e segurança jurídica: a insólita opção estatal pelo 'viver perigosamente'", in Aires Fernandino Barreto *et alii* (Orgs.), *Segurança jurídica na tributação e Estado de Direito*, São Paulo, Noeses, 2005, p. 319.

[9]Miguel Reale, "Prefácio", in Theophilo Cavalcanti Filho, *O problema da segurança no Direito*, São Paulo, Ed. RT, 1964, p. IV.

[10]Héctor Villegas, "Principio de seguridad jurídica en la creación y aplicación del tributo", *RDT* 66, p. 10, São Paulo, s.d.

[11]Franz Petermann, *Psychologie des Vertrauens*, 3rd ed., Göttingen, Hogrefe, 1996.

[12]Tanja Ripperger, *Ökonomik des Vertrauens*, 2nd ed., Tübingen, Mohr Siebeck, 2003; Martin Schweer e Barbara Thies, *Vertrauen als Organisationsprinzip*, Bern, Hans Huber, 2003.

the complexity of society, as in Kaufmann, Luhmann and Geiger;[13] *Philosophy*, inquiring into the value of trust as a spiritual phenomenon or moral value, as proposed by Lagerspetz and Köhl;[14] and *Politics*, analyzing the processes of reliability formed among citizens in governmental systems, as in Offe.[15]

Certainty also refers to the protection of individual or collective assets, such as life, health, freedom or property. This sense of certainty is implicit in the English phrase "public security or safety," which is both internal and external and is assured by preventive and repressive strategies.[16] Certainty here refers to the avoidance of threats to law and order.[17] Although there can be no public security or safety unless the law is enforced, public security and safety are not to be confused with "legal certainty": whereas the former concerns actions the state must perform to protect individual and social goods, the latter refers to properties, content, processes, methods and results that must be present if the law is to serve as an instrument to guarantee fundamental rights.

Certainty can also be conceived of as protection against threats to the essential conditions for survival. From this angle, certainty can refer to social security, i.e. the system of publicly or privately funded institutions that provide services to protect people from social risks such as maternity, disease, occupational accidents, job loss, old age, death, permanent injury, loss of a spouse, and so on.[18]

In all such cases, what is at issue is not legal certainty properly speaking but simply certainty, usually in the sense of trust. Legal certainty takes the stage only when we transcend the individual psychological dimension and enter the socio-axiological but not merely behavioral dimension: thus legal certainty represents

---

[13]Franz-Xaver Kaufmann, *Sicherheit als soziologisches und sozialpolitisches Problem*, 2nd ed., Stuttgart, 1973, p. 10; Niklas Luhmann, *Vertrauen – Ein Mechanismus der Reduktion sozialer Komplexität*, 4th ed., Stuttgart, Lucius & Lucius, 2000; Theodor Geiger, *Vorstudien zu einer Soziologie des Rechts*, 4th ed., Berlin, Duncker und Humblot, 1987, pages 63 and following.

[14]Olli Lagerspetz, "Vertrauen als geistiges Phänomen", in Martin Hartmann e Claus Offe (Orgs.), *Vertrauen: Die Grundlage des sozialen Zusammenhalts*, Frankfurt, Campus, 2001, pages 85–113; Harald Köhl, "Vertrauen als zentraler Moralbegriff?", in Martin Hartmann e Claus Offe (Orgs.), *Vertrauen: Die Grundlage des sozialen Zusammenhalts*, Frankfurt, Campus, 2001, pages 114–140.

[15]Claus Offe, "Wie können unseren Mitbürgern vertrauen?", in Martin Hartmann e Claus Offe (Orgs.), *Vertrauen: Die Grundlage des sozialen Zusammenhalts*, Frankfurt, Campus, 2001, pages 241–294.

[16]Markus Möstl, *Die staatliche Garantie für die öffentliche Sicherheit und Ordnung*, Tübingen, Mohr Siebeck, 2002, pages 654 and 659; Jutta Limbach, *Ist die kollektive Sicherheit der Feind der individuellen Freiheit?*, Köln, Carl Heymanns, 2002, p. 4; Ricardo Lobo Torres, "Liberdade, segurança e justiça", in Paulo de Barros Carvalho (Org.), *Justiça tributária*, São Paulo, Max Limonad, 1998, p. 704.

[17]Christian Calliess, "Die Staatsaufgabe der Äußeren Sicherheit im Wandel: Staatstheoretische Grundlagen und völkerrechtliche Konsequenzen", in Christian Calliess (Org.), *Äußere Sicherheit im Wandel – Neue Herausforderungen an eine alte Staatsaufgabe*, Baden-Baden, Nomos, 2005, p. 15.

[18]Alexia Bierweiler, *Soziale Sicherheit als Grundrecht in der Europäischen Union*, Stuttgart, Boorberg, 2007, p. 135.

certainty as an intersubjective value event associated with the law of a given society, either as a norm or as a value, and with the legal as its object or instrument.[19] The distinction is also important with regard to non-legal certainty as opposed to legal certainty: someone may be psychologically safe, protected from external threats such as cold or violence, but lacking in legal certainty if the state prevents him from freely planning and performing actions based on law.[20]

However, this definition is still not sufficient because legal certainty can have more than one meaning even though in every case it represents a value and is somehow linked to law. The second step in this process of progressive semantic delimitation is an examination of the several meanings of "legal certainty".[21]

References

ARCOS RAM´iREZ, Federico. *La seguridad jurídica: una teoría formal.* Madrid: Dykinson, 2000.

von ARNAULD, Andreas. *Rechtssicherheit.* Tübingen: Mohr Siebeck, 2006.

BIERWEILER, Alexia. *Soziale Sicherheit als Grundrecht in der Europäischen Union.* Stuttgart: Boorberg, 2007.

CACHO, José L. Mezquita del. *Seguridad jurídica y sistema cautelar,* v. 1, "Teoría de la seguridad jurídica". Barcelona: Bosch, 1989.

CALLIESS, Christian. "Die Staatsaufgabe der Äußeren Sicherheit im Wandel: Staatstheoretische Grundlagen und völkerrechtliche Konsequenzen". In: CALLIESS, Christian (Org.). *Äußere Sicherheit im Wandel – Neue Herausforderungen an eine alte Staatsaufgabe.* Baden-Baden: Nomos, 2005.

DOUET, Frédéric. *Contribution à l'étude de la sécurité juridique en Droit Interne Français.* Paris: LGDJ, 1997.

EVERS, Adalbert; NOWOTNY, Helga. *Über den Umgang mit Unsicherheit. Die Entdeckung der Gestaltbarkeit von Gesellschaft.* Frankfurt am Main: Suhrkamp, 1987.

FREUD, Sigmund. *Abriß der Psychoanalyse.* Frankfurt am Main, 1960.

GEIGER, Theodor. *Vorstudien zu einer Soziologie des Rechts,* 4th ed. Berlin: Duncker und Humblot, 1987.

KAUFMANN, Franz-Xaver. *Sicherheit als soziologisches und sozialpolitisches Problem.* 2nd ed. Stuttgart, 1973.

KÖHL, Harald. "Vertrauen als zentraler Moralbegriff?". In: HARTMANN, Martin; OFFE, Claus (Orgs.). *Vertrauen: Die Grundlage des sozialen Zusammenhalts.* Frankfurt: Campus, 2001.

LAGESPETZ, Olli. "Vertrauen als geistiges Phänomen". In: HARTMANN, Martin; OFFE, Claus (Orgs.). *Vertrauen: Die Grundlage des sozialen Zusammenhalts.* Frankfurt: Campus, 2001.

LIMBACH, Jutta. *Ist die kollektive Sicherheit der Feind der individuellen Freiheit?.* Köln: Carl Heymanns, 2002.

LUHMANN, Niklas. *Vertrauen – Ein Mechanismus der Reduktion sozialer Komplexität.* 4th ed. Stuttgart, Lucius & Lucius, 2000.

[19]Franz-Xaver Kaufmann, *Sicherheit als soziologisches und sozialpolitisches Problem*, 2nd ed., Stuttgart, 1973, pages 140 and following.

[20]Andrea Schrimm-Heins, "Gewissheit und Sicherheit: Geschichte und Bedeutungswandel der Begriffe 'certitudo' und 'securitas'" (*Teil* 2), *Archiv für Begriffsgeschichte* 35, p. 209, 1992.

[21]Federico Arcos Ramírez, *La seguridad jurídica: una teoría formal*, Madrid, Dykinson, 2000, p. 3; Andreas von Arnauld, *Rechtssicherheit*, Tübingen, Mohr Siebeck, 2006, p. 79.

MATHIEU, Bertrand. "La sécurité juridique: un principe constitutionnel clandestin mais efficient". In: FRAISSEIX, Patrick (Org.). *Mélanges Patrice Gélard – Droit Constitutionnel*. Paris: Montchrestien, 1999.

MÖSTL, Markus. *Die staatliche Garantie für die öffentliche Sicherheit und Ordnung*. Tübingen: Mohr Siebeck, 2002.

OFFE, Claus. "Wie können unseren Mitbürgern vertrauen?". In: HARTMANN, Martin; OFFE, Claus (Orgs.). *Vertrauen: Die Grundlage des sozialen Zusammenhalts*. Frankfurt: Campus, 2001.

PETERMANN, Franz. *Psychologie des Vertrauens*. 3rd ed., Göttingen: Hogrefe, 1996.

REALE, Miguel. "Prefácio". In: CAVALCANTI FILHO, Theophilo. *O problema da segurança no Direito*. São Paulo: Ed. RT, 1964.

RIPPERGER, Tanja. *Ökonomik des Vertrauens*. 2nd ed. Tübingen: Mohr Siebeck, 2003.

SCHRIMM-HEINS, Andrea. "Gewissheit und Sicherheit: Geschichte und Bedeutungswandel der Begriffe 'certitudo' und 'securitas'" (Teil 1). *Archiv für Begriffsgeschichte* 34, 1991.

SCHWEER, Martin; THIES, Barbara. *Vertrauen als Organisationsprinzip*. Bern: Hans Huber, 2003.

TORRES, Ricardo Lobo. "Liberdade, segurança e justiça". In: CARVALHO, Paulo de Barros (Org.). *Justiça tributária*. São Paulo: Max Limonad, 1998.

VIEIRA, José Roberto. "Medidas provisórias tributárias e segurança jurídica: a insólita opção estatal pelo 'viver perigosamente'". In: BARRETO, Aires Fernandino. *Et alii* (Orgs.). *Segurança jurídica na tributação e Estado de Direito*. São Paulo: Noeses, 2005.

VILLEGAS, Héctor. "Principio de seguridad jurídica en la creación y aplicación del tributo", *RDT* 66, São Paulo, s.d.

Legal Certainty

Abstract The various meanings of legal certainty are examined. The aim is to demonstrate that legal certainty is a principle, in its preponderant normative meaning, in the sense that it establishes a state of affairs that ought to be sought through behavior that contributes to its gradual advancement. This prevalent normative meaning of legal certainty does not exclude the existence of other normative dimensions that perform different efficacy-related functions. Furthermore, the chapter demonstrates that besides being a legal principle, legal certainty can manifest itself as a legislatively established legal rule; a principle recognized by the courts as a rule; a *metanorm* for the interpretation and application of other norms; or a subjective right resulting from reflexive application of the legal certainty principle itself.

1 Certainty as Defining Element

Legal certainty can refer to an element in the definition of law and as such it can be a structural condition of any legal order. Thus a legal order void of certainty cannot be considered "legal" by definition. This conception has been advocated by many authors, some of whom are highlighted in what follows. Radbruch states that legal certainty, alongside justice and fitness for purpose, is a key element of the law, without which it cannot exist.[1] For Bobbio, legal certainty is not only a requirement for orderly coexistence among men, but also an "intrinsic element of the law" whose function is to debar arbitrariness and assure equality, so that a legal order without minimal certainty is unimaginable.[2] Fuller argues that without legal certainty law itself simply cannot exist and lists several elements that are part of what he calls legal morality, a social environment in which individuals know where they stand and whom they can count on thanks to reciprocity of expectations based on knowledge of the rules in force.[3] Coing emphasizes the need for lasting institutions and relations to assure legal certainty, noting that these are consolidated

[1]Gustav Radbruch, *Rechtsphilosophie. Studienausgabe*, 2nd ed., Heidelberg, C. F. Müller, 2003 (1932), p. 73.

[2]Norberto Bobbio, "La certezza del Diritto é un mito?", *Rivista Intenazionale di Filosofia del Diritto* 28, pp. 150–151, 1951.

[3]Lon Fuller, *Anatomy of the Law*, Connecticut, Greenwood, 1968, p. 73.

© Springer International Publishing Switzerland 2016
H. Ávila, *Certainty in Law*, Law and Philosophy Library 114,
DOI 10.1007/978-3-319-33407-3_3

only over long periods of time, and goes as far as to say that law is not law at all when young.[4] Rawls also presents the law as a structure that can enable social cooperation by assuring reciprocal expectations.[5] Hart also defends certainty about primary and secondary rules and the rule of recognition as a defining element of law that defines it in opposition to other systems.[6] Mezquita del Cacho alludes to legal certainty as the "cornerstone of the General Theory of Law."[7] Along the same lines, Carvalho acknowledges that "legal certainty is at the very root of what ought to be, it is embodied in the deontic, and one cannot imagine it without specific determination."[8]

Finally, some scholars discuss legal certainty but do not mention the mechanisms to promote it; others mention the instruments to realize it without making direct reference to it. In any event, for both groups legal certainty is an "element" in a definition and thus a metalinguistic proposition concerning law as a historical phenomenon.[9] In other words, what is under discussion is a *defining concept* of legal certainty. A case in point is Recaséns Siches, for whom legal certainty is a quality "without which there could be no law of any kind, good or bad."[10]

It is also important to stress that legal certainty, seen from this perspective, is not a norm but a concept or an element of a concept. In this light, it is defined as a "superordinate" idea (*übergeordneter Idee*) or as a "hypernym" (*Überbegriff*).[11] It should noted that on this view legal certainty is an element of doctrinal metalinguistics and not a norm to which it applies.

2 Certainty as Fact

Legal certainty may refer to a factual state of affairs, i.e., a given concrete reality that can be verified.[12] In this sense, legal certainty does not concern how people ought to behave or an ideal state of affairs that ought to be achieved. Instead, it is bound to

[4]Helmut Coing, *Grundzüge der Rechtsphilosophie*, 5th ed., Berlin, Walter de Gruyter, 1993, p. 149.

[5]John Rawls, *A Theory of Justice*, Cambridge, Belknap, 1971, pages 235 and 310 and following.

[6]H. L. Hart, *The Concept of Law*, Oxford, Clarendon, 1991 (1961), pages 90 and following.

[7]José L. Mezquita del Cacho, *Seguridad jurídica y sistema cautelar*, v. 1, "Teoría de la Seguridad Jurídica", Barcelona, Bosch, 1989, p. 41.

[8]Paulo de Barros Carvalho, *Curso de Direito Tributário*, 21st ed., São Paulo, Saraiva, 2009, p. 165; idem, *Direito Tributário, linguagem e método*, São Paulo, Noeses, 2008, p. 265.

[9]Rubén Asorey, "Seguridad jurídica y Derecho Tributario", *RDT* 52, p. 28, São Paulo, 1990; José L. Mezquita del Cacho, *Seguridad jurídica y sistema cautelar*, v. 1, "Teoría de la seguridad jurídica", Barcelona, Bosch, 1989, p. 11.

[10]L. Recaséns Siches, *Tratado general de Filosofía del Derecho*, México, Porrúa, 1961, p. 224.

[11]Andreas von Arnauld, *Rechtssicherheit*, Tübingen, Mohr Siebeck, 2006, p.7.

[12]Gianmarco Gometz, *La certezza giuridica come prevedibilità*, Torino, Giappichelli, 2005, pp. 12, 25, 37; Letizia Gianformaggio, "Certezza del Diritto", in Enrico Diciotti e Vito Velluzzi (Orgs.), *Filosofia del Diritto e ragionamento giuridico*, Torino, Giappichelli, 2008, p. 83.

a factual reality that is assumed to exist.[13] In this respect, therefore, the expression "legal certainty" denotes an assessment about that which is perceived as existing in reality. The expression "there is no legal certainty in Brazil because courts do not confirm the expectations held for most of their decisions" represents this meaning. On this view, legal certainty means the ability to foresee the legal consequences of facts or behavior in a concrete case. For taxpayers, legal certainty means the ability to know beforehand what will actually happen. In short, it is the ability to predict an actual situation or to foresee a situation effectively. Hence this is the *realist view* of legal certainty, which presupposes a *descriptive concept*.[14]

3 Certainty as Value

Legal certainty may also denote an assertion about a desirable state, i.e., a state that is defined as worthy to be sought for social, cultural or economic reasons, though not specifically by normative imposition. In this sense, the expression "legal certainty" is an *axiological assessment* about that which is thought good according to a *given system of values*.[15] The sentence "a predictable order is much better for economic development that an unpredictable order" indicates that legal certainty is a substantive value of human life.[16] Moreover, legal certainty denotes value because it embodies the general features of all values, such as bipolar implication, referrability, preferability, hierarchy, incommensurability, inexhaustibility, objectivity, and historicity.[17]

---

[13]Federico Arcos Ramírez, *La seguridad jurídica: una teoría formal*, Madrid, Dykinson, 2000, p. 63; Antonio Enrique Perez Luño, *La seguridad jurídica*, Barcelona, Ariel, 1991, p. 21.

[14]Otto Pfersmann, "Constitution et sécurité juridique – Autriche", *Annuaire International de Justice Constitutionnelle 1999*, Paris, Economica.

[15]Franz-Xaver Kaufmann, *Sicherheit als soziologisches und sozialpolitisches Problem*, 2nd ed., Stuttgart, 1973, p. 32; Antonio Enrique Perez Luño, *La seguridad jurídica*, Barcelona, Ariel, 1991, p. 104; Gianmarco Gometz, *La certezza giuridica come prevedibilità*, Torino, Giappichelli, 2005, p. 36; José Souto Maior Borges, "O princípio da segurança jurídica na criação e aplicação do tributo", *RDDT* 22, p. 24, São Paulo, 1997.

[16]Eduardo García de Enterría, *Justicia y Seguridad Jurídica en un Mundo de Leyes Desbocadas*, Madrid, Civitas, 1999, p. 48.

[17]Miguel Reale, *Filosofia do Direito*, 12th ed., São Paulo, Saraiva, 1987, pages 189 and following; Paulo de Barros Carvalho, "O princípio da segurança jurídica no campo tributário", *RDT* 94, pp. 26–27, São Paulo, s.d.; idem, *Curso de Direito Tributário*, 21st ed., São Paulo, Saraiva, 2009, p. 162; Ricardo Lobo Torres, "Segurança jurídica e as limitações ao poder de tributar", in Roberto Ferraz (Org.), *Princípios e limites da tributação*, São Paulo, Quartier Latin, 2007, p. 430; idem, "Limitações ao poder impositivo e segurança jurídica", in Ives Gandra da Silva Martins (Org.), *Limitações ao poder impositivo e segurança jurídica*, São Paulo, Ed. RT/CEU, 2007, p. 75; idem, *Tratado de Direito Constitucional, Financeiro e Tributário*, v. 2, "Valores e princípios constitucionais tributários", Rio de Janeiro, Renovar, 2005, p. 168; idem, "Liberdade, segurança e justiça", in Paulo de Barros Carvalho (Org.), *Justiça Tributária*, São Paulo, Max Limonad, 1998, p. 680.

As an *axiological concept*, legal certainty may equally denote a political ideal, such as an ideal of justice or legal policy with which a given order can be compared. With this meaning it can be used to judge how well legal orders measure up against such an ideal.

4 Certainty as Principle Norm

Legal certainty can also embody a legal norm, i.e., a normative prescription establishing directly or indirectly that something is allowed, forbidden or mandated. This is the view I develop throughout this book. Here legal certainty concerns a state of affairs that ought to be brought about by behaving in such a way as to produce effects that contribute to its promotion, and thus denotes a *prescriptive assessment* about that which ought to be done according to a *given legal order*. The sentence "the efficacy of legal decisions ought to be assured" illustrates this meaning. From this perspective, therefore, legal certainty does not mean the *possibility* of predicting the legal consequences of facts or behaviors, but a prescription for behaving so as to increase the degree of predictability. On this view, legal certainty is positive law.[18] But this *positivist understanding* of legal certainty is argumentative (and hence post-positivist): as will be clarified later, while legal certainty is seen here as a duty of positive law, this view also maintains that its realization depends on the reconstruction of normative meanings through argumentative and hermeneutical structures, rather than the mere impartial description of meanings external to the cognizing subject.

All these considerations show that legal certainty as fact (factual dimension) is not to be confused with legal certainty as value (strictly axiological dimension) or norm (normative dimension): it is one thing to state as a *fact* that judges apply the legal order in order to confirm the predictions made for most of their decisions; it is quite another to say that a predictable order is far *better* than an unpredictable one; and it is entirely different again to say that judges must apply the legal order so as to increase the probability that users of the law can predict their decisions. These are different levels, subject to different assessments: legal certainty as fact is the ability to predict a real situation; legal certainty as value is the manifestation of approval or disapproval about legal certainty; legal certainty as norm is a prescription to behave so as to assure the realization of a more or less diffused real situation and an extension of the capacity to predict the legal consequences of action.[19] In sum, the *actual conditions* in which citizens are able to predict the legal effects of present actions is one thing; a *norm* requiring norms to be created and enforced so as to

---

[18] José Souto Maior Borges, "O princípio da segurança jurídica na criação e aplicação do tributo", *RDDT* 22, p. 24, São Paulo, 1997.

[19] Gianmarco Gometz, *La certezza giuridica come prevedibilità*, Torino, Giappichelli, 2005, pages 12 and 46.

increase the ability of citizens to predict the future legal effects of present acts is another thing: whereas legal certainty in the former case relates to a fact, in the latter case it concerns a *principle norm*.[20]

However, despite the above distinctions these meanings are necessarily *correlated*. It is crucial to notice this. On one hand, legal certainty as norm represents positive law and thus embodies value.[21] Similarly, in presupposing the possibility of realizing a given state of affairs it relates to a factual situation. Otherwise it would encompass, for instance, the command to "touch the sky with a finger."[22] As Luzzati well notes, the principle of legal certainty presupposes the possibility of realizing legal certainty as an effective practice at least in part.[23] On the other hand, as a factual situation it also involves some sort of positive valuation and thus embodies both normative and valorative aspects.[24] Finally, the understanding that legal certainty is a defining element of law, a mere element of a *definiens*, is based on the importance of the principle of legal certainty to the creation and enforcement of legal norms. In this sense, legal certainty as a defining element presupposes that it has scientific value as a legal principle. These observations are intended to stress both that *analytically differentiating* between the several ways of analyzing legal certainty does not eliminate their *concrete relationship* or even their *semantic interrelationship* and, conversely, that the interdependence of the three concepts does not preclude their analytical differentiation.

It must be added that legal certainty as fact, value or norm (i.e. at a doctrinal metalevel) can be used in different ways: for example, it can be described ("there is legal certainty in Brazil") or valorized ("legal certainty is a fundamental requirement"), or both together.[25]

All the above observations aim to show that it is possible to believe one is treating the same object from an identical perspective while actually examining different objects from the same or different standpoints, so that delimiting an object and the standpoint from which it is analyzed is an indispensable prerequisite for effectively understanding it. The examination of legal certainty is no exception to these epistemological conditions.

In this book, legal certainty is examined primarily as a legal norm in the "principle" category, i.e. as a prescription addressed to the legislative, judicial and executive branches determining the pursuit of a state of reliability and calculability of the legal order based on its knowability. As will be explained in detail, this

---

[20]Claudio Luzzati, *La vaghezza delle norme*, Milano, Giuffrè, 1990, p. 421.

[21]Paulo de Barros Carvalho, "O princípio da segurança jurídica no campo tributário", *RDT* 94, pages 26–27, São Paulo, s.d.; Ricardo Lobo Torres, *Tratado de Direito Constitucional, Financeiro e Tributário*, v. 2, "Valores e Princípios Constitucionais Tributários", Rio de Janeiro, Renovar, 2005, p. 168.

[22]Gianmarco Gometz, *La certezza giuridica come prevedibilità*, Torino, Giappichelli, 2005, p. 43.

[23]Claudio Luzzati, *l'interprete e il legislatore*, Milano, Giuffrè, 1999, p. 254; Federico Arcos Ramírez, *La seguridad jurídica: una teoría formal*, Madrid, Dykinson, 2000, p. 66.

[24]Gianmarco Gometz, *La certezza giuridica come prevedibilità*, Torino, Giappichelli, 2005, p. 37.

[25]Gianmarco Gometz, *La certezza giuridica come prevedibilità*, Torino, Giappichelli, 2005, p. 42.

normative concept of legal certainty connotes certain properties (states of affairs realizable in varying degrees) whose subsistence depends on the implementation of certain legal conditions. Hence it is a normative concept that is indicative of certain properties and that relates to states of affairs realized to a greater or lesser extent.

As a legal principle, legal certainty ought to be differentiated from rules. These are norms that describe what is allowed, forbidden and mandated.[26] Thus they consist of a hypothesis (assumption or antecedent), coupled with a mandate, consequence or mandatory provision whose associative form is a deontic copula, which characterizes normative imputation.[27] A simple example: Anyone who earns income in a given fiscal year in Brazil must pay income tax to the federal government at a rate of 27.5 %. Given the fact, the consequence applies. Hence it is said that regular deontic logic is represented by an "if-then" structure.

In this model of rules consisting of a hypothesis and a consequence, several aspects relating to each of these two parts must be examined in order to choose the appropriate conduct. Regarding the hypothesis, it is necessary to identify the expected behavior (the material aspect), time frame (the temporal aspect) and location (the spatial aspect). Regarding the consequence, what matters is who the active and passive subjects are (the personal aspect) and how much tax is due based on taxable income and the applicable tax rate (the quantitative aspect).[28] In other words, given the normative structure of the rules, the questions essential to understanding their meaning and scope are, regarding the hypothesis, "what," "when" and "where", and concerning the consequence, "who" and "how much." The expression "incidence matrix rule", which designates the key elements of the tax rule, is designed to enable the identification and detailed knowledge of its core unit through the presentation of an operative and practical formal schema.[29]

It is at once apparent that the procedure for interpreting and applying rules primarily involves a terminal operation of *concept matching* between the aspects mentioned earlier and each actual situation. Hence the importance of breaking down the tax rule into hypothesis (operative fact) and consequence in order to interpret and apply it properly. However, in the case of legal principles such as legal certainty, no such procedure of interpretation and application exists.

This is because legal principles are norms which determine an ideal state of affairs requiring behavior that produces effects that contribute to its realization. They are therefore said to involve an end (a state of affairs) and the means to that end (the required behavior).[30] As a simple illustration we can say that assuring a state of morality requires serious, fair, motivated and continuous conduct. In sum, it is necessary to choose behavior (means) whose effects contribute to the achievement

[26] Aulis Aarnio, *Reason and authority*, Dartmouth, Ashgate, 1997, pages 174 and following; Ota Weinberger, *Norm und Institution*, Wien, Manz, 1988, p. 87.

[27] Paulo de Barros Carvalho, *Curso de Direito Tributário*, 21st ed., São Paulo, Saraiva, 2009, p. 262.

[28] Idem, p. 263.

[29] Idem, p. 381.

[30] Humberto Ávila, *Teoria dos princípios*, 12th ed., São Paulo, Malheiros Editores, 2011, p. 61.

of this end. Thus it is possible to assert that the logic of legal principles is symbolized by the logical structure "in order for A to be the case, then it is necessary that B . . . "

As evidenced by the above, the procedure followed to interpret and apply principles primarily covers the assessment of the correlation between *states of affairs*, *effects* and *conduct*. The elements to be considered and verified are therefore different from those that concern rules. The key point often overlooked by legal doctrine is that this does not mean principles do not need a model by which to identify and know their structural elements, i.e., those elements without whose identification and knowledge they cannot be rationally understood and applied. Carvalho is absolutely right to say that objectivity is impossible when dealing with principles, which are always characterized by subjectivity: "No one should be disheartened because principles cannot be objective. That will never happen. If it did, they would no longer be principles."[31] Indeed, if the concept of objectivity utilized is the *semantic concept* according to which the objective is something external to the subject that can be apprehended by means of description, then principles cannot really be examined objectively as they involve the analysis of effects and purposes, which cannot be described beforehand. Thus owing to their structural distinctness the elements of principles have no *parallel* with those of rules: whereas rules comprise a "hypothesis" (describing a fact) and a "consequence" (prescribing a legal relationship), principles comprise an "end" (describing an ideal state of affairs) and "means" (prescribing behavior that contributes to the achievement of such a state of affairs). The content of a principle is made up of the means to actualize the result it is designed to accomplish.[32]

However, besides *semantic objectivity*, which consists in knowledge without intuition or feeling of anything external to the subject, *metaphysical objectivity*, which is present when there is something real in the world regardless of whether it is known, and *logical objectivity*, which arises from propositions that possess formal consistency and lack of vagueness, there is a different kind of objectivity relating to the ability to control the elements and operation of a given normative species, so that it is indeed possible to speak of a species of objectivity in dealing with legal principles: *discursive or methodological objectivity*, based on neutrality and equality in interpretation and application, as stressed by Marmor, or *objectivity in a weak or modest sense*, grounded in discourse that consists mainly of public and intersubjective principles for the justification of its cognitive intentions, as argued by Villa.[33]

---

[31]Paulo de Barros Carvalho, "O princípio da anterioridade em matéria tributária", *RDT* 63, p. 104, São Paulo, s.d.

[32]César García Novoa, *El principio de seguridad jurídica en materia tributaria*, Madrid, Marcial Pons, 2000, p. 43.

[33]Andrei Marmor, *Positive Law and objective values*, Oxford, Clarendon, 2001, pages 112 and following, especially pages 119 and 153; idem, "An essay on the objectivity of law", in Brian Bix (Org.), *Analyzing Law – New Essays in Legal Theory*, Oxford, Clarendon, 1998, pages 4–6; Vittorio Villa, *Costruttivismo e teorie del Diritto*, Torino, Giappichelli, 1999, p. 161.

The essential point in this search for discursive objectivity in dealing with principles is that several aspects relating to each of their structural elements must be specified in order to verify which kinds of conduct will promote the state of affairs whose realization they determine. With regard to the end or purpose (finalistic aspects), the aspects to be specified are the meaning assigned to the state of affairs (substantive aspect), the object it refers to (objective aspect), the benchmark to be used (subjective aspect), the moment to be considered (temporal aspect) and the extent to which the end must be achieved (quantitative aspect). With regard to the means (instrumental aspects), the relevant aspects are the conduct required to achieve the end (substantive aspect) and who should perform it (subjective aspect). To summarize, the normative structure of principles means that the questions essential to understanding their meaning and scope are different: instead of a hypothesis and a consequence, there is an end and the means needed to achieve it. Legal certainty, as will be shown below, is a principle norm, which establishes an end of the law.[34] To take legal certainty as an example, the fundamental questions are these: Certainty in what sense? – finalistic-substantive aspect; certainty of what? – finalistic-objective aspect; certainty for whom, in whose view, and by whom? – finalistic-subjective aspect; certainty to be realized when and assessed when? – finalistic-temporal aspect; certainty in what measure? – finalistic-quantitative aspect; certainty in which way? – instrumental-substantive aspect; certainty by whom? – instrumental-personal aspect. As I will make clear throughout this book, lack of configuration of these elements has contributed to a paradoxical uncertainty in dealing with legal certainty on a metatheoretical scientific plane and in the theoretical plane of the prohibition of argumentative arbitrariness.

As I shall show, strictly speaking it is impossible to understand the normative content of legal certainty without first specifying the above aspects.[35] This can be illustrated by more questions. Certainty in what way – as knowability or as determination? As reliability or immutability? As calculability or predictability? If predictability, for instance, is it absolute or relative? Absolute or relative in what sense? Predictability based on norms or maxims of experience? Certainty of what – knowability, reliability or calculability of a general norm, of a decision, of the legal order, of the science of law, of law itself, of one's own conduct, of someone else's conduct, of an omission, of a fact, or of normative consequences? Of law as norm or as argumentative activity? Of a decision as fundamentally provided or as enforced by the agents of the state? Certainty for whom, in whose view, and by whom? For the state or for the taxpayer? In the view of a layman or a specialist? By the legislative, judiciary or executive? Certainty to be realized when – today, yesterday or tomorrow? To be assessed when – today or tomorrow? Tomorrow at what time? Tomorrow by what instrument or against what benchmark? Certainty in what measure – as total predictability for all or as partial predictability for

[34] Anne-Laure Valembois, *La constitutionnalisation de l'exigence de sécurité juridique en Droit Français*, Paris, LGDJ, 2005, p. 4.

[35] Gianmarco Gometz, *La certezza giuridica come prevedibilità*, Torino, Giappichelli, 2005, p. 193.

most? Certainty in what way – through behavior or through the effects of behavior? What behavior? What effects? Effects to be assessed how? Certainty through whose behavior – that of the state or that of its agents? Which agents?

These questions, to which others will be added and all of which will be addressed in due course, are enough to demonstrate that the problem of legal certainty – and that of legal principles in general, especially if substantive – depends on the progressive specification of its several aspects. Two examples may illustrate this point.

First example: Some jurists claim that legal certainty is impossible (an illusion, a myth or a chimera), whereas others consider it attainable. The debate between Frank and Bobbio referred to in the Introduction to this book offers an eloquent case in point. Frank argues that legal certainty is a basic myth or illusion deriving from men's childish desire to replace the feeling of paternal certainty with an institution that apparently has a similar effect. Thus, in his precise terms: "Why do men seek unrealizable certainty in the Law? Because, we reply, they have not relinquished the childish need for an authoritative father and unconsciously have tried to find in the law a substitute for those attributes of firmness, sureness, certainty and infallibility ascribed in childhood to the father."[36] Bobbio, in contrast, not only considers legal certainty possible but also dismisses Frank's book as "simplistic one-sided scientism" and goes on to call legal certainty the constitutive element of the very notion of law.[37] A more detailed analysis of the doctrinal remarks concerned shows that strictly speaking Frank refers to legal certainty as the duty to pursue an ideal of absolute certainty or total predictability, assured only by "final, certain and mechanical" application; on the other hand, Bobbio is discussing the duty of achieving an ideal of relative certainty or high calculability. In sum, each is making a statement about a different object: one about legal certainty in a strictly personal dimension, as a fact at the level of being, i.e. the ability to forecast what will occur exactly and concretely, the other about the social and historical dimension of legal certainty as a norm, at the level of what ought to be, as a factual state that is more or less attainable, i.e. as the general duty to observe a set of rules for a given normative field.[38]

Second example: Some scholars see legal certainty as a principle opposed to the democratic principle because it freezes institutions[39]; others see it as perfectly

[36] Jerome Frank, *Law and the modern mind*, New Brunswick, Transaction, 2009, p. 22 (1st ed., New York, Brentano's Inc., 1930; 2nd rev. ed., New York, Coward-McCann, 1949).

[37] Norberto Bobbio, "La certezza del Diritto è un mito?", *Rivista Intenazionale di Filosofia del Diritto* 28, pages 150–151, 1951.

[38] Gianmarco Gometz, *La Certezza giuridica come prevedibilità*, Torino, Giappichelli, 2005, p. 20. Sobre os equívocos de Frank, ver: Theophilo Cavalcanti Filho, *O problema da segurança no Direito*, São Paulo, Ed. RT, 1964, pages 144 and following.

[39] Anna Leisner, *Kontinuität als Verfassungsprinzip*, Tübingen, Mohr Siebeck, 2002, pages 376 and following.

compatible with the democratic ideal.[40] A deeper examination of these doctrinal statements reveals that the former are actually referring to legal certainty as the duty to pursue an ideal of normative immutability through the absolute prohibition of legislative changes in certain areas, whereas what the latter are discussing is the duty to reach an ideal of continuity of the legal order through gradual change that preserves legitimate expectations. In other words, each group of scholars is discussing a different object.

These two examples, to which others could be added, show that without the above analytical process of ambiguity reduction the principle of legal certainty not only can be manipulated arbitrarily, but also can give rise to merely apparent debates or simple verbal disputations, creating confusion and constituting a veritable dialogue of the deaf.[41] This is because the expression "legal certainty," like others such as "freedom," is extremely vague, given the large number of intrinsically uncertain objects that may or may not be included in the category to which the expression refers (extensional vagueness) or the high degree of indeterminacy of the set of properties that connote such objects (intensional vagueness).[42] Without this process of ambiguity reduction, to which other problems should be added, neither "the end" nor "the means" needed to realize the principle of legal certainty can be defined. In other words, the conditions for realizing legal certainty cannot be created, nor can it be treated with the clarity and precision required by scientific discourse.[43]

Essentially, without investigating the several aspects of legal certainty one cannot understand its meaning or scope. To state – as do Cavalcanti Filho, Pintore and Jori, for example – that legal certainty is a subject's capacity to know before acting how the legal order will evaluate his or her actions, however important, is not enough.[44] "Know" in what respect – material access to the norm or intellectual access to its content? Is such intellectual access absolute or relative, in one case or all, for all or for some? "Evaluate" in what sense – by ascribing concrete consequences or as a merely abstract qualification? "Legal order" in what sense – as a set of normative texts, as a set of abstract norms set forth generally in the Constitution and legislation, or as individual decisions by the judiciary and decision-making bodies of the executive branch? In short, the above definition, used here merely as a representative example[45] of many others, shows that unless the concept of legal

---

[40]Christian Waldhoff, "Vertrauensschutz im Steuerrechtsverhältnis", in Heinz-Jürgen Pezzer (Org.), *Vertrauensschutz im Steuerrecht*, v. 27, Deutsche Steuer-juristische Gesellschaft, Köln, Otto Schmidt, 2004, p. 142.

[41]Gianmarco Gometz, *La certezza giuridica come prevedibilità*, Torino, Giappichelli, 2005, pages 15 and 162.

[42]Gianmarco Gometz, *La certezza giuridica come prevedibilità*, Torino, Giappichelli, 2005, p. 15.

[43]Idem, pages 13 and 29.

[44]Theophilo Cavalcanti Filho, *O problema da segurança no Direito*, São Paulo, Ed. RT, 1964, p. 59; Mario Jori e Anna Pintore, *Manuale di Teoria Generale del Diritto*, 2nd ed., Torino, Giappichelli, 1995, p. 194.

[45]Federico Arcos Ramírez, *La Seguridad Jurídica: una teoría formal*, Madrid, Dykinson, 2000, p. 32.

certainty is progressively specified it will itself become a source of legal uncertainty. The same can be said of attempts to define legal certainty as the way in which the law performs its necessary function of ordering and normatively structuring a community's social and political relations, as exemplified by Arcos Ramírez, albeit in preliminary fashion.[46] This kind of definition is so vague it cannot even be understood. What is meant by performing the function of ordering or normatively structuring social relations? Performing in what sense and in what measure? What exactly is an ordering function? What is the meaning of "social relations"? This concept, like many similar ones, is so indeterminate that it cannot be put to any kind of practical use, not even for scientific falsification. It is worth recalling that such indeterminacy occurs in tax law, where it is far from unusual to find definitions of legal certainty like Douet's, as the duty to ensure that tax liability is so determined that taxpayers can predict and calculate it themselves,[47] without any semantic reduction of the terms "ensure," "predict," "calculate" or "liability." All such definitions suffer, so to speak, from some sort of "analytical anemia."

Although as noted above the principle of legal certainty has the finalistic structure common to all principles, it also has elements not found in other principles and rules: thus it presupposes the intermediation of a legal reality. For example, a tax rule describes in its hypothesis a fact whose occurrence triggers a tax obligation. Its interpretation requires a correspondence between the concept of the norm and the concept of the factual situation. Its application therefore requires linking a normative element to a factual element; or, in an elliptical explanation that is not rigorous but more direct, linking "a norm to a fact." A substantive principle such as the principle of protecting the private sphere requires the search for a state of respect for individualities whose realization entails behavior that contributes to its promotion, such as respecting the inviolability of the home. Its application requires correlating the effects of conduct with the state of affairs to be realized thereby. A normative element therefore correlates with a factual element, or, to put it more simply, "a norm with a fact." Thus the substantive principle operates on a reality that is the object of normatization. In the case of the principle of legal certainty, however, something subtly different happens.

Indeed, application of the legal certainty principle requires a link to a *legal reality*, or in simpler language it presupposes a comparison between one norm (the legal certainty principle itself) and another norm (which may be legal, administrative or judicial). This entails verifying whether the inferior norm accords with the legal certainty principle; for instance, whether a legal norm is retroactive, whether a law contains transitional rules, whether a normative act oversteps the bounds set by the law it is supposed to be interpreting, whether a court decision matches the legitimate expectations of the citizenry, and so on. In other words, it is necessary to check the

---

[46]Federico Arcos Ramírez, *La seguridad jurídica: una teoría formal*, Madrid, Dykinson, 2000, p. 32.

[47]Frédéric Douet, *Contribution à l'étude de la sécurité juridique en Droit interne français*, Paris, LGDJ, 1997, p. 11.

compatibility of an inferior norm with the legal certainty principle. This principle therefore concerns a given configuration of reality *by means of legal institutions*: its application does not entail analyzing the subsumption of a factual presupposition to a norm, but contrasting a constitutional norm with a legal reality, whether it be a norm or the application of a norm.[48] The distinction resides in the interposition of a norm between the superior norm and factual reality: whereas any substantive principle requires a correlation between the effects of an act and the state of affairs it aims to realize, the principle of legal certainty requires a correlation between the effects of a norm and the state of affairs whose realization it ordains. The object of the legal certainty principle is not, so to speak, directly to configure reality, but to configure the law or a right as an instrument with which to configure reality. As we will see in due course, this is precisely why it is defined in its capacity as norm as an "instrumental principle" and, in its capacity as right, as a kind of "guarantee right": its function is to serve as an instrument for the realization of principles or rights. However, this distinction does not change the fact that the legal certainty principle consists of a state of affairs which depends for its realization on the adoption of means (legal if need be) to produce effects that contribute to that realization.

In sum, the legal certainty principle must be structured by means of an analytical process capable of progressively reducing its ambiguities, especially by indicating its dimensions, aspects and elements. One last reservation is required. It is of the highest importance.

The aim of constructing this "matrix principle" of the legal certainty principle is the same clarifying purpose as the analytical organization of rules, although without the same rigor and precision, which is not and could not be intended. Thus for example the point of decomposing jurisdiction rules into several aspects, given their function of configuring the state's power to tax, is to demonstrate the elements without which the state has no jurisdiction. If the ownership of goods within a state's territory cannot be conveyed, the state can have no jurisdiction to tax the movement of goods; without paid human effort deriving from economic activity within a city, the city can have no jurisdiction to tax services – and so on. The occurrence of facts that fit the hypothesis (operative fact) of the tax rule is a condition without which there is no state jurisdiction to be exercised. In the case of principles, especially the legal certainty principle, that is not so.

Indeed, as will become clearer throughout this book, the configuration of each element is never "yes or no," but always "more or less." For instance, the certainty of orientation assumes knowability of the norms, which depends on the amount of information supplied to the addressees. However, "too much information" causes complexity, and complexity does not orient, while "too little information" does not guide behavior and does not orient either. *Dosis facit venenum*.[49] Furthermore, the presence of an element must always be coordinated with that of another. For

---

[48] César García Novoa, *El principio de seguridad jurídica en materia tributaria*, Madrid, Marcial Pons, 2000, pages 43 and 45.

[49] Andreas von Arnauld, *Rechtssicherheit*, Tübingen, Mohr Siebeck, 2006, p. 690.

instance, to make the law reliable the state must guarantee fundamental rights by protection and non-restriction. To discharge its duties of protection the state needs normative instruments and information. However, the more it uses such instruments, the more it limits the exercise of individual freedom. If it protects too much, it constrains; if too little, it cannot provide guarantees.[50]

These brief considerations aim only to show that although the elements that make up legal certainty are structured they must be *individually measured* and *jointly coordinated*, which is not the case with the structural examination of rules of incidence. However paradoxical it may seem, the absolutization of legal certainty could spell its death sentence as an instrument for guaranteeing freedom, equality and dignity.

Having demonstrated the indispensability of a structural examination of the legal certainty principle, we can now proceed to an investigation of its various aspects. This first approximation analyzes the possible meanings of each aspect, leaving the question of which meanings to adopt until after the normative foundations of legal certainty have been discussed.

5 Finalistic Aspects: The State of Affairs to Be Promoted

5.1 Substantive Aspect (What Is the Content of Legal Certainty?)

5.1.1 Meanings of the Word "Certainty"

5.1.1.1 Concerning the End

5.1.1.1.1 In a Static, Atemporal Perspective: Determination vs. Knowability

Concerning knowledge of the law, there are two views that can be contrasted for didactic purposes. According to one view, legal certainty requires that citizens have an accurate understanding of the normative content of norms, be they general or individual. In this sense we speak of the determinacy and (absolute) certainty of law or of the "univocity of results."[51] It is also in this sense that some jurists, especially Kelsen in his early work but also Frank, call legal certainty an "illusion," a "myth" or a "chimera."[52] This also is the sense in which legal scholars, mainly of tax law, but also of administrative law, refer to the principle of "strict" legality

[50]Christoph Gusy, "Gewährleistung von Freiheit und Sicherheit im Lichte unterschiedlicher Staats- und Verfassungsverständnisse", *VVDStRL* 63, p. 160, Berlin, 2004.

[51]César García Novoa, *El principio de seguridad jurídica en materia tributaria*, Madrid, Marcial Pons, 2000, p. 113.

[52]Hans Kelsen, *Reine Rechtslehre. Studienausgabe der 1. Auflage 1934* (Herausgegeben und eingeleitet von Matthias Jestaedt (Org.), Tübingen, Siebeck, 2008, p. 109. Jerome Frank, *Law and*

and "closed" material typicality as an absolute prerequisite of normative content.[53] The best word to express this is "determinacy" (*Bestimmtheit*), meaning the capacity for total knowledge of normative content. As emphatically put by Frank, "the law, ready-made, pre-exists the judicial decisions."[54]

On the other hand, it can be argued that legal certainty requires that citizens fully understand all the possible meanings of a normative text from core significations that have to be reconstructed by means of intersubjectively controllable argumentative processes. It is in this sense that we can speak of the determinability and (relative) certainty of the law. It is also in this sense that some jurists claim that legal certainty is something to be achieved progressively. In later work Kelsen no longer uses the term "illusion", but employs the term "fiction" to describe an ideal that can be "approximately realizable" (*annährungsweise realisierbar*).[55] It is also in this sense that scholars, notably of tax law, refer to the principle of "strict" legality or "open" material typicality.[56] The best word for this, instead of "determinacy" (*Bestimmtheit*), is the "determinability" (*Bestimmbarkeit*) of normative content. The requirement of determinability is very restricted, however, as it does not necessarily encompass aspects relating to the substantive existence of the source from which the legal norm will be reconstructed, so "knowability" or "comprehensibility" can be used to refer to the formal or substantive ability to know the possible normative content of a given normative text or to know the argumentative practices used to reconstruct them. These terms are broader than "determinability," covering substantive aspects relating to the accessibility of content (such as publication and notification) and its scope, as well as its intelligibility (clarity and determinability, for example).

5.1.1.1.2 In a Dynamic Intertemporal Perspective

5.1.1.1.2.1 Backward Looking: Immutability vs. Reliability

With regard to changes in the law and references to norms prior to the change, there are two possible interpretations of legal certainty. One is that legal certainty

the modern mind, New Brunswick, Transaction, 2009, p. 35 (1st ed., New York, Brentano's Inc., 1930; 2nd ed. rev., New York, Coward-McCann, 1949).

[53] Alberto Xavier, *Os princípios da legalidade e da tipicidade da tributação*, São Paulo, Ed. RT, 1978, p. 92. More recently with similar arguments: idem, *Tipicidade da tributação, simulação e norma antielisiva*, São Paulo, Dialética, 2001, p. 18.

[54] Jerome Frank, *Law and the modern mind*, New Brunswick, Transaction, 2009, p. 35 (1st ed., New York, Brentano's Inc., 1930; 2nd ed. rev., New York, Coward-McCann, 1949).

[55] Hans Kelsen, *Reine Rechtslehre*, 2nd ed., Wien, Franz Deuticke, 1960, p. 353.

[56] Marciano Seabra de Godoi, "O quê e o porquê da tipicidade tributária", in Ricardo Lodi Ribeiro e Sérgio André Rocha (Orgs.), *Legalidade e tipicidade no Direito Tributário*, São Paulo, Quartier Latin, 2008, p. 96; Fernando Aurélio Zilvetti, "Tipo e linguagem: a gênese da igualdade na tributação", in Ricardo Lodi Ribeiro e Sérgio André Rocha (Orgs.), *Legalidade e tipicidade no Direito Tributário*, São Paulo, Quartier Latin, 2008, pages 30–51.

involves an ideal of immutability of certain norms. It is in this sense that we speak of the "immutability of the law" and it is also in that sense that publicists use the term "stability" or even the sometimes derogatory expression "petrification of the law."[57] In this sense, legal certainty inexorably binds future law to past law. As Gutierrez puts it, immutability as the property of that which cannot be changed is closely connected to the notion of intangibility.[58]

On the other hand, however, legal certainty can be understood as a requirement of "stability in change," i.e. as the protection of subjective situations already assured individually and the requirement of continuity of the legal order by means of transitional rules and equity clauses. The most consistent word to designate this meaning is "reliability," understood as the requirement of a legal order that protects expectations and guarantees stable change. This reciprocal relationship between stability and change is skillfully formulated by Cavalcanti Filho: "It is therefore inevitable that the law should have some scope for uncertainty and insecurity, as otherwise it would become an instrument of social stagnation. But this uncertainty and insecurity are the price of human progress and the search for juster forms of social organization."[59]

In this second meaning, legal certainty only establishes requirements relating to the transition from past law to future law. Thus it refers not to immutability, but to change with stability or rationality, and hence without abruptness.[60] To quote Vedel, "an airplane can be stable even as it travels the fastest route."[61] However paradoxical this may seem, movement is a condition of stability. When you ride a bicycle, you fall over if you stop. If you skate on a thin layer of ice, you will sink if you stand still. Similarly, while the law should not be changed frequently, suddenly and drastically, it must adapt to new realities lest it become a check to economic activity itself.[62]

---

[57] Antonio Enrique Perez Luño, *La seguridad jurídica*, Barcelona, Ariel, 1991, p. 33.

[58] Monica Madariaga Gutierrez, *Derecho Administrativo y Seguridad Jurídica*, Santiago do Chile, Editorial Jurídica de Chile, 1965, pages 7 and 49.

[59] Theophilo Cavalcanti Filho, *O Problema da Segurança no Direito*, São Paulo, Ed. RT, 1964, p. 162.

[60] Anne-Laure Valembois, *La constitutionnalisation de l'exigence de sécurité juridique en Droit Français*, Paris, LGDJ, 2005, p. 17; César García Novoa, *El principio de seguridad juridica en materia tributaria*, Madrid, Marcial Pons, 2000, p. 88; Jean-Baptiste Racine e Fabrice Siiriainen, "Sécurité juridique et Droit Économique. Propos introductifs", in Laurence Boy, Jean-Baptiste Racine e Fabrice Siiriainen (Orgs.), *Sécurité Juridique et Droit Économique*, Bruxelles, Larcier, 2008, p. 13.

[61] Georges Vedel, "Discontinuité du Droit Constitutionnel et continuité du Droit Administratif: le rôle du juge", in *Le juge et le Droit. Mélanges offerts à Marcel Waline*, v. 2, Paris, LGDJ, 1974, p. 779.

[62] Jean-Baptiste Racine & Fabrice Siiriainen, "Sécurité juridique et Droit Économique. Propos introductifs", in Laurence Boy, Jean-Baptiste Racine e Fabrice Siiriainen (Orgs.), *Sécurité juridique et Droit Economique*, Bruxelles, Larcier, 2008, p. 21.

Thus the goal must be certainty in movement.[63] The key is for "the evolutionary nature of law to repel crystallization and stagnation", as Machado Derzi rightly puts it.[64]

5.1.1.1.2.2 Forward Looking: Predictability vs. Calculability

With regard to the law's future efficacy, two heuristic concepts are also available. On one view, legal certainty can be said to prescribe the complete capacity to predict the legal consequences of any act (one's own or someone else's).[65] This meaning is embodied in "predictability" and "absolute certainty." In this sense, legal certainty ensures that citizens have a right today to know tomorrow's law exactly, anticipating the content of a future decision that will legally qualify an act performed today.

On the other hand, however, it can be argued that legal certainty only requires a significant capacity to foresee the legal consequences of legal acts or facts on the part of most people. In this sense, legal certainty ensures that alternative interpretations and normative effects of legal norms are largely predictable. The best word for this is not "predictability" (*Voraussehbarkeit*) but "calculability" (*Berechenbarkeit*).[66] Calculability here means the capacity to foresee the limits of state intervention in one's acts to a large extent, through prior knowledge of the state's discretionary powers.[67]

5.1.1.2 Concerning the Foundations

5.1.1.2.1 Certainty as a Result of the Idea of Law

Legal certainty is often associated with the very idea of law, regardless of its positivation in a given legal order. For instance, despite initially stating that the central notion of law is justice (*Gerechtigkeit*), Radbruch later says legal certainty (*Rechtssicherheit*), the rule of law (*Sicherheit des Rechts*) and fitness for purpose

---

[63] Cármen Lúcia Antunes Rocha, "O princípio da coisa julgada e o vício de inconstitucionalidade", in Cármen Lúcia Antunes Rocha (Org.), *Constituição e segurança jurídica: direito adquirido, ato jurídico perfeito e coisa julgada. Estudos em homenagem a José Paulo Sepúlveda Pertence*, Belo Horizonte, Fórum, 2004, p. 168; Leandro Paulsen, *Segurança jurídica, certeza do direito e tributação*, Porto Alegre, Livraria do Advogado, 2006, p. 26.

[64] Misabel de Abreu Machado Derzi, *Modificações da jurisprudência no Direito Tributário*, São Paulo, Noeses, 2009, p. 284.

[65] José Luis Palma Fernández, *La seguridad jurídica ante la abundancia de normas*, Madrid, Centro de Estudios Políticos y Constitucionales, 1997, p. 38.

[66] Andreas von Arnauld, *Rechtssicherheit*, Tübingen, Mohr Siebeck, 2006, p. 391; Sylvia Calmes, *Du principe de protection de la confiance légitime en Droits Allemand, Communautaire et Français*, Paris, Dalloz, 2001, p. 159.

[67] Gianmarco Gometz, *La certezza giuridica come prevedibilità*, Torino, Giappichelli, 2005, p. 224; Eros Roberto Grau, *O Direito posto e o Direito pressuposto*, 7th ed., São Paulo, Malheiros Editores, 2008, p. 103.

or utility (*Zweckmässigkeit*) are also essential.[68] On this view legal certainty is a value that, next to justice and social peace, inspires any legal order as a whole.[69] Likewise, Fuller lists several elements that are part of the "morality of law" and aim among other things to assure social traffic based on reciprocity of expectations, i.e., an environment where citizens know the rules in force and can therefore act with foresight of how others will act.[70] Luhmann does something similar by presenting law united with legal certainty in essence and concept: Owing to the complexity of the social world (there are always more possibilities for action than can be actually pursued) and contingency (experience may not match expectations), citizens must choose, on one hand, and risk frustration, on the other hand, so that the law can reduce complexity and contingency by guaranteeing expectations common to all citizens.[71]

What matters is that on this view legal certainty, more than a positive value, is a notion inherent in the very idea of law.[72] Legal certainty is a constitutive value of law, since without a minimum of certainty, efficacy and lack of arbitrariness we cannot speak of a legal system strictly speaking.[73] The primary function of law is that of ensuring.[74] Hence the statement that legal certainty, especially in tax law, embodies a pleonasm: Assuring certainty is the essence of the law.[75]

It should be noted that the concern of these scholars is with definitions, i.e. demonstrating the extent to which legal certainty is part of the very concept of law. However, simply accepting this connection, important as it is, does not help very much to clarify how legal certainty ought to be realized. To do so, as advocated here, it does not suffice to accept the "idea" of certainty as connected to the "idea" of law. Legal certainty has to be defined so as to make it operational – which in turn

[68]Gustav Radbruch, *Rechtsphilosophie. Studienausgabe*, 2nd ed., Heidelberg, C. F. Müller, 2003 (1932), p. 73. Sobre o assunto, ver: Theophilo Cavalcanti Filho, *O problema da segurança no Direito*, São Paulo, Ed. RT, 1964, p. 75.

[69]Anne-Laure Valembois, *La constitutionnalisation de l'exigence de sécurité juridique en Droit Français*, Paris, LGDJ, 2005, p. 6.

[70]Lon Fuller, *Anatomy of Law*, Connecticut, Greenwood, 1968, p. 73.

[71]Niklas Luhmann, *Vertrauen – Ein Mechanismus der Reduktion sozialer Komplexität*, 4th ed., Stuttgart, Lucius & Lucius, 2000, p. 27; Federico Arcos Ramírez, *La seguridad jurídica: una teoría formal*, Madrid, Dykinson, 2000, p. 24.

[72]Sylvia Calmes, *Du principe de protection de la confiance légitime en Droits Allemand, Communautaire et Français*, Paris, Dalloz, 2001, p. 112.

[73]Federico Arcos Ramírez, *La seguridad jurídica: una teoría formal*, Madrid, Dykinson, 2000, p. 120.

[74]Gérard Farjat, "Observations sur la sécurité juridique, le lien social et le Droit Économique", in Laurence Boy, Jean-Baptiste Racine e Fabrice Siiriainen (Orgs.), *Sécurité Juridique et Droit Économique*, Bruxelles, Larcier, 2008, p. 47.

[75]Frédéric Douet, *Contribution à l'étude de la sécurité juridique en Droit Interne Français*, Paris, LGDJ, 1997, p. 1; Jacques Chevallier, "Le Droit Économique: l'insécurité juridique ou nouvelle sécurité juridique?", in Laurence Boy, Jean-Baptiste Racine e Fabrice Siiriainen (Orgs.), *Sécurité juridique et Droit Économique*, Bruxelles, Larcier, 2008, p. 559.

requires both an analytical perspective to bring to the fore its many dimensions and aspects, and a dogmatic perspective to demonstrate which of the many dimensions and aspects should be adopted for a given legal order.

5.1.1.2.2 Certainty as a Product of Positive Law

Precisely for this reason, legal certainty can be explained as a specific norm of a given legal order and not simply as a notion inherent in the idea of law. The difference lies in the fact that legal certainty as a norm already has more precise contours, since the legal order itself provides answers to the questions necessary to the progressive reduction of its indeterminacy: questions regarding the ideals that ground it, the objects to which it refers, the subjects it protects, and its weight compared with other norms, among others. Moreover, if it makes sense to discuss the legal efficacy of legal certainty only as a norm, the same cannot be said about it as a defining element, fact, political ideal or value.

The consideration of legal certainty as a norm of a given legal order does not exclude its qualification as an essential element to the very idea of law. What it does is define the content of legal certainty according to the direct and indirect foundations of a specific legal order. In other words, its appreciation as a norm – which this book aims to demonstrate – shows that although legal certainty is inherent in the idea of law, it is not externalized in the same manner in all legal orders. A case in point is the Brazilian legal order, on which this book focuses: Here legal certainty is accorded high systemic importance and several of its specific sub-elements are detailed in rules. Understanding legal certainty as a norm enables an assessment of how and to what extent it ought to be realized.

Having analyzed the possible meanings of the word "certainty," we must now investigate the meaning of the word "legal."

5.1.2 Meanings of the Word "Legal"

5.1.2.1 With Reference to "Law"

First, legal certainty can be understood as certainty of law (*Rechtssicherheit, securité juridique, certezza del Diritto, segurança jurídica, seguridad del Derecho*), both in the sense that for the law itself to be considered "reliable law" it must have objective qualities such as clarity and determinacy, and in the sense that for the law to be held "certain" it must be applied by means of impersonal and uniform processes.[76]

---

[76]César García Novoa, *El principio de seguridad jurídica en materia tributaria*, Madrid, Marcial Pons, 2000, p. 25; Federico Arcos Ramírez, *La seguridad jurídica: una teoría formal*, Madrid, Dykinson, 2000, p. 29; José Afonso da Silva, "Constituição e segurança jurídica", in Cármen Lúcia Antunes Rocha (Org.), *Constituição e segurança jurídica: direito adquirido, ato jurídico perfeito e coisa julgada. Estudos em homenagem a José Paulo Sepúlveda Pertence*, Belo Horizonte,

This dimension attempts to answer the following question: "Is law itself certain?" Note that here the word "law" is the subject, i.e. the element about which something is said, whereas "certain" acts as nominal predicate by means of an adjective that describes a property of the subject. Thus certainty is a property, an attribute of the law.

This view of legal certainty (as certainty of the norms or certainty of their application) highlights aspects termed objective, inasmuch as it encompasses several features the legal order ought to have regardless of its concrete efficacy in specific areas, as will be shown below in the examination of accessibility, scope and comprehensibility of legal norms. Certainty of law, or "certainty of meaning" (*Bedeutungssicherheit*), however, emphasizes the static elements the legal order must have initially, regardless of the future elements to be generated during the application process. Law held certain, or "certainty of application" (*Anwendungssicherheit*), on the other hand, focuses on dynamic aspects to be addressed in the application process.

However, this definition of legal certainty as certainty of law says nothing about how it should be understood. This is because even if defined in this way it can be understood as *an end in itself* or as a *means to guarantee other ends*: in the first case, when legal certainty, regardless of indirectly guaranteeing other values, is itself considered important (*certainty for its own sake*)[77]; in the second case, when legal certainty is an instrument to guarantee other values, such as freedom, property and dignity.[78]

Second, legal certainty can be understood as certainty *through* law, in the sense that law ought to be an instrument to assure certainty *through the content of its norms*, as well as in the sense that law should be the means to assure expectations, *through the procedures that it determines* (*Sicherheit durch Recht, securité par le Droit, certezza per il Diritto, segurança pelo Direito, seguridad por el Derecho*).[79] Legal certainty in this sense represents a way of guaranteeing certainty, i.e. an "assurance" of rights and obligations.

The question at the foundation of this meaning is the following: "Is there certainty through law?" Note that here the word "law" is part of an adverbial predicate ("through law"). This way of understanding legal certainty heightens the formal

Fórum, 2004, p. 17; Christof Münch, "Rechtssicherheit als Standortfaktor. Gedanken aus Sicht der vorsorgenden Rechtspflege", in Albrecht Weber (Org.), *Währung und Wirtschaft. Das Geld im Recht. FS für Hugo J. Hahn*, Baden-Baden, Nomos, 1997, p. 674.

[77] Frederick Schauer, *Profiles, probabilities and stereotypes*, Cambridge, Belknap, 2003, p. 261.

[78] Federico Arcos Ramírez, *La Seguridad Jurídica: una Teoría Formal*, Madrid, Dykinson, 2000, p. 15; Andreas von Arnauld, *Rechtssicherheit*, Tübingen, Mohr Siebeck, 2006, p. 79.

[79] Andreas von Arnauld, *Rechtssicherheit*, Tübingen, Mohr Siebeck, 2006, p. 89; José L. Mezquita del Cacho, *Seguridad Jurídica y Sistema Cautelar*, v. 1, *Teoría de la seguridad jurídica*, Barcelona, Bosch, 1989, p. 67; José Afonso da Silva, "Constituição e segurança jurídica", in Cármen Lúcia Antunes Rocha (Org.), *Constituição e segurança jurídica: direito adquirido, ato jurídico perfeito e coisa julgada. Estudos em homenagem a José Paulo Sepúlveda Pertence*, Belo Horizonte, Fórum, 2004, p. 24.

and procedural instrumental aspect: formal because it sees law as an instrument to guarantee given expectations, whatever they may be; procedural because it acknowledges administrative and judicial procedures as the means to assure given values. In this sense, we can speak of "procedural certainty" (*Verfahrenssicherheit*). Here it is law that is instrumental for certainty. And certainty is neutral: law can assure many kinds of certainty (of law, of rights, of a right), as will be analyzed later on.

Within this second meaning – certainty through law – legal certainty can be understood on one hand as certainty *of rights*, in the sense that law can be the instrument to "assure" any other rights, such as freedom, property and equality, or even the right to legal certainty. This way of understanding legal certainty highlights its dynamic aspect, as it includes the effects of the application of laws for citizens in general. Certainty in this context means guaranteeing rights against manifestations of the law itself.[80] This meaning is derived from the answer to the question: "Are rights certain or secured?" Note that here the word "rights" (indicating a set of subjective rights) operates as the subject, i.e. the element of which something is said, while "certain" acts as adjectival predicate, denoting that which is said about the subject and defining it by indicating a property. Thus certainty is a quality of rights. it is important to note that "rights" is plural: this is not about the right of any subject, but about all the rights pertaining to a legal order. This is one of the senses Torres ascribes to legal certainty: "Legal certainty is certain and guaranteed rights," meaning above all "certainty of fundamental rights."[81]

On the other hand, still within the meaning of certainty *through law*, legal certainty can be used in a sense subtly different from the previous one: certainty as it refers not to law in general, or even to the rights of citizens collectively, but instead as it refers to "a right" specific to a given person in a concrete case. As we will see later, this meaning relates not exactly to the principle of legal certainty as an objective norm that requires the realization of a state of reliability and calculability of law based on its knowability, but to the reflexive efficacy of this norm relative to a given subject. Therefore it is the subjective right to protection of legitimate trust.[82] This meaning derives from the answer to the question: "Is the right certain?"

[80]Gianmarco Gometz, *La certezza giuridica come prevedibilità*, Torino, Giappichelli, 2005, p. 257; José Afonso da Silva, "Constituição e segurança jurídica", in Cármen Lúcia Antunes Rocha (Org.), *Constituição e segurança jurídica: direito adquirido, ato jurídico perfeito e coisa julgada. Estudos em homenagem a José Paulo Sepúlveda Pertence*, Belo Horizonte, Fórum, 2004, p. 17.

[81]Ricardo Lobo Torres, "Segurança jurídica e as limitações ao poder de tributar", in Roberto Ferraz (Org.), *Princípios e limites da tributação*, São Paulo, Quartier Latin, 2007, p. 430; idem, "Limitações ao poder impositivo e segurança jurídica", in Ives Gandra da Silva Martins (Org.), *Limitações ao poder impositivo e segurança jurídica*, São Paulo, Ed. RT/CEU, 2007, p. 74; idem, *Tratado de Direito Constitucional, Financeiro e Tributário*, v. 2, *Valores e Princípios Constitucionais Tributários*, Rio de Janeiro, Renovar, 2005, p. 168; idem, "Liberdade, segurança e justiça", in Paulo de Barros Carvalho (Org.), *Justiça Tributária*, São Paulo, Max Limonad, 1998, p. 686.

[82]Sylvia Calmes, *Du principe de protection de la confiance légitime en Droits Allemand, Communautaire et Français*, Paris, Dalloz, 2001, p. 171.

Note that the word "right" (singular, as a subjective right and not law or an objective order) is the subject, while "certain" is an adjectival predicate. Certainty in this sense may refer to both a quality of a specific right of a given subject and to an instrument for its protection. In both cases, however, certainty is an instrument to guarantee a right. The protection of acquired rights, completed legal acts and res iudicata is located within this scope.

Third, legal certainty can be understood as certainty *before the law*, both in the sense that the law ought to offer procedural conditions for individuals to protect themselves from its own manifestations by means of administrative or court procedures that can be used to oppose the exercise of power by a given authority, for instance, and in the sense that the law should meet certain requirements for individuals to be able to protect themselves from the law itself, by means of publication and notification of acts, for instance.[83] This meaning derives from the answer to the question: "Is there certainty before the Law?" Here "law" does not operate as an instrument to guarantee certainty, but as an object that causes it. Paradoxically, legal instruments are required to deal with the uncertainty caused by the law. Here the law is both cause and solution of legal certainty. This is how Lambert understands legal certainty when he says the principle of legal certainty works to protect citizens "against" a threat from law itself.[84]

Fourth, legal certainty can be understood as certainty of the individual *under the individual protection of the law*. Here the focus is not on general and abstract norms but on individual norms that assure something for someone, such court rulings or administrative decisions. Hence this is a version of certainty through law and certainty of rights.

Fifth, legal certainty can be used not to refer "to the law," "to rights" or "to a right," but instead "as a right". That is, instead of referring to the object of certainty, the word "legal" refers to the normative characterization of certainty. This meaning only shows that the legal certainty principle can function, from the concrete and subjective point of view, as a subjective right: As legal norm it creates obligations and prohibitions for the state, albeit indirectly, and where procedurally legitimate, citizens can go to court over these. Thus it is possible to speak of the "right to legal certainty."[85] This characterization is evidently not uncontroversial. Some legal scholars argue that "there is no subjective right to legal certainty. Indeed, granting a subjective right to legal certainty might (certainly would!) be the equivalent of opening Pandora's box."[86] Far from allowing overindulgence, however, defining

[83]Federico Arcos Ramírez, *La seguridad jurídica: una teoría formal*, Madrid, Dykinson, 2000, pages 3, 16 and 159.

[84]Pierre Lambert, "Le principe général de la sécurité juridique et les validations législatives", *Les Cahiers de l'Institut d'Études sur la Justice* 4, p. 6 ("Sécurité Juridique et Fiscalité"), Bruxelles, Bruyant, 2003.

[85]César García Novoa, *El principio de seguridad jurídica en materia tributaria*, Madrid, Marcial Pons, 2000, pages 41–42.

[86]Jean-Baptiste Racine and Fabrice Siiriainen, "Sécurité juridique et Droit Économique. Propos introductifs", in Laurence Boy, Jean-Baptiste Racine and Fabrice Siiriainen (Orgs.), *Sécurité*

legal certainty as a right is nothing more than the subjective reflection of the objective principle of legal certainty. While on one hand, it is true that legal certainty is positivated as an end to be realized by the state in the legitimate exercise of its freedom of configuration – so that individuals cannot legitimately sue for specific public policies to protect it – on the other hand it is no less true that if the state fails to perform the duty of protecting it, legal certainty may be normatively densified to the point of creating not general claims to public policies, but individual claims to realize it minimally.[87] A subjective right arises as to "whether" the state will act, rather than "how".[88] Notwithstanding this observation, it can be said – as does Torres – that legal certainty is "a true *fundamental right*."[89] In the course of this book I will clarify the contours of the rights that can be generated from the efficacy of the legal certainty principle – such as rights to the protection of legitimate trust or to the establishment of transitional rules or equity clauses, for example.

Sixth, legal certainty may denote a state of certainty not through law but through a specific *right*, such as the right to a fair hearing, for instance. In this very specific sense, one can say that a citizen's right to be notified of the inclusion of new evidence in a suit, for instance, increases this citizen's state of calculability of the opposite party's position. This meaning can be stated as follows: "I experience greater certainty thanks to the right to respond." The audi alteram partem principle guarantees that citizens are not surprised by a judgment based on a document of whose complete content they have not been notified so that they can duly respond. This is certainty through a right. A right is an instrument of legal certainty. It is, so to speak, legal certainty (through a procedural right) assuring legal certainty (of a right, of rights, or of law).

Lastly, legal certainty can indicate not exactly certainty "of" or "through law," but certainty "in" law. As will become clearer in due course, understanding the law as a previously given object placed before a judge facilitates the understanding of legal certainty as certainty "of" law: certainty is intrinsic to the law or its norms,

---

juridique et Droit Économique, Bruxelles, Larcier, 2008, p. 12; Ingo Wolfgang Sarlet, "A eficácia do direito fundamental à segurança jurídica: dignidade da pessoa humana, direitos fundamentais e proibição de retrocesso social no Direito Constitucional brasileiro", in Cármen Lúcia Antunes Rocha (Org.), *Constituição e segurança jurídica: direito adquirido, ato jurídico perfeito e coisa julgada. Estudos em homenagem a José Paulo Sepúlveda Pertence*, Belo Horizonte, Fórum, 2004, p. 92.

[87] Winfried Brugger, "Gewährleistung von Freiheit und Sicherheit im Lichte unterschiedlicher Staats- und Verfassungsverständnisse". *VVDStRL* 63, p. 132, Berlin, 2004; Markus Möstl, *Die staatliche Garantie für die öffentliche Sicherheit und Ordnung*, Tübingen, Mohr Siebeck, 2002, p. 652.

[88] Jutta Limbach, *Ist die kollektive Sicherheit der Feind der individuellen Freiheit?*, Köln, Carl Heymanns, 2002, p. 5.

[89] Ricardo Lobo Torres, "Segurança jurídica e as limitações ao poder de tributar", in Roberto Ferraz (Org.), *Princípios e limites da tributação*, São Paulo, Quartier Latin, 2007, p. 433; idem, *Tratado de Direito Constitucional, Financeiro e Tributário*, v. 2, "Valores e Princípios Constitucionais Tributários", Rio de Janeiro, Renovar, 2005, p. 170; idem, "Liberdade, segurança e justiça", in Paulo de Barros Carvalho (Org.), *Justiça Tributária*, São Paulo, Max Limonad, 1998, p. 687.

something it "contains" or "conveys." In this sense, we can say that the law is or is not certain. This reasoning is grounded in an understanding of law itself as an object to be described by scientists or understood by its users through a sheer abstract act of knowledge. However, if the law is not considered something previously given whose existence precedes the interpretative process, but instead is viewed as something to be realized whose existence depends on the process of interpretation and application, then we ought to speak of certainty "in" law rather than "of" law: legal certainty is an ideal state that is *achieved* during the very process of interpretation and application of the law.[90] This last expression – certainty "in" law – somehow covers the previous notions, on which it depends for its realization. It can therefore be said to denote legal certainty in the broadest sense.[91]

All the above senses are not parallel, however. Certainty through law, assuring a state of certainty by means of law, can be realized by guaranteeing "a right" (acquired rights are guaranteed), "rights" (citizens' rights to a minimum wage are guaranteed) or "a right via a right" (a right is guaranteed by means of the right to respond). This means only that the different senses are not really separate, but outward manifestations that intersect with one another. Even definitions that can be analytically separated are not functionally separate. For instance, the concept of certainty *of* law can be separated from that of certainty *through* law, but how can legal certainty be assured if not by norms and hence through law? Conversely, how can certainty through law be preserved if law itself is not certain? Thus all these concepts – "certainty of law," "certainty through law," "certainty of a right," "certainty of rights," "certainty before the law," "certainty under law," "certainty as a right," "certainty through a right" – are intertwined, albeit analytically separable.

It is also important to note that several of these concepts of legal certainty concern the concrete realization of the legal certainty principle as certainty of law. This is the case, for instance, for "certainty of a right," "certainty of rights," "certainty as a right" and "certainty by means of a right." From a different angle, this means that while there are several concepts of legal certainty, they are not parallel but related as a genus to its species, or as the general to the concrete.

For all these reasons, to speak of the *principle of legal certainty* is not to refer a single mode of legal certainty (certainty of law, through law, as a right, before law, under law, of a right or rights, as a right, or in law). However, if a single definition had to be chosen as the broadest characterization of legal certainty as advocated in this book, it should be "certainty in law", because this best illustrates the idea that legal certainty is not an intrinsic quality of law or its norms, and hence dependent upon prior determination, but a product whose existence to a greater or lesser extent depends upon a combination of criteria and argumentative structures used in the process of applying the law. This will become clearer when the several meanings of "law" are examined.

---

[90] Stefano Bertea, *Certezza del Diritto e argomentazione giuridica*, Soveria Manelli, Rubbertino, 2002, pages 19, 23 and 55.

[91] Markus Möstl, *Die staatliche Garantie für die öffentliche Sicherheit und Ordnung*, Tübingen, Mohr Siebeck, 2002, p. 66.

5.1.2.2 The Meanings of "Law"

The above examination of the several meanings of "legal" in the phrase "legal certainty" is still not enough, because having said that it refers to law we must now define "law", at least in general terms.

First, "law" can refer to an *object*. This classification of legal certainty corresponds to an *objectivist concept of interpretation* that focuses on the *result*, in the sense that through a static and deterministic activity centered on exclusively semantic aspects the interpreter has the duty merely to reveal normative content prior to the interpretation process itself. The normative concept, which can be assessed in advance and in its entirety, corresponds to a point, which either does or does not conform to reality. On this view, law is a given object regardless of the subject and the process of interpretation and application. Each rule corresponds to a possible interpretation or normative meaning ($R = A$). Thus the problem of legal certainty is substantially a *semantic problem* circumscribed to the predetermination of meaning. Legal certainty is the need for ex ante knowledge of the material limits of the legislative exercise of jurisdiction.[92] It is an objectivist concept of interpretation based on substantive rules (*rule-dependent certainty of law*).[93] Consequently, the very concept of legal certainty is dual, as it is based on the poles "certainty/uncertainty."[94] On this view, law is independent of the interpretative and argumentative processes that realize it and hence legal certainty is defined as the need for semantic predetermination of something that precedes and is independent of such subsequent processes.

Second, "law" can refer to law not as an object, but as a practice: in this case an argumentative practice. This non-classificatory concept of legal certainty corresponds to an *argumentative conception of interpretation*, based on the *process* through which a result is reached, in the sense that through dynamic and intermediate activity centered not only on semantic aspects but also on argumentative structures the interpreter has a duty to reconstruct normative content from minimal general semantic cores. The normative content, which can be assessed in advance only regarding the possible alternative interpretations, and the criteria to delimit it correspond to a spectrum that matches reality to a greater or lesser extent. On this view, law is an activity that depends on the process of interpretation and application. Each rule corresponds to several possible interpretations or normative meanings ($R = A,\ B\ or\ C$), to be determined through argumentative structures supplied by metanorms of interpretation, such as the postulates of proportionality,

[92] Stefano Bertea, *Certezza del Diritto e argomentazione giuridica*, Soveria Manelli, Rubbertino, 2002, p. 47.

[93] Stefano Bertea, *Certezza del diritto e argomentazione giuridica*, Soveria Manelli, Rubbertino, 2002, p. 14; Antonio Enrique Perez Luño, *La Seguridad Jurídica*, Barcelona, Ariel, 1991, p. 100.

[94] Gianmarco Gometz, *La certezza giuridica come prevedibilità*, Torino, Giappichelli, 2005, p. 30.

coherence and reasonableness. Thus the problem of legal certainty is substantially an *argumentative problem* circumscribed to the predetermination of possible minimal meanings through defined argumentative structures and their correlation with concrete elements by means of applied normative postulates. This is a procedural conception of interpretation based on rational procedures (*procedure-dependent certainty of law*).[95] Consequently, the factual states relating to legal certainty are not seen as dual but as gradual, encompassing a spectrum that ranges between the poles of total uncertainty and total certainty, so that it is possible to speak of "a great deal of certainty" "little certainty" or "no certainty" from a factual standpoint.[96] The bottom line is that law is not merely described or revealed, but reconstructed from core meanings of normative provisions, which in turn must be connected to factual elements in the application process. The normative material is therefore not totally but partially given. On this view, then, legal certainty is not the need for mere knowledge of total content given in advance, but the duty to reconstruct and apply normative meanings according to rules of argumentation, hermeneutical postulates (substantive and formal coherence) and principles of application (proportionality and reasonableness).

5.2 *Objective Aspect (Legal Certainty of What?)*

5.2.1 The Object of Legal Certainty

5.2.1.1 Normative Certainty

5.2.1.1.1 Certainty of Norms

The object of legal certainty is usually deemed to include the legal consequences of acts or facts: There is legal certainty when citizens are able to know and calculate the results that law will ascribe to their acts.[97] This is the general finding. Since the principle of legal certainty concerns all three branches of government, its application may be embodied in a general, statutory or regulatory norm, an administrative act, or an administrative decision or court ruling. In this sense, the ideals of reliability and calculability based on knowability inform each of these objects.

[95] Stefano Bertea, *Certezza del diritto e argomentazione giuridica*, Soveria Manelli, Rubbertino, 2002, p. 301; Gianluigi Palombella, *Dopo la Certezza – Il Diritto in equilibrio tra Giustizia e Democrazia*, Bari, Dedalo, 2006, p. 12.

[96] Gianmarco Gometz, *La certezza giuridica come prevedibilità*, Torino, Giappichelli, 2005, p. 30; Federico Arcos Ramírez, *La seguridad jurídica: una teoría formal*, Madrid, Dykinson, 2000, p. 68.

[97] Gianmarco Gometz, *La certezza giuridica come prevedibilità*, Torino, Giappichelli, 2005, p. 204.

5.2.1.1.1.1 Certainty of the Legal Order

In some situations, the object of legal certainty is not a norm but the legal order: Knowability informs the legal order in general, in the sense that it ought to be formally and substantively intelligible in its entirety; stability can also refer to the order in general in the sense that considered as a whole it ought to have durability; and calculability can also refer to the legal order in the sense that in its entirety it cannot be the object of abrupt, drastic and incoherent modifications. On this view legal certainty as an objective principle, without any reference to its concrete subjectivation, relates to the legal order as a whole.[98]

This reference to the legal order in general has repercussions regarding the elements to be analyzed as well as the evidence to be produced. As I will explain in detail in due course, legal certainty has two dimensions: one is objective and refers to qualities that law as such ought to have; the other is subjective and refers to the concrete and objective efficacy it ought to display. The objective dimension of legal certainty requires stability and credibility of the legal order, so that to argue restriction it is necessary to demonstrate that a given rule, act or decision will severely undermine the regular credibility of law as an institution from the viewpoint of most people and according to average criteria of rationality. A case in point would be a legal decision that diverges from all precedents and thereby affects a large number of citizens who placed trust in the previous interpretation, resulting in general and abstract distrust on the part of the legal community with regard to the judiciary and the law as social institutions.

In contrast, legal certainty can be subjective, in which case its object is not the legal order but concrete application of the principle to a specific case and person. The subjective dimension of legal certainty entails the intangibility of subjective situations, so that to argue restriction it is necessary to demonstrate that by relying on a given rule, act or decision someone has concretely performed acts that dispose of their rights to freedom and property. A case in point would be a legal decision that diverges from all precedents and thereby affects a specific person who has invested significantly as a result of the precedents now altered, which not only could but actually did guide their past actions, causing a significant and unforeseen individual and concrete restriction of their rights of freedom and property.[99]

These two examples show that legal certainty may concern both the legal order as a totality and from a collective perspective, and its individual and concrete application from the viewpoint of a given individual. They also show that to know the object of certainty it is not enough to make the analytical distinctions needed for a better understanding, but the analysis must also extend to the requirements and the evidence required for its application.

---

[98] Willy Zimmer, "Constitution et sécurité juridique – Allemagne", *Annuaire International de Justice Constitutionnelle 1999*, Paris, Economica.

[99] Bodo Viets, *Rechtsprechungsänderung und Vertrauensschutz*, Bern, Herbert Lang, 1976, p. 203.

5.2.1.1.1.2 Certainty of a Norm

Given the multiplicity of partial ideas that make it up, legal certainty can refer to a norm only rather than to the legal order in general, as shown above. The requirement of knowability, as the duty to make the law accessible and intelligible, may refer to the legal order in general or to a specific norm. In this case, the debate about determinable tax liability, also known as "material typicality", precisely involves a requirement addressed to a norm, i.e. the tax rule, which (depending, naturally, on how one understands such a requirement) must determine tax liability clearly enough to serve as effective guidance for taxpayers. The requirement of reliability, as the duty to make the law durable and stable, may also refer to the legal order in general or to a specific norm. In this case, the discussion about the intangibility of subjective situations based on the principle of protecting legitimate expectations precisely involves a requirement addressed to the application of a previous norm, which cannot be revised if it has been the basis for dispositional acts.

The object of legal certainty may also be an administrative or normative act rather than the legal order or even a general norm. The importance of defining the object in this case derives from the fact that realizing or restricting the legal certainty principle varies depending on whether an act is administrative or normative. In the case of an administrative act, which is defined by its concrete effects, the requirement of knowability encompasses notification, pertinence and legal basis; the requirement of reliability concerns the possible intangibility of subjective situations that prevent revocation or annulment in individual and concrete cases; and the requirement of calculability imposes transitional rules or equity clauses to attenuate the change in administrative interpretation. In the case of a normative act, however, knowability concerns publication and sufficient determination; reliability refers to the possible intangibility of subjective situations that prevent retroactive effects; and calculability imposes transitional rules or equity clauses to protect trust in the administrative interpretation at the general and abstract levels.

Similarly, the object of legal certainty may be an administrative or court decision with general or individual effects, in which case the requirements deriving from it are different again: Knowability refers to notification or publication, pertinence, and legal basis; reliability concerns the duty of assigning prospective efficacy based on the prohibition of jurisprudential retroactivity if retroactive efficacy would jeopardize the credibility of the legal order or affect subjective situations unjustifiably; and calculability aims to impose prospective effects, transitional rules or equity clauses to temper past achievements with future perspectives.

What is important about distinguishing between certainty "of the order," "of norms," "of norms as acts" and "of decision norms" is that these not only permit identification of the object of legal certainty, and thus the requirements necessary to its application in each case, but also show that the existence of legal certainty relative to one object is not necessarily bound to the existence of certainty relative to another. For example, there may be both certainty "of norms" without certainty "of the order", as in the case when legal norms are highly unstable albeit accessible and intelligible, and certainty "of the order" without certainty "of a norm", as in the opposite case, when legal norms are stable yet incomprehensible owing to excessive indeterminacy or too much detail, lack of clarity, or a large number of cross-references. These distinctions show that one cannot truly speak of legal certainty without a clear indication of the object it refers to.

5.2.1.1.2 Certainty of the Application of Norms

The object of legal certainty may also be not a norm itself, but its uniform and non-arbitrary application. Hence the expression "certainty of application of norms" instead of "certainty of norms." Such certainty depends on argumentative and procedural elements. Argumentative elements concern the use of clear and objective structures of argument, with clear premises and conclusions grounded in the legal order and constructed in accordance with rational criteria based on formal consistency and substantive coherence.[100] Procedural elements concern administrative or judicial procedures that allow and take into consideration the right to a full defense and a fair hearing, as well as guaranteeing a logical written justification of decisions. All this is analyzed in greater detail below.

This distinction is also relevant because a norm can be considered certain insofar as it is accessible and intelligible, yet may be applied arbitrarily, without objective and uniform criteria, and without proper justification and legal basis. Without certainty of application, the legal certainty of a norm is overridden by the uncertainty of its application. Thus with due poetic license, we would have to say that certainty comes in the door but flies out the window.

5.2.1.2 Behavioral Certainty

5.2.1.2.1 Certainty of One's Own (In)action

Besides normative certainty, there is also behavioral certainty. Indeed, legal certainty can be defined as the possibility of predicting the reaction of legal bodies to the behavior of citizens – and of taxpayers in the case of tax law.[101] This conception may refer to the effects of action itself: A taxpayer who sells goods must be able to know beforehand whether a sales tax applies and, if so, at what tax rate.

It should be noted that behavioral certainty can refer to both normative certainty and social certainty, understood as certainty "of social relations" rather than

[100] Theophilo Cavalcanti Filho, *O problema da segurança no Direito*, São Paulo, Ed. RT, 1964, p. 7.

[101] Gianmarco Gometz, *La certezza giuridica come prevedibilità*, Torino, Giappichelli, 2005, pages 13 and 204.

"of law." In this respect, the French language has two different terms: *sécurité*, meaning certainty (*Sicherheit*); and *sûreté*, meaning reliability (*Verlässlichkeit*) in social relations.[102]

5.2.1.2.2 Certainty of Someone Else's (In)action

Instead of or together with the above, the same legal certainty may involve the possibility of predicting the reactions of judicial bodies to the actions of third parties. This sense of certainty concerns the anticipation of someone else's conduct rather than one's own. Because our own actions have normative consequences, which nevertheless depend on legal qualifications established wholly or partly by judicial bodies (including tacit approval), legal certainty can correctly be considered the ability to predict the reaction of judicial bodies to one's own actions. Thus Torres emphasizes that legal certainty "becomes the fundamental value of the rule of law, since capitalism and liberalism need certainty, calculability, legality and objectivity in *legal relations* and predictability *in state action*."[103] In this sense legal certainty serves as a parameter for predicting what others can do and demand.[104]

It is worth recalling that the object of certainty can also include inaction by judicial bodies, i.e. a legal consequence of lack of state reaction to a given act.[105] This is important, for example, if a citizen, based on the alternative interpretations of a tax rule, purposely and effectively performs an act that does not coincide with any of the alternatives provided for in the tax rule. In this case, the principle of legal certainty would be infringed by a decision to tax the act in question, given the frustration and surprise resulting from such a decision for the taxpayer.

In this regard, indeed, it is important to bear in mind that the acts to which legal certainty could be referring may be real or imaginary: Citizens must be able to foresee the legal consequences not only of their real actions, past, present or future, but also of any actions they may imagine. This is because for a citizen calculability has to involve precisely the ability to weigh up possible options in order best to decide what to do. This circumstance explains the existence of tax queries, for example, when a taxpayer asks an administrative body to say whether planned or

[102]Sylvia Calmes, *Du principe de protection de la confiance légitime en Droits Allemand, Communautaire et Français*, Paris, Dalloz, 2001, p. 157.

[103]Ricardo Lobo Torres, "Segurança jurídica e as limitações ao poder de tributar", in Roberto Ferraz (Org.), *Princípios e limites da tributação*, São Paulo, Quartier Latin, 2007, p. 430; idem, "Limitações ao poder impositivo e segurança jurídica", in Ives Gandra da Silva Martins (Org.), *Limitações ao poder impositivo e segurança jurídica*, São Paulo, Ed. RT/CEU, 2007, p. 74; idem, *Tratado de Direito Constitucional, Financeiro e Tributário*, v. 2, "Valores e Princípios Constitucionais Tributários", Rio de Janeiro, Renovar, 2005, p. 168; idem, "Liberdade, segurança e justiça", in Paulo de Barros Carvalho (Org.), *Justiça Tributária*, São Paulo, Max Limonad, 1998, p. 686 (emphasis added).

[104]Theophilo Cavalcanti Filho, *O problema da segurança no Direito*, São Paulo, Ed. RT, 1964, p. 7.

[105]Gianmarco Gometz, *La certezza giuridica come prevedibilità*, Torino, Giappichelli, 2005, p. 225.

actual actions in connection with a project will give rise to a tax liability. Thus calculability must include the consequences not only of actual acts or facts, but also of acts (one's own, or someone else's, by omission or commission) or facts that have not occurred or which would have had certain consequences if they had occurred. In sum, calculability entails predictability relative not only to the effective reaction of judicial bodies to acts or facts, but also to their expected reaction should they be invested with the power to decide about acts that could have been performed or facts that could have happened. In this framework, legal certainty concerns not only acts or facts that have actually occurred, are in dispute, and face coercive effects that are heteronomously imposed, but also with acts or facts that are possible, are not in dispute, and whose effects are self-imposed and spontaneously qualified.[106]

5.2.1.3 Factual Certainty

Legal certainty includes not only acts, but also facts, which are events that do not directly depend on human intervention.[107] An example is normal wear and tear to a machine, which is relevant to knowing the rules for calculating depreciation; another is the simple passage of time, which is decisive to test the statute of limitations in tax law – and so on.

What matters is that the spectrum of meanings of legal certainty include the ability to know and foresee the legal consequences that judicial bodies may assign not only to acts – one's own or someone else's – but also to facts that may occur and directly or indirectly impact a taxpayer's legal sphere.

5.2.1.4 Jurisprudential Certainty

There is one last significant version of certainty: jurisprudential certainty. Indeed, the examination of legal certainty usually involves an analysis of the requirements for law to be considered certain (certainty of law), or for law to be an instrument to assure rights (certainty through law and of rights). Legal certainty so to speak imbues law and rights, the prescriptive statements, whether general or individual, that make up the object language in the various normative manifestations of law. However, legal certainty can also be used to refer not to law but to the *way it is treated,* and many do so without realizing it. Legal certainty in this sense imbues the descriptive-explanatory or reconstructive statements that make up the metalanguage of jurisprudence.

On this view, therefore, legal certainty refers to the clarity, scope, consistency (formal) and coherence (substantive) not of norms (object language), but of the

[106]Gianmarco Gometz, *La certezza giuridica come prevedibilità*, Torino, Giappichelli, 2005, p. 243–244.

[107]Idem, p. 228.

jurisprudential statements that imbue them (metalanguage), even where they refer to the principle of legal certainty itself. This explains why some scholars state that legal certainty has been treated "insecurely" by jurisprudence, which focuses so obsessively on certainty that it ends up neither eliminating nor minimally decreasing uncertainty for lack of clear definitions and intelligible criteria.[108] In sum, this is legal certainty as certainty of the "science of law."

Part of the uncertainty with which legal certainty has been treated arises from the fact that it is not a rule norm but a principle norm, and as such it does not have a dual structure of hypothesis and consequence but a connection between ends and means whose analysis depends on the investigation of effects and the promotion of states of affairs. In other words, the uncertainty with which the principle of legal certainty has been treated is also a consequence of its own structure: to expect to examine it and find a deontic structure of fact and consequence is to risk frustration at finding a norm with a structure than involves ends and means and the production of effects. As already stated, however, this kind of negative assessment derives from a semantic conception of objectivity, based on the idea that objectivity only exists when knowledge of something external exists, regardless of who knows it. However, if instead of this conception we adopt a discursive notion of objectivity such as the semantic-argumentative controllability of practical legal discourse advocated in this book, the jurisprudential certainty required is of a different kind.

5.2.2 How to Understand the Object of Legal Certainty

5.2.2.1 Regarding the Character of Understanding

5.2.2.1.1 Univocal Conception of the Object

However, merely stating that legal certainty involves knowledge and calculability of a norm is simply a circumvention of the core problem, which is the meaning of "knowing and calculating the content of a norm": Does this mean to be able to know and predict the *sole outcome totally and exactly* or to be able to know and predict a *range of generic alternative results* compatible with the normative text? In other words, the problem of the object of legal certainty lies not primarily in the normative source, whether statutory, administrative or judicial, but rather in the type of result attributed to it, i.e. *univocal* or *alternative*. Since court decisions and administrative acts, given their individuality, have a higher level of concretization than statutes, the problem resides most intensely in the definition of what it means to know and calculate the content of a statutory norm.[109] In this respect, two conceptions can be contrasted.

[108]Massimo Corsale, "Il problema della certezza del Diritto in Italia dopo il 1950", in Flavio Lopez de Oñate, *La certezza del Diritto*, Milano, Giuffrè, 1968, p. 288.

[109]Gianmarco Gometz, *La certezza giuridica come prevedibilità*, Torino, Giappichelli, 2005, p. 208.

One is that what ought to be understood and calculated has only one meaning: Rule “X” has meaning “A” ($X = A$). This approach is based on the assumption that legal norms carry objective and unique meanings. Thus to speak of determination and predictability is to refer to the ability of citizens in general, and of taxpayers specifically, to know the content of any norm they will obey and predict the content it will be given by the executive and judiciary. Here “determination” means the ability to know the *only meaning of the norm*, while predictability is a general ability to predict the *exact meaning of future normative decisions*. This is the position taken by Lièvre-Gravereaux, for whom predictability means that “the structure and wording of the text ought to tend to allow for a univocal interpretation and qualification of the facts.”[110] It is also the view long criticized by Frank as a basic illusion or myth.[111] Thus on this view legal certainty is a guarantee that citizens can *know generally and foresee precisely* the consequences that law will ascribe to their acts. Their predictions are successful when the judicial or administrative interpretation is exactly what could have already been deduced from the statutory rule.

In tax law this understanding is manifested in the debate about the content of the legality principle, which from the standpoint of the state is the lawmaker's duty, when instituting a tax rule, to determine unequivocally all elements of the tax obligation, and from that of the taxpayerthe ability to understand the rule's meaning correctly. It is in this context that some jurists defend the “closed typicality principle” as, to quote Xavier, the obligation that the tax rule “contain within itself all the necessary elements with which to assess the facts and produce effects, with no need to resort to external elements and or accept any assessment that replaces or adds to that contained by the type enshrined in the rule.”[112] In this respect, legal certainty means “univocal determination”[113] or “objective determination” of tax obligations.[114]

[110] Amélie Lièvre-Gravereaux, *La rétroactivité de la loi fiscale: une nécessite en matière de procédures*, Paris, Harmattan, 2007, p. 33. Similarly, on clarity: Antonio Enrique Perez Luño, *La seguridad jurídica*, Barcelona, Ariel, 1991, p. 24. Critics on the issue: Gianmarco Gometz, *La certezza giuridica come prevedibilità*, Torino, Giappichelli, 2005, pages 13, 205 and 209.

[111] Jerome Frank, *Law and the modern mind*, New Brunswick, Transaction, 2009, p. 37 (1st ed., New York, Brentano's Inc., 1930; 2nd rev. ed., New York, Coward-McCann, 1949).

[112] Alberto Xavier, *Os princípios da legalidade e da tipicidade da tributação*, São Paulo, Ed. RT, 1978, p. 92. More recently, in a similar sense: idem, *Tipicidade da tributação, simulação e norma antielisiva*, São Paulo, Dialética, 2001, p. 18.

[113] Wilhelm Hartz, “Mehr Rechtssicherheit im Steuerrecht. Ziele, Wege, Grenzen”, *StbJb*, p. 77, 1965/1966.

[114] Frédéric Douet, *Contribution à l'étude de la sécurité juridique en Droit Interne Français*, Paris, LGDJ, 1997, p. 17.

5.2.2.1.2 Alternative Conception of the Object

It can also be argued that what ought to be understood and calculated has alternative meanings. The alternative understanding of the object, however, can take different forms.

First, alternation can be stated in the form rule "X" may have possible meanings "A," "B" and "C" ($X = A$, B *or* C).[115] This can be termed the indeterminate conception of interpretation, as it argues that the language of rules is entirely or broadly indeterminate and that the interpreter therefore cannot either know or predict the meaning of a legal rule. It is a radical conception, which when taken to an extreme rejects the very notion of a legal rule because if all rules are meaningless before a decision is made, only a legal decision has value. This is the extreme realism espoused by Frank.[116] Adopting this conception entails an acceptance that every legal decision is retroactive, because before it there was nothing. Moreover, it implicitly rejects the very possibility of realizing the principle of irretroactivity.

Second, alternation can be defended from another angle, by stating that rule "X" embodies a notion ($X = A$) but this notion in turn comprises several elements that do not need to be entirely present and can be dispensed with, as the presence of one or several of them (depending on the case) is enough. This can be called the *typological conception of interpretation*, as it is grounded in the idea that rules contain not classificatory concepts whose verification depends on the necessary existence of all the abstractly stipulated elements ($A = a + b + c$), but types, i.e. general valorative notions whose verification depends on the concrete configuration of the general idea – and thus on the existence of one or more elements, but not necessarily all ($A = a$, b *and/or* c).[117]

Third, alternation can be seen from yet another angle, by stating that rule "X" calls for a concept ($X = A$) but despite a halo of certainty or core of meaning this concept may leave room for indeterminacy to some extent ($A = A+$ *or* $A-$), depending on the kind of rule (conceptual or finalistic) and the principles relating to it (legal certainty or justice). This can be termed the *determinable conception of interpretation*, as it is based on the idea that while rules contain concepts, language makes them indeterminate to some extent and determinate to some extent (usually because of jurisprudential practice or doctrinal consensus) or determinable (case by case, based on the normative and factual context). These cores of meaning, intersubjectively fixed by doctrine or jurisprudence, cannot be ignored by the interpreter.

---

[115]Tércio Sampaio Ferraz Jr., "Segurança jurídica, coisa julgada e justiça", *Revista do Instituto de Hermenêutica Jurídica*, v. 1, n. 3, p. 264, Porto Alegre, 2005.

[116]Jerome Frank, *Law and the modern mind*, New Brunswick, Transaction, 2009, pages 37 and following. (1st ed., New York, Brentano's Inc., 1930; 2nd rev. ed., New York, Coward-McCann, 1949).

[117]Ricardo Lobo Torres, "O princípio da tipicidade no Direito Tributário", in Ricardo Lodi Ribeiro e Sergio André Rocha (Orgs.), *Legalidade e tipicidade no Direito Tributário*, São Paulo, Quartier Latin, 2008, p. 137.

The latter two views, albeit different, start from the common assumption that legal norms translated into language are necessarily indeterminate to some extent.[118] They may therefore have alternative meanings.[119] Hence instead of "determinacy" and "predictability," the words "determinability" and "calculability" are used to refer to the ability of citizens in general and taxpayers specifically to know the possible meanings of any norm they will obey, and to control how the executive and judiciary will concretize it. Here determinability means the ability to know the alternative meanings of the norm, and calculability means the ability to control the alternative meanings of future normative decisions.[120] Thus legal certainty is the assurance that citizens can know and calculate the alternative consequences the law may ascribe to acts or facts, so that the consequence actually applied in future falls *within* those reduced and anticipated alternatives. Prediction of a consequence is successful not when the meaning eventually ascribed by a judicial or administrative body is precisely the only one expected, but when the decision made falls within the *scope* of the predictable alternative interpretations and abstractly foreseen consequences. The substantive limitation represented by the constitutional order works as a valuable tool to delimit the possible normative contents of the legislation.[121] However, such meanings, albeit alternative, may be packed into a single meaning by a legal decision, thus creating a true normative expectation of behavior for all cases in the same group, as noted by Machado Derzi.[122]

This last conception is the most recommendable, given the impossibility of a univocal meaning. However, this means the main axis of legal certainty is no longer predictability of content, but controllability of decisions.[123] The pair "predictability *vs.* determinacy" is replaced by "controllability *vs.* non-arbitrariness." This is the overall approach taken by Gianformaggio, Habermas and Palombella, to name but a few,[124] albeit without adequately specifying their criteria.

---

[118] Joseph Raz, "The rule of law and its virtue (1977)", in *The authority of Law. Essays on Law and Morality*, Oxford, Oxford, 1979, p. 215. On the open texture of language, see mostly: H. L. Hart, *The Concept of Law*, Oxford, Clarendon, 1991 (1961).

[119] Gianmarco Gometz, *La Certezza giuridica come prevedibilità*, Torino, Giappichelli, 2005, pages 13 and 205; Misabel de Abreu Machado Derzi, *Modificações da jurisprudência no Direito Tributário*, São Paulo, Noeses, 2009, p. 72.

[120] Gianmarco Gometz, *La Certezza giuridica come prevedibilità*, Torino, Giappichelli, 2005, pages 13 and 208.

[121] Luigi Ferrajoli, "The past and the future of the rule of law", in Pietro Costa e Danilo Zolo (Orgs.), *The rule of Law – History, theory and criticism*, Dordrecht, Springer, 2007, p. 329.

[122] Misabel de Abreu Machado Derzi, *Modificações da jurisprudência no Direito Tributário*, São Paulo, Noeses, 2009, p. 188.

[123] Federico Arcos Ramírez, *La seguridad jurídica: una teoría formal*, Madrid, Dykinson, 2000, p. 326; Letizia Gianformaggio, "Certezza del Diritto", in Enrico Diciotti e Vito Velluzzi (Orgs.), *Filosofia del Diritto e ragionamento giuridico*, Torino, Giappichelli, 2008, p. 85.

[124] Letizia Gianformaggio, "Certezza del Diritto", in Letizia Gianformaggio (Org.), *Studi sulla giustificazione giuridica*, Torino, Giuppichelli, 1986; Jürgen Habermas, *Faktizität und Geltung*, Darmstadt, Wissenschaftliche Buchgesellschaft, 2002, pp. 239–291; Gianluigi Palombella, *Dopo la certezza – Il Diritto in equilibrio tra Giustizia e Democrazia*, Bari, Dedalo, 2006, p. 8.

In tax law this understanding is also manifest in the debate concerning the content of the legality requirement, seen from the state's viewpoint as the lawmaker's duty to determine the general parameters of a tax obligation with the highest determinability possible when instituting a tax rule, and from the taxpayer's viewpoint as the ability to understand the possible alternative meanings of the rule. It is in this context that the existence of the "principle of open typicality" is defended.[125]

So far we have examined the meaning of "knowing" and "calculating" in the sphere of law. The next step is to resume our examination of the term "law." This is because, depending on the theory of knowledge and law adopted, knowledge and calculability may not refer exclusively to a norm but instead to a rational procedure for (re)constructing a norm – which is subtly different. Thus if it is admitted that legal consequences are encapsulated in the legal norm and must be extracted by the interpreter, then legal certainty indeed has a norm as its object. However, if it is accepted that legal consequences essentially depend on an *argumentative process* that reconstructs normative meaning, then the object of legal certainty is not a norm, or at least not only a norm; instead, its object is an argumentative process. In this respect, therefore, legal certainty can be seen as existing when citizens are able to know and calculate law as the semantic content of legal norms, or as the structure and criteria of the arguments needed to reconstruct the content of legal norms. These two conceptions regarding the object of understanding and calculation by citizens are analyzed below.

5.2.2.2 Regarding the Object of Understanding

5.2.2.2.1 The Objectivist Conception of Law

On this view law is perceived as an object to be entirely revealed by the interpreter. The legal norm has a meaning, and hence the interpreter must discover the predetermined meaning of the norm through a static and deterministic activity. From this perspective, law above all involves a semantic problem, while interpretation involves an objectivist activity and legal certainty a problem of "certainty of the object": Law is ready-made and placed before the interpreter, who passively reveals it.

5.2.2.2.2 The Argumentative Conception of Law

On this other view law is understood as an argumentative structure through which the possible semantic alternatives of a norm are reconstructed by means of

---

125 Ricardo Lobo Torres, "O princípio da tipicidade no Direito Tributário", in Ricardo Lodi Ribeiro e Sergio André Rocha (Orgs.), *Legalidade e tipicidade no Direito Tributário*, São Paulo, Quartier Latin, 2008, p. 137.

hermeneutical criteria. In general, a legal norm does not have a single meaning, but semantic alternatives and cores of meaning, so that the interpreter must reconstruct decisional alternatives dynamically and argumentatively. From this perspective, law above all involves an argumentative problem, while interpretation involves an intermediate activity and legal certainty a problem of "certainty of argumentation." Thus in this case legal certainty is not certainty of the object but rational and argumentative certainty.[126]

These considerations – to which we will return – are sufficient to show that the expression "legal certainty" may refer to two different objects: on one hand, certainty of the object (a result revealed by a norm); on the other, certainty of an activity relative to an object (a means by which a normative meaning is reconstructed).[127]

5.3 Subjective Aspect (Who Are the Subjects of Certainty?)

5.3.1 Preliminary Considerations

As Pacteau states, "certainty for some is not certainty for others."[128] In other words, depending on the *perspective* used to analyze the states of knowability, reliability and calculability, they may exist, not exist or exist in different degrees. A law may be obvious to an expert but not to an ordinary citizen.[129] A law or administrative act can be clearly void for some and valid for others.[130] That is precisely why at bottom the issue of legal certainty involves a subjective aspect.[131] Consequently, a study of legal certainty that leaves out its personal aspect is uncertain in its treatment.

[126]Neil MacCormick, "Rhetoric and rule of law", in David Dyzenhaus (Org.), *Recrafting the rule of Law – The Limits of Legal Order*, Oxford, Hart, 1999, p. 163.

[127]Stefano Bertea, *Certezza del Diritto e argomentazione giuridica*, Soveria Manelli, Rubbertino, 2002, p. 294.

[128]Bernard Pacteau, "La sécurité juridique, un principe que nous manque?", *AJDA* 20, 1995, p. 154.

[129]Federico Arcos Ramírez, *La seguridad jurídica: una teoría formal*, Madrid, Dykinson, 2000, p. 260.

[130]Almiro do Couto e Silva, "O princípio da segurança jurídica (proteção à confiança) no Direito Público brasileiro e o direito da Administração Pública de anular os seus próprios atos: o prazo decadencial do art. 54 da Lei do Processo Administrativo da União (Lei n. 9.784/99)", *RDA* 237, p. 300, Rio de Janeiro, 2004.

[131]Antonio Perez Luño, *La Seguridad Jurídica*, Barcelona, Ariel, 1991, p. 22.

5.3.2 Perspective of Who Will Benefit from Legal Certainty (Certainty for Whom?)

5.3.2.1 Legal Certainty for a Citizen

The first element to be studied in the subjective aspect concerns the perspective of who will benefit from legal certainty. Clarity of norms denotes an objective requirement because precision can be evaluated objectively. However, the same is not true of intelligibility, which is largely subjective as it is evaluated from the viewpoint of the addressee; a norm can be more or less intelligible depending on who analyzes it.[132] This is due to the subjectivation of certainty, by virtue of which it is possible to tell whether something is certain or seems certain *for someone*.[133]

Legal certainty can take on a strictly individual dimension when its use aims to protect an individual's private interests.[134] The legal order contains several norms that protect this dimension, such as protection for acquired rights, completed legal acts, and res iudicata, in which legal certainty acts in a concrete and reflexive manner towards a given subject. Individual matters are analyzed rather than collective ones.

5.3.2.2 Legal Certainty for Citizens

Legal certainty can also take on a collective dimension, however, when its use has the purpose of preserving the legal order as a whole for the entire collectivity. The legal order also contains several norms that protect this dimension, such as the Brazilian Supreme Court's powers of judicial review and constitutional control, whereby it has the authority to modulate the effects of a declaration of unconstitutionality on the basis of legal certainty. This is also the case in diffuse control of constitutionality, when a general consequence is acknowledged at the appeal level. In these cases, as we will see later, general questions are examined relating to the effectiveness of the legal order overall or of a particular sector.

5.3.2.3 Legal Certainty for the State?

A very important question is whether the state can benefit from legal certainty. Here the first step is to define in what sense "legal certainty" is used.

---

[132] Anne-Laure Valembois, *La constitutionnalisation de l'exigence de sécurité juridique en Droit Français*, Paris, LGDJ, 2005, p. 287.

[133] Christoph Gusy, "Gewährleistung von Freiheit und Sicherheit im Lichte unterschiedlicher Staats- und Verfassungsverständnisse", *VVDStRL* 63, p. 159, Berlin, 2004.

[134] Anne-Laure Valembois, *La constitutionnalisation de l'exigence de sécurité juridique en Droit Français*, Paris, LGDJ, 2005, p. 19.

If by legal certainty is meant an objective principle, then knowability, reliability and calculability of the legal order in general are obviously indispensable to the state. Abstraction and typification are technical instruments that assure the certainty function inherent in the concept of legal certainty and assessable from the perspective of the issuer of normative commands, as noted by Ferraz Jr.[135] Hence the expression *Funktionsfähigkeit des Staates* used by legal scholars to denote the idea that the functionality of the state cannot be assured without rationality.[136]

In light of the above, it is possible to postulate, for instance, the prospective efficacy (*ex nunc* effect) of a Supreme Court decision by arguing that normal retroactive efficacy (declaratory *ex tunc* effect) would cause significant normative or institutional instability, and might even prevent the state from "functioning". As we will see later on, this possibility depends not only on the effective demonstration of such instability, but also on weighing all the consequences for the principle of certainty itself of choosing one or the other attribution of efficacy to the decision: In some situations, maintaining the past effects of a norm or act that is vitiated by unconstitutionality will protect the stability of the legal order without causing calculability problems; in others, however, maintaining past effects paradoxically contributes to a loss of credibility, stability and calculability for the legal order. This is the case, to be detailed below, when opting for the prospective efficacy of a decision in the name of the stability of the legal order does not devalue the issuance of an unconstitutional norm and thus encourages the state to issue other unconstitutional norms in future, given the benefit accruing from unlawfulness. In this case, in the name of legal certainty (in its dynamic dimension, from the objective standpoint of reliability through stability) even more uncertainty is created (in its dynamic dimension, from the objective standpoint of reliability through credibility and efficacy, and of reliability through continuity).

If instead legal certainty is used in a subjective sense, as the reflexive application of the principle of legal certainty relative to some subject, there are already serious normative obstacles to its consideration in favor of the state. These obstacles are of two kinds.

First, and in general, the reflexive and subjective efficacy of the principle of legal certainty as protection of trust is developed under the aegis of fundamental rights and not primarily of the principle of the rule of law. And fundamental rights can be used in their defensive and protective efficacy only by citizens, not the state. The state lacks the requisite personal substrate, connection with the exercise of freedom, relationship with human dignity and positioning as addressee of norms. It is an objective institution, not a human being; it does not exercise freedom, only jurisdiction and power; it has no dignity; it is not an addressee but the issuer of norms. Therefore the state cannot use the principle of protection of trust to make

[135] Tércio Sampaio Ferraz Jr., "Segurança jurídica e normas gerais tributárias", *RDT* 17–18, p. 55, São Paulo, 1981.

[136] Paul Kirchhof, *Schrifte des Instituts Finanzen und Steuern*, n. 362, p. 28, Bonn, 1998.

past effects intangible, by claiming to have trusted that the norm later declared unconstitutional would be upheld, since this principle is built upon the fundamental rights of freedom and property, of which it is the owner.

On the other hand, specifically in the case of tax law, as we will see, the principle of legal certainty becomes protective of citizens, because its foundations relating to taxation (legality, anteriority, irretroactivity, protection of trust, equality) are designed not to further but to limit state action. The state therefore cannot invoke the trust protection principle within the scope of tax law to make past effects intangible, since this principle in this sphere benefits the taxpayer and not the state, as will be justified later.

5.3.3 Perspective of Who Serves as a the Criterion for Measuring Legal Certainty (Certainty in Whose View?)

5.3.3.1 Legal Certainty from the Viewpoint of Ordinary Citizens

Besides knowing who benefits from legal certainty, the subjective aspect also involves examining who serves as the *criterion* for measuring it. First, legal certainty can involve knowledge of, trust in and calculation of the law by an ordinary citizen. This understanding is a consequence of the fact that citizens are the addressees of norms, whose main purpose is to provide guidance to anyone subject to normative prescriptions.[137]

In the case of tax law, this requirement affects the very concepts used by lawmakers: There will be knowability, for instance, when taxpayers themselves, not their lawyers or accountants, are able to access the norm they must obey and to understand its content. This perspective is also important in showing whether the taxpayer's trust is protected when the trust-generating base (a law, administrative act, administrative decision or court order) is clearly illegal or lacks clarity. Thus the doctrine first of civil law and then of administrative law developed the image of "average citizens" (*citoyens moyens*) or "good parents" (*bons pères de famille*) to represent the ordinary citizen, who is not an expert in law but is prudent, well informed and lacking in bad faith.[138] In this respect, citizens should be able to understand a norm "without intellectual gymnastics", as Pfersmann puts it.[139]

The perspective of who will assess normative quality is therefore essential, because it is impossible to know whether an act is evidently or manifestly illegal without knowing in whose view illegality is to be established. Some flaws are

[137]Gianmarco Gometz, *La certezza giuridica come prevedibilità*, Torino, Giappichelli, 2005, pp. 202–203; Katharina Sobota, *Das Prinzip Rechtsstaat*, Tübingen, Mohr Siebeck, 1997, p. 155.

[138]Sylvia Calmes, *Du principe de protection de la confiance légitime en Droits Allemand, Communautaire et Français*, Paris, Dalloz, 2001, pages 367 and 378.

[139]Otto Pfersmann, "Constitution et sécurité juridique – Autriche", *Annuaire International de Justice Constitutionnelle 1999*, Paris, Economica.

reasonably predictable for a specialist in tax law but imperceptible to the layperson. This is why Duong refers to certainty as reasonable inasmuch as it depends upon the content of the text in question, the domain it covers, and the number and quality of its addressees.[140]

5.3.3.2 Legal Certainty from the Viewpoint of Operators of the Law

Second, legal certainty may involve knowledge, trust and calculation of the law by an expert in the object of regulation. This understanding arises from the content of norms, which cannot be suitably regulated without the use of precise technical terms.

In the sphere of tax law this understanding also affects the concepts used by lawmakers: for example, there will be knowability if technicians can decode tax concepts, regardless of whether taxpayers can do so without help.

5.3.3.3 Legal Certainty from the Viewpoint of the State?

The question whether legal certainty can be assessed from the viewpoint of the state must be answered in the negative, since the norms that create taxes are addressed to taxpayers, not the state. The state issues the norms taxpayers must obey. That being so, it is entirely inappropriate to assess knowability, reliability and calculability from the viewpoint of the issuer of norms rather than of those who must obey them and hence have to understand, trust and calculate based on them.

5.3.4 Perspective of Who Guarantees Legal Certainty (Certainty Guaranteed by Whom?)

5.3.4.1 Legal Certainty Guaranteed by the Legislative

The subjective aspect also includes knowing who ought to guarantee legal certainty. At this level all three branches of government, legislative, executive and judiciary, ought to assure legal certainty.[141] As each of them plays a different role, the realization of legal certainty is also different.

---

[140] Lémy Duong, "La sécurité juridique et les standards du Droit Économique: la notion de raisonnable", in Laurence Boy, Jean-Baptiste Racine e Fabrice Siiriainen (Orgs.), *Sécurité juridique et Droit Économique*, Bruxelles, Larcier, 2008, pages 217 and 229.

[141] Maria Sylvia Zanella Di Pietro, "Os princípios da proteção à confiança, da segurança jurídica e da boa-fé na anulação do ato administrativo", in Fabrício Motta (Org.), *Direito Público atual: Estudos em homenagem ao Professor Nélson Figueiredo*, Instituto de Direito Administrativo de Goiás (IDAG), Belo Horizonte, Fórum, 2008, p. 297; José Joaquim Gomes Canotilho, *Direito Constitucional e Teoria da Constituição*, 7th ed., 6th reprint, Coimbra, Livraria Almedina, 2004,

The activity of the legislative is typically forward-looking, as laws deal with facts that will occur after their enactment. Lawmakers are concerned with the future and aim to construct "new" law with what normally happens as their compass.[142] This is why laws are written as general and abstract norms addressed to an indeterminate number of people and situations. This assures uniform treatment of citizens in general, and taxpayers in particular. However, owing to the social and legal factors presented in the Introduction to this book, legislation has caused problems of knowability, reliability and calculability: knowability because of the indeterminacy and complexity of laws; reliability because of their instability and the limited number of previously consolidated situations or of even guaranteed expectations; and calculability because changes are not smooth and the development of the legal order lacks coherence.

Because of these problems, the legislative has the duty to preserve legal certainty by several means, including setting a standard for the determinability of the hypotheses of incidence, prohibiting restrictions on acquired rights, completed legal acts and res iudicata, prohibiting retroactive legislation that harms legitimate trust, including transitional rules or equity clauses – and so forth.

5.3.4.2 Legal Certainty Guaranteed by the Executive

The primary activity of the executive is to enforce the laws. Thus public administrators are concerned with the present and aim to concretize law case by case.[143] However, at times this function is performed not only contrary to legal provisions, but also by issuing administrative acts, normative acts or administrative contracts that also cause problems of knowability, reliability and calculability of law: knowability because if they are contrary to legal provisions, they prevent taxpayers from knowing what to obey, or because they are excessively detailed or in breach of published normative acts; reliability because of administrative acts that revoke or void others under whose aegis past situations were consolidated, or because of interpretative normative acts that aim to interpret previous legal provisions with retroactive effects; and calculability because of a lack of transitional rules covering changes in administrative interpretation, for example.

Because of such hindrances, the executive must also fulfill various duties in order to preserve legal certainty, among which are not revoking or voiding previous acts on the basis of which a taxpayer may have performed disposals, issuing transitional rules when interpretations change abruptly – and so forth.

---

p. 257; Andreas Vonkilch, *Das Intertemporale Privatrecht*, Wien, Springer, 1999, p. 336; Xavier Philippe, "Constitution et sécurité juridique", *Annuaire International de Justice Constitutionnelle 1999*, Paris, Economica, 2000, p. 81; José L. Mezquita del Cacho, *Seguridad jurídica y sistema cautelar*, v. 1, *Teoría de la Seguridad Jurídica*, Barcelona, Bosch, 1989.

[142]Gehard Husserl, *Recht und Zeit*, Frankfurt am Main, Vittorio Klostermann, 1995, p. 54.

[143]Gehard Husserl, *Recht und Zeit*, Frankfurt am Main, Vittorio Klostermann, 1995, p. 52.

5.3.4.3 Legal Certainty Guaranteed by the Judiciary

The primary activity of the judiciary is backward-looking because its decisions relate to prior facts narrated by the parties. Judges are concerned with the past, basing their decisions on the norms in force and the facts that have already occurred.[144] As explained by Machado Derzi, the fact that the efficacy of the judiciary's manifestations focuses on the past does not mean they do not have effects on the present and the future: depending on the intended efficacy (declaratory, constitutive or condemnatory), they do indeed have an impact on the present and the future. Multidimensional efficacy is inherent in every decision, given the way it blends past and future.[145]

However, for the social and legal reasons outlined in the Introduction to this book, the judiciary has also caused problems of knowability, reliability and calculability: knowability because decisions lack a sound legal basis or even because of divergence between decisions, bodies or courts; reliability because of changes to firm legal precedents with retroactive efficacy even for those who acted under the former interpretations in accordance with their fundamental rights; and calculability because changes in interpretation are not smooth or lack coherence.

In light of these problems, the judiciary must also fulfill various duties to preserve legal certainty, including the duty to ground its decisions in a sufficient and rational legal basis, not making retroactive changes to precedents in such a way as to affect legitimate trust, using moderation mechanisms to change precedents – and so forth.

The key point is that the legal certainty principle applies to all three branches, each of which contributes substantially to its realization.

5.4 *Time Aspect (or Legal Certainty When?)*

5.4.1 The Moment of Realizing the Ideal State

The temporal aspect of legal certainty is usually addressed by taking time into consideration merely as the perspective in which the sub-elements of the legal certainty principle are examined. For example, it is said that the requirement of stability of the law through the intangibility of certain situations concerns the past, whereas the duty to guarantee the predictability of state actions concerns the future. Time – past, present and future – operates only as the perspective in which the sub-elements of legal certainty are analyzed, thus serving a predominantly classificatory purpose. What I mean to show here is different: My point is that an examination of the temporal aspect can – and as will be justified later on, *ought to* –

[144]Gehard Husserl, *Recht und Zeit*, Frankfurt am Main, Vittorio Klostermann, 1995, p. 58.

[145]Misabel de Abreu Machado Derzi, *Modificações da jurisprudência no Direito Tributário*, São Paulo, Noeses, 2009, pages 236 and 246.

operate as a criterion for testing the extent to which the legal certainty principle is effectively *realized*. This can be best explained by means of the following examples.

The first example consists of the possible *alternatives for the internal content of decisions* in the diffuse control of constitutionality. When presented with an administrative act performed by an authority lacking competence on a matter lying outside its jurisdiction, the Supreme Court may declare the act and its effects null and void, or may instead uphold its validity and effects. Let us assume the Court decides to uphold the validity of the act and preserve its effects based on the principle of legal certainty, arguing that the apparent legality of the administrative act and the long time elapsed since it was issued have consolidated a de facto situation which must become legally intangible in accordance with the legal certainty principle. In this case, the Court upholds the validity of the act and preserves its effects.

In a second example, let us imagine the *alternatives for the external efficacy of decisions* in the concentrated control of constitutionality. When presented with an infraconstitutional norm incompatible with the Constitution, the Supreme Court may declare it null and void *ex tunc*, or may instead declare it invalid *ex nunc* or *pro futuro*. Let us assume the Court decides to declare the norm unconstitutional only for the future and to keep intact the effects produced by the norm in the past based on the principle of legal certainty, arguing that if it declared the norm null and void, it would cause a "state of legal uncertainty." In this case, the Court declares the norm to be incompatible with the Constitution but limits the effects of its decision to the future.

In these two examples the reasoning underscored represents the "state of legal uncertainty" and by extension the legal certainty principle in the contrasted pair "certainty *vs.* uncertainty" but does not take due note of a circumstance I shall go on to highlight, which is that the realization of legal certainty *in one period* might cause it to be restricted *in another period.*

Indeed, to return to the first example, if the validity and effects of the administrative act are upheld, the problem of uncertainty is resolved concerning past action, but uncertainty is simultaneously created concerning the present and future: *concerning the present*, because the decision creates a lack of certainty about the validity and enforcement of norms, either because citizens will not know for sure which norms to obey, given that invalid norms may produce effects, or because the administrative authorities will not know the exact limits of their jurisdiction, given that even acts lacking it may at times have efficacy; *concerning the future*, because the decision creates a lack of certainty about the effects the legal order will ascribe to present acts, both for citizens – who will no longer be able to foresee the future effects of such acts, given that even invalid acts may produce effects – and for administrative authorities – who might feel encouraged to act outside their jurisdiction, judging that doing so will nevertheless produce effects in the future.

A similar situation occurs in the second example. If a declaration of unconstitutionality produces effects for the future only, the problem of uncertainty is likewise resolved concerning the past, but at the same time and in the same manner uncertainty is created concerning the present and the future: *concerning the present*, because the decision creates a lack of certainty about the general efficacy of legal decisions, either because citizens will not know for sure which norms to obey, given that even unconstitutional laws may produce effects, or because administrative authorities will not exactly know the boundaries of their jurisdiction, given that unconstitutional acts may generate effects; *concerning the future*, because this modulation of the effects of the decision creates a lack of certainty concerning the effects the legal order will ascribe in future to acts performed outside a given constitutional jurisdiction, either because citizens will not be able to foresee the future effects of such acts, given that even unconstitutional laws may produce effects, or because the legislative may occasionally feel encouraged to enact unconstitutional laws, given the lack of negative consequences ascribed by the judiciary to violation of the Constitution.

These two examples show that the legal certainty principle cannot be realized by doing what is advisable only analytically, for the sake of comprehension: *splitting* past, present and future. Instead, application of the law requires an analysis of the temporal dimension from a *single* perspective encompassing all three periods: certainty today, yesterday and tomorrow. As Machado Derzi brilliantly states, trust and reliability involve the past as well as the present and the future: the fact of trust situated in the past; the trust that lives on in the present; and the trust that is projected into the future.[146]

5.4.1.1 Legal Certainty Today

Present certainty requires an analysis of the static or structural aspect of legal certainty to assess the existence of a greater or lesser degree of substantive knowability, via the accessibility and scope of norms, and greater or lesser intellectual knowability, via normative determinability and clarity.

In this dimension, the citizen's capacity to understand the norms they must obey is investigated. Thus any decision that may restrict the "certainty of existence and enforcement" and the "certainty of content", both of which we will examine in greater depth later on, is a decision that restricts "the present dimension of the state of certainty." Besides this dimension, however, there are two others, past and future.

5.4.1.2 Legal Certainty Yesterday

Past certainty requires an analysis of the dynamic or intertemporal aspect of legal certainty to assess whether the conditions for the intangibility of past situations exist. A global understanding of the temporal aspect of legal certainty is not

[146]Misabel de Abreu Machado Derzi, *Modificações da jurisprudência no Direito Tributário*, São Paulo, Noeses, 2009, p. XXIV.

problematic as far as the past is concerned because it is typically past decisions that aim to realize a "state of certainty." The real problem is the possible consequences of pursuing certainty in the past for certainty in the present and future.

5.4.1.3 Legal Certainty Tomorrow

Future certainty requires an analysis, still within the dynamic aspect of legal certainty, of whether the preservation of certainty in the past will cost the realization of certainty in the future. In some situations, maintaining the effects of norms, whether general or individual, that are contrary to the legal order (or to a part of it, usually its formal principles or rules of jurisdiction) encourages their addressees, particularly the state, to behave unlawfully because they believe the legal effects of their unlawful acts will nonetheless be preserved. This is undoubtedly the worst problem of all: A past decision to uphold a norm or the effects of a norm may restrict the state of certainty in the present and future to a greater or lesser extent, for the simple reason that this kind of decision contains a "counterorder".

This "counterorder" is manifested by the existence of a later order (upholding the effects of an invalid norm) which opposes a previous order (excluding the effects of an invalid act). Simply put, the counterorder is externalized as a restriction of the certainty of guidance and application resulting from the upholding of the effects of unlawful acts. If norms serve as guidance for citizens and as a constraint on and foundation for the exercise of power by the authorities, whenever an act is upheld that runs counter to norms that are valid and in force at the time, the effect is to validate yesterday's unlawfulness today and potentially to encourage unlawfulness tomorrow. The law misleads instead of leading, and this creates a restriction for its observance tomorrow. A conflict is thereby created regarding the consequence that addressees of the norm should expect: They can expect either that unconstitutional norms will be declared null and thus void of effects, or that they will be declared valid and their effects upheld. However – and this is the problem in all its gravity – if citizens do not know what to expect, they cannot foresee; and if they cannot foresee, they cannot find guidance in the law. If that happens, certainty in the past is obtained at the expense of uncertainty in the future. Under the rule of law, citizens ought to be able legitimately to expect that unconstitutional norms be declared as such, and that this declaration entails their effective eviction from the legal order.[147] If citizens who expect unconstitutionality find constitutionality, or receive stones instead of bread ("des pierres à la place de pain"), the law will begin to lose part of its efficacy and consequently part of the legal certainty it aims to preserve.[148] And if the state sees no concrete confirmation of the consequences

[147] César García Novoa, *El principio de seguridad jurídica en materia tributaria*, Madrid, Marcial Pons, 2000, p. 183.

[148] Anne-Laure Valembois, *La constitutionnalisation de l'exigence de sécurité juridique en Droit Français*, Paris, LGDJ, 2005, p. 226.

abstractly provided for and wagers that present unconstitutional acts will be upheld in future, it will be tempted to raise unconstitutional taxes in order to fill the public coffers.[149]

These observations, to which we will return in due course, have the utmost practical importance, because they show that the "state of certainty" can only be examined *as a whole*, even though it can and should be analytically broken up into conceptually separate time units. This is crucial in the case of tax law, as will be shown later in the section of this book on the content of legal certainty, because upholding the effects of unconstitutional tax laws under the pretext of promoting legal certainty may actually restrict it further.

These considerations justify the thesis advanced in this book that the meaning of legal certainty must be analyzed in every dimension and, as far as the temporal dimension is concerned, for past, present and future alike. The "ambivalent nature" of the certainty principle, requiring at once continuity and innovation, firmness and flexibility, cannot be disregarded.[150] Precisely for this reason, if only one temporal dimension is scrutinized, any of the following problems will necessarily result: If our sole concern is the present, the narrative coherence of law and the very justification of decisions in time are lost; considering the past alone risks immobility and may encourage future non-compliance with the laws; focusing solely on the future blurs the reality of law because the future benefits from the present and the past.[151] As we will see in due course, this risk arises most of all when unlawful administrative acts and unconstitutional laws are upheld with the argument that declaring them void would create a state of instability. Assuring stability by upholding the past effects of acts contrary to the law risks encouraging opposition to it in future.

5.4.2 The Moment of Verifying or Predicting the Ideal State

The time factor also works as a benchmark to analyze the moment of verifying calculability. In this sense, it is important to emphasize that the reaction time in applying consequences is a key element to increase the degree of normative calculability. This is because the more citizens are able to predict the moment of definition of a legal consequence applicable to acts and facts, the greater their capacity to plan the actions required to carry out their intentions.[152] For example, if taxpayers know that administrative procedures take a long time, they may decide not

---

[149] Gerhardt Habscheidt, *Der Anspruch des Bürgers auf Erstattung verfassungswidriger Steuern*, Köln, Otto Schmidt, 2003, p. 54.

[150] Heike Pohl, *Rechtsprechungsänderung und Rückanknüpfung*, Berlin, Duncker und Humblot, 2005, p. 178.

[151] Gehard Husserl, *Recht und Zeit*, Frankfurt am Main, Vittorio Klostermann, 1995, p. 50.

[152] Gianmarco Gometz, *La certezza giuridica come prevedibilità*, Torino, Giappichelli, 2005, p. 229.

to pursue them but instead to file a lawsuit immediately; if they know the judicial procedure takes a long time, they may choose legal remedies that protect them against the passage of time, such as opting for a judicial deposit to avoid future interest expense on cumulative tax arrears.

This observation is extremely valuable to an understanding of legal certainty. For if calculability is defined as the mere capacity to predict legal consequences, legal certainty will be greatest when the least time elapses between prediction of the consequences and their definition. The ideal calculability is that of a legal system in which consequences are foreseen and decided almost instantly. In that sense, there would be no calculability in systems with long administrative or legal processes. However, if calculability is defined as the ability to foresee the *range of consequences* and the *time frame* needed to define them, there will be more legal certainty, since the ability to foresee consequences and their moment of definition is greater. In this other sense, there can be calculability even when administrative or legal processes take a long time to reach a final solution.[153]

Given these considerations, legal certainty as a requirement of calculability ought to be defined as the ability of citizens to foresee the range of consequences attributable to acts or facts and the time frame within which the applicable consequence will be defined.

Having examined the temporal aspect of legal certainty, we must now examine its quantitative aspect.

5.5 Quantitative Aspect (or Legal Certainty in What Measure?)

5.5.1 Regarding the Unit of Measure

5.5.1.1 Certainty as Predictability

Legal certainty is associated, for instance, with the ideal of predictability. Citizens ought to be able to predict the legal consequences of their actions. A doctrinal statement of this ideal, however, reveals very little about its content because it says nothing about the meaning of "prediction" or which "actions" it refers to. In this scenario, certainty can be understood as the realization *in every case* and *in their entirety* of the ideals that represent it: always predicting everything, in the case of predictability. Alternatively it can be understood as the realization of those ideals *in most cases* and *in great measure*: predicting *a great deal* of *almost everything*, in the case of predictability. Thus legal certainty can be absolute or relative.[154]

[153]Gianmarco Gometz, *La certezza giuridica come prevedibilità*, Torino, Giappichelli, 2005, p. 231.

[154]Gianmarco Gometz, *La certezza giuridica come prevedibilità*, Torino, Giappichelli, 2005, p. 13.

Indeed, legal certainty is often represented as an ideal state of (absolute) predictability, such that citizens can predict exactly the content of the norms to which they are and will be subject, and the exact consequences of their actions. On this conception, certainty means sureness of normative content and accurate predictability of the consequences to be attributed to the acts performed, as illustrated by the redundant expression "absolutely sure." It is classificatory, "all or nothing", with no room for indeterminacy.[155]

This classifying conception of legal certainty corresponds to an *objectivist concept of interpretation* that focuses on the *result*, in the sense that the duty of the interpreter, through static and deterministic activities concerned solely with semantic aspects, is to reveal the normative content that precedes the interpretation process. The normative content is totally knowable in advance and corresponds to a point, which reality will or will not match. From this perspective, law is a *given object*, regardless of the subject and its process of interpretation and application. To each rule corresponds an interpretation or normative meaning ($R = A$). Thus the problem of legal certainty is substantially a *semantic problem* circumscribed to the predetermination of meaning. As noted above, this is an objectivist view of interpretation based on substantive rules (*rule-dependent certainty of law*).[156] The underlying conception of legal certainty is dual, as it is based on the extremes certainty/uncertainty (sureness/unsureness).[157] Moreover, it blurs the distinction between norms and decision norms, which are entirely different things.[158]

In tax law, this conception corresponds directly or indirectly to the understanding that the principle of legality requires absolute determinacy of the essential elements of a tax obligation, also known as the *principle of closed typicality*. The taxpayer is able to recognize normative meaning in advance by interpreting the tax rule, and the lawmaker's duty is to materialize it comprehensively in the hypothesis of incidence.

5.5.1.2 Certainty as Determinability

From a different perspective, legal certainty represents an ideal state of (relative) sureness, such as the possibility that citizens can predict, with a high degree of determinacy, the content of substantive and procedural norms to which they are and will be subject, or the argumentative structure through which the content of such norms is determined. This conception of certainty is associated with determinability of the content of norms through prior argumentative processes of determination, or with predetermination of the argumentative structure through which norms will

---

[155] Idem, p. 11.

[156] Stefano Bertea, *Certezza del Diritto e argomentazione giuridica*, Soveria Manelli, Rubbertino, 2002, p. 14.

[157] Gianmarco Gometz, *La certezza giuridica come prevedibilità*, Torino, Giappichelli, 2005, p. 30.

[158] Eros Roberto Grau, *Ensaio e discurso sobre a interpretação/aplicação do Direito*, 5th ed., São Paulo, Malheiros Editores, 2009, p. 28.

be interpreted and applied, by the clear indication of criteria and argumentative structures, as represented by the oxymoron "relatively sure." With regard to normative content, it is a non-classificatory conception of certainty, inevitably leaving room for indeterminacy.[159] Concerning the process of legal argumentation, this conception of certainty is argumentative, based on intersubjectively controllable criteria.[160] Legal certainty in this sense is above all rational control of argumentative arbitrariness.[161]

This non-classificatory conception of legal certainty corresponds to an *argumentative conception of interpretation*, based on the *process* through which a result is reached, in the sense that by means of a dynamic and intermediate activity focusing not only on semantic aspects but also on argumentative structures, the interpreter must reconstruct normative content from minimal general semantic cores. Normative content cannot be apprehended in advance except as to its possible interpretations, so that it corresponds to a spectrum which reality matches to a greater or lesser extent. On this conception, law is perceived as an *activity*, dependent on the process of interpretation and application. To each norm correspond several interpretations or normative meanings ($R = A$, B *or* C), to be determined by means of argumentative structures furnished by interpretational metanorms, such as the postulates of proportionality, coherence and reasonableness. Here the problem of legal certainty is essentially an *argumentative problem* circumscribed to the predetermination of minimal possible meanings by means of defined argumentative structures. This is a procedural conception of interpretation based on rational procedures (*procedure-dependent certainty of law*).[162] The underlying conception of legal certainty is therefore not dual but *gradual*, in that it encompasses a range between the poles of total uncertainty and total certainty. Hence it is appropriate to speak of "little," "a great deal of" or "no" certainty from a factual viewpoint.[163]

In tax law, this conception corresponds directly or indirectly to the understanding that the principle of legality requires determinability of the essential elements of the tax obligation. Thus taxpayers can only acknowledge beforehand the reduced normative meanings made possible by interpretation of the tax rule. The legislative's duty is to materialize a concept of the hypothesis of incidence, while the judiciary's is to use rational procedures of application to decide which meaning is correct whenever there is disagreement over more than one relating to a specific situation. This seldom occurs since the language used will have been determined by prior argumentative processes, be they statutory, precedential or jurisprudential. As noted by Dourado, "in fairly mature legal orders indeterminacy is not as frequent

[159] Gianmarco Gometz, *La certezza giuridica come prevedibilità*, Torino, Giappichelli, 2005, p. 12.

[160] Stefano Bertea, *Certezza del Diritto e argomentazione giuridica*, Soveria Manelli, Rubbertino, 2002, p. 295.

[161] Aulis Aarnio, *The rational as reasonable*, Dordrecht, Reidel, 1987, p. 3.

[162] Stefano Bertea, *Certezza del Diritto e argomentazione giuridica*, Soveria Manelli, Rubbertino, 2002, p. 301.

[163] Gianmarco Gometz, *La certezza giuridica come prevedibilità*, Torino, Giappichelli, 2005, p. 30.

as skeptics may fear, because among all instances of indeterminacy (missing disciplines in poor legal systems, contradictory laws in very rich or complex legal systems, laws that do not assure a single answer to a particular case), only in *difficult cases* will laws normally be found where the arguments do not justify a single answer. . . "[164]

As will be clearer below, understanding law as an argumentative practice, and accepting that norms involve not a single meaning but alternative normative meanings, a point to which we will also return later, does not prevent the pursuit of the ideals of knowability, reliability and calculability. This is because on one hand the argumentative nature of law is limited by hermeneutical and applicative postulates that above all reduce the scope of decisions, such as the postulates (or applicational metanorms) of proportionality and reasonableness; and on the other hand the range of alternative normative consequences is limited by jurisprudence and precedents, so that over time certain meanings are deemed more correct or more strongly supported by the constitutional order. The realist conception, according to which a judge's decision depends on frivolous aspects such as whether the judge had a good night's sleep or enjoyed a good breakfast, is indeed completely unrealistic, because decisions never operate in a vacuum but are surrounded by meanings intersubjectively assimilated into language and centuries of interpretations and meanings shared by the operators of the law, among other factors.[165] Cardozo is incomparable in his presentation of the issue:

> Even when a judge is free, he is not entirely free. He cannot innovate for his enjoyment. He is not a free ranger, voluntarily theorizing in search of his own ideal of beauty or goodness. He ought to seek inspiration in consecrated principles. He is not there for spasmodic feelings, for vague and unregulated benevolence. He ought to exercise discretion as informed by the tradition, regulated by analogy, disciplined by the system, and subordinated to the 'prime necessity of order in social life.'[166]

Finally, it should be noted, in Grau's words, that "the 'openness' of legal texts, albeit sufficient to allow the law to remain in the service of reality, is not unbounded. Any interpreter will always be permanently tied by them. Any rupture in this relationship caused by the authentic interpreter will result in subversion of the text."[167]

So far we have examined two opposed concepts of legal certainty with regard to unit of measure – predictability (absolute) or calculability (relative). However, saying that legal certainty involves calculability as the ability to predict legal consequences to a greater or lesser extent is still not enough. How much greater

[164] Ana Paula Dourado, *O princípio da legalidade fiscal – Tipicidade, conceitos jurídicos indeterminados e margem de livre apreciação*, Coimbra, Livraria Almedina, 2007, p. 767.

[165] Alex Kozinski, "What I ate for breakfast and other mysteries of judicial decision making", in David M. O'Brien (Org.), *Judges on judging*, New Jersey, Chatham, 1997, p. 74.

[166] Benjamin N. Cardozo, *The nature of judicial process*, New York, 1921, p. 141.

[167] Eros Roberto Grau, *Ensaio e discurso sobre a interpretação/aplicação do Direito*, 5th ed., São Paulo, Malheiros Editores, 2009, p. 56.

or lesser? To speak of legal certainty at all, we need at least an approximate measure of the *degree of calculability*. Here it is necessary to distinguish between the *depth* and the *breadth* of predictability.[168]

On one hand, the *quantificative depth* or *vertical dimension* of anticipation has to do with the effectiveness, accuracy and duration of predictions. Thus the ability to calculate future normative consequences is greatest when an individual is in a position to predict *a limited number of comprehensible consequences within a reasonable period* – defined as long enough to permit decisions based on legally oriented strategic planning, depending on the action considered.

On the other hand, the *breadth* or *horizontal dimension* of anticipation has to do with the diffusion of certainty across a given class of predictors. On this view, the calculability of future normative consequences is greatest when – to use tax law as an example – *most taxpayers* are in a position to predict a limited number of comprehensible consequences within a reasonable period. A legal norm that is particularly complex, even for scholars, or whose operative facts can be interpreted in multiple ways does not allow for such calculability. It is worth stressing that calculability does not concern the prediction of future events. Only the past and present exist; the future does not, by definition.[169] Calculability in the sense relevant here is not the anticipation of events, but the ability to predict with reasonable depth and breadth the legal consequences whose implementation the legal order requires. Thus it is a matter of predicting not the future but the normative meaning of the present in the future or, more technically, the normative meaning of present action or inaction as interpreted by a decision to be issued in the future.

5.5.2 Regarding Measurement

5.5.2.1 Factual Analysis

Besides defining the meanings of intelligibility and calculability, we must ask yet another question: How is the degree of knowability and calculability of law to be measured? Didactically speaking, two approaches can be distinguished.

On one hand, the degree of legal certainty can be examined by comparing past predictions with future decisions, if any, and measuring the degree to which the predicted consequence matches that which was actually executed. This examination is statistical and based on facts: The more confirmed predictions there are, the more legal certainty there is. Whether or not there is legal certainty can only be known *a posteriori*.

---

[168]Gianmarco Gometz, *La certezza giuridica come prevedibilità*, Torino, Giappichelli, 2005, p. 269.

[169]Mark van Hoecek, "Time and law. Is it the nature of law to last? A conclusion", in François Ost and Mark van Hoecke (Orgs.), *Temps et Droit. Le Droit a-t-il pour vocation de durer?*, Bruxelles, Bruylant, 1998, p. 452.

5.5.2.2 Normative Analysis

On the other hand, the degree of legal certainty can be examined by analyzing certain theoretical normative conditions that are abstractly predictable. This method is therefore juridical: The more abstractly predicted conditions are met, the more legal certainty there is. In this sense, whether or not there is legal certainty can be known *ex ante*.

As I hope to prove during the course of this book, the proposed concept of legal certainty involves the definition of states of affairs (ends) whose existence depends on types of behavior (means) whose effects contribute to its promotion. Thus the definitions of ends and means constitute the requirements for showing whether legal certainty exists, and to what extent. To take an example that will only later become clearer, legal certainty can be said to require the existence of a state of normative knowability; normative knowability exists when norms are accessible and intelligible; normative accessibility exists when taxpayers are able to know the norms they must obey, and intelligibility when they can minimally understand the content of norms; taxpayers can know the norms when they have material access to those norms they must obey, and can minimally understand the content of those norms when they are clear and determinable; and – to finalize this long but necessary chain of elements – taxpayers have material access to the norms they must obey when the norms are published or they are personally notified of the decisions that issue the norms, and the content of norms is determinable when the alternative interpretations are limited, reduced, and comprehensible to ordinary citizens. In sum – and this is the point – legal certainty exists as a state of knowability when there is publication, notification, accessible language and a small number of predicted consequences. Thus in order to confirm whether or not legal certainty exists, it is not necessary – to use the same example – to find out whether taxpayers know the legal norms, and if so how many, but instead to verify whether the legal order has rules regarding the publication, notification, language and scope of the laws.[170]

In sum, it is possible to identify doctrinally the theoretical conditions whose subsistence leads to the existence of ends to be achieved by means of principles.

5.5.3 Regarding the Sufficient Measure

5.5.3.1 Little Uncertainty

A very important issue is the sufficient measure of uncertainty that must be avoided or tolerated. Legal certainty in the sense of an objective principle involves the

[170]Christof Münch, "Rechtssicherheit als Standortfaktor. Gedanken aus Sicht der vorsorgenden Rechtspflege", in Albrecht Weber (Org.), *Währung und Wirtschaft. Das Geld im Recht. FS für Hugo J. Hahn*, Baden-Baden, Nomos, 1997, p. 675.

requirements of knowability, reliability and calculability of law in general. On this conception, a norm that is not very clear, or a legal order that is a little unstable or not totally predictable, can be understood as a violation of the legal certainty principle. Legal certainty in a subjective sense involves the protection of acts that dispose of the rights of freedom and property based on a norm (a rule, administrative act, normative act or administrative or court order). And on this interpretation any sort of frustration of expectation can be perceived as legitimating the application of the principle of protection of trust.

Thus in this respect any restriction on the ideals of normative knowability, reliability and calculability represents in itself a violation of the legal certainty principle. The low degree of uncertainty needed to violate the principle corresponds to an *absolute concept* of legal certainty.

5.5.3.2 A Great Deal of Uncertainty

On the other hand, it can be considered that only a highly indeterminate norm, or an excessively unstable or highly unpredictable legal order, can lead to a violation of the objective dimension of the legal certainty principle, and only a significant frustration of expectation is able to legitimate the application of the principle of protection of trust.

In this specific sense, therefore, it is not any restriction of the ideals of normative knowability, reliability and calculability that leads to a violation of the legal certainty principle. The high degree of uncertainty needed to violate the principle corresponds to a *relative concept* of legal certainty.

In sum, defining the measure of uncertainty that is sufficient to violate the principle of legal certainty is crucial. For instance, can the state, in the name of legal certainty, propose to modulate the effects of an unconstitutionality ruling for the future, alleging that any constraint on past effects would cause instability? What instability, or better yet, "how much" instability is needed to justify ignoring the rule of *ex tunc* efficacy of decisions? Does a massive financial loss constitute "instability" for the legal order? Another example: Can taxpayers claim unfairness and violation of trust by the state if it minimally and gradually changes a tax rule to adjust it to the needs of foreign trade? In sum, these questions and others need to be answered in order to verify whether the legal certainty principle has been violated.

5.6 Justificatory Aspect (Legal Certainty for What and Why?)

5.6.1 Certainty with Functional Value

Legal certainty can be analyzed as having value in itself (merely functional value) or as being an instrument for the realization of other values (instrumental value). Purely functional values do not have any additional value besides that which is embodied in the function they perform.[171] Thus a knife can be good merely because it is sharp and capable of cutting anything, so that it is valuable for its sharpness, regardless of any other element; or it can be considered good because it can cut certain specific things, so that it is valuable or worthless according to the value of what it can cut. Valuing a knife simply because it is sharp, with no other value, is to ascribe *merely functional value*; adding value for the objects it can cut ascribes *instrumental value*. For a knife in this simple illustrative example we can substitute legal certainty. Legal certainty can be valued simply because it assures intelligibility, reliability and calculability, with no other value, or it can be valued for the values whose realization it serves. In the first case, its value is merely functional – it is important simply because it operates as an assumption to guide people; in the second case, its value is instrumental – it is valuable because by serving as a guiding assumption it permits respect for the exercise of freedom and the dignified treatment of human beings.

Thus functional value is ascribed to legal certainty when it is perceived as carrying value in itself, i.e. when it embodies a requirement that has value regardless of being an instrument of other values: A legal order that offers legal certainty is desirable in itself. In this respect, legal certainty can be understood in two ways.

On one hand, legal certainty can have intrinsic value regardless of justice value. This conclusion results from the understanding that certainty is a value in itself. This is often called certainty for its own sake. This understanding is proper to normative formalism, defined as a conception of law according to which a bad rule is better than no rule. In other words, it defends certainty despite injustice because certainty is a form of justice in general. A predictable, stable and sure system is important, especially to avoid arbitrariness, casuistry and breaches of expectations.[172]

On the other hand, legal certainty can have the sort of intrinsic value that adds other values, in the sense that even in an unjust order the existence of legal certainty provides *one more* value. In spite of injustice, at least there would be certainty. The idea is that even when there is injustice the existence of legal certainty offers citizens *additional* advantages, in the sense that they can take strategic action to avoid practices that are even *more unjust*. This observation externalizes an intrinsic value of legal certainty in the sense that an unjust system with legal certainty is better than an unjust system without it. This seems to be the position taken by both MacCormick and Summers.[173] Legal certainty in an unjust system would at least serve to avoid greater injustice.[174]

---

[171]Andrei Marmor, *Law in the age of pluralism*, Oxford, OUP, 2007, p. 9.

[172]Brian Z. Tamanaha, *Law as a means to an end – Threat to the rule of Law*, Cambridge, Cambridge University Press, 2006, p. 230.

[173]Neil MacCormick, *Legal reasoning and legal theory*, Oxford, Clarendon, 1978, p. 63; Robert Summers, *Lon L. Fuller*, Londres, Edward Arnold, 1984, p. 66.

[174]Federico Arcos Ramírez, *La seguridad jurídica: una teoría formal*, Madrid, Dykinson, 2000, p. 170.

5.6.2 Certainty with Instrumental Value

On the other hand, legal certainty can be considered an instrument to assure other rights that involve individual autonomy.[175] Thus we can speak of life, freedom and property "in" certainty, given its role in stabilizing and assuring the necessary conditions for the exercise of freedom.[176] Individual autonomy assumes knowledge of existing and valid norms as well as their stability over time because without these elements people are no longer able to plan and conceive their future.[177] This explains why Rümelin always analyzes legal certainty in connection with the interests of citizens, the interests of determination and equality, freedom, assurance of proof, stability and continuity.[178] Treating it from the angle of interest is a subjective and hence instrumental way of examining legal certainty. This is why Recaséns Siches says "law is not an end in itself, but a special means placed at the service of the realization of several ends."[179] Similarly, Reale places it in the class of "means values" as opposed to "end values," the latter being exemplified by justice.[180] Legal certainty, then, is at the service of individual autonomy.[181] This is evidenced in Ataliba's radiant words:

> The predictability of state action, due to the rigid framework of the Constitution, and the representativeness of the legislative body assure citizens, more than the rights listed in Article 5, of the peace and climate of trust that give them psychological conditions to work, develop, affirm themselves, and expand their personality.[182]

Because legal certainty has to exist so that other rights may also exist, Grau calls it a "scope value" and others call it "guarantee right."[183] Not a guarantee

---

[175] Gianmarco Gometz, *La certezza giuridica come prevedibilità*, Torino, Giappichelli, 2005, pages 220 and 228; Andreas von Arnauld, *Rechtssicherheit*, Tübingen, Mohr Siebeck, 2006, p. 668.

[176] Winfried Brugger, "Gewährleistung von Freiheit und Sicherheit im Lichte unterschiedlicher Staats- und Verfassungsverständnisse", *VVDStRL* 63, p. 102, Berlin, 2004; Christoph Gusy, "Gewährleistung von Freiheit und Sicherheit im Lichte unterschiedlicher Staats- und Verfassungsverständnisse", *VVDStRL* 63, p. 162, Berlin, 2004.

[177] Joseph Raz, "The rule of law and its virtue (1977)", in *The authority of Law. Essays on Law and Morality*, Oxford, Oxford, 1979, p. 221; Neil MacCormick, "Diritto, *rule of law* e democrazia", in Paolo Comanducci and Riccardo Guastini (Orgs.), *Analisi e Diritto*, Torino, Giappichelli, 1994, p. 194.

[178] Max Rümelin, *Die Rechtssicherheit*, Tübingen, Mohr Siebeck, 1924, pages 9–10 and 12–13.

[179] L. Recaséns Siches, *Filosofía del Derecho*, México, Porrúa, 1959, p. 222. Also: Theophilo Cavalcanti Filho, *O problema da segurança no Direito*, São Paulo, Ed. RT, 1964, p. 84.

[180] Miguel Reale, "Prefácio", in Theophilo Cavalcanti Filho, *O problema da segurança no Direito*, São Paulo, Ed. RT, 1964, p. VI.

[181] Hanns Uhlrich, "La sécurité juridique en Droit Économique allemand: observations d'un privatiste", in Laurence Boy, Jean-Baptiste Racine and Fabrice Siiriainen (Orgs.), *Sécurité juridique et Droit Économique*, Bruxelles, Larcier, 2008, p. 92.

[182] Geraldo Ataliba, *República e Constituição*, 3rd ed., São Paulo, Malheiros Editores, 2011, p. 167.

[183] Eros Roberto Grau, *O Direito posto e o Direito pressuposto*, 7th ed., São Paulo, Malheiros Editores, 2008, p. 186; Anne-Laure Valembois, *La constitutionnalisation de l'exigence de sécurité juridique en droit français*, Paris, LGDJ, 2005, pages 53, 55 and 456.

in the sense of protection, such as a writ of mandamus or habeas corpus, in the words of the 1988 Constitution, because a guarantee is an external and typically procedural instrument to protect a right. Instead, it is a "guarantee right," i.e. a right whose realization serves to realize another right.[184] Mindful of this subtlety, Torres states that the subprinciples of the principle of legal certainty, such as statutory legality, irretroactivity and anteriority, embody "guarantees of principles".[185] He also argues that the legal certainty principle is not to be confused with procedural instruments such as the writ of mandamus or procedural guarantees such as the right to a full defense, or even with institutional guarantees such as the judiciary.[186] If the term "certainty" is used here to refer to a guarantee, it is merely to illustrate the instrumental character of legal certainty relative to the protection of other rights. This is because "guarantee" means nothing more than an instrument to secure rights.[187] Thus the essential point is that on this view the predictability of state action enables citizens to plan future action because they can be sure in their knowledge of the legal discipline required, as noted by Carvalho.[188]

It must be noted at this point that accepting legal certainty as an instrument says nothing regarding the values whose realization it is instrumental for; nor does it say anything about the value of such instrumentality, i.e. whether it is sufficient by itself to assure such values. Hence the need to seek foundations in the legal order that will bind legal certainty to specific instruments. It must be stressed that this move is fundamental to prevent certainty from becoming the instrument of any conception. A tract by the Nazi general Hermann Göring, published in the suggestive year of 1935, is instructive in this regard. According to Göring, legal certainty was an exclusive instrument of the "people's community" (*Volksgemeinschaft*) and could never serve an individual's egotistical purposes.[189]

---

[184]Paul Roubier, *Théorie Générale du Droit*, 2nd ed., Paris, Sirey, 1951, p. 334; Anne-Laure Valembois, *La constitutionnalisation de l'exigence de sécurité juridique en droit français*, Paris, LGDJ, 2005, p. 53.

[185]Ricardo Lobo Torres, "Limitações ao poder impositivo e segurança jurídica", in Ives Gandra da Silva Martins (Org.), *Limitações ao poder impositivo e segurança jurídica*, São Paulo, Ed. RT/CEU, 2007, p. 64.

[186]Ricardo Lobo Torres, "Segurança jurídica e as limitações ao poder de tributar", in Roberto Ferraz (Org.), *Princípios e limites da tributação*, São Paulo, Quartier Latin, 2007, p. 434; idem, *Tratado de Direito Constitucional, Financeiro e Tributário*, v. 2, "Valores e Princípios Constitucionais Tributários", Rio de Janeiro, Renovar, 2005, p. 172; idem, "Liberdade, segurança e justiça", in Paulo de Barros Carvalho (Org.), *Justiça Tributária*, São Paulo, Max Limonad, 1998, p. 687.

[187]José Souto Maior Borges, "O princípio da segurança jurídica na criação e aplicação do tributo", *RDDT* 22, p. 25, São Paulo, 1997.

[188]Paulo de Barros Carvalho, *Curso de Direito Tributário*, 21st ed., São Paulo, Saraiva, 2009, p. 166.

[189]General Hermann Göring, "Die Rechtssicherheit als Grundlage der Volksgemeinschaft", in Hans Frank (Org.), *Schriften der Akademie für Deutsches Recht*, Hamburg, Hanseatische Verlagsanstalt, 1935, p. 6.

With regard to the first aspect, as will be emphasized in due course, this book argues that legal certainty serves as an instrument to realize the values of freedom, equality and dignity: freedom because the more citizens are assured of material and intellectual access to the norms they must obey, and the greater the stability of those norms, the better citizens will be able to grasp the present and plan for the future; equality because the more general and abstract the norms and the more uniformly they are applied, the more equally will citizens be treated; and dignity because the more accessible and stable the norms and the sounder the justification for their application, the more intensely citizens will be treated as being able to define themselves autonomously, both by present respect for the autonomy they have exercised in the past and by future respect for the autonomy they exercise in the present. Hence legal certainty functions as a guarantee.[190]

With regard to the second aspect, even if the instrumental value of legal certainty relatively to other values is accepted, this instrumentality can be assigned different values: Legal certainty can be understood as a necessary and sufficient value to assure freedom, in the sense that if legal certainty is assured then freedom is automatically protected, as per Hayek[191]; but legal certainty can also be conceived as a necessary but insufficient value, in the sense that law, albeit predictable, can include content that runs counter to the independent exercise of freedom, as sustained by Rawls and Waldron.[192] On the latter view, it is possible to say that although there cannot be freedom without legal certainty, legal certainty does not necessarily entail freedom.

Nevertheless, it must be noted that, as will become clear later on, this latter conception holds water only when legal certainty means certainty of law through structural requirements of the legal order: Law can be foreseeable and stable, yet not allow for the independent and free exercise of freedom if, for example, it is applied arbitrarily. However, under a broader concept of legal certainty involving not only static and structural elements of the legal order, but also dynamic and functional elements, such as the requirement of continuity and the prohibition of arbitrariness, a higher degree of legal certainty will yield a higher measure of freedom. Without reliability and calculability, as Ataliba stresses, there can be neither work, production, entrepreneurship nor action in a market economy.[193] For the time being, suffice it to reaffirm the idea that legal certainty is a precondition of freedom. Or in Gusy's suggestive phrasing: "Certainty is a constitutional precondition; freedom is

[190] Stefano Bertea, *Certezza del Diritto e argomentazione giuridica*, Soveria Manelli, Rubbertino, 2002, p. 69.

[191] Friedrich A. Hayek, *The Constitution of liberty*, Oxford, Clarendon, 1961, p. 155.

[192] John Rawls, *Theory of Justice*, Cambridge, Belknap, 1971, pages 235 and following; Jeremy Waldron, "The rule of law in contemporary liberal theory", *Ratio Juris*, v. 2, n. 1, p. 85, 1989.

[193] Geraldo Ataliba, *República e Constituição*, 3rd ed., São Paulo, Malheiros Editores, 2011, p. 175.

constitutional content."[194] Thus legal certainty is an essential value without which other values are unlikely to be realized, as noted by Villegas.[195]

Having finished this initial examination of the finalistic aspects that make up the structure of the principle of legal certainty, we now need to move on to the analysis of its instrumental aspects, defined as the aspects relating to the means required to bring ideal states into being.

6 Instrumental Aspects: Means Needed to Promote the Ends

6.1 Material Aspect

6.1.1 Human Behavior

Legal certainty as a normative species is defined above as a principle; and as such it requires the realization of a state of affairs whose gradual promotion depends on certain types of behavior, such as publishing an act or setting forth transitional rules, which create the "means," "factual conditions" or "juridical goods" necessary to realize a state of legal certainty.[196] Thus there is, as it were, a chain of elements to be considered: The principle of legal certainty imposes the realization of ideal states (of knowability, reliability and calculability); the promotion of these ideal states depends on the existence of certain factual conditions; the existence of such conditions depends on certain types of behavior; these types of behavior are determined either indirectly by the concrete establishment of rules (decisions) or directly by the abstract establishment of rules that concretize the principle of legal certainty.

These elements (behavior → conditions → state of affairs → legal certainty) form the structure of the legal certainty principle. It can therefore be said that legal certainty is a legal norm that determines the performance of types of human behavior whose effects contribute to the promotion of a state of knowability, reliability and calculability of law, whose realization depends on abstract or concrete rules. In other words, legal certainty is a *norm* that determines the realization of a *state of affairs* characterized, as stated earlier, by the individual's capacity to plan action strategically in a juridically informed and respected manner, and with dignity.

---

[194] Christoph Gusy, "Gewährleistung von Freiheit und Sicherheit im Lichte unterschiedlicher Staats- und Verfassungsverständnisse", *VVDStRL* 63, p. 154, Berlin, 2004.

[195] Héctor Villegas, "Principio de seguridad jurídica en la creación y aplicación del tributo", *RDT* 66, p. 15, São Paulo, s.d.

[196] Gianmarco Gometz, *La certezza giuridica come prevedibilità*, Torino, Giappichelli, 2005, p. 252.

6.1.2 Effects

The application of a rule involves an examination of the correspondence between the definition of the fact or act contained in the normative hypothesis and the fact that has occurred or the act that has been performed. Proper behavior is directly or indirectly defined in the hypothesis. However, this is not the case with principles. Proper behavior is not defined a priori, but must be ascertained by its *effects* relative to a state of affairs. Thus it is defined not as a description, but as an effect. In other words, the required types of behavior are those that contribute to the promotion of the desired state of affairs and whose performance is justified by the duty to promote it. In the case of the legal certainty principle, therefore, the question is what types of behavior contribute to the promotion of the factual conditions that constitute the ideal states of knowability, reliability and calculability of law.

The entire first chapter of the Second Part of this book is devoted to delimiting these types of behavior, some of which are already the object of abstract rules, while the rest depend on concrete decisions: publication of laws; notification of administrative acts and decisions; definition of the general parameters of tax obligations; exclusion of normative innovations relative to acquired, consolidated and guaranteed rights; the establishment of transitional rules; deferred and prospective effects in the case of administrative or judicial changes – and so on. What matters for the time being is that such types of behavior are as mandatory as those set forth in legal rules. The normatization of behavior by *implied efficacy* is no less mandatory than that achieved by *hypothetical description*. These are merely different and complementary ways of normatizing human conduct through norms.

6.2 *Personal Aspect*

6.2.1 Addressee of the Duty to Act

The types of behavior that help to promote the ideals that make up legal certainty ought to be performed by each of the three branches of government in the exercise of power.[197]

Thus when the legislative enacts laws, it must assure the determinability of the incidence hypothesis, exclude from the law's normative scope both acquired rights and rights guaranteed by legitimate trust, avoid surprise by means of transitional rules and equity clauses – and so forth. The executive must not revoke or void previous acts that have been the basis for taxpayers to dispose of rights; it must issue transitional norms when sudden changes of interpretation occur – and so on.

[197] Maria Sylvia Zanella Di Pietro, "Os princípios da proteção à confiança, da segurança jurídica e da boa-fé na anulação do ato administrativo", in Fabrício Motta (Org.), *Direito Público atual: Estudos em homenagem ao Professor Nélson Figueiredo*, Instituto de Direito Administrativo de Goiás (IDAG), Belo Horizonte, Fórum, 2008, p. 297.

The judiciary must ground its decision rationally and sufficiently, avoid retroactive jurisprudential changes, use mechanisms to temper or moderate changes to precedents – and so on. The key point at this moment is simply that all three branches of government, each within its own sphere of jurisdiction, are co-responsible for the types of behavior that contribute to the promotion of the ideals of normative knowability, reliability and calculability, by establishing rules that concretize them.

6.2.2 Beneficiary of the Duty to Act

The counterpart of the addressee of the duty to act is its beneficiary. Although the entire collectivity is the ultimate addressee of the principle of certainty, both its objective dimension and its reflexive application can be required by anyone who can prove that it has not been realized. Obviously, given that legal certainty is normatively established as an end whose realization depends on configuration by all three branches of government, each in its own sphere of jurisdiction, individuals cannot demand in court compliance with general public policies that are supposed to protect them. However, this does not prevent those affected by failure to perform the specific types of behavior that constitute the content of such policies from demanding their performance in court. For example, anyone affected by an administrative act that alters a situation made intangible by time or an acquired right, anyone affected by a law whose incidence hypothesis includes a past taxable event or an irreversible act of induced freedom, and anyone who is affected by a court decision that disregards consolidated precedents has the right to expect the court to exclude their situation from the scope of such norms. The beneficiaries of the duty to act as necessary to protect the principle of certainty are the holders of rights capable of forcing its realization.[198]

So far we have discussed what legal certainty "may mean", examining all its aspects and all the meanings they may have. This process of ambiguity reduction shows that without progressive delimitation of the several aspects and dimensions of legal certainty, it cannot be appropriately defined and consequently applied. In other words, a scientific examination of legal certainty presupposes the decomposition of its several aspects (material, objective, subjective, temporal, quantitative and justificatory).

However, while our focus so far has been on what legal certainty "may mean", it is now necessary to investigate what it "ought to mean". In other words, based on the several meanings legal certainty may have within each aspect, our focus from now

---

[198]Ricardo Lobo Torres, "Segurança jurídica e as limitações ao poder de tributar", in Roberto Ferraz (Org.), *Princípios e limites da tributação*, São Paulo, Quartier Latin, 2007, p. 433; idem, *Tratado de Direito Constitucional, Financeiro e Tributário*, v. 2, *Valores e princípios constitucionais tributários*, Rio de Janeiro, Renovar, 2005, p. 170; idem, "Liberdade, segurança e justiça", in Paulo de Barros Carvalho (Org.), *Justiça Tributária*, São Paulo, Max Limonad, 1998, p. 687; Winfried Brugger, "Gewährleistung von Freiheit und Sicherheit im Lichte unterschiedlicher Staats- und Verfassungsverständnisse", *VVDStRL* 63, p. 132, Berlin, 2004.

on will be on which of them *ought to* be chosen. We must redirect the discussion from the hermeneutical "head" to its constitutional "feet", to borrow a metaphor from Vonkilch, following Schneider.[199] This procedure depends on an analysis of its foundation in the legal order: In this case, the 1988 Constitution of the Federative Republic of Brazil will define the meanings to be chosen from so many possibilities.

This analysis begins overleaf.

References

AARNIO, Aulis. *Reason and authority*. Dartmouth: Ashgate, 1997.

_____. *The rational as reasonable*. Dordrecht, Reidel: 1987.

ANTUNES ROCHA, Cármen Lúcia Antunes. "O princípio da coisa julgada e o vício de inconstitucionalidade". In: Idem. (Org.). *Constituição e segurança jurídica: direito adquirido, ato jurídico perfeito e coisa julgada. Estudos em homenagem a José Paulo Sepúlveda Pertence*. Belo Horizonte: Fórum, 2004.

ARCOS RAM´iREZ, Federico. *La seguridad jurídica: una teoría formal*. Madrid: Dykinson, 2000.

von ARNAULD, Andreas. *Rechtssicherheit*. Tübingen: Mohr Siebeck, 2006.

ASOREY, Rubén. "Seguridad jurídica y Derecho Tributario", *RDT* 52, São Paulo, 1990.

ATALIBA, Geraldo. *República e Constituição*. 3rd ed. São Paulo, Malheiros Editores, 2011.

ÁVILA, Humberto. *Teoria dos princípios*, 12th ed. São Paulo, Malheiros, 2011.

BERTEA, Stefano. *Certezza del Diritto e argomentazione giuridica*. Soveria Manelli: Rubbertino, 2002.

BOBBIO, Norberto. "La certezza del Diritto é un mito?", *Rivista Intenazionale di Filosofia del Diritto* 28, pp. 150–151, 1951.

BORGES, José Souto Maior. "O princípio da segurança jurídica na criação e aplicação do tributo", *RDDT* 22, São Paulo, 1997.

BRUGGER, Winfried. "Gewährleistung von Freiheit und Sicherheit im Lichte unterschiedlicher Staats- und Verfassungsverständnisse". *VVDStRL* 63. Berlin, 2004.

CACHO, José L. Mezquita del. *Seguridad jurídica y sistema cautelar*, v. 1, "Teoría de la Seguridad Jurídica". Barcelona: Bosch, 1989.

CALMES, Sylvia. *Du principe de protection de la confiance légitime en Droits Allemand, Communautaire et Français*. Paris: Dalloz, 2001.

CANOTILHO, José Joaquim Gomes. *Direito Constitucional e Teoria da Constituição*. 7th ed., 6th reprint. Coimbra: Livraria Almedina, 2004.

CARDOZO, Benjamin N. *The nature of judicial process*, New York, 1921.

CARVALHO, Paulo de Barros. *Curso de Direito Tributário*, 21st ed. São Paulo: Saraiva, 2009.

_____. *Direito Tributário, linguagem e método*. São Paulo: Noeses, 2008.

_____. "O princípio da segurança jurídica no campo tributário", *RDT* 94, São Paulo, s.d.

_____. "O princípio da anterioridade em matéria tributária", *RDT* 63, São Paulo, s.d.

CAVALCANTI FILHO, Theophilo. *O problema da segurança no Direito*. São Paulo: Ed. RT, 1964.

CHEVALLIER, Jacques. "Le Droit Économique: l'insécurité juridique ou nouvelle sécurité juridique?". In: BOY, Laurence; RACINE, Jean-Baptiste; SIIRIAINEN, Fabrice (Orgs.). *Sécurité Juridique et Droit Économique*. Bruxelles: Larcier, 2008.

COING, Helmut. *Grundzüge der Rechtsphilosophie*, 5th ed., Berlin, Walter de Gruyter, 1993.

CORSALE, Massimo. "Il problema della certezza del Diritto in Italia dopo il 1950". In: OÑATE, Flavio Lopez de. *La certezza del Diritto*. Milano: Giuffrè, 1968.

[199] Andreas Vonkilch, *Das Intertemporale Privatrecht*, Wien, Springer, 1999, p. 312.

COUTO E SILVA, Almiro do Couto e Silva. "O princípio da segurança jurídica (proteção à confiança) no Direito Público brasileiro e o direito da Administração Pública de anular os seus próprios atos: o prazo decadencial do art. 54 da Lei do Processo Administrativo da União (Lei n. 9.784/99)", *RDA* 237, Rio de Janeiro, 2004.

DI PIETRO, Maria Sylvia Zanella. "Os princípios da proteção à confiança, da segurança jurídica e da boa-fé na anulação do ato administrativo". In: MOTTA, Fabrício (Org.). *Direito Público atual: Estudos em homenagem ao Professor Nélson Figueiredo*. Instituto de Direito Administrativo de Goiás (IDAG). Belo Horizonte: Fórum, 2008.

DOUET, Frédéric. *Contribution à l'étude de la sécurité juridique en Droit interne français*. Paris: LGDJ, 1997.

DUONG, Lémy. "La sécurité juridique et les standards du Droit Économique: la notion de raisonnable". In: BOY, Laurence; RACINE, Jean-Baptiste; SIIRIAINEN, Fabrice (Orgs.). *Sécurité Juridique et Droit Économique*. Bruxelles: Larcier, 2008.

ENTERRIA, Eduardo García de. *Justicia y Seguridad Jurídica en un Mundo de Leyes Desbocadas*. Madrid: Civitas, 1999.

FARJAT, Gérard. "Observations sur la sécurité juridique, le lien social et le Droit Économique". In: BOY, Laurence; RACINE, Jean-Baptiste; SIIRIAINEN, Fabrice (Orgs.). *Sécurité Juridique et Droit Économique*. Bruxelles: Larcier, 2008.

FERNANDEZ, José Luis Palma. *La seguridad jurídica ante la abundancia de normas*. Madrid: Centro de Estudios Políticos y Constitucionales, 1997.

FERRAJOLI, Luigi. "The past and the future of the rule of law". In: COSTA, Pietro; ZOLO, Danilo Zolo (Orgs.). *The rule of Law – History, theory and criticism*, Dordrecht, Springer, 2007.

FERRAZ JR., Tércio Sampaio. "Segurança jurídica, coisa julgada e justiça", *Revista do Instituto de Hermenêutica Jurídica*, v. 1, n. 3, Porto Alegre, 2005.

FRANK, Jerome. *Law and the modern mind*, New Brunswick: Transaction, 2009 (1st ed., New York, Brentano's Inc., 1930; 2nd ed. rev., New York, Coward-McCann, 1949).

FULLER, Lon. *Anatomy of Law*. Connecticut: Greenwood, 1968.

GIANFORMAGGIO, Letizia. "Certezza del Diritto". In: DICCIOTTI, Enrico; VELLUZZI, Vito (Orgs.). *Filosofia del Diritto e ragionamento giuridico*. Torino: Giappichelli, 2008.

GODOI, Marciano Seabra de. "O quê e o porquê da tipicidade tributária". In: RIBEIRO, Ricardo Lodi; ROCHA, Sérgio André (Orgs.). *Legalidade e tipicidade no Direito Tributário*. São Paulo: Quartier Latin, 2008.

GOMETZ, Gianmarco. *La certezza giuridica come prevedibilità*. Torino: Giappichelli, 2005.

GÖRING, General Hermann Göring. "Die Rechtssicherheit als Grundlage der Volksgemeinschaft". In: FRANK, Hans (Org.). *Schriften der Akademie für Deutsches Recht*. Hamburg: Hanseatische Verlagsanstalt, 1935.

GRAU, Eros Roberto. *O Direito posto e o Direito pressuposto*. 7th ed. São Paulo: Malheiros, 2008.

_____. *Ensaio e discurso sobre a interpretação/aplicação do Direito*. 5th ed. São Paulo: Malheiros Editores, 2009.

GUSY, Christoph. "Gewährleistung von Freiheit und Sicherheit im Lichte unterschiedlicher Staats- und Verfassungsverständnisse", *VVDStRL* 63, Berlin, 2004.

GUTIERREZ, Monica Madariaga. *Derecho Administrativo y Seguridad Jurídica*. Santiago do Chile: Editorial Jurídica de Chile, 1965.

HABERMAS, Jürgen. *Faktizität und Geltung*. Darmstadt: Wissenschaftliche Buchgesellschaft, 2002.

HABSCHEIDT, Gerhardt. *Der Anspruch des Bürgers auf Erstattung verfassungswidriger Steuern*. Köln: Otto Schmidt, 2003.

HART, H. L. *The Concept of Law*. Oxford: Clarendon, 1991. (1961).

HARTZT, Wilhelm. "Mehr Rechtssicherheit im Steuerrecht. Ziele, Wege, Grenzen", *StbJb*, 1965/1966.

HAYEK, Friedrich A. *The Constitution of liberty*, Oxford: Clarendon, 1961.

von HOECEK, Mark. "Time and law. Is it the nature of law to last? A conclusion". In: OST, François Ost; von HOECEK, Mark (Orgs.). *Temps et Droit. Le Droit a-t-il pour vocation de durer?*. Bruxelles: Bruylant, 1998.

HUSSERL, Gehard. *Recht und Zeit*. Frankfurt am Main: Vittorio Klostermann, 1995.

KAUFMANN, Franz-Xaver. *Sicherheit als soziologisches und sozialpolitisches Problem*. 2nd ed. Stuttgart, 1973.

KELSEN, Hans. *Reine Rechtslehre. Studienausgabe der 1. Auflage 1934* (Herausgegeben und eingeleitet von Matthias Jestaedt (Org.). Tübingen: Siebeck, 2008.

KIRCHHOF, Paul. *Schrifte des Instituts Finanzen und Steuern*, n. 362, Bonn, 1998.

KOZINSKI, Alex. "What I ate for breakfast and other mysteries of judicial decision making". In: O'BRIEN, David M. (Org.). *Judges on judging*. New Jersey: Chatham, 1997.

JORI, Mario; PINTORE, Anna. *Manuale di Teoria Generale del Diritto*. 2nd ed., Torino: Giappichelli, 1995.

LAMBERT, Pierre. "Le principe général de la sécurité juridique et les validations législatives", *Les Cahiers de l'Institut d'Études sur la Justice* 4, p. 6 ("Sécurité Juridique et Fiscalité"). Bruxelles: Bruyant, 2003.

LEISNER, Anna. *Kontinuität als Verfassungsprinzip*. Tübingen: Mohr Siebeck, 2002.

LIÈVRE-GRAVEREAUX, Amélie. *La rétroactivité de la loi fiscale: une nécessite en matière de procédures*. Paris: Harmattan, 2007.

LIMBACH, Jutta. *Ist die kollektive Sicherheit der Feind der individuellen Freiheit?*. Köln: Carl Heymanns, 2002.

LUHMANN, Niklas. *Vertrauen – Ein Mechanismus der Reduktion sozialer Komplexität*. 4th ed. Stuttgart: Lucius & Lucius, 2000.

LUÑO, Antonio Enrique Perez. *La seguridad jurídica*. Barcelona: Ariel, 1991.

LUZZATI, Claudio. *La vaghezza delle norme*. Milano: Giuffrè, 1990.

_____. *L'interprete e il legislatore*. Milano: Giuffrè, 1999.

MacCORMICK, Neil. *Legal reasoning and legal theory*. Oxford: Clarendon, 1978.

_____. "Rhetoric and rule of law". In: DYZENHAUS, David (Org.). *Recrafting the rule of Law – The Limits of Legal Order*. Oxford: Hart, 1999.

_____. "Diritto, *rule of law* e democrazia". In: COMANDUCCI, Paolo; GUASTINI, Riccardo (Orgs.). *Analisi e Diritto*. Torino: Giappichelli, 1994.

MARMOR, Andrei. *Positive Law and objective values*. Oxford: Clarendon, 2001.

_____. *Law in the age of pluralism*. Oxford: OUP, 2007.

_____. "An essay on the objectivity of law". In: BIX, Brian (Org.). *Analyzing Law – New Essays in Legal Theory*. Oxford: Clarendon, 1998.

MACHADO DERZI, Misabel de Abreu. *Modificações da jurisprudência no Direito Tributário*. São Paulo: Noeses, 2009.

MÖSTL, Markus. *Die staatliche Garantie für die öffentliche Sicherheit und Ordnung*. Tübingen: Mohr Siebeck, 2002.

MÜNCH, Christof. "Rechtssicherheit als Standortfaktor. Gedanken aus Sicht der vorsorgenden Rechtspflege". In: WEBER, Albrecht (Org.). *Währung und Wirtschaft. Das Geld im Recht. FS für Hugo J. Hahn*. Baden-Baden: Nomos, 1997.

NOVOA, César García. *El principio de seguridad jurídica en materia tributaria*. Madrid: Marcial Pons, 2000.

PACTEAU, Bernard. "La sécurité juridique, un principe que nous manque?", *AJDA* 20, 1995.

PALOMBELLA, Gianluigi. *Dopo la Certezza – Il Diritto in equilibrio tra Giustizia e Democrazia*. Bari: Dedalo, 2006.

PAULSEN, Leandro. *Segurança jurídica, certeza do direito e tributação*. Porto Alegre: Livraria do Advogado, 2006.

PFERSMANN, Otto. "Constitution et sécurité juridique – Autriche". *Annuaire International de Justice Constitutionnelle*. Paris: Economica, 1999.

PHILIPPE, Xavier. "Constitution et sécurité juridique". *Annuaire International de Justice Constitutionnelle 1999*, Paris, Economica, 2000.

POHL, Heike. *Rechtsprechungsänderung und Rückanknüpfung*. Berlin: Duncker und Humblot, 2005.

RACINE, Jean-Baptiste; SIIRIAINEN, Fabrice. "Sécurité juridique et Droit Économique. Propos introductifs". In: BOY, Laurence; RACINE, Jean-Baptiste; SIIRIAINEN, Fabrice (Orgs.). *Sécurité Juridique et Droit Économique*. Bruxelles: Larcier, 2008.

RADBRUCH, Gustav. *Rechtsphilosophie. Studienausgabe*, 2nd ed. Heidelberg: C. F. Müller, 2003 (1932).

RAZ, Joseph. "The rule of law and its virtue (1977)". In: *The authority of Law. Essays on Law and Morality*. Oxford: Oxford, 1979.

RAWLS, John. *A Theory of Justice*. Cambridge: Belknap, 1971.

REALE, Miguel. *Filosofia do Direito*. 12th ed. São Paulo: Saraiva, 1987.

ROUBIER, Paul. *Théorie Générale du Droit*. 2nd ed. Paris, Sirey, 1951.

RÜMELIN, Max. *Die Rechtssicherheit*. Tübingen: Mohr Siebeck, 1924.

SARLET, Ingo Wolfgang. "A eficácia do direito fundamental à segurança jurídica: dignidade da pessoa humana, direitos fundamentais e proibição de retrocesso social no Direito Constitucional brasileiro". In: ANTUNES ROCHA, Cármen Lúcia. (Org.). *Constituição e segurança jurídica: direito adquirido, ato jurídico perfeito e coisa julgada. Estudos em homenagem a José Paulo Sepúlveda Pertence*. Belo Horizonte: Fórum, 2004.

SCHAUER, Frederick. *Profiles, probabilities and stereotypes*. Cambridge: Belknap, 2003.

SICHES, L. Recaséns. *Filosofía del Derecho*. México: Porrúa, 1959.

______. *Tratado general de Filosofía del Derecho*. México: Porrúa, 1961.

SILVA, José Afonso da. "Constituição e segurança jurídica". In: ANTUNES ROCHA, Cármen Lúcia. (Org.). *Constituição e segurança jurídica: direito adquirido, ato jurídico perfeito e coisa julgada. Estudos em homenagem a José Paulo Sepúlveda Pertence*. Belo Horizonte: Fórum, 2004.

SOBOTA, Katharina. *Das Prinzip Rechtsstaat*. Tübingen: Mohr Siebeck, 1997.

SUMMES, Robert. *Lon L. Fuller*. Londres: Edward Arnold, 1984.

TAMANAHA, Brian Z. *Law as a means to an end – Threat to the rule of Law*. Cambridge: Cambridge University Press, 2006.

TORRES, Ricardo Lobo Torres "Segurança jurídica e as limitações ao poder de tributar". In: FERRAZ, Roberto (Org.), *Princípios e limites da tributação*. São Paulo: Quartier Latin, 2007.

_____. "Limitações ao poder impositivo e segurança jurídica". In: MARTINS, Ives Gandra da Silva (Org.). *Limitações ao poder impositivo e segurança jurídica*. São Paulo: Ed. RT/CEU, 2007.

_____. *Tratado de Direito Constitucional, Financeiro e Tributário*, v. 2, "Valores e princípios constitucionais tributários". Rio de Janeiro: Renovar, 2005.

_____. "Liberdade, segurança e justiça". In: CARVALHO, Paulo de Barros (Org.). *Justiça Tributária*. São Paulo: Max Limonad, 1998.

UHLRICH, Hanns. "La sécurité juridique en Droit Économique allemand: observations d'un privatiste". In: BOY, Laurence; RACINE, Jean-Baptiste; SIIRIAINEN, Fabrice (Orgs.). *Sécurité Juridique et Droit Économique*. Bruxelles: Larcier, 2008.

VALEMBOIS, Anne-Laure. *La constitutionnalisation de l'exigence de sécurité juridique en Droit Français*. Paris: LGDJ, 2005.

VEDEL, Georges. "Discontinuité du Droit Constitutionnel et continuité du Droit Administratif: le rôle du juge". In: *Le juge et le Droit. Mélanges offerts à Marcel Waline*, v. 2, Paris: LGDJ, 1974.

VIETS, Bodo. *Rechtsprechungsänderung und Vertrauensschutz*. Bern: Herbert Lang, 1976.

VILLA, Vittorio. *Costruttivismo e teorie del Diritto*. Torino: Giappichelli, 1999.

VILLEGAS, Héctor. "Principio de seguridad jurídica en la creación y aplicación del tributo", *RDT* 66, São Paulo, s.d.

VOLKILCH, Andreas. *Das Intertemporale Privatrecht*. Wien: Springer, 1999.

VONKILCH, Andreas. *Das Intertemporale Privatrecht*. Wien: Springer, 1999.

WALDHOFF, Christian. "Vertrauensschutz im Steuerrechtsverhältnis". In: PEZZER, Heinz-Jürgen (Org.), *Vertrauensschutz im Steuerrecht*, v. 27, Deutsche Steuer-juristische Gesellschaft. Köln: Otto Schmidt, 2004.

WALDRON, Jeremy. "The rule of law in contemporary liberal theory", *Ratio Juris*, v. 2, n. 1, 1989.

WEINBERGER, Ota. *Norm und Institution*. Wien: Manz, 1988.

XAVIER, Alberto. *Os princípios da legalidade e da tipicidade da tributação*. São Paulo: Ed. RT, 1978.

_____. *Tipicidade da tributação, simulação e norma antielisiva*. São Paulo: Dialética, 2001.

ZILVETTI, Fernando Aurélio. "Tipo e linguagem: a gênese da igualdade na tributação". In: RIBEIRO, Ricardo Lodi; ROCHA, Sérgio André (Orgs.). *Legalidade e tipicidade no Direito Tributário*. São Paulo: Quartier Latin, 2008.

ZIMMER, Willy. "Constitution et sécurité juridique – Allemagne". *Annuaire International de Justice Constitutionnelle*. Paris, Economica, 1999.

Part II
Justification of Legal Certainty

> Law, from any viewpoint one may wish to consider it, is a foundation of certainty. (Carmignani, *Teoria delle leggi della sicurezza sociale*, v. 1, Pisa, 1831, p. 151)

> ... observance of the rule of law is necessary if the law is to respect human dignity. Respecting human dignity entails treating humans as people capable of planning and plotting their future. Thus, respecting people's dignity includes respecting their autonomy, their right to control their future. (Joseph Raz, *The authority of Law: Essays on Law and Morality*, Oxford, Clarendon, 1979, p. 221)

> Our laws are not generally known; they are the secret of a small group. We are convinced that these old laws will be followed, but it is extremely odd to be ruled by laws one does not know. (Franz Kafka, *Zur Frage der Gesetze – Fragment*, 1920/22)

> Justice must not only be done. It must also be seen to be done. (Eivind Smith, "Constitution et securite juridique – Norvège", *Annuaire International de Justice Constitutionnelle 1999*, Paris, Economica, p. 2)

In the words of Cavalcanti Filho, "the fundamental reason for law is the requirement of sureness and certainty in the relations formed in society."[1] Legal certainty is inherent in law and is therefore justified by the very notion of law and does not require positive justification. While this statement is true, it is insufficient to indicate the meanings that the expression "legal certainty" can and ought to bear, as I will show in due course. In other words, although legal certainty is indeed intrinsic to the idea of law, only the legal order can densify it normatively as a legal principle so that it can effectively limit state action.

The word "certainty" is expressly listed in the catalogue of fundamental rights (1988 Constitution, article 5), as well as a number of other provisions: the right to receive information from public bodies, save that information indispensable to the "security of society and the state" (article 5, XXXIII); the right to protection from occupational hazards by means of health and "safety" norms (article 6, XXII); empowering the local, regional and central governments to establish and implement a "traffic safety" education policy (article 23, XII); defining acts against "homeland

[1]Theophilo Cavalcanti Filho, *O Problema da segurança no direito*, São Paulo, Ed. RT, 1964, p. 52.

security as an abuse of presidential office (article 85, IV); empowering the National Defense Council to propose criteria and conditions for the use of areas indispensable to "the security of the national territory" (article 91, §1, III); empowering the Supreme Court to issue precedential rulings to avoid grave "legal uncertainty" (article 103-A, §1); provision for norms relating to "public safety" (article 144); requiring the state to perform economic activities for reasons of "national security" (article 173); conditions for booking expenses, except those relating to "national defense and security" (ADCT, article 35, §1, II); provision for emphyteusis on land located within the "shoreline security strip" (ADCT, article 49, §3).

The Brazilian Supreme Court has reaffirmed the constitutional priority of the principle of legal certainty more than once. Suffice it to note the statement by Justice Gilmar Mendes that the legal certainty principle, "as is well known, is at the summit of the constitutional hierarchy among us as well." "As far as legal certainty is concerned, there seems to be no doubt that it is expressed in the very principle of the rule of law, and that this is broadly accepted in Brazilian and foreign jurisprudence."[2]

It might therefore seem unnecessary to inquire into the foundation for legal certainty. It is apparently a given, and there is no need for the interpreter to construct or even reconstruct it. It is entirely ready, so that there is not the least need to invent it. This initial impression is undone, however, as soon as the following questions are posed: Does the term "*segurança*" used in the 1988 Constitution refer to legal certainty as a guiding idea for law, or physical security to guarantee protection of citizens from external threats or of the territory from foreign invasion? If it means the legal certainty principle, and even if it is acknowledged by the Supreme Court, we must still ask this: What does it require exactly? Does it require certainty of law, through law, before the law, under law, of rights, for a right, as a right or in the law? If certainty of law, in what sense does it require "certainty"? As absolute predictability or only as relative knowledge of its norms? If certainty through law, does it require certainty to assure freedom for citizens or to enable the state to attain its goals, or both? We can only begin to answer these questions and others like them after considering the foundations of legal certainty. Moreover, simply stating that the 1988 Constitution literally guarantees "*segurança*" does not answer some fundamental related questions: What certainty? Certainty of what? Certainty how? Certainty by whom? Certainty for whom? Certainty in whose view? Certainty when? Certainty with what weight? Certainty verified how?

An examination of these provisions shows how complex the Brazilian Constitution is: differently from other Constitutions, it not only contains express protection of "*segurança*," whatever its meaning, but also establishes several elements typically ascribed to certainty by legal doctrine – guarantees of legality, irretroactivity

[2]HC n. 82.959, Full Court, Reporting Justice. Marco Aurélio, *DJ* 1 Sep 2006. Opinion by Justice Gilmar Mendes, pages 64 and 76. Likewise: Order Issue on Pet #2.900, 2nd Panel, Reporting Justice Gilmar Mendes, *DJ* 1 Aug 2003; MS n. 24.268, Full Court, Reporting Justice Gilmar Mendes, *DJ* 17 Sep 2004.

and anteriority, the duties of publication and morality, and the right to a full defense and due process of law, for example.[3] Among this plethora of provisions, therefore, we must choose a point of reference to help us find its foundations. After all, one can only look for something if one knows what it is. The search for foundations depends on first determining what exactly is being sought, paradoxical though this may seem.[4] To some extent, finding precedes seeking, so to speak. One cannot conduct a search for nothing, but only for something. In other words, the definition precedes the finding.

In light of the above, this discussion starts with a minimal preliminary definition of legal certainty which, as shown in the previous chapter, pivots on what Rümelin refers to, albeit without specifying either foundation or criteria, as the three pillars of legal certainty: intelligibility, reliability or seriousness, and calculability of law.[5] Thus the notion of legal certainty is linked to the ideas of stability and predictability.[6] From this initial reference point, therefore, we must search the 1988 Constitution for the legal norms that directly provide for the means to realize this state of reliability and calculability (rules), or that point to such states, leaving to the applier the choice of means from among those needed to realize the states concerned (principles). Within this framework, a revealing normative archetype can be constructed, as it were, from the normative affluents that form and define the large river of legal certainty. The main point at present is that legal certainty does not necessarily require a written support, a fact which by no means removes its constitutional foundations.[7]

An analysis of this kind may seem trivial, but actually it is complex, since the 1988 Constitution establishes direct and indirect foundations to justify legal certainty, as preliminarily defined above. The direct foundations comprise express protection for "*segurança*" (article 5), as well as protection for the reflexive efficacy of the same principle of legal certainty in the form of guarantees for acquired rights, completed legal acts and res iudicata (article 5, XXXVI). The indirect justifications

[3]Paulo de Barros Carvalho, "Segurança jurídica e modulação dos efeitos", *Revista da Fundação Escola Superior de Direito Tributário* 1, p. 207, Porto Alegre, 2008; Ingo Wolfgang Sarlet, "A eficácia do direito fundamental à segurança jurídica: dignidade da pessoa humana, direitos fundamentais e proibição de retrocesso social no Direito Constitucional brasileiro", in Cármen Lúcia Antunes Rocha (Org.), *Constituição e segurança jurídica: direito adquirido, ato jurídico perfeito e coisa julgada. Estudos em Homenagem a José Paulo Sepúlveda Pertence*, Belo Horizonte, Fórum, 2004, p. 91.

[4]Max Rümelin, *Die Rechtssicherheit*, Tübingen, Mohr Siebeck, 1924, pages 9, 12 and 14.

[5]Max Rümelin, loc. cit. Likewise: Oscar Adolf Germann, "Rechtssicherheit (1935)", in idem, *Methodische Grundfragen*, 6. Aufsätze, Basel, 1946, p. 55; Sylvia Calmes, *Du principe de protection de la confiance légitime en Droits Allemand, Communautaire et Français*, Paris, Dalloz, 2001, p. 114; Andreas von Arnauld, *Rechtssicherheit*, Tübingen, Mohr Siebeck, 2006, p. 104; Rafael Maffini, *O princípio da proteção substancial da confiança no Direito Administrativo brasileiro*, Porto Alegre, Verbo Jurídico, 2007, p. 50.

[6]Odete Medauar, "Segurança jurídica e confiança legítima", in Humberto Ávila (Org.), *Fundamentos do Estado de Direito*, São Paulo, Malheiros Editores, 2005, p. 115.

[7]Gianmarco Gometz, *La certezza giuridica come prevedibilità*, Torino, Giappichelli, 2005, p. 47.

consist of rules and principles that, depending on the viewpoint from which they are analyzed, at times refer to less comprehensive means or ends from which the structuring elements of legal certainty may be induced, and at other times translate more comprehensive ends from which these same elements may be deduced. The constitutional order establishes these indirect foundations in many ways.[8]

First, the Constitution requires a search for broader ends (the rule of law and the social rule of law), which allow for the deduction of narrower ends necessary to their realization (knowability, reliability and calculability). In this context, rather than establishing narrower means or ends, the Constitution defines broader goals that in turn allow for the deduction of narrower goals, which as a whole translate the ideals of reliability and calculability of (and by) the legal order. Here the elements of legal certainty are discovered by deduction from superprinciples that impose the realization of broader goals relatively to legal certainty (graphically illustrated as: rule of law → legal certainty → knowability, reliability and calculability).[9] In this respect, legal certainty serves as the means to realize other ends.

Second, the Constitution determines the realization of specific ends (states of protection of freedom, property and equality), which allow for the deduction of narrower ends necessary to their realization (knowability, reliability and calculability). Thus instead of directly stipulating the narrower means or ends, the Constitution defines specific goals that in turn are fully realized only via the existence of requirements that in aggregate reveal legal certainty. Here the elements of legal certainty are discovered by induction from specific principles that require realization of the elements of legal certainty (graphically illustrated as: freedom, property, equality → legal certainty → knowability, reliability and calculability). In this respect, legal certainty serves as an instrumental requirement for the realization of other purposes.

Third, the Constitution requires the search for narrower goals (states of morality and administrative publicity), which on one hand allow for the deduction of the types of behavior necessary for their realization (behaving seriously and loyally, publishing general and individual norms, and notifying citizens of whatever concerns them) and on the other hand allow for the induction of broader ends that make up the state of reliability and calculability of (and by) the legal order. By means of this normatization, instead of establishing the means that will contribute to the existence of the elements that make up legal certainty, the Constitution establishes narrower goals which in turn serve as means to realize the broader goal of assuring and preserving legal certainty. Here the elements of legal certainty are discovered by induction from subprinciples as ends narrower than that whose realization is determined by the legal certainty principle (graphically illustrated as: publication

[8] Anne-Laure Valembois, *La constitutionnalisation de l'exigence de sécurité juridique en Droit Français*, Paris, LGDJ, 2005, p. 380.

[9] Otto Pfersmann, "Constitution et sécurité juridique – Autriche", *Annuaire International de Justice Constitutionnelle 1999*, Paris, Economica, 2000, p. 114.

and notification → morality, publicity → knowability, reliability and calculability → legal certainty). In this respect, legal certainty also serves as an end.

Fourth, the Constitution prescribes some types of behavior (enacting statutes to create taxes, waiting until the beginning of the following fiscal year to levy taxes, including in the normative hypothesis only events that occur after the statute that institutes the tax enters into force) that produce effects that contribute to the promotion of the state of reliability and calculability of (and by) the legal order, based on their knowability. By means of this kind of normatization, the Constitution defines the means that, once adopted, contribute to the existence of the structuring elements of legal certainty. Here the elements of legal certainty are discovered by induction from rules (graphically illustrated as: legality, anteriority and irretroactivity → knowability, reliability and calculability → legal certainty). Legal certainty is "built from the inside out", so to speak, using these rules.[10] In this respect, legal certainty again serves as an end.

The above considerations aim to show that construction of the legal certainty principle, albeit highly complex, can be clearly explained by means of deductive and inductive operations that reveal the foundations of its structuring elements. In other words, the Constitution protects legal certainty in several ways at the same time: by protecting it directly, by determining the search for ideals that require it, by establishing ideals that give it instruments, and even by predicting the types of behavior required for the realization of the partial ideals that comprise it.

The examination of foundations as set out in this book is necessary for three main reasons.

First, none of the foundations examined below is an exclusive foundation for all the structuring elements of legal certainty.[11] Only their analysis in aggregate can result in construction of the totality. And knowledge of all the foundations shows the existence of reciprocal relationships whose importance will be acknowledged when the efficacy of legal certainty is examined. This is because the broader and more independent the foundations for a principle, the stronger its constitutional support and hence the greater its weight compared with other principles.[12]

Another reason is that plenty of practical consequences flow from an analysis of foundations, however secondary it may seem. On one hand, if the only foundation for legal certainty is a norm that guarantees an individual fundamental right, its efficacy will be limited to the protection of citizens whose freedom or property is restricted. Therefore, the efficacy of legal certainty will be merely reflexive and individual. If, however, legal certainty is rooted in norms that establish requirements for the production of general or individual legal norms, or that prescribe certain types of loyal behavior by public agents, its efficacy will go beyond the individual dimension to reach an objective dimension in which, for instance, a norm can be

[10] Andreas von Arnauld, *Rechtssicherheit*, Tübingen, Mohr Siebeck, 2006, p. 662.

[11] Stefan Muckel, *Kriterien des verfassungsrechtlichen Vertrauensschutzes bei Gesetzesänderungen*, Berlin, Duncker und Humblot, 1989, pages 29–58.

[12] Aleksander Peczenick, *Scientia Juris*, Dordrecht, Springer, 2005, p. 144.

declared null and void even if it has no reflexive subjective efficacy regarding a given individual. On the other hand, if legal certainty is grounded in norms that guarantee individual rights as well as norms that establish state purposes, it will be necessary to examine the emphasis placed on each of these foundations by the Constitution so that they can be appropriately weighted. For example, it will then be possible to verify whether legal certainty can protect only individual aspirations or state aspirations as well, as in the case of an attempt to limit the effects of a declaration of unconstitutionality of tax rules to the future, based on the argument that the federated entity had trusted the constitutionality of the tax and the revenues to be obtained from it.

The third reason is that since the expression "legal certainty" carries several meanings, only an examination of the constitutional order will reveal its normative dimension (fact, value or norm), its normative species (rule or principle), the meaning of "certainty" (knowability or determination, reliability or immutability, calculability or predictability), the meaning of "legal" (whether "of," "by," "before" or "under" law, "of rights," "as a right," "in law"), which object it refers to (the legal order, a norm or a type of behavior), what subject it protects (taxpayers, the state, or both), from what perspective it is conceived (a common citizen's or a specialist's), who ought to protect it (the legislative, the executive or the judiciary), when it ought to be realized (today or tomorrow), in what measure it ought to be assured (relatively or absolutely) and why it is protected (as end or means). Only a detailed examination of the legal order will provide answers to these indispensable questions, without which the investigation is like a fencing match against gusts of wind, to coin a phrase.

However, the "foundations" of the principle of legal certainty should not be confused with its "elements." The former concern the normative basis that justifies its consideration as a legal principle, answering the question: What is the origin of the legal certainty principle, or what is the basis on which it is built? The latter concern the states of affairs whose realization is determined by the principle, answering the question: What does the legal certainty principle involve? This explains why the legal certainty principle is not identical with the rule of legality or the principle of publicity, although in circular fashion it derives from them and is realized in them.

In sum, an investigation of the foundations of legal certainty is indispensable as a first step in constructing its content, dimensions and effects. This investigation, on which we will now embark, must be performed on the legal order as a totality and on its parts.

Foundations in the Constitutional Superstructure: As a Totality

Abstract Among the possible meanings that can be assigned to legal certainty as a principle, the normative order indicates which of the analytically discernible meanings should be taken into consideration for its structuring aspects, by examining its superstructure (the whole) and its constitutional structure (the parts). Analysis of the constitutional superstructure shows that the Brazilian Constitution not only protects legal certainty, but also embodies legal certainty itself: It establishes more rules than principles, and insists on stipulating the competent authorities, which laws should be enacted, the content to be implemented, the procedures to be followed, and the subjects to be covered, favoring through such provisions the ideals of normative knowability, reliability and calculability.

An examination of the foundations of legal certainty must begin with the following question: What constitutional norms directly or indirectly protect the knowability or determinacy, reliability or immutability, calculability or predictability of the legal order? Or more simply: What constitutional norms are designed to enable citizens to know to a greater or lesser extent which norm is valid and applicable to their case, and what is its content, and to guarantee that once known and valid the norm will effectively be applied, binding and stable? A reading of Brazil's 1988 Constitution in order to answer these questions produces a first major surprise: It is not only a Constitution that protects legal certainty; it is a Constitution that embodies legal certainty itself. In other words, it is not only a Constitution *for* legal certainty; it is a Constitution *of* legal certainty par excellence. What I mean by this is that, more than empowering the implementation (at an infraconstitutional level) of a system of certainty, the Constitution itself institutes such a system (at a constitutional level). In sum, more than assigning the task of realizing certainty, it takes the burden upon itself to a large extent, although not entirely. This perception explains why Pizzorusso, speaking of the Italian Constitution, but in a manner even more intensely applicable to the Brazilian Constitution, says that legal certainty "is a fundamental principle that, albeit not expressly and specifically contained in any article, characterizes the entire Constitution."[1]

[1] Alessandro Pizzorusso e Paolo Passaglia, "Constitution et sécurité juridique – Italie", *Annuaire International de Justice Constitutionnelle*, Paris, Economica, 1999, pages 221–222.

© Springer International Publishing Switzerland 2016

H. Ávila, *Certainty in Law*, Law and Philosophy Library 114,
DOI 10.1007/978-3-319-33407-3_4

An examination of the constitutional superstructure leads to this discovery. From the standpoint of its breadth, the 1988 Constitution is a Constitution of rules more than of principles. After an introduction that sets out the fundamental principles of the Federative Republic of Brazil (article 1), as well as individual and social rights and guarantees (articles 5 and 6), which incidentally are mostly guaranteed by rules, the Constitution unfurls a long catalogue of rules establishing jurisdictions, procedures and guarantees. If truth be told, in its emphasis it is not a Constitution of principles but a regulatory Constitution. It insists on defining all the competent authorities, all the types of act that can be issued, all the kinds of content that must be regulated, all the procedures to be followed, all the subjects to be treated – and so forth. In short, it is so detailed in terms of normative production that it seeks itself to answer the questions: Who? What? How? When? In what measure? The entire constitutional system in general, and the National Tax System in particular, are designed to provide answers to these questions – answers embodying solutions that are designed precisely to guarantee knowability, reliability and calculability of and through the legal order. Instead of leaving the answers regarding the exercise of power and the efficacy of the rights of freedom, property and equality to other norms, it supplies the answers itself and constitutes a system of legal certainty complete with a myriad rules and principles bordering on casuistry.[2]

Indeed, by establishing the rules of the legislative process, for instance, determining jurisdictions, defining procedures and specifying sources and subjects for normative production, the Constitution favors the ideals that make up legal certainty: When citizens know who can produce norms and what procedures must be followed, they not only know and better understand the norms to which they are subject, but can more easily anticipate and obey future modifications. As a result they can calculate today the future consequences of their acts. By determining rules for the activity of the executive branch, likewise creating jurisdictions, determining procedures and specifying sources and subjects for administrative actions, the Constitution also protects the knowability, reliability and calculability of the legal order. In other words, because citizens know which authority can and must act, what it can and must do, and which procedure it must follow, they know and understand better the norms they ought to obey and the acts that can restrict or condition their activities, and they can anticipate future administrative actions and plan their own activities with enhanced autonomy. By establishing the rules for the judiciary, again determining jurisdictions and procedures for judicial activities, the Constitution again promotes the knowability, reliability and calculability of the legal order: Citizens know who will judge their cases and how, so that they not only know and understand the options available to further their interests, but above all they know beforehand that they cannot be arbitrarily surprised by a restriction of their activities except by due process of law with all the guarantees already specified.

[2]Roque Antonio Carrazza, *Curso de Direito Constitucional Tributário*, 27th ed., São Paulo, Malheiros Editores, 2011, pages 418–419.

In sum, these simple observations, to which might be added others (almost as long as the text of the Constitution), only reveal the system of certainty created by the Constitution. Unlike others, the framers of Brazil's 1988 Constitution chose a system of predictability through the minutely detailed regulation of jurisdictions, subject-matters, procedures and sources.[3] As a result, the Constitution enables citizens to know the limits to the exercise of their freedom.[4] The lawmaker's power of configuration is not theoretical, but juridico-dogmatic: The concrete scope of legislative freedom is a direct consequence of substantive constitutional rules.[5]

This system is even more clearly evidenced in the sphere of taxation. The National Tax System comprises a set of norms that stipulate what taxes may be created (articles 145, 148, 149, 153, 155, 156 and 195), how they can be levied (article 150, I), when they can be required (articles 150, I and III) and in what measure they may restrict taxpayers' fundamental rights (article 150, II and IV). In sum, the system seeks to make state powers and taxpayers' guarantees predeterminable at the constitutional level. "What," "how," "when," and "in what measure" are questions the Constitution asks and itself answers through legal rules.[6] By doing so, it promotes knowability, reliability and calculability of the legal order: When taxpayers know who can create taxes, how taxable events are defined, what procedures can be used to create new taxes, when they can start being levied, and in what measure, they not only know and understand better the taxes they will pay, and how and when they can be levied, but can also better exercise their fundamental rights of freedom, property and equality, and more accurately anticipate future taxation.

In other words, legal certainty is a consequence of the constitutional system as a whole. It should be noted, however, that one of its foundations is not contained in the Constitution; it is the Constitution itself. Put yet another way, legal certainty is not only a result of what the Constitution ordains, but also of how it does so. To use metaphors that have been subjected to extensive wear and tear by usage and time but still provide powerful explanations, on one hand the legal order can be compared to a forest and its norms to the trees; on the other hand, it resembles a building whose pillars are its norms. Pursuing the same metaphorical language, we can say that legal certainty is protected not only by the trees, but also by the forest; not only by the pillars, but by the very architecture of the building.

This "system of legal certainty," visible through the analysis of the constitutional order in its entirety, is also externalized by means of its parts, as demonstrated in what follows.

---

[3]Geraldo Ataliba, *Sistema Constitucional Tributário Brasileiro*, São Paulo, Ed. RT, 1968, p. 39.

[4]Andreas von Arnauld, *Rechtssicherheit*, Tübingen, Mohr Siebeck, 2006, p. 20.

[5]Anja Bräunig, *Die Gestaltungsfreiheit des Gesetzgebers in der Rechtsprechung des Bundesverfassungsgerichts zur deutschen Wiedervereinigung*, Berlin, Duncker und Humblot, 2007, p. 177.

[6]Roque Antonio Carrazza, *Curso de Direito Constitucional Tributário*, 27th ed., São Paulo, Malheiros Editores, 2011, p. 482.

References

von ARNAULD, Andreas. *Rechtssicherheit*. Tübingen: Mohr Siebeck, 2006.

ATALIBA, Geraldo. *Sistema Constitucional Tributário Brasileiro*. São Paulo: Ed. RT, 1968.

BRÄUNIG, Anja. *Die Gestaltungsfreiheit des Gesetzgebers in der Rechtsprechung des Bundesverfassungsgerichts zur deutschen Wiedervereinigung*. Berlin: Duncker und Humblot, 2007.

CARRAZZA, Roque Antônio. *Curso de Direito Constitucional Tributário*. 27th ed. São Paulo: Malheiros Editores, 2011.

PIZZORUSSO, Alessandro; PASSAGLIA, Paolo. "Constitution et sécurité juridique – Italie". *Annuaire International de Justice Constitutionnelle*. Paris: Economica, 1999.

Foundations in the Constitutional Structure: In Terms of Its Parts

Abstract The constitutional structure of legal certainty is analyzed using the Brazilian Constitution as an example. The structure of the Constitution shows that legal certainty is an unequivocal positive principle, which protects it directly by "ensuring certainty" as a "right" and as a "value". Moreover, the Constitution also protects legal certainty in many of its dimensions, i.e., as certainty of law, before law, of rights, and as a right. The Constitution not only protects legal certainty in all of its manifestations but does so by assigning a high priority to legal certainty in the constitutional order. This is done through the way legal certainty is assured by the totality of the constitutional order and by its parts, through the insistence with which the Constitution protects legal certainty, through the independence of its foundations, and through the reciprocal efficacy of these same foundations. Finally, the Constitution protects legal certainty in favor of citizens and against the state.

1 Direct Foundations

1.1 General Protection of "Certainty"

As noted above, the Brazilian Constitution expressly provides for the protection of "certainty." Its "Preamble" says the representatives of the Brazilian People have convened in a National Constitutional Assembly to institute a Democratic State "that aims to ensure... certainty, well-being, development, equality and justice as supreme values of a fraternal, pluralist and prejudice-free society founded on social harmony and committed to the peaceful solution of disputes at home and abroad..." Let us examine this opening statement more closely. It can be summarized as saying that the Constitution institutes a democratic state committed to "assuring certainty, well-being, development, equality and justice as supreme values of a society founded on social harmony and order."[1] Legal certainty is present

[1]Maria Sylvia Zanella Di Pietro, "Os princípios da proteção à confiança, da segurança jurídica e da boa-fé na anulação do ato administrativo", in Fabrício Motta (Org.), *Direito Público atual: Estudos em Homenagem ao Professor Nélson Figueiredo*, Instituto de Direito Administrativo de Goiás (IDAG), Belo Horizonte, Fórum, 2008, p. 296.

© Springer International Publishing Switzerland 2016
H. Ávila, *Certainty in Law*, Law and Philosophy Library 114,
DOI 10.1007/978-3-319-33407-3_5

here at least five times: "assuring" means making certain; "certainty" means a state worthy of protection; "value" is something worthy of being assured; "social harmony" refers to a state of stability, predictability, and hence certainty; and "order" also denotes a desired state of stability and therefore certainty.[2] Thus the Constitution can be said already to "raise certainty to the fifth power" in its "Preamble", establishing with emphatic redundancy a state of affairs that can be summarized as "certainty secured as worthy of being assured in a society of certainty."

Moreover, the "Preamble" establishes an intertemporal commitment, which claims to be perpetual and is manifestly linked to the idea of continuity of the legal order, while at the same time stating its obedience to the newly established order and thus instituting a promise of stability.[3] The creation of a new order implies certainty because it presupposes there is something to seek and uphold.[4] There is no sense in creating a norm or establishing an order that is not expected to last.[5]

Furthermore, article 5 states that "all persons are equal before the law without distinction, Brazilians and foreign residents being assured of the inviolable right... to *segurança*...", among other things.[6]

The *segurança* to which the "Preamble" refers is clearly a social value. The Constitution is unequivocal: It institutes a Democratic State with the aim of "assuring certainty as a value". This expression denotes the use of legal certainty as "certainty through law" because law must serve as an instrument to guarantee certainty (or security). This begs the following question: Which certainty – non-legal certainty, i.e., security (*segurança*) to protect the nation against external threats, or legal certainty? By instituting a democratic state that assures "certainty as a value," i.e., as something that transcends individuals and has axiological content for society as a whole, the Constitution seems to adopt the second meaning, i.e., legal certainty. In sum, the "Preamble" to the Constitution directly protects legal certainty through law. This certainty is viable only if law itself is certain, as we will demonstrate in due course, so that ultimately the Constitution also indirectly protects certainty as certainty of law.

Article 5 is not as clear as the "Preamble" in its use of the term. Its guarantee of the inviolable "right to *segurança*" clearly refers to an individual right opposable to the state and guaranteed by it, given the chapter in which the expression is placed. Initially, however, it is not clear whether the term "*segurança*" refers to physical

---

[2]Theophilo Cavalcanti Filho, *O problema da segurança no Direito*, São Paulo, Ed. RT, 1964, pages 8 and 39.

[3]Anne-Laure Valembois, *La constitutionnalisation de l'exigence de sécurité juridique en Droit Français*, Paris, LGDJ, 2005, pages 381 and 390.

[4]Federico Arcos Ramírez, *La seguridad jurídica: una teoría formal*, Madrid, Dykinson, 2000, p. 20.

[5]Mark van Hoecek, "Time and law. Is it the nature of law to last? A conclusion", in François Ost e Mark van Hoecke (Orgs.), *Temps et Droit. Le Droit a-t-il pour vocation de durer?*, Bruxelles, Bruylant, 1998, p. 466.

[6]Geraldo Ataliba, *República e Constituição*, 3rd ed., São Paulo, Malheiros Editores, 2011, p. 179.

protection of the individual, i.e., security, or legal certainty, i.e., the requirement of a knowable, reliable and calculable order. Indeed, this provision guarantees the "right to *segurança*" without any adjectives to qualify the term "*segurança*." The truth is that several of the values and rights listed in these provisions are highly ambiguous. They may denote physical as well as valorative aspects: Protection of the right to life may mean the protection of biological life as well as the preservation of a group of juridical goods necessary to life with dignity; the right to freedom may mean the right to freedom of movement as well as the right to live one's life independently. The open phrasing, without any restriction of meaning, favors the interpretation according to which the term "*segurança*" means both non-legal certainty (safety or security) and legal certainty.

A reading of article 5 in its entirety, however, leads to the conclusion that the term "*segurança*" is used in the strict sense of legal certainty. First because the right to "*segurança*" is guaranteed alongside the right to freedom, equality and property. Since freedom, equality and property are objective social values, and not merely individual psychological states, the protection of "*segurança*" *in parallel with* the assurance of those other values is a clear indicator that the term is used in the sense of legal certainty, because physical security does not share such attributes. Second, because the fundamental rights listed under article 5 include both many rights relating to physical and individual safety or security (such as protection of the home and the institution of habeas corpus against abusive restrictions of freedom) and specific types of freedom (freedom of thought, freedom of opinion and belief, freedom of intellectual, artistic and scientific inquiry, or freedom of association), the conclusion must be that for the opening paragraph of the article to mean anything at all, it can only refer to certainty in every possible sense including legal certainty, certainty of law or certainty through law. If the indents include a guarantee of physical integrity, the reference to *segurança* in the opening paragraph of the same article has meaning only if it protects a different good. Thus Ataliba is right that the root element unifying all provisions of article 5 and making them fully meaningful is legal certainty.[7]

It must also be pointed out that even if the term "*segurança*" were interpreted restrictively, only as freedom from fear, dangers and external threats, this meaning would still contribute to the construction of legal certainty. This is because external security is one of the basic building blocks of legal certainty: Individuals are initially concerned with averting danger and external threats to their physical integrity, but soon seek psychological freedom from other surprises. Security then incorporates an internal element (a feeling) that creates a state of trust in citizens and eventually expands from the personal domain to become a social and legal value, at which time its realization depends on legal and institutional preconditions.[8]

The above considerations demonstrate that the guarantee of "*segurança*" in the "Preamble" and the opening paragraph of article 5 indeed means protection of *legal*

---

[7]Geraldo Ataliba, *República e Constituição*, 3rd ed., São Paulo, Malheiros Editores, 2011, p. 179.

[8]Andreas von Arnauld, *Rechtssicherheit*, Tübingen, Mohr Siebeck, 2006, p. 63.

certainty as certainty *of* law and certainty *through* law, protection for the *citizen from* the state, to be realized *by* the state through rules, acts and procedures that make certainty effectively an *individual right* and a *social value*.

1.2 Specific Protection of "Legal Certainty"

The Constitution expressly mentions legal certainty in only one provision, added by Constitutional Amendment 45/2004. Article 103-A authorizes the Supreme Court to issue precedential rulings on its own initiative or when petitioned, provided two-thirds of its members concur and in response to several prior decisions on a constitutional matter. These rulings must be published by the official press to be binding on all other instances of the judiciary and on the federal, state and city governments at all levels. Paragraph 1 states that the object of such precedential rulings "will be to review the validity, interpretation and efficacy of norms disputed by judicial bodies or between such bodies and governmental bodies, so as to cause *grave legal uncertainty* and significant proliferation of lawsuits on the same subject" (emphasis added).

Obviously, the phrase "legal certainty" is used without being defined. Nevertheless, an examination of the normative scope into which it has been inserted helps delimit its content: If the purpose of such precedential rulings is to "review the validity, interpretation and efficacy of norms disputed by judicial bodies or between such bodies and governmental bodies," then the phrase refers to two main substantive aspects: knowability of the legal order, requiring clarity and intelligibility of the norms and their application; and calculability of the legal order, requiring predictability and normative binding. This means that the 1988 Constitution, albeit by a constitutional amendment, acknowledges legal certainty as a fundamental element and defines it as required to assure the knowability and calculability of law in terms of both guidance and application.

1.3 Protection of One of the Effects of Legal Certainty

By ordaining that "the law shall not prejudice acquired rights, completed legal acts and res iudicata," (article 5, XXXVI), the Constitution protects legal certainty in the efficacy of one of its partial elements – reliability of the legal order.

The protection of acquired rights, completed legal acts and res iudicata is a manifestation of the principles of protection of trust and good faith, which in turn translate the reflexive efficacy of the legal certainty principle oriented to a specific subject and a specific concrete case.[9] By protecting these rights, it is as if through

[9] Stefan Muckel, *Kriterien des verfassungsrechtlichen Vertrauensschutzes bei Gesetzesänderungen*, Berlin, Duncker und Humblot, 1989, p. 63; Constantin Yannakopoulos, *La notion de droits acquis*

a rule the Constitution guaranteed the reflexive efficacy of the objective principle of legal certainty, applying it so as to uphold something won through law in the past. This rule governs the past-oriented subjective aspect of a principle which in addition to its objective dimension protects supraindividual interests, and may even oppose a given individual interest, as when a subjective right expires owing to limitation or prescription for lack of use.[10] Thus the Constitution provides in some sense a "guarantee of the past," as noted by Carvalho and Carrazza.[11]

In other words, express protection for these rights, which we examine in detail below, shows that the Constitution assures legal certainty, as certainty of law and certainty through law, for any citizen with regard to the state and to be realized by the state by means of rules, acts and procedures to enforce the individual rights arising from the reflexive efficacy of certainty as an objective principle of the legal order.

2 Indirect Foundations

2.1 By Deduction

2.1.1 Objective Structuring Principles

2.1.1.1 Principle of the Rule of Law

Besides providing for certainty directly, the Constitution also requires a search for broader ends from which more restricted ends necessary for its realization can be deduced and which as a whole translate the ideals of reliability and calculability of (and through) the legal order. Here the elements of legal certainty are discovered by *deduction* from superprinciples that impose the realization of broader ends relative to legal certainty.[12]

The Constitution begins by establishing that "the Federative Republic of Brazil, formed by the indissoluble union of its states, municipalities and the Federal District, is constituted as a democratic state based on the rule of law ..." (article 1). This is not the place to examine the principle of the rule of law in its entirety, but it

en Droit Administratif Français, Paris, LGDJ, 1997, p. 53; Enrico Riva, *Wohlerworbene Rechte – Eigentum – Vertrauen*, Bern, Stämpfli, 2007, p. 79; Miguel Reale, *Revogação e anulamento do ato administrativo*, 2nd ed., Rio de Janeiro, Forense, 1980, p. 81.

[10]Andreas von Arnauld, *Rechtssicherheit*, Tübingen, Mohr Siebeck, 2006, pages 153 and 156.

[11]Paulo de Barros Carvalho, *Curso de Direito Tributário*, 21st ed., São Paulo, Saraiva, 2009, p. 166; Roque Antonio Carrazza, *Curso de Direito Constitucional Tributário*, 27th ed., São Paulo, Malheiros Editores, 2011, pages 456 and 981–982.

[12]Katharina Sobota, *Das Prinzip Rechtsstaat*, Tübingen, Siebeck, 1997, p. 411; Willy Zimmer, "Constitution et sécurité juridique – Allemagne", *Annuaire International de Justice Constitutionnelle 1999*, Paris, Economica, 2000, p. 114.

is appropriate at this juncture to assess in what measure the principle of the rule of law contributes to the content of the principle of legal certainty – and in that sense it is decisive.

Indeed, the legal certainty principle is usually deduced from the principle of the rule of law.[13] In Carrazza's words, it "lies at the very heart of the democratic law-based state."[14] It is not only linked to the universality and non-arbitrariness of law, but also to the requirement that state actions be governed by general rules that are clear, known, relatively constant over time, prospective and non-contradictory.[15] The rule of law is also characterized by the ideal of protection for rights and state responsibility, an ideal that can be achieved only by means of an intelligible, reliable and predictable order. State activity is not founded in and limited by law if powers and procedures are not provided for, stable and controllable (certainty of law). Moreover, fundamental rights are not minimally effective if citizens lack advance knowledge of the limits within which they can fully exercise their freedom (certainty of rights), and lack instruments to assure their expectations (certainty through law) and the efficacy of those rights in the event of unjustified restrictions (certainty under law). If the rule of law is the protection of the individual against arbitrariness, only an accessible and understandable order can play this role.[16] Either the rule of law is certain, or it is not the rule of law. As Raz rightly points out, "observance of the rule of law is necessary if the law is to respect human dignity. Respecting human dignity entails treating humans as persons capable of planning and plotting their future. Thus, respecting people's dignity includes respecting their autonomy, their right to control their future."[17] These considerations show how right Maior Borges is to say

[13]Klaus Stern, "Der Rechtsstaat", in *Kölner Universitätsreden*, Krefeld, Scherpe, 1971, p. 8; Andreas von Arnauld, *Rechtssicherheit*, Tübingen, Mohr Siebeck, 2006, pages 665 and 671; Philip Kunig, *Das Rechtsstaatsprinzip*, Tübingen, Siebeck, 1986, pages 163 and 390 and following; idem, "Der Rechtsstaat", in Peter Badura e Horst Dreier (Orgs.), *FS 50 Jahre Bundesverfassungsgericht. Klärung und Fortbildung des Verfassungsrechts*, v. 2, Tübingen, 2001, p. 440; Delf Buchwald, *Prinzipien des Rechtsstaats*, Aachen, Shaker, 1996, pages 181 and following; Katharina Sobota, *Das Prinzip Rechtsstaat*, Tübingen, Siebeck, 1997, p. 422; Karl Albert Schachtschneider, *Prinzipien des Rechtsstaates*, Berlin, Duncker und Humblot, 2006, p. 359; Lúcia Valle Figueiredo, "Planejamento, Direito Tributário e segurança jurídica", *RTDP* 12, p. 14, São Paulo, 1995; Carlos Alberto Alvaro de Oliveira, "O formalismo valorativo no confronto com o formalismo excessivo", *RF* 15, p. 388, separata, s.d.

[14]Roque Antonio Carrazza, "Segurança jurídica e eficácia temporal das alterações jurisprudenciais – Competência dos Tribunais Superiores para fixá-la – Questões conexas", in Tércio Sampaio Ferraz Jr. *et alii* (Orgs.), *Efeito "ex nunc" e as decisões do STF*, São Paulo, Manole, 2008, p. 41.

[15]Jeremy Waldron, "The rule of law in contemporary liberal theory", *Ratio Juris*, v. 2, n. 1, p. 84, 1989; Hans-Wolfgang Arndt, "Das Rechtsstaatsprinzip", *JuS* 27, pages L41-L44, 1987.

[16]Sylvia Calmes, *Du principe de protection de la confiance legitime en droits Allemand, Communautaire et Français*, Paris, Dalloz, 2001, p. 115.

[17]Joseph Raz, "The rule of law and its virtue (1977)", in *The authority of law. Essays on law and morality*, Oxford, Oxford, 1979, p. 221.

of legal certainty, "without it, Brazil could not even define itself as a democratic law-based state."[18]

Indeed, the principle of the rule of law is related to the legal certainty principle in both of its dimensions. Its formal dimension concerns the separation of powers, the hierarchy of norms and jurisdictional protection.[19] The separation of powers favors control of the exercise of power and its allocation through rules of jurisdiction – elements which contribute to an increase in knowability, reliability and calculability of the legal order. As the source of general and abstract norms properly directed to an indeterminate number of people and situations, the law favors the stability of the order, since it is not necessary to change norms because of changes in people or circumstances. Under the rule of law, the rulers agree to be ruled by the law rather than their own will.[20] The hierarchy of norms, with each norm requiring a justification for its validity in a superior norm, helps enhance the predictability and control of state action. This formal structure promotes normative accessibility, since citizens know, for instance, that a lower-ranking norm must be in accordance with a higher-ranking norm, which in turn must be in accordance with an even higher one, and so on up to the Constitution. Thus while the grounding of laws in the Constitution may cause uncertainty on one hand, given that their validity depends on vertical constitutional compatibility, which is not always easy to assess, on the other hand it contributes to certainty by limiting their possible meanings.[21] Jurisdictional protection, in turn, serves as an instrument to assure rights and the effectiveness of the legal order as a whole.

Thus formal structuring of law is an element that assures the realization of legal certainty. All these elements of a formal conception of the rule of law contribute to the ideals of legal certainty, such as clarity, sureness, precision, intelligibility, generality and abstraction.[22] Evidently, such elements of the rule of law are only *necessary* to create a state of legal certainty, not *sufficient*: Rules of jurisdiction may conflict with one another; the legality rule requires only that new obligations be instituted in formal sources of law and thus cannot prevent a margin of indeterminacy, which is inevitable in the use of language, or the argumentative process of interpretation; normative hierarchy may give rise to uncertainty due to the existence of not one but multiple norms, many containing highly indeterminate

[18]José Souto Maior Borges, "Segurança jurídica: sobre a distinção entre competências fiscais para orientar e autuar o contribuinte", *RDT* 100, p. 20, São Paulo, s.d.

[19]Robert Summers, "A formal theory of the rule of law", in *Essays in Legal Theory*, Dordrecht, Kluwer, 2000, p. 169; Brian Z. Tamanaha, *On the rule of law*, Cambridge, Cambridge University Press, 2004, p. 91; Manoel Gonçalves Ferreira Filho, *Estado de Direito e Constituição*, 4th ed., São Paulo, Saraiva, 2007, pages 86 and following.

[20]Roque Antonio Carrazza, *Curso de Direito Constitucional Tributário*, 27th ed., São Paulo, Malheiros Editores, 2011, p. 422.

[21]Luigi Ferrajoli, "The past and the future of the rule of law", in Pietro Costa e Danilo Zolo (Orgs.), *The Rule of Law – History, theory and criticism*, Dordrecht, Springer, 2007, p. 329.

[22]Anne-Laure Valembois, *La constitutionnalisation de l'exigence de sécurité juridique en Droit Français*, Paris, LGDJ, 2005, pages 35 and 39.

legal concepts – and so on. In sum, the principle of the rule of law is ambiguous with regard to legal certainty: For example, the legality principle requires that laws be enacted whenever freedom is restricted in any way, but ultimately leads to an indiscriminate increase in the number of laws; the duty of equality means disparities must be considered either in laws or in their application, making legislation complex and jeopardizing the uniformity of application – and so on.[23] None of this, however, detracts from the fundamental significance of the rule-of-law principle's role in shaping the entire legal system.

The substantive dimension of the rule of law also favors the ideals of legal certainty. Since this dimension aims to protect a set of rights, legal certainty acts as a principle to assure these same rights. Hence the creation of the term "guarantee rights" (or "supporting rights," "rights that guarantee rights" or "tutorial rights"), i.e., rights that aim to assure others, such as freedom of expression and communication, for instance, which are instruments to make the principle of legal certainty effective.[24] In a way the legal certainty principle is a "guarantee right" because its realization precedes the actual exercise of certain fundamental rights. These rights, it must be stressed, serve to enable individuals to exercise their autonomy. For this reason, the very conception of the rule of law must be "robust", in the sense of involving material aspects without which the rule of law does not serve as an instrument for the realization of human dignity.[25]

It is also worth underscoring that the rule of law rather than the so-called police state or legal state operates as an instrument to assure legal certainty: a police state cannot do so because it lacks checks on the exercise of power and is therefore unpredictable and oppressive; while a "legal state" requires only statutory provision without the constraints resulting from fundamental rights, making the legislative virtually omnipotent and not preventing the arbitrary exercise of power through the incorporation of substantive fundamental rights, such as equality in the law.[26]

These observations, to which others could be added, explain why Brazil's Supreme Court considers the legal certainty principle a subprinciple of the rule of law, as exemplified in the following excerpt from the opinion of Justice Gilmar Mendes in MS (Writ of Mandamus) no. 24268–0:

> Today the subject is considered a key element of our Constitution (principle of the rule of law), and is partially codified at the federal level in Law 9784 of 29 Jan 1999 (e.g., art. 2). As

[23]Klaus-Michael Groll, *In der Flut der Gesetze: Ursachen, Folgen, Perspektiven*, Düsseldorf, Droste, 1985, pages 32 and following.

[24]Anne-Laure Valembois, *La constitutionnalisation de l'exigence de sécurité juridique en Droit Français*, Paris, LGDJ, 2005, p. 50.

[25]Sebastián Urbina, *Legal method and the rule of law*, Dordrecht, Kluwer, 2002, p. 227.

[26]Anne-Laure Valembois, *La constitutionnalisation de l'exigence de sécurité juridique en Droit Français*, Paris, LGDJ, 2005, p. 36; Michel Troper, "Le concept d'État de Droit", *Cahiers de Philosophie Politique et Juridique* 24, p. 28, 1993.

we have seen, in fact, as a subprinciple of the rule of law legal certainty has unique value in the legal system and plays an especially significant role in the realization of material justice.[27]

In short, institution of the rule-of-law principle demonstrates that the Constitution, having set forth a broader ideal to be sought, ensures *legal* certainty as certainty *of* law, *through* law *before* law, and *rights*, and certainty *of the citizens against* the state, to be realized *by* the state through rules, acts and procedures implement individual rights and assure the legitimate exercise of power by the state. The entire theory of the rule of law, in the words of Chevallier, was constructed to limit and circumscribe the power of the state.[28] A state that is not regulated by law is unpredictable and arbitrary – in other words, it causes legal uncertainty.

In light of the above it is clear that founding the legal certainty principle on the rule-of-law principle has a significant impact on its content. This is because, as its name suggests, the rule-of-law principle is preliminarily contrary to the maintenance of acts that violate law: The maintenance of illegal or unconstitutional acts affects the knowability and calculability of state actions because it may encourage more illegal acts, thus preventing citizens from anticipating governmental acts; it contributes to state arbitrariness, given the lack of objective criteria to regulate state activity; it decreases the control of state actions by upholding irregular acts; it undermines uniformity of treatment by allowing for the possibility of differentiated treatment depending on whether legal proceedings are instituted.[29] All that is meant here is that founding the legal certainty principle on the rule of law significantly restricts its meaning. In the name of legal certainty alone, as a subprinciple of the rule of law, and without any other foundation, no state action can be supported unless it is governed by general, clear, known rules that are relatively constant over time, forward-looking and non-contradictory.

2.1.1.2 Principle of the Social Rule of Law

Although nominally speaking the Constitution institutes only a "democratic state based on the rule of law" (article 1), it contains a number of provisions that in aggregate create an ideal we can call a state based on the social rule of law: The "Preamble" refers to the institution of a democratic state in which social and individual rights, equality and justice are guaranteed as *supreme values* of a fraternal, pluralist and prejudice-free society, founded on *social harmony*; article 3 establishes the fundamental objectives of the Federative Republic of Brazil, among which are the construction of a free, just and solidary society, the eradication

[27] MS n. 24.268, Tribunal Pleno, Relator Ministro Gilmar Mendes, *DJ* 17 Sep 2004, p. 183 of the decision.

[28] Jacques Chevallier, *L'État de Droit*, 2nd ed., Paris, Montchrestien, 1994, p. 11.

[29] Robert Summers, "A formal theory of the rule of law", in *Essays in legal theory*, Dordrecht, Kluwer, 2000, p. 169.

of poverty and marginalization, and the reduction of social inequalities; article 5 guarantees the right to full and free legal aid for those who prove insufficiency of resources, for example; article 6 guarantees the social rights to education, health, work, shelter, leisure, *segurança*, social security, protection of mother and child, and assistance for the destitute. And in the chapter on the general principles of economic activity, the Constitution guarantees an economic order founded on the value of work so that all citizens live with dignity, in accordance with the precepts of social justice (article 170).

The connection between the principle of the social rule of law and legal certainty is that a social order is one that assures social certainty, i.e., an order that permits not only the creation but also the maintenance of institutions and measures that remedially or preventively guarantee citizens the means of subsistence with dignity.[30] From this normative content, it is possible to deduce the duty of taking the citizens' positions and expectations into consideration.[31] Thus the principle requires that citizens must not be surprised, without a grave national justification, by risks greater than those life presents and from which social security ought to protect them, so as not to place them in a situation incompatible with the minimal social conditions of survival.[32]

In reality, however, since the principle of the social rule of law is not predominantly one of protection, it does not guarantee expectations, a role played by the principle of the rule of law. What ends up happening is precisely an opposition between these principles: The social rule of law requires the state to abide by its function of planning and driving social change, especially redistribution of wealth; whereas the rule of law operates to balance and assure expectations, preventing certain changes.[33] What the principle of the social state requires is a sort of stable change of the legal order: a compromise between innovation and continuity.[34] And continuity is indeed one of the elements of legal certainty. In this respect, it is important to remember that in the era of the social state, although the state acts more intensely, not least to correct inequalities and imbalances, it must remain impartial and ban the arbitrariness proper to general and abstract norms, lest it corrupt social justice itself.[35] Thus, either the principle of the social state is harmonized with the

[30] Alexia Bierweiler, *Soziale Sicherheit als Grundrecht in der Europäischen Union*, Stuttgart, Boorberg, 2007, p. 135. Likewise: Wilhelm Hartz, "Mehr Rechtssicherheit im Steuerrecht. Ziele, Wege, Grenzen", *StbJb*, 1965/1966, p. 89.

[31] Stefan Muckel, *Kriterien des verfassungsrechtlichen Vertrauensschutzes bei Gesetzesänderungen*, Berlin, Duncker und Humblot, 1989, p. 31.

[32] Anna Leisner, *Kontinuität als Verfassungsprinzip*, Tübingen, Mohr Siebeck, 2002, p. 300; Ricardo Lobo Torres, *O Direito ao mínimo existencial*, Rio de Janeiro, Renovar, 2009, p. 83.

[33] Stefan Muckel, *Kriterien des verfassungsrechtlichen Vertrauensschutzes bei Gesetzesänderungen*, Berlin, Duncker und Humblot, 1989, p. 33; Federico Arcos Ramírez, *La seguridad jurídica: una teoría formal*, Madrid, Dykinson, 2000, p. 351.

[34] Anna Leisner, *Kontinuität als Verfassungsprinzip*, Tübingen, Mohr Siebeck, 2002, p. 2.

[35] Federico Arcos Ramírez, *La seguridad jurídica: una teoría formal*, Madrid, Dykinson, 2000, p. 361.

principle of the rule of law – and therefore with legal certainty – or the balanced, non-arbitrary realization of the principle of the social state will be compromised. Schoueri rightly advocates, for this reason, that there ought to be an adjustment to the principle of legal certainty so as to uphold the classical guarantees of the liberal state while creating mechanisms that allow for some needed flexibility to reach the goal sought by the economic order.[36]

In addition, the social-rule-of-law principle establishes a certain prevalence of human life over other values, and considers certain rights innate in human beings, thus not only limiting the exercise of economic activities by private individuals but also requiring services and redistribution from the state.[37] These functions also impact on the states of normative reliability and calculability. Respect for human dignity, for example, disqualifies the institution of norms that treat humans as mere objects, as in the case of retroactive inductive laws, which under the pretext of influencing human behavior also affect past behavior that by definition cannot be influenced.

To summarize, institution of the social-rule-of-law principle shows that by establishing a broader ideal to be sought the Constitution protects *legal* certainty as certainty *by* law, certainty *of rights*, and certainty *of citizens before* the state, to be realized *by* the state by means of rules, acts and procedures that create the minimal social conditions required to implement individual rights.

2.1.1.3 Principle of the Functional Division of Powers

The principle of the division of powers requires that functions and tasks be shared between the legislative, executive and judiciary. However, this is only possible if the law is minimally able to constrain them as a heterolimitation: Only accessible, intelligible and stable law can ensure that the judiciary acts *predominantly* in a declarative, non-creative manner, and that the executive acts according to an agenda previously set by the legislative.[38]

Thus when the Constitution refers to the principle of separation of powers in article 2, it requires minimal accessibility, intelligibility and stability of law. This absolutely does not mean that the minimal meanings of normative texts do not have to be put into context from the normative and factual viewpoints. What it does mean is that there are semantic limits that the judiciary must not disregard when performing normative reconstruction.

---

[36] Luís Eduardo Schoueri, "Segurança na ordem tributária nacional e internacional: tributação do comércio exterior", in Aires Fernandino Barreto *et alii* (Orgs.), *Segurança jurídica na tributação e Estado de Direito*, São Paulo, Noeses, 2005, pages 382–383.

[37] Francisco González Navarro, *El Estado Social y Democrático de Derecho*, Pamplona, EUNSA, 1992, pages 61 and 98 and following.

[38] Federico Arcos Ramírez, *La seguridad jurídica: una teoría formal*, Madrid, Dykinson, 2000, p. 86; Christoph Möllers, *Gewaltenteilung*, Tübingen, Mohr Siebeck, 2005, p. 133; idem, *Die drei Gewalten*, Göttingen, Velbrück, 2008, pages 118 and 153; Eros Roberto Grau, *O Direito posto e o Direito pressuposto*, 7th ed., São Paulo, Malheiros Editores, 2008, p. 226.

2.1.2 Democratic Principle

The democratic principle has a connection with the legal certainty principle, because it is based on and requires a relation of trust between the citizens and their elected representatives, so that the latter must avoid frustrating the formers' expectations in order to win the next election.[39] Precisely for this reason, besides requiring and assuming trust the democratic principle also promotes stability, since continued trust perpetuates the structures of power. As illustratively noted by Redor, "the state keeping its word may be the high point of democracy."[40] Thus the democratic principle contributes especially to the ideal of reliability that is a component of the principle of legal certainty.

Moreover, by requiring the participation of citizens in the formulation and implementation of public policies, the democratic principle assures state transparency: Citizen participation is effective in controlling state activities only when there is transparency regarding results, processes, content, and responsibilities.[41] Thus the democratic principle is the basis for the requirement of transparency of information, which contributes to the realization of the ideal of knowability of state actions, including financial transparency.

2.1.3 Subjective Principles of Freedom

2.1.3.1 Property-Related

2.1.3.1.1 Principle of Protection of Property

Besides ordaining these broader ideals, from which the elements of legal certainty can be deduced, the Constitution also determines the realization of more specific goals that presuppose the existence of knowability, reliability and predictability of the legal order to assure their efficacy. The principles of protection of property and freedom are particularly highly valorized by the Constitution, as stressed by Carrazza.[42]

The inviolability of the right to property is guaranteed in article 5 (opening paragraph and indents XXII and XXIII). The same right to property is also established as a principle of the economic order (in article 170, II and III). This right is important for legal certainty when perceived as protection for certain legal positions regarding property: Citizens can exercise legal positions effectively if they can trust the stability of the legal relations that concern them – this is why the

[39] Anne-Laure Valembois, *La constitutionnalisation de l'exigence de sécurité juridique en Droit Français*, Paris, LGDJ, 2005, p. 61.

[40] Marie-Joële Redor, *De l'État legal à l'État de Droit*, Paris, Economica, 1992, p. 291.

[41] Jürgen Bröhmer, *Transparenz als Verfassungsprinzip*, Tübingen, Mohr Siebeck, 2004, p. 377.

[42] Roque Antonio Carrazza, *Curso de Direito Constitucional Tributário*, 27th ed., São Paulo, Malheiros Editores, 2011, p. 464.

protection of trust in the permanence of property is *immanent* in the right to property itself.[43] However, the protection of trust based on the right to property does not preclude protection for immaterial rights grounded in other principles.

What is essential to the specific point examined here is that the protection of property involves *a claim of durability*: An available property sphere is protected so that citizens are free to use it, presupposing a claim to durability of this state of intangibility since if the sphere in question could be constantly and unjustifiably changed, its owner would not be able to use it freely.[44] The right of property so clearly assumes permanence that the Constitution allows for restrictions to this right only through specific procedures, including compulsory purchase in extraordinary cases, also requiring preconditions that are not easily met and with proportional compensation. Thus even the restriction of property rights must occur in a predictable manner. Moreover, the explicit determination of inheritance rights is also an indirect form of preservation of continuity: The right to transfer assets to heirs is a form of permanence of the deceased in other persons.[45]

These considerations show, on one hand, that the partial ideals of legal certainty can be deduced from the durability claim inherent in property rights. In protecting the property sphere as a rule to which exceptions can be made only through a rigorous procedure and under highly specific conditions, the Constitution indirectly protects the reliability and calculability of the legal order. Because they know the rule that this right cannot be restricted, citizens can plan their activities with greater autonomy, so that the right becomes the means to realize freedom. Thus legal certainty is protected as certainty *of* law, *through* law and *of rights*. On the other hand, the above considerations also show that the ideals of reliability and predictability become conditions for full exercise of the fundamental right to property: Without a knowable, reliable and calculable legal order, property-related rights and freedoms cannot be minimally exercised with autonomy.[46] Thus legal certainty as certainty *of rights* is protected on the basis of certainty *of* law.

In addition, the fundamental right to property connects with the fundamental right to freedom as the foundation for protecting the past exercise of this right: Anyone who has configured property based on state guidance will deserve the protection of trust, as long as the requisite preconditions exist.[47]

---

[43] Stefan Muckel, *Kriterien des verfassungsrechtlichen Vertrauensschutzes bei Gesetzesänderungen*, Berlin, Duncker und Humblot, 1989, p. 41; Paul Kirchhof, "Rückwirkung von Steuergesetzen", *StuW*, 2000, p. 230.

[44] Johanna Hey, *Steuerplanungssicherheit als Rechtsproblem*, Köln, Otto Schmidt, 2002, p. 136; Anna Leisner, *Kontinuität als Verfassungsprinzip*, Tübingen, Mohr Siebeck, 2002, p. 290.

[45] Anna Leisner, *Kontinuität als Verfassungsprinzip*, Tübingen, Mohr Siebeck, 2002, p. 292.

[46] Andreas von Arnauld, *Rechtssicherheit*, Tübingen, Mohr Siebeck, 2006, p. 663.

[47] Johanna Hey, *Steuerplanungssicherheit als Rechtsproblem*, Köln, Otto Schmidt, 2002, p. 152.

2.1.3.1.2 *Principles of Freedom to Exercise Professional and Economic Activities*

As early as the chapter about fundamental rights, the Constitution states that the Federative Republic of Brazil is established as a democratic state based on the rule of law and that its foundations include the social values of work and free enterprise (article 1). Later on, the list of individual rights and guarantees includes the freedom to engage in any occupational activity, craft or profession (article 5, XIII). Furthermore, in the chapter on the general principles of economic activity, it guarantees an economic order founded on the value of work and free enterprise (article 170), also "assuring" the free exercise of any economic activity regardless of authorization by public bodies, except in cases defined by law. Even with regard to the National Tax System, the Constitution does not allow distinctions based on professional activity (article 150, II), which by ellipsis protects the exercise of any kind of professional activity.

Freedom to engage in any kind of work or economic activity serves as an instrument for citizens to plan their own lives. It is through work and economic activity that citizens independently build their individuality. Thus these fundamental rights are invested with core relevance for self-determination and self-fulfillment with dignity. Freedom functions as a kind of status: Only the *continuous* protection of the capacity to act permits the effective exercise of freedom and self-formation of personality. Unlike property, which often changes hands, an occupation or trade is a lasting capability and remains with individuals for their entire lives, so that it can be considered a constantly developing object. A trade or profession is neither more nor less than the lasting realization of a foundation for life.[48] The fundamental right to a trade or profession therefore assumes a temporal dimension characterized by a claim to permanence: The state has a duty of *continuously* protecting and not restricting it.[49] This claim to stability appears again in the use of the examination of proportionality for the constitutional control of restrictions on rights and freedoms, including those relating to work and professional activities: Restriction is considered constitutional only if appropriate, necessary and proportional. With respect to the point we are investigating, this means that the conditions for exercising a trade or profession must remain stable, unless there is a reason that proportionally justifies a restriction.[50]

The same is true for the fundamental right to the free exercise of economic activities: Because it presupposes free choice and free exercise of a given activity, it precludes sudden legislative or administrative changes.[51] The predictability of the effects of future decisions and their stability are necessary conditions for the rational

---

[48] Anna Leisner, *Kontinuität als Verfassungsprinzip*, Tübingen, Mohr Siebeck, 2002, p. 315.

[49] Johanna Hey, *Steuerplanungssicherheit als Rechtsproblem*, Köln, Otto Schmidt, 2002, pages 163–164; Anna Leisner, *Kontinuität als Verfassungsprinzip*, Tübingen, Mohr Siebeck, 2002, p. 314.

[50] Anna Leisner, *Kontinuität als Verfassungsprinzip*, Tübingen, Mohr Siebeck, 2002, p. 318.

[51] Johanna Hey, *Steuerplanungssicherheit als Rechtsproblem*, Köln, Otto Schmidt, 2002, p. 171.

and functional exercise of freedom, especially considering that autonomy is founded on the law and exercised within its limits.[52] In the sphere of economic activity durability is a requirement deriving from certain specific factors: Investment in real estate or manufacturing, for example, makes economic sense only over time, so that investment decisions cannot be made unless judgments and calculations according to tax law are feasible for the long term.[53]

The above demonstrates that the durability claim is also inherent in the right to free exercise of professional and economic activities, from which the partial ideals of legal certainty can be deduced. In protecting the individual's sphere of action in terms of profession or economic activity, and prohibiting the state from creating disproportional or excessive restrictions, the Constitution indirectly preserves the reliability and calculability of the legal order: Citizens enjoy an active right to self-determination and can act and plan their activities. Thus legal certainty is guaranteed as certainty of rights through certainty *of* law, and even *before* the law. More than assuring durability of the legal order, the concrete exercise of freedom can generate subjective application of the legal certainty principle through the protection of trust: In specific cases, which we will discuss later, those who exercise their freedom in the manner directed by law cannot be harmed.[54]

2.1.3.2 Not Property-Related

2.1.3.2.1 Principle of Protection of Freedom

The Constitution repeatedly protects freedom not only as a whole, as we have seen, but also in its parts. In the "Preamble" it institutes a democratic state designed to guarantee freedom. The chapter on individual rights and guarantees starts by assuring citizens of the inviolability of the right to freedom and then lists a number of more specific rights (freedom of expression, thought, opinion and belief, freedom of intellectual, artistic and scientific inquiry, freedom of communication, and freedom of association for lawful purposes), as well as certain specific guarantees to make freedom effective (e.g., receiving information from public bodies, or filing for a writ of mandamus or habeas corpus).

It is unnecessary to repeat everything that has already been said about the principles of free exercise of professional and economic activities. As far as the principle of freedom in general is concerned, all of the above applies, but even

[52]Hanns Uhlrich, "La sécurité juridique en Droit Économique allemand: observations d'un privatiste", in Laurence Boy, Jean-Baptiste Racine e Fabrice Siiriainen (Orgs.), *Sécurité juridique et Droit Économique*, Bruxelles, Larcier, 2008, p. 77.

[53]Karl Heinrich Friauf, "Steuerrechtsänderungen und Altinvestitionen. Zum Verfassungsgebot der steuerlichen Investitionssicherheit", *StbJb*, 1986/1987, p. 279; Herbert Wiedemann, "Rechtssicherheit – ein absoluter Wert? Gedanken zum Bestimmtheitserfordernis zivilrechtlicher Tatbestände", in Gotthard Paulus *et alii* (Orgs.), *FS für Karl Larenz*, München, Beck, 1973, pages 204–205.

[54]Johanna Hey, *Steuerplanungssicherheit als Rechtsproblem*, Köln, Otto Schmidt, 2002, p. 162.

more broadly: Besides subsidiary protection against any restriction not prohibited by specific principles of freedom, this general principle of freedom protects self-affirmation and self-determination (the capacity to define one's own identity), and self-protection (the capacity to protect oneself and to withdraw, both legally, into privacy and intimacy, and physically, into the home), as well as protecting against self-exposure (the capacity to abstain from exposure considered harmful to one's own person and to decide what to make public concerning one's own self).[55] Thus legal freedom means the *freedom to choose* forms of behavior that avoid or lessen legal risks, i.e., legal consequences that can be foreknown and controlled, and that will affect individual decisions.[56] Freedom therefore involves autonomy, as opposed to a life of *forced choices* or *no choice at all*.[57]

By examining the content of the principles of freedom we can prove that the ideals of reliability and calculability serve as preconditions for their efficacy. Without a knowable, reliable and calculable legal order, property-related freedoms cannot be minimally exercised with independence; nor can freedom of self-determination: In order to work or exercise an economic activity, citizens need to know who can produce the norms that will regulate their activities, how such norms can be enacted, what their content is, and how they condition or restrict their choice of profession or activity and its continued exercise. Without knowing what the norms are and what authorities can enact them, and if such norms are not minimally stable and binding on the authorities, in actuality citizens lack minimal conditions to act and plan with freedom.[58] Hence it can justly be said that reliability and calculability of state action embody the foundations for individual action and planning, including in the economic sphere.[59] The necessary correlation between freedom and certainty also derives from this. As von Arnauld puts it, "leading a life with autonomy means being able to plan it."[60] Or in the words of Vogel, "*legal certainty is a precondition for the certainty of subjective rights*."[61] Or again, to quote Hey, "freedom only prospers in trust, and trust only prospers in freedom."[62] In sum, the protection of freedom is an indirect guarantee of legal certainty as certainty *of rights* by means of certainty *of* law.

---

[55] Pieroth/Schlink, *Staatsrecht II*: *Grundrechte*, 23rd ed., Heidelberg, C. F. Müller, 2007, p. 87.

[56] Christoph Gusy, "Gewährleistung von Freiheit und Sicherheit im Lichte unterschiedlicher Staats- und Verfassungsverständnisse", *VVDStRL* 63, p. 155, Berlin, 2004.

[57] Joseph Raz, *The Morality of Freedom*, Oxford, Clarendon, 1986, p. 371.

[58] Christoph Gusy, "Gewährleistung von Freiheit und Sicherheit im Lichte unterschiedlicher Staats- und Verfassungsverständnisse", *VVDStRL* 63, p. 164, Berlin, 2004.

[59] Andreas von Arnauld, *Rechtssicherheit*, Tübingen, Mohr Siebeck, 2006, pages 37, 118, 155 and 162.

[60] Idem, p. 668.

[61] Klaus Vogel, "Rechtssicherheit und Rückwirkung zwischen Vernunftrecht und Verfassungsrecht", *Juristen Zeitung*, n. 43, 1988, p. 833.

[62] Johanna Hey, *Steuerplanungssicherheit als Rechtsproblem*, Köln, Otto Schmidt, 2002, p. 120; Anna Leisner, *Kontinuität als Verfassungsprinzip*, Tübingen, Mohr Siebeck, 2002, p. 280.

The fundamental rights to freedom and property are pivotal to an assessment of the reflexive efficacy of the legal certainty principle. In some situations, even if the credibility of the legal order is not entirely compromised, taxpayers have already disposed of their assets and freedom with such intensity and duration that any change capable of harming them is unjustifiable. Moreover, the problem often concerns not only dispositional acts performed freely and spontaneously by taxpayers, but also action by the state to encourage, attract or even force taxpayers to undertake certain activities. In such situations, questions pertaining to retroactivity ought to be solved with property rights and basic freedoms in mind rather than simply based on the retroactive or prospective efficacy of the modifying norm. What this means is that consideration of the fundamental rights of the taxpayer significantly changes how the legal certainty principle must be understood. If it means not only protection of continuity of the legal order, but also protection of the exercise of some fundamental rights, then problems arising from changes to the legal order can no longer be solved only from the mere perspective of the relations among norms over time, by testing whether the taxpayer consummated an action while the previous legislation was in force; instead, they have to be solved from the perspective of the restriction of fundamental rights, by examining the intensity of the restriction and the weight of the justification given for this restriction, even in cases where actions have not been consummated in the past. In other words, grounding the legal certainty principle in fundamental rights changes the criteria for verifying the validity of normative changes, which are no longer based exclusively on the rule of law but instead on fundamental rights and the principles that shape state action. This refounding of the legal certainty principle affects an examination of the means for its realization in specific ways. For example, instead of a concept of irretroactivity linked to the incidence hypothesis (*tatbestandsbezogener Rückwirkungsbegriff*), a new concept linked to behavior must be constructed (*handlungsbezogener Rückwirkungsbegriff*); rather than being unlimited, administrative powers to change administrative acts must be limited to the disposition of freedom and property – and so forth.[63]

Grounding legal certainty in fundamental rights affects the value of elements that are not necessarily relevant from the perspective of the incidence hypotheses or operative facts for taxation rules. In many situations, the actions of taxpayers will be relevant from the perspective of legal certainty even if, from the perspective of constitutional rules of irretroactivity, the acts performed were not consummated while the previous norm was in force.

2.1.3.2.2 *Principle of Protection of the Family*

Besides establishing that the family must be afforded special state protection (article 226), the Constitution lists a number of family-related rights and guarantees, such

[63] Johanna Hey, *Steuerplanungssicherheit als Rechtsproblem*, Köln, Otto Schmidt, 2002, pages 215 and 237.

as protection for marriage and civil union (article 226), protection for family farms (article 5, XXVI), a guaranteed minimum wage sufficient to assure subsistence of the family (article 7, IV), child allowance (article 7, XII), and social assistance to protect the family (article 203, I), among others. From a broader perspective, protection of the family involves guaranteeing permanence and protecting trust against restrictions that harm the family as an institution and as a fundamental right – which presupposes minimal and, more importantly, stable social conditions.[64] Protection of the family means the duty of creating conditions to maintain one.[65]

Again, the protection of stable social institutions, such as family and marriage, presupposes the creation of a state of institutional stability that defines precisely one of the elements of the legal certainty principle: reliability through permanence. In protecting the family, the Constitution protects legal certainty as certainty of law and rights.

All the above considerations regarding property-related and other rights and freedoms confirm that by establishing specific ideals to be sought, the Constitution protects *legal* certainty as certainty *of rights*, which assumes certainty *of* law and *of any citizen before* the state, to be realized *by* the state through rules, acts and procedures capable of assuring individual rights.

2.1.4 Principle of Equality

After the "Preamble" instituting a democratic state designed to guarantee equality, the chapter on individual rights and guarantees affirms the inviolability of the right to equality (article 5) in general, and equality of rights and obligations between men and women (article 5, I), especially alongside other indirect manifestations. Surprising though this may seem, protecting equality is an indirect way of protecting legal certainty.

That happens mostly in two ways. One is the duty of equality before the law: All norms, general and abstract, must be applied uniformly and impersonally, regardless of the person, so that citizens of equivalent standing must receive the same treatment.[66] Being general and abstract, norms provide fixed parameters of behavior for their addressees, who are thereby enabled to anticipate the consequences of their actions and the behavior of other citizens. That being so, knowledge of an administrative act or of a judicial or administrative decision creates an expectation

[64] Stefan Muckel, *Kriterien des verfassungsrechtlichen Vertrauensschutzes bei Gesetzesänderungen*, Berlin, Duncker und Humblot, 1989, p. 48; Paul Kirchhof, "Rückwirkung von Steuergesetzen", *StuW*, 2000, p. 229.

[65] Misabel de Abreu Machado Derzi, "A família e o Direito Tributário", *RDT* 65, p. 162, São Paulo, s.d.

[66] Federico Arcos Ramírez, *La seguridad jurídica: una teoría formal*, Madrid, Dykinson, 2000, p. 160.

among citizens that a similar case will have an identical solution.[67] From this demand of applicational uniformity, which is a result of equality, the elements of reliability and calculability that make up legal certainty can be deduced: reliability because the duty of uniform application creates the duty to maintain the same decision for equal cases, thus favoring stability and bindingness of law; calculability because citizens can predict the same solution for equal cases, so that they can plan their activities based on the knowledge that if they perform the same act, the consequence will be identical.[68]

On the other hand, given the duty of equality in time, because citizens must be treated equally unless there is a justification for unequal treatment, they know that barring substantial changes in the situations that formed the basis for passing an administrative act or for issuing an administrative or judicial decision, the act and the decision ought to be upheld. From this requirement of equality over time, or systematic equality, resulting from equality, the elements of reliability and calculability that make up legal certainty can again be deduced: reliability since the duty to uphold the act or decision, barring reasons that justify the change, favors the ideals of stability and bindingness of law; calculability because citizens can predict maintenance of the act or decision in the absence of any new reason to justify the change. Thus equality is an instrument of certainty through the uniformity and impartiality that result from reliability and calculability.[69]

In addition, several questions related to the calculability of law also represent a problem of equality. Let us take retroactivity as an example: If two people, *A* and *B*, are in the same legal situation at a given moment, but one of them, *A*, adopts a type of behavior whose consequence is later changed, whereas the other person, *B*, does not, the position of *B* is more favorable than that of *A*, for reasons beyond their control.[70] That is to say, retroactivity unequalizes legally equal people: The only difference between the person affected by the new rule and the other is time, as the behavior of both is the same.[71]

It can easily be concluded, therefore, that the protection of equality leads to *legal* certainty as certainty *of* law and *of rights*, *for any citizen before* the state, to be realized *by* the state through coherent and consistent application of the legal order to all those who are in equivalent situations.

---

[67] Misabel de Abreu Machado Derzi, "Mutações, complexidade, tipo e conceito, sob o signo da segurança e da proteção da confiança", in Heleno Torres (Org.), *Estudos em homenagem a Paulo de Barros Carvalho*, São Paulo, Saraiva, 2007, p. 284.

[68] Michael Reinhardt, *Konsistente Jurisdiktion*, Tübingen, Mohr Siebeck, 1997, p. 499.

[69] Anne-Laure Valembois, *La constitutionnalisation de l'exigence de sécurité juridique en Droit Français*, Paris, LGDJ, 2005, p. 386.

[70] Ake Frändberg, "Retroactivity, simulactivity, infraactivity", in Jes Bjarup e Mogens Blegvad (Orgs.), *Time, Law and Society*, *ARSP*, v. 64, Stuttgart, Franz Steiner, 1995, p. 70.

[71] Ben Juratowitch, *Retroactivity and the Common Law*, Oxford, Hart, 2008, p. 212.

2.1.5 Principle of Human Dignity

Including the principle of human dignity among the foundations of the legal certainty principle may seem excessive. A more careful analysis, however, will show that it has a close connection with the requirements of knowability, reliability and calculability of law.

Indeed, these partial ideals that make up the greater ideal of legal certainty are the conditions for human fulfillment: Without a minimally intelligible, stable and predictable legal order, self-determination is impossible, so that people cannot shape the present and plan for the future with freedom and autonomy. Without these conditions, therefore, human beings cannot define themselves as subjects with autonomy and dignity. This is why legal certainty constitutes the legal condition for the realization of human dignity. Thus human dignity can be considered an indirect foundation of legal certainty, without which human dignity, as active and co-responsible participation in the destiny of one's own existence and life in common with other human beings, is severely restricted.[72]

Furthermore, disrespect for legal certainty also causes violation of the principle of human dignity. A case in point is the retroactive efficacy of legislation. For individuals to be able to shape the present and plan the future freely and independently, they must be guided by the rules in force at the time they act. However, when legislative changes have retroactive effects, their actions are judged on the basis of rules that did not exist at the time they acted. The rules no longer act on their will because the rules arise only after their will has been manifested. They act under the influence of laws in force at the time, but are judged by laws that did not exist at the time. They are manipulated, as they act based on one norm but are judged by a different one. They are also deceived, for they act in the belief they will be judged by one norm, but end up judged by another. In short, they are treated like objects rather than human beings worthy of respect who are free to make their own choices within the normative framework they know. These considerations explain Della Vale's statement that normative retroactivity *in peius* (for the worse) degrades man from "subject to object."[73] The reason for this degradation is clear: If the principle of human dignity requires the establishment of conditions for people to be able to develop their personality in a responsible, free and rational manner, retroactive efficacy is simply opposed to it, because it simply prevents them from deciding and reacting.[74]

---

[72]Ingo Wolfgang Sarlet, "A eficácia do direito fundamental à segurança jurídica: dignidade da pessoa humana, direitos fundamentais e proibição de retrocesso social no Direito Constitucional brasileiro", in Cármen Lúcia Antunes Rocha (Org.), *Constituição e segurança jurídica: direito adquirido, ato jurídico perfeito e coisa julgada. Estudos em homenagem a José Paulo Sepúlveda Pertence*, Belo Horizonte, Fórum, 2004, p. 94.

[73]Eugenio Della Vale, *Affidamento e certezza del Diritto Tributario*, Milano, Giuffrè, 2001, p. 92.

[74]Heike Pohl, *Rechtsprechungsänderung und Rückanknüpfung*, Berlin, Duncker und Humblot, 2005, p. 198.

Moreover, *rational* people choose how to behave by examining the consequences of the many alternative forms of conduct. Some of these consequences are assigned by the legal order. Thus a given individual's actions may change owing to the consequences assigned to certain types of behavior. If the legal order ascribes a certain consequence to certain behavior at a given moment but then changes it after the act is performed, it automatically changes the normative rationale for the action. Had the individual been aware of the consequences that would come into force after their action, they might not have taken the same course of action. Human dignity is restricted because the addressee *is* affected by a consequence that was *not* expected, and is *not* affected by the consequence that was expected. It is as if the lawmaker were playing games with the addressees, as if they were objects, especially owing to the destruction of their autonomy, since they can no longer change their behavior once they have acted based on the norm then in force, in order to adjust it to the norm that came into force only later. As the consequences that affect them have already been completely determined by the course of action already chosen, they are denied the ability to make different plans that take into consideration the new legal consequences.[75] This is why Marmor calls a retroactive norm an offense to human dignity and freedom. People deserve to be treated in a rational and dignified manner, and the law must therefore determine models of behavior beforehand, so that citizens can freely decide whether to obey or disobey.[76] Thus it can be said that respect for the autonomy of individuals involves respect for their ability to plan, and this in turn requires respect for the ability of individuals to base their actions on the law. This respect prevents the law from being different than at the time the action was performed.[77]

Another case in point is the absence of procedural certainty when the right to a full defense and a fair hearing (audi alteram partem) is not guaranteed. The claim to legal protection requires parties to be informed of all actions performed throughout the proceedings and of all elements of the case, so that they can make their statements about the factual and legal elements and have their arguments considered in a neutral, impartial and properly justified manner. When these guarantees are not observed, i.e., when citizens are taken by surprise by decisions or acts that restrict their rights, and are unable to react autonomously, not only are they restricted in their right to procedural legal certainty (through lack of knowability, reliability and calculability of judicial or administrative acts), but also their dignity is unjustifiably affected. Here it is worth quoting the welcome remarks made by Justice Cézar Peluso in the judgment of MS no. 24268 concerning the right to a fair hearing and full defense. The case involved cancellation of a pension granted for a long period because of alleged fraud: "The party must be heard, because not hearing

[75] Ake Frändberg, "Retroactivity, simulactivity, infraactivity", in Jes Bjarup e Mogens Blegvad (Orgs.), *Time, Law and Society, ARSP*, v. 64, Stuttgart, Franz Steiner, 1995, p. 70.

[76] Andrei Marmor, *Law in the age of pluralism*, Oxford, OUP, 2007, p. 20.

[77] Ben Juratowitch, *Retroactivity and the Common Law*, Oxford, Hart, 2008, p. 49.

the party under the pretext of an alleged appearance of fraud, changes the person into an object, disposing of them without affording an opportunity to be heard and considered as a subject."[78]

Finally, it must be said that these fundamental rights (property, freedom, equality and dignity) are mentioned in the first part of the Constitution, immediately after the fundamental principles. Moreover, paragraph 1 of article 5 assures immediate applicability – which implies self-application, in the words of Maior Borges.[79] In this sense, as explained by Machado Derzi, the Constitution itself has assigned them self-applicability, prevalence, integrity, irreversibility and perpetuity.[80] It is also quite telling that to a large extent these fundamental rights are instituted through categorical expressions in order to avoid limitations (e.g., "is inviolable") or to ensure their efficacy (e.g., "fully guaranteed"). The way in which the Constitution has established these fundamental rights is an indicator of the efficacy with which its framers intended to qualify them objectively.

2.2 *By Induction*

2.2.1 Administrative Principles

2.2.1.1 Morality Principle

Besides setting forth specific overarching ideals from which the structural elements of legal certainty can be deduced, the Constitution also requires a search for more restricted ideals from which it is possible to induce major ends comprised in the state of reliability and calculability of (and through) the legal order. In this case, it behooves the jurist to examine "the principles which, when combined, form the foundations on which is erected" legal certainty, to quote Carvalho's eloquent formulation.[81]

In addition to fundamental principles, the Constitution institutes administrative principles that also impact on the legal certainty principle. Among them is the principle of administrative morality (article 37). Despite its breadth, from this principle can be inferred the requirement of serious and loyal behavior on the part of civil servants: serious in the sense of well-grounded and justifiable; loyal in the sense

---

[78] Writ MS n. 24.268, Full Court, Reporting Justice Gilmar Mendes, *DJ* 17 Sep 2004, p. 189 of the decision.

[79] José Souto Maior Borges, "Segurança jurídica: sobre a distinção entre competências fiscais para orientar e autuar o contribuinte", *RDT* 100, p. 20, São Paulo, s.d.

[80] Misabel de Abreu Machado Derzi, *Modificações da jurisprudência no Direito Tributário*, São Paulo, Noeses, 2009, p. 463.

[81] Paulo de Barros Carvalho, "Segurança jurídica e modulação dos efeitos", *Revista da Fundação Escola Superior de Direito Tributário* 1, p. 206, Porto Alegre, 2008.

of respecting the trust and legitimate expectations of citizens.[82] It is precisely these requirements of seriousness and loyalty that make up the ideal of legal certainty. They result to a greater or lesser extent in the pursuit of the authentic public interest, which is not to be confused with the interest of the state apparatus or treasury, in respect for private interests and in observance of objective good faith.[83]

Indeed, the requirement of seriousness is a means to attain a state of reliability and calculability of the legal order based on its knowability: The administration's duty to behave seriously, i.e., with sound foundations and justifications, means citizens have access to administrative acts and the conditions for understanding their motivation, so that they can organize and plan their own activities;the administration's duty to behave loyally, in the sense of creating an environment of reciprocal reliability between state and citizens, means the latter can act without being surprised in the exercise of their freedom.

Thus the morality principle plays two roles: for the state it serves to avoid disloyal and unjustified behavior; for citizens, it serves as a guide to the right conduct to avoid frustration and surprise. The morality principle can therefore be said to have an individual component and a state component. This duality also gives the legal certainty principle, which is founded on it, a hybrid nature, in the sense that it both protects citizens and regulates state actions. While this simple observation may appear insignificant, it is particularly relevant to effective delivery of the legal certainty principle. For example, as we will see in discussing the temporal dimension of legal certainty, legitimate trust is protected only when there is a sound basis for such trust, perceived as state manifestations so unequivocal as to create expectations. According to legal doctrine, there can be no legitimate expectations when the basis for trust is imprecise and obscure, or even invalid.[84] Trust cannot be protected when the norms are unclear; the more obscure the law, the less protected the expectation of citizens who act on the basis of law. However, this understanding is incompatible with the morality principle: If the protection of trust is made impossible simply by the mere lack of normative clarity, the state is encouraged to adopt obscure legislation and will also benefit from its adoption, in manifest violation of the duty to behave seriously and loyally.

With regard to the maintenance of unlawful acts, the efficacy of the trust protection principle is ambiguous. On one hand, the lapse of a long period of time creates an appearance of lawfulness which, if modified, leads to contradictory behavior by the state: the longer the time elapsed, the greater the expectation that

[82]Celso Antônio Bandeira de Mello, "Legalidade e moralidade", *RDT* 69, p. 183, São Paulo, s.d.

[83]Marçal Justen Filho, "O princípio da moralidade pública e o Direito Tributário", *RTDP* 11, pages 52 and following, 1995.

[84]Anne-Laure Valembois, *La constitutionnalisation de l'exigence de sécurité juridique en Droit Français*, Paris, LGDJ, 2005, p. 252; Kyrill-A. Schwarz, *Vertrauensschutz als Verfassungsprinzip*, Baden-Baden, Nomos, 2002, p. 301.

the act is valid and that the state does not consider it unlawful.[85] The revision of administrative acts after a long period of time is an example of disloyal conduct by the administration.[86] On the other hand, the same principle of state morality is opposed to the preservation of acts contrary to law: the law requires loyal, serious and justified behavior by the state, so that action contrary to law is disloyal, especially when the actor is aware of its unlawfulness from the start. This ambiguity is surmounted by the annulment of unlawful acts whenever the authorities who perform them or the individuals who benefit from them knew or can reasonably be assumed to have known that the acts concerned were unlawful, except where, whether or not this is the case, another element is present that can make up for the deficiencies of the normative base, such as the passage of a long period of time or the synallagmatic nature of the relationship with the administration, as will be analyzed in due course.

This and other examples show that the morality principle changes the configuration of the legal certainty principle by attributing to it the function of shaping state actions and protecting citizens' expectations.

2.2.1.2 Publicity Principle

The Constitution establishes not only that the public administration must observe the publicity principle (article 37), but also that a law may restrict the publicity of procedural acts only when required to do so to protect privacy or the social interest (article 37, LX). In this way the Constitution institutes ideals that are part of the ideals of knowability, reliability and calculability of the legal order.[87]

Thus the requirement to seek a state of publicity depends, on one hand, on certain types of behavior that contribute to its promotion, such as issuing normative and administrative acts in writing, publishing statutes and administrative acts, notifying the addressees of administrative and procedural acts, and providing a full justification for all administrative acts. In other words, the institution of the publicity principle entails the prescription of the types of behavior necessary to its realization. Publicity is the *end* from which the means needed to realize it must be deduced.

On the other hand, the duty of achieving a state of publicity is part of the broader ideal of assuring a state of reliability and calculability of the legal order, based on its knowability. Indeed, the duty of publicity contributes to increased intelligibility

---

[85] Johannes Mainka, *Vertrauensschutz im öffentlichen Recht*, Bonn, Ludwig Röhrscheid, 1963, p. 32.

[86] Fritz Ossenbühl, *Die Rücknahme fehlerhafter begünstigender Verwaltungsakte*, 2nd ed., Berlin, Walter de Gruyter, 1965, p. 99.

[87] Jürgen Bröhmer, *Transparenz als Verfassungsprinzip*, Tübingen, Mohr Siebeck, 2004, pages 159 and following.

of the legal order because, through publication and notification, citizens have better access to norms and better means to understand them.[88] Publicity is the *means* from which one of the partial ideals that comprise legal certainty is deduced.

In sum, the establishment of morality and publicity as administrative principles leads to a guarantee of *legal* certainty as certainty *of* law and *through* law, *of citizens before* the state, to be realized *by* the state in the serious, loyal and transparent exercise of administrative jurisdiction.

2.2.2 Procedural Principles

The Constitution ordains that no law shall preclude from appreciation by the judiciary any violation of or threat to rights (article 5, XXXV), that no one shall be prosecuted or sentenced except by the competent authority (article 5, LIII), that no one shall be deprived of freedom or personal property without due process of law (article 5, LIV), and that parties to lawsuits or administrative procedures, and defendants in general, are assured of the right to adversarial proceedings and a full and fair hearing, with all the requisite means and resources (article 5, LV). In doing so, it also provides for the promotion of legal certainty in its dimension of certainty *through* law as well as that of certainty *before* law. Certainty through law is promoted through the creation of procedures whereby citizens can defend their rights, such as due process of law, adversarial proceedings and a fair hearing, including the right to a full defense in all litigation matters.

The institution of rules that delimit the powers of the state and rules that guarantee procedural rights promotes the ideals of reliability and calculability of the legal order: reliability because citizens cannot be surprised by restrictions on their rights without the ability to defend themselves, so that the stability of the legal order is enhanced; calculability because citizens can predict state actions and protect themselves through appropriate procedural instruments.[89] Because of this connection between legal certainty and procedural instruments of protection, we can speak of a "principle of instrumental legal certainty" (*Grundsatz der Rechtsmittelsicherheit*): Citizens cannot be surprised by a change in the procedural rules in which they have trusted and with which they can protect their fundamental rights. Thus any change must be measured in terms of the extent to which it restricts such rights and pass the tests of proportionality and reasonableness.[90]

[88] Alessandro Pizzorusso e Paolo Passaglia, "Constitution et sécurité juridique – Italie", *Annuaire International de Justice Constitutionnelle 1999*, Paris, Economica, 2000, p. 202

[89] E. Schmidt-Aßmann, "Verwaltungsverfahren", in Paul Kirchhof e Josef Isensee (Orgs.), *Handbuch des Staatsrechts*, 2nd ed., v. 3, Heidelberg, C. F. Müller, 1996, p. 634.

[90] Michael Koch, *Die Grundsätze des intertemporalen Rechts im Verwaltungsprozess – Vertrauensschutz im verwaltungsgerichtlichen Verfahren*, Berlin, Duncker und Humblot, 2009, p. 256.

In sum, the determination of procedural rights and competence rules leads to the assurance of *legal* certainty as certainty *through* law and *before* law, of *citizens before* the state, to be realized *by* the state in the non-arbitrary exercise of administrative competence and the enforcement of procedural rights.

2.2.3 Rules

2.2.3.1 Prohibition of Constitutional Change

The Constitution determines specific conditions for amendments. On one hand, certain formalities are required: Amendments must be proposed by at least one-third of the Chamber of Deputies or the Federal Senate, the lower and upper houses of Congress respectively (article 60, I), by the President of the Republic (article 60, II), or by a relative majority in more than half the state legislatures (article 60, III); in Congress they must be debated and voted on by each house in two rounds, and cannot be passed with a majority of less than three-fifths (article 60, paragraph 2). On the other hand, the Constitution stipulates certain rules regarding content: No amendments to abolish the federation, direct, secret, universal and regular elections, the separation of powers or individual rights and guarantees may be debated (article 60, paragraph 4). These safeguards built into the Constitution indirectly protect legal certainty by promoting the ideals of reliability and predictability of the legal order: reliability because the rules regarding form and content contribute to the stability of the order, either by preventing amendments to certain topics or by making amendments conditional upon the observance of certain formal requirements; foresee ability because the rules regarding form and content enable citizens to know beforehand what can and what cannot be changed.

In other words, the promulgation of a Constitution that cannot be amended without the observance of laborious procedures implies a claim to permanence and thus posits the ideal of legal certainty. As argued by Barroso, the "Constitution thus delimits public and private spaces, organizing political power and defining fundamental rights. It has a vocation for permanence and it is endowed with rigidity."[91]

2.2.3.2 Statutory Legality

Besides establishing ideals from which it is possible to deduce narrower or broader ideals that justify certain types of state behavior, the Constitution also directly prescribes certain types of behavior that will contribute to the reliability and predictability of (and through) the legal order based on its intelligibility.

---

[91] Luís Roberto Barroso, "A segurança jurídica na era da velocidade e do pragmatismo", *RTDP* 43, p. 53, São Paulo, 2003.

By establishing that no one shall be obliged to do or refrain from doing anything except by virtue of the law (article 5, II), and that there is no crime *without a prior law* defining it, and no punishment other than that laid down by law (article 5, XXXIX), the Constitution elliptically determines that the state can impose taxes only by statute.[92] Even so the chapter on the National Tax System specifies that taxes may be neither introduced nor increased without the enactment of a statute (article 150, I), and forbids the granting of tax benefits without specific statutory provision (article 150, paragraph 6).

The requirement of statutory provision is itself an instrument of legal certainty because by demanding general and abstract norms addressed to an indeterminate number of people and situations it helps avoid the surprises arising from a lack of public written norms or from decisionism and *ad hoc* circumstantial decisions. It also promotes the stability of law because current legislation can be modified only by specific procedures.[93] The requirement of statutory legality fosters the ideal of democratic participation, and offers citizens peace, trust and certainty regarding taxation.[94]

The rule that taxes may be neither introduced nor increased without the enactment of a statute promotes the ideals of reliability and predictability of (and through) the legal order. The requirement of a statute fosters: the intelligibility of the legal order by enhancing taxpayers' access to the norms they must follow and understanding of their content; the reliability of the legal order by prohibiting alteration of legal norms except by modification of other legal norms and hence contributing to their stability; and the calculability of the order, as taxpayers are better able to predict future tax obligations. It should be noted that the generality of law is not a condition of predictability, since on one hand an individual norm serves as a far more efficient planning tool for addressees, while on the other hand a general norm that is not known and stable is not an adequate means for individuals to pursue their own ideals.[95] Generality is in fact a planning instrument for all, and not just for some, based on the preservation of the requirement of statutory legality along with that of equality.

2.2.3.3 Anteriority

The Constitution forbids the introduction or raising of taxes in the same fiscal year as the statute that introduces or raises them is published (article 150, III, "b") and

[92]Roque Antonio Carrazza, *Curso de Direito Constitucional Tributário*, 27th ed., São Paulo, Malheiros Editores, 2011, pages 263 and following.

[93]Federico Arcos Ramírez, *La Seguridad Jurídica: una Teoría Formal*, Madrid, Dykinson, 2000, p. 220.

[94]Sacha Calmon Navarro Coelho, "Princípios retores da tributação: legalidade e tipicidade", *RDT* 33, p. 206, São Paulo, 1985.

[95]Jeremy Waldron, "The rule of law in contemporary liberal theory", *Ratio Juris*, v. 2, n. 1, p. 82, 1989.

within 90 days of the date of publication (article 150, III, "c"). In doing so, it indirectly protects legal certainty.[96]

Indeed, prohibition of the sudden introduction of taxes contributes both to promotion of the intelligibility of the legal order, since taxpayers are better able to understand the content of the legal norms they must obey, and to realization of its predictability, since taxpayers are better able to foresee future changes.[97]

It is worth stressing here that these guarantees of statutory legality and anteriority do not hinder change, as they leave room for attenuation of some taxes. This is the case with compulsory loans, and with taxes on imports, exports, manufactured goods and financial operations, whose rates can be changed by decree for enforcement in the same fiscal year within certain statutorily defined conditions and limits (articles 150, paragraph 1 and 153, paragraph 1). In other words, while guaranteeing predictability the Constitution also preserves sufficient flexibility to enable the state to act for the general good.[98]

2.2.3.4 Irretroactivity

By establishing that events occurring before the statute that introduced or raised a tax entered into force are not taxable (article 150, III, "a"), the Constitution also promotes the ideals of reliability and predictability of (and through) the legal order: If the effects of legal norms that are valid today cannot be changed by future norms, taxpayers are better able to trust the continuity of norms and their effects as well as the binding character of the legal order as a whole.[99]

All the above observations regarding constitutional rules show that by requiring certain types of behavior the Constitution protects *legal* certainty as certainty of law, of *citizens before* the state, to be realized *by* the state through the creation and collection of taxes. The prohibition of retroactivity is no exception to the rule, as shown below. So much so that according to Supreme Court Precedent no. 654 "the guarantee of irretroactivity set forth in article 5, XXXVI, of the Constitution of the Republic, cannot be invoked by any state entity that enacts a law."

---

[96] Francisco Pinto Rabello Filho, *O princípio da anterioridade da lei tributária*, São Paulo, Ed. RT, 2002, p. 83.

[97] Eduardo Maneira, *Direito Tributário – Princípio da não-surpresa*, Belo Horizonte, Del Rey, 1994, p. 161.

[98] Luís Eduardo Schoueri, "Segurança na ordem tributária nacional e internacional: tributação do comércio exterior", in Aires Fernandino Barreto *et alii* (Orgs.), *Segurança jurídica na tributação e Estado de Direito*, São Paulo, Noeses, 2005, p. 389.

[99] Maria Luíza Vianna Pessoa de Mendonça, *O Princípio constitucional da irretroatividade da lei – A irretroatividade da lei tributária*, Belo Horizonte, Del Rey, 1996, p. 74.

2.2.3.5 Prohibition of Taxation with Confiscatory Effects

By prohibiting the creation of taxes with confiscatory effects, the Constitution indirectly enhances calculability for the taxpayer. The competence rules enable the taxpayer to know which events are taxable and the prohibition of confiscatory effects guarantees that taxation cannot encroach on the minimal conditions for exercising freedom and owning property.[100]

Thus taxpayers can rely in advance on an unassailable margin of freedom within which they cannot be surprised. Although they may not know the exact result of future taxation, they can at least predict the limits of state intervention in their rights and freedoms.

It should be noted on this subject that all the norms referred to here – statutory legality, anteriority, irretroactivity and prohibition of taxation with confiscatory effects – not only are included in the National Tax System but also are constitutionally defined as "limitations on the power to tax", so that they are eminently protective of the citizen before the state. Thanks to this, tax law can be said, with Machado Derzi's teachings in mind, to reinforce legal certainty, in contrast with other systems.[101]

2.2.3.6 Restrictions on Supplementary Laws

The Constitution reserves the following functions for supplementary laws: establishing how tax competence disputes between or among the Union, the states, the Federal District and municipalities are resolved (article 146, I); and establishing general legal norms in matters relating to tax law (article 146, III), especially to define types of tax and their essential elements (article 146, III, "a") and to set fundamental guidelines for the start and end of tax obligations (article 146, III, "b"). Moreover, the Constitution prohibits the Union from creating a tax that is not *uniform* across the national territory or entails any distinctions or preferences for a state, the Federal District or a municipality to the detriment of another (article 151). In doing so, it also prescribes the promotion of the ideals of knowability (through the normative accessibility, scope and intelligibility arising from the general norms applicable nationally to all members of the federation), reliability (through the

[100]Cassiano Menke, *A proibição aos efeitos de confisco no Direito Tributário*, São Paulo, Malheiros Editores, 2008, pages 110 and following; Estevão Horvath, *O Princípio do Não-Confisco no Direito Tributário*, São Paulo, Dialética, 2002, pages 41 and following and 118.

[101]Misabel de Abreu Machado Derzi, *Modificações da jurisprudência no Direito Tributário*, São Paulo, Noeses, 2009, p. 469; idem, "A irretroatividade do Direito, a proteção da confiança, a boa-fé e o RE n. 370.682-SC", in Valdir de Oliveira Rocha (coord.), *Grandes questões atuais do Direito Tributário*, v. 11, São Paulo, Dialética, 2007, p. 317.

stability arising from the difficulty of changing general norms) and calculability (through the substantive bindingness of the general norms.)[102]

To elaborate, the rule requiring supplementary laws and stipulating that they must be passed by absolute majority (article 69) favors stability of the order, by making any changes to the order conditional upon compliance with rules that are relatively hard to obey. The function of avoiding competence disputes among members of the federation contributes to the intelligibility of the legal order, both for states and cities, whose tax competence disputes are typically resolved, and for taxpayers, who are better able to know to which federated entity they must pay their taxes. And the function of setting the fundamental guidelines to introduce and extinguish tax obligations, to be observed nationwide by all members of the federation, favors the intelligibility of the legal order by making norms more accessible, comprehensive and understandable.

Consequently, the inclusion of a rule restricting the use of supplementary laws to certain subjects and purposes leads to the assurance of *legal* certainty as certainty *of* law and *through* law, guaranteeing reciprocal trust not only between citizens and federated entities, but also among federated entities themselves.

2.2.3.7 Financial Activities of the State

The Constitution also includes a number of rules governing the financial activities of the state, such as the rules for passing the federal budget, Budget Guidelines Laws and multiyear plans (articles 165 and ff). These rules require state actions to be planned, thus favoring the ideals of knowability, reliability and calculability of law: knowability because they allow citizens to know, in a broad and accessible manner, the sources of state revenue and expenditure; reliability because they make the state's activities more stable through continuity over more than one financial year; and calculability because they permit advance control by taxpayers of future administrative actions.

These financial norms also serve to control and publicize the activities of government, enabling the legislative and citizens to control the state's financial activities.[103]

However, it must be emphasized that these rules govern the organization and control of the revenue obtained but say nothing about how to obtain it. The norms that govern the raising of revenue are the tax rules, whose function is precisely to set limits on the power to tax by describing the substantive aspects of their incidence

[102] Fábio Canazaro, *Lei complementar tributária na Constituição de 1988*, Porto Alegre, Livraria do Advogado, 2005, p. 108; Frederico Araújo Seabra de Moura, *Lei complementar tributária*, São Paulo, Quartier Latin, 2009, pages 331 and following.

[103] Anne-Laure Valembois, *La constitutionnalisation de l'exigence de sécurité juridique en Droit Français*, Paris, LGDJ, 2005, p. 266; Ricardo Lobo Torres, "O orçamento na Constituição", in *Tratado de Direito Constitucional, Financeiro e Tributário*, 3rd ed., Rio de Janeiro, Renovar, 2008, pages 173 and 203.

hypotheses. The point here is to underscore the fact that although the budgetary rules contribute to the ideals of knowability, reliability and calculability of the legal order, they are an instrument not for legitimating the *raising* of revenue, which is *the previous moment*, but to control the use of revenue, which is a *later moment*. This observation is highly valuable because it clearly refutes any connection between the legal certainty principle and budget management, so that it is impossible to claim that the revenue projections contained in the budget are sufficient in themselves to justify the legitimate expectation of raising revenues in the specified amount, even against the rules of competence, which cannot be frustrated by declaring tax laws unconstitutional *ex tunc*. As will be made clear below by the discussion of the Supreme Court's modulation of the effects of its unconstitutionality rulings, budgetary reasons cannot be assimilated to the concept of legal certainty, and even less to tax law certainty.

2.2.3.8 State Intervention

Besides providing guarantees for taxpayers, from which the ideal of predictability can be constructed, the Constitution also guarantees the coherence and predictability necessary to the indicative planning required by article 174.[104] As noted by Schoueri, this entails a systematic correction of the concept of legal certainty solely as regards predictability because if tax guarantees require predictability, the state requires flexibility in order to pursue the general good by making the positive and negative adjustments needed to keep the economic domain on the path chosen by the framers of the Constitution. This is precisely why the Constitution also establishes competences to regulate the economy from a tax perspective (article 146-A).

2.2.3.9 Legitimation of Petitions for Judicial Review

The Constitution empowers only a few entities or institutions to file a petition with the Supreme Court for judicial review of laws passed by Congress, known as *Ação Direta de Inconstitucionalidade* (ADIN): the President of the Republic, the secretariats of the Senate, Chamber of Deputies or state legislatures, state governors, the Attorney General of the Republic, the Federal Council of the Brazilian Bar Association, political parties with seats in Congress, labor union confederations, and nationwide professional or industrial associations. Individual citizens cannot do so directly. One of the justifications for this limitation relates to continuity of the legal order.

[104] Luís Eduardo Schoueri, "Segurança na ordem tributária nacional e internacional: tributação do comércio exterior", in Aires Fernandino Barreto *et alii* (Orgs.), *Segurança Jurídica na Tributação e Estado de Direito*, São Paulo, Noeses, 2005, p. 376.

Because an ADIN typically leads to a Supreme Court ruling that an infraconstitutional general norm is unconstitutional, thus changing the legal order itself, the Constitution restricts the number of people empowered to cause such a change as a means of evidencing the importance of a stable legal order. Thus one of the ideas underpinning this restriction on active procedural legitimacy is the need to guarantee the continuity of the legal order: An order that could be changed on the initiative of any citizen, at any moment, would be unstable and hence insufficiently certain.[105]

3 Partial Conclusions

All in all, the above examination of the foundations for legal certainty enables us to draw some important general conclusions.

The first is that the Constitution protects "legal certainty." It does so directly when it "ensures certainty" as a "right" and as a "value" or when it regulates its reflexive efficacy through the protection of acquired rights, completed legal acts and *res iudicata*; and indirectly when it provides for types of behavior that promote the ideals of calculability and reliability, a key part of legal certainty, and establishes ideals, whether broad, restricted or specific, whose realization presupposes or implies the existence of the ideals of legal certainty. In sum, it is an unequivocal positive principle of the Constitution.

Second, our analysis of the foundations demonstrates that the Constitution not only assures legal certainty, but also protects it in several of its dimensions. In short, the rules and related principles it establishes lead to the assurance of legal certainty as certainty *of* law, *through* law, *before* law and *of* rights. Each of these dimensions requires the existence of the elements of knowability, reliability and calculability of the legal order.

Third, our examination of the foundations shows that the Constitution not only protects legal certainty in all of its manifestations, but also assigns high priority to legal certainty in the constitutional order. It does so in several ways:

- Through the way legal certainty is assured by the totality of the constitutional order and by its parts: The constitutional superstructure expresses legal certainty and the constitutional structure requires legal certainty either as a fundamental principle or as a fundamental right.
- Through the *insistence* with which the Constitution protects legal certainty: Not just one provision but an extensive set of provisions directly or indirectly lead to the ideals of reliability and calculability of and through the legal order, based on its knowability.
- Through the *independence* of its foundations: Legal certainty is protected in different ways and by several provisions, so that it remains effective even if one

[105] César García Novoa, *El principio de seguridad jurídica en materia tributaria*, Madrid, Marcial Pons, 2000, p. 50.

or several of its foundations are removed; it is as if legal certainty were a building erected on and supported by so many beams that if one or even more than one were to be removed, its structure would remain unshakable.
- Through the *reciprocal efficacy* of these same foundations: For instance, the efficacy of the rule of law principle presupposes the existence of individual rights and the guarantees of statutory legality and irretroactivity, while the efficacy of individual rights and the guarantees of statutory legality and irretroactivity presuppose the existence of the rule of law. Since both the rule of law principle and these rights and guarantees are expressly provided for, the interpretation of the one depends on simultaneously considering the others, and the interpretation of the others depends on simultaneously considering the one, so that it is possible to speak of a reciprocal efficacy that generates and interprets the foundations of legal certainty.

The fourth conclusion to be drawn from the foregoing investigation of the foundations for legal certainty in the Constitution is that it protects legal certainty in such a way that we know what certainty is protected, whose legal certainty is safeguarded, who must enforce it and how, and for whom it is instituted. When we analyze all the foundations of legal certainty, we are justified in concluding that the Constitution insists on instituting legal certainty for the citizen before the state, in contrast with what could possibly be said about other systems, where legal certainty provides leeway for state action.[106] This protective connotation of legal certainty is present in both the form and content of its foundations:

- In the *form* because the foundations embody individual rights and guarantees with a protective connotation, some guarantees even being tagged as "limitations on the power to tax"; administrative principles that tend to restrict the arbitrary exercise of power; and structuring principles that also place constraints on power and protect individual rights.
- In the *content* because as predictions of types of behavior or ideals the foundations imply or presuppose certainty in favor of freedoms and rights for the individual.

In sum, a detailed examination of the foundations for legal certainty leads to the conclusion that the Constitution protects all its dimensions, and moreover that the manner and insistence with which independent foundations are established assigns a high priority to legal certainty as a constitutional principle that protects individuals and assures a state of reliability and calculability of and through the legal order, based on its knowability.

All these observations are extremely important both to an understanding of the content of the constitutional principle of legal certainty and to the delimitation of its efficacy. It bears repeating that the Constitution not only protects legal certainty but *superprotects* it. Such superprotection is closely linked to the rule of law principle

[106] Amélie Lièvre-Gravereaux, *La rétroactivité de la loi fiscale: une necessité en matière de procédures*, Paris, Harmattan, 2007, p. 43.

both in its formal dimension, which involves regulating and separating the powers of the state, and in its substantive dimension, which involves limiting the exercise of power through the protection of fundamental rights.[107]

These considerations also play a key role inasmuch as they give meaning to certain infraconstitutional norms whose application depends on how the expression "legal certainty" is interpreted. For example, Law 9868/98 determines in article 27 that the Supreme Court, when declaring a statute or normative act unconstitutional, and "for reasons of legal certainty or exceptional social interest," may restrict the effects of this declaration or decide that it will come into force only once it is res iudicata or at some other moment.

Finally, it is necessary to stress that the examination of the foundations of legal certainty also leads to some important conclusions about tax law certainty: The states of knowability, reliability and calculability are not only especially relevant in the tax subsystem, but also have a *more protective import*. This conclusion derives from an examination of the norms of the National Tax System. Specific norms emphatically assure: the intelligibility of law via the determinability of incidence hypotheses (the legality rule and the system of competence rules); the reliability of law through stability over time (the rule restricting the use of supplementary laws to prescription and limitation), period of validity (the rule prohibiting retroactivity) and procedure (rules that expressly apply rights and guarantees not specified in the tax subsystem, such as protection for acquired rights, completed legal acts and res iudicata); and the calculability of law through non-surprise (the anteriority rule). There is a reiteration at the tax level that "thickens" its content, so to speak, to quote Maior Borges, or an insistence on protecting legal certainty in tax law that translates as a "reinforced guarantee", to quote Machado Derzi.[108]

This reinforcement of legal certainty in the sphere of taxation lies mostly in the tendency of the guarantees established to favor the taxpayer. The most direct foundations of legal certainty in the National Tax System chapter of the Constitution consist not only of guarantees that favor taxpayers, but also of others arising out of constitutional principles and rights. The definition of guarantees that favor taxpayers links tax law certainty as a principle to the fundamental rights of taxpayers. Thus several issues that could be resolved solely on the basis of the rule of law principle must be resolved from the perspective of fundamental rights. Elements that could be considered irrelevant from the perspective of tax norms therefore become decisive from the perspective of fundamental freedoms and property rights. A case in point is the disposal of rights under laws that are later changed.

[107] Anne-Laure Valembois, *La constitutionnalisation de l'exigence de sécurité juridique en Droit Français*, Paris, LGDJ, 2005, p. 32.

[108] José Souto Maior Borges, "O princípio da segurança jurídica na criação e aplicação do tributo", *RDDT* 22, p. 25, São Paulo, 1997; Misabel de Abreu Machado Derzi, "Mutações, complexidade, tipo e conceito, sob o signo da segurança e da proteção da confiança", in Heleno Torres (Org.), *Estudos em Homenagem a Paulo de Barros Carvalho*, São Paulo, Saraiva, 2007, pages 275–276.

In sum, if it is true that the legal certainty principle requires a state of certainty that leans toward the citizen, it can equally be argued that the principle of tax law certainty requires a state of certainty that leans even more intensely toward the taxpayer.

References

ALVARO DE OLIVEIRA, Carlos Alberto. "O formalismo valorativo no confronto com o formalismo excessivo". *RF* 15.

von ARNAULD, Andreas. *Rechtssicherheit*, Tübingen: Mohr Siebeck, 2006.

ARNDT, Hans-Wolfgang. "Das Rechtsstaatsprinzip". *JuS* 27, 1987.

ATALIBA, Geraldo. *República e Constituição*. 3rd ed. São Paulo: Malheiros Editores, 2011.

BANDEIRA DE MELLO, Celso Antônio. "Legalidade e moralidade". *RDT* 69, São Paulo: s.d.

BARROSO, Luís Roberto. "A segurança jurídica na era da velocidade e do pragmatismo". *RTDP* 43, São Paulo: 2003.

BIERWEILER, Alexia. *Soziale Sicherheit als Grundrecht in der Europäischen Union*. Stuttgart: Boorberg, 2007.

BRÖHMER, Jürgen. *Transparenz als Verfassungsprinzip*. Tübingen: Mohr Siebeck, 2004.

BUCHWALD, Delf. *Prinzipien des Rechtsstaats*. Aachen: Shaker, 1996.

CALMES, Sylvia. *Du principe de protection de la confiance legitime en droits Allemand. Communautaire et Français*. Paris: Dalloz, 2001.

CANAZARO, Fábio. *Lei complementar tributária na Constituição de 1988*. Porto Alegre: Livraria do Advogado, 2005.

CARRAZZA, Roque Antônio. "Segurança jurídica e eficácia temporal das alterações jurisprudenciais – Competência dos Tribunais Superiores para fixá-la – Questões conexas". In:

____. CARRAZZA, Roque Antônio. *Curso de Direito Constitucional Tributário*. 27th ed. São Paulo: Malheiros Editores, 2011.

CARVALHO, Paulo de Barros, "Segurança jurídica e modulação dos efeitos". *Revista da Fundação Escola Superior de Direito Tributário* 1, Porto Alegre, 2008.

____. *Curso de Direito Tributário*. 21st ed. São Paulo: Saraiva, 2009.

CAVALCANTI FILHO, Theophilo. *O problema da segurança no Direito*. São Paulo: Ed. RT, 1964.

CHEVALLIER, Jacques. *L'État de Droit*. 2nd ed. Paris: Montchrestien, 1994.

DELLA VALE, Eugenio. *Affidamento e certezza del Diritto Tributario*. Milano: Giuffrè, 2001.

DI PIETRO, Maria Sylvia Zanella. "Os princípios da proteção à confiança, da segurança jurídica e da boa-fé na anulação do ato administrativo". In: MOTTA, Fabrício. (Org.). *Direito Público atual: Estudos em Homenagem ao Professor Nélson Figueiredo*. Instituto de Direito Administrativo de Goiás (IDAG). Belo Horizonte: Fórum, 2008.

FERRAJOLI, Luigi Ferrajoli. "The past and the future of the rule of law". In: COSTA, Pietro; ZOLO, Danilo.(Orgs.). *The Rule of Law – History, theory and criticism*. Dordrecht: Springer, 2007.

FERRAZ JR, Tércio Sampaio. "Irretroatividade e jurisprudência judicial". In FERRAZ JÚNIOR, Tércio Sampaio; CARRAZZA, Roque; NERY JÚNIOR, Nelson (Orgs.). *Efeito "ex nunc" e as decisões do STF*. São Paulo: Manole, 2008, pp. 1–32.

FERREIRA FILHO, Manoel Gonçalves. *Estado de Direito e Constituição*. 4th ed. São Paulo: Saraiva, 2007.

FIGUEIREDO, Lúcia Valle. "Planejamento, Direito Tributário e segurança jurídica". *RTDP* 12. São Paulo, 1995

FRÄNDBERG, Ake. "Retroactivity, simulactivity, infraactivity". In: BJARUP, Jes; BLEGVAD, Mogens (Orgs.). *Time, Law and Society. ARSP*. v. 64. Stuttgart: Franz Steiner, 1995.

FRIAUF, Karl Heinrich. "Steuerrechtsänderungen und Altinvestitionen. Zum Verfassungsgebot der steuerlichen Investitionssicherheit". *StbJb*, 1986/1987.

GRAU, Eros Roberto. *O Direito posto e o Direito pressuposto*. 7th ed. São Paulo: Malheiros Editores, 2008.

GROLL, Klaus-Michael. *In der Flut der Gesetze: Ursachen, Folgen, Perspektiven*. Düsseldorf: Droste, 1985.

GUSY, Christop. "Gewährleistung von Freiheit und Sicherheit im Lichte unterschiedlicher Staats- und Verfassungsverständnisse". *VVDStRL* 63. Berlin, 2004.

HARTZ, Wilhelm. "Mehr Rechtssicherheit im Steuerrecht. Ziele, Wege, Grenzen". *StbJb*. 1965/1966.

HEY, Johanna. *Steuerplanungssicherheit als Rechtsproblem*. Köln: Otto Schmidt, 2002.

van HOECKE, Mark. "Time and law. Is it the nature of law to last? A conclusion". In: OST, François; van HOECKE, Mark (Orgs.). *Temps et Droit. Le Droit a-t-il pour vocation de durer?*, Bruxelles: Bruylant, 1998.

HORVATH, Estevão. *O Princípio do Não-Confisco no Direito Tributário*. São Paulo: Dialética, 2002.

JURATOWITCH, Ben. *Retroactivity and the Common Law*. Oxford: Hart, 2008.

JUSTEN FILHO, Marçal."O princípio da moralidade pública e o Direito Tributário". *RTDP* 11. 1995.

KIRCHHOF, Paul. "Rückwirkung von Steuergesetzen" *StuW*, 2000.

KOCH, Michael. *Die Grundsätze des intertemporalen Rechts im Verwaltungsprozess – Vertrauensschutz im verwaltungsgerichtlichen Verfahren*. Berlin: Duncker und Humblot, 2009.

KUNIG, Philip. Das Rechtsstaatsprinzip. Tübingen: Siebeck, 1986.

_____. "Der Rechtsstaat". In: BADURA, Peter; DREIER, Horst. (Orgs.). *FS 50 Jahre Bundesverfassungsgericht. Klärung und Fortbildung des Verfassungsrechts*. v. 2. Tübingen, 2001.

LEISNER, Anna. *Kontinuität als Verfassungsprinzip*. Tübingen: Mohr Siebeck, 2002.

LIÈVRE-GRAVEREAUX, Amélie. *La rétroactivité de la loi fiscale: une necessité en matière de procédures*. Paris: Harmattan, 2007.

MACHADO DERZI, Misabel de Abreu. "Mutações, complexidade, tipo e conceito, sob o signo da segurança e da proteção da confiança". In: TORRES, Heleno (Org.). *Estudos em homenagem a Paulo de Barros Carvalho*. São Paulo: Saraiva, 2007.

_____. Modificações da jurisprudência no Direito Tributário. São Paulo: Noeses, 2009.

_____. "A irretroatividade do Direito, a proteção da confiança, a boa-fé e o RE n. 370.682-SC". In: ROCHA, Valdir de Oliveira (coord.). Grandes questões atuais do Direito Tributário. v. 11. São Paulo: Dialética, 2007.

_____. "A família e o Direito Tributário". *RDT* 65. São Paulo: s.d.

MAINKA, Johannes. *Vertrauensschutz im öffentlichen Recht*. Bonn: Ludwig Röhrscheid, 1963.

MAIOR BORGES, José Souto. "O princípio da segurança jurídica na criação e aplicação do tributo". *RDDT* 22. São Paulo: 1997.

_____. "Segurança jurídica: sobre a distinção entre competências fiscais para orientar e autuar o contribuinte". *RDT* 100. São Paulo: s.d.

MANEIRA, Eduardo. *Direito Tributário – Princípio da não-surpresa*. Belo Horizonte: Del Rey, 1994.

MARMOR, Andrei. *Law in the age of pluralism*. Oxford: OUP, 2007.

MENKE, Cassiano. *A proibição aos efeitos de confisco no Direito Tributário*. São Paulo: Malheiros Editores, 2008.

MÖLLERS, Christoph Möllers. *Gewaltenteilung*. Tübingen: Mohr Siebeck, 2005.

_____. *Die drei Gewalten*. Göttingen: Velbrück, 2008.

MUCKEL, Stefan. *Kriterien des verfassungsrechtlichen Vertrauensschutzes bei Gesetzesänderungen*. Berlin: Duncker und Humblot, 1989.

NAVARRO, Francisco González. *El Estado Social y Democrático de Derecho*. Pamplona: EUNSA, 1992.

NAVARRO COELHO, Sacha Calmon. "Princípios retores da tributação: legalidade e tipicidade". *RDT* 33. São Paulo: 1985.

NOVOA, César García. *El principio de seguridad jurídica en materia tributaria*. Madrid: Marcial Pons, 2000.

OSSENBÜHL, Fritz. *Die Rücknahme fehlerhafter begünstigender Verwaltungsakte*. 2nd ed. Berlin: Walter de Gruyter, 1965.

PESSOA DE MENDONÇA, Maria Luíza Vianna. *O Princípio constitucional da irretroatividade da lei – A irretroatividade da lei tributária*. Belo Horizonte: Del Rey, 1996.

PIEROTH/SCHLINK, *Staatsrecht II: Grundrechte*. 23rd ed. Heidelberg, C. F. Müller, 2007.

PIZZORUSSO, Alessandro; PASSAGLIA, Paolo. "Constitution et sécurité juridique – Italie". *Annuaire International de Justice Constitutionnelle 1999*. Paris: Economica, 2000.

POHL, Heike. *Rechtsprechungsänderung und Rückanknüpfung*. Berlin: Duncker und Humblot, 2005.

RABELLO FILHO, Francisco Pinto. *O princípio da anterioridade da lei tributária*. São Paulo: Ed. RT, 2002.

RAM´iREZ, Federico Arcos. *La seguridad jurídica: una teoría formal*. Madrid: Dykinson, 2000.

RAZ, Joseph. "The rule of law and its virtue (1977)". In: *The authority of law. Essays on law and morality*. Oxford: Oxford, 1979.

_____. *The Morality of Freedom*. Oxford: Clarendon, 1986.

REALE, Miguel. *Revogação e anulamento do ato administrativo*. 2nd ed. Rio de Janeiro: Forense, 1980.

REDOR, Marie-Joële. *De l'État legal à l'État de Droit*. Paris: Economica, 1992.

REINHARDT, Michael. *Konsistente Jurisdiktion*. Tübingen: Mohr Siebeck, 1997.

RIVA, Enrico. *Wohlerworbene Rechte – Eigentum – Vertrauen*. Bern: Stämpfli, 2007.

SARLET, Ingo Wolfgang. "A eficácia do direito fundamental à segurança jurídica: dignidade da pessoa humana, direitos fundamentais e proibição de retrocesso social no Direito Constitucional brasileiro". In: ANTUNES ROCHA, Cármen Lúcia (Org.). *Constituição e segurança jurídica: direito adquirido, ato jurídico perfeito e coisa julgada. Estudos em homenagem a José Paulo Sepúlveda Pertence*. Belo Horizonte: Fórum, 2004.

SCHACHTSCHNEIDER, Karl Albert. *Prinzipien des Rechtsstaates*. Berlin: Duncker und Humblot, 2006.

SCHMIDT-ABMANN, Eberhard. Schmidt-Aßmann, "Verwaltungsverfahren". In: KIRCHHOF, Paul; ISENSEE, Josef (Orgs.). *Handbuch des Staatsrechts*. 2nd ed. v. 3. Heidelberg: C. F. Müller, 1996.

SCHOUERI, Luís Eduardo. "Segurança na ordem tributária nacional e internacional: tributação do comércio exterior". In: BARRETO, Aires Fernandino *et alii* (Orgs.). *Segurança jurídica na tributação e Estado de Direito*. São Paulo: Noeses, 2005.

SCHWARZ, Kyrill-A. *Vertrauensschutz als Verfassungsprinzip*. Baden-Baden: Nomos, 2002.

SEABRA DE MOURA, Frederico Araújo. *Lei complementar tributária*. São Paulo: Quartier Latin, 2009.

SOBOTA, Katharina. *Das Prinzip Rechtsstaat*. Tübingen: Siebeck, 1997.

STERN, Klaus. "Der Rechtsstaat". In: *Kölner Universitätsreden*. Krefeld: Scherpe, 1971.

SUMMERS, Robert. "A formal theory of the rule of law". In: *Essays in Legal Theory*. Dordrecht: Kluwer, 2000.

TAMANAHA, Brian Z. *On the rule of law*. Cambridge: Cambridge University Press, 2004.

TORRES, Ricardo Lobo. *O Direito ao mínimo existencial*. Rio de Janeiro: Renovar, 2009.

_____. "O orçamento na Constituição". In: *Tratado de Direito Constitucional, Financeiro e Tributário*. 3rd ed. Rio de Janeiro: Renovar, 2008.

TROPER, Michel. "Le concept d'État de Droit". *Cahiers de Philosophie Politique et Juridique* 24, 1993.

UHLRICH, Hanns. "La sécurité juridique en Droit Économique allemand: observations d'un privatiste". In: BOY, Laurence; RACINE, Jean-Baptiste; SIIRIAINEN Fabrice (Orgs.). *Sécurité juridique et Droit Économique*. Bruxelles: Larcier, 2008.

URBINA, Sebastián. *Legal method and the rule of law*. Dordrecht: Kluwer, 2002.

VALEMBOIS, Anne-Laure. *La constitutionnalisation de l'exigence de sécurité juridique en Droit Français*. Paris: LGDJ, 2005.

VOGEL, Klaus. "Rechtssicherheit und Rückwirkung zwischen Vernunftrecht und Verfassungsrecht". *Juristen Zeitung*, n. 43, 1988.

____. "The rule of law in contemporary liberal theory". *Ratio Juris*. v. 2, n. 1, 1989.

WIEDAMNN, Herbert. "Rechtssicherheit – ein absoluter Wert? Gedanken zum Bestimmtheitserfordernis zivilrechtlicher Tatbestände". In: PAULUS, Gotthard *et alii* (Orgs.). *FS für Karl Larenz*. München: Beck, 1973.

YANNAKOPOULOS, Constantin. *La notion de droits acquis en Droit Administratif Français*. Paris: LGDJ, 1997.

ZIMMER, Willy."Constitution et sécurité juridique – Allemagne". *Annuaire International de Justice Constitutionnelle 1999*. Paris: Economica, 2000.

Part III
Definition of Legal Certainty

The law always has been, is now, and will ever continue to be, largely vague and variable. (Jerome Frank, *Law and the modern mind*, New Brunswick, Transaction, 2009, p. 6; 1st ed., New York, Brentano's Inc., 1930; 2nd ed., New York, Coward-McCann, 1949).

. . . Law is certain or is not even law. (Norberto Bobbio, "La certezza del diritto é un mito?", in *Rivista Internazionale di Filosofia del Diritto*, n. 28, p. 150, 1951)

Ultimately we are in agreement: We want the foundations of legal certainty, so that Law is certain and secure against the interference of arbitrariness and unjust disposition. (Friedrich Carl von Savigny, *Vom Beruf unserer Zeit für Gesetzgebung und Rechtswissenschaft*, Heidelberg, Mohr und Zimmer, 1814, p. 161)

. . . men need certain, approved and acknowledged norms; otherwise there is no freedom, certainty or property. (Romagnosi, *Assunto primo della scienza del Diritto Naturale*, 3rd ed., 1832, p. 127)

In chapter "Legal Certainty", we analyzed the various meanings of "legal certainty" depending on the aspect examined. In chapter "Foundations in the Constitutional Superstructure", we investigated the foundations of the legal certainty principle according to the Brazilian constitutional order. Thus we are now in a position to conclude which of all such possible meanings the Constitution actually assigns to legal certainty, given each aspect considered. It *can* mean many things, but what *ought* it to mean according to the Constitution?

In this framework, it is necessary to summarize the answers that have already been partially given to the following questions: What is the normative dimension of legal certainty according to the Constitution? Fact, value or norm? If norm, of what kind – rule or principle? What is the substantive aspect of legal certainty according to the Constitution – regarding the word "certainty," does it mean a state of knowability or determination, reliability or immutability, calculability or predictability? And does the word "legal" mean certainty "of," "through," "before" or "under" law, "of rights," "as" a right, or "in" law? What is the objective aspect of legal certainty based on the Constitution – certainty of the legal order, of a norm or of behavior? If a norm, is it a general or individual norm? If behavior, is it one's own behavior or someone else's? What is the subjective aspect of legal certainty according to the Constitution? Regarding the beneficiary, is it meant to protect the taxpayer or the state? Regarding the subject used as a parameter to assess certainty, is legal certainty to be assured from the perspective of an average citizen or an expert in tax law? Regarding the subject that ought to assure it, is it the responsibility of the legislative, executive or judiciary? What is the time aspect of legal certainty according to the Constitution? Is legal certainty to be sought yesterday, today or tomorrow? What is the quantitative aspect of legal certainty? Is total or partial legal certainty to be assured? Finally, what is the justificatory aspect of legal certainty? Is certainty an end in itself or an instrument to realize other ends? These questions are crucial. Let us now discuss the answers to them.

Concept of Legal Certainty

Abstract This chapter sets out to establish a concept of legal certainty, defining legal certainty as a guarantee of observance founded on the paradigm of semantic-argumentative controllability. Such control, it is argued, depends on elements, dimensions and aspects to be jointly assessed. Accordingly, legal certainty entails processes of determination, legitimation, argumentation and justification that assure the semantic-argumentative controllability of state action, on one hand, and the respectability of the individual's law-based actions on the other, as well as reflexively grounding the argumentation referring to such actions.

The concept of legal certainty as conceived in this book depends on the answers to a number of questions that together make up the finalistic aspects of certainty. In this sense, the core questions that will shape the concept of legal certainty are addressed below.

What is the meaning of the word "**certainty*****" in the Constitution? Does it refer to "legal" or "physical" certainty?***

It refers to *legal certainty*. First, because when the Constitution institutes a democratic state based on the rule of law with the aim of "assuring certainty as a value" in article 1, it refers to a social objective that transcends the merely psychological or physical dimension.

Second, because when article 5 assures the "right to certainty" *alongside* the right to freedom, equality and property, which are qualified as objective social values and not merely individual psychological states, it ends up protecting certainty in parallel to the assurance of these other values, i.e., as legal values.

Third, because among the fundamental rights listed in the indents to article 5 several relate to physical and individual security (protection of the home and guaranteed habeas corpus against abusive restrictions of freedom), or to specific forms of freedom (of thought, opinion and belief, of intellectual, artistic and scientific inquiry, of communication and expression, and of association for lawful purposes), presupposing a broader scope for the provision in the article's opening paragraph.

What is the normative dimension of legal certainty according to the Constitution – fact, value or norm? If norm, what kind of norm – rule or principle?

© Springer International Publishing Switzerland 2016

H. Ávila, *Certainty in Law*, Law and Philosophy Library 114,
DOI 10.1007/978-3-319-33407-3_6

Legal certainty is qualified as a legal norm of the species "principle norm" because an examination of its structure and constituent parts reveals that it determines the protection of an ideal state of affairs whose realization depends on specific types of behavior, many of which are expressly determined. All the foundations referred to above, whether direct or indirect, obtained by deduction or induction, not only express the bindingness of the ideals of knowability, reliability and calculability established by the Constitution, but also define every aspect of these ideals. To say that legal certainty is a legal norm is by no means to devalue the axiological aspect of the principle. It merely indicates that as a principle legal certainty embodies and positivates a value at a higher level of concretization.[1]

What is the material aspect of legal certainty according to the Constitution? – Does the word "certainty" mean a state of knowability or determination? Reliability or immutability? Calculability or predictability?

A state of knowability, reliability and calculability.

Knowability for both theoretical and normative reasons. The theoretical reasons that lead to knowability instead of determination concern the indeterminacy of language: Language evidently cannot have *entirely* ready-made meanings before interpretation begins and hence it is impossible to argue for a univocal conception of interpretation. However, and this is fundamental, normative language nonetheless can have cores of meaning gradually determined by doctrine and jurisprudence.[2] Thus when ruling on the incidence of a service tax, for example, there can be indecision about which cases fit the concept of service, but there is a high degree of consensus among scholars and judges that a "service" involves an obligation to do something, not to deliver something physical. In this case the idea of knowability corresponds to a guarantee of physical and intellectual access by taxpayers to the normative concept, while bearing in mind that despite its halo of certainty or core of meaning (services are obligations to act) there is nevertheless room for indeterminacy to a greater or lesser extent (does a leasing operation involve a service or not?). A determinable conception of interpretation is therefore adopted, in the sense that rules contain concepts which are to some extent indeterminate because of language, but have core meanings that are intersubjectively determined through use by doctrine or jurisprudence, and the interpreter must not depart from these meanings.

The normative reasons that lead to knowability have to do with legal norms that are opposed to determinacy in some way: The legality rule must be coupled with several principles, such as democracy and the separation of powers, which presuppose limited scope for configuration by the executive and require the legislative to establish normative standards without involvement in technical aspects of administrative competence. In light of this, knowability must be interpreted as the material and intellectual ability to understand the interpretative alternatives and the

[1]Ricardo Lobo Torres, "Valores e princípios constitucionais tributários", in *Tratado de Direito Constitucional Financeiro e Tributário*, v. 2, Rio de Janeiro, Renovar, 2005, p. 198.

[2]José Souto Maior Borges, *Curso de Direito Comunitário*, São Paulo, Saraiva, 2005, p. 10.

criteria indispensable to their realization, rather than determinacy as the ability to know the only previous normative meaning. In sum, as noted by Grau, "there are no previously structured solutions to legal problems, as if we were dealing with semi-manufactured parts on an assembly line."[3]

Reliability instead of immutability because the Constitution contains both entrenched clauses, making changes difficult but possible, and the principle of the state based on the social rule of law, which requires the state to perform a planning function and act for the general good by driving social change, mostly through the distribution of wealth. Such change, however, must assure normative stability and continuity, since property rights and freedoms presuppose minimal permanence of rules as a condition for people to plan their own lives freely, and the right to a job, trade or profession depends on stable conditions of living. Given that the ideal of reliability of law is required by the legal certainty principle, it cannot be said, as Seiller does based on Rivero, that "legal certainty is necessarily sacrificed in the name of presumed progress of law."[4]

And *calculability* rather than (absolute) predictability, as the total capacity to anticipate normative content, because although the Constitution contains a number of rules designed to permit the anticipation of state actions, such as the legality and anteriority rules, as we will see in detail in Part Two the nature of law, especially the intense use of indeterminate language that depends on argumentative processes to reconstruct meanings, prevents its enunciations from being univocal. For this reason, it is more correct to speak of calculability in two dimensions.

With regard to the normative content assigned to the norms in force at the time of acting, calculability consists of the ability to foresee the range of legal consequences that can be abstractly assigned to facts and to one's own acts or those of others, as well as the time frame within which consequences will be defined, through a process of argumentative reconstruction of the minimal meanings of the law's provisions. Thus predictability is not understood here as the ability to anticipate completely the content of legal norms and final state action.

With regard to the modifiability of norms, calculability should be understood as a high degree of foreseeability of the range of legal consequences that future norms may assign to facts regulated by past norms: Although the legislative is empowered to innovate, fundamental rights will be effectively respected only if innovations are not sudden, drastic or unfair. Thus while taxpayers should be aware that a norm may change in future, there is no calculability when they cannot tell how or how much it may change. Changing a tax rate by 5 % cannot be compared to changing it by 600 % because in the latter case not only are taxpayers are placed in an irreversible position, but they might refrain from acting at all if they knew the change would be so intense.

---

[3]Eros Roberto Grau, *Ensaio e discurso sobre a interpretação/aplicação do Direito*, 4th ed., São Paulo, Malheiros Editores, 2006, p. 36.

[4]Bertrand Seiller, "Le procès de la rétroactivité", in Bertrand Seiller, *La rétroactivité des décisions du juge administratif*, Paris, Economica, 2007, p. 17.

In sum, calculability involves the ability to predict the range of consequences to which a taxpayer will be subject in future. This requirement is not met when taxpayers know only that norms can change but have no idea how much.[5]

An alternative conception of calculability must therefore be preferred. Ideally one should be able to predict all the ways in which the law-applying bodies may reconstruct legal norms, define the small number of legal qualifications that can be attributed to the existing factual situation, and calculate most of the abstract legal consequences assignable to any of these qualifications.[6] In other words, taxpayers must be able to reconstruct the facts and abstract legal qualifications, and fairly accurately predict not the one actual consequence of any action but the few applicable alternative consequences flowing from their actions and the time frame within which the actual consequence will be defined.

It should be stressed at this point that the adoption of a concept of legal certainty connected to a state of calculability does not imply an absence of control over predictions. On one hand, although interpretation involves some degree of indeterminacy it is not free or independent from criteria of legitimation, such as proportionality and reasonableness.[7] On the other, because the choice of a meaning also depends on external structures given by substantive and procedural rules, such as rules of administrative or court jurisdiction, and administrative or court procedures.[8] Moreover, interpretation is a reconstructive activity in the sense that although it is creative, this creativity cannot be discretionary because decisional norms are constrained by the meanings of the text.[9] Even acceptance of room for indeterminacy in language cannot justify an interpretative "free for all" or "à *la diable*" manipulation of normative elements, to quote Machado Derzi, because the law applier is obliged to refer to the internal elements of the legal system, and to do so in a well-grounded manner. Not to do so would be a violation of the rule of law and the separation of powers.[10] At the same time, it must never be forgotten that the application of norms, including tax norms, involves a greater or lesser degree of uncertainty arising from indeterminacy, multiple relations among norms, and complex links with the facts of the case.[11]

---

[5]Johanna Hey, *Steuerplanungssicherheit als Rechtsproblem*, Köln, Otto Schmidt, 2002, p. 285.

[6]Gianmarco Gometz, *La certezza giuridica come prevedibilità*, Torino, Giappichelli, 2005, p. 211.

[7]Ricardo Lobo Torres, "Valores e princípios constitucionais tributários", in *Tratado de Direito Constitucional Financeiro e Tributário*, v. 2, Rio de Janeiro, Renovar, 2005, pages 203 and following.

[8]Anne-Laure Valembois, *La constitutionnalisation de l'exigence de sécurité juridique en Droit français*, Paris, LGDJ, 2005, p. 81.

[9]Eros Roberto Grau, *Ensaio e discurso sobre a interpretação/aplicação do Direito*, 4th ed., São Paulo, Malheiros Editores, 2006, pages 28, 66. Misabel de Abreu Machado Derzi, *Modificações da jurisprudência no Direito Tributário*, São Paulo, Noeses, 2009, p. 106.

[10]Misabel de Abreu Machado Derzi, *Modificações da jurisprudência no Direito Tributário*, São Paulo, Noeses, 2009, pages 105, 110.

[11]César García Novoa, *El principio de seguridad jurídica en materia tributaria*, Madrid, Marcial Pons, 2000, p. 122.

In this respect, the conception of legal certainty advocated here follows a conception of law that is *intermediate* between the objectivist and argumentative conceptions. For the former, law is a previously given object whose content depends mostly on knowledge activities that reveal predetermined meanings. For the latter, law is an activity whose realization depends, at its core, on argumentative structures to be used in the decision making process.[12] The understanding advocated here is that law is a harmonious blend of semantic and argumentative activities. The activity of legal operators begins with the reconstruction of normative meanings through rules of argumentation, but application depends on hermeneutical and applicative postulates. Thus law is neither a mere object whose realization has no need for argumentative structures, nor is it a merely argumentative activity without heterolimitation by normative meanings that precede it; it is a sort of "object-activity", as its realization requires the reconstruction of meanings and argumentative structures of legitimation and justification. After all, the argumentative character of law is undeniable. As MacCormick puts it:

> Law is an argumentative discipline. Whatever question or problem one thinks about, if we pose it as a legal question or problem we seek a solution or answer in terms of a proposition that seems sound as a matter of law, at least arguably sound, though preferably conclusive. To check whether it is sound or genuinely arguable, or perhaps even conclusive, we think through the arguments that could be made for the proposed answer or solution.[13]

Dworkin follows the same path when he states that "legal practice, unlike many other social phenomena, is *argumentative*. Every actor in the practice understands that what it permits or requires depends on the truth of certain propositions that are given sense only by and within the practice; the practice consists in large part in deploying and arguing about these propositions."[14]

Consequently, legal certainty ceases to be a mere requirement of predetermination and becomes a standard of rational and argumentative control. This change of perspective shows that legal certainty involves elements that ought to permeate the process of applying law and not simply be part of its result. Hence the unequivocal statement by Habermas that legal certainty does not mean "certainty of the result" (*Ergebnissicherheit*), but the discoursive clarification of normative and factual elements to be realized through a due legal process capable of indicating the arguments that lead to the decision. Because legal certainty is connected to both a logical-semantic dimension and a pragmatic dimension of the argumentative process of justification, it should be understood as procedurally dependent legal certainty

---

[12]Aulis Aarnio, *The Rational as Reasonable*, Dordrecht, Reidel, 1987, p. 4. Stefano Bertea, *Certezza del Diritto e argomentazione giuridica*, Soveria Manelli, Rubbertino, 2002, pages 13 and following.

[13]Neil MacCormick, "Rhetoric and the Rule of Law", in David Dyzenhaus (Org.), *Recrafting the rule of Law – The Limits of Legal Order*, Oxford, Hart, 1999, p. 163.

[14]Ronald Dworkin, *Law's Empire*, Cambridge, Belknap, 1986, p. 13.

(*verfahrensabhängige Rechtssicherheit*).[15] As Neves well states, justification in law ceases to be merely semantic and becomes discoursive, so that it involves the question of the rational acceptability of decisions through a procedure of legal production that generates legitimacy.[16]

This concept of legal certainty brings it closer to the requirement of state transparency. However, the legal certainty principle cannot be totally assimilated into the transparency principle. This is so because the core concept of the requirement of transparency is linked to the idea of information, in the sense that all state procedures must be sufficiently open to assure their comprehension and effectiveness.[17] The concept of legal certainty proposed here also presupposes transparency but is not centered on the mere question of information. Instead it centers on reasoning and argumentation: more than informing, the legal certainty principle aims to assure rationality and effectiveness for law as a whole.

And does the word "legal" designate certainty "of," "through," "before" or "under" law, "of rights," "as a right" or "in law"?

It designates each of these hypotheses, depending on the context and perspective.

Of law because by instituting legality, anteriority and irretroactivity rules the Constitution creates conditions for law itself to become more certain, through clarity of its enunciations and anticipation of its norms. For example, by establishing the principles of morality and publicity, it makes justification and publication requisites for the validity of legal norms.

Through law because by instituting a democratic state whose aim is to "assure certainty as a value" in article 1, the Constitution determines that law must serve as an *instrument to guarantee* certainty; on the other hand, because the institution of procedures through which citizens can defend their rights, such as due process of law and the right to a full and fair hearing, or even the writ of mandamus and habeas corpus, enables citizens to use law as an instrument to protect their rights.

Before law because the state can only act by exercising powers established in competence rules and using sources and procedures provided for in law, and cannot affect the rights individuals have acquired according to law.

Of rights because the protection of acquired rights, completed legal acts and res iudicata in article 5, XXXVI, translates the reflexive efficacy of the legal certainty principle, directed to a specific subject and a specific concrete case, assuring the exercise of specific rights.

As a right because the reflexive efficacy of the objective principle of legal certainty creates, for a given subject, the right to a given type of state behavior without which the states of knowability, reliability and calculability are not minimally realized.

---

[15] Jürgen Habermas, *Faktizität und Geltung*, Darmstadt, Wissenschaftliche Buchgesellschaft, 2002, pages 270, 277.

[16] Marcelo Neves, *Entre Têmis e Leviatã: uma relação difícil – O Estado Democrático de Direito a partir e além de Luhmann e Habermas*, São Paulo, Martins Fontes, 2006, pages 107, 112, 118.

[17] Jürgen Bröhmer, *Transparenz als Verfassungsprinzip*, Tübingen, Mohr Siebeck, 2004, p. 376.

In law given that legal certainty as defined in this study centers not on the requirement of knowledge of entirely and previously determined content, but on the controllability of argumentative structures required to reconstruct and apply normative meanings. Thus legal certainty is revealed in the course of realizing law.[18] This view of certainty *in* law illustrates more broadly the general meaning of the legal certainty principle, which rather than being confined to prior knowledge of legal effects, extends especially to the controllability of argumentative processes.[19]

What is the objective aspect of legal certainty according to the Constitution – certainty of the legal order, of a norm or of behavior? If a norm, is it a general or individual norm? If behavior, is it one's own or someone else's?

Certainty of the order, of a norm and of behavior. Again, these meanings are not mutually exclusive. Each one exists according to the context in which legal certainty is applied.

Of the order because several principles, such as the rule of law or the social rule of law, concern the whole of the legal order and not one of its specific manifestations.

Of a norm, both *general*, because several rules impose conditions of validity for the creation of norms, such as the tax rule prohibiting retroactivity, and *individual*, because several rules protect individual situations guaranteed by court rulings or administrative acts, such as the rule that protects completed legal acts, res iudicata and acquired rights.

Of behavior, especially state behavior, because in addition to the principles of publicity and morality the Constitution also contains a number of procedural and substantive rules that favor the knowledge and justification of state activities. These principles, when allied to competence rules (regarding exercise, substantive limitation and procedural limitation), enable taxpayers to anticipate the consequences that the legal order will ascribe to their behavior.

Who must guarantee legal certainty: the legislative, executive or judiciary?

All three.[20] The *legislative* because the Constitution contains rules about the production of norms, such as legality, anteriority and irretroactivity, that require the legislative to create obligations through formal laws, take into account facts that will happen after a certain period of time, and legislate for situations that will occur only after laws come into force.

The executive because the Constitution establishes norms regarding uniform application of the legislation, such as the principle of equality, and observance of the rules determined by the legislative, such as legality.

---

[18] Arthur Kaufmann, "Die ontologische Struktur des Rechts", in *Die ontologische Begründung des Rechts*, Darmstadt, Wissenschaftliche Buchgesellschaft, 1965, p. 482.

[19] Stefano Bertea, *Certezza del Diritto e argomentazione giuridica*, Soveria Manelli, Rubbertino, 2002, p. 113.

[20] Bertrand Mathieu, "Constitution et sécurité juridique – France", in *Annuaire International de Justice Constitutionnelle, 1999*, Paris, Economica, 2000.

And the *judiciary* because in addition to requiring the institution of general rules to be applied uniformly, the Constitution contains a number of rules designed to assure proper foundations and publicity for judicial activities.

All three branches are also key to legal certainty because of the immediate efficacy of the fundamental rights relating to them, in accordance with article 5 of the Constitution.[21]

Regarding the beneficiary, is the aim of legal certainty to protect taxpayers or the state?

Taxpayers inasmuch as the aim of constitutional norms is, on one hand, to permit the anticipation of state action, as evidenced by the principles of morality and publicity, and on the other to permit knowledge of the consequences assignable to taxpayers' acts, as illustrated by the rules governing competence as well as the tax anteriority and irretroactivity rules. In this respect, legal certainty is "not a two-way street", as Machado Derzi pointedly asserts. Irretroactivity, protection of trust and good faith cannot be invoked to protect the public coffers from the effects of changes in jurisprudence, for instance.[22]

Regarding the subjective criteria to assess certainty, should legal certainty exist from the perspective of ordinary citizens or experts in tax law?

From the perspective of *ordinary citizens* because the rule of law presupposes that all citizens know the norms, not least as an instrument of democratic participation, and the publicity and morality principles do not have specific addressees but address all citizens. The purpose of legal norms – and particularly of tax norms– is to allow, prohibit or require certain types of behavior. Thus in order to have practical effects they need to be understood by those who are able to, prohibited from or required to do something. Given that norms are designed to serve as guidance for their addressees, the perspective from which they are considered must be that of the addressees, not least as a condition for certainty to serve as an instrument of individual autonomy.[23] Thus because citizens must be the yardstick against which the clarity and intelligibility of norms are measured, and norms must be "user-friendly" (*Benutzerfreundlich*) and "addressee-comprehensible" (Adressatenverständlich).[24]

In the field of tax law, it must be noted that the National Tax System instituted by the Constitution contains specific rules on knowability, reliability and calculability from the taxpayer's perspective. Thus the legality, anteriority and irretroactivity rules are defined as "limitations on the power to tax" and serve as instruments to

[21]Roque Antonio Carrazza, *Curso de Direito Constitucional Tributário*, 27th ed., São Paulo, Malheiros Editores, 2011, p. 430.

[22]Misabel de Abreu Machado Derzi, *Modificações da jurisprudência no Direito Tributário*, São Paulo, Noeses, 2009, p. 160. Idem. "Mutações jurisprudenciais, em face da proteção da confiança e do interesse público no planejamento da receita e da despesa do Estado", in Roberto Ferraz (Org.), *Princípios e limites da tributação 2 – Os princípios da ordem econômica e a tributação*, São Paulo, Quartier Latin, 2009, p. 746.

[23]Gianmarco Gometz, *La certezza giuridica come prevedibilità*, Torino, Giappichelli, 2005, p. 202.

[24]Andreas von Arnauld, *Rechtssicherheit*, Tübingen, Mohr Siebeck, 2006, p. 230.

protect taxpayers from the state. Moreover, these rules are termed "guarantees," understood as norms designed to assure individual rights before the state. The definition of these norms as "limitations on the power to tax" and as "guarantees" clearly reveals the concern embodied by the Constitution that taxpayers, and no other subject, be the yardstick with which to measure the states of knowability, reliability and calculability of law.

Finally, it must be kept in mind that general tax norms, of which the rules in the National Tax Code are examples, provide for taxpayers themselves to calculate and anticipate payment of taxes directly (article 150) and prohibit penalties for taxpayers who take action in advance of any enforcement or surveillance measure by the authorities (article 100). In doing so they assume taxpayers will spontaneously obey the tax norms, regardless of participation by lawyers in administrative or court cases, or by authorities in administrative procedures. Thus legal certainty must be assessed from the perspective of the addressee. In tax law this means there is certainty when taxpayers are able to gain detailed knowledge of the laws, rely on and trust them, and calculate their effects. Determinability will be all the greater in proportion to the constraints imposed on fundamental freedoms, property rights and equality.[25] This is precisely the case of tax law because tax norms effectively induce behavior and place a burden on the citizen.

One reservation must be noted, however: Because legal certainty involves not one aspect but many, its existence is not always analyzed from the taxpayer's perspective. Depending on the objective and subjective substantive aspects, it may be necessary to consider not only one taxpayer, but several or even all taxpayers, or even the executive. Thus if the problem is one of intelligibility, the tax norm in question may be addressed to the taxpayer or to the tax authorities, although in this case strictly speaking such a norm would be predominantly administrative. If the problem is one of reliability, what matters most is whether it is an issue of individual stability, in which case only the viewpoint of the taxpayer affected ought to be considered by the reflexive application of legal certainty, or whether it is a problem relative to the legal order as a whole, in which case the perspective of all taxpayers should be adopted. In sum, these considerations show that tax law certainty must be gauged from the perspective of the addressee unless there is a reason to see it from a different perspective.

Regarding the subjective scope of certainty, ought there to be legal certainty for an individual and for an individual right, or for the collectivity, or for the legal order as a whole?

The answer to this question depends on the applicable norms. Legal certainty can be considered both an objective principle of the legal order and reflexively applicable to a specific subject. Thus it can be said that legal certainty has an objective and impersonal dimension relating to the general or collective interest in the maintenance of law and order, as well as a strictly personal dimension

[25]Federico Arcos Ramírez, *La seguridad jurídica: una teoría formal*, Madrid, Dykinson, 2000, p. 263.

associated with individual interests.[26] What is at stake is the legal certainty principle in the former case, and the principle of protection of legitimate trust (*Vertrauensschutzprinzip*) in the latter. Though related, they are different: The legal certainty principle concerns the legal order in a general and abstract way, regardless of anyone's specific interests, and can even be used against individual interests; the trust protection principle refers to a concrete and subjective situation, and aims solely to uphold a legal situation favorable to a given subject.[27] In this sense, it can be said that the legal certainty principle serves as an instrument to protect "trusts" (of citizens in general, before the legal order considered as a whole), whereas the trust protection principle is a means to assure "trust" (of a citizen in response to a particular manifestation of the legal order). In fact, the trust protection principle does not so much protect "stability of law for all," as does the legal certainty principle, but "someone's trust in the stability of a manifestation of law," *in light of which* the citizen has performed some activity, which is subtly different. The legal certainty principle, as Calmes points out, aims to avoid unpredictability, especially retroactivity, "whatever it is" (*quoi qu'il soit*), and the instability of the order in general, whatever it is.[28] Hence, strictly speaking it is more correct to speak of a *subjective right* to the protection of legitimate trust than of a principle of protection of legitimate trust.[29]

In order to know when legal certainty aims to protect individual interests and when its objective is to protect collective interests, the normative and factual context in which it is used must be analyzed. For example, when what is at stake is the protection of acquired rights, completed legal acts, res iudicata and legitimate trust, the legal certainty principle is reflexively applied to private interests, either because the norms that protect such situations are qualified as "individual guarantees" or because they deal with individual circumstances. However, in the case of the rule instituted by article 27 of Law 9868/98, which allows the Supreme Court in the concentrated control of constitutionality to declare a statute or normative act unconstitutional and, "for reasons of legal certainty or exceptional social interest", modulate the effects of its declaration of unconstitutionality, the legal certainty principle aims to protect the reliability and calculability of the legal order as a whole,

[26] Sylvia Calmes, *Du principe de protection de la confiance légitime en Droits allemand, communautaire et français*, Paris, Dalloz, 2001, p. 170. Anne-Laure Valembois, *La constitutionnalisation de l'exigence de sécurité juridique en Droit français*, Paris, LGDJ, 2005, p. 19. Rafael Maffini, *O princípio da proteção substancial da confiança no Direito Administrativo brasileiro*, Porto Alegre, Verbo Jurídico, 2007, pp. 55, 61. This authorassimilates the concept of protection to that of legal certainty by arguing that the former aims to realize a state of stability, predictability and calculability.

[27] Sylvia Calmes, *Du principe de protection de la confiance légitime en Droits allemand, communautaire et français*, Paris, Dalloz, 2001, p. 167. Anne-Laure Valembois, *La constitutionnalisation de l'exigence de sécurité juridique en Droit français*, Paris, LGDJ, 2005, p. 237.

[28] Sylvia Calmes, *Du principe de protection de la confiance légitime en Droits allemand, communautaire et français*, Paris, Dalloz, 2001, p. 170.

[29] Katharina Sobota, *Das Prinzip Rechtsstaat*, Tübingen, Mohr Siebeck, 1997, p. 507.

because the rule refers to the concentrated control of constitutionality, in which the constitutionality of a law is analyzed in theory, without primordially considering private interests, and also because in concentrated control there is no way to prove observance of the requirements indispensable to application of the trust principle (existence of a basis for trust, of trust, of a causal nexus between the basis and the trust, of the exercise of trust and of the frustration of trust), given that this proof can be obtained only in diffuse control and through a broad and thorough process of discovery.

As will be seen in the second part of this book, the fact that legal certainty may have both an individual normative dimension and a transindividual dimension does not mean that these dimensions are unrelated to each other or, more importantly, that they should not be harmonized. For example, when analyzing the existence of requisites to configure the intangibility of a de facto situation, although concrete and individual requisites must be examined, it is necessary to verify whether the individual protection of legal certainty might compromise the collective realization of legal certainty. In theory this could happen when the effects of invalid administrative acts are upheld under such circumstances that, given their potential for repetition, upholding them may encourage administrative authorities to exceed their competence in future. In this case, protecting the stability of individual acts would eventually compromise the calculability of the legal order, as many administrative authorities could be encouraged to practice acts in violation of the competence rules, assuming future intangibility by virtue of the time elapsed. In short, individual stability would be achieved at the expense of general calculability.[30] In other words, protection of certainty (through stability) would cause loss of certainty (through calculability). Legal certainty would thus cause legal uncertainty. As will be seen later in the discussion of the efficacy of legal certainty, legal certainty sometimes conflicts with itself. The thesis advanced in this book is that although one dimension of legal certainty may take priority depending on the normative context, it must never be realized at the expense of another, and the realization of one must never entail failure to realize them all. This explains why the principle of legal certainty is defined as the requirement to realize a state of "more" certainty.

What is the time aspect of legal certainty according to the Constitution? – Should legal certainty be sought for past, present or future?

All three time dimensions, analyzed separately.

Present because the Constitution establishes lawmaking rules designed to enable citizens to know the norms they must obey in the current exercise of their activities. As will be shown in the next chapter, the Constitution institutes a number of duties regarding the existence of norms (such as publication and notification), their enforcement (such as anteriority and irretroactivity) and their content (such as clarity and determinability), thus assuring a static "certainty of orientation."

[30] Anne-Laure Valembois, *La constitutionnalisation de l'exigence de sécurité juridique en Droit français*, Paris, LGDJ, 2005, p. 20.

Past because the Constitution establishes norms that protect situations already protected by law in the past, such as the guarantees of acquired rights, completed legal acts and res iudicata. As will be specified in the next chapter, the Constitution institutes a number of rules regarding changes to the laws, thus assuring a dynamic "rhythmic certainty."

Future because the Constitution establishes norms about the bindingness of law so that citizens know today how binding norms will be tomorrow. As also detailed in the next chapter, the Constitution institutes several norms governing anteriority and normative efficacy, thus assuring "certainty of application."

What is the quantitative aspect of legal certainty? – Should total or partial certainty be guaranteed?

Total. This is a highly complex question, as will be shown later, and cannot be understood in terms of polar dualities such as "absolute vs. relative". Instead, the aim is to demonstrate that legal certainty ought to be *more* promoted than restricted. Because it involves not a single uniform ideal but a *multifaceted complex of ideals*, internal conflicts between different aspects may arise. For example, assuring stability of law through protection for someone's legitimate expectations may jeopardize both the intelligibility of law for all other citizens, who will not be sure what the legal order allows or forbids, and the bindingness of law, given that a formal principle is made temporarily ineffectual; similarly, assuring the stability of legitimate expectations protects certainty for the past but jeopardizes certainty for the future by potentially encouraging wagers that the effects of unlawful acts may be protected by the upholding of a consolidated situation.

These examples, to which others will be added, show that legal certainty can conflict "with itself" in the sense of contradictions between aspects of legal certainty such as reliability and calculability, certainty of law and certainty through law, past certainty and future certainty and so on. This is a very good reason to advocate use of the legal certainty principle only when on average its use leads more to its promotion than to its restriction. In other words, the legal certainty principle should be the foundation for a decision only when it can be rationally and argumentatively demonstrated that its use promotes greater overall certainty on average for all aspects. For example, a decision that makes the effects of a past unlawful act intangible for a subject but weakens the binding force of the legal order for most citizens only apparently promotes legal certainty because to protect past legal certainty for one citizen it restricts future legal certainty for most citizens. In short, legal certainty is greatly restricted by being minimally protected. A limb is protected, and the body is forgotten. Thus the legal certainty principle is promoted only when the *synthesis* of its aspects reveals its *greater* promotion as a whole. Hence the figurative saying that either legal certainty is total or it is not legal certainty.

And, lastly, what is the justificatory aspect of legal certainty? – Is certainty an end in itself or a means to other ends?

It is a *means to other ends*: on one hand, fundamental freedoms and property rights because without stability and calculability of state action, individuals cannot exercise the right to free self-determination and a decent life; on the other, state purposes, given that the exercise of state action and planning in the medium and long term (articles 70 and ff) presupposes the permanence of valid rules. However, this permanence is not for the benefit of the state, but for the benefit of individuals, who can control state activity and plan their activities. This instrumentality is even more visible within the scope of tax law because in the National Tax System grounded in the Constitution the principles and rules relating to legal certainty, are instituted as "guarantees" and "limits to the power to tax," so that they tend to protect the taxpayer rather than the state.

The instrumentality of legal certainty leads to a very important *adjustment* to the concept of knowability and calculability, without which the principle of certainty loses such instrumentality. Knowability has been defined as the ability to understand the *alternative meanings* that lead back to a normative text, and calculability as the ability to anticipate the *range of consequences* possibly applicable to acts or facts and the *time frame* within which the consequence will be effectively applied. The question that arises in this context, however, is: Will there be knowability if there are too many alternative normative meanings? Will there be calculability if the ranges of consequences and time frames are too broad? In other words, is there knowability when citizens have the ability to know that there are ten alternative meanings for a given norm and is there calculability when citizens have the ability to foresee ten legal consequences that can be assigned to their actions over a period of 10 years? If legal certainty is understood as the necessary instrument for individuals to be able to plan and conceive their future and increase their range of free action, the answer is no: Individuals cannot plan or conceive their future if the range of normative consequences assignable to acts or facts is too broad, or too discrepant, and the time frame within which there will be a confirmation of the applicable consequence is too long.[31] This is so because one cannot autonomously and freely achieve legally informed strategic planning when the normative consequences are limitless or too broad and too different from one another. Broad uncertainty concerning the normative consequences of action leads to inaction due to a lack of minimal control over the future. When a prediction is too general, it leads to lack of information and that tends to make planning impossible.

Thus what matters is not being able to predict normative consequences, but being able to predict a *small* number of *not very different* normative consequences. If someone can foresee only two consequences for an act, one of which is a fine of 500 dollars and the other life imprisonment, there is actually no calculability at all, since they lack the means to *measure* the consequences of their actions. Similarly, if taxpayers can predict only two consequences for a given act, one of which is a tax liability of 500 dollars and the other a tax liability of half a million dollars, there is no calculability at all. In sum, calculability encompasses alternative normative consequences but assumes that they are neither too extensive nor too different from one another, and that their application does not exceed a reasonable

[31] Gianmarco Gometz, *La certezza giuridica come prevedibilità*, Torino, Giappichelli, 2005, p. 232.

period. Predicting a small number of unsure consequences or a large number of sure consequences is not calculating. Therefore, unlimited calculability or excessive calculability regarding the *number* and *variability* of consequences, or the *time frame* for their definition, is not calculability. This is also why calculability depends on reasonable process length, as we will see later.

Given these considerations, calculability must be defined as a state of affairs in which citizens are largely able to *anticipate* and *measure* a *limited* and *fairly invariable* range of consequences abstractly assignable to their own or others' actions, and to facts, and a *short* time frame within which the final consequence will be applied. Without this reservation, calculability becomes unpredictability. This explains why requiring calculability through continuity of the legal order avoids *sudden* but not drastic changes, as well as *drastic* but not sudden changes. Change is acceptable depending on the case, but must be carried out respectfully, with protection of trust, transitional rules and equity clauses, or it is "*trop brutal*", to quote Ost.[32]

One more point must be highlighted. There may be an ability to *anticipate* and *measure* a *limited* and *fairly invariable* range of consequences abstractly assignable to acts or facts and a *short* time frame within which the final consequence will be applied and yet no calculability. This is because although citizens may know there are two consequences assignable to the practice of an act (say X and Y), they may know the exact meaning of these ($X = A$ and $Y = B$), and they may know the time frame within which the applicable consequence will be defined (say between *T1* and *T5*), they nevertheless may not know whether either consequence (X or Y) will *actually* be implemented by the state. Legal efficacy, or legal effectiveness, must therefore be part of the concept of legal certainty.[33]

Given the above, calculability ought to be defined as the ability to anticipate and measure the limited and fairly invariable range of consequences abstractly assignable to acts or facts, and a short time frame within which the final consequence will be *effectively* applied. This legal efficacy depends on access to the judiciary and on the existence of procedural guarantees, such as the writ of mandamus.

All these aspects will be explored further in the second part of this book, which deals with the content and efficacy of the legal certainty principle. At this stage, however, we can already outline a concept of legal certainty in general and of tax law certainty in particular.

Given all previous considerations, legal certainty can be defined as a *principle norm that requires the legislative, executive and judiciary to adopt forms of behavior that contribute more to the existence, for the benefit of citizens and from their perspective, of a state of legal calculability and reliability based on knowability,*

---

[32]François Ost, *Le temps du Droit*, Paris, Odile Jacob, 1999, p. 291.

[33]Gianmarco Gometz, *La certezza giuridica come prevedibilità*, Torino, Giappichelli, 2005, p. 237. Erhard Denninger, "Rechtsstaat oder Rule of Law – was is das heute?", in Cornelius Prittwitz *et alii* (Orgs.), *FS für Klaus Lüderssen*, Baden-Baden, Nomos, 2002, p. 49. Niklas Luhmann, *Ausdifferenzierung des Rechts – Beiträge zur Rechtssoziologie und Rechtstheorie*, Frankfurt am Main, Suhrkamp, 1999, p. 271.

through the juridico-rational controllability of argumentative structures that reconstruct general and individual norms, as an instrument that guarantees respect for their capacity to shape the present in a worthy and responsible manner and to plan the future strategically in a legally informed manner, without deceit, frustration, surprise or arbitrariness.

In this definition, *knowability* means a state of affairs in which citizens have to a high degree the material and intellectual capacity to understand argumentative structures that reconstruct general and individual substantive and procedural norms that are minimally effective by virtue of their accessibility, breadth, clarity, determinability and executability. *Reliability*, in turn, means a state of affairs in which the acts that dispose of fundamental rights and freedoms are respected through law, thanks to the existence of stability, durability and irretroactivity of the legal order. *Calculability* means a state of affairs in which citizens have to a high degree the capacity to approximately anticipate and measure a limited and fairly invariable range of criteria and argumentative structures that define consequences to be assigned, heteronomously and coercively or autonomously and spontaneously, to their actions or those of others, or to facts that have actually occurred or might occur in future, whether or not they are in dispute, and the reasonable time frame within which the final consequence will be applied, through anteriority and continuity of change and the bindingness of the general and individual norms.

It is important to stress that the definition of legal certainty proposed here does not refer to an intrinsic quality of a norm. On the contrary, it concerns an ideal state of affairs that is determined by a legal norm and depends for its existence to a greater or lesser extent on a complex of normative, factual and rational conditions. What this amounts to is "de facto legal certainty", as it were, which depends on "theoretical normative conditions" that include both semantic and argumentative aspects.

The concept expounded above, as already mentioned in the Introduction, is a *non-classificatory legal concept* constructed by means of an *analytical process* of ambiguity reduction.

It is *non-classificatory* because instead of the duality "certainty/uncertainty" that conceives of either state as "all or nothing", as in bivalent classificatory concepts, it is based on abstract requisites that refer to factual conditions to be verified gradually.

It is *legal* not only because it is based on the constitutional order and implies normative prescriptions, but also because it does not indicate elements whose *verification* depends on *effective* and *factually observable* prediction of states of affairs, as factual and empiricist concepts do. Instead it connotes properties whose *controllability* depends on the observance of certain *theoretical conditions* capable of indicating the *potential* to promote a certain state of affairs.

And its construction involves an *analytical process* of ambiguity reduction. Indeed, this book eschews a detailed examination of its evolution in history and legal doctrine to focus instead on decomposing the various aspects of legal certainty that can be discerned, and on clarifying their meanings and dimensions.

Given the several dimensions of legal certainty, the following questions inevitably arise: Which of these dimensions is the one that denotes the "true" core of legal certainty? If none, then which is the most important?

The thesis advocated in this text does not see legal certainty as having a single dimension, or even a primary dimension. On the contrary, if legal certainty is to be truly certain as well as legal it must include *all* the dimensions analyzed. In other words, legal certainty is certainty *of* and *through* law, and certainty *of rights before* law. If the various dimensions of legal certainty are not combined, it is impossible to achieve a minimal state of reliability and calculability of the legal order based on its knowability, because the state of certainty attained by one dimension will be undermined by the absence of another dimension. In other words, there is a *nexus of presuppositions* and *reciprocities* across the various dimensions of legal certainty, so that one does not work without the other. After all, can law guarantee certainty without itself being certain: that is, can law assure expectations without being minimally knowable, reliable and calculable? Can it be certain without guaranteeing other values with certainty: that is, can law be knowable, reliable and calculable if these elements are at the service of other values? Can law guarantee certainty without permitting certainty before law itself: that is, can law assure reliability and calculability without meeting certain prerequisites for individuals to protect themselves from it? And so on. Answering these questions is one of the goals of this book.

This global understanding of legal certainty explains why analyzing it partially produces an impression that studying it is futile: When an examination of legal certainty is limited to one of its dimensions, not always properly described, the minimal conditions for efficacy are not created. Thus for example, an understanding of legal certainty based on the pair "determination/predictability" has lost importance over time and is now considered counterproductive: To seek legal certainty in a single dimension, perceived as absolute, while disregarding all others, is to expect what no dimension alone can offer. Hence the attempt to present a global view of legal certainty based on other foundations.

The result of all this is a more complex and overarching concept of legal certainty, which is not circumscribed to one of its elements, one of its dimensions or one of its aspects, but presents it as a norm made up of a multiplicity of ideals, dimensions and aspects to be considered *together* and *in a balanced manner*. Thus the concept of legal certainty proposed does not hang exclusively on the idea of sureness but instead hinges on the concept of *balance*, similarly to what Palombella proposes, albeit apologetically.[34] The requirement of balance derives from the multifacetedness of the legal certainty principle, so that it can be analyzed from many perspectives according to the aspect under investigation. For this reason it is compared to Janus, the Roman god with two or even four faces looking in different directions at once.[35]

---

[34]Gianluigi Palombella, *Dopo la Certezza – Il Diritto in Equilibrio tra Giustizia e Democrazia*, Bari, Dedalo, 2006, p. 9.

[35]Andreas von Arnauld, *Rechtssicherheit*, Tübingen, Mohr Siebeck, 2006, p. 671. Jutta Limbach, *Ist die kollektive Sicherheit der Feind der individuellen Freiheit?*, Köln, Carl Heymanns, 2002, p. 77.

When a holistic analysis of legal certainty is advocated, therefore, all its aspects and perspectives must necessarily be encompassed. With regard to time, for example, a synthetic and balanced consideration of all three perspectives, past, present and future, is required: not only present, without past and future; not only past, without present and future; and not only future, without present and past. As noted with precision by Machado Derzi, based on Heidegger, the analysis of time should be four-dimensional: past, present and future, and the unity of these three dimensions.[36] Even more than these dimensions, the analysis could extend to the instant, duration, eternity, or even relations of simultaneity ("at the same time") or successiveness ("one after the other").[37] Indeed, the indispensability of analyzing all three dimensions from a unified perspective, i.e., in four, could be compared to working in colors. The phenomenon of color cannot be analyzed without paying attention to every color, because to do so would result in black, or the absence of color. Nor is it possible to investigate only the primary colors, blue, red and yellow separately; ideally, the set of all colors represented by the color white should be examined. This simultaneous analysis, applied to all three temporal perspectives, should be applied to each of the perspectives of each of the aspects of legal certainty: material, objective, subjective, quantitative and instrumental.

It is also important to stress that the concept proposed herein promotes a shift in several aspects of the discussion regarding legal certainty. Instead of proposing a concept of legal certainty linked solely to sureness through knowledge of the previous and abstract determination of legal hypotheses and measurable by the *description* of language – for which law is the creation of the judiciary alone and precedes its application as something entirely given, the concept of legal certainty presented centers on argumentative control and is verifiable through the use of language, by means of the knowledge of hermeneutical structures and criteria, in which law is a product of experience and results from a combination of the objective and subjective aspects inherent in its application. Thus at bottom legal certainty ceases to be a mere linguistic factor based on the prior determination of legal hypotheses, and instead centers on a set of processes of determination, legitimation, argumentation, and justification of premises, methods and results involved in the definition of general and individual norms. Instead of something ready-made ("law as certainty"), legal certainty denotes something to be constructed ("a right to certainty"); instead of "semantic certainty," "argumentative controllability"; instead of "descriptive activity," a "set of reconstructive and decisional activities." The goal is to go beyond the comprehension of legal certainty as an *assurance of content* based on the paradigm of determination, to arrive at legal certainty

[36] Misabel de Abreu Machado Derzi, *Modificações da jurisprudência no Direito Tributário*, São Paulo, Noeses, 2009, p. 197.

[37] François Ost, "Conclusions générales: le temps, la justice et le droit", in Simone Gaboriau and Hélène Pauliat (Orgs.), *Le Temps, la Justice et le Droit*, Limoges, Pulim, 2003, p. 359.

as an *assurance of respect* founded on the paradigm of semantic-argumentative controllability and whose realization depends on elements, dimensions and aspects to be assessed together, synthetically and in balance.

Finally, one point must be highlighted again. Shifting the core of legal certainty from semantics to argumentation does not mean accepting state arbitrariness. At first sight it may seem that the requirement of sureness is incompatible with the argumentative character of law. MacCormick clearly explains why this is not so:

> Many people, and certainly I for one, find attractive both thesis and antithesis as stated above. I do believe in the argumentative quality of law, and find it admirable in an open society. We should look at every side of every important question, not come down at once on the side of prejudice or apparent certainty. We must listen to every argument, and celebrate, not deplore, the arguable quality that seems built in to law. But I also believe in the rule of law, and think that our life as humans in community with others is greatly enriched by it. Without it, there is no prospect of realising the dignity of human beings as independent though interdependent participants in public and private activities in a society. Dignity of that sort and independence-in-interdependence are, to my way of thinking, fundamental moral and human values. How is it possible to believe in both? Can this be anything other than wishful believing? These are the questions that lie before us. Can we reconcile the commonplace of the 'Arguable Character of Law' with the ideology of the 'Rule of Law'?[38]

However, this apparent contradiction disappears when it is realized that the argumentative nature of law is controllable by means of the processes of determination, legitimization, argumentation and justification mentioned earlier. And the argumentativeness of these processes depends on conditions of *rationality* as well as *coherence. Rationality* is assured by rational rules of argumentation, including the necessity of justification and universalization. Thus no assertion can be made without the addition of an argument.[39] This justification in turn depends on its capacity for universality: Every time a certain fact occurs, a certain consequence is to be applied, and the same happens in every case with the same characteristics. *Coherence* is assured by referring decisions to a set of principles and rules that is internally consistent in form and substance, especially owing to the substantive support furnished by fundamental principles.[40] This avoids the need for a fresh start from scratch in each new case, as well as making arbitrary and *ad hoc* decisions less likely. If rules regarding determination, legitimation, argumentation and justification are added to these rules of argumentative rationality and substantive coherence, the level of control becomes quite high. With these precautions, the argumentative character of law can be made compatible with the requirements of knowability and calculability of law that derive from the legal certainty principle.

[38]Neil MacCormick, "Rhetoric and Rule of Law", in David Dyzenhaus (Org.), *Recrafting the Rule of Law – The Limits of Legal Order,* Oxford, Hart, 1999, pages 165–166.

[39]Robert Alexy, *Theorie der juristischen Argumentation*, Frankfurt am Main, Suhrkamp, 1983, pages 261 and following. Neil. MacCormick, *Legal Reasoning and Legal Theory*, Oxford, Clarendon, 1995, pages 272–274.

[40]Neil MacCormick, "Rhetoric and Rule of Law", in David Dyzenhaus (Org.), *Recrafting the Rule of Law – The Limits of Legal Order*, Oxford, Hart, 1999, pages 166, 169.

What must not be done – and here we reach the crucial point of the discussion – is to ignore, in the name of legal certainty, the fact that the duty of determining the legal incidence hypotheses, even if terms already exist from previous connotation processes, cannot totally neutralize the several problems inherent in its concrete application, as MacCormick demonstrates.[41]

First, problems of *proof*: A tax liability arises when a taxable event occurs, but in order to be "deemed to have occurred," the event's occurrence must be proven in accordance with article 142 of the National Tax Code. For example, the duty to pay tax on services arises only if it is proven that services have been rendered.

Second, problems of *qualification*: That which is deemed to have occurred has to be "characterized" or "qualified" from a legal viewpoint. Using the same example, it is necessary to know whether the human activity deemed to have occurred can be qualified as a service for the purpose of being taxed as a service.

Third, problems of *interpretation*: The qualification of facts that have provenly occurred depends on prior conceptual determination, without which they cannot be legally defined. Thus in order to qualify an activity as a service, the meaning of "rendering services" has to be defined from a normative standpoint, and "what occurred" has to be defined from a factual standpoint. In order to know whether a leasing operation creates an obligation to pay tax on services, the meanings of both leasing and service have to be defined.

Fourth, problems of *relevance*: Among many factual elements, some will have to be assigned a level of importance to the detriment of others in order to reach a legal description of what has occurred. To know whether leasing is a service, greater or smaller importance will have to be assigned to elements such as the constitution of a financial fund, credit analysis, the drafting of a contract, signature of a contract, delivery of a vehicle, use of the vehicle, monthly payment for use of the vehicle, and the existence of a purchase option, among others. The relevance assigned to each of these elements will not only indicate the existence of "services rendered" but also show where they were rendered.

All these issues demonstrate that although the incidence hypothesis may be stated in words whose meanings have a high level of determinacy (they are clear for the easy cases, which are greater in number), such determinacy still does not assure absolute predictability regarding the effects that will be assigned to acts that may be performed by taxpayers because such acts have to be proven, qualified, interpreted and considered in a due legal process. Moreover, interpretation also depends on adaptations to previous interpretations, just as it often requires connections between several fragments of provisions.[42] Among other things, this means that the impossibility of absolute predictability results not from the ambiguity and vagueness inherent in language, as is normally argued, but above all from the problems of proof, qualification, interpretation and relevance inherent in the very

[41] Neil MacCormick, "Rhetoric and Rule of Law", in David Dyzenhaus (Org.), *Recrafting the Rule of Law – The Limits of Legal Order*, Oxford, Hart, 1999, p. 175.

[42] Andrei Marmor, *Interpretation and Legal Theory*, Clarendon, Oxford, 1992, p. 126.

application of law. The initial syllogistic alternatives ($X = A$, B or C) provide only a "putative certainty" to be confirmed by a decision through a long process of argumentation and proof, as described by MacCormick.[43] This decision – and this is the point – must not only fall within the few basically similar initial alternatives, but also undergo careful rational and argumentative control, as well as later justification. It is for no other reason that Günther states:

> The certainty of expectation of participants in institutionalized application discourses should be shifted from legal certainty, which is assured through stable meanings and paradigms, to procedural certainty, which is assured through a dense network of procedural rights.[44]

These considerations show that arbitrariness is not avoided merely by requiring determination of the operative facts or legal hypothesis. If the application of this hypothesis cannot be argumentatively questioned, then there is arbitrariness, paradoxical though this may seem. It is an illusion to think there is no arbitrariness whenever a given fact engenders a consequence if there is no possibility of argumentative questioning of the definition of the "fact" and the proof of its occurrence, as well as the definition of the "consequence" and the delimitation of its extent. However, this leads to the conclusion that the argumentative quality of law is not against legal certainty but one of its premises: If the occurrence of a taxable event and its normative consequence cannot be questioned through rational (universal and coherent) argumentation, the result is arbitrariness, given the impossibility of disputing that which is ontologically inherent in law – proof, qualification, interpretation and relevance. It bears repeating therefore that the argumentative character of law is not a barrier but a prerequisite of legal certainty. MacCormick defines this point accurately, using the example of an accusation to stress the argumentative challenges inherent in problems of proof, characterization, interpretation and relevance: "There is no security against arbitrary government unless such challenges are freely permitted, and subjected to adjudication by officers of state separate from and distanced from those officers who run prosecutions."[45] Thus arbitrariness is not a result of the argumentative character of law but arises when this character is denied, as if it did not exist. Contradictory as it may seem, this means there would be arbitrariness if tax obligations resulted from the occurrence of taxable events without taxpayers being able to question the "occurrence" of such "taxable events" argumentatively through due process of law. This is also why the belief that legal certainty is achieved by determining legal

[43]Neil MacCormick, "Rhetoric and Rule of Law", in David Dyzenhaus (Org.), *Recrafting the Rule of Law – The Limits of Legal Order*, Oxford, Hart, 1999, p. 175.

[44]Klaus Günther, "Universalistische Normbegründung und Normanwendung in Recht und Moral", in *Generalisierung und Individualisierung im Rechtsdenken, ARSP* n. 45, p. 75, Stuttgart, Franz Steiner, 1992. On this subject, see: Tobias Lieber, *Diskursive Vernunft und formelle Gleichheit*, Tübingen, Mohr Siebeck, 2007, p. 318.

[45]Neil MacCormick, "Rhetoric and Rule of Law", in David Dyzenhaus (Org.), *Recrafting the Rule of Law – The Limits of Legal Order*, Oxford, Hart, 1999, p. 176.

incidence hypotheses is "ingenuous" according to Torres.[46] It must be insisted that conceptual determination is still important, since argumentative processes precede the interpretation and application of some provisions whose usage has already conceptually determined the terms used by lawmakers. However, to continue placing the foundations of legal certainty – exclusively, it bears repeating – on the requirement of conceptual determination despite the argumentative character of law and as if it were pathological, is to build it on clear and determinate feet… of clay. To switch metaphors, it is to let a plastic balloon shoot down … an airplane.

It should also be mentioned that the idea that any degree of indeterminacy causes arbitrariness assumes that indeterminacy not only is contrary to legal certainty but also necessarily involves arbitrariness by leaving room for subjectivity, inconsistency and uncertainty. However, this assumption must be revisited. If language is always vague to a certain extent, then law, which is expressed through language, is also necessarily vague. However, and this is the point at issue, precision is not necessarily good, nor does precise formulation always make law precise as well. Precision can have negative effects, if for example, instead of inserting the phrase "within a reasonable time" for information to be filed or a procedure to be completed, lawmakers specify a precise period whose application may be unreasonable when the amount of information required or the situation is abnormal, so that an increase in precision may paradoxically increase arbitrariness, in the sense of irrationality. Furthermore, the precise formulation of a rule does not lead to sureness of law when it is applied flexibly, so that an increase in precision does not necessarily lead to an increase in uniformity of treatment.[47] Thus if law is necessarily vague, the ideal of certainty as the absence of vagueness is unattainable. This conclusion will be different, however, if instead of complete bindingness, consistency and predictability to guide behavior in each and every situation, the legal certainty principle simply advocates the rational and reasonable application of law.[48]

It bears repeating that these remarks should not be taken to dispense with a high degree of determinacy for normative hypotheses, notably those regarding the main tax obligations when there are terms whose meaning has already been determined by previous processes of conceptual delimitation. What is meant by this is that realization of the legal certainty principle cannot be defended exclusively via the ideal of absolute determinacy because, besides being unattainable, it does not necessarily eliminate arbitrariness in the production and application of law.

In sum, this conception of legal certainty as a *guarantee of respect* founded on the paradigm of semantic-argumentative controllability, and whose realization

---

[46] Ricardo Lobo Torres, "Legalidade tributária e riscos sociais", *Revista Dialética de Direito Tributário*, São Paulo, n. 59, pages 101, 103, 2000. On the subject, see: Ricardo Lodi Ribeiro, *A segurança jurídica do contribuinte*, Rio de Janeiro, Lumen Juris, 2008, pages 31 and following.

[47] Timoty A. O. Endicott, "Law is necessarily vague", *Legal Theory* n. 7, pages 379–380, 2001.

[48] Idem, "The Impossibility of the Rule of Law", *Oxford Journal of Legal Studies*, v. 19, n. 1, pages 4, 19, 1999. Idem, *Vagueness in Law*, Oxford, OUP, 2003, pages 183 and following.

depends on elements, dimensions and aspects to be assessed in aggregate assumes observation of the following factors:

- Whether the Constitution establishes infraconstitutional preconstitutional concepts, or presupposes them by incorporation, by virtue of previous processes of conceptual determination, in which case legislative and administrative activity must take them into account; conceptual reconstruction, which is supposed to act as a foundation for the external justification of legal reasoning, must prioritize the linguistic, systematic, genetic, historical and pragmatic arguments most strongly supported by the principles of the rule of law and legal certainty, which implies the prevalence of linguistic and systematic arguments, always ultimately supported by the substantive coherence of the arguments.
- Whether in the situation being normatized there are terms that have already been connoted and whose utilization is appropriate to its regulation; expressions whose meaning is relatively indeterminate must be used only in cases where, first of all, there are no conceptual presuppositions in the Constitution and, second, there is no legal use of terms that have undergone previous argumentative processes of determination, and even so only provided their use is necessary and proportional, in which case, however, the reasonableness of administrative concretization must be more rigorously controlled.
- Whether the normative concretization performed by any of the three branches of government has considered and assessed counter-arguments presented by the taxpayers, and whether the problems of proof, qualification, interpretation and relevance have been properly addressed. This presupposes both an authentic rational justification, i.e. one that preserves universalization and coherence in argumentation and is therefore capable of indicating the elements to be assessed and the intersubjectively controllable criteria necessary for their assessment, and a due legal process that assures transparency, which occurs when there is impartiality, publicity, a full and fair hearing of all parties, and justification.
- Whether all previous processes were justified in clear, logically connected and highly informative language in the assessment of the addressees.

In sum, the legal certainty principle entails processes of determination, legitimation, argumentation and justification that assure the semantic-argumentative controllability of state action, on one hand, and the respectability of taxpayers' law-based actions on the other, as well as reflexively grounding the argumentation referring to such actions. Indeed, the requirement of argumentative transparency makes application of the law visible. The legal certainty principle, as stressed by Ferraz Júnior in a discussion of the decisional process, requires "predictable development of decisional activity."[49] Here it is useful to recall an elucidatory

---

[49] Tércio Sampaio Ferraz Júnior, "Segurança jurídica, coisa julgada e justiça", *Revista do Instituto de Hermenêutica Jurídica*, Porto Alegre, v. 1, n. 3, p. 271, 2005.

remark by Smith: "Justice must not only be done. It must also be seen to be done."[50] Along similar lines one could say that the legal certainty principle, in this sense of respect not only for the action but for the pertinent argumentation, requires not only respectability, but also *transparency of respectability* for the taxpayer. From this angle, it is possible to speak of discoursive objectivity in dealing with principles so as to guarantee the intelligibility of disagreements in intersubjective discourse, as stressed by Marmor.[51]

References

AARNIO, Aulis. *The rational as reasonable*. Dordrecht, Reidel: 1987.

ALEXY, Robert. *Theorie der juristischen Argumentation*. Frankfurt am Main: Suhrkamp, 1983.

ARCOS RAM´iREZ, Federico. *La seguridad jurídica: una teoría formal*. Madrid: Dykinson, 2000.

von ARNAULD, Andreas. *Rechtssicherheit*. Tübingen: Mohr Siebeck, 2006.

BERTEA, Stefano. *Certezza del Diritto e argomentazione giuridica*. Soveria Manelli: Rubbertino, 2002.

BORGES, José Souto Maior. *Curso de Direito Comunitário*, São Paulo: Saraiva, 2005.

BRÖHMER, Jürgen. *Transparenz als Verfassungsprinzip*. Tübingen: Mohr Siebeck, 2004.

CALMES, Sylvia. *Du principe de protection de la confiance légitime en Droits Allemand, Communautaire et Français*. Paris: Dalloz, 2001.

CARRAZZA, Roque Antonio. *Curso de Direito Constitucional Tributário*. 27th ed. São Paulo: Malheiros Editores, 2011.

DENNINGER, Erhard. "Rechtsstaat oder Rule of Law – was is das heute?". In: PRITTWITZ, Cornelius. *et alii* (Orgs.). *FS für Klaus Lüderssen*. Baden-Baden: Nomos, 2002.

DERZI, Misabel de Abreu Machado Derzi, *Modificações da jurisprudência no Direito Tributário*. São Paulo: Noeses, 2009.

______. "Mutações jurisprudenciais, em face da proteção da confiança e do interesse público no planejamento da receita e da despesa do Estado". In: FERRAZ, Roberto (Org.). *Princípios e limites da tributação 2 – Os princípios da ordem econômica e a tributação*. São Paulo: Quartier Latin, 2009.

DWORKIN, Ronald. *Law's Empire*. Cambridge: Belknap, 1986.

ENDICOTT, Timoty A. O. "Law is necessarily vague". *Legal Theory* n. 7, s.d.

______. "The Impossibility of the Rule of Law", *Oxford Journal of Legal Studies*, v. 19, n. 1, 1999.

______. *Vagueness in Law*. Oxford: OUP, 2003.

FERRAZ JR., Tércio Sampaio. "Segurança jurídica, coisa julgada e justiça", *Revista do Instituto de Hermenêutica Jurídica*, v. 1, n. 3, Porto Alegre, 2005.

GOMETZ, Gianmarco. *La certezza giuridica come prevedibilità*. Torino: Giappichelli, 2005.

GRAU, Eros Roberto. *Ensaio e discurso sobre a interpretação/aplicação do Direito*. 4th ed. São Paulo: Malheiros Editores, 2006.

GÜNTHER, Klaus. "Universalistische Normbegründung und Normanwendung in Recht und Moral". In: *Generalisierung und Individualisierung im Rechtsdenken, ARSP* n. 45, Stuttgart: Franz Steiner, 1992.

[50] Eivind Smith, "Constitution et sécurité juridique – Norvège", *Annuaire International de Justice Constitutionnelle, 1999*, Paris, Economica, p. 234.

[51] Andrei Marmor, "An Essay on the Objectivity of Law", in Brian Bix (Org.), *Analysing Law. – New Essays in Legal Theory*, Oxford, Clarendon, 1998, p. 31.

HABERMAS, Jürgen. *Faktizität und Geltung*. Darmstadt: Wissenschaftliche Buchgesellschaft, 2002.

HEY, Johanna. *Steuerplanungssicherheit als Rechtsproblem*. Köln: Otto Schmidt, 2002.

KAUFMANN, Arthur. "Die ontologische Struktur des Rechts". In: *Die ontologische Begründung des Rechts*. Darmstadt: Wissenschaftliche Buchgesellschaft, 1965.

LIEBER, Tobias. *Diskursive Vernunft und formelle Gleichheit*. Tübingen: Mohr Siebeck, 2007

LIMBACH, Jutta. *Ist die kollektive Sicherheit der Feind der individuellen Freiheit?*. Köln: Carl Heymanns, 2002.

LUHMANN, Niklas. *Ausdifferenzierung des Rechts – Beiträge zur Rechtssoziologie und Rechtstheorie*. Frankfurt am Main: Suhrkamp, 1999.

MacCORMICK, Neil. *Legal reasoning and legal theory*. Oxford: Clarendon, 1978.

______. "Rhetoric and rule of law". In: DYZENHAUS, David (Org.). *Recrafting the rule of Law – The Limits of Legal Order*. Oxford: Hart, 1999.

MAFFINI, Rafael. *O princípio da proteção substancial da confiança no Direito Administrativo brasileiro*. Porto Alegre: Verbo Jurídico, 2007.

MARMOR, Andrei. *Interpretation and Legal Theory*. Clarendon: Oxford, 1992.

______. "An essay on the objectivity of law". In: BIX, Brian (Org.). *Analyzing Law – New Essays in Legal Theory*. Oxford: Clarendon, 1998.

MATHIEU, Bertrand Mathieu, "Constitution et sécurité juridique - France". In *Annuaire International de Justice Constitutionnelle, 1999*, Paris, Economica, 2000.

NEVES, Marcelo. *Entre Têmis e Leviatã: uma relação difícil – O Estado Democrático de Direito a partir e além de Luhmann e Habermas*. São Paulo: Martins Fontes, 2006.

NOVOA, César García. *El principio de seguridad jurídica en materia tributaria*. Madrid: Marcial Pons, 2000.

OST, François. *Le temps du Droit*. Paris: Odile Jacob, 1999.

______. "Conclusions générales: le temps, la justice et le droit". In: GABORIAU, Simone; PAULIAT, Hélène (Orgs.). *Le Temps, la Justice et le Droit*. Limoges: Pulim, 2003.

PALOMBELLA, Gianluigi. *Dopo la Certezza – Il Diritto in equilibrio tra Giustizia e Democrazia*. Bari: Dedalo, 2006.

RIBEIRO, Ricardo Lodi. *A segurança jurídica do contribuinte*. Rio de Janeiro: Lumen Juris, 2008.

SEILLER, Bertrand. "Le procès de la rétroactivité". In: Idem. *La rétroactivité des décisions du juge administratif*, Paris, Economica, 2007.

SMITH, Eivind. "Constitution et sécurité juridique – Norvège". *Annuaire International de Justice Constitutionnelle, 1999*, Paris, Economica.

SOBOTA, Katharina. *Das Prinzip Rechtsstaat*. Tübingen: Mohr Siebeck, 1997.

TORRES, Ricardo Lobo Torres. "Legalidade tributária e riscos sociais", *Revista Dialética de Direito Tributário*, São Paulo, n. 59.

______. "Valores e princípios constitucionais tributários". In: *Tratado de Direito Constitucional Financeiro e Tributário*, v. 2. Rio de Janeiro: Renovar, 2005.

VALEMBOIS, Anne-Laure. *La constitutionnalisation de l'exigence de sécurité juridique en Droit Français*. Paris: LGDJ, 2005.

The Concept of Tax-Law Certainty

Abstract The concept of legal certainty defined in the previous chapter is now applied to taxation. The concept of legal certainty in tax law does not differ from the general concept of legal certainty but emphasizes the mostly protective character that certainty has within this normative field owing to the existence of tax norms that establish a defensive perspective toward the individual's constitutional rights, albeit in balance with moderate interference by the state in exercising its power to tax.

The concept of legal certainty applies equally to tax law.[1] There are not two principles of legal certainty, one general and one for tax. The legal certainty principle applies to the legal sector as whole. Nevertheless, there are subtle differences due to the way legal certainty is positivated by the Constitution in the sphere of tax law and to the very nature of the tax obligation relationship. These nuances give a *special* character to the principle of tax law certainty.

First, as stressed in the earlier discussion concerning the foundations of legal certainty, the states of knowability, reliability and calculability not only are particularly relevant in the tax subsystem but also have a *more protective* meaning. This is because there are specific and emphatic norms in the National Tax System that serve as instruments to assure the intelligibility of law through the determinability of incidence hypotheses (the legality rule and the system of competence rules); the reliability of law through stability over time (the rule restricting the use of supplementary laws to prescription and limitation), periods of validity (the rule prohibiting retroactivity), and procedure (rules that expressly apply rights and guarantees not in the tax subsystem, such as the protection for acquired rights, completed legal acts and res iudicata); and the calculability of law through non-surprise (the anteriority rule). These specific rules endow the ideals whose realization is determined by the legal certainty principle with an *aspect of resistance* or *protection*. As a result they give it what could be called *qualified content*.[2] Moreover, they delimit the "possible

[1] César García Novoa, *El principio de seguridad jurídica en materia tributaria*, Madrid, Marcial Pons, 2000, pages 91 and 104.

[2] Leandro Paulsen, *Segurança jurídica, certeza do direito e tributação*, Porto Alegre, Livraria do Advogado, 2006, p. 74.

© Springer International Publishing Switzerland 2016

H. Ávila, *Certainty in Law*, Law and Philosophy Library 114,
DOI 10.1007/978-3-319-33407-3_7

content" of laws, to quote Carrazza's nicely turned phrase.[3] It bears repeating that tax law is usually a right of legal certainty. Above all its purpose is "to limit state power", as well stressed by Machado.[4]

The fact that the tax law certainty principle protects the interests of taxpayers does not mean it should not be treated in its concrete reflexive aspect. It is important not to confuse an "objective principle that protects citizens" with "concrete protection of citizens based on an objective principle." The subjective orientation of an objective principle is one thing; the subjective dimension as a reflexive and concrete application of an objective principle is quite another. In this respect, assigning a protective character to the tax law certainty principle is intended only to demonstrate that the ideal states whose realization it determines are protectively oriented, which changes its efficacy, as will be seen later.

Second, this protective effect gives special significance to the states whose realization is determined by the legal certainty principle when external conflicts need to be addressed. In other words, should tax law certainty conflict with another principle, the former's abstract preponderance means that the prevalence of the other principle depends on a differentiated argumentative burden, as discussed below in the part on the efficacy of the legal certainty principle.

Third, the juridical goods restricted by concretization of the tax obligation relationship, usually in respect of freedom, property and equality, have an even more prominent claim to protection when the restriction of fundamental rights intensifies.[5] As Asorey notes, "if tax law is a constitutionally expressed form of exaction law, it follows that the fundamental character of the legal certainty principle makes it especially important in the field of taxation."[6] Thus, as shown throughout this book, even greater weight should be given to the protective character of the legal certainty principle depending on the *object*, *intensity* and *purpose* of the limitations placed on fundamental rights. This is the case, for example, when taxation has a non-fiscal purpose: If taxpayers end up performing an activity because of the guidance provided by the state, although they should expect future change and there are therefore reasons for their trust not to be legitimate, the trust they exercise ought to be protected. This example – to which others will be added – only shows that tax norms require special treatment because of the many purposes they may serve and the many different effects they may have.

What should be made clear is that the legal certainty principle must be all the more protected because it is also grounded in fundamental rights and taxation

[3]Roque Antonio Carrazza, *Curso de Direito Constitucional Tributário*, 27th ed., São Paulo, Malheiros Editores, 2011, p. 448.

[4]Hugo de Brito Machado, *Curso de Direito Tributário*, 30th ed., São Paulo, Malheiros Editores, 2009, p. 6.

[5]Herbert Wiedemann, "Rechtssicherheit – ein absoluter Wert? Gedanken zum Bestimmtheitserfordernis zivilrechtlicher Tatbestände", in Gotthard Paulus *et alii* (Orgs.), *FS für Karl Larenz*, München, Beck, 1973, p. 212.

[6]Rubén Asorey, "Seguridad jurídica y Derecho Tributario", *RDT* 52, p. 36, São Paulo, 1990.

restricts these rights to a greater or lesser extent, depending on the fundamental right and the intensity with which it is restricted. In some situations, personal income tax may restrict the fundamental right to raise a family, given the lack of relief for taxpayers with children or of deduction for education costs. In other situations, corporate income tax may restrict the fundamental right to property, by affecting not the results but the basis of a business, or by overlooking prior investment for lack of transitional rules. In yet other situations, it may restrict the fundamental right to a craft, trade or profession and the freedom to exercise such activities by affecting a specific profession without any justification for discrimination – and so on.[7] These considerations only show that the financially onerous nature of tax law affects fundamental rights relating to dignity, family, freedom, property and equality, so that special protection by the legal certainty principle is required. And this is particularly so because these fundamental rights cannot be minimally effective without normative reliability and calculability.

The concept of tax law certainty, therefore, can be defined as a principle norm that requires the legislative, executive and judiciary to behave in ways that contribute more to the existence of a higher state of legal calculability and reliability based on complete knowability, from the perspective of taxpayers and for their benefit, through the juridico-rational controllability of argumentative structures that reconstruct general and individual norms, as an instrument that guarantees respect for their capacity to shape the present in a worthy and responsible manner and to plan the future strategically in a legally informed manner, without deceit, frustration, surprise or arbitrariness.

It must be stressed yet again that this concept evidences on one hand that in the field of tax law the legal certainty principle is no different in the formal structure of its elements and dimensions; and on the other hand that it is indeed different in its foundations and efficacy, because of the different norms applicable to the sector and because of the specific purpose and effects these norms may have. In the field of tax law, the exercise of private autonomy is not an issue as it is in private law, where subjects create limitations on themselves, and the states of knowability, reliability and calculability relate to *self-restriction* of property and freedom. In the tax law sphere, in contrast, individuals are subject to *heterorestrictions* on their fundamental rights imposed for various different purposes, and the object of knowledge, trust and calculation changes as a result. If the legal certainty principle requires *state respect* for the private exercise of freedom, as discussed in detail below, the content and efficacy of that principle will be different when the exercise of freedom is also subject to certain differences, as it is in the case of tax law.

Having qualified legal certainty as a *guarantee of respect* founded on the paradigm of semantic-argumentative control and whose realization depends on elements, dimensions and aspects to be assessed together, we must now examine these elements, dimensions and aspects with precision as they apply in the sphere of tax law.

This is the focus for what follows.

[7]Paul Kirchhof, "Rückwirkung von Steuergesetzen", *StuW*, 2000, pages 229–231.

References

ASOREY, Rubén. "Seguridad jurídica y Derecho Tributario", *RDT* 52, São Paulo, 1990.

CARRAZZA, Roque Antonio. *Curso de Direito Constitucional Tributário.* 27th ed. São Paulo: Malheiros Editores, 2011.

KIRCHHOF, Paul. "Rückwirkung von Steuergesetzen", *StuW*, 2000.

MACHADO, Hugo de Brito. *Curso de Direito Tributário.* 30th ed. São Paulo: Malheiros Editores, 2009.

NOVOA, César García. *El principio de seguridad jurídica en materia tributaria.* Madrid: Marcial Pons, 2000.

PAULSEN, Leandro. *Segurança jurídica, certeza do direito e tributação.* Porto Alegre: Livraria do Advogado, 2006.

WIEDEMANN, Herbert. "Rechtssicherheit – ein absoluter Wert? Gedanken zum Bestimmtheitserfordernis zivilrechtlicher Tatbestände". In: PAULUS, Gotthard. *et alii* (Orgs.). *FS für Karl Larenz.* München: Beck, 1973.

Part IV
Content of Legal Certainty

How can one believe in people who do not know what they want, constantly change their own creations, have no trust in themselves, offer not the remotest certainty that anything whatever still absolutely exists at any moment? But from those in whom I place no trust, in whom I do not believe, I ask nothing, I rely on them for nothing, I do nothing for them. (Robert von Mohl, "Staatsrecht", in *Völkerrecht, Politik*, v. 1, Tübingen, 1860)

The need for behavior to be predictable and valued is the reason why the law does not think particular and present things, but general and future things, according to Aristotle's ingenious intuition. In doing so, the law makes continuity possible, so that present action is linked to future action, which connects men to one another. (Piero Calamandrei, "La certezza del diritto e le responsabilità della dottrina", *Rivista di Diritto Commerciale* 1, p. 341, 1942)

The Content of Legal Certainty (or What Does the Legal Certainty Principle Presuppose and Require?)

. . . where this essential value of legal certainty has disappeared, no other value can subsist. (Paul Roubier, *Théorie Générale du Droit*, 2nd ed., Paris, Sirey, 1951, p. 334)

Because in the first sense [*as value*], the ability to predict legal decisions (and the disappointment following a prediction proven wrong) would be as beautiful as the ability to predict the beginning and end of a war, the ups and downs of exchange rates, the progress of production, tomorrow's weather, or the winning number in a lottery. (Letizia Gianformaggio, "Certezza del Diritto", in Enrico Diciotti & Vito Velluzzi (eds.), *Filosofia del Diritto e ragionamento giuridico*, Torino, Giappichelli, 2008, p. 85 (orig. *Studi sulla giustificazione giuridica,* Torino, Giappichelli, 1986, pages 157–169)

What men call stability is not immobility, but the slow and uniform movement of everything that allows the subsistence of some general form of the things to which they are accustomed. (Maurice Hauriou, *Précis de Droit Constitutionnel*, Paris, Sirey, 1929, p. 6)

The notion of legal certainty is so broad that we can make it say whatever we want. (S. Boissard, "Comment garantir la stabilité des situations juridiques sans priver l'autorité administrative de tous moyens d'action et sans transiger sur le respect du principe de legalité? Le difficile dilemme du juge administratif", *Les Cahiers du Conseil Constitutionnel* 11, p. 70, 2001)

Legal certainty in the several aspects examined so far can be better understood if analyzed in two dimensions: a static dimension, which consists of examining the content of law; and a dynamic dimension focusing on the investigation of the force of law, along the lines proposed by Mathieu and Valembois, albeit with different content.[1] Most authors do not differentiate between these dimensions; some even confuse "dimensions" with "parts." Others follow a similar orientation to the one adopted here but do not always include the same elements in each dimension and, while also conceptually separating the static and dynamic dimensions of legal certainty and time in law, do so differently and from vantage points that are not always comparable, speaking for example of dimensions that are static and pragmatic (Carvalho), relating to orientation and realization (Geiger, Novoa) or to source, application and interpretation (Mesquita del Cacho), structural and functional (Perez Luño), qualitative and temporal (Mathieu, Calmes, Zimmer), synchronic or structural and diachronic or historical (Jackson), synchronic and diachronic (Della Valle), intrinsic and extrinsic or referential (Azoulai), formal and substantial (Aarnio, Peczenick, Reis), objective and subjective.[2]

---

[1]Anne-Laure Valembois, *La constitutionnalisation de l'exigence de sécurité juridique en Droit Français*, Paris, LGDJ, 2005, pages 13 and 16; Bertrand Mathieu, "Constitution et sécurité juridique – France", *Annuaire International de Justice Constitutionnelle*, Paris, Economica, 1999, p. 157.

[2]Paulo de Barros Carvalho, "Segurança jurídica e modulação dos efeitos", *Revista da Fundação Escola Superior de Direito Tributário* 1, p. 206, Porto Alegre, 2008; Theodor Geiger, *Vorstudien zu einer Soziologie des Rechts*, 4th ed., Berlin, Duncker und Humblot, 1987, pages 64–65; César García Novoa, *El principio de seguridad jurídica en materia tributaria*, Madrid, Marcial Pons, 2000, p. 81; José L. Mezquita del Cacho, *Seguridad jurídica y sistema cautelar*, v. 1, *Teoría de la seguridad jurídica*, Barcelona, Bosch, 1989, pages 87 and following; A. Perez Luño, *La seguridad jurídica*, Barcelona, Ariel, 1991, pages 22 and following; Bertrand Mathieu, "Constitution et sécurité juridique – France", *Annuaire International de Justice Constitutionnelle 1999*, Paris, Economica, 2000, p. 157; Sylvia Calmes, *Du principe de protection de la confiance légitime en Droits Allemand, Communautaire et Français*, Paris, Dalloz, 2001, p. 158; Willy Zimmer, "Constitution et sécurité juridique – Allemagne", *Annuaire International de Justice Constitutionnelle 1999*, Paris, Economica, 2000, p. 94; Bernard Jackson, "On the atemporality of legal time", in François Ost e Mark van Hoecke (Orgs.), *Temps et Droit. Le Droit a-t-il pour vocation de durer?*, Bruxelles, Bruylant, 1998, p. 225; Eugenio Della Valle, *Affidamento e certezza del Diritto Tributario*, Milano, Giuffrè, 2001, p. 1; Loïc Azoulai, "La valeur normative de la sécurité juridique", in Laurence Boy, Jean-Baptiste Racine e Fabrice Siiriainen (Orgs.), *Sécurité juridique et Droit Économique*, Bruxelles, Larcier, 2008, p. 26; Aulis Aarnio, *Reason and authority*, Dartmouth, Ashgate, 1997, pages 189–193; idem, *The rational as reasonable*, Dordrecht, Reidel, 1987, pages 189–193; idem, *The Rational as Reasonable*, Dordrecht, Reidel, 1987, pages 3–8, 44; Aleksander Peczenick, *On Law and reason*, Dordrecht, Kluwer, 1989, p. 31; Patrice Reis, "Les méthodes d'interprétation, analyse formelle, analyse substancielle et sécurité juridique", in Laurence Boy, Jean-Baptiste Racine e Fabrice Siiriainen (Orgs.), *Sécurité juridique*

So let us see. The *static* dimension concerns the *problem of knowledge* of law, or the *problem of communication* in law, and reveals what *qualities* it must have in order to be considered "certain" and hence serve as a *guide* to citizens in general and taxpayers in particular. In this respect, law must be understandable and effective.[3]

Understandable in the sense that citizens can know the laws substantively and intellectually. If the laws are to be obeyed, they must be able to guide the behavior of their subjects and this is possible only if the latter know what it means and act based on such knowledge.[4] Knowability in this sense exists only if the laws are accessible and intelligible, and if what is understood is then *put into effect*.[5]

Thus the *static* dimension concerns certainty "of law" (*Rechtssicherheit*) more than certainty "through law" (*Rechtssicherung*). It therefore deals with the qualities law must have for citizens to consider it certain, i.e. "*seguro*", which in this context means the same as the Latin term *certus*.[6] And with regard to laws and other norms legal certainty means "certainty of validity" (*certezza della sua vigenza*), "certainty of sufficiency" (*certezza della sua sufficienza*) and "certainty of meaning" (*certezza del suo significato*), so as to assure the validity, clarity and content of the norms to be obeyed.[7] It is therefore a sort of certainty for the individual both before law and obtained through law itself, to quote Arcos Ramirez.[8]

The *dynamic* dimension, in turn, concerns the *problem of action* over time and prescribes which ideals must be assured if law is to "guarantee" citizens' rights and thus serve them as an *instrument of protection*. In this sense, law must be reliable and calculable.

Reliable in the sense of enabling citizens to know *which* changes can be made and which cannot, thus preventing *frustration* of their rights. This reliability exists only if citizens see that the effects guaranteed by law yesterday are assured today,

---

et Droit Économique, Bruxelles, Larcier, 2008, p. 193; Lémy Duong, "La sécurité juridique et les standards du Droit Économique: la notion de raisonnable", in *Sécurité juridique et Droit Économique*, cit., p. 9; Rubén Asorey, "Seguridad jurídica y Derecho Tributário", *RDT*, n. 52, p. 34, São Paulo, 1990.

[3]Max Rümelin, *Die Rechtssicherheit*, Tübingen, Mohr Siebeck, 1924, p. 9; A. Perez Luño, *La Seguridad Jurídica*, Barcelona, Ariel, 1991, p. 106; Federico Arcos Ramírez, *La seguridad jurídica: una teoría formal*, Madrid, Dykinson, 2000, p. 38; Frédéric Douet, *Contribution à l'étude de la sécurité juridique en Droit Interne Français*, Paris, LGDJ, 1997, p. 2; Sylvia Calmes, *Du principe de protection de la confiance légitime en Droits Allemand, Communautaire et Français*, Paris, Dalloz, 2001, p. 158; Andreas von Arnauld, *Rechtssicherheit*, Tübingen, Mohr Siebeck, 2006, p. 167.

[4]Joseph Raz, "The rule of law and its virtue (1977)", in *The authority of Law. Essays on Law and Morality*, Oxford, Oxford, 1979, p. 214.

[5]Anne-Laure Valembois, *La constitutionnalisation de l'exigence de sécurité juridique en Droit Français*, Paris, LGDJ, 2005, p. 16.

[6]Theodor Geiger, *Vorstudien zu einer Soziologie des Rechts*, 4th ed., Berlin, Duncker und Humblot, 1987, p. 64.

[7]Guido Alpa, *La certezza del Diritto nell'età dell'incertezza*, Napoli, Scientifica, 2006, p. 37.

[8]Federico Arcos Ramírez, *La seguridad jurídica: una teoría formal*, Madrid, Dykinson, 2000, p. 16.

i.e. if they can "presentify the past," make the past certain in the present. In other words, there must be "certainty of the past", or more exactly, without the ellipsis, there must be stability of the legal effects assigned by law to acts performed in the past. As I will show, this depends on the existence of a state of intangibility of past situations, durability of the legal order and irretroactivity of present norms.

Calculable in the sense of enabling citizens to know *how* changes can be made and *when* they will be effected, so they are not *surprised*. This calculability exists only if citizens can control today the effects law will assign tomorrow, i.e. if they can "presentify the future" (*Zukunft vergegenwärtigen*), make the future certain in the present so as to increase their possibilities for action.[9] In other words, there must be "certainty of the future", or more rigorously, without the ellipsis, there must be calculability of the future legal effects of present acts. This consideration justifies Kaufmann's statement that the future is the "dimension of freedom": People can be considered "free" only when they have a "future," which in turn is the case only when they can strategically "see" what is to come even if they cannot act on this vision.[10] For the same reason, Blegvad says "all social order implies a tendency to 'bind' the future."[11] As we will see, this "closing" of the future depends on the existence of a state of normative binding and continuity. Without it, men's actions have no sense, prompting Pessoa's melancholy thoughts: "I always live in the present. The future I do not know. The past I no longer have. The one weighs on me as the possibility of everything, the other as the reality of nothing. I have neither hope nor nostalgia."[12]

The dynamic dimension self-evidently deals with certainty "through law" (*Rechtssicherung*) more than certainty "of law" (*Rechtssicherheit*),. It concerns the conditions that must be met for law to "guarantee" rights and expectations. "Certain" in this context, like "*seguro*", corresponds to the Latin word *securus*, not *certus*.[13] And legal certainty with regard to norms means "certainty of duration" (*certezza della sua durata*), guaranteeing the stability of the norms to be obeyed.[14] This dimension must enable citizens to say, as Rümelin puts it: "My right, in which I have trusted, must remain mine. It must be protected by the community and cannot be arbitrarily taken from me or restricted."[15]

---

[9]Niklas Luhmann, *Vertrauen – Ein Mechanismus der Reduktion sozialer Komplexität*, 4ª ed., Stuttgart, Lucius & Lucius, 2000, p. 15; Francis Delpérée, Rasson-Roldand e Marc Verdussen, "Constitution et sécurité juridique – Belgique", *Annuaire International de Justice Constitutionnelle 1999*, Paris, Economica, 2000, p. 121.

[10]Franz-Xaver Kaufmann, *Sicherheit als soziologisches und sozialpolitisches Problem*, 2ª ed., Stuttgart, 1973, p. 159.

[11]M. Blegvad, "Preface", in J. Bjarup e M. Blegvad (Orgs.), *Time, Law and Society*, *ARSP*, v. 64, Stuttgart, Franz Steiner, 1995, p. 7.

[12]Fernando Pessoa, *Livro do desassossego*, São Paulo, Companhia das Letras, 1997, p. 129.

[13]Theodor Geiger, *Vorstudien zu einer Soziologie des Rechts*, 4th ed., Berlin, Duncker und Humblot, 1987, p. 65.

[14]Guido Alpa, *La certezza del Diritto nell'età dell'incertezza*, Napoli, Scientifica, 2006, p. 37.

[15]Max Rümelin, *Die Rechtssicherheit*, Tübingen, Mohr Siebeck, 1924, p. 1.

In aggregate, the static and dynamic dimensions of the legal certainty principle reveal the ideal states to be sought: knowability, reliability and calculability. These ideals, however, are not located on the same horizontal plane in parallel with one another. Instead, their general relationship is one of means to ends. Thus the ideal of knowability is a precondition for concretizing the ideals of reliability and calculability, in the sense that past law and future law can be assured in the present only if citizens are able to know the laws, their rights and the instruments to realize them, and to force their realization if it does not occur spontaneously. Rümelin is therefore right to argue that the determinacy of law is a "presupposition" of legal certainty.[16] In sum, it is correct to state that the static dimension of the legal certainty principle is a precondition or presupposition of the dynamic dimension: Reliability and calculability cannot exist without knowability, because one cannot rely on respect for, or calculate the permanence of, that which is not known or enforceable.

This relationship of presupposition between the ideals is an internal one of means to ends, as noted earlier. However, it is not always one-way. In some cases, which will be discussed in due course, the relationship of presupposition is reciprocal. Thus, while it is usually correct to state that the knowability of the legal order is a presupposition of its reliability, the reverse may also be true. An example will clarify the argument: For law to be stable it has to be known, because that which is unknown cannot be trusted; however, if law is highly unstable, its addressees can hardly know it to a reasonable extent. It can therefore be said both that knowability of the legal order is a presupposition of its reliability and that its reliability is a condition of its knowability. This *reciprocal relationship* between the elements is also evidenced by an examination of the requirements for the existence of each one. For example, for the legal order to be stable it has to be knowable; to be knowable it must be clear; to be stable it has to respect the citizens' legitimate expectations; however, these expectations will be respected only when there is a reliable basis for trust, which will exist only if this basis is clear and precise. In other words, lack of clarity in the basis for trust prevents its protection.[17] Thus the requirements for applying the elements of each dimension of the legal certainty principle are also interdependent in terms of content: without knowability, no reliability; without reliability, no knowability.

By synthesizing the static and dynamic dimensions of the legal certainty principle, we can show that in aggregate its aim is to assure an ideal state of respect for human beings and protection against deceit, frustration, surprise and arbitrariness. To recall yet again the formulation propounded by Raz, respecting human dignity means treating humans as persons capable of planning and plotting their future.[18]

---

[16]Max Rümelin, *Die Rechtssicherheit*, Tübingen, Mohr Siebeck, 1924, p. 9. Likewise: Antonio Enrique Perez Luño, *La seguridad jurídica*, Barcelona, Ariel, 1991, p 20.

[17]Anne-Laure Valembois, *La constitutionnalisation de l'exigence de sécurité juridique en Droit Français*, Paris, LGDJ, 2005, p. 252.

[18]Joseph Raz, "The rule of law and its virtue (1977)", in *The authority of Law. Essays on Law and Morality*, Oxford, Oxford, 1979, p. 221.

Precisely because the legal certainty principle serves as an instrument to guarantee respect for individuals – avoiding deceit, frustration, and surprise regarding the laws – it is associated with the prohibition of arbitrariness in their institution and application.[19] It is for no other reason that legal certainty, as the core of the rule of law principle, serves to assure consideration and respect for men and women as citizens.[20] As correctly noted by Sypnowich when she refers to the rule of law in the sense of legal certainty as an ethic of civility: "It directs government to be civil to its citizens, to treat citizens with a concern which is generalised and abstract, unintrusive and aloof."[21] This is why Garlicki mentions that legal certainty in Poland incorporates what jurisprudence calls the "principles of decent legislation."[22]

These considerations allow us to say that the legal certainty principle aims in its dynamic dimension to guarantee a respectful transition from past to present and from present to future through knowledge of law. It is an instrument for "seeing ahead" but also for "seeing in retrospect," in the suggestive words of Carnellutti based on the work of Onãte.[23] Or for "knowing" and "predicting" according to Pacteau.[24] Or finally for gaining control of future-related results and certainty of the present situation, in Luhmann's expression.[25]

Whichever perspective is adopted, what matters is that the static (or structural or systemic) dimension cannot be separated from the dynamic (or functional or operative) dimension of legal certainty.[26] It can be said – based on Ferraz Jr. – that both dimensions, from the perspective of duration in time, aim to prevent a past from suddenly becoming strange, a future from becoming opaque and unsure, and duration from becoming a collection of life-destabilizing surprises.[27] Time in law, it must be stressed, is not the objective time of the mind ("it's 8 o'clock," "the trip

---

[19]Anne-Laure Valembois, *La constitutionnalisation de l'exigence de sécurité juridique en Droit Français*, Paris, LGDJ, 2005, p. 4; Federico Arcos Ramírez, *La seguridad jurídica: una teoría formal*, Madrid, Dykinson, 2000, p. 35.

[20]José Roberto Vieira, "Medidas provisórias tributárias e segurança jurídica: a insólita opção estatal pelo 'viver perigosamente'", in Aires Fernandino Barreto *et alii* (Orgs.), *Segurança jurídica na tributação e Estado de Direito*, São Paulo, Noeses, 2005, p. 317.

[21]Christine Sypnowich, "Utopia and the rule of law", in David Dyzenhaus (Org.), *Recrafting the rule of Law – The Limits of Legal Order*, Oxford, Hart, 1999, p. 194.

[22]Leszek Garlicki, "Constitution et sécurité juridique – Pologne", *Annuaire International de Justice Constitutionnelle 1999*, Paris, Economica, 2000, p. 241.

[23]Francesco Carnellutti, "La certezza del Diritto", in Flavio Lopez Onãte, *La certezza de Diritto*, Milano, Giuffrè, 1968, p. 195.

[24]Bernard Pacteau, "La sécurité juridique, un principe que nous manque?", *AJDA* 20, p. 154, 1995.

[25]Niklas Luhmann, *Vertrauen – Ein Mechanismus der Reduktion sozialer Komplexität*, 4th ed., Stuttgart, Lucius & Lucius, 2000, p. 17.

[26]Anne-Laure Valembois, *La constitutionnalisation de l'exigence de sécurité juridique en Droit Français*, Paris, LGDJ, 2005, pages 13 and following; César García Novoa, *El principio de seguridad jurídica en materia tributaria*, Madrid, Marcial Pons, 2000, p. 81.

[27]Tércio Sampaio Ferraz Jr., "Anterioridade e irretroatividade no campo tributário", *RDDT* 56, p. 125, São Paulo, 2001; idem, "Segurança jurídica, coisa julgada e justiça", *Revista do Instituto de Hermenêutica Jurídica*, v. 1, n. 3, p. 264, Porto Alegre, 2005; idem, "Coisa julgada em matéria

lasts 3 h") or subjective time ("a 1-min kiss between lovers lasts 1 h," "stepping on burning coals for a minute lasts an eternity"). On the contrary, it is social-historic time, established through meanings assigned to time and to its duration.[28]

In light of these reflections we can conclude that in this text the legal certainty principle is not a norm that prescribes a search for the ideals of knowability, reliability and calculability, placed in parallel and in sequence, but is redefined as a norm that prescribes a search for the ideals of reliability and calculability of law, with these ideals as the ends that characterize its internal presupposition *based on* its knowability. These dimensions and ideals will be examined in the following sections.

It must also be stressed that such ideals not only are not juxtaposed or superimposed, but are part of the "static vs. dynamic" binary rather than the "formal vs. material" binary. Leaving aside other reasons that will be examined in depth below, the use of the word "formal" to denote normative qualities that are entirely independent of the content of norms, qualifying the requirements of normative accessibility and intelligibility, would lead to the idea that legal certainty is implemented by technical means regardless of the content of legal norms. This is not true of legal certainty as defined in this book.

First because strictly speaking it is impossible to know whether a norm has been published and whether it is determinate without analyzing subjective aspects, since publicity and determinacy can be verified only from a subjective perspective even though they are objective qualities of norms. Defining whether a norm can be known presupposes defining *by whom* and *in what conditions*. Defining whether a norm is determinate presupposes defining *in whose view* and *to what extent*. This is why the above discussion of the meaning of legal certainty examined the several meanings that can be adopted in the subjective aspect of legal certainty and, among these, which one is in fact adopted by the legal order (as a rule, the perspective of the taxpayer as addressee).

Second, it is impossible to verify the fulfillment of normative qualities if the purposes served by those qualities can be known in advance. Knowing whether a norm is *determinate* presupposes knowing what purpose determinacy serves, as this is the only way to find out what information must be understood in order for a given state of affairs to be realized. Content is not a blind spot, but an element that serves as an instrument for a given action provided it is known. This is why the above discussion of the meaning of legal certainty examined the several meanings that can be adopted in the axiological aspect of legal certainty and, among these, which one is in fact adopted by the legal order (legal certainty as an instrument to realize the fundamental rights to freedom, equality and dignity).

---

tributária e as alterações sofridas pela legislação da contribuição social sobre o lucro (Lei n. 7.689/88)", *RDDT* 125, p. 73, São Paulo, 2006.

[28] François Ost, "Conclusions générales: le temps, la justice et le Droit", in Simone Gaboriau e Hélène Pauliat (Orgs.), *Le temps, la Justice et le Droit*, Limoges, Pulim, 2003, p. 359.

These observations justify my division of the content of legal certainty into "static and dynamic" parts instead of "formal and material" dimensions. Similar reasons serve to reject the division into objective and subjective elements adopted by some scholars.[29] Although some elements can be described as objective, in the sense of objectively regulated by the legal order (e.g. decay or protection of acquired rights), they refer to modes of reflexive application of the legal certainty principle oriented to specific subjects, so that they can also be considered subjective elements. Of course, this kind of labeling depends on the meanings chosen for the terms "objective" and "subjective", and on the perspectives chosen to analyze them, so that any element can be called objective or subjective depending on meaning and perspective. This is what happens with the requirement of stability of the legal order: Gomes Canotilho calls it an objective element of legal certainty, whereas von Arnauld refers to stability as a category within which the protection of legitimate trust belongs as an essentially subjective element.[30] The reason is the different perspectives these authors adopt: The former examines the objectivity of the requirements; the latter assesses the subjectivity of the effects. Focusing on the static and dynamic dimensions circumvents this problem and shows that some elements are neutral relative to objective or subjective, formal or material aspects.

The above considerations also show why I prefer an approach that can appropriately be called material or substantive.[31] Because the ideal of knowability depends on subjective perspectives and criteria supplied by the fundamental rights to freedom, equality and dignity, the realization of legal certainty is not independent from the content of norms. The requirements of legal certainty are met only when legal norms have the qualities indispensable to the realization of certain content.

These observations are the preamble to the analysis of the static and dynamic dimensions of legal certainty that follows.

---

[29] Antonio Enrique Perez Luño, *La seguridad jurídica*, Barcelona, Ariel, 1991, p. 69; Federico Arcos Ramírez, *La seguridad jurídica: una teoría formal*, Madrid, Dykinson, 2000, p. 71.

[30] José Joaquim Gomes Canotilho, *Direito Constitucional e Teoria da Constituição*, 7th ed., Coimbra, Almedina, 2004, p. 256; Andreas von Arnauld, *Rechtssicherheit*, Tübingen, Mohr Siebeck, 2006, p. 284.

[31] Joseph Raz, "The rule of law and its virtue (1977)", in *The authority of Law. Essays on Law and Morality*, Oxford, Oxford, 1979, p. 221; Robert Summers, "A formal theory of the rule of law", *Ratio Juris*, v. 6, n. 2, pages 127–142, 1993; Federico Arcos Ramírez, *La seguridad jurídica: una teoría formal*, Madrid, Dykinson, 2000, p. 3.

Static Dimension

Abstract This chapter deals with the static dimension of legal certainty. The static dimension concerns the problem of knowledge of law, of knowing or communicating law, and the qualities law must have to be considered "certain" and thus act as an instrument of orientation for citizens. Accordingly, the discussion covers the ideal of knowability, a state of affairs in which citizens have the material and intellectual capacity to understand the argumentative structures that reconstruct general and individual substantive and procedural norms. Such norms are minimally effective by virtue of their accessibility, breadth, clarity, determinability and executability.

1 Initial Considerations

The static dimension of the legal certainty principle concerns the structural requirements law must have in order to serve as a guiding instrument. It therefore encompasses all the preconditions without which citizens are not able to obey the laws. Thus it refers fundamentally to the problems of *knowledge* and *communication*, seeking to answer the following question: What elements are necessary for citizens to be able to shape the present with dignity in compliance with the laws, autonomously, freely and without deception?

The analysis of this aspect focuses on the conditions or qualities that enable law to be an object of knowledge from both the substantive and intellectual viewpoints: To be able to obey a legal norm, citizens must have access to it, through the observance of requirements that enable them to consider it as existing and in force; they must also understand what it determines, prohibits or allows. Precisely for this reason, as will be demonstrated, norms must be accessible, broad, clear and sufficiently determinate. Law, and hence all legal norms individually, must be "certain", as must the legal order as a whole.[1]

An interesting question is whether it is *norms* or *normative texts* that must be comprehensible. If norms are the interpreted texts, obviously they are the object of comprehension. Whether a norm is the understood text or the meaning of the text,

[1] Theodor Geiger, *Vorstudien zu einer Soziologie des Rechts*, 4th ed., Berlin, Duncker und Humblot, 1987, p. 64.

© Springer International Publishing Switzerland 2016

H. Ávila, *Certainty in Law*, Law and Philosophy Library 114,
DOI 10.1007/978-3-319-33407-3_8

the phrase "comprehensible norm" is a tautology, since it refers to the requirement of understanding what has been understood. In this sense, the object of the knowability requirement is in fact the normative texts. However, if the normative knowability requirement involves not mere "understanding", i.e. the ability to capture meanings, but genuine "comprehension" defined as the ability to act according to something understood, then the object of comprehension is not the texts per se, but the legal norms as minimal meanings of normative texts. As can be seen, it is a matter of stipulation.

In any case, the use of the expression "static dimension" ought to be understood as structural, not immovable. This is because the examination of its elements also requires movement, so to speak, and hence involves a dynamic element: Normative accessibility and intelligibility, for example, illustrate the ability of addressees to comprehend the meaning of normative texts, which to some extent presupposes a transition from text to norm. These observations suffice to show that the term "static dimension" as opposed to "dynamic dimension" in the sense defined here represents the structural elements law must have in order to serve as a guide for conduct and as a foundation for and constraint on the exercise of power.

Although legal certainty is usually associated with the presuppositions of determinacy and clarity, and indeed is sometimes associated solely with them, the analysis below shows the need for a review of these elements.

2 Substantive Knowability: "Certainty of Existence and Validity" Through Accessibility, Scope and the Possibility of Normative Identification

2.1 Normative Accessibility

2.1.1 Normative Provisions

2.1.1.1 Publication

In order to understand, one needs to know; in order to know, one must have access.[2] People cannot be guided by norms unless they are aware of their existence.[3] These two dimensions are therefore inseparable: Substantive access is meaningless without intellectual access, and the latter is impossible without the former. The necessary condition for accessibility is publicity, which depends on publication. Publicity therefore must not be confused with publication, which is a technical procedure

[2] Ben Juratowitch, *Retroactivity and the Common Law*, Oxford, Hart, 2008, p. 130.

[3] Andrei Marmor, *Law in the age of pluralism*, Oxford, OUP, 2007, p. 7.

of a formal legal nature that serves as the means to achieve the end of publicity.[4] Without previous public existence, law cannot act as a guide. The concept of legal certainty must therefore include an element relating to "certainty of existence" and "certainty of validity": no one can be oriented by what is not known to exist or be valid.[5] Indeed, this is why Novoa treats these requirements as part of the normative certainty of guidance and hence of the ideal of knowability.[6]

The ideal of publicity thus becomes an element of legal certainty, and publication one of the conditions not only for knowability but also reliability and calculability of law.[7] Case law follows this line of reasoning in Brazil.[8] Thus if the newspaper that prints an announcement or notice does not have a large circulation, it is not acceptable as a means of publication;[9] if the matter is not actually secret, there is no reason to allow an exception to the rule requiring publicity for judicial decisions;[10] an administrative order that interrupts publicity services causes serious harm to public order[11] – and so forth.

All the above considerations show that publicity, through publication, is an important factor in legal certainty.[12] However, this function can be realized only if it is combined with two fictions.

One of these is that once publication and *vacatio legis* are complete, the laws are fully known to their addressees. *Ignorantia legis neminem excusat*. Without this fiction, strictly speaking there can be no certainty of law regarding the legal consequences that the legal order can assign to the actions of third parties. Hence the need for citizens to trust that everyone will obey the laws, whether or not they *effectively* know them. This trust would disappear if the efficacy of norms could be realized only if their addressees *actually* knew their content.[13]

---

[4]Federico Arcos Ramírez, *La seguridad jurídica: una teoría formal*, Madrid, Dykinson, 2000, p. 246.

[5]Federico Arcos Ramírez, *La seguridad jurídica: una teoría formal*, Madrid, Dykinson, 2000, p. 37.

[6]César García Novoa, *El principio de seguridad jurídica en materia tributaria*, Madrid, Marcial Pons, 2000, p. 77.

[7]Anne-Laure Valembois, *La constitutionnalisation de l'exigence de sécurité juridique en Droit Français*, Paris, LGDJ, 2005, pages 14 and 190; Federico Arcos Ramírez, *La seguridad jurídica: una teoría formal*, Madrid, Dykinson, 2000, pages 36 and 249.

[8]AgR in REsp n. 753.469-SP, 1st Panel, Reporting Justice Luiz Fux, *DJ* 27 Mar 2006, p. 203; ED in AgR in REsp n. 572.642-RS, 1st Panel, Reporting Justice Luiz Fux, *DJ* 29 Aug 2005, p. 148.

[9]AgR in Ag n. 650.055-PR, 2nd Panel, Reporting Justice Humberto Martins, *DJ* 20 Apr 2007, p. 332; AgR in Ag n. 650.055-PR, 2nd Panel, Reporting Justice Humberto Martins, *DJ* 20 Apr 2007, p. 332.

[10]HC n. 91-DF, 3rd Section, Reporting Justice Arnaldo Esteves Lima, *DJ* 16 Apr 2005, p. 164.

[11]AgR in STA n. 29, Reporting Justice Edson Vidigal, *DJ* 6 Dec 2004, p. 180.

[12]Hugo de Brito Machado, "Os princípios da anterioridade e da irretroatividade das leis tributárias e a publicação da lei", *Cadernos de Direito Tributário e Finanças Públicas* 8, p. 107, São Paulo, 1994.

[13]Federico Arcos Ramírez, *La seguridad jurídica: una teoría formal*, Madrid, Dykinson, 2000, p. 249.

Acceptance of this fiction, which is positivated in the Law of Introduction to the Rules of Brazilian Law, causes a sort of internal conflict within legal certainty: On one hand, it establishes that knowledge is a presupposition of the validity of law, while on the other it ignores knowledge as a condition for this same validity. Thus knowledge is now relevant, now irrelevant, to the intelligibility of law.[14] This observation shows that strictly speaking not knowledge of law but knowability is a presupposition of legal certainty, i.e., the possibility of physical and intellectual access to the laws, which is quite different.

On the other hand, publicity also depends on the existence of another fiction, which concerns the completeness of the legal order. This is the notion that the legal order is a universal method for solving all conflicts of interest that arise socially, albeit not directly, for if law is to operate as a generator of sureness and trust concerning its contents and functioning, it cannot leave any conflict of interests unanswered.[15] Acceptance of this fiction does not imply agreement with the idea that each and every conflict of interests has a specific answer ready in a given abstract norm in particular. Such a conception would entail accepting the theory of the univocity of normative declarations. This theory cannot be accepted, since "not even Judge Hercules [Dworkin] can find a true answer for every case because there is simply no such thing as the right answer."[16] What it does mean is that law as a whole and in all its various manifestations, not a specific norm from a specific source, must be the wellspring from which the criteria are found to solve any conflict through the acts of a competent authority. In other words, *dynamic* rather than static *completeness* of law is necessary in order for legal certainty to exist as intelligibility.

2.1.1.2 Notification

Notification is the externalization of the need for knowability and calculability on the individual and procedural planes. Without knowledge of acts or facts that concern them, citizens cannot genuinely comply with the laws or, if necessary, exercise their right to a full defense. Indeed, due procedural process of law assumes that parties will be *informed* of all acts performed in the proceedings and of all their elements so that they can make their views heard about the factual and legal elements of the case and have their arguments considered in a neutral, impartial and justified manner. This has in fact been the subject of a ruling by the Brazilian Supreme Court.[17]

---

[14] Federico Arcos Ramírez, *La seguridad jurídica: una teoría formal*, Madrid, Dykinson, 2000, p. 250.

[15] Ibidem, p. 283.

[16] Eros Roberto Grau, *Ensaio e discurso sobre a interpretação/aplicação do Direito*, 5th ed., São Paulo, Malheiros Editores, 2009, p. 40.

[17] MS n. 24.268, Full Court, Reporting Justice Gilmar Mendes, *DJ* 17 Sep 2004, p. 189 of the decision.

If citizens are not notified of administrative or judicial acts and procedures, they will be taken by surprise by decisions or acts that restrict their rights and will be unable to react autonomously. When this happens, the right to procedural legal certainty is restricted by lack of knowability, reliability and calculability of judicial or administrative manifestations of law. Indirectly, moreover, dignity is unjustifiably affected because it is disposed of without any opportunity for manifestation, reaction or defense, so that instead of being autonomous subjects who can shape their lives actively and responsibly, citizens are struck by something to which they cannot react, making them into objects.

2.1.2 Validity

Citizens' actions cannot be guided by retroactive laws because they did not exist at the time they acted.[18] Thus besides knowing the norms they must obey, citizens must be aware they are in force. This is why the Constitution includes an anteriority rule, as will be discussed in due course, enabling taxpayers to know beforehand when the tax norms they must obey will enter into force.

For the same reason, articles 101 and ff. of the National Tax Code establish norms concerning the applicability of tax rules to cases in which the norm itself does not specify a validity period. Moreover, even though the legal norms relative to validity in general apply to tax law, to forestall all doubts article 103 of the Code establishes specific rules for the cases in which tax norms do not specify when they enter into force: Administrative acts are valid from the publication date; the normative effects of administrative decisions 30 days after publication; interstate agreements on the date they themselves specify.

Because certainty of validity is an aspect of knowability, which is one of the elements of legal certainty, one point must once again be stressed: Citizens must be able to know which norm to obey or they cannot be guided. In other words, without certainty of content and validity there can be no legal certainty of guidance. And without that, there can be no autonomous and responsible exercise of the fundamental rights to freedom and property.

2.2 *Normative Scope*

2.2.1 Codification

Codification is one of the main instruments of normative comprehensiveness because it groups general provisions together logically and in a single document

[18] Joseph Raz, "The rule of law and its virtue (1977)", in *The authority of Law. Essays on Law and Morality*, Oxford, Oxford, 1979, p. 214; César García Novoa, *El principio de seguridad jurídica en materia tributaria*, Madrid, Marcial Pons, 2000, p. 76.

from the perspective of matter and scope of application.[19] The connection between codification and the ideals of knowability and calculability of the legal order can easily be seen: Grouping into a single document favors material accessibility because easier access and comprehensiveness enhances the ability to know where to find the applicable legal provision; the systematic arrangement of the parts, in turn, serves as an instrument of intellectual accessibility by enabling citizens to have a clearer idea of the content of the norms they must obey. Codification based on criteria of authenticity, completeness and presentation is a means that contributes to the promotion of legal certainty.[20] Hence von Savigny's advocacy of codification as an instrument to ensure greater "assurance" (*Gewissheit*).[21] In order for law to be known, it must be concentrated rather than dispersed. Münch therefore inserts "legal concentration" (*Rechtskonzentration*) as an element of the legal certainty principle itself, next to determinacy, understandability, effectiveness and continuity.[22]

Accepting codification as an important factor in legal certainty does not entail agreeing that it provides legal certainty in and of itself. It is only one means among several to increase the knowability, reliability and calculability of law.[23] And today this means is as valuable as were the codifications produced in the 19th century. Their aim was to unify the dispersed common law to assure normative accessibility and intelligibility; the same issue arises today, given the large number of special, circumstantial and transitory laws, which together produce a "legal maze" and make the contemporary and pre-modern orders highly similar, as noted by Ferrajoli.[24]

2.2.2 General Norms

The Constitution reserves to supplementary statutes the function of establishing general tax norms, mainly regarding tax obligations, credits, prescription and limitation. The main function of general norms is to assure certainty and stability in

[19] Anne-Laure Valembois, *La constitutionnalisation de l'exigence de sécurité juridique en Droit Français*, Paris, LGDJ, 2005, p. 289; Eugenio Della Valle, *Affidamento e certezza del Diritto Tributario*, Milano, Giuffrè, 2001, p. 32.

[20] Andreas von Arnauld, *Rechtssicherheit*, Tübingen, Mohr Siebeck, 2006, pages 211 and 214.

[21] Friedrich Carl von Savigny, *Vom Beruf unserer Zeit für Gesetzgebung und Rechtswissenschaft*, Heidelberg, Mohr und Zimmer, 1814, p. 20 (reprinted Goldbach, Keip, 1997).

[22] Christof Münch, "Rechtssicherheit als Standortfaktor. Gedanken aus Sicht der vorsorgenden Rechtspflege", in Albrecht Weber (Org.), *Währung und Wirtschaft. Das Geld im Recht. FS für Hugo J. Hahn*, Baden-Baden, Nomos, 1997, p. 675.

[23] Eduardo García de Enterría, *Justicia y seguridad jurídica en un mundo de leyes desbocadas*, Madrid, Civitas, 1999, p. 32.

[24] Luigi Ferrajoli, "The past and the future of the rule of law", in Pietro Costa e Danilo Zolo (Orgs.), *The Rule of Law – History, Theory and Criticism*, Dordrecht, Springer, 2007, p. 342.

a federation, both among federal entities and between them and taxpayers.[25] They do so by guaranteeing two intertwined objectives: uniformity and diversity.

Uniformity resides in the unitary normative treatment of autonomous federal entities: All such entities must obey the same (general) norms. Thus the rules on prescription and limitation, for example, are not non-uniform but receive a common treatment that assures normative unity within the diversity of federal entities. By assuring normative homogeneity, the requirement of general tax norms favors the partial ideals whose realization is required by the legal certainty principle for taxpayers and federal entities in parallel relationships with other entities or vertical relationships with taxpayers: knowability, since each federal entity has easier material and intellectual access to the rules that govern their relations with other entities by delimiting areas of conflict within the federation, and their relations with taxpayers with regard to the duties of both parties; reliability, given the stability of norms assured by the qualified statutory reservation that makes it harder to amend them; and calculability through the continuity of general norms assured by the difficulty of amending them and by their bindingness, which arises from the ban on federal entities exercising legislative competence in violation of the general norms, regardless of financial difficulties.

Federative uniformity is particularly important in the Brazilian case. This is because there are three tiers to the federation – the federal, state and municipal – and many federal entities – 26 states plus the Federal District and more than 5,500 municipalities. Moreover, the federal entities are profoundly unequal in geographical, social and economic terms. This is enough to demonstrate that normative uniformity operates as a centripetal force around egalitarian normative ideals. For present purposes it is important to stress that these ideals contribute to better intelligibility, stability and predictability of the norms to which federal entities and taxpayers are subject in the tax relationships established.

Diversity resides in the normative treatment of the federative autonomy enjoyed by federal entities: Each entity must submit to the same norms, yet each one is free to exercise the normative competences established by the Constitution. Municipalities may set different tax rates for services rendered in their territory, provided they observe the limits established by supplementary statutes; states may tax the sale of goods in their territory differently, provided they obey the guidelines defined by general norms – and so on. However, it should be noted that this autonomy is limited, since the creation, collection and execution of tax credits must obey the general norms established in supplementary laws. Unlimited autonomy is not autonomy but sovereignty. Federal entities do not have tax sovereignty precisely because the exercise of their constitutional competences must be uniform, and this uniformity is assured by the observance of common general norms.

[25] Fábio Canazaro, *Lei complementar tributária na Constituição de 1988*, Porto Alegre, Livraria do Advogado, 2005, p. 108; Frederico Araújo Seabra de Moura, *Lei complementar tributária*, São Paulo, Quartier Latin, 2009, pages 331 and following.

It can be seen clearly enough that the ideals of federative diversity and uniformity are intertwined because increasing one entails decreasing the other: Too much uniformity ultimately annihilates the autonomy of federal entities, changing the federation into a unitary state; too much diversity ultimately obliterates uniformity, turning federal entities into independent states. Although there is no formula that can exactly determine the point at which a federated state ceases to be federal, in the abstract it can be said that neither ideal must be pursued too far. In the many configurations of federated states that have taken shape throughout history, diversity has had to be harmonized with uniformity.

The general norms governing the creation and discharge of tax obligations have been consolidated into the National Tax Code, instituted by an ordinary statute classified by the Constitution as a supplementary law because the Code plays the role constitutionally assigned to this normative source. The Code groups together the basic rules governing the birth, life and death of tax obligations, so to speak. This does not mean there are no other supplementary laws with a general scope. Indeed, the laws that assure uniformity of purpose with regard to specific taxes have already been mentioned. A pertinent example is the supplementary law that establishes general rules regarding state taxes levied on the sale of goods and on transportation and communications services (Supplementary Law 87/96), as is the supplementary law governing the exercise of municipal competence to tax services of all kinds (Supplementary Law 116/2003).

For present purposes what matters is that general norms are indispensable mechanisms to assure the states of knowability, reliability and calculability of the legal order. They are means at the service of the *sureness function*, through abstraction and typification, and of the *equality function*, through generality in terms of distinctions between jurisdictions in concretizing the relations between taxpayers and a given federal entity or among the latter, alongside the wider function of rationalizing the exercise of tax competences, thus avoiding an unrealizable spontaneous order.[26] Without them – and this is enough to demonstrate their importance – taxpayers cannot exercise their economic activity in the present or plan for the future in a strategic and legally informed manner throughout the territory of the Federative Republic of Brazil, owing to a lack of comprehensiveness, accessibility, stability and predictability of the legal order. This is precisely why general norms also perform an often overlooked complementary or *expletory ("filling out") function*.

Indeed, a careful reading of the provisions of the National Tax Code, for instance, may lead to the conclusion that many of them are superfluous.[27] A few examples will suffice to show why.

---

[26] Tércio Sampaio Ferraz Jr., "Segurança jurídica e normas gerais tributárias", *RDT* 17–18, pages 53 and 55, São Paulo, 1981.

[27] On the subject, see, for all: Ricardo Lobo Torres, *Normas de interpretação e integração do Direito Tributário*, 3rd ed., Rio de Janeiro, Renovar, 2000, pages 21 and following.

Some provisions can be deemed *tautological*, such as those stating that the Code implements the National Tax System (articles 1 and 2) or the provision that introduces the chapter on the interpretation and application of tax norms by establishing that tax norms will be interpreted and applied according to the provisions of that chapter (article 107). With apologies for the quibble, these provisions are like a housepainter's sign that reads "Houses painted at home."

Similarly, some provisions can be deemed *repetitive*, merely repeating articles already found in the Constitution: Articles 9 through 11 reproduce the limitations on the power to tax established in articles 150 and ff. of the Constitution; articles 19 through 85 of the Code repeat the incidence hypothesis aspects of the competence rules set out in articles 153 through 156; article 97 reproduces the legality rule found in article 150, I; article 104 repeats article 150, III, "b"; and articles 105 and 106 reproduce the provisions of article 150, III, "a".

The Code can also be said to contain provisions that establish *implied norms*, i.e., norms whose content can be deduced by systematic interpretation of the Constitution itself: The provision in articles 6 and 7 that tax competence cannot be delegated and must not be confused with the tax collection function arises from the nature of the competence rule and the basic principle that the Constitution is supreme; the provision in article 14 that immunity depends on the observance of constitutional requirements arises from the content of the rules in the paragraphs of article 150 of the Constitution; the content of paragraphs 1 and 2 of article 108 indicating that analogy cannot justify collection of a tax not created by statute and that equity does not justify waiving a tax liability is a specification that arises from the legality rule established by article 150, I, of the Constitution; the provision in article 109 that private law concepts cannot be used to change tax effects arises from the superiority of the competence rules in the Constitution and the special character of tax norms; the provision in article 110 that constitutional concepts cannot be altered by the framers of tax laws arises from the limiting nature of the competence rules and the supremacy of the Constitution; the provision in article 111 of the Code that tax benefits must be interpreted literally can be construed by examining the exceptional character of tax incentives, as set forth in article 150, indent I and paragraph 6, of the Constitution; the provision in article 112 that penalties must be interpreted in the defendant's favor can be inferred from the criminal retroactivity established in article 5 of the Constitution; the provision in article 142 according to which tax assessments are binding can be construed from the legality rule and the administrative principles in article 37 of the Constitution, mainly the requirements of legality, impersonality and morality; and so forth.

Strictly speaking, the provisions relating to the concept of tax (article 3) and the elements to be considered in delimiting types of tax (article 4) can also be considered mere substantive implications of constitutional norms: On one hand, an overview of the tax rules in the Constitution shows that the concept of tax involves the payment of monies defined by statute and is not to be confused with sanctions for unlawful acts; on the other hand, based on the elements of the competence rules it is perfectly possible to specify which elements are legally relevant to configure each type of tax, from facts ("*impostos*", direct taxes in a strict sense) to presuppositions ("intervention contributions" and "compulsory loans") and purposes ("social contributions"), separately or as a whole.

If we leave aside the tautological, repetitive, implied and concretizing provisions, as well as others that are merely conceptual or didactic, such as those that define the concept of "tax legislation" (article 96), "complementary norms" (article 100), "taxable event," "main obligation" and "accessory obligation" (article 113), or simply incorporate private law concepts, such as those that discipline "responsibility" (articles 128 and ff.), the question remains: What is the National Tax Code for?

I am well aware that the institution of a code of general norms is a distraction from the fundamental normative instrument, which is the Constitution. The endeavors of Ataliba and Carrazza furnish ample proof of this.[28] It is equally true that the repetition and concretization of constitutional provisions have negative effects. Suffice it to think of articles that are repetitions but omit part of the repeated provision, such as articles 21 and 25 of the National Tax Code, which in referring to taxes on foreign trade densify what was to be the content of article 150, paragraph 1, of the Constitution. Indeed, instead of merely indicating the executive's prerogative to change the "rates" of such taxes, these articles of the Code extend the same power to the "tax base," conflicting with the Constitution now in force. Another case in point is article 110, which prevents the framers of tax laws from altering "private law" concepts used in the Constitution to define or limit competences but does not mention public law concepts (salary) or even tax law concepts (sales) used in the Constitution for the same purpose. In sum, repetition was supposed to help but ended up being harmful.

Even considering this risk, it is essential not to undervalue the guiding function of general norms – here at last is the point to be stressed. The purpose of general norms is to increase physical and intellectual access to tax norms for everyone who has recourse to law, whether they are experts in tax law, taxpayers that call all types of tax by the same name or refer to the former financial transactions contribution as "the check tax," or even public agents with experience in administrative law but no specialist knowledge of tax law. In this respect, the "expletory function" is an instrument of legal certainty. After all, how many addressees of tax norms can easily understand that the non-delegability of tax competence derives from the federative tax structure itself? Or that the ban on modifying tax concepts arises from the constraints imposed by the competence rules and the supremacy of the Constitution? According to Sousa, the National Tax Code is an instrument of knowability and calculability of tax law through the definition of "certain general principles that must be obeyed by federal, state and city tax statutes"[29] – in sum, neither more nor less

[28]Geraldo Ataliba, *Sistema Constitucional Tributário Brasileiro*, São Paulo, Ed. RT, 1968, p. 15; Roque Antonio Carrazza, *Curso de Direito Constitucional Tributário*, 27ª ed., São Paulo, Malheiros Editores, 2011, p. 56.

[29]Rubens Gomes de Sousa, *Compêndio de legislação tributária*, posthumous edition, São Paulo, Resenha Tributária, 1975, p. 190.

than an instrument of tax law certainty. Maior Borges is categorical on this point: "The National Tax Code is a repository of general norms of tax law at the service of legal certainty."[30] Ferraz Jr. follows the same path in acknowledging that "the presence of general tax norms is fundamental for legal certainty, from the viewpoint of both the issuer (sureness function) and the addressee (equality function)."[31]

This observation about the superfluousness of some provisions of the National Tax Code can also be made about the Constitution. It too contains provisions which, when rigorously interpreted, merely complement or reproduce norms already implicitly or explicitly provided for in the constitutional order. A few examples will suffice to make this point. The provision in article 145, paragraph 1, banning federal entities from treating taxpayers in equivalent situations unequally or discriminating between them on the basis of their job or occupation is a necessary consequence of the general principle of equality already set forth in the body of article 5; the provision in article 145, paragraph 1, according to which taxpayers must be treated according to economic capacity is also a consequence of the equality principle, which requires the choice of differentiating criteria that are reasonably pertinent to the purpose of the differentiation; the provision in article 150, I, that only a statute can create or raise taxes is a consequence of the rule of law principle and the separation of powers, which require state action to comply with the provisions of general and abstract rules and are already positivated in articles 1 and 2; the provision in article 150, III, "a", banning federal entities from levying taxes on taxable events that occur before the statute that created or raised them enters into force is an indirect consequence of the rule of law and legal certainty principles established in articles 1 and 5 respectively; the provision in article 150, IV, that federal entities cannot tax with confiscatory effects is a logical implication of the positivation of the fundamental rights to freedom and property, which cannot be restricted without loss of efficacy; the provision in article 151, I banning the creation of a tax that is not uniform across the entire national territory or that implies a distinction or preference for a state, the Federal District, or a municipality to the detriment of another is a consequence of the federative principle set forth in article 1; and so on.

Nor am I unaware that such instances can also have negative effects. As will be shown later, the irretroactivity rule linked to taxable events can be mistakenly understood as authorizing retrospective effects whenever the taxable event has not yet occurred. The ban on confiscatory taxes can be misinterpreted as meaning that the Constitution allows excessive fines. Nevertheless, and again this is the point to be stressed, the Constitution has a valuable guiding function with regard to the exercise of power provided for in the competence rules, since not all authorities or taxpayers

[30] José Souto Maior Borges, "Segurança jurídica: sobre a distinção entre competências fiscais para orientar e autuar o contribuinte", *RDT* 100, p. 24, São Paulo, s.d.

[31] Tércio Sampaio Ferraz Jr., "Segurança jurídica e normas gerais tributárias", *RDT* 17–18, p. 55, São Paulo, 1981.

in this vast federation comprising thousands of federal entities have reasonable conditions to acquire clear advance knowledge of norms that only complex logical implication can reveal.

2.2.3 Pertinence

One of the problems that hinder the intelligibility of norms is the introduction of norms on completely different themes into a single legislative document. Known as "omnibus laws", these often have a final part dealing randomly with several subjects and may even include indeterminate or complex repealing provisions ("all contrary provisions are hereby repealed"; "the provisions of all acts enumerated below are hereby repealed . . ."). This practice clearly conflicts with the duty to assure the intelligibility of law by maintaining a high degree of uncertainty.[32]

Within this framework, for legislative novelties to accord with the legal certainty principle, each legislative text must address a single topic instead of several. With regard to tax benefits, the Constitution expressly requires their creation by a statute devoted exclusively to this topic (article 150, paragraph 6). If this requirement is valid for tax relief it must apply equally to taxation. Supplementary Law 95/98 also requires that all laws, except codes, must deal with a single subject and contain nothing foreign or disconnected from that subject in terms of affinity or pertinence (article 7, I and II). On the other hand, as was once required in Spain, new provisions must expressly cite all previous provisions that are totally or partially repealed.[33] The same requirement is also established by Supplementary Law 95/98, which (as amended by Supplementary Law 107/2001) states that repealing clauses must expressly enumerate all acts and legal provisions repealed.

2.3 *Possibility of Normative Identification*

2.3.1 Applicable Norm

Citizens may know that norms in general exist and are in force without being minimally sure about which norm to obey in the vast universe of modern legal orders. They may have doubts regarding which legislative norm to follow when norms contradict each other. In some cases they may even be sure which norm to be obey, but sureness turns into doubt when judicial decisions invalidate the applicability of the norm concerned by declaring it unconstitutional for all citizens or for one in particular. In such cases, the legislative norm is defined, but its validity

[32]Eduardo García de Enterría, *Justicia y seguridad jurídica en un mundo de leyes desbocadas*, Madrid, Civitas, 1999, pages 78 and 84.

[33]Ibidem, p. 94.

is not defined. In more emblematic cases there are opposing judicial positions on the validity of the applicable norm. Such antagonism is sometimes synchronic: At a given moment there are two contradictory decisions issued by different panels of the same court or different courts. At other times the conflict is diachronic: The same body issues a decision at a given moment and later issues a different decision on the same legislative norm. In these situations the addressee knows which norm to obey but does not know whether it is legally worthy of obedience, given the unsettled question of its validity at a given moment or during a given period. This can be illustrated by the following example.

Law 9430, passed in 1996, contained a provision (article 56) repealing a previous exemption granted by Supplementary Law 70/91, in article 6, II. Thus starting in 1996 firms constituted as civil law partnerships to provide regulated professional services were required by the applicable legislative norm to pay the social contribution on revenue. From a legislative viewpoint, therefore, the applicable norm was clear. However, this norm was judicially contested, and in 2002 and 2003 the High Court (STJ) found for the unconstitutionality of the tax, arguing that there was a hierarchy between supplementary and ordinary laws, so that no provision in the latter could repeal provisions in the former.[34] In 2003 this finding became Precedent No. 276, according to which taxpayers did not have to pay the contribution on revenue.[35] In 2007, however, Supreme Court rulings on injunctions and later extraordinary appeals found that there was no hierarchy between supplementary and ordinary laws when the subject-matter was not reserved to supplementary laws by the Constitution.[36] Hence civil law partnerships that provide regulated professional services must pay the contribution on revenue. In 2008 this understanding was reaffirmed by a decision issued in a direct unconstitutionality suit.[37]

This case – studied here in its general aspects, leaving aside matters relevant to other problems – demonstrates the uncertainty regarding the applicability of legislative norms. Between 1996 and 2003 there was a clear legislative norm requiring taxpayers to pay the social contribution on revenue; in 2002 the STJ began to find that payment was not required, undermining the assumption that the tax law concerned was constitutional; in 2003 the STJ issued an abstract unifying the positions of its two tax law panels to establish a precedent that the contribution was

[34]REsp n. 227.939, 1st Panel, Reporting Justice Milton Luiz Pereira, *DJ* 12 Mar 2001; REsp n. 260.960, 1st Panel, Reporting Justice Humberto Gomes de Barros, *DJ* 26 Mar 2001; AgR in REsp n. 297.461, 1st Panel, Reporting Justice Francisco Falcão, *DJ* 3 Sep 2001; REsp n. 422.741, 1st Panel, Reporting Justice José Delgado, *DJ* 9 Sep 2002; ED in AgR in REsp n. 422.342, 1st Panel, Reporting Justice Paulo Medina, *DJ* 17 Mar 2003; REsp n. 221.710, 2nd Panel, Reporting Justice Peçanha Martins, *DJ* 18 Feb 2002; ED in AgR in REsp n. 258.630, 2nd Panel, Reporting Justice Eliana Calmon, *DJ* 9 Sep 2002.

[35]Súmula no. 176, 1a Seção, *DJ*, 2.6.2003.

[36]ACi-MC-AgR n. 1.717, 2nd Panel, Reporting Justice Gilmar Mendes, *DJ* 28 Sep 2007; RE n. 377.457, Full Court, Reporting Justice Gilmar Mendes, j. 19 Sep 2008, *DJe* 19 Dec 2008; RE n. 381.964, Full Court, Reporting Justice Gilmar Mendes, j. 17 Sep 2008, *DJe* 29 Sep 2008.

[37]ADI n. 4.071, Full Court, Reporting Justice Menezes Direito, *DJe* 13 Oct 2008.

unlawful; and in 2007 the Supreme Court ruled that the legislative norm enacted in 1996 was constitutional. So what is the applicable norm? Is it the legal norm, presumably valid and never declared unconstitutional by the Supreme Court? Or is it the legal norm as interpreted by the STJ, which found it incompatible with a supposedly superior supplementary law? After all, from the viewpoint of the addressee, what is the applicable norm: the legal norm or the court-interpreted legal norm? If the latter, interpreted by which court – the STJ or the Supreme Court?

These considerations, to which others could be added, demonstrate that substantive knowability depends not only on knowledge of the applicable norms, but also on knowledge of the norms regarding their application. In other words, there must be clarity not only regarding first-degree norms (object norms), but also concerning the norms that regulate conflicts among norms (antinomy rules), structure their application (normative postulates) and confirm their meaning and validity (judicial decisions). Besides clarity regarding the norms, there must be clarity concerning the *norms of norms*, so to speak. If there is certainty that a norm exists and is in force, but no certainty of identification, strictly speaking it is impossible to know with a minimum of certainty what norm is applicable to a case.[38]

The "legal order" cannot be obeyed, even with regard only to "principles", by complying with specific tax obligations. Just as one cannot say "Look!" without pointing to the object to be observed, since it is impossible to observe everything, a behavioral obligation cannot be discharged unless it is required by some rule of the legal order.[39] Thus the applicable norm must be that which is *presumably valid* and *directly applicable* to the behavior that is questioned. This conclusion is reached by observing the legality rules established by the Constitution – both the general rule according to which something can or cannot be done only according to the law (article 5, I), and the tax rule according to which a tax can be created or raised only by statute (article 150). In other words, taxpayers must obey the law.

Where there is a conflict between legal rules, a solution should be sought in the rules for solving antinomies: A superior norm repeals an inferior norm (the hierarchical criterion); a later norm repeals an earlier norm, as per article 2 of the Law of Introduction to the Rules of Brazilian Law (the chronological criterion); and a special norm repeals a general norm (the speciality criterion). This is not the place to discuss the tortuous issue of antinomies. For present purposes, however, it is relevant to establish that the valid special legal rule is presumed to be applicable. This is the rule addressees should obey, except of course if a judicial decision with general efficacy or specific to the addressee determines otherwise. Thus the criteria that determine the applicable norm are *normative force* (legal or judicial norms with general efficacy) and *speciality* (a specific rule or individual decision relating to the addressee).

---

[38] Andreas von Arnauld, *Rechtssicherheit*, Tübingen, Mohr Siebeck, 2006, p. 106.

[39] José Souto Maior Borges, *Obrigação tributária – Uma introdução metodológica*, São Paulo, Saraiva, 1984, p. 7.

Although there can be a special legal rule that is valid because it has not yet been declared unconstitutional with *erga omnes* efficacy by the Supreme Court, the presumption that it is constitutional may be questioned, in which case the addressee will no longer know whether to obey the legal norm proper or the legal norm as judicially interpreted. In such situations it is necessary to know when judicial decisions must serve as a guide not only for the parties to the respective proceedings but also for citizens in general – the Constitution itself answers this question.

The only decisions with general efficacy are judicial review decisions issued in concentrated control of constitutionality (direct unconstitutionality suits or ADIs, and constitutionality declaration suits, or ADCs) or in diffuse control of constitutionality regarding a statute that has been the object of a Senate resolution to suspend its efficacy or of a binding precedent or *stare decisis* ruling binding on all lower courts and the entire public administration. These decisions have prescriptive force, in the sense that they create obligations subject to judicial lien. In the event of a conflict, which strictly speaking may only be apparent, between a legal norm and a binding judicial decision, there can be no doubt that citizens must obey the judicial decision for the simple reason that it is binding on everyone and in that sense replaces or densifies the content of the legal norm previously applicable.

However, there are decisions that lack general efficacy yet offer collective guidance. For example, some bodies and courts issue decisions specifically to guide lower courts directly, and the addressees of the interpreted norms indirectly, by means of uniformization. They include decisions issued by sections of the STJ in appeals against split decisions and STJ precedents. Their purpose is not only to resolve disputes between parties, but also to offer guidance to judicial bodies and citizens on the interpretation of a specific legal norm. As Alvaro de Oliveira stresses, "the instruments primarily designed to make precedents uniform evidence the value of certainty most vividly against threats to the principle of equality for similar or identical cases."[40]

Nevertheless, the point being which norm is applicable and hence must be obeyed by the addressee, it is important to note that the Constitution itself defines it as the specific, existing, valid norm that is in force, unless it has been excluded by an ADI, ADC or extraordinary appeal, or suspended by Senate resolution or binding precedent – that is the rule.

There are also decisions that lack general efficacy, yet nevertheless have certain features that make them trustworthy to the addressees, such as a claim to correctness, being part of a chain of similar decisions, the provision of guidance, and so on. Although non-binding, such decisions can produce effects for agents who have performed acts that dispose of their fundamental rights to freedom and property based on the decisions concerned. These elements will be investigated in the part of this book that deals with the subjective aspect of the requirement of reliability of law.

---

[40]Carlos Alberto Alvaro de Oliveira, *Do formalismo no Processo Civil*, 3rd ed., São Paulo, Saraiva, 2009, p. 81.

2.3.2 Value of the Applicable Norm

For certainty of guidance to exist, addressees must know not just which norm to obey but also the *value* of the norm to be obeyed. We will return to this issue later, in the discussion of reliability through legal efficacy, but the connection between knowability and reliability should be made clear now.

Knowability of law requires clarity regarding the general consequence of not complying with the applicable legal norms. This is not a matter of legal efficacy, via the existence of institutional and procedural conditions to enforce the laws, nor of the effectiveness or social efficacy of the legal order, perceived as average obedience to legal norms by their addressees. Instead, what is at stake is the standard of clarity with regard to the *abstract* and *general* consequences applicable to non-compliance with legal norms: Even if addressees are aware of the applicable norms, knowability of law does not exist if they do not minimally know the effects assigned to lack of compliance.

The point at issue concerns both the upholding of invalid administrative acts and the preservation of past effects of unconstitutional acts through modulation of effects in the control of constitutionality. Both cases will be analyzed in the part of this book that deals with reliability of law. What matters in this step is only one aspect of the discussion. The institutionalized upholding of invalid acts in diffuse control of constitutionality and of the effects of unconstitutional acts or norms through modulation of the efficacy of decisions in concentrated or diffuse control of constitutionality, either via their transformation into rules instead of exceptions or via lack of clarity regarding the guiding criteria and the cases to be used, creates a problem of knowability of the legal order. The addressees will no longer clearly know whether the rule applies and hence whether they should obey the rule or risk wagering that no effects will be assigned to their non-compliance in future.

In this respect, the rule must continue to be that failure to comply with a legal norm always triggers application of the consequence abstractly and generally provided for. Only exceptional cases can justify abandoning the normal consequence of non-compliance with the applicable statutory norm: in the case of administrative acts, only those involving circumstances that are unlikely to recur, such as acts that are applied with a presumption of legitimacy for a long period or that create an onerous or synallagmatic relationship; in the case of statutes, only those that have already caused effects that can no longer be undone, for example, or whose loss of efficacy would certainly compromise the aggregate protection of fundamental rights and the credibility of the legal order itself, as analyzed in the chapter on the reliability of law.

What is essential for the existence of knowability of law is the existence of rules and exceptions, as long as the exceptions can be perceived using minimally objective and controllable criteria in most cases. However, when an exception is institutionalized, or slowly but steadily transformed into the rule, addressees no longer know which norm to follow, whether the specific applicable norm or another one possibly determined by the Judiciary. Ultimately, right and wrong can no longer be told apart. And when that happens, as noted with rigor by Machado Derzi, law loses one of its fundamental functions, which is to generalize and stabilize normative expectations of behavior through the binary code lawful/unlawful.[41] What distinguishes law is that it is the bearer of the binary code lawful/unlawful, so that it is operationally closed but cognitively open.[42] This distinction is negated by the transformation in practice of what is unlawful into what is lawful. Preiser's words are opportune on this subject: "The more exceptions a state makes to its duty to protect the confidence of its citizens in the validity of its laws, the more it loses the trust of its citizens and the further it gets from the essence of the rule of law."[43]

3 Intellectual Knowability: "Certainty of Content" Through Normative Intelligibility

3.1 Intelligibility Through Normative Clarity

Normative prescriptions can guide human conduct only if their addressees can understand what they prescribe.[44] Certainty, as Aquinas said, is related to man's cognitive ability: "*certitudo est proprietas cognitivae virtutis*".[45] Thus it is best to avoid excessively generic descriptions, as well as too much detail.[46]

In this respect, it should be borne in mind that the generality or universality of the addressee is an important instrument of normative intelligibility, but it is not a necessary or sufficient condition to permit predictability. If known and stable, a private norm addressed to a single person can be of more help to the individual concerned in planning their life than a general and abstract norm.[47] However, this can be accepted only if legal certainty is considered an instrument of predictability

[41] Misabel de Abreu Machado Derzi, *Modificações da Jurisprudência no Direito Tributário*, São Paulo, Noeses, 2009, p. 308.

[42] Niklas Luhmann, *Ausdifferenzierung des Rechts. Beiträge zur Rechtssoziologie und Rechtstheorie*, Frankfurt am Main, Suhrkamp, 1999, p. 140; Marcelo Neves, *Entre Têmis e Leviatã: uma relação difícil – O Estado Democrático de Direito a partir e além de Luhmann e Habermas*, São Paulo, Martins Fontes, 2006, pages 80–81.

[43] Friedrich Preiser, "Rechtsstaatswidrige Rechtsunsicherheit. Vorschläge zur Erzielung von Rechtsunsicherheit", *DVBl* 83, p. 545, 1968.

[44] Andrei Marmor, *Law in the Age of Pluralism*, Oxford, OUP, 2007, p. 7.

[45] St Thomas Aquinas, *apud* Andrea Schrimm-Heins, "Gewissheit und Sicherheit: Geschichte und Bedeutungswandel der Begriffe 'certitudo' und 'securitas'" (Teil 1), *Archiv für Begriffsgeschichte* 34, pages 169, 1991.

[46] César García Novoa, *El principio de seguridad jurídica en materia tributaria*, Madrid, Marcial Pons, 2000, p. 79; J. J. Ferrero Lapatza, "El principio de seguridad jurídica en la creación y aplicación del tributo", *CT*, p. 52, 1968; Jacques Chevallier, "Le Droit Économique: l'insécurité juridique ou nouvelle sécurité juridique?", in Laurence Boy, Jean-Baptiste Racine e Fabrice Siiriainen (Orgs.), *Sécurité juridique et Droit Économique*, Bruxelles, Larcier, 2008, p. 564.

[47] Federico Arcos Ramírez, *La seguridad jurídica: una teoría formal*, Madrid, Dykinson, 2000, p. 227.

for individuals regarding the consequences of their own actions. If instead what is at stake is the predictability of the consequences of someone else's actions, not one's own, then generality becomes essential. While a private norm known only to the addressee may be a planning tool for that addressee, knowing how the addressee will behave is of no use to others. Generality is therefore an indispensable instrument of legal certainty and of certainty of rights for everyone. This does not mean the existence of private norms is incompatible with certainty, provided they are written in accordance with general norms about their production and modification.[48] This is precisely the case in Brazil, thanks to the requirement of general norms.

Clarity is achieved only through a measure of information. Lack of information causes uncertainty: If a norm does not properly specify the conduct to be adopted, addressees are unable to obey it, because it does not define the required behavior. Addressees know they must do something, but this something is undefined. Excessive information also causes uncertainty: Too many specifications that overlap with and contradict one another, depending on the angle from which they are analyzed, prevent addressees from obeying a commandment, for lack of determinacy as to which commandment to obey. Addressees know they must do something, but this something is defined contradictorily. Hence von Arnauld's conclusion that neither "too much information" nor "too little information" serves as a guide to behavior. The measure has to be right: *dosis facit venenum*.[49]

3.2 *Intelligibility Through Normative Determinability*

3.2.1 Of Norms

3.2.1.1 Clarity of Language

If law serves to guide people, they ought to be able to know what it means. Its content ought to be clear, inasmuch as ambiguous, vague, obscure or imprecise law eventually deceives or at least confuses those who wish to be guided by it.[50] Thus the intelligibility of norms requires clarity and precision, the latter being a condition of the former.[51] It is for no other reason that Supplementary Law 95/98 sets forth criteria to increase both the clarity and the precision of norms (article 11, I and II respectively).

[48] Joseph Raz, "The rule of law and its virtue (1977)", in *The Authority of Law. Essays on Law and Morality*, Oxford, Oxford, 1979, p. 215.

[49] Andreas von Arnauld, *Rechtssicherheit*, Tübingen, Mohr Siebeck, 2006, p. 690.

[50] Joseph Raz, "The rule of law and its virtue (1977)", in *The authority of Law. Essays on Law and Morality*, Oxford, Oxford, 1979, p. 214.

[51] Anne-Laure Valembois, *La constitutionnalisation de l'exigence de sécurité juridique en Droit Français*, Paris, LGDJ, 2005, p. 15.

Such clarity, however, depends on the extent of normative particularization: Too much precision leads to complexity and thus prevents intelligibility, as well as compromising the generality of the norm, which in its turn restricts its stability; too little precision prevents law from exercising its guiding function, besides preventing citizens from predicting the effects assigned to their acts. This is why Zimmer says clarity depends on the "golden mean" (*juste milieu*).[52]

The clarity required by legal certainty, however, cannot be confused with univocity,[53] since there is not a single possible meaning, but a scale from what is most obvious to what is most contestable.[54]

3.2.1.2 Determinability of Content

Besides clarity, norms must also have "sufficient density" for addressees and appliers of law to be able to abide by them.[55] Jurisprudence has at last incorporated the understanding that tax norms must determine all elements of a tax obligation with precision. Tax laws are subject to an especially intense requirement of determinacy, the argument goes, although its terms may vary. Some decisions of Brazil's High Court (STJ) illustrate this point.

> It is a well-known fact that the legality principle, highlighted in the tax field by article 150, I, of the Constitution, embodies the requirement that the law define types of tax in a very detailed manner. This key principle of tax law encompasses that of closed typicality, according to which written laws in the formal substantive sense must contain all the structural elements of a tax, i.e. the incidence hypothesis, based on material, spatial, temporal and personal criteria, and the respective legal consequence, as determined by article 97 of the National Tax Code.[56]
>
> In compliance with the legality and closed typicality principles inherent in tax law, the Administration can impose the burden of taxation on taxpayers only when there is a perfect fit between the fact and the legal incidence hypothesis, i.e., the tax type description, such as we find in this case.[57]
>
> The Brazilian tax system has adopted the legality and closed typicality principles, i.e., all elements of the tax type (*Tatbestand*) must be defined by law *stricto sensu* (article 97 of the National Tax Code).[58]
>
> The legality principle enshrined in the constitutional text stresses that no one shall be obliged to do or refrain from doing anything except by virtue of the law (article 5, II). In tax

[52]Willy Zimmer, "Constitution et sécurité juridique – Allemagne", *Annuaire International de Justice Constitutionnelle 1999*, Paris, Economica, p. 100.

[53]Federico Arcos Ramírez, *La seguridad jurídica: una teoría formal*, Madrid, Dykinson, 2000, p. 259.

[54]Neil MacCormick, *Legal reasoning and legal theory*, Oxford, Clarendon, 1978, p. 197.

[55]José Joaquim Gomes Canotilho, *Direito Constitucional e Teoria da Constituição*, 7th ed., 6th reprint, Coimbra, Almedina, 2004, p. 258.

[56]REsp n. 724.779-RJ, STJ, 1st Panel, Reporting Justice Luiz Fux, *DJ* 20 Nov 2006, p. 278.

[57]AgR in REsp n. 636.377-SP, 2nd Panel, Reporting Justice Humberto Martins, *DJ* 2 Oct 2006, p. 248.

[58]REsp n. 395.143-RS, 2nd Panel, Reporting Justice Laurita Vaz, *DJ* 27 May 2002, p. 165.

> law this means taxes cannot be created, repealed, raised or reduced except by law (article 150, I, of the Constitution and article 97 of the National Tax Code). That is the principle of strict statutory legality.[59]

To some extent these decisions reflect the longstanding discussion concerning strict legality in the sphere of tax law, founded mainly, but not only, on the work of Xavier.[60] However, there are two positions that should be considered, that of Machado Derzi and that of Torres. A summary of each position follows.

For Machado Derzi, the classificatory conceptual tendency predominates in tax law, given the tax principles relating to legal certainty.[61] Her analysis is based on a distinction between "type" and "concept". Type is a notion with alternative properties, not all of which need exist in each concrete case; what is decisive is the totality, the general idea. In contrast, concept connotes properties that must be present and without which it would not exist.[62] A number of issues are worthy of analysis here, but one in particular deserves emphasis. The author draws attention to the fact that the legal certainty principle in the field of tax law prohibits incidence hypotheses containing elements that may or may not be present for the creation of a tax obligation, without denying that there are more or less indeterminate conceptual halos and typological residues, although it is legitimate to speak of a classificatory conceptual tendency.[63] "The fact that classifying concepts are admitted in law does not mean rejecting its historicity or the openness of the system as a whole," she explains.[64] However, if lawmakers prefer a classifying concept in legal fields where the need for certainty is greatest, and if the normative hypothesis calls for "a, b and c", there can be subsumption only if all of these elements are present in the actual situation.[65] This is so, among other factors, because the legal system needs operating closure so as to permit behavioral agendas that can generate reliability. Thus the legislative and judiciary have to be backward-looking, given the bindingness of the Constitution and other laws.[66]

Running the risk always posed by an excessively synthetic analysis, we can say that the author deploys the legal certainty principle "on the inside," i.e., as a principle that axiologically overlies the constitutional competence rules and the

---

[59] REsp n. 1.015.855-SP, 1st Panel, Reporting Justice José Delgado, *DJ* 30 Apr 2008.

[60] Alberto Xavier, *Os Princípios da legalidade e da tipicidade da tributação*, São Paulo, Ed. RT, 1978, p. 92. More recently, in a similar sense: idem, *Tipicidade da tributação, simulação e norma antielisiva*, São Paulo, Dialética, 2001, p. 18.

[61] Misabel de Abreu Machado Derzi, *Direito Tributário, Direito Penal e tipo*, São Paulo, Ed. RT, 1988, pages 191 and 248.

[62] Misabel de Abreu Machado Derzi, *Modificações da jurisprudência no Direito Tributário*, São Paulo, Noeses, 2009, pages 77 and following.

[63] Misabel de Abreu Machado Derzi, *Direito Tributário, Direito Penal e tipo*, São Paulo, Ed. RT, 1988, pages 195 and 264. Idem, *Modificações da Jurisprudência no Direito Tributário*, São Paulo, Noeses, 2009, pages 122, 124 and 144.

[64] Idem, *Modificações da jurisprudência no Direito Tributário*, São Paulo, Noeses, 2009, p. 120.

[65] Ibidem, p. 71.

[66] Ibidem, p. 57.

statutory competence hypotheses, "tightening" the interpretation of its content not only in the sense of not tolerating analogies or extensive interpretation of the norms that create or raise taxes, but also by demonstrating that its normative structure cannot be compatible with elements that are not abstractly defined. The illustrious scholar is quite right: Normative hypotheses must have fixed elements; otherwise it will be impossible to realize a minimum of knowability, one of the elements of the legal certainty principle.

Torres, in turn, demonstrates the impossibility in the linguistic plane of capturing the world in complete hypotheses because of the necessarily indeterminate nature of language.[67] His analysis starts with the impossibility of absolute linguistic determinacy, so that legal certainty cannot be satisfied by a naive belief in the possibility of closed legal concepts. At the same time, he argues from the necessity that in a society of risk, characterized by ambivalence, uncertainty, and a re-designing of the relationship between the powers of state institutions and society, it may even be inconceivable to expect incidence hypotheses to contain closed concepts, especially in the case of earmarked taxes, social contributions and taxes levied on extremely complex and technologically changing activities, which therefore repel classificatory conceptual rigidity.[68] This does not lead Torres to disregard the importance of the legal certainty principle or accept totally indeterminate incidence hypotheses – far from it. Yet again risking an excessively synthetic analysis, we can say that this author deploys the legal certainty principle "on the outside" and in connection with what he calls "principles of legitimation," such as proportionality and reasonableness. In other words, he understands that legal certainty, as a general principle of the legal order, needs principles to restrict the indeterminacy of legal hypotheses in the development and application of norms, limiting the arbitrariness of state power. Some taxes can justifiably be more indeterminate, as is the case of local rates and contributions, which require the applier to take into account changing realities that cannot be captured by classificatory concepts, whereas others, such as property taxes, must be more determinate. The key point is that there cannot be uniformity of determinacy in the legal incidence hypotheses because taxes refer to different realities and cannot always be adapted in the same manner to social change and the protection of diffuse interests. Moreover, the fact that some taxes have more indeterminate hypotheses does not mean their concretization

[67]Ricardo Lobo Torres, "Legalidade tributária e riscos sociais", *RDDT* 59, pages 95–112, São Paulo, 2000; idem, "O princípio da tipicidade no Direito Tributário", *RDA* 235, p. 207, 2004. Likewise: Ricardo Lodi Ribeiro, "Legalidade tributária, tipicidade aberta, conceitos indeterminados e cláusulas gerais tributárias", *RDA* 229, pp. 313–333, 2002; Sérgio André Rocha, "Existe um princípio da tipicidade no Direito Tributário?", *RDDT* 136, pages 68–79, São Paulo, 2007.

[68]Ricardo Lobo Torres, "Legalidade tributária e riscos sociais", *RDDT* 59, pages 101 and 103, São Paulo, 2000; idem, "Interação entre princípios constitucionais tributários e princípios da ordem econômica", in Roberto Ferraz (Org.), *Princípios e limites da tributação 2 – Os princípios da Ordem Econômica e a tributação*, São Paulo, Quartier Latin, 2009, p. 504. On the subject, see: Ricardo Lodi Ribeiro, *A segurança jurídica do contribuinte*, Rio de Janeiro, Lumen Juris, 2008, pages 31 and following.

cannot be controlled: The requirements of proportionality and reasonableness place limits on state regulatory action to assess whether indeterminacy is necessary and whether enforcement instruments make reasonable distinctions between the situations normatized.[69]

These brief comments, to which I could add a number as vast as the outstanding works of these authors, have a modest goal. What I mean to show is simply that the state of knowability, rather than determinacy, a state whose realization is required by the legal certainty principle, can be achieved in more than one way. Indeed, its realization can be based on the incidence hypotheses of tax rules, by highlighting the incompatibility between indeterminate hypotheses (due to their elements being alternative or indeterminate) and the ideal of normative intelligibility, or on mechanisms of legitimation that temper the inevitable indeterminacy of norms with other ends that the state also needs to attain. These are not opposing but complementary approaches. Language is inevitably indeterminate, and the indeterminacy of the norms therefore depends on the situation to be regulated and the structure of the tax which will deal with it. The indeterminacy of the incidence hypothesis is matched by greater control of the executive's and judiciary's activities via the postulates of proportionality and reasonableness.

Note that behind this debate are several ways of understanding law itself: It can be understood as an *object* – and thus examined in terms of the realization of legal certainty through the prior duty of assuring the greatest semantic closure possible, so that highly indeterminate norms are rejected, although there will always be an insurmountable margin of indeterminacy; from another perspective, it can be seen as *argumentative practice*, and hence analyzed in terms of the realization of legal certainty first through the prior duty of the greatest possible semantic determinacy, accepting a wider margin of indeterminacy if content mutability and diffusion do not allow for greater semantic closure, and second through control of legitimacy and argumentation in the normative regulation and application process. The point of these brief comments is that both stances, albeit by different routes, reject (excessive or unnecessary) indeterminacy of the incidence hypotheses and advocate control of state arbitrariness: the first mostly through semantic control; and the second primarily through argumentative control.

Far from choosing the comfortable path of eclecticism, this thesis opts for a proposition that combines semantic and argumentative elements, based on the foundations already presented. According to this approach, legal certainty involves a sort of argumentative-semantic controllability through the following methods:

1. *Legitimation* – Because they refer to different normative realities, normative hypotheses cannot have a uniform degree of determinacy, as some realities are more complex and unstable than others, and in some cases cannot be apprehended by means of classificatory concepts. Thus legitimation must be

[69] Ricardo Lobo Torres, "Legalidade tributária e riscos sociais", *RDDT* 59, p. 105, São Paulo, 2000.

controlled through the postulates of proportionality and reasonableness, so that relatively indeterminate legal incidence hypotheses can be adopted.

The duty of proportionality requires state actions to be appropriate, necessary and proportional in a strict sense. Appropriateness is a consequence of the positivation of an end to be attained and requires that the means used produce effects that contribute to its gradual promotion; necessity arises from the positivation of several ends to be achieved simultaneously and requires that, from all the equally appropriate means to a given end, the least restrictive means relative to other ends be chosen; proportionality results from the positivation of a set of ends to be globally attained and requires that the positive effects resulting from the promotion of an end be proportional to the negative effects resulting from the restriction of other goals.[70] In the case of the determinacy of normative hypotheses, the duty of proportionality prescribes that hypotheses bearing more indeterminate concepts can only be chosen by lawmakers when there are no terms that connote more precise properties. Otherwise, indeterminacy will be unnecessary and therefore illegitimate. Thus, for example, certain environmental taxes designed to protect the environment may have more indeterminate legal hypotheses. However, that does not mean they can be realized arbitrarily. The postulate of reasonableness must be used to control the existence of congruence, equivalence and equity in its concretization.

Among other requirements, the duty of reasonableness requires that concretization of the concept take into account the specifics of the concrete case, without unreasonable treatment of subjects in equivalent situations.[71] Thus the fact that the hypothesis is more indeterminate does not necessarily lead to arbitrariness in its application. This is because the executive has to concretize the (less) determinate concept through secondary normative instruments that take into account the specifics of concrete cases and make a reasonable distinction between taxpayers, so that the entire process of concretization is subject to jurisdictional control. Thus secondary normative acts, embodied in acts that interpret legislation (*norminterpretierende Verwaltungsvorschriften*), to help clarify facts (*Verwaltungsvorschriften der Sachverhaltermittlung*), typify the facts (*Typisierungsvorschriften*) and guide the administration's discretionary appreciation (*ermessenslenkende Verwaltungsvorschriften*), must accord with the ideals of equality and equity.[72]

2. *Determinacy* – The interpreter must reconstruct the minimum meanings of the expressions used by the Constitution in order to verify whether the terms utilized do not have concepts that have already been the object of argumentation

[70]Ricardo Lobo Torres, "A legitimação dos direitos humanos e os princípios da ponderação e da razoabilidade", in idem (Org.), *Legitimação dos direitos humanos*, 2nd ed., Rio de Janeiro, Renovar, 2007, pages 502 and following.

[71]Ibidem, p. 498.

[72]Johanna Hey, *Steuerplanungssicherheit als Rechtsproblem*, Köln, Otto Schmidt, 2002, pages 21, 28 and 48.

processes. For example, in using the term "*salário*" the Constitution ultimately retrieves the concept of wage or salary already sedimented in the labor laws and in labor law doctrine; in using the term "*faturamento*" (sales) it harks back to a concept used by pre-constitutional ordinary legislation, especially Decree-Law 2397/87 and the Corporations Law (*Lei das SA*). In this sense, interpretative activity is not free because it works from concepts that have already been highly determined by previous argumentative use, so that the use of certain expressions points to a process of concept incorporation that the interpreter cannot avoid. This rejects the conception according to which a norm is constructed exclusively for each case, as if there were no prior intersubjective meanings which the interpreter must take into account. Barzotto is therefore right to say this:

> If law is interpretation, we must identify law and interpretation, the laws and their interpretation. But where is the object to be interpreted, if it is given by the interpretation? And if the object is given by the interpretation, how can we distinguish between the interpretation of the Bible, a cookbook, and the Constitution, since we cannot argue for an objective difference between Bible, cookbook and Constitution before we interpret them? If the object to be interpreted is its interpretation, then we cannot distinguish between good and bad interpretations by reference to the object, because it does not exist outside of the interpretation. The question is no longer: 'What is the best interpretation of *x*?' because this formulation assumes that *x* is different from the interpretation of *x*.[73]

In sum, the interpretative activity is neither totally constructive nor entirely descriptive, but reconstructive and situational, producing minimal meanings of normative provisions.

This process of incorporation, however, is feasible only if allowed by the *constitutional context*, i.e., if there is constitutional room for the concept to be incorporated. Room will exist if the incorporation is allowed by the tax competence rules, on one hand, and by the general competence rules, on the other. Incorporation will be allowed if the overall interpretation of *tax competence* rules does not imply a different concept. This is because the Constitution also indirectly fixes concepts by *implication* when, in empowering a federal entity to tax only *one event*, it indirectly empowers a different federal entity to tax *another event*. Thus, for example, if the Constitution empowers states to tax sales of goods, in accordance with the concept of the "obligation to deliver something" under the civil legislation, in empowering municipalities to tax services it can only be acknowledging their competence to tax the "obligation to do something." Because the Constitution institutes a Federative Republic (article 1), which presupposes legislative autonomy of the federal entities and uniformity of their actions, each entity is empowered to tax certain events but the concept of these events may not "coincide" with those pertaining to another entity. This means first that there will be constitutional room for the intended incorporation of concepts if the context of tax competence rules does not have comparable terms whose simultaneous utilization causes conceptual divergence.

---

[73]Luís Fernando Barzotto, *Filosofia do Direito: os Conceitos fundamentais e a tradição jusnaturalista*, Porto Alegre, Livraria do Advogado, 2009, pages 130–131.

Furthermore, incorporation will be allowed if the overall interpretation of *general* competence rules does not imply a different concept. This is because the Constitution often uses similar terms in other competence rules, so that the concept assigned to the term found in the tax competence rule must be different. For example, before passage of the 20th Amendment (1998), the term "*salário*" was used in the Constitution to empower the federal government to create social contributions. Strictly speaking, however, there was not one but two concepts of *salário*: wage or salary, referred to in the labor legislation as "remuneration"; and shadow salary, referred to in the social security legislation as "contribution salary", i.e. the basis for calculating pensions and benefits. In deciding which of the two was adopted by the Constitution, the Supreme Court understood that the term "*salário*" was used with the meaning defined in the labor laws because when the framers of the Constitution wished to connote properties other than those embodied by this concept, as in article 201, paragraph 5, they used the expression "contribution salary" instead of the simple word "salary," just as the term "worker" is used instead of "employee" in other provisions.[74] Second, therefore, there will be constitutional room for the intended incorporation if the concept to be incorporated is in accordance with the set of general competence rules, i.e., if the context of general competence rules does not contain comparable terms whose simultaneous use implies different conceptualizations.

The key point to retain from all that has been said is that the use of terms that have been the object of previous connotation practices determines conceptual parameters that lawmakers cannot disregard.

3. *Argumentation* – Although reference to certain terms institutes a process of incorporation of concepts already sedimented by prior argumentative use, and thus limits the interpreter's freedom through semantic factors, it does not exclude argumentation itself. This is because other elements are not semantically predetermined. For example, although the Constitution uses the term "*faturamento*" to refer to sales for social security purposes in article 195, it should be noted that at least three concepts of "*faturamento*" are found in Brazilian law: the 1850 Commercial Code uses the term to mean billings; the 1976 Corporations Act (*Lei das SA*) uses the term to mean operating revenue; and Decree-Law 2397/87, which deals with corporate income tax, refers to the revenue earned from the provision of services and sale of goods. When it had to choose between the commercial, corporate and tax concepts, the Supreme Court preferred the tax concept in Decree-Law 2397/87. While it did not explicitly justify this choice, the Court presumably considered the concept in the Commercial Code too old and out of date, adopting the concept in Decree-Law 2397/87 coupled with the term's meaning in the Corporations Act because the former was more current than the latter and thus more appropriate to the competence rule that used it, which

[74]RE n. 166.772-9, Full Court, Reporting Justice Marco Aurélio, j. 12 May 94, *DJ* 16 Dec 94, p. 34.896.

was a tax competence rule.[75] This shows that in order to know which concept is presupposed in the Constitution, we must select criteria for the solution of antinomies, choosing the existing criteria that best match the specific competence rule provided for.

In sum, the incorporation of concepts from the pre-1988 infraconstitutional order must be compatible with the general and tax competence rules. Concepts incompatible with the new constitutional order cannot be incorporated. Such decisions are not straightforward, however, but *result* from a process of contextualization of the concepts assignable to the terms found in the constitutional provisions. This contextualization process, it bears repeating, is permeated with arguments with multiple dimensions: linguistic, systematic, genetic, historical and pragmatic.[76] Given an issue to be resolved, the use of arguments and the prevalence of one over another in the intended normative construction will need to be justified.[77] The main rule is that prevalence be given to arguments leading back to the principles of the democratic law-based state, which means preferring linguistic and systematic arguments over others.[78]

Lastly, it should be noted that argumentation is not limited to the normative plane, but also targets the facts. Factual elements are not ready-made before the process of application, but depend on value judgments oriented by the legal order. Even though the normative concept may be clear, there may be uncertainty regarding the factual situation. For instance, there may be no doubt about the obligation to do something embodied in the concept of a service, yet uncertainty might nevertheless be justified as to whether a service was in fact performed, given the difficulty of assessing which of the several factual elements should be considered preponderant. A case in point is the taxation by municipalities of leasing or custom manufacturing as services. Although there is agreement on the concept of services as involving an obligation to do something, whether such an obligation can be discerned on the factual plane is disputed. This is because of the already mentioned issues of proof, qualification, interpretation and relevance that are inherent in law and transcend merely semantic and strictly conceptual questions.[79]

4. *Justification* – The processes of legitimation, determination and argumentation, however, must be the object of a rational written discourse capable of assuring access to the reasons that justify normative reconstruction, on one hand, and to the evidence that demonstrates the occurrence of the factual elements to which

[75] RE n. 150.755-1, Full Court, Reporting Justice Carlos Velloso, Opinion of the Court by Justice Sepúlveda Pertence, j. 18 Nov 92, *DJ* 20 Aug 93, p. 16.322.

[76] Juha Raitio, *The Principle of Legal Certainty in EC Law*, Dordrecht, Kluwer, 2003, p. 307.

[77] Humberto Ávila, "Juristische Theorie der Argumentation", in Andreas Heldrich *et alii* (Orgs.), *FS für Claus-Wilhelm Canaris zum 70. Geburtstag*, München, Beck, 2007, pages 963–989.

[78] Juha Raitio, *The Principle of Legal Certainty in EC Law*, Dordrecht, Kluwer, 2003, p. 316.

[79] Neil MacCormick, "Rhetoric and rule of law", in David Dyzenhaus (Org.), *Recrafting the rule of Law – The Limits of Legal Order*, Oxford, Hart, 1999, p. 175.

they refer, on the other. It bears repeating that the application of the laws, especially the tax laws, intertwines norms and facts. The construction of facts through language depends on the perspective from which the applier analyzes them. A norm initially considered applicable may ultimately prove inapplicable in light of the facts as ultimately understood.[80] Thus both the normative and factual pieces require justification, including details of how the decision was reached and the foundations used to justify it.

What is meant by the above commentary is that legal certainty as described here does not revolve *exclusively* around semantics but is grounded in a *combination* of argumentative and semantic elements, which act as factors of legitimation, determination, argumentation and justification. In sum, instead of a notion of legal certainty based solely on a discoursive method of conceptual determination of normative premises, the concept of legal certainty proposed here is grounded in a metadiscoursive and applicative method of semantic-argumentative controllability, which controls legitimation, determination, argumentation and justification not only of the premises but also of the methods and results of norms. Thus instead of an *atomistic* conception, what is proposed here is a *holistic* notion of legal certainty, based on a *balance* among various elements.[81]

It is important to stress that the above considerations do not lead to dismissal of the typicality principle. As stated earlier, the duty to determine the hypothesis as clearly as possible remains valid.[82] As long as the topic can be legislated for using terms whose properties have undergone a prior process of conceptual fixation, a federal entity is duty-bound to choose such terms, reducing the margin of arbitrariness as much as possible. If this is the case, once the elements of a tax obligation having been defined by statute, administrative action must not overstep their bounds.[83] It is crucial to bear in mind that the rules and the concepts that their words may connote also "crystallize" values, as stressed by Machado Derzi, especially the values of certainty and equality.[84] What must also be understood, however, is that the requirement of determinacy is not absolute and uniform for each and every sector of reality. In some cases, there may be less determinacy,

[80]Jürgen Habermas, *Faktizität und Geltung*, Darmstadt, Wissenschaftliche Buchgesellschaft, 2002, p. 268.

[81]Gianluigi Palombella, *Dopo la Certezza – Il Diritto in equilibrio tra Giustizia e Democrazia*, Bari, Dedalo, 2006, p. 7.

[82]Luís Eduardo Schoueri, "Tributação e indução econômica: os efeitos econômicos de um tributo como critério para sua constitucionalidade", in Roberto Ferraz (Org.), *Princípios e limites da tributação 2 – Os Princípios da Ordem Econômica e a Tributação*, São Paulo, Quartier Latin, 2009, p. 163.

[83]Roque Antonio Carrazza, *Curso de Direito Constitucional Tributário*, 27th ed., São Paulo, Malheiros Editores, 2011, pages 458–459.

[84]Misabel de Abreu Machado Derzi, *Modificações da jurisprudência no Direito Tributário*, São Paulo, Noeses, 2009, p. 186.

although these are rare; in others, the vast majority in fact, there must be more.[85] To underscore the point once more, the unnecessary use of terms with a high degree of indeterminacy, when for the sector being normatized there are terms whose properties have already undergone argumentative processes of connotation, is a violation of the legal certainty principle. Nevertheless, it is quite wrong to continue arguing that the legal certainty principle is concretized exclusively or mostly through the determination of incidence hypotheses, and ignoring the fact that some realities in a modern society cannot be "grasped" conceptually.[86]

If legal certainty is understood as requiring determinability instead of absolute determinacy, as advocated here, it follows that the application of penalties must be reviewed in cases where a taxpayer's behavior corresponds to one of the possible interpretations of the norm concerned. After all, the calculability dimension of legal certainty requires a state in which taxpayers are highly likely to be able to predict alternative meanings. So how can taxpayers be punished if the alternative they choose, albeit different from the one later preferred by the applier, was one of the possible interpretations of the abstract norm? Thus if the legal certainty principle is understood as requiring knowability and calculability, the norm in article 100 of the National Tax Code must be reinterpreted. Although it points in the right direction by assuring that penalties are not imposed when an administrative decision legitimates a taxpayer's behavior, it does not rule out the application of penalties for the exercising of activities compatible with one of a tax norm's possible semantic interpretations. If this possibility were explicitly ruled out beyond a shadow of doubt, taxpayers would no longer feel the need to take preventive measures to eliminate uncertainty or the risk of being penalized for tax arrears, such as applying for an advance tax ruling or filing for an injunction to suspend the assessment or collection of a tax.

So far we have examined the prerequisites for the existence of intellectual accessibility to norms. Nothing has been said about whether and to what extent rules and principles are types of norms that are compatible with legal certainty. As legal certainty requires knowability, reliability and calculability, a system made up exclusively of principles is incompatible with it, for lack of minimally comprehensible behavioral hypotheses to assure what is known as "certainty of orientation."[87] A system made up of principles alone would become minimally intelligible only after its continuous, uniform and justified application by the judiciary. In this case, however, not the principles but their careful application through concrete rules of prevalence would be the instruments that guaranteed

[85]Ricardo Lobo Torres, "Legalidade tributária e riscos sociais", *RDDT* 59, pages 101 and 102, São Paulo, 2000.

[86]Ricardo Lodi Ribeiro, *A segurança jurídica do contribuinte*, Rio de Janeiro, Lumen Juris, 2008, pages 58 and 261.

[87]Theodor Geiger, *Vorstudien zu einer Soziologie des Rechts*, 4ª ed., Berlin, Duncker und Humblot, 1987, p. 64; Theophilo Cavalcanti Filho, *O problema da segurança no Direito*, São Paulo, Ed. RT, 1964, p. 50; Frederick Schauer, *Thinking like a Lawyer: a New Introduction to Legal Reasoning*, Cambridge, Harvard University Press, 2009, p. 190.

knowability. Thus legal certainty would derive from the rules that concretized the principles, rather than from the principles themselves. Hence the statement that legal certainty is incompatible with models of decision not based on prior general norms and limited to the pursuit of individualized case-by-case justice.[88] That is, a legal system made up mostly of rules, not principles. Among the many reasons for this, two stand out: on one hand, the fact that rules favor the intelligibility of law by describing what is forbidden, allowed or mandatory; on the other, the circumstance that by hypothesis the rules, if assigned some degree of rigidity, both include the reasons to be considered in their application and exclude those not to be considered.[89] The inclusion and exclusion of elements to be considered favor the ideals that make up legal certainty: knowability, insofar as citizens know what they ought and ought not to consider; calculability, since the application of norms focuses on predetermined elements and hence cannot be merely subjective, capricious, and therefore arbitrary. We will come back to this point in the discussion of calculability of law.

3.2.2 Of the Legal Order

3.2.2.1 Coherence

The legal certainty principle as defined in this study requires, among other things, the realization of a state of affairs in which citizens are capable of a high degree of intellectual comprehension of argumentative structures that reconstruct the *possible normative content* of a norm, and of anticipating and measuring the *range of consequences assignable* to acts or facts. This concept presupposes the alternativity of normative content and consequences. One of the factors that decisively contribute to increased knowability of normative content and calculability of the consequences is the coherence of the legal order, also known as *material consistency*.

Coherence, from the static point of view, means the gradual relationship of support a given alternative receives from the legal order as a whole and, from the dynamic point of view, the requirement of uniform application of norms.[90] The static dimension helps reduce uncertainty as to which alternative interpretation is correct, indicating which of the alternatives compatible with the provision being interpreted is most strongly supported by the legal order, especially its fundamental principles. The dynamic dimension helps reduce uncertainty as to which normative

---

[88]Federico Arcos Ramírez, *La seguridad jurídica: una teoría formal*, Madrid, Dykinson, 2000, p. 220.

[89]Federico Arcos Ramírez, *La seguridad jurídica: una teoría formal*, Madrid, Dykinson, 2000, p. 230.

[90]Anne-Laure Valembois, *La constitutionnalisation de l'exigence de sécurité juridique en Droit Français*, Paris, LGDJ, 2005, p. 199; Susanne Bracker, *Kohärenz und juristische Interpretation*, Baden-Baden, Nomos, 2000, p. 177; Aleksander Peczenik, ***Scientia Juris*** . *Legal doctrine as knowledge of Law and as a source of Law*, Dordrecht, Springer, 2005, pages 115 and following.

consequence is most likely to be imposed in future, since the duty of uniform application allows citizens, knowing the normative consequences assigned to analogous acts or facts, to foresee the imposition of the same consequence to similar acts they may perform. We will return to this point when analyzing the requirement of calculability of law.

3.2.2.2 Consistency

The duty of consistency or formal coherence means the requirement of non-contradiction between norms in both the stage of enactment by the legislative and the application stage.[91]

It also contributes to the knowability and calculability of the legal order: Because norms cannot conflict with one another, the possible semantic alternatives are restricted to those that are compatible with the axiologically overlying norms; because the application of these norms cannot contradict the solutions given previously, citizens can foresee the future consequences to be assigned to acts they may practice with a greater degree of approximation. Hence the level of congruence and harmony among normative propositions is clearly part of the of legal certainty principle.[92]

4 Final Considerations

These comments permit the conclusion, first, that for legal certainty to exist as a requirement of knowability of law the addressees must have a minimum of knowledge about the existence, validity, enforceability and efficacy of norms; they must know that a norm exists, is presumably valid, is producing effects and will probably be enforced institutionally if it is not obeyed spontaneously. For this to happen, the addressees need to understand the norm, comprehend its meaning and extent, and know its value and the consequences of non-compliance. Thus either knowability is complete and connected with its efficacy, or it does not guarantee legal certainty. A simple example will illustrate this point.

Imagine the case of a Brazilian coming home after a trip abroad and arriving at customs, where a system of randomly changing colored lights is used, with "green" meaning you can pass uninspected and "red" meaning you must stop for your baggage to be checked by customs officials. In this situation, normative knowability exists only if the following requirements are met: The addressees must understand

[91] Anne-Laure Valembois, *La constitutionnalisation de l'exigence de sécurité juridique en Droit Français*, Paris, LGDJ, 2005, p. 198.

[92] Paulo de Barros Carvalho, "Segurança jurídica e modulação dos efeitos", *Revista da Fundação Escola Superior de Direito Tributário* 1/206, Porto Alegre, 2008.

"what the norm is" – which in this case means they must know that inspection depends on the color shown; they must comprehend "what the norm means" – which in this case corresponds to knowing that "green" signals no inspection and "red" signals inspection; they must comprehend "the extent of the norm" regarding their actions – which in this case means that "green" translates as "go ahead" and "red" as "open your bags please." However, as the next part of this book will make clear, understanding and comprehending the meaning and extent of the norm is not enough to assure certainty. The addressee must also know the value of the norm and the consequences of disobeying it. To continue with the same example, the addressee must know whether "red" really is "red", or might perhaps be deemed "green" for a modest consideration, or whether, even if the official thinks it is "red", the institutional body in charge of applying the rule might eventually change the color code and assign the same effects to "red" and "green." In other words, there is no legal certainty if the addressee knows "green" means pass uninspected and "red" means stop, knows "green" means "go ahead" and "red" means "open your bags please," but does not know whether "red" will be considered "red" or "green" by the duty official or whether "red" can be assigned the same effects as "green" by the law-applying body. Thus for legal certainty to exist, it is essential that what is guaranteed by compliance with the requirement of knowability of law is not frustrated by failure to comply with the duty of reliability. Or, to use a metaphor, it is essential that what comes in at the door does not end up flying out of the window. "Certainty of existence and validity" without "certainty of application" is not legal certainty. Once again, as constantly reiterated throughout this book, either legal certainty is complete or it is not legal certainty.

References

ARCOS RAM´iREZ, Federico. *La seguridad jurídica: una teoría formal*. Madrid: Dykinson, 2000.

von ARNAULD, Andreas. *Rechtssicherheit*. Tübingen: Mohr Siebeck, 2006.

ATALIBA, Geraldo. *Sistema constitucional tributário brasileiro*. São Paulo: Ed. RT, 1968.

ÁVILA, Humberto. "Juristische Theorie der Argumentation". In HELDRICH, Andreas *et alii* (Orgs.). *FS für Claus-Wilhelm Canaris zum 70. Geburtstag*. München: Beck, 2007, pp. 963–989.

BARZOTTO, Luis Fernando. *Filosofia do Direito – Os conceitos fundamentais e a tradição jusnaturalista*. Porto Alegre: Livraria do Advogado, 2009.

BORGES, José Souto Maior. *Obrigação tributária – Uma introdução metodológica*. São Paulo: Saraiva, 1984.

_____."O princípio da segurança jurídica na criação e aplicação do tributo", *RDDT* 22, São Paulo, 1997.

CANAZARO, Fábio. *Lei Complementar Tributária na Constituição de 1988*. Porto Alegre: Livraria do Advogado, 2005.

CARRAZZA, Roque Antonio. *Curso de Direito Constitucional Tributário*. 27ª ed. São Paulo: Malheiros Editores, 2011.

CARVALHO, Paulo de Barros. "Segurança jurídica e modulação dos efeitos". *Revista da Fundação Escola Superior de Direito Tributário*, n. 1, Porto Alegre, 2008, pp. 203–216.

CAVALCANTI FILHO, Theophilo. *O problema da segurança no Direito*. São Paulo: Ed. RT, 1964

CHEVALLIER, Jacques. "Le Droit Économique: l'insécurité juridique ou nouvelle sécurité juridique?". In: BOY, Laurence; RACINE, Jean-Baptiste; SIIRIAINEN, Fabrice (Orgs.). *Sécurité Juridique et Droit Économique*. Bruxelles: Larcier, 2008.

DELLA VALLE, Eugenio. *Affidamento e certezza del Diritto Tributario*. Milano: Giuffrè, 2001.

ENTERRIA, Eduardo García de. *Justicia y Seguridad Jurídica en un Mundo de Leyes Desbocadas*. Madrid: Civitas, 1999.

FERRAJOLI, Luigi. "The past and the future of the rule of law". In: COSTA, Pietro; ZOLO, Danilo Zolo (Orgs.). *The rule of Law – History, theory and criticism*, Dordrecht, Springer, 2007.

FERRAZ JR., Tércio Sampaio. "Segurança jurídica, coisa julgada e justiça", *Revista do Instituto de Hermenêutica Jurídica*, v. 1, n. 3, Porto Alegre, 2005.

_____. "Segurança jurídica e normas gerais tributárias", *RDT* 17–18, São Paulo, 1981.

FERRERO LAPATZA, J. J. "El principio de seguridad jurídica en la creación y aplicación del tributo". *CT* 1968.

GEIGER, Theodor. *Vorstudien zu einer Soziologie des Rechts*. 4ª ed. Berlin: Duncker und Humblot, 1987.

GOMES CANOTILHO, José Joaquim. *Direito Constitucional e Teoria da Constituição*. 7ª ed. 6ª reimp. Coimbra: Almedina, 2004.

GRAU, Eros Roberto. *Ensaio e discurso sobre a interpretação/aplicação do Direito*. 5th ed. São Paulo: Malheiros Editores, 2009.

HABERMAS, Jürgen. *Faktizität und Geltung*. Darmstadt: Wissenschaftliche Buchgesellschaft, 2002.

HEY, Johanna. *Steuerplanungssicherheit als Rechtsproblem*. Köln: Otto Schmidt, 2002.

JURATOWITCH, Ben. *Retroactivity and the Common Law*. Oxford: Hart, 2008.

LUHMANN, Niklas. *Ausdifferenzierung des Rechts – Beiträge zur Rechtssoziologie und Rechtstheorie*. Frankfurt am Main: Suhrkamp, 1999.

MacCORMICK, Neil. *Legal reasoning and legal theory*. Oxford: Clarendon, 1978.

_____. "Rhetoric and rule of law". In: DYZENHAUS, David (Org.). *Recrafting the rule of Law – The Limits of Legal Order*. Oxford: Hart, 1999.

MACHADO, Hugo de Brito Machado, "Os princípios da anterioridade e da irretroatividade das leis tributárias e a publicação da lei", *Cadernos de Direito Tributário e Finanças Públicas* 8, São Paulo, 1994.

MACHADO DERZI, Misabel de Abreu. *Direito Tributário, Direito Penal e tipo*. São Paulo, Ed. RT, 1988.

____. *Modificações da jurisprudência no Direito Tributário*. São Paulo: Noeses, 2009.

MARMOR, Andrei. *Law in the age of pluralism*. Oxford: OUP, 2007.

MÜNCH, Christof. "Rechtssicherheit als Standortfaktor. Gedanken aus Sicht der vorsorgenden Rechtspflege". In: WEBER, Albrecht (Org.). *Währung und Wirtschaft. Das Geld im Recht. FS für Hugo J. Hahn*. Baden-Baden: Nomos, 1997.

NEVES, Marcelo. *Entre Têmis e Leviatã: uma relação difícil – O Estado Democrático de Direito a partir e além de Luhmann e Habermas*. São Paulo: Martins Fontes, 2006.

NOVOA, César García. *El principio de seguridad jurídica en materia tributaria*. Madrid: Marcial Pons, 2000.

OLIVEIRA, Carlos Alberto Alvaro de. *Do formalismo no Processo Civil*. 3rd ed. São Paulo: Saraiva, 2009.

PALOMBELLA, Gianluigi. *Dopo la Certezza – Il Diritto in equilibrio tra Giustizia e Democrazia*. Bari: Dedalo, 2006.

PECZENIK, Aleksander. *"Scientia Juris". Legal Doctrine as Knowledge of Law and as a Source of Law*. Dordrecht: Springer, 2005.

PREISER, Friedrich. "Rechtsstaatswidrige Rechtsunsicherheit. Vorschläge zur Erzielung von Rechtsunsicherheit". *DVBl*, n. 83, 1968, pp. 545–549.

RAITIO, Juha. *The Principle of Legal Certainty in EC Law*. Dordrecht: Kluwer, 2003.

RAZ, Joseph. "The Rule of Law and its Virtue" (1977). In *The Authority of Law. Essays on Law and Morality*. Oxford: Oxford, 1979, pp. 210–229.

RIBEIRO, Ricardo Lodi. "Legalidade tributária, tipicidade aberta, conceitos indeterminados e cláusulas gerais tributárias", *RDA* 229, pp. 313–333, 2002.

_____. *A segurança jurídica do contribuinte*. Rio de Janeiro: Lumen Juris, 2008.

ROCHA, Sérgio André. "Existe um princípio da tipicidade no Direito Tributário?", *RDDT* 136, pp. 68–79, São Paulo, 2007.

von SAVIGNY, Friedrich Carl. *Vom Beruf unserer Zeit für Gesetzgebung und Rechtswissenschaft*. Heidelberg: Mohr und Zimmer, 1814.

SCHAUER, Frederick. *Thinking like a lawyer: a new introduction to legal reasoning*. Cambridge: Harvard University Press, 2009.

SCHOUERI, Luís Eduardo. "Tributação e indução econômica: os efeitos econômicos de um tributo como critério para sua constitucionalidade". In FERRAZ, Roberto (Org.). *Princípios e Limites da Tributação 2 – Os Princípios da Ordem Econômica e a Tributação*. São Paulo: Quartier Latin, 2009, pp. 140–164.

SCHRIMM-HEINS, Andrea. "Gewissheit und Sicherheit: Geschichte und Bedeutungswandel der Begriffe 'certitudo' und 'securitas'" (Teil 1). *Archiv für Begriffsgeschichte*, v. 34, 1991, pp. 123–213.

SEABRA DE MOURA, Frederico Araújo. *Lei Complementar Tributária*. São Paulo: Quartier Latin, 2009.

SOUSA, Rubens Gomes de. *Compêndio de legislação tributária*. Edição póstuma. São Paulo: Resenha Tributária, 1975.

_____. *Tipicidade da tributação, simulação e norma antielisiva*. São Paulo: Dialética, 2001.

TORRES, Ricardo Lobo. "O princípio da tipicidade no Direito Tributário". In RIBEIRO, Ricardo Lodi; ROCHA, Sergio André (Orgs.). *Legalidade e Tipicidade no Direito Tributário*. São Paulo: Quartier Latin, 2008, pp. 137–184.

_____. "Legalidade tributária e riscos sociais", *RDDT* 59, pp. 95–112, São Paulo, 2000.

_____. "Interação entre princípios constitucionais tributários e princípios da ordem econômica". In FERRAZ, Roberto (Org.). *Princípios e limites da tributação 2 – Os princípios da ordem econômica e a tributação*. São Paulo: Quartier Latin, 2009, pp. 491–516.

_____. "A legitimação dos direitos humanos e os princípios da ponderação e da razoabilidade". In TORRES, Ricardo Lobo (Org.). *Legitimação dos direitos humanos*. 2ª ed. Rio de Janeiro: Renovar, 2007, pp. 467–520.

_____. *Normas de interpretação e integração do Direito Tributário*. 3ª ed. Rio de Janeiro: Renovar, 2000.

VALEMBOIS, Anne-Laure. *La constitutionnalisation de l'exigence de sécurité juridique en Droit Français*. Paris: LGDJ, 2005.

XAVIER, Alberto. *Os princípios da legalidade e da tipicidade da tributação*. São Paulo: Ed. RT, 1978.

_____. *Tipicidade da tributação, simulação e norma antielisiva*. São Paulo: Dialética, 2001.

ZIMMER, Willy. "Constitution et sécurité juridique – Allemagne". *Annuaire International de Justice Constitutionnelle 1999*. Paris: Economica, 2000, pp. 91–107.

Dynamic Dimension

Abstract The discussion now turns to the dynamic dimension of legal certainty. The dynamic dimension concerns the problem of action in time and the ideals that must be guaranteed if law is to "assure" citizens of rights and thus act as an instrument of their protection. The chapter therefore deals with the ideals of reliability and calculability. Reliability means the ideal state in which citizens can know which changes are allowed or prohibited, avoiding frustration of their rights. Thus reliability exists only if citizens can be assured today of the effects that law assured them yesterday, which in turn depends on the inviolability of past situations, the durability of the legal order, and the irretroactivity of present norms. Calculability means the ideal state in which citizens know how and when changes can be made, so that they are not surprised. Thus calculability exists only if citizens can control today the effects law will assign tomorrow, which is the case only when they can anticipate and measure a fairly invariable range of criteria and argumentative structures that define consequences to be assigned, heteronomously and coercively or autonomously and spontaneously, to their own actions or those of others, or to facts that have actually occurred or might occur in future, whether or not they are in dispute, as well as the reasonable time frame within which the final consequences will be applied.

1 Initial Considerations

So far we have examined the static dimension of the legal certainty principle, i.e., the part concerned with the structural requisites law must have in order to serve as a guide for citizens to shape the present with dignity, without deception, freely, and autonomously according to law. Having addressed the problem of knowledge of law, we must now turn to the dynamic dimension of legal certainty, which has to do especially with problems of realization of law. We will seek to answer the following question: What elements are necessary for citizens to assure the legal effects of freedom exercised in the past, and freely and autonomously to plan the future in a legally informed manner without frustration or surprise? Rather than focusing on requirements relating to *norms*, here we must examine the requirements relating to

© Springer International Publishing Switzerland 2016

H. Ávila, *Certainty in Law*, Law and Philosophy Library 114,
DOI 10.1007/978-3-319-33407-3_9

the *acts* indispensable to their application.[1] Whereas the static dimension concerns the problems of knowledge and quality of law, the dynamic dimension concerns the problems of action in time and transition in law.

The first step is to analyze the conditions for realization of law: Citizens need to be able to know whether the freedom they legally exercised yesterday will be respected today, and whether the freedom they exercise today will be respected tomorrow. "Citizens gain trust in the laws they are entrusted with", as Kirchhof argues.[2] However, what must be inserted as an element of reliability or calculability depends on stipulative definitions, since frustration and surprise, albeit conceptually connected to the notion of time, are not necessarily bound to a *past-* or *future-oriented* analysis of time. This explains, for example, why the requirement of continuity is part of the requirement of reliability through stability for some, such as Arcos Ramírez, whereas for others, such as Hey, it is part of the requirement of calculability through the duties of systematic coherence and equality over time.[3] This occurs because terms such as "stability," "continuity" and "permanence" are indeterminate relative to *content* and to the *temporal perspective* from which they can be analyzed: stable, in the sense of something that is set and does not change, relating to an event in the past that cannot be changed in the present or an event in the present that cannot be changed in future. The use of the terms "continuous" and "permanent" is similar, because it can be asked whether what happened yesterday ought to continue or remain permanent today, as well as whether what is happening today should continue or remain permanent tomorrow. It is precisely for this reason that the prohibition of retroactivity can be both inserted as an element of reliability of law for its stability, in the sense of illustrating the duty of maintaining today what was valid yesterday, and described as an element of calculability of law for its bindingness, in the sense of requiring that what is valid today will be upheld tomorrow. Hence Calmes treats irretroactivity as part of the ideal of predictability of the legal order,[4] while von Arnauld considers it part of the ideal of stability.[5] Because of this diversity of perspectives, Ost refers to the past as "memory" and to the future as "promise," arguing that memory is a *retrospective* or *past-oriented projection* of promise, and promise is a *prospective* or *future-oriented projection* of memory.[6]

---

[1] Federico Arcos Ramírez, *La seguridad jurídica: una teoría formal*, Madrid, Dykinson, 2000, p. 54.

[2] Paul Kirchhof, "Rückwirkung von Steuergesetzen", *StuW*, 2000, p. 222.

[3] Federico Arcos Ramírez, *La seguridad jurídica: una teoría formal*, Madrid, Dykinson, 2000, p. 269. Johanna Hey, *Steuerplanungssicherheit als Rechtsproblem*, Köln, Otto Schmidt, 2002, p. 189.

[4] Sylvia Calmes, *Du principe de protection de la confiance légitime en Droits Allemand, Communautaire et Français*, Paris, Dalloz, 2001, p. 159.

[5] Andreas von Arnauld, *Rechtssicherheit*, Tübingen, Mohr Siebeck, 2006, p. 324.

[6] François Ost, *Le Temps du Droit*, Paris, Odile Jacob, 1999, p. 34. Idem, "L'instantané ou l'institué? L'institué ou l'intantuant? Le Droit a-t-il pour vocation de durer?", in François Ost

It could also be said that reliability is a past-oriented projection of calculability, and the latter is a future-oriented projection of reliability – two sides of the same coin.

In sum, without a *semantic agreement* regarding the object, the perspective and the emphasis, terms such as "continuity," "permanence," "stability" and "duration" are entirely interchangeable, as they do not specify "what" continues, remains, stabilizes or lasts, or "with regard to what", or "why." Thus it is necessary to specify whether the "direction in time" is retrospective or prospective.[7]

Because the terms concerned are exchangeable depending on the meaning they are given, let us stipulate the meanings of the terms "reliability" and "calculability" as used here. "Reliability" (*Verlässlichkeit*) is used *retrospectively* (*mit Blick in die Vergangenheit, perspectiva retrospectiva*), to refer to the past or the transition from past to present (*ex post, par renvoi au passé*) while *focusing on permanence* and *on the object*, and thus encompassing the elements that prohibit modification or a specific modification in the present of something gained in the past; "calculability" (*Berechenbarkeit*) is used prospectively (*mit Blick in die Zukunft, perspectiva prospectiva*), to refer to the future or the transition from present to future (*ex ante, par renvoi au futur*) while *focusing on change* and *its mode*, and thus encompassing the elements that prescribe the pace of future change in what is being realized in the present. In other words, the term "reliability" is used to denote elements from the past that must remain in the present of law, while "calculability" is used to denote elements from the present that must be maintained in the transition to its future. In line with Ost's argument, reliability is law's "memory" mitigated by "forgiveness" and calculability its "promise" tempered by "adaptation": against forgetfulness, tradition; against the uncertainty of the future, promise.[8] These stipulations in no way diminish the fact that legal certainty necessarily involves the issue of time and moreover does so in a dialectical way, simultaneously looking backward and forward, and that jurists are duty-bound to acknowledge that legal certainty must sometimes be analyzed retrospectively, and sometimes prospectively.[9]

Besides enabling a clear distinction to be made between the two dynamic dimensions of legal certainty, this semantic option harmonizes with the more traditional use of the terms: "Reliability" is usually associated with the idea of prohibition of change, and hence with subjective inviolability and objective durability; "calculability" is traditionally linked to the concept of slow or constant change, and hence to continuity.[10]

---

and Mark van Hoecke (Orgs.), *Temps et Droit. Le Droit a-t-il pour vocation de durer*?, Bruxelles, Bruylant, 1998, p. 14.

[7]Mark van Hoecke, "Time and law. Is it the nature of law to last? A conclusion", in François Ost and Mark van Hoecke (Orgs.), *Temps et Droit. Le Droit a-t-il pour vocation de durer*?, Bruxelles, Bruylant, 1998, p. 469.

[8]François Ost, *Le Temps du Droit*, Paris, Odile Jacob, 1999, p. 37.

[9]Paulo de Barros Carvalho, "Segurança jurídica e modulação dos efeitos", *Revista da Fundação Escola Superior de Direito Tributário* 1, pages 208–209, Porto Alegre, 2008.

[10]Anna Leisner, *Kontinuität als Verfassungsprinzip*, Tübingen, Mohr Siebeck, 2002, p. 1. Johanna Hey, *Steuerplanungssicherheit als Rechtsproblem*, Köln, Otto Schmidt, 2002, p. 190.

The analysis now continues, beginning with the duty of permanence relative to the freedom legally exercised in the past and that cannot be changed in the present, i.e. with reliability, as just stipulated.

2 Normative Reliability and the Problem of Permanence: "Certainty of Transition from Past to Present" Through Normative Stability and Efficacy

2.1 Normative Stability

2.1.1 Initial Considerations

For certainty of law and certainty through law to exist, certain presuppositions need to be met. These may concern law itself or they may refer to subjective situations. Because of this ambiguity, it is absolutely impossible to discuss this matter without a semantic agreement on this particular aspect as well. This is because the word "stability" is itself ambiguous: it may refer to objective or subjective aspects, and to static or dynamic aspects. Hence the crucial importance of stipulating the several meanings that the term "stability" may have.

In light of this, I have opted on one hand for using the term "permanence" (*Dauerhaftigkeit, permanência*) to represent the requirement of objective stability of the legal order as a whole; and on the other hand, for using the generic term "reliability" (*Verlässlichkeit, confiabilidade*) with two meanings: one objective, synonymous with "credibility" and relating more to objects, and another subjective, relating more to people.

2.1.2 Objective Dimension

2.1.2.1 Permanence of the Legal Order

2.1.2.1.1 Via the Maintenance of Content: Entrenched Clauses

By prohibiting constitutional amendments on specific subjects in article 60, paragraph 4, the Constitution indirectly assures stability of the legal order: A substantial portion of its fundamental principles is likely remain intact.[11] Indeed, the institution of entrenched clauses has several repercussions. The first concerns the resulting syntactic hierarchy: In prohibiting the modification of some norms, the Constitution

[11] Maria Sylvia Zanella Di Pietro, "Os princípios da proteção à confiança, da segurança jurídica e da boa-fé na anulação do ato administrativo", in Fabrício Motta (Org.), *Direito Público atual: Estudos em homenagem ao Professor Nélson Figueiredo*, Instituto de Direito Administrativo de Goiás (IDAG), Belo Horizonte, Fórum, 2008, p. 297.

assigns greater importance to them. And this axiological preponderance influences the very interpretation of law: The interpretation of constitutional principles and rules must gravitate around the fundamental principles.

With regard to legal certainty, the institution of entrenched clauses reflects resistance to changing the axiological core of the Constitution, which cannot be the object of constitutional amendments. Thus albeit indirectly, the Constitution institutes an ideal that harmonizes permanence and change: The Constitution has a part that cannot be changed and a part that can, provided amendments are passed by a specific procedure involving an unusually large majority.

2.1.2.1.2 Via the Maintenance of Norms: Durability of the Legal Order

For law to guide human conduct not just in the short term but also in the medium and long term, the legal order must be minimally stable, lasting, continuous and permanent. If it is frequently changed, citizens will have difficulty knowing which norms to obey and will be reluctant to act because they will not be sure whether the norms they know will remain valid. Continuous modification prevents planning.[12] Raz therefore states that stability of the legal order (permanence, durability) is a condition for law to serve as a long-term guide to conduct.[13] That being so, law must be born with a vocation for lasting validity, not as a contingency solution to momentary problems.[14]

However, the requirement of durability as a duty of permanence over time is not to be confused with the requirement of immutability of the legal order.[15] Indeed, while it is true that repeatedly changing the legal order hinders knowledge of it and leads to distrust, due to loss of authority for lawmakers and constant frustration of the citizens' trust in general, so that continuous change is contrary to the requirements of knowability and reliability, it is also true that complete lack of change leads to loss of effectiveness, since law can no longer keep pace with social evolution and hence can no longer be accepted as an instrument to guide action. In other words, "too much" change causes ignorance and distrust, but "too little" change creates ineffectiveness. It is for no other reason that both Aarnio and

---

[12] Johanna Hey, *Steuerplanungssicherheit als Rechtsproblem*, Köln, Otto Schmidt, 2002, p. 189.

[13] Joseph Raz, "The rule of law and its virtue (1977)", in *The Authority of Law. Essays on Law and Morality*, Oxford, Oxford, 1979, p. 215.

[14] Eros Roberto Grau, *O Direito posto e o Direito pressuposto*, 7th ed., São Paulo, Malheiros Editores, 2008, p. 185. Federico Arcos Ramírez, *La seguridad jurídica: una teoría formal*, Madrid, Dykinson, 2000, p. 265. Johanna Hey, *Steuerplanungssicherheit als Rechtsproblem*, Köln, Otto Schmidt, 2002, p. 193.

[15] Eros Roberto Grau, *O Direito posto e o Direito pressuposto*, 7th ed., São Paulo, Malheiros Editores, 2008, p. 188. Federico Arcos Ramírez, *La seguridad jurídica: una teoría formal*, Madrid, Dykinson, 2000, p. 269. Johanna Hey, *Steuerplanungssicherheit als Rechtsproblem*, Köln, Otto Schmidt, 2002, p. 193. Christof Münch, "Rechtssicherheit als Standortfaktor. Gedanken aus Sicht der vorsorgenden Rechtspflege", in Albrecht Weber (Org.), *Währung und Wirtschaft. Das Geld im Recht. FS für Hugo J. Hahn*, Baden-Baden, Nomos, 1997, p. 677.

Peczenik include in their definitions of legal certainty not only *lack of arbitrariness* (legal certainty in a formal sense), but also the *existence of acceptability* (legal certainty in a substantive sense).[16] For the same reason, Habermas includes in the concept of law both *consistency in deciding* (similar cases are decided in the same manner based on the legal order) and *rational acceptability* (decisions are rationally justified so that addressees can receive them as rational decisions).[17]

It should be made clear that the requirement of permanence is discussed here in the objective sense, i.e., as the duty of assuring stability of the legal order as a whole to enable citizens to exercise freedom. Thus stability through durability of the legal order is a fundamental condition to guarantee freedom and the proper functioning of the institutions.[18] This is because the exercise of freedoms presupposes the *credibility* of normative conditions and legal institutions. As Hey emphasizes, freedom prospers only in trust, and trust only in freedom, which is why, in this sense, the durability of the legal order has value "per se," regardless of the exercise of any specific freedom.[19] In sum, the permanence of the order is a condition for legal certainty to begin to exist.

The requirement of durability of the legal order, therefore, derives from the objective dimension of legal certainty, relates to the legal order and benefits freedoms of all kinds, regardless of whether they can be shown to be effectively exercised in individual cases. Hence its utilization is the polar opposite of change, because in itself it affects the *institutional credibility* of law as a precondition for the *potential* exercise of freedoms. Or, in the words of Zanella Di Pietro, "The idea is to protect the belief that the acts performed by the state comply with the laws."[20] Another issue, to be discussed below, is the requirement to protect trust, which is the subjective dimension of the legal certainty principle and relates to the exercise of someone's freedom. Its use is not contrary to change strictly speaking, but to the production of normative effects that may adversely affect the past exercise of one or more freedoms.[21] This does not mean the trust of citizens cannot be considered part of the objective dimension of legal certainty. In this case, however, it is not a

[16]Aulis Aarnio, *Reason and Authority*, Dartmouth, Ashgate, 1997, pages 189–193. Idem, *The rational as reasonable*, Dordrecht, Reidel, 1987, pages 3–8 and 44. Aleksander Peczenick, *On Law and reason*, Dordrecht, Kluwer, 1989, p. 31.

[17]Jürgen Habermas, *Faktizität und Geltung*, Darmstadt, Wissenschaftliche Buchgesellschaft, 2002, p. 243.

[18]Rudolf Mellinghoff, "Vertrauen in das Steuergesetz", in Heinz-Jürgen Pezzer (Org.), *Vertrauensschutz im Steuerrecht. Deutsche Steuerjuristische Gesellschaft* 27, Köln, Otto Schmidt, 2004, p. 30. Johanna Hey, *Steuerplanungssicherheit als Rechtsproblem*, Köln, Otto Schmidt, 2002, p. 129.

[19]Johanna Hey, *Steuerplanungssicherheit als Rechtsproblem*, Köln, Otto Schmidt, 2002, pages 120–121, 129 and 182.

[20]Maria Sylvia Zanella Di Pietro, "Os princípios da proteção à confiança, da segurança jurídica e da boa-fé na anulação do ato administrativo", in Fabrício Motta (Org.), *Direito Público atual: Estudos em homenagem ao Professor Nélson Figueiredo*, Instituto de Direito Administrativo de Goiás (IDAG), Belo Horizonte, Fórum, 2008, p. 303.

[21]Johanna Hey, *Steuerplanungssicherheit als Rechtsproblem*, Köln, Otto Schmidt, 2002, p. 134.

question of how normative change may already have affected or may in future affect someone's past exercise of freedom, but of analyzing the presumptive past exercise of all the freedoms protected by the changed norm and the significance of frustrated trust for the credibility of the legal order. In such cases, it is better to speak not of individual trust but of systematic credibility – or, in the words of Carvalho, of a "grave threat to the entire legislative system in force."[22]

This being so, it is not just any threat to the stability and credibility of the legal order that can be considered a violation of the legal certainty principle, but only a restriction capable of jeopardizing the institutional credibility of law. A severe restriction, in other words, as highlighted above in our discussion of the quantitative aspect.

2.1.2.2 Inviolability of Individual Situations for Objective Reasons

2.1.2.2.1 Via the Passage of Time

2.1.2.2.1.1 Prescription

In contrast with other legal systems, article 146 of Brazil's Constitution reserves for supplementary laws the competence to create general tax norms, "especially concerning (...) prescription and limitation". Thus the Constitution itself acknowledges the importance of determining a general time frame within which to assure the knowability and calculability of the legal order in the federal sphere.

In exercising this competence, the National Tax Code contains rules setting a time limit for the state's right to collect back taxes, especially in articles 150 and 173. If the tax authorities do nothing before the specified period expires, the state loses its right to collect back taxes owing to prescription. The term for this is *decadência*, a legal effect instituted by an infraconstitutional rule that embodies the unconditional prevalence of legal certainty over justice: Citizens may owe tax, and know they owe tax, but prescription prevents the competent authorities from demanding payment after a specified period.[23]

Prescription and limitation are included in the part of this book that deals with the inviolability of individual situations for objective reasons, rather than the chapter on the application of the principle of protection of trust. This is because prescription and limitation depend on the lapse of time and may benefit or burden even those who

[22]Paulo de Barros Carvalho, "Segurança jurídica e modulação dos efeitos", *Revista da Fundação Escola Superior de Direito Tributário* 1, p. 203, Porto Alegre, 2008.

[23]On the subject of prescription and limitation in German law, see: Johanna Hey, *Steuerplanungssicherheit als Rechtsproblem*, Köln, Otto Schmidt, 2002, p. 786. Annette Guckelberger, *Die Verjährung im Öffentlichen Recht*, Tübingen, Mohr Siebeck, 2004, pp. 376 and ff.. Andreas Piekenbrock, *Befristung, Verjährung, Verschweigung und Verwirkung*, Tübingen, Mohr Siebeck, 2006, pp. 346 and ff.

do not manifest trust. This is precisely the reason why *decadência* can be considered an objective consequence of the objective principle of legal certainty.[24]

The point is that statutes of limitations favor the stability of legal situations and the elimination of uncertainty. In other words, they reinforce the legal certainty principle.[25] In this respect, the National Tax Code is categorical, establishing that the right to demand payment of back tax expires 5 years after the respective taxable event. This provision is in fact misdrafted. In article 156, V, *decadência* is stipulated as one of the ways in which a tax liability may expire, whereas actually the tax liability never materializes if the specified period elapses before it has been assessed.[26] However, what matters for present purposes is that in order to have it perform what was to become its constitutional role the framers of the National Tax Code inserted a rule that categorically establishes the loss of the state's right to constitute a tax credit after a lapse of 5 years. Because *decadência* is also required by private law, the National Tax Code explicitly includes provisions designed to eliminate any doubts regarding the consolidation of a given situation due to the state's failure to exercise the right to constitute a tax credit via assessment. Moreover, the Code also clearly states that the time frame for *decadência* applies even in cases of fraud, willful misconduct or sham transactions, save that it starts on the first day of the fiscal year following that in which the taxable event occurred, as per article 173. Thus the Code places predictability and uniformity above other values, such as justice (or more accurately, considers it fair to deny a prerogative if it is not exercised within a reasonable period of time).

2.1.2.2.1.2 Limitation

The situation is similar with regard to the right to take legal action. In accordance with article 146 of the Constitution, article 156, V, and article 174 of the National Tax Code institute a limitation (*prescrição*) on legal action to recover back tax. Thus even if the state assesses back tax within the specified time limit, under the general rule it loses the right to execute the debt unless it takes the necessary legal action within 5 years.

In the original language of the Code, the limitation clock started running with a tax assessment and stopped when the debtor was summonsed, as per article 174. Thus limitation applied if the tax authorities filed for execution within the 5-year period but the debtor was not served until later. The logic behind this was that

[24] Johanna Hey, *Steuerplanungssicherheit als Rechtsproblem*, Köln, Otto Schmidt, 2002, p. 785.

[25] Maria Sylvia Zanella Di Pietro, "Os princípios da proteção à confiança, da segurança jurídica e da boa-fé na anulação do ato administrativo", in Fabrício Motta (Org.), *Direito Público atual: Estudos em homenagem ao Professor Nélson Figueiredo*, Instituto de Direito Administrativo de Goiás (IDAG), Belo Horizonte, Fórum, 2008, p. 311.

[26] Paulo de Barros Carvalho, *Curso de Direito Tributário*, 18th ed., São Paulo, Saraiva, 2007, pages 481 and following. Luciano Amaro, *Direito Tributário Brasileiro*, 15th ed., São Paulo, Saraiva, 2009, p. 406. Sacha Calmon Navarro Coelho, *Curso de Direito Tributário*, 9th ed., Rio de Janeiro, Forense, 2006, pages 831 and following.

the state is unitary albeit divided into several bodies and must exercise its right to execute by a given time limit or forfeit that right. However, the situation was changed by Supplementary Law 118/2005, which stipulates that the limitation clock is halted when a court orders that the debtor in a tax execution proceeding be summonsed. While salutary to avoid the penalization of state action determining execution, this change is harmful inasmuch as it indefinitely prolongs the collection of back tax, which may take much longer than the period the original wording was intended to set for the resolution of litigation.

For the limited subject under discussion at this point, what matters is that the Code stipulates limitation as specifically as prescription, and does so with the purpose of establishing in a general and indistinct manner the period within which the state must exercise its claims. In this way it favors a state of reliability: Taxpayers can know that if a claim is not exercised within the legal time limit, it can no longer be exercised, even if the state theoretically has the right to do so. In other words, the framers of the Code weighed the conflict between certainty and justice, and opted to have the former prevail over the latter in this case (or rather, qualified the former as an option for the latter, if justice is understood as inviolability for objective reasons).

2.1.2.2.2 Via Legal Consolidation of the Status Quo

2.1.2.2.2.1 Initial Considerations

Unlike other constitutions, the Brazilian Constitution explicitly prohibits any restriction of completed legal acts, acquired rights and *res iudicata*. Precisely for this reason, its application is *inflexible*: In any of these hypotheses, retroactive effects are banned by the rule itself, so that any other reasons, such as public interest claims, are powerless to avoid its application by means of weighing. As Couto e Silva argues, in these cases the weighing was done by the framers of the Constitution, making past situations inviolable and invalidating any further judicial weighing to permit retroactive effects.[27] To cite Weber-Dürler, the Constitution "preempted the weighing of interests" by instituting a rule to resolve the conflict in advance.[28] Thus not even reasons of public order, which are commonly claimed in Brazil, can overcome the rigidity ordained by the 1988 Constitution.[29] As notably clarified in an opinion written by Justice Sepúlveda Pertence, the key point is that the notion

[27]Almiro do Couto e Silva, "O princípio da segurança jurídica (proteção à confiança) no Direito Público brasileiro e o direito da Administração Pública de anular os seus próprios atos: o prazo decadencial do art. 54 da Lei do Processo Administrativo da União (Lei n. 9.784/99)", *RBDP* 6, pages 7–59, Porto Alegre, Jul-Sep/2004.

[28]Beatrice Weber-Dürler, Vertrauensschutz im öffentlichen Recht, Basel/Frankfurt a.M., Helbing & Lichtenhahn, 1983, p. 125.

[29]Carlos Mário da Silva Velloso, "O princípio da irretroatividade da lei tributária", *RTDP* 15, p. 18, São Paulo, 1996. Luís Roberto Barroso, "Em algum lugar do passado: segurança jurídica, Direito Intertemporal e o novo Código Civil", in Cármen Lúcia Antunes Rocha (Org.), *Constituição e segurança jurídica: direito adquirido, ato jurídico perfeito e coisa julgada. Estudos em homenagem a José Paulo Sepúlveda Pertence*, Belo Horizonte, Fórum, 2004, p. 149.

that these rules can be superseded for reasons of public interest is "the result of overhasty importing of jurisprudential lessons based on legal orders in which they are not safeguarded at the constitutional level."[30]

Despite its rules governing inviolability hypotheses, the Constitution is ambiguous in including in the same provision both acquired rights and completed legal acts and *res iudicata*, because strictly speaking this places a genus (acquired rights) on the same level as its species (completed legal acts and *res iudicata*). The difference between these hypotheses is that acquired rights are derived from the laws, whereas a completed legal act results from a law-based contractual arrangement and *res iudicata* from the principle that a matter may not be relitigated once it has been judged on the merits.[31] Both the latter are in fact law-based and can be considered analogous in that respect.[32] In other words, the difference between these two species concerns the source of the rights, which is either directly statutory or directly contractual or judicial, albeit grounded in law. In all cases, however, there are acquired rights, whether they derive from a statute, a legal agreement or a court decision.[33] Hence it must be acknowledged that although the Constitution attempts to assure the inviolability of known institutes without weakening its protection for others, it confuses *genus* with *species* and *source* with *effect* by equating completed legal acts with acquired rights. Moreira Alves is right to conclude that what the Constitution's framers intended, albeit non-technically, was only to assure the inviolability of known hypotheses, as it was possible to take a position on these, leaving the rest to be resolved case by case.[34]

Regardless of these conceptual questions, what matters for the issue at hand is that the Constitution establishes inviolability rules by defining the requisites for rights to exist, whether they derive from statutes, private agreements or judicial decisions.

Having made this initial observation, we must now analyze the hypotheses encompassed by the constitutional rule, starting with completed legal acts.

2.1.2.2.2.2 Completed Legal Acts

According to article 1, paragraph 1, of the Law of Introduction to the Rules of Brazilian Law, a completed legal act is any action consummated in accordance

[30] RE 226.855, Full Court, Rep. Justice Moreira Alves, *DJ* 13 Oct 2000.

[31] José Afonso da Silva, "Constituição e segurança jurídica", in Cármen Lúcia Antunes Rocha (Org.), *Constituição e segurança jurídica: direito adquirido, ato jurídico perfeito e coisa julgada. Estudos em homenagem a José Paulo Sepúlveda Pertence*, Belo Horizonte, Fórum, 2004, p. 21.

[32] Jacques Petit, *Les conflits de lois dans le temps en Droit Public Français*, Paris, LGDJ, 2002, pages 145 and following.

[33] Luís Roberto Barroso, "Em algum lugar do passado: segurança jurídica, Direito Intertemporal e o novo Código Civil", in Cármen Lúcia Antunes Rocha (Org.), *Constituição e segurança jurídica: direito adquirido, ato jurídico perfeito e coisa julgada. Estudos em homenagem a José Paulo Sepúlveda Pertence*, Belo Horizonte, Fórum, 2004, p. 155.

[34] José Carlos Moreira Alves, "Direito adquirido", *Fórum Administrativo* 15, p. 582, 2002.

with the laws in force at the time. Thus the clause protecting consummated legal acts can be understood as prohibiting the establishment of new norms that change the requisites for legal acts already completed by means of the fulfillment of all the elements necessary to their existence according to the norms in force at the time.[35]

2.1.2.2.2.3 Acquired Rights

The clause on acquired rights can be understood as prohibiting the application of a new norm relative to rights created by the concretization of the legal requisites for the efficacy of facts or legal acts based on a previous norm in force at that time.

The protection of acquired rights aims to prevent a later norm from changing the effects created by completion of the facts required for a subjective right to be generated according to the previous norm. This protection derives from the broad efficacy of the right to the protection of property resulting from the fundamental rights and freedoms. Because the legislative branch established certain conditions for the birth of a subjective right, so that when these conditions are met they produce the specified effects, it instituted a basis for trust that protects trust from future legislative changes to a considerable extent. In this case, to accept that a new statute prevents the formation of a right or restricts its effects when its conditions of efficacy are met would be tantamount to accepting that legislators can turn citizens into mere objects of their own fickle will.[36] Bluntly worded, it would be like allowing legislators to make fools of their fellow-citizens.

In light of this brief consideration, it is clear that the protection of acquired rights derives from the fundamental rights to freedom and property, as well as the right to dignity. Even so, to preempt any possibility of restriction via a weighing of the principles of freedom and property against some public purpose, the Constitution expressly establishes the prevalence of legal certainty by guaranteeing the inviolability of acquired rights.[37] Thus unlike other legal orders where acquired rights may be overruled by the prevalence of public interest, the Brazilian order excludes this possibility.

The point is that the inviolability of the individual situation derives from the fact that the legal effect created by an act that may be deemed unconstitutional has become the addressee's property. Hence the Supreme Court's decision in RE no. 122.202-6, for example, regarding the validity of payments made to an employee

---

[35]Limongi França, *Direito Intertemporal Brasileiro*, 2nd ed., São Paulo, Ed. RT, 1968, pages 426 and following.

[36]Martin Stötzel, *Vertrauensschutz und Gesetzesrückwirkung*, Frankfurt am Main, Peter Lang, 2002, p. 189.

[37]Almiro do Couto e Silva, "O princípio da segurança jurídica (proteção à confiança) no Direito Público brasileiro e o direito da Administração Pública de anular os seus próprios atos: o prazo decadencial do art. 54 da Lei do Processo Administrativo da União (Lei n. 9.784/99)", *RBDP* 6, pages 7–59, Porto Alegre, Jul-Sep/2004.

based on a statute that was later found to be unconstitutional. In that case the Court's understanding was that the payments received ought not to be returned as they had been incorporated into the addressee's property.[38]

2.1.2.2.2.4 Res iudicata

This constitutional provision bars the application of a new norm to the effects of acts or facts covered by a court decision that cannot be appealed. The core meaning of *res iudicata* is that all the means of contestation regularly admitted in law must have been exhausted. The principle serves to ensure that disputes do not last forever and to promote the stability of legal relations and the certainty of state acts.[39] Thus the point of this provision is simply to end the dispute, even if the reasons given for modifying a decision are based on arguments of justice. The justification for *res iudicata* is precisely that it interrupts a chain of decisions that could perpetuate litigation, with the last being revised by another and so on. In order to avoid this *recursiveness*, *res iudicata* acts as an objective limit to the reopening of a dispute even if arguments relating to the fairness of a decision can be marshaled. As stressed by Ferraz Jr., therefore, the assurance of *res iudicata* is a manifestation of legal certainty according to which the normative meaning resulting from a previous court decision cannot be altered, and which thus confers certainty, through stability, on the legal relationship that is the object of the decision, preventing a continuation of the dispute.[40]

This does not mean, however, that there are no situations in which a grave state of inequality may arise in the case of continuing relations, by virtue of a decision favoring or harming a certain taxpayer more than others. In such cases *res iudicata* itself may have to be reassessed if a later decision of the Supreme Court declares the tax (un)constitutional.[41] Thus if a final decision on the merits has been handed down to a taxpayer declaring a tax constitutional and the taxpayer then applies for judicial review to the Supreme Court, which later revises that decision, either in concentrated control of constitutionality or in diffuse control, along with some measure to magnify the subjective efficacy of its ruling (suspension of the statute by the Senate, or a binding precedent), the validity of the *res iudicata* principle embodied by the individual court decision is upheld, and only its *future effects* are

[38]RE 122.202-6, 2nd Panel, Rep. Justice Francisco Rezek, *DJ* 8 Apr 94.

[39]Cármen Lúcia Antunes Rocha, "O princípio da coisa julgada e o vício de inconstitucionalidade", in idem (Org.), *Constituição e segurança jurídica: direito adquirido, ato jurídico perfeito e coisa julgada. Estudos em homenagem a José Paulo Sepúlveda Pertence*, Belo Horizonte, Fórum, 2004, pages 173 and 178.

[40]Tércio Sampaio Ferraz Jr., "Coisa julgada em matéria tributária e as alterações sofridas pela legislação da contribuição social sobre o lucro (Lei n. 7.689/88)", *RDDT* 125, p. 74, São Paulo, 2006.

[41]Luiz Guilherme Marinoni, *Coisa julgada inconstitucional*, São Paulo, Ed. RT, 2008, pages 137 and following. Gustavo Sampaio Valverde, *Coisa julgada em matéria tributária*, São Paulo, Quartier Latin, 2004, pages 140 and following.

limited by the Supreme Court ruling.[42] If it is diffuse judicial review, with subjective efficacy restricted to the parties in the suit, no individual norms are created for third parties, and thus the *res iudicata* principle embodied in the final decision is not affected.[43]

This position results from a combination of two factors.[44]

One is article 471 of the Code of Civil Procedure, according to which no judge shall re-decide a claim that has already been litigated, unless continued legal relations are involved and there has been a change in the facts or in the law, in which case the decision can be appealed. Thus if the decision concerns a momentary relationship and a taxable event considered instantaneous, as exemplified by real estate transfer tax, the future effects of a *res iudicata* are not altered. However, if the decision concerns a continuous relationship in the sense of a relationship that involves taxes classified as recurring, i.e. paid in every new fiscal period, such as income tax or the social contribution on revenue, the future effects (and only these) of a *res iudicata* will be limited by the interference of Supreme Court judicial review in concentrated control of constitutionality, or by a new individual decision based on article 471, I, of the Code of Civil Procedure. The application of this provision presupposes that such a Supreme Court ruling constitutes some sort of change in the "state of law". This is the view underlying Supreme Court Precedent no. 239, according to which "a decision that deems undue the collection of a tax in a given fiscal period does not constitute *res iudicata* for later periods."

On the other hand, this understanding derives from a reconciling of the legal certainty principle, through *res iudicata*, with the equality principle, through judicial review. Harmonization along these lines rejects both the extreme solution of upholding the future effects of a *res iudicata* – regardless of the state of inequality it causes by obliging someone to pay what no one else will have to pay, or allowing someone not to pay what everyone else will have to pay – as well as the solution of completely voiding a *res iudicata* regardless of the trust placed in it by the party it benefits. Upholding the validity of a *res iudicata*, with the mere limitation of its future effects in the case of continuing relations, preserves both values without undermining the stability of the judicial decision, which is what matters most for present purposes.

The essential point is that *res iudicata*, limited to judicial certainty relative to the suit and cause of action that defines the legal situation presented in a judgment,

---

[42] José Souto Maior Borges, "Limites constitucionais e infraconstitucionais da coisa julgada tributária (contribuição social sobre o lucro)", *Cadernos de Direito Tributário e Finanças Públicas* 27, p. 191, 1999.

[43] Tércio Sampaio Ferraz Jr., "Coisa julgada em matéria tributária e as alterações sofridas pela legislação da contribuição social sobre o lucro (Lei n. 7.689/88)", *RDDT* 125, p. 77, São Paulo, 2006. Gustavo Sampaio Valverde, *Coisa julgada em matéria tributária*, São Paulo, Quartier Latin, 2004, p. 169.

[44] Tércio Sampaio Ferraz Jr., "Coisa julgada em matéria tributária e as alterações sofridas pela legislação da contribuição social sobre o lucro (Lei n. 7.689/88)", *RDDT* 125, p. 77, São Paulo, 2006.

must prevail in the absence of continuing relations and action by the executive or judiciary to revise it based on a Supreme Court ruling.[45] This respects not only the constitutional rule establishing the inviolability of *res iudicata*, but also the state of reliability of law through the stabilization of decisions, as required by the Supreme Court. Simply pushing aside *res iudicata* through a Supreme Court ruling in diffuse control of constitutionality is incompatible with the legal certainty principle.[46] Hence the doubtful constitutionality of provisions inserted into the Code of Civil Procedure by Law 11,232/05 (article 475-L, paragraph 1, and article 741, sole paragraph) to allow that a debt instrument may be deemed unenforceable based solely on a declaration of unconstitutionality issued by the Supreme Court in diffuse control, even in the absence of an exhaustive process of judicial cognition.[47] The above considerations make clear the connection between the institute of *res iudicata* and the legal certainty principle: The individuals affected by the subjective efficacy of *res iudicata* trust its validity.[48] This explains why, in some legal orders where it is not expressly warranted, *res iudicata* is protected by case law precedents: Its constitutional basis is legal certainty directly, and the protection of fundamental rights indirectly, and there is no need to protect it with a specific provision.[49]

2.1.2.2.2.5 Past Taxable Events

As we will see later in the discussion of the tax irretroactivity rule, the Supreme Court has developed case law based on article 150, III, "a", of the Constitution, according to which the power to tax does not apply to "taxable events that occurred before the enactment of a statute that creates or raises them."[50] This jurisprudence, examined in detail below, disregards – wrongly, as I will show – other situations in

[45]Humberto Theodoro Jr., "Notas sobre sentença, coisa julgada e interpretação", *RePro* 167, p. 19, 2009.

[46]Tércio Sampaio Ferraz Jr., "Coisa julgada em matéria tributária e as alterações sofridas pela legislação da contribuição social sobre o lucro (Lei n. 7.689/88)", *RDDT* 125, p. 79, São Paulo, 2006.

[47]Carlos Alberto Alvaro de Oliveira, *Do formalismo no Processo Civil*, 3rd ed., São Paulo, Saraiva, 2009, p. 82.

[48]Luiz Guilherme Marinoni, *Coisa julgada inconstitucional*, São Paulo, Ed. RT, 2008, pages 67–68.

[49]Enrico Riva, *Wohlerworbene Rechte – Eigentum – Vertrauen*, Bern, Stämpfli, 2007, pages 8 and 38.

[50]RE n.181.664, Full Court, Rep. Justice Ilmar Galvão, *DJ* 19 Dec 97. Likewise: AgR in AI n.333.209-9, 1st Panel, Rep. Justice Sepúlveda Pertence, j. 22 Jun 2004; RE n.194.612, 1st Panel, Rep. Justice Sydney Sanches, *DJ* 8 May 98; ED in AgR in RE n.278.466, 2nd Panel, Rep. Justice Maurício Corrêa, *DJ* 6 Feb 2003; AgR in AI n.511.024, 1st Panel, Rep. Justice Eros Grau, j. 14 Jun 2005. Likewise: RE n.254.459, 1st Panel, Rep. Justice Ilmar Galvão, *DJ* 10 Aug 2000. With dissenting opinion by Justice Carlos Velloso, see: AgR in RE n.433.878, Rep. Justice Carlos Velloso, j. 1 Feb 2005; AgR in RE n.305.212, 2nd Panel, Rep. Justice Carlos Velloso, j. 17 Sep 2002.

which a taxable event has not yet been consummated as stipulated by law yet the effects of facts started but not completed under the aegis of a previous statute should nevertheless be protected.

What matters at this point is simply to highlight that the inviolability analyzed here results from the straightforward application of the rule itself, regardless of any subjective element relating to the taxpayer, such as trust and good faith, or any objective or concrete element, such as the exercise of acts to dispose of property and freedom. Inviolability operates exclusively by force of the irretroactivity rule, which is applicable when the taxable event has already occurred. Strictly within this scope, the rule is sovereign and no horizontal weighing can be justified.

2.1.2.2.3 Via Factual Consolidation of Situations

In some extraordinary situations, given the lack of a norm that supports the production of legal effects, strictly speaking there are no acquired rights or completed legal acts. Nevertheless, owing to the passage of time or the lack of alternative mechanisms the situation may have become consolidated to such an extent that in factual terms its effects cannot be retrospectively undone from the standpoint of law properly speaking.

In these cases, the Supreme Court's jurisprudence argues that the "situation is consolidated" by the "normative force of the facts," which law cannot disregard. Strictly speaking, it is not a matter of acquired rights, completed legal acts, or the applicability of the specific rules on prescription and limitation. Even so, these situations have particular features, usually but not only time-related, and undoing them or their effects would eventually cause legal uncertainty.

For example, in judging an application for an injunction the Supreme Court examined the case of a pensioner who had been adopted by her own great-grandfather as his daughter 1 week before he died of cancer so that she would be entitled to a survivor's pension after his death, and did indeed receive it for 18 long years until it was unilaterally and summarily suspended by the Federal Court of Audit. The Supreme Court granted the injunction with the effect that due process of law must also be observed at the administrative level.[51] During the discussion, however, the justices debated the applicability of the legal certainty principle to the case, given the passage of 18 years between the start of disbursement and interruption of the pension by the Court of Audit, and the passage of 20 years until the Supreme Court ruled the interruption invalid without due process of law. The summary of the decision quotes Justice Gilmar Mendes as advocating application of "the legal certainty principle as a subprinciple of the rule of law". It also refers to the "possibility of revoking administrative acts that cannot last indefinitely", "power of annulment subject to a reasonable time limit", and the "need for stability in administratively created situations." What matters for present purposes is that, even considering the statement by the rapporteur, Justice Ellen Gracie, that "this is

[51]MS n.24.268, Full Court, Rep. Justice Gilmar Mendes, *DJ* 17 Sep 2004.

a crystal-clear case of fraud" (p. 186 of the decision), and Justice Carlos Britto's remark that "fraud was committed, there can be no doubt of this" (p. 196), the Supreme Court ordered the Court of Audit to review the case owing to failure to observe due process of law, with all justices stressing the need to preserve the stability of legal situations over the course of time.

In this situation, it can be seen that the lack of a basis for trust, and even of subjective trust, given the apparent simulation of the adoption of a great-granddaughter by her great-grandfather 1 week before he died, was no hindrance to inviolability because the situation was temporally consolidated: The pension was received for 18 years and the recipient, who was no longer young, had no source of income. Thus what actually created the inviolability was not the protection of legitimate trust, but the consolidation of a de facto situation whose preservation over a long period of time does not depend even on the good faith of the beneficiary. In this decision, legal certainty is clearly connected with other principles, notably the principles and fundamental rights of the person.[52]

The decisive factor in general terms is that the passage of time can consolidate a situation even if it is illegal or based on a norm declared to be unconstitutional. This is the understanding expressed by the Supreme Court in RE 217,141.[53] In this case a public servant retired on April 11, 1984, while holding the position of Divisional Director, to which he had been promoted based on Supplementary Law 317/83. However, some years later (September 2, 1987) the Supreme Court declared that statute unconstitutional, with the usual *ex tunc* effects. This raised the question whether the annulment of the public servant's retirement 8 years later, on March 21, 1992, was compatible with the legal certainty principle. The Court ruled that it was not, mainly because more than 5 years had passed between the date of his retirement and the start of the annulment procedure. In this respect, Justice Gilmar Mendes distinguished between the scope of the ruling that the law was unconstitutional and the concrete scope of its application, clearly stating that "the acts performed on the basis of the unconstitutional statute that can no longer be reviewed are not affected by the declaration of unconstitutionality". And he concluded that "the legal certainty principle requires that the administrative act that authorized his retirement must be upheld" (p. 699 of the decision). Strictly speaking, the Court did not modulate the effects of this ruling or consider the existence of acquired rights. It simply understood that the legal situation was inviolable because a reasonable amount of time elapsed before annulment.

A similar situation happened when the Supreme Court analyzed the hiring of employees by a semi-public company without a public competitive examination. The Court understood that "the existence at the time of the hirings of a dispute

[52] Judith Martins-Costa, "Almiro do Couto e Silva e a ressignificação do princípio da segurança jurídica na relação entre Estado e cidadãos", in Humberto Ávila (Org.), *Fundamentos do Estado de Direito – Estudos em homenagem a Almiro do Couto e Silva*, São Paulo, Malheiros Editores, 2005, p. 134.

[53] RE n.217.141, 2nd Panel, Rep. Justice Gilmar Mendes, *DJ* 4 Aug 2006.

about the requirement of public competitive examinations for public companies and semi-public companies, and the fact that the dispute was settled only after the employment contracts were signed, cannot invalidate the legitimacy of the hirings, which complied with the legislation then in force". It therefore declined to declare the acts unconstitutional. On the contrary, because it considered them consummated and thus stable, the Court found that it could not judge them unlawful. It thus preserved the stability of legal relations "in observance of the legal certainty principle".[54]

The Supreme Court decided likewise in AgR no. 328,232-8, which concerned the maintenance of a productivity bonus granted to employees under an unconstitutional state law that was eventually received by the new constitutional order.[55] Justice Carlos Velloso grasped the issued clearly:

> The principle of legal certainty is founded mainly on good faith and the need for stability of the situations created administratively. It bears repeating that in the present case an administrative act was based on the principle of good faith, both by the administrative body that granted the benefit and above all by the public servant, in light of which we should uphold the effects of the act. In any event, as mentioned earlier, those effects were validated by the 1988 Constitution. (p. 433 of the decision)

As can be seen, in this case the Supreme Court upheld the effects of the acts, despite their incompatibility with the Constitution at the time they were performed, by virtue of the passage of time and the existence of good faith. Thus this an instance of the simultaneous application of the objective and subjective aspects of the legal certainty principle.

2.1.2.2.4 Via the Absence of Injury

In other cases, what makes the situation inviolable is not predominantly time but the absence of injury: Although an act has been performed illegally, a legal end is indirectly reached, and none of the parties involved suffers any injury.

There are several older decisions of the Supreme Court along these lines. For example, asked in RE no. 78,209 to rule on the validity of acts performed by contractors acting as bailiffs in accordance with a statute that the Supreme Court later declared unconstitutional, the Court found that the contractors were de facto public servants and recognized as "valid the attachment by agents of the executive, acting on a court order, in accordance with an unnumbered law of São Paulo State dated December 3, 1971, especially if no harm resulted to the debtor."[56] Similarly, in RE no. 78,594 the Supreme Court upheld the validity of acts by de facto public

[54] MS n.22.357-DF, Full Court, Rep. Justice Gilmar Mendes, j. 27 May 2004, *DJ* 5 Nov 2004, p.6; RE/AgR/AgR/AgR/AgR n.348.364-RJ, 1st Panel, Rep. Justice Eros Grau, *DJ* 11 Mar 2005, p. 19.

[55] AgR in RE n.328.232-8, 2nd Panel, Rep. Justice Carlos Velloso, *DJ* 2 Sep 2005.

[56] RE n.78.209, 1st Panel, Rep. Justice Aliomar Baleeiro, *DJ* 9 Oct 1974.

servants improperly acting as bailiffs because the acts did not affect the defense or create irreparable or harmful damage to the attachment creditor.[57]

What matters in these cases is that lack of injury serves to stabilize the disputed act, whose effects are upheld in the name of the permanence and durability of law. The legal certainty principle operates in its objective dimension, insofar as it does not depend on subjective interests or any other elements apart from the simple absence of harm.

2.1.3 Subjective Dimension: Inviolability of Individual Situations for Subjective Reasons

2.1.3.1 General Considerations on the Protection of Trust

The trust protection principle, as it is called, serves as an instrument to defend individual interests in cases where citizens not protected by acquired rights or completed legal acts in any sphere, including the tax sphere, exercise their freedom to a greater or lesser extent by trusting in the validity (or appearance of validity) of a known general or individual normative act and whose trust is frustrated when its efficacy is discontinued, by a simple change, or by revocation or annulment, or by a declaration of its invalidity. Thus the trust protection principle entails the existence of (a) a basis for trust, (b) trust in this basis, (c) the exercise of trust in the basis that created it, and (d) its frustration by a later contradictory act of a public authority.

Because this principle requires the trust of a private citizen in a manifestation of a public authority (whether regular or irregular, as we will see), by definition its application involves tension with other principles that are also part of the legal certainty principle: with the democratic principle, whereby the legislative enjoys freedom of configuration, i.e. the ability to institute new rules or change prior rules to adapt them to reality, potentially leading to discontinuation of the application of prior rules; with the principle of the separation of powers, which grants each branch of government including the executive the prerogative of concretizing the legally defined public interest within its jurisdiction but based on criteria of convenience and opportunity – which may also lead to an interruption of the continuity of the effects produced previously, either via the annulment or revocation of a previous norm or via the enactment of a new norm; and similarly with other principles that in some manner allow the state to introduce new rules or change prior rules. After all, private individuals do not have the right to postulate the maintenance of the legal order as it is at present, because the legislative is empowered to change normative reality.[58] In other words, the scope of application of the trust protection principle

[57] RE n.78.594, 2nd Panel, Rep. Justice Bilac Pinto, *DJ* 30 Oct 1974.

[58] Kyrill-A. Schwarz, *Vertrauensschutz als Verfassungsprinzip*, Baden-Baden, Nomos, 2002, pages 296 and 299.

involves a struggle between the old and the new within the state itself, to quote Couto e Silva, or, as noted by Martins-Costa, a tension between permanence and rupture, stability and change, what may be eternal and what tends to perpetual change.[59]

The scope of application of the trust protection principle, therefore, does not only include acts based on valid normative acts that were changed without protection for the private citizen through assurance of acquired rights, completed legal acts and *res iudicata*. It also extends to acts, whether consummated or merely commenced, that are based on normative acts that are merely apparently legal, or not even that, and whose annulment from scratch would frustrate the individual expectations placed on them. Thus whenever the trust protection principle is applied, either a conflict arises with the democratic principle or the principle of the separation of powers, enabling the state to change its orientation, or tension is created with the constitutional competence rules, which require statutes and administrative acts to comply with requisites of form and content in order to be valid.

However, unlike acquired rights, completed legal acts and *res iudicata*, which are protected by an express constitutional rule, legitimate trust regarding acts commenced (but not completed from the viewpoint of the immediately applicable rule) is not protected by any express constitutional rule. This might lead to the conclusion that by protecting only some situations that involve the past exercise of legally oriented freedom but not others the Constitution withholds protection for justified expectations. Such a conclusion would be mistaken.

This is because the list of individual rights and guarantees expressly states that "the rights and guarantees expressed in this Constitution do not exclude others that result from the regime and principles adopted by it, or from international treaties to which the Federative Republic of Brazil is a party" (article 5, paragraph 2). This final reservation, therefore, is unambiguous in incorporating *other rights and guarantees* that result from the principles the Constitution adopts, as is the case precisely of the rights and guarantees deriving from the legal certainty principle and the fundamental rights explicitly named in the list. That being so, and because trust protection is a reflexive effect of the legal certainty principle, in conjunction with the fundamental rights of freedom and property and the principles that define state action, there is no reason to pre-exclude trust protection from the list of rights and guarantees established by the Constitution. The fact that it is not expressly listed means only that it depends on a concrete weighing against other principles with which it might

[59] Almiro do Couto e Silva, "O princípio da segurança jurídica (proteção à confiança) no Direito Público brasileiro e o direito da Administração Pública de anular os seus próprios atos: o prazo decadencial do art. 54 da Lei do Processo Administrativo da União (Lei n. 9.784/99)", *RDA* 237, p. 276, Rio de Janeiro, 2004. Judith Martins-Costa, "Almiro do Couto e Silva e a ressignificação do princípio da segurança jurídica na relação entre Estado e cidadãos", in Humberto Ávila (Org.), *Fundamentos do Estado de Direito – Estudos em homenagem a Almiro do Couto e Silva*, São Paulo, Malheiros Editores, 2005, p. 131. Likewise: Rudolf Mellinghoff, "Vertrauen in das Steuergesetz", in Heinz-Jürgen Pezzer (Org.), *Vertrauensschutz im Steuerrecht. Deutsche Steuerjuristische Gesellschaft* 27, Köln, Otto Schmidt, 2004, p. 27.

collide and its relationship with the fundamental rights of freedom, property and equality, in contrast with the rules that protect acquired rights, completed legal acts, *res iudicata* and taxable events that are legally deemed to have occurred.

The principle of protection of trust, or protection of legitimate expectations (*Vertrauensschutzprinzip, principe de protection de la confiance légitime, princípio da proteção da confiança*) is distinguished from the legal certainty principle by the following criteria: (a) *normative sphere* – whereas the legal certainty principle is concerned with the legal order as a whole, focusing on the macrolegal view, the principle of legitimate expectations relates to a normative aspect of the legal order, focusing on a microlegal view; (b) *personal sphere* – whereas the legal certainty principle represents an objective norm, not necessarily linked to a specific subject, the legitimate expectations principle protects the interest of a specific person; (c) *concretization level* – whereas the legal certainty principle refers primarily to the abstract plane, the legitimate expectations principle presupposes a concrete level of application; (d) *subjective scope of protection* – whereas the legal certainty principle serves as an instrument of protection of collective interests, the legitimate expectations principles serves as a means of protection of individual interests; (e) *individual protectivity* – whereas the legal certainty principle is neutral regarding the interests of citizens, so that it may be used for or against them, the legitimate expectations principle is used only to protect the interests of those who consider themselves harmed by the past exercise of legally oriented freedom.[60]

The systemization of these differences evidences that the legal certainty principle, from the macrolegal angle, defines an objective, abstract norm that protects collective interests and therefore serves as an instrument to protect "legitimate expectations" or "the set of all expectations" in the legal order, whereas the legitimate expectations principle represents a reflexive, subjective, concretely oriented application of the objective principle of legal certainty and is a vehicle to protect "an expectation." Thus the legal certainty principle can be said to reveal the general face of legal certainty, protecting the interests of all, possibly against the interests of some; whereas the legitimate expectations principle protects the interests of one or a few, possibly against those of all. The former is therefore linked to general justice; the latter to individual justice. If this is so, however, some relevant consequences cannot be disregarded.

First, the application of these principles may lead to opposite results, thus creating an internal conflict within legal certainty itself, considered as the greater principle: If the legal certainty principle is *the whole* and the legitimate expectations principle is *the part*, assuring the latter might lead to restricting the former, and vice-versa. Thus it is said that strictly speaking the legitimate expectations principle is not a mere deductive derivation of the legal certainty principle, but rather a

[60] Sylvia Calmes, *Du principe de protection de la confiance légitime en Droits Allemand, Communautaire et Français*, Paris, Dalloz, 2001, pages 167–171.

limitation or *limiting corollary* of this principle.[61] For this reason, as has already been explained in discussing the meaning of legal certainty and will be detailed below, it is necessary to find criteria that harmonize these principles, so as to produce *more* certainty than uncertainty; or in other words, so that the protection of legitimate expectations, representing the past dimension of legal certainty from the individual perspective, does not end up doing even greater damage to the present and future dimensions of legal certainty from the collective standpoint, in which case legal certainty ends up being diminished, under the pretext of augmenting it. Or, to use the distinction being made here, so that the protection of legitimate expectations does not lead to the loss of legal certainty; or, more precisely and strictly, so that the individual subjective dimension of legal certainty is not preserved at the expense of losing its transindividual objective dimension.

Second, because these principles differ in normative scope, personal applicability, level of concretization and range of protection, they also differ in content, moment of verification, and the evidence needed for their realization. This point is of fundamental importance. Because the legitimate expectations principle represents a reflexive, subjective and concrete application of an objective principle, the demonstration of the requisites necessary for its realization (basis for trust, trust, exercise of trust, and frustration of trust) depends on concrete evidence produced and exhaustively examined in judicial proceedings, and thus cannot be discussed in proceedings that examine the theoretical constitutionality of a statute in an abstract concentrated manner. In sum, the requirements of the legitimate expectations principle can only be shown to exist in ordinary lawsuits and in the diffuse control of constitutionality, which analyzes the concrete violation of the Constitution by an administrative or court order; not in constitutionality declaration suits, which involve the concentrated control of constitutionality, examining the theoretical violation of the Constitution by a normative act, because such control lacks cognition of the concrete elements whose configuration densifies the legitimate expectations principle.

This observation shows that in citing "reasons of legal certainty" as a justification for the Supreme Court to modulate the effects of a declaration of unconstitutionality in concentrated control, article 27 of Law 9868/98 refers not to the legitimate expectations principle, as "subjectivated certainty," but to the legal certainty principle in its objective dimension and in its personal aspect relating to the collective interest. The legitimate expectations principle depends on the *exercise* of trust (*Betätigung des Vertrauens* or *Vertrauensdisposition*), whereas the legal certainty principle must be assured independently of any *concrete action* (*tatsächliche Betätigung*).[62] Thus, to claim in a constitutionality declaration suit that a citizen trusted or had a legitimate expectation in a specific administrative act or judicial decision, and hence that declaring a statute unconstitutional with general efficacy can only create

[61] Sylvia Calmes, *Du principe de protection de la confiance légitime en Droits Allemand, Communautaire et Français*, Paris, Dalloz, 2001, p. 181.

[62] Johanna Hey, *Steuerplanungssicherheit als Rechtsproblem*, Köln, Otto Schmidt, 2002, p. 129.

effects for the future, considering concrete individual harm, is to bring into the case elements that cannot be proven, and further to confuse issues relating to the internal content of the decision with external issues relating to its effects.

However, that does not mean that the trust and expectations *of all* or *of the majority*, or even trust *itself* as a configuring element of the ideals of permanence and continuity of the *legal order*, cannot be assessed in the concentrated judicial review process, albeit presumed, or even in diffuse control, when declaring a statute null and void has transindividual effects, as the Supreme Court admits.[63] In this case, however, what must be demonstrated is not that the change unjustifiably affects *someone's concrete exercise of freedom*, but that it unjustifiably restricts *everyone's abstract right to freedom*. Nevertheless, strictly speaking what is under analysis here is the objective face of the protection of trust and legitimate expectations – i.e. no less than the legal certainty principle itself.

It must be repeated that the legitimate expectations principle is a "subjectivated" application of the legal certainty principle.[64] This does not merely mean that the legitimate expectations principle refers to a concrete individual dimension of the legal certainty principle; it also means this principle is founded on the fundamental rights of the individual, especially the right to freedom and the right to engage in an economic activity. These rights, together with the rule of law, protect the legitimate expectations put into practice by citizens with a causal basis in both the legal norms and the credibility of state actions, with which their expectations and the configuration of their freedom are linked.[65]

These rights are even more relevant in the sphere of tax law because the incentive and disincentive effects of taxation impinge with varying degrees of intensity on taxpayers' rights relating to the configuration of freedom and the use of property, so that a later change that retroactively or even retrospectively affects a taxpayer's past actions usually entails restrictions on the past exercise of freedom, which was necessarily guided by the norms in force at the time.[66] Taxpayers do not act based on future norms: *In praeteritum non vivitur*. Their actions are based on present norms. And precisely because fundamental rights become the yardstick for protecting legitimate expectations, the logic of the argument is reversed: It is not taxpayers who must find a reason to invalidate the past effects of a new normative orientation,

[63] RE n.197.917-8, Full Panel, Rep. Justice Maurício Corrêa, *DJ* 7 May 2004.

[64] Johanna Hey, *Steuerplanungssicherheit als Rechtsproblem*, Köln, Otto Schmidt, 2002, p. 110.

[65] Kyrill-A. Schwarz, *Vertrauensschutz als Verfassungsprinzip*, Baden-Baden, Nomos, 2002, pages 145 and following. Rudolf Mellinghoff, "Vertrauen in das Steuergesetz", in Heinz-Jürgen Pezzer (Org.), *Vertrauensschutz im Steuerrecht. Deutsche Steuerjuristische Gesellschaft* 27, Köln, Otto Schmidt, 2004, p. 28. Sylvia Calmes, *Du principe de protection de la confiance légitime en Droits Allemand, Communautaire et Français*, Paris, Dalloz, 2001, p. 391.

[66] Rudolf Mellinghoff, "Vertrauen in das Steuergesetz", in Heinz-Jürgen Pezzer (Org.), *Vertrauensschutz im Steuerrecht. Deutsche Steuerjuristische Gesellschaft* 27, Köln, Otto Schmidt, 2004, p. 29.

but the state, which is obligated to produce a proportional justification for restricting fundamental rights.[67]

Finally, it must be highlighted that the protection of legitimate expectations, representing the reflexive efficacy of legal certainty, also serves to protect citizens from the state. This is why Machado Derzi is absolutely right to say that the protection of legitimate expectations in a vertical relationship such as taxation can only be considered unilaterally, i.e., in favor of the taxpayer, not the state.[68]

2.1.3.2 Requisites of Application

2.1.3.2.1 Basis for Trust

2.1.3.2.1.1 General Considerations

The basis for trust is expressed in the norms that served as a foundation for individual (in)action.[69] This basis may be general and abstract, such as a statute, or individual and concrete, such as an administrative act or judicial decision. Moreover, it may be either *positive*, through voluntary and active means, as in the case of a clear and precise court ruling, a conclusive administrative act that bears a promise, a uniform repeated practice of the administration, or a legislative normative act; or *negative*, passive and at times involuntary, as exemplified by administrative tolerance or a long lack of exercise of an administrative prerogative whose use does not expire by prescription or limitation.[70] *Knowledge* of the basis for trust that can generate trust is therefore the first element of the trust protection principle and of the protection of legitimate expectations.

The issue of the basis for trust is far from being uncontroversial. A few questions suffice to demonstrate this: Can a manifestly unconstitutional norm be a basis for trust? Or a confusing and obscure norm? A norm that contains a reservation on amendment? A norm concerning a short-term economic matter? A norm that is part of a normative environment known to be unstable? Does a warning that the legislation will change or the news of a proposed bill undermine trust in the legislation currently in force? These and other questions show that to study the basis for trust it is necessary to know not only which elements can configure it, but also how these elements interact with one another to create in aggregate a "relationship of trust."

---

[67] Johanna Hey, *Steuerplanungssicherheit als Rechtsproblem*, Köln, Otto Schmidt, 2002, p. 134.

[68] Misabel de Abreu Machado Derzi, *Modificações da jurisprudência no Direito Tributário*, São Paulo, Noeses, 2009, p. 266.

[69] Sabine Altmeyer, *Vertrauensschutz im Recht der Europäischen Union und im deutschen Recht*, Baden-Baden, Nomos, 2003, p. 43.

[70] Sylvia Calmes, *Du principe de protection de la confiance légitime en Droits Allemand, Communautaire et Français*, Paris, Dalloz, 2001, p. 324.

The position advocated here is that the basis is defined by its *fitness as a justification for the exercise of civil liberties and property rights*, rather than any objective requisites it might have. This will be clear later from the demonstration that even invalid administrative acts and unconstitutional statutes enacted without the necessary objective requirements can create expectations deserving of protection.[71]

That does not mean that all bases are equally fit to create trust. This is because the nature of the expectations created by the normative base is fundamental and not all normative bases have the same degree of reliability. The key therefore lies in finding *guiding criteria* that show which bases generate legitimate trust and which do not, so that case law can be less variable and consequently less uncertain.[72]

Legal doctrine usually presents a stark division between legitimate and illegitimate bases for trust. The theory is that trust is not protected when the basis for trust is legally non-existent or manifestly invalid, contains a reservation clause limiting future modification, is merely experimental or conjunctural, or is part of a normative environment known to be unstable. In all such cases, the basis for trust is said not to be reliable, so that citizens cannot count on its permanence, but should instead count on its changing. Thus the theme is studied by indicating the intrinsic properties the basis for trust must have to create trust, i.e. validity and a claim to permanence. The analysis is strictly formal.

However, an examination of case law, as outlined below, shows that the basis for trust merits reliability even when it has some features that at first sight seem to disqualify it as a source of trust. For instance, it is said that an unconstitutional statute or a null act does not generate trust.[73] But if a citizen has acted for a long period on the basis of a statute or act and the status quo is irreversible, is there no protection? If the citizen acted because of the state's induction through an act that was eventually considered null, and did so onerously, for a long time and in close cooperation with the state to further the public interest, even so is there no protection? On the contrary, an investigation of legal doctrine reveals precisely that case law protects such acts or their effects in some situations.[74]

---

[71] Johanna Hey, "Vertrauen in das fehlerhafte Steuergesetz", in Heinz-Jürgen Pezzer (Org.), *Vertrauensschutz im Steuerrecht. Deutsche Steuerjuristische Gesellschaft* 27, Köln, Otto Schmidt, 2004, pages 91–127.

[72] Fritz Ossenbühl, *Die Rücknahme fehlerhafter begünstigender Verwaltungsakte*, 2nd ed., Berlin, Walter de Gruyter, 1965, p. 33. Rudolf Mellinghoff, "Vertrauen in das Steuergesetz", in Heinz-Jürgen Pezzer (Org.), *Vertrauensschutz im Steuerrecht. Deutsche Steuerjuristische Gesellschaft* 27, Köln, Otto Schmidt, 2004, p. 42. Johanna Hey, *Steuerplanungssicherheit als Rechtsproblem*, Köln, Otto Schmidt, 2002, p. 230.

[73] Kyrill-A. Schwarz, *Vertrauensschutz als Verfassungsprinzip*, Baden-Baden, Nomos, 2002, p. 297. Stefan Muckel, *Kriterien des verfassungsrechtlichen Vertrauensschutzes bei Gesetzesänderungen*, Berlin, Duncker und Humblot, 1989, p. 84.

[74] Almiro do Couto e Silva, "O princípio da segurança jurídica (proteção à confiança) no Direito Público brasileiro e o direito da Administração Pública de anular os seus próprios atos: o prazo decadencial do art. 54 da Lei do Processo Administrativo da União (Lei n. 9.784/99)", *RDA* 237, p. 300, Rio de Janeiro, 2004.

These considerations point to the need to transcend the idea that it suffices to classify acts into those that merit protection and those that do not. The right approach takes other elements into account and also provides criteria to harmonize them. Thus it must be borne in mind that there are several elements to consider, not just one, that the elements may vary, and that distinctions must be made as to which aspect of the basis for trust they are concerned with. Indeed, some elements refer to objective qualities intrinsic to the basis for trust – such as the degree of bindingness, permanence, onerousness, efficacy over time or effectiveness – and some elements that concern subjective effects of the basis for trust – such as the appearance of lawfulness, behavioral incentives, or the extent to which the citizen depends on the public authorities. What is decisive is that the fitness of these elements to assign reliability to the basis for trust is also a result of the *effects* they actually or potentially have on the scope of protection for the fundamental rights involved and the constitutional principles relating to state action. For example, an onerous agreement with extrafiscal purposes that solidifies a relationship of close cooperation between state and taxpayer in pursuit of the public interest, and stimulates the taxpayer's behavior in such a manner that that the acts already performed and the expenses already incurred place the taxpayer in an irreversible de facto situation, calls for the application of the principles of liberty and property, on one hand, and morality, on the other. The greater the citizen's cooperation with the state, the greater the claim to permanence of the legal effects of the citizen's action.[75] In other words, from one perspective the protection of legitimate expectations is a type of reflexive application of the legal certainty principle, built upon the principles that protect fundamental rights and qualify state action, and from another angle it is a type of reflexive application of those very principles. Lehner is therefore right to say that the conflict between protection of trust and retroactivity, hitherto seen as requiring verification of the existence of acts completed in the past according to legal requirements, should now be considered linked to the actions of taxpayers and the state.[76] The focus has changed – and with it, the preconditions for configuring the trust protection principle. The nub of the principle is no longer the validity of the basis for trust, the consummation of facts according to the previous law or the mere intertemporal relationship between norms, but the exercise of fundamental rights and state action, so that the validity of the basis for trust and the consummation of facts according to the previous law cannot preclude protection by themselves.[77]

[75]Christof Münch, "Rechtssicherheit als Standortfaktor. Gedanken aus Sicht der vorsorgenden Rechtspflege", in Albrecht Weber (Org.), *Währung und Wirtschaft. Das Geld im Recht. FS für Hugo J. Hahn*, Baden-Baden, Nomos, 1997, p. 677.

[76]Moris Lehner, "Das Rückwirkungsproblem im Spiegel der Abschnittsbesteuerung", in Paul Kirchhof, Karsten Schmidt e Wolfgang Schön (Orgs.), *FS für Arndt Raupach. Steuer- und Gesellschaftsrecht zwischen Unternehmerfreiheit und Gemeinwohl*, Köln, Otto Schmidt, 2006, p. 67.

[77]Martin Stötzel, *Vertrauensschutz und Gesetzesrückwirkung*, Frankfurt am Main, Peter Lang, 2002, p. 119.

In other words, the protection of trust now reflects less the intrinsic aspects relating to the formal regularity of state acts and more those that concern their *effects* on the principles associated with freedom, property, equality, and state actions themselves. Thus what is essential is not whether the basis for trust is regular, definitive, unequivocal, precise, positive or conclusive, as jurisprudence generally affirms,[78] but the *effects* of the basis for trust on fundamental rights and principles, even when that basis is irregular, temporary, mistaken, imprecise, negative or inclusive. As will be demonstrated later, trust is protected if it is justified by the *inter-relation* between the elements of this basis and their *connection* with fundamental rights.

An analysis of traditional legal doctrine, however, shows that for a long time, and to some extent even today, the principle of certainty applied to legislative acts through the prohibition of retroactivity, applied to administrative acts through completed legal acts or acquired rights, and applied to judicial acts through *res iudicata*, has always focused, as far as the state is concerned, on the *formal regularity* of the act and, as far as individual citizens are concerned, on the *conclusiveness or completion of the normative preconditions*. Indeed, the constitutional rules on the matter refer to conclusiveness or completion: Article 5, XXXVI protects *acquired* rights, *completed* legal acts and *res* iudicata, while article 150, III, "b", forbids the retroactivity of statutes relative to taxable events that *occurred* before they enter in force. The framers gave no thought to the application of the principles of freedom and administrative principles or their restriction. Consummation or completion as a technical and formal standard accepts only "yes" or "no" for an answer, never "more or less."[79]

However, case law has steadily broadened the field of protection, initially based on the theory of consolidated facts, and more recently using the principle of subjectivated legal certainty itself to protect the trust of citizens in cases where acts have not been completed or state action lacks formal regularity.[80] If the focus of the debate shifts toward the behavior of taxpayers, and it evolves over time, normative changes never begin from nothing, but from a moment when behavior may have been adopted, so that the concept of retroactivity or change must involve not only a qualitative but also a quantitative problem; not "yes or no," but "more or less"; not a "point," but a "scale".[81]

Even so, the cases in which the Supreme Court explicitly or implicitly uses the trust protection or legitimate expectations principle by name, as it has recently

---

[78] Sylvia Calmes, *Du principe de protection de la confiance légitime en Droits Allemand, Communautaire et Français*, Paris, Dalloz, 2001, pages 305–332.

[79] Johanna Hey, *Steuerplanungssicherheit als Rechtsproblem*, Köln, Otto Schmidt, 2002, p. 235.

[80] Almiro do Couto e Silva, "O princípio da segurança jurídica (proteção à confiança) no Direito Público brasileiro e o direito da Administração Pública de anular os seus próprios atos: o prazo decadencial do art. 54 da Lei do Processo Administrativo da União (Lei n. 9.784/99)", *RDA* 237, p. 302, Rio de Janeiro, 2004.

[81] Johanna Hey, *Steuerplanungssicherheit als Rechtsproblem*, Köln, Otto Schmidt, 2002, pages 238 and 243.

started to do, or via the consolidation of de facto situations, as it has long done, involve more or less extreme situations relating to administrative activity, in which the passage of long periods of time plays a decisive role in declarations of the inviolability of acts and their effects. In other situations, however, where the issue is legislative action and it is subject to constitutional rules, the Supreme Court has admitted the retrospective efficacy of norms relative to acts or facts commenced but not completed, arguing that only acts completed under the aegis of a previous norm merit protection. It is therefore necessary to move forward in our investigation of the trust protection principle in this sphere.

The questions asked above show, on the other hand, that there is a *scale* of intensity of realization of the elements configured in the basis for trust. However, this scale cannot be delimited on the basis of *fixed dual verification* criteria (yes or no). Instead, it can only be constructed on the basis of *gradual verification* criteria (more or less). Moreover, as we will see later, there will be protection of trust when there are, relative to the several criteria, *more reasons* to protect trust than not to protect it. This is the proposal advocated here: verifying the basis for trust with gradual verification criteria, whose sum, also to be gradually examined, will indicate whether there are more justifications for the protection of trust than otherwise. The examination of these criteria will permit the construction of general rules to confirm or refute the basis for trust.

As can be seen and will be further clarified later, the elements to be verified do not fit a rigid classificatory conception in the sense of pointing to requisites that must be present, but are merely indicative.[82] These elements more closely resemble a typological representation, defined as differing from concepts by involving elements that are not individually necessary or sufficient, but depend for their configuration on a view of the whole, so that a basis for trust can exist despite the lack of one or more of its elements. However, it is not a question of analyzing case law to construct real types, i.e., a typology that indicates which cases normally or exceptionally deserve protection by *describing* what has usually been decided in case law, as Stötzel does.[83] Instead, it is a matter of indicating which elements and legal criteria must be considered in applying the trust protection principle in cases where facts that have already occurred or acts performed in the past were not completed according to the previous law, so that in the presence of such elements the applier must use the criteria indicated. In other words, what must be constructed is not real types but a material typology, along the lines advocated by Hey.[84]

The need to indicate the elements to be considered for the configuration of the basis for trust, and the manner in which they are configured and interact, also result from the requirement of legal certainty in the application of law. It

---

[82]Fritz Ossenbühl, *Die Rücknahme fehlerhafter begünstigender Verwaltungsakte*, 2nd ed., Berlin, Walter de Gruyter, 1965, pages 92–93.

[83]Martin Stötzel, *Vertrauensschutz und Gesetzesrückwirkung*, Frankfurt am Main, Peter Lang, 2002, pages 149 and following.

[84]Johanna Hey, *Steuerplanungssicherheit als Rechtsproblem*, Köln, Otto Schmidt, 2002, p. 245.

is not enough, as often found in theoretical writings, simply to claim that the state's interest in changing the applicable norms based on the democratic principle should be weighed against or balanced with the private interest in maintaining their past effects, based on the protection of legitimate expectations. It is essential to go further by asking such questions as: What are the relevant elements of these interests? Based on what criteria? With what weight? Without first specifying the object and criteria of the weighing exercise, weighing is an instrument of arbitrariness and therefore incompatible with the legal certainty principle in its dynamic dimension.[85] And leaving everything to case-by-case weighing is also insufficient.[86] The criteria presented in this book are therefore the product of an effort to create secure weighing parameters. Unless this precaution is taken, a curious paradox results: The prevalence of legal certainty, through the upholding of past norms or acts, or their past effects, is achieved through a weighing exercise that lacks intersubjectively controllable criteria and is therefore arbitrary and offensive to legal certainty. In other words, either weighing is oriented by universal and legally justifiable criteria or, under the pretext of assuring legal certainty (in its dynamic dimension as reliability in its subjective aspect of trust protection) on one hand, the same legal certainty is restricted on the other hand (in its dynamic dimension as calculability in its objective aspect of prohibiting arbitrariness). Once again, we return to the general proposition that permeates this entire study: Either legal certainty is whole, or it is not legal certainty; or more rigorously, either the efficacy of legal certainty is examined as a whole or, under the pretext of assuring legal certainty, its *effective* and *verified* restriction is made to be greater than its *desired* and *proclaimed* realization.

2.1.3.2.1.2 Configuration Criteria

The criteria, or methods, that configure the basis for trust at times concern each and every state manifestation, and at times concern only the statutes and administrative or judicial acts. The following list initially reflects the requisites applicable to any state manifestation, and ends with those that concern individual state manifestations.

Basis Bindingness Criterion (Binding Basis ↔ Non-binding Basis)
The more binding a normative basis, the more the trust placed in it must be protected. This requisite results from the fact that not all norms are equally binding: Some laws are coercive and require, while other laws are dispositional and permit; there are administrative acts with external efficacy, aimed at individuals, such as interpretative normative acts, and administrative acts with internal efficacy, such as service orders; there are Supreme Court decisions in concentrated control of constitutionality with *erga omnes* efficacy, decisions in diffuse control of

[85] Matthias Jestaedt, "Die Abwägungslehre – ihre Stärken und ihre Schwächen", in Otto Depenhauer *et alii* (Orgs.), *Staat im Wort – FS für Josef Isensee*, Heidelberg, C. F. Müller, 2007, pages 265 and 267.

[86] Bodo Pieroth, *Rückwirkung und Übergangsrecht*, Berlin, Duncker und Humblot, 1981, p. 147.

constitutionality with suspension of a law by resolution of the Federal Senate, and decisions in the diffuse control of constitutionality with *inter partes* efficacy; there are decisions of the Superior Court of Justice (STJ), Brazil's highest non-constitutional appellate court, that constitute precedents or are issued by the Section of the Court with jurisdiction over the issue at hand, and there are decisions by one of its Panels; there are decisions of lower courts issued by Civil Groups, and decisions issued by Chambers – and so on indefinitely. What matters is that these acts are not equally binding: Some have formal binding force (laws and decisions by the Supreme Court in concentrated control, or in diffuse control with suspension of a law by resolution of the Federal Senate, or binding precedents); others have material force (administrative acts that standardize a position of the executive, repeated decisions of higher courts, issued by their Plenaries or by the bodies charged with standardizing case law, non-binding precedents); others still do not have final binding force but produce immediate efficacy (first-instance administrative decisions or injunctions granted by courts of first or second instance).

In this sense, and because the ability to create trust is the distinctive criterion for its basis, the efficacy of a binding act cannot match that of a non-binding act in terms of creating trust, nor can that of a materially binding act match that of an act that is not materially binding. This is because the more binding the act, the greater its reliability for citizens, ranging from formal bindingness at one extreme (where there must be obedience, rather than trust, which assumes dispositional capacity and freedom of action) to merely material bindingness at the other (where there must be mere trust to a greater or lesser degree). In sum, provided an act admits some degree of disposition by the citizen, then the more binding it is the greater the citizen's expectation regarding its future fulfillment, given the diminishing capacity to choose what decision to make and the lesser presence of circumstances that justify sharing the risk in the decision-making process.

It must be kept in mind that the legal certainty principle, in the aspect examined here, is an instrument of respect for the freedom exercised in the past under the guidance of law itself. That being so, the more citizens follow the guidance provided by law the more this principle must protect them. The same applies to the bindingness of the act that creates trust, for the more binding it is, the greater the influence of law on the exercise of freedom.

Apparent Basis Legitimacy Criterion (Valid Basis ↔ Invalid Basis)

The more legitimate a basis appears to be, the greater must be the protection of the trust deposited in it. This rule results, on one hand, from the requirements of knowability and legal efficacy that make up the legal certainty principle: In order for law to serve as a guide for citizens, it must be known and enforceable; for it to be known and minimally efficacious, however, citizens need to *trust* in the validity of the normative acts that have been published or served, never considering them suspect. In other words, the legality principle works, and laws are minimally efficacious, only if underpinned by an assumption of validity.[87] This assumption, however, has its price: Citizens who trust in the validity of state actions cannot suffer injury for that very reason at a later stage. There is no reliability without the assumption of validity. Without reliability, there is no obedience. And without obedience there cannot be minimal effectiveness. Thus the price of effectiveness is the protection of those who, trusting in the validity of state acts, follow the guidance offered by such acts even if they are later declared unlawful.

Acts that appear valid are more robust precisely thanks to the reliability, and more specifically the credibility, law must merit. Hence acts manifestly devoid of validity, such as non-existent acts, meaning exceptional acts so grossly and obviously irregular that their flaws are immediately apparent, do not merit any trust at all, on this criterion at least.[88]

In fact, like all the other criteria the apparent validity criterion is not definitive in the sense of necessary and sufficient for the protection of trust, nor is its configuration straightforward. In some situations it will not be possible to distinguish between a non-existent act and a null and void act or even a voidable act, or to distinguish between a constitutional and an unconstitutional law.[89] Thus the key is the *appearance* of legitimacy of the act, rather than legitimacy properly speaking. The appearance of legitimacy depends in turn on issues connected to (i) the subjects of the act (the higher the rank of the authority issuing the act, and the more subjects involved in the composition of its content, the more it is assumed to be in accordance with law, given the presupposition that higher authorities make fewer mistakes) and (ii) the form of the act (the more publicity given to it and the more democratic participation in its elaboration, the more it is assumed to be correct, given that public acts presumably do not aim to hide flaws and that participation by more people should anyway mean fewer flaws), among other elements.[90] The point is that the protection of trust cannot be invalidated purely and simply because the basis for trust is irregular from some perspective, as legal theory would have it.[91] The

[87] Fritz Ossenbühl, *Die Rücknahme fehlerhafter begünstigender Verwaltungsakte*, 2nd ed., Berlin, Walter de Gruyter, 1965, p. 65.

[88] Almiro do Couto e Silva, "O princípio da segurança jurídica (proteção à confiança) no Direito Público brasileiro e o direito da Administração Pública de anular os seus próprios atos: o prazo decadencial do art. 54 da Lei do Processo Administrativo da União (Lei n. 9.784/99)", *RDA* 237, p. 301, Rio de Janeiro, 2004. Sylvia Calmes, *Du principe de protection de la confiance légitime en Droits Allemand, Communautaire et Français*, Paris, Dalloz, 2001, pages 334 and 341.

[89] Rudolf Mellinghoff, "Vertrauen in das Steuergesetz", in Heinz-Jürgen Pezzer (Org.), *Vertrauensschutz im Steuerrecht. Deutsche Steuerjuristische Gesellschaft* 27, Köln, Otto Schmidt, 2004, p. 35.

[90] Fritz Ossenbühl, *Die Rücknahme fehlerhafter begünstigender Verwaltungsakte*, 2ª ed., Berlin, Walter de Gruyter, 1965, p. 99.

[91] Sabine Altmeyer, *Vertrauensschutz im Recht der Europäischen Union und im deutschen Recht*, Baden-Baden, Nomos, 2003, p. 45.

knowledge of some *visible* unconstitutionality may *limit* the protection of trust but does not automatically exclude it.[92]

Similarly, effective knowledge of a flaw in an act, especially when it is evident, militates against the creation of legitimate trust. More so when the citizen participates in creating the flaw, acting with criminal intent, or engaging in coercion or bribery, for example, or supplying false or inaccurate information.[93] Hence it is said that without subjective good faith, understood as a lack of any intent to deceive, there is no objective good faith, understood as protection of the order relative to acts, regular or irregular, that create rights for citizens.[94]

However, it must again be emphasized that even in such situations enough of the basis for trust may be present to compensate for the absence of an element, as explained below. For example, a long period of time may have elapsed between the act and the identification of the flaw or the individual's dependency on its effects, even in cases of bad faith. So much so that the legislation itself assures the upholding of flawed acts once a stipulated time limit for prescription or limitation has elapsed. This is the case in tax law: Article 173 of the National Tax Code simply defers until the beginning of the following fiscal year the date from which the time to prescription is measured if the passive subject acts with intent to deceive, although the tax authorities still lose the right to execute and collect the tax debt.

Legal doctrine excludes the existence of a trust legitimating basis in some situations, three of which are worth highlighting: obscurity, previous announcement of modification, and unlawfulness.[95] In none of these three cases, however, can the basis for trust be *automatically* disregarded.

In the case of obscurity of the basis for trust, it is said that citizens cannot base their conduct on a norm that is not clear enough to guide their behavior in the course effectively taken. Without clarity there is no protection of trust. This understanding, however, ignores the fact that a citizen may have actually trusted one of the alternative meanings of the norm, and moreover cannot be held responsible for its obscurity. If the protection of trust is excluded when the basis for trust is somehow obscure, a paradox results: The state neglects its duty of assuring "certainty of guidance" through the issuance of norms that are clear and free of

---

[92] Martin Stötzel, *Vertrauensschutz und Gesetzesrückwirkung*, Frankfurt am Main, Peter Lang, 2002, p. 174.

[93] Almiro do Couto e Silva, "O princípio da segurança jurídica (proteção à confiança) no Direito Público brasileiro e o direito da Administração Pública de anular os seus próprios atos: o prazo decadencial do art. 54 da Lei do Processo Administrativo da União (Lei n. 9.784/99)", *RDA* 237, p. 305, Rio de Janeiro, 2004.

[94] Sylvia Calmes, *Du principe de protection de la confiance légitime en Droits Allemand, Communautaire et Français*, Paris, Dalloz, 2001, p. 363. Almiro do Couto e Silva, "O princípio da segurança jurídica (proteção à confiança) no Direito Público brasileiro e o direito da Administração Pública de anular os seus próprios atos: o prazo decadencial do art. 54 da Lei do Processo Administrativo da União (Lei n. 9.784/99)", *RDA* 237, p. 304, Rio de Janeiro, 2004.

[95] César García Novoa, *El principio de seguridad juridica en materia tributaria*, Madrid, Marcial Pons, 2000, p. 179. Sylvia Calmes, *Du principe de protection de la confiance légitime en Droits Allemand, Communautaire et Français*, Paris, Dalloz, 2001, p. 305.

contradictions, yet benefits from its own fault when the time comes to realize "certainty of application." On this point it must not be forgotten that tax planning is also a consequence of the complexity and instability of the legislation, which disorients taxpayers instead of orienting them.[96]

Besides creating a hypothesis of benefit resulting from non-fulfillment of a duty, this interpretation is incompatible with both the legal certainty principle and the morality principle. It is irreconcilable with the legal certainty principle because it creates a state of greater uncertainty than otherwise, as citizens, who ought to follow the state's directions by virtue of the requirement of reliability through normative efficacy, will be penalized precisely for doing so. This has the effect of discouraging obedience to norms with some degree of indeterminacy, violating both the requirement of reliability and that of calculability of law. And the interpretation is incompatible with the principle of administrative morality because the state benefits from obscurity even though it must be held responsible for that same obscurity, which contradicts its previous behavior of requiring compliance with the norms it enacts. Invalidating the protection of trust would therefore create a conflict: The state would be obligated to enact clear norms and not punished but rewarded for defaulting on this obligation. The state would be obligated to issue clear norms and at the same time encouraged to do just the opposite.

In the case of a previous announced possibility of modification, it is said that citizens cannot expect to have their trust protected in future if a change that occurs has been announced in advance.[97] This understanding cannot be accepted either. As seen above, one of the elements of the requirement of knowability of the law is certainty about the existence and validity of a norm the individual is required to obey. Thus there is legal certainty only if citizens have the ability to know which norm they ought to obey. The understanding that the announcement of a possible future modification of the legal order eliminates the protection of trust conflicts with this element because it leads to doubt as to which norm the citizen must obey, the norm currently in force or the norm that might possibly come into force in future. It also forces the citizen to analyze the many plans to change the legislation, which are not always published.

Such duality of norms from which to seek guidance conflicts not only with the knowability of law, but also with its reliability: The legal order is designed to last a long time, not to be frequently and repeatedly changed. Denying the protection of trust when the state announces the intention of changing the legislation contradicts the principle of continuity of the order not by virtue of effective changes, because they are not yet in force, but instead because of a mere political desire to change the legislation. Denying the protection of trust when a change to the legislation is announced means giving credence to "possible future law" rather than "law as it

[96]Frédéric Douet, *Contribution à l'étude de la sécurité juridique en Droit Interne Français*, Paris, LGDJ, 1997, p. 47.

[97]César García Novoa, *El principio de seguridad jurídica en materia tributaria*, Madrid, Marcial Pons, 2000, p. 179.

is in force now." In other words, it means assigning greater weight to changes in the legal order than to its permanence, manifestly contradicting the requirements of normative stability and continuity inherent in the legal certainty principle. Hence the dictum that the valid legislation in force ought to be the only parameter on which to base guidance for the citizen.[98]

The understanding that the reliability of the order is undermined when a desire for change is announced also militates against comprehension of the legal certainty principle as an instrumental principle of freedom, since lack of definition regarding the applicable rules restricts individuals' abilities to conceive of the present and shape the future. An individual cannot plan freely and autonomously without minimal certainty of orientation. A person who does not know which norm to obey hesitates before acting, or acts with uncertainty, not knowing the limits to the exercise of freedom.[99] To accept that draft legislation whose final result is completely unpredictable erodes the protection of trust would be tantamount to saying that the reliability of law is grounded not in laws but in their absence.[100] Machado Derzi is therefore absolutely right to reject transposition of the so-called "announcement effect" to the Brazilian legal order.[101]

In the case of an unlawful basis for trust, the argument is that citizens cannot derive guidance for action from an unlawful normative basis.[102] Without lawfulness there is no protection of trust. However, this understanding overlooks the fact that the key to the protection of trust, as noted above, is not the formal regularity of state action but the restriction of fundamental rights. Thus there may have been some exercise of freedom or use of property that justifies restricting the effects of the new law to the future in order to protect these fundamental rights, even if there is an unlawful normative basis. Instead of excluding the protection of trust, the unlawfulness of the basis for trust ought to be an element in weighing the reasons to protect trust against the reasons to deny such protection.[103]

It must also be mentioned that the unlawfulness of an act is usually declared after the private citizen has performed acts of disposition. But in performing such acts the individual believed the basis for trust was legitimate. The obligation to obey the laws must therefore be matched by protection of trust in their constitutionality.

---

[98] Johanna Hey, *Steuerplanungssicherheit als Rechtsproblem*, Köln, Otto Schmidt, 2002, pages 126 and following.

[99] Franz-Xaver Kaufmann, *Sicherheit als soziologisches und sozialpolitisches Problem*, 2nd ed., Stuttgart, 1973, p. 22. John Rawls, *Theory of Justice*, Cambridge, Belknap, 1971, p. 407.

[100] Kyrill-A. Schwarz, *Vertrauensschutz als Verfassungsprinzip*, Baden-Baden, Nomos, 2002, p. 305.

[101] Misabel de Abreu Machado Derzi, *Modificações da jurisprudência no Direito Tributário*, São Paulo, Noeses, 2009, p. 448.

[102] Stefan Muckel, *Kriterien des verfassungsrechtlichen Vertrauensschutzes bei Gesetzesänderungen*, Berlin, Duncker und Humblot, 1989, p. 54.

[103] Johanna Hey, *Steuerplanungssicherheit als Rechtsproblem*, Köln, Otto Schmidt, 2002, p. 183.

The *appearance of a norm* creates as much trust as the *norm itself*.[104] Both lawful and unlawful state acts produce concrete effects that cannot be simply disregarded: Those who trust a state act without negligence or fault, and consequently dispose of their freedom and property in an intense and irreversible manner, must be protected, whether or not the act is unlawful.[105]

Basis Changeability Criterion (Basis with a Strong Claim to Permanence ↔ Basis with a Weak Claim to Permanence)
The greater the permanence of the basis, the greater must be the protection of the trust placed in it. This is because there are: *acts with a claim to permanence*, such as a statute that does not stipulate its own expiration; *merely provisional acts*, whose definitive efficacy depends on a subsequent act, such as *medidas provisórias*, the Brazilian version of executive orders that must be ratified by Congress, or intermediate administrative decisions; and *acts lacking definitiveness* because another authority is empowered to change them for economic policy reasons, such as taxes, whose rates can be changed by presidential decree. These acts indeed have differing degrees of permanence – some are born to last and others are destined from the start to a temporary, if not ephemeral, existence.

If the distinctive quality of the basis is its capacity to generate trust, an act with a claim to permanence has incomparably more of this quality than a merely transitory and circumstantial act.[106] This is because the greater the claim to permanence, the greater the reliability for citizens, from definitiveness at one extreme to ephemerality at the other. It is relevant to recall in this context that the legal certainty principle is a means of protecting the respectability of the freedom exercised in the past under the guidance of law itself. If so, however, the more citizens *could* trust the guidance offered by law, the more the legal certainty principle should protect them. And it will do so all the more in proportion to the claim to continuity of the trust-generating act, for the greater the claim, the more citizens should take into account the manifestation of law in the exercise of freedom.

Finally, it must also be pointed out that, as noted above, the legal certainty principle aims to assure the respectability of the free, autonomous and legally oriented exercise of freedom. Freedom is autonomously exercised when citizens are responsible for their decisions to some extent, even when acting within the limits of the law. In other words, the legal certainty principle must protect the responsible exercise of freedom. This is not the case with the protection of trust in an act that is or should be known to be distinctly transient and therefore subject to future

[104] Martin Stötzel, *Vertrauensschutz und Gesetzesrückwirkung*, Frankfurt am Main, Peter Lang, 2002, p. 204.

[105] Fritz Ossenbühl, *Die Rücknahme fehlerhafter begünstigender Verwaltungsakte*, 2ª ed., Berlin, Walter de Gruyter, 1965, pages 66 and 91.

[106] Kyrill-A. Schwarz, *Vertrauensschutz als Verfassungsprinzip*, Baden-Baden, Nomos, 2002, p. 297. Martin Stötzel, *Vertrauensschutz und Gesetzesrückwirkung*, Frankfurt am Main, Peter Lang, 2002, p. 167.

modification. In this case, while trust can be deemed to exist, it will not be legitimate trust and the basis for trust will be too weak to justify any claim of frustration or surprise. The term surprise is appropriate only when something a citizen does not expect happens without warning. There is no surprise when whatever happens is expected, in which case the affected party should have counted on its changing (*mit der Änderung rechnen müsste*).[107] Thus the key question is not whether the individual trusted, but whether she *could* have trusted.[108] A person who foresees a future change is not surprised but has the appropriate expectation. Justice Cézar Peluso was right to aver, in examining an alleged change in case law where the "modified decision" was not yet *res iudicata* and was therefore provisional, that "the grounds for validity of the annulled act (credit) were provisional because the decision was appealable; neither reversal nor existence can be considered an unexpected consequence."[109] Expectation is confirmed by a future change to the present norm. The legitimate expectation in this case is the expectation of change, not permanence; protecting trust therefore means assisting change, not stability.

However, the degree of reliability created by a norm with a weak claim to permanence is not to be confused with a norm with a time-limit for enforcement, which creates a high degree of reliability, inasmuch as citizens trust that it will remain in force until its scheduled expiration. This means that, unlike norms with a weak claim to permanence, on whose permanence citizens cannot rely, norms with a time limit for enforcement allow citizens to rely on their permanence.[110] This is why article 178 of the National Tax Code establishes that exemptions granted "for a fixed period" and under strict conditions are irrevocable.

To repeat the first axiom, which applies to the examination of all these elements: Neither a norm's low claim to permanence nor the reservation of repeal suffices in itself to undermine the protection of trust, as some scholars have argued.[111] The taxpayer may know a norm is transitory, without knowing *to what extent* it will be modified – which rules out the calculability of the future consequences of her acts. It is of little use to know that a norm may be changed without knowing *to what extent* it can be changed. This would be akin to the "certainty of uncertainty," which is

---

[107] Josef Isensee, "Vertrauensschutz für Steuervorteile. Ein Folgeproblem der Wirtschaftslenkung durch Steuer des §3a EStG", in Paul Kirchhof, Klaus Offerhaus e Horst Schöberle (Orgs.), *Steuerrecht, Verfassungsrecht, Finanzpolitik. FS für Franz Klein*, Köln, 1994, p. 627. Johanna Hey, *Steuerplanungssicherheit als Rechtsproblem*, Köln, Otto Schmidt, 2002, p. 127. Martin Stötzel, *Vertrauensschutz und Gesetzesrückwirkung*, Frankfurt am Main, Peter Lang, 2002, p. 167.

[108] Johanna Hey, *Steuerplanungssicherheit als Rechtsproblem*, Köln, Otto Schmidt, 2002, p. 127.

[109] RE n.370.682-9, Full Court, Rep. Justice Ilmar Galvão, *DJ* 19 Dec 2007, p. 562 of the opinion.

[110] Martin Stötzel, *Vertrauensschutz und Gesetzesrückwirkung*, Frankfurt am Main, Peter Lang, 2002, pages 171 and 200.

[111] Sylvia Calmes, *Du principe de protection de la confiance légitime en Droits Allemand, Communautaire et Français*, Paris, Dalloz, 2001, p. 344.

incompatible with the requirement of calculability of law. Moreover, the knowledge that change is possible does not eliminate the restriction of fundamental rights or the need to justify any changes.[112]

It will therefore be necessary to verify whether other qualities of the basis for trust compensate for the lack of permanence. In exceptional cases, there may be protection of trust even when a private citizen can count on future modification.[113]

Basis Efficacy Lastingness Criterion (Short-Lived Efficacy ↔ Lasting Efficacy) The longer the efficacy of the basis lasts, the more protection is merited by the trust placed in it. This is because the *passage of time* steadily strengthens the appearance of legitimacy of the basis, typically of administrative acts: The longer the production of effects lasts, the fewer doubts remain about the validity of the act. Time "creates" or "reinforces" the citizen's trust in the normative basis. Reale is therefore quite correct to say that "when the inertia of the administration has allowed the formation of situations with a strong appearance of lawfulness, to the point of creating a conviction of their legitimacy, it would be absurd to grant the authorities an indefinite power of self-supervision on pretext of the state's eminence."[114] On this point it can be said, first, that the repeated application of an act tends to reinforce its validity and may cause individuals to act accordingly[115]; and second that repeated application may give citizens the idea that the administration will not revoke the act. Even if there is no statute of limitations for the revision of administrative acts, the passage of time without any kind of state action may jeopardize the administration's right to revise it.[116] This is the sense of the ban on penalty and interest when the taxpayer trusts the administration's reiterated practice, as per the National Tax Code, article 100, sole paragraph.

What is essential is that repeated application be capable of giving citizens the impression the act is valid, so that any future interruption in the production of effects may be perceived as unfair. The relationship between the basis for trust and time is inversely proportional in this manner: The longer an act's efficacy lasts, the less strong its basis for trust needs to be; the less an act's efficacy lasts, the stronger the basis for trust has to be.[117]

---

[112] Johanna Hey, *Steuerplanungssicherheit als Rechtsproblem*, Köln, Otto Schmidt, 2002, p. 288.

[113] Martin Stötzel, *Vertrauensschutz und Gesetzesrückwirkung*, Frankfurt am Main, Peter Lang, 2002, p. 168.

[114] Miguel Reale, *Revogação e anulamento do ato administrativo*, 2nd ed., Rio de Janeiro, Forense, 1980, p. 86.

[115] Johanna Hey, *Steuerplanungssicherheit als Rechtsproblem*, Köln, Otto Schmidt, 2002, p. 737. Beatrice Weber-Dürler, *Vertrauensschutz im öffentlichen Recht*, Basel/Frankfurt a.M., Helbing & Lichtenhahn, 1983, p. 102.

[116] Fritz Ossenbühl, *Die Rücknahme fehlerhafter begünstigender Verwaltungsakte*, 2nd ed., Berlin, Walter de Gruyter, 1965, p. 108.

[117] Roland Kreibich, *Der Grundsatz von Treu und Glauben im Steuerrecht*, Heidelberg, C. F. Müller, 1992, p. 162. Martin Stötzel, *Vertrauensschutz und Gesetzesrückwirkung*, Frankfurt am

One more observation is necessary. This study distinguishes between two dimensions regarding the protection of individual situations: on one hand, the objective dimension of the reflexive application of legal certainty, revealed by the inviolability of individual situations for objective reasons resulting from factual consolidation; on the other hand, the subjective dimension of the reflexive application of legal certainty, externalized by the inviolability of individual situations for subjective reasons originating in the exercise of trust. Conceptually speaking these two kinds of protection are different: It is one thing to uphold the legal effects of an illegal or unconstitutional act because the passage of time has made them irreversible, regardless of whether the act was practiced in good faith and whether the individual knew or should have known it was unlawful; it is quite another to preserve the legal effects of an unconstitutional act by virtue of the exercise of trust in cases where the individual trusted the legitimacy of the act without knowledge of its unlawfulness or any duty to have such knowledge. In the former case, trust is irrelevant; in the latter, it is relevant. *Conceptually*, therefore, a consolidated situation ought not to be confused with a case involving protection of trust. The difference between them, however, is not limited to a point, but continuous: The transition from one to the other is like the passage from day to night, where there is no doubt about the distinction between the two states, but it is hard to be sure of the exact moment when one replaces the other. This happens because the consolidated situation and the protection of trust have a point in common, which is time: Time can operate both as a *factor that creates factual or legal irreversibility* and a *factor that generates trust*. The passage of time steadily legitimates the normative basis, to such an extent that its addressees start to believe in its validity even if they are aware of its invalid birth, thanks to the long and concrete production of effects. That being so, while a factually consolidated situation is not to be confused with legitimate trust, in borderline cases it is impossible to know exactly whether intangibility is assured for one reason or the other. On this point, Zanella Di Pietro is absolutely right to state that in reality several aspects of the legal certainty principle may apply simultaneously in some cases: "In all such situations, the *stability of legal relations*, i.e., the legal certainty principle in its objective aspect, is protected; the citizen's *trust*, i.e. the legal certainty principle in its subjective aspect, or the principle of legitimate expectations, is protected; and *good faith* is protected."[118]

Basis Effectiveness Criterion (Effective Basis ↔ Non-effective Basis)

The greater the degree to which the purpose underlying an allegedly violated rule is realized, the more the effects of the act marred by illegality must be protected. This axiom is arrived at by observing that the formal requirements applied to statutes

Main, Peter Lang, 2002, p. 225. Eugenio Della Valle, *Affidamento e certezza del Diritto Tributario*, Milano, Giuffrè, 2001, p. 102.

[118]Maria Sylvia Zanella Di Pietro, "Os princípios da proteção à confiança, da segurança jurídica e da boa-fé na anulação do ato administrativo", in Fabrício Motta (Org.), *Direito Público atual: Estudos em homenagem ao Professor Nélson Figueiredo*, Instituto de Direito Administrativo de Goiás (IDAG), Belo Horizonte, Fórum, 2008, p. 305.

and administrative acts are not ends in themselves, but in most cases the means to assure the realization of certain ends. The requirement that a tax benefit can be created only by law, for instance, serves the purpose of avoiding a waste of public funds, combating inequality and assuring fair competition. The requirement of public competitive examinations to enter public service is an instrument to avoid inappropriate filling of positions, assure equality of conditions among applicants, and combat arbitrariness in the selection process.

However, when the end underlying a formal rule is met, even if the behavior required by its incidence hypothesis is not observed, there will be a reason that may lead, alongside others, to the upholding of the invalid act. A case in point, analyzed below, involved a recruiting process for positions in a semi-public company: Although there was no public competitive examination, the Supreme Court decided to uphold the process, arguing that the selection process was so rigorous, and equality of opportunity for all applicants so intensely assured, that there was no sense in voiding it. In other words, what the Court did was to uphold an act marred by invalidity because the purpose of the rule was indirectly met with no harm to the general stability of the legal order.[119]

In the field of tax law, such reasoning is extremely relevant, because there are acts that indirectly achieve their ends even though they are not performed in accordance with the formal rules. This can be said of sectoral tax benefits granted onerously to specific taxpayers in exchange for investment considered to be in the public interest. In this situation, while the tax benefits are granted without a statute (or an interstate agreement), no harm is done to the state because the public interest is furthered; any competitive imbalance (given the cost of the benefit) can be extenuated and the protection of trust is not ruled out *ipso facto*.[120]

Basis Conduciveness Criterion (Conducive Basis ↔ Neutral Basis)

The greater the conduciveness of the basis, the more the trust relating to it merits protection. This is because not all norms operate in the same manner as a foundation for individual action: Some are more foundational than others. Conducive norms are a case in point: Citizens who obey them act not just within a *scope of action permitted* by legislation that establishes a mere framework for action, but also within *a scope of action stimulated* by legislation, and hence by the state, which conduces to such action.[121] Conducive norms are not only conditions for action, but also appeal to it and are its object, operating as the foundation for activity; they are not

[119]MS n.22.357, Full Court, Rep. Justice Gilmar Mendes, *DJ* 5 Nov 2004.

[120]Beatrice Weber-Dürler, *Vertrauensschutz im öffentlichen Recht*, Basel/Frankfurt a.M., Helbing & Lichtenhahn, 1983, p. 224.

[121]Federico Arcos Ramírez, *La seguridad jurídica: una teoría formal*, Madrid, Dykinson, 2000, p. 265. Martin Stötzel, *Vertrauensschutz und Gesetzesrückwirkung*, Frankfurt am Main, Peter Lang, 2002, p. 183.

limits to action, but offer it and model it.[122] Thus permission to exercise freedom and laws that allow action must be distinguished from the stimulating of freedom and conducive laws. Moreover, lack of foresight regarding freedom freely conceived within the limits of permission must be distinguished from surprise relating to freedom exercised by stimulation within the limits of what has become mandatory. In the former case, the taxpayer is *surprised* as a consequence of the legislative or administrative prerogative of effecting changes; in the latter case, the taxpayer is *deceived* as a consequence of *unfair behavior* by the authorities, who encourage one day and disregard the next. Hence the importance of distinguishing between levels of surprise: The effect of surprise may be to prohibit retroactive effects of a new norm on activities commenced in the past, when the degree of normative conduciveness is highest, or to require transitional rules, exceptions or equity clauses, when the degree of conduciveness is lowest. This avoids unfairness and prevents not only violation of the legal certainty principle, but also to the administrative morality principle.

In the sphere of tax law, therefore, normative acts that affect only the tax burden (*Belastungswirkung*) and are based on norms that aim to share that burden equitably (*Lastenausteilungsnormen*) must be distinguished from normative acts designed to drive a change in behavior (*Gestaltungswirkung*) and grounded in norms that aim to have conducive effects (*Lenkungsnormen*).[123] Conducive norms cause *higher* expectations of permanence. This does not mean that norms with tax purposes, which in many cases are hard to distinguish from norms with extrafiscal purposes, cannot create expectations, since taxes can cause or inhibit behavior to a greater or lesser extent and hence serve as a foundation for planning.[124] "Norms with conducive purposes" must not be confused with "norms with conducive effects": Norms that do not have conducive purposes may produce conducive effects on the behavior of taxpayers, in the sense that they do or refrain from doing something because of a greater or smaller tax burden. Thus norms with tax purposes can produce conducive effects and qualify as "behavior-influencing norms with tax purposes" (*verhaltensbeeinflussende Fiskalzwecknorm*).[125] What matters is not only

[122]Josef Isensee, "Vertrauensschutz für Steuervorteile. Ein Folgeproblem der Wirtschaftslenkung durch Steuer des §3a EStG", in Paul Kirchhof, Klaus Offerhaus e Horst Schöberle (Orgs.), *Steuerrecht, Verfassungsrecht, Finanzpolitik. FS für Franz Klein*, Köln, 1994, p. 611.

[123]Kyrill-A. Schwarz, *Vertrauensschutz als Verfassungsprinzip*, Baden-Baden, Nomos, 2002, p. 298. Luís Eduardo Schoueri, "Segurança jurídica e normas tributárias indutoras", in Maria de Fátima Ribeiro (Org.), *Direito Tributário e segurança jurídica*, São Paulo, MP, 2008, pages 117–146.

[124]Rudolf Mellinghoff, "Vertrauen in das Steuergesetz", in Heinz-Jürgen Pez-zer (Org.), *Vertrauensschutz im Steuerrecht. Deutsche Steuerjuristische Gesellschaft* 27, Köln, Otto Schmidt, 2004, p. 37.

[125]Johanna Hey, *Steuerplanungssicherheit als Rechtsproblem*, Köln, Otto Schmidt, 2002, p. 215. Paul Kirchhof, "Rückwirkung von Steuergesetzen", *StuW*, 2000, p. 226.

the objective *purpose* of the norm, but also its *effect*: the greater the conduciveness, the greater the protection of trust ought to be. This applies equally to norms with tax purposes and norms with extrafiscal purposes.

The key point is that conducive norms, by purpose or effect, produce behavioral results and hence create a *greater* expectation that their efficacy will last. Indeed, without this they would become entirely meaningless, especially since in such cases the state does not simply exercise top-down power by means of taxation, but also stimulates taxpayers to cooperate in a relationship that is also economic.[126] In such cases the state does not simply indicate but also incites, in the sense that in addition to signaling its ends it aims to engage private enterprise in achieving them.[127] It not only directs but also stimulates behavior.[128] And by deploying means to stimulate behavior (*verhaltensmotivierende Vorschriften*) in order to achieve some public purpose, it ends up "instrumentalizing citizens" to act in the public interest, and more than simply instituting a rule, it engages in true "partnerships with the addressees of the norm" (*kooperative Hand-in-Hand-Arbeiten von Staat und Normadressaten*).[129] Moreover, in such cases norms resemble legal transactions with synallagmatic efficacy, because addressees play their part with the expectation that the state will do likewise. What is at stake is a contract of the type *do ut des*, "I give so that you may give," establishing reciprocal relationships proper to a cooperative society.[130]

Lastly, it must be observed that norms with extrafiscal purposes aim to achieve social and economic purposes in a broad sense, by stimulating behavior. That being so – and this is essential – if their goal is to influence the behavior of taxpayers, they must be in force before, never afterwards. A conducive norm instituted after the behavior it aims to stimulate is a contradiction in terms: Behavior that has already happened cannot be influenced. A retroactive conducive norm is therefore an oxymoron because it juxtaposes contradictory words.[131] By definition, a legal norm

[126]Johanna Hey, *Steuerplanungssicherheit als Rechtsproblem*, Köln, Otto Schmidt, 2002, p. 313. Josef Isensee, "Vertrauensschutz für Steuervorteile. Ein Folgeproblem der Wirtschaftslenkung durch Steuer des §3a EStG", in Paul Kirchhof, Klaus Offerhaus e Horst Schöberle (Orgs.), *Steuerrecht, Verfassungsrecht, Finanzpolitik. FS für Franz Klein*, Köln, 1994, p. 614. Kyrill-A. Schwarz, *Vertrauensschutz als Verfassungsprinzip*, Baden-Baden, Nomos, 2002, p. 306.

[127]Lúcia Valle Figueiredo, "Planejamento, Direito Tributário e segurança jurídica", *RTDP* 12, p. 12, São Paulo, 1995.

[128]Luís Eduardo Schoueri, *Normas tributárias indutoras e intervenção econômica*, Rio de Janeiro, Forense, 2005, pages 43 and following.

[129]Martin Stötzel, *Vertrauensschutz und Gesetzesrückwirkung*, Frankfurt am Main, Peter Lang, 2002, p. 194.

[130]Josef Isensee, "Vertrauensschutz für Steuervorteile. Ein Folgeproblem der Wirtschaftslenkung durch Steuer des §3a EStG", in Paul Kirchhof, Klaus Offerhaus e Horst Schöberle (Orgs.), *Steuerrecht, Verfassungsrecht, Finanzpolitik. FS für Franz Klein*, Köln, 1994, p. 628. John Rawls, *Theory of Justice*, Cambridge, Belknap, 1971, p. 235.

[131]Andrei Marmor, *Law in the Age of Pluralism*, Oxford, OUP, 2007, p. 20.

cannot influence past behavior, only future actions.[132] People cannot be guided by a norm that does not exist at the time of their action.[133] A will already manifested in the past cannot be influenced by a norm that as yet is non-existent.[134] From the perspective of fundamental rights and principles that delimit state activity, retroactive efficacy of conducive norms is not just a contradiction in terms. It is arbitrary and deceitful: *arbitrary* because application to past behavior, however conclusive the normative consequences from a legal standpoint, is unjustified, given the impossibility of realizing the legal purpose of such norms, which is to achieve economic or social objectives by stimulating certain types of behavior; and *deceptive* because it embodies utterly unfair state action, which first encourages behavior and then legally disregards it, so that the original conducive purposes are replaced by a mere desire to collect taxes.

Indeed, if the objective of a conducive norm is to influence future behavior and it affects past behavior, it simply fails to yield the desired effect: Past behavior cannot be influenced; only future behavior can. Thus to apply a conducive norm to past behavior is to use a norm with an extrafiscal purpose for a merely fiscal purpose. The taxpayers have already acted, so that the purpose of applying the new norm to the effects of their behavior can only be to tax instead of to foster certain types of behavior. Thus the retroactive or retrospective efficacy of conducive norms with regard to final taxpayer behavior involves a deviation from purpose: They are instituted as an incentive, but tax without motivating. Hence the justification for conducive norms disappears. For example, if an increase in the rate of import tax intended to discourage imports of foreign automobiles and protect domestic industry is also applied to already completed imports encouraged by a previous reduction in the rate, under the argument that the taxable event had not yet occurred through customs clearance of the imported merchandise, means not only frustrating and deceiving the taxpayer, but also applying a conducive rule to behavior that can no longer be influenced. Past imports cannot be discouraged, whether the taxable event has happened or not – this is the point. The behavior has already occurred, which is what matters in the case of this type of norm. The occurrence of the taxable event does not coincide with the occurrence of the encouraged behavior. Thus whenever there is no *temporal identification* between the moment when the taxable event occurs and the moment when the behavior to be stimulated occurs, or between the moment when the taxable event occurs and the intensity of the trust created, neither retroactive nor retrospective efficacy of modificatory conducive norms can be accepted.

[132] Thomas Berger, *Zulässigkeitsgrenzen der Rückwirkung von Gesetzen*, Frankfurt am Main, Peter Lang, 2002, p. 33.

[133] Joseph Raz, "The rule of law and its virtue (1977)", in *The authority of Law. Essays on Law and Morality*, Oxford, Oxford, 1979, p. 214.

[134] Martin Stötzel, *Vertrauensschutz und Gesetzesrückwirkung*, Frankfurt am Main, Peter Lang, 2002, p. 104.

Retroactively applying legal consequences to activities that have already begun in the past is therefore an affront to the fundamental rights of taxpayers and the principles that shape state activity. This explains why German case law requires both clarity of the law (*Normenklarheitsgebot*) and truth of the law (*Normenwahrheitsgebot*): Lawmakers must not only institute norms such that taxpayers know the taxes and to what extent they must pay them, but also remain *faithful* to a *recognizable* legal objective.[135]

Basis Individuality Criterion (Individual Basis ↔ General Basis)
The greater the proximity of an act, the more the trust placed in it should be protected. This is because there are acts of individual efficacy addressed to specific citizens, and sometimes to them only, such as agreements or administrative contracts, and acts of general efficacy, such as statutes. Because these acts do not have the same degree of individuality, they create different bases for trust. If the aptitude to create trust is the distinctive criterion for the basis, the trust-making efficacy of an act addressed specifically to one citizen will never equal that of an act addressed to everyone, without any subjective elements. This is because the more individual the act, the greater its reliability should be for the citizen, because the "relationship of trust" created will be stronger.[136] Individualized acts produce in their addressees the idea that the rights involved are "theirs." Thus an act addressed to a given taxpayer, signed by the state governor and finance secretary – the highest tax authorities in the state concerned – and containing elements that relate to the same taxpayer, cannot be compared with an act that makes no distinctions regarding its addressees. The greater the proximity between the authorities and the citizens, the stronger the loyalty and the greater the deception arising from any later changes. In such cases, the usual distance between state and taxpayer is replaced by proximity.[137]

In this respect, it must be recalled that the morality principle both performs an autonomous efficacy function relative to the legal certainty principle and serves as one of its foundations. Among other requirements, the morality principle prohibits unfair government behavior, defined as an act found to be disloyal to the commitments undertaken. The individuality of an act externalizes a *commitment* between government and citizen; any violation of this commitment is a case of unfairness and hence *disloyalty*, breaching the administrative morality principle,

---

[135] *BVerfGE* v. 19.3.2003. Rudolf Mellinghoff, "Vertrauen in das Steuergesetz", in Heinz-Jürgen Pezzer (Org.), *Vertrauensschutz im Steuerrecht. Deutsche Steuerjuristische Gesellschaft* 27, Köln, Otto Schmidt, 2004, p. 37.

[136] Kyrill-A. Schwarz, *Vertrauensschutz als Verfassungsprinzip*, Baden-Baden, Nomos, 2002, p. 299.

[137] Josef Isensee, "Vertrauensschutz für Steuervorteile. Ein Folgeproblem der Wirtschaftslenkung durch Steuer des § 3a EStG", in Paul Kirchhof, Klaus Offerhaus e Horst Schöberle (Orgs.), *Steuerrecht, Verfassungsrecht, Finanzpolitik. FS für Franz Klein*, Köln, 1994, p. 614.

which requires respect for both the public interest and, more importantly for present purposes, private interests.[138]

Basis Onerousness Criterion (Onerous Basis ↔ Gratuitous Basis)
The more onerous the basis, the more the trust placed in it must be protected. This rule is arrived at by observing that there are acts that create an onus for individuals, such as agreements or administrative contracts containing clauses that create obligations for citizens, and gratuitous acts, which are not subject to conditions and do not create obligations. The difference in onerousness creates different bases for trust because the greater the onerousness, the stronger the commitment assumed by the citizen toward the state and, if the terms and conditions are synallagmatic, the stronger the commitment to the public interest. In this situation, the trust placed in the state must also be more protected as long as the citizens concerned are discharging their obligations.[139] In this case, there is no opposition of public and private interests, but a conflict internal to public interest itself (*In-sich-Konflikt*).[140] Thus an agreement whereby a company undertakes to invest and to create jobs and technology in exchange for a tax benefit cannot be considered equal to gratuitous forgiveness of tax debts. The maintenance of bindingness in such cases results not from lower interests, but from the public interest itself.[141] In the case of onerous acts, the expectation that the state will discharge its obligations results not from the normative act that creates them, but from the synallagmatic nature of the relationship: If taxpayers discharge their obligations, they can legitimately expect the state to do likewise.

In this context, it is also necessary to recall the influence of the morality principle, which bans not only state unfairness or disloyalty but also the illicit enrichment of public entities. Thus an onerous act also entails a greater commitment by the individual, who cannot be encouraged one moment and disregarded the next, on pain of violating the morality principle along with the legal certainty principle.

Internal Relations Among the Criteria
The criteria for testing the elements of the basis for trust outlined above show that its configuration depends on several elements, rather than just one. Each criterion entails a scale: the basis for trust intensifies in proportion to the intensity of the element concerned. In other words, the degree of inviolability of an act intensifies in

---

[138] Marçal Justen Filho, "O princípio da moralidade pública e o Direito Tributário", *RTDP* 11, p. 52, 1995.

[139] Josef Isensee, "Vertrauensschutz für Steuervorteile. Ein Folgeproblem der Wirtschaftslenkung durch Steuer des § 3a EStG", in Paul Kirchhof, Klaus Offerhaus e Horst Schöberle (Orgs.), *Steuerrecht, Verfassungsrecht, Finanzpolitik. FS für Franz Klein*, Köln, 1994, p. 614.

[140] Beatrice Weber-Dürler, *Vertrauensschutz im öffentlichen Recht*, Basel/Frankfurt a.M., Helbing & Lichtenhahn, 1983, p. 118.

[141] Almiro do Couto e Silva, "Problemas jurídicos do planejamento", *RDA* 170, p. 15, Rio de Janeiro, 1987. Joachim Burmeister, "Selbstbindung der Verwaltung. Zur Wirkkraft des rechtsstaatlichen Übermaßverbots, des Gleichheitssatzes und des Vertrauensschutzprinzips", *DÖV* 34, p. 505, 1981.

proportion to the intensity of the elements mentioned earlier. Of all these elements, the importance of time is inversely proportional to all others: The longer the time elapsed, the lower the requirements for the other elements, to the point where even a manifestly null and void act is validated after an extremely long period of time has passed.[142]

However, the problem is that the criteria described above can conflict with one another. A few examples will illustrate this argument. An act may have a very high degree of efficacy with a low intensity of permanence, as in the case of a preliminary injunction, which is temporary but produces immediate effects; an act may not be very binding but may have a high degree of proximity and onerousness, as in the case of an agreement that creates an onerous tax benefit; an act may display a low appearance of validity with a high degree of duration and dependency, as in the case of a pension granted through simulation but received for decades – and so on. The citizen's dependency on state action becomes the decisive factor for the protection of trust in such hypotheses.[143]

These cases show there may be conflicts in the assessment of the various criteria proposed. The thesis advocated here is precisely that low intensity of any element must be offset by high intensity of others, so that in sum it is possible to point to a *greater presence* of elements that favor the existence of a "reliable basis for trust". Such a "criterion of criteria" is arrived at by considering that the essential conditions to configure the basis for trust are the capacity to create trust, on one hand, and protection of fundamental rights, especially freedom, property and equality, on the other. Meeting such criteria depends on a set of factors, rather than just one.

To this end, low intensity of one element has to be *offset* by high intensity of the presence of the others. To use a metaphor, the relationships between the elements of the basis for trust resemble a system of "communicating vessels": Whatever is syphoned off from one vessel flows into another, so that there is a compensating balance among them, and the lowering of liquid in one is offset by the rise in another. Supreme Court case law confirms the rules expounded here.

A preventive injunction was requested by a law student, who had earlier won injunctive relief from a first-instance federal court guaranteeing his right to transfer enrollment from one public university to another and was about to graduate after successfully completing the degree course. In the meantime, however, the Fourth Circuit Federal Court of Appeal had set aside the lower court's decision, and the student petitioned the Supreme Court to suspend the appeal court's ruling based on legal certainty. The Supreme Court granted the motion precisely because in its view the legal certainty principle was evoked by the case.[144] This is a good example of

---

[142]Roland Kreibich, *Der Grundsatz von Treu und Glauben im Steuerrecht*, Heidelberg, C. F. Müller, 1992, p. 166.

[143]Misabel de Abreu Machado Derzi, *Modificações da jurisprudência no Direito Tributário*, São Paulo, Noeses, 2009, p. 398.

[144]MC n.2.900, Rep. Justice Gilmar Mendes. Likewise, see: RMS n.13.807 (*RTJ* 37, p. 248); RMS 17.144 (*RTJ* 45, p. 589).

how a basis with a weak claim to permanence (a provisional decision by a court of first instance) can be offset by a high degree of efficacy over time, behavioral conduciveness and the creation of dependency (the lower court's decision produced effects for years, allowing the student to complete the course credits, and he now depended on its proper conclusion). Thus it can be said that voiding the original decision to guarantee the transfer would have created more injustice than justice.

In another case involving a request for injunctive relief, the Supreme Court examined a selection process without public competitive examinations to fill positions in a semi-public company (Infraero). This infringed article 37, I-II, of the Constitution but at the time it was widely felt that public competitive examinations night not be required for semi-public companies; so much so that the Court of Audit accepted the procedure adopted, simply suggesting that an open competitive examination should be held in future. The Supreme Court upheld the validity of the selection process, citing the legal certainty principle.[145] This case exemplifies a basis with an ambiguous appearance of legitimacy (while article 37, I-II, requires public competitive examinations for career government employees, the Constitution also says in article 173, paragraph 1, that semi-public companies are subject to private law in matters relating to employment), offset by high levels of permanence, addressee dependency and realization of the underlying purpose (the selection was public and rigorous, and the successful applicants were placed on the company's payroll and gainfully employed for several years). The justification for the decision, however, was the legal certainty principle, given the "need for stability of administratively created situations".

The above considerations show that the analysis of the basis for trust requires the use of several criteria to gauge interacting elements that are always linked to the fundamental rights of freedom, property and equality, on one hand, and to the principles applicable to state activity, on the other. This observation is enormously important in tax law, a field where, to use a representative example, the tax war between states makes tax benefits based on private agreements with companies commonplace, in breach of the Constitution: Article 150, paragraph 6, requires a specific statute to grant tax benefits, and article 155, paragraph 2, XII, "g", requires the observance of conditions determined by a supplementary law, which in turn requires an interstate agreement. In such cases, the absence of a law alone cannot prevent the benefits from producing effects. It is also necessary to take into account the degree of permanence, individuality, onerousness, efficacy over time, fitness for purpose, appearance of legitimacy, address dependency and behavioral conduciveness in the normative acts that grant the benefits. The Supreme Court recently granted "general repercussion" status (similar to *certiorari* in the U.S.) to an appeal contesting ICMS sales tax credits in cases where the original operation is taxed in a state that unilaterally grants a tax incentive.[146] Besides having to analyze whether the tax measure in question constitutes a breach of the principles

[145] MS n.22.357, Full Court, Rep. Justice Gilmar Mendes, *DJ* 5 Nov 2004.

[146] RE n.628075-RS, Supreme Court, Rep. Justice Joaquim Barbosa, *DJ* 01 Dec 2011.

of the separation of powers, universality of jurisdiction, statutory legality and non-cumulativity, the Supreme Court will also have to consider the criteria discussed above, since the lack of a statute cannot by itself invalidate the existence of a basis for trust. The issue is controversial and also involves the separation of powers, since the nub of the matter is where states can use their autonomy to retaliate against each other, invading the exclusive competence of the judiciary. While the Supreme Court's case law has protected the trust of citizens in cases relating to the inviolability of the effects of administrative acts, in the field of tax law the justices tend to prioritize the criterion of consummation of the taxable event, or of acts or facts, as is the case with the guarantees covering completed legal acts and *res iudicata*, ignoring other elements that might be considered. We will come back to this subject in due course.

What must be made clear is that these criteria concern fundamental rights and the principles of state action involved: On one hand, the basis for trust stimulates varying degrees of behavioral changes relating to work, the exercise of freedom and use of property; on the other hand, it externalizes the type of action deployed by the public administration, which may be fair or unfair, serious or arbitrary. Thus the existence of a basis for trust results from the application of the legal certainty principle under the influence of the fundamental rights of freedom, property and equality, and the principles pertaining to state actions. Hence the protection of trust cannot be invalidated simply because an individual acts in accordance with an invalid act, a contract covering a matter reserved for statutes, or an act without legal force, such as an administrative regulation. It is necessary to analyze the other elements that concern the fundamental rights involved and the guidelines for action by the public administration. Even an invalid act cannot be annulled if it causes individuals to dispose of their rights of freedom and property intensely, actively and irreversibly, and if its reversal will cause them substantial damage.[147]

2.1.3.2.2 Trust

For protection of trust to exist, private individuals must have trusted the "basis for trust." And for that to happen, first and foremost individuals must know the basis for trust. Here it should be noted that reliability is required alongside the knowability of law: Individuals must know the basis for trust through publication or notification.[148]

Precisely because individuals ought to be guided by valid statutes in force or by normative acts that produce effects, trust begins with the publication of a statute, or service of an administrative decision or act. Mere bills brought before the

[147] Fritz Ossenbühl, *Die Rücknahme fehlerhafter begünstigender Verwaltungsakte*, 2nd ed., Berlin, Walter de Gruyter, 1965, p. 132.

[148] Kyrill-A. Schwarz, *Vertrauensschutz als Verfassungsprinzip*, Baden-Baden, Nomos, 2002, p. 302.

legislative, or administrative manifestations not yet reduced to writing and served on the addressees, do not create trust.[149]

The degree of trust, however, is not linear: At times, it is greater; at other times, it is smaller. The variability in the intensity of trust depends on the relationship between trust and its basis, which can be gauged using the above criteria concerning the basis for trust, such as bindingness, appearance of legitimacy, permanence, durability and individuality. Trust depends on the normative weight of the basis for trust.[150]

Thus, for example, the degree of trust will be smaller: the more freely a normative act allows citizens to act, as is often the case with normative acts of disposition; the more citizens should count on changes, which are frequent in the case of provisional normative acts; the more fragile the appearance of legitimacy of an act, as is the case with acts by an authority manifestly lacking jurisdiction; the shorter the time during which a normative act has produced effects, as occurs mostly in the case of acts issued very recently; and the more general the act, as is the case with general statutes. It bears repeating that these criteria are only pointers to the intensity of trust, especially because they can conflict with one another and lack of intensity in one can be offset by a high degree of realization in one or more others.

2.1.3.2.3 Exercise of Trust

For protection of trust to exist, it is also necessary that trust is exercised, i.e., that citizens have "put trust into practice" (*ins Werk gesetzt*) by concretely exercising their freedom.[151] Legal doctrine is unstable as to whether the exercise of trust is a true requisite for the protection of trust: Some scholars say it is;[152] others say it is not.[153] The Supreme Court's case law, at least in the sphere of administrative law, points in the direction that there must be concrete acts based on trust, as exemplified in building permits, where for the sake of protection it is required that the citizen concerned has started to build.[154]

---

[149] Rudolf Mellinghoff, "Vertrauen in das Steuergesetz", in Heinz-Jürgen Pezzer (Org.), *Vertrauensschutz im Steuerrecht. Deutsche Steuerjuristische Gesellschaft* 27, Köln, Otto Schmidt, 2004, p. 38.

[150] Kyrill-A. Schwarz, *Vertrauensschutz als Verfassungsprinzip*, Baden-Baden, Nomos, 2002, p. 306.

[151] Kyrill-A. Schwarz, *Vertrauensschutz als Verfassungsprinzip*, Baden-Baden, Nomos, 2002, p. 307. Johanna Hey, *Steuerplanungssicherheit als Rechtsproblem*, Köln, Otto Schmidt, 2002, p. 126. Rudolf Mellinghoff, "Vertrauen in das Steuergesetz", in Heinz-Jürgen Pezzer (Org.), *Vertrauensschutz im Steuerrecht. Deutsche Steuerjuristische Gesellschaft* 27, Köln, Otto Schmidt, 2004, p. 38.

[152] Kyrill-A. Schwarz, *Vertrauensschutz als Verfassungsprinzip*, Baden-Baden, Nomos, 2002, p. 308.

[153] Beatrice Weber-Dürler, *Vertrauensschutz im öffentlichen Recht*, Basel/Frankfurt a.M., Helbing & Lichtenhahn, 1983, p. 98. Stefan Muckel, *Kriterien des verfassungsrechtlichen Vertrauensschutzes bei Gesetzesänderungen*, Berlin, Duncker und Humblot, 1989, p. 83.

[154] RE n.85.002, Rep. Justice Moreira Alves, *RDA* 130, p. 252.

In this respect, it is necessary to distinguish between the requirement of stability as the duty to ensure that the legal order as a whole is stable and lasting, because this is the condition for citizens to exercise freedom, and the requirement of stability as the prohibition of frustration and deceit in respect of a given manifestation of the legal order that affects someone's exercise of freedom. This distinction is of the highest importance.

Indeed, there are two questions: Whether frequent, intense and inconsistent normative change, or even one specific normative change, affects (or may presumably affect) the credibility of the legal order as a whole for the exercise of freedom by most people is one thing; it is quite another whether a given normative change restricts the exercise of a certain person's freedom. In some situations, a change may shake the institutional credibility of law with regard to a given matter, normative sphere, sector or region; in other situations, although it does not have such an impact, it may unjustifiably restrict someone's past exercise of legally oriented freedom. Hence stability, because of the durability and credibility of the legal order, is an *objective* requirement of the legal certainty principle, whereas the inviolability of subjective individual situations through protection of trust is a reflexive and limited application of the legal certainty principle in decisive connection with fundamental rights and property rights.

If these two requirements are different, so are their founding justifications: Whereas the durability of the order is founded on the principles of the rule of law and the objective, holistic and abstract consideration of fundamental rights and freedoms, the protection of trust is based on the relationship between the legal certainty principle and fundamental rights, as will be examined later. This differentiation becomes relevant insofar as the requisites to be demonstrated for the configuration of one requirement or another are different – and here lies the core question. Indeed, if the problem concerns the legal order as a whole, a normative change must be shown to have effects that compromise the maintenance of a stable legal order, capable of offering minimal conditions for the collective exercise of individual freedoms. In this case, it is unnecessary to prove that someone's specific interest has been harmed, that someone's freedom has been exercised in this or that manner, with this or that intensity, and that there was legitimate trust to be protected. What is essential is a general demonstration, based on the rule of law principle and on the objective dimension of the legal certainty principle, that accepting the validity of the change will shake the credibility of the legal order for all citizens.

However – and from this perspective the axis of justification is changed – if the issue is the protection of someone's individual interest, then proof is required that the effects of normative change have unjustifiably compromised the past exercise of a legally oriented freedom. In this case it is indispensable to prove the exercise of freedom in this or that manner, with such and such intensity. Individual demonstration is imperative, based on fundamental rights and on the subjective dimension of the legal certainty principle, that accepting the validity of the change will unjustifiably restrict someone's rights to freedom, property or equality.

If the above considerations are true, the question whether the exercise of freedom is an indispensable requirement for the protection of trust is answered first by verifying the intended *type of stability*: It can concern the legal order as a whole, based on the objective face of the legal certainty principle, which requires normative durability (reliability through permanence) and stable, moderate and consistent normative development (calculability through continuity); or it can concern a concrete situation, based on the reflexive application of the legal certainty principle, which bans unjustified restrictions on the past exercise of legally oriented freedom (reliability through protection of trust). Second, and as a consequence, it is necessary to verify whether the intended stability is founded on individual fundamental rights. Thus, if the issue concerns the objective requirements of permanence and continuity of the legal order, it is unnecessary and irrelevant to require proof of the past exercise of freedom. However, if what is at stake is the inviolability of individual rights, the exercise of trust is a precondition for the protection of trust.[155]

These considerations demonstrate that the exercise of trust requirement depends on whether the claim to protection is or is not founded on the protection of individual fundamental rights. When this is indeed the justification for the claim to protection, it suffices to know the extent to which freedom must be exercised in order for trust to be protected: Whether a decision to act, not followed by effective action, is enough; whether any kind of action, such as preparatory action or a project, is enough; or whether instead an action qualified by intensity, onerousness and permanence is required.[156]

As explained earlier, the thesis advanced here is that there is a connection between the various criteria mentioned, among which are precisely the onerousness, permanence and reversibility of a citizen's actions. The greater the cost imposed, the longer the efficacy of the basis lasts and the more difficult it is to reverse the effects produced, the more intensely the citizen's fundamental rights to property and freedom will be restricted, and consequently the greater will be the duty to protect trust and to justify any relinquishment of it.

From this perspective, a lack of intensely onerous or lasting action is not a reason to preclude the protection of trust. Low intensity of these elements, however, must be offset by a more intense presence of others. Trust must be protected, for example, when taxpayers sign a cooperation agreement with the highest authorities of the state with the purpose of obtaining tax benefits in exchange for investment and job creation, and, although they have not yet made the investment, they have not only invested in preparatory actions (such as projects and hirings), but have also irreversibly altered their strategic plan.[157] In this case, a low degree of exercise of trust is offset by the irreversibility of their actions and by the effect that discontinuity of the effects may have on the credibility of state action.

155 Johanna Hey, *Steuerplanungssicherheit als Rechtsproblem*, Köln, Otto Schmidt, 2002, p. 128. Beatrice Weber-Dürler, *Vertrauensschutz im öffentlichen Recht*, Basel/Frankfurt a.M., Helbing & Lichtenhahn, 1983, p. 97.

156 Johanna Hey, *Steuerplanungssicherheit als Rechtsproblem*, Köln, Otto Schmidt, 2002, p. 406.

157 Fritz Ossenbühl, *Die Rücknahme fehlerhafter begünstigender Verwaltungsakte*, 2nd ed., Berlin, Walter de Gruyter, 1965, pages 89–90.

2.1.3.2.4 Frustration of Trust

The trust protection principle is justified only when the trust created by a previous state act is later frustrated by a contradictory new state manifestation. In other words, there has to be frustration of trust. However, not every frustration justifies the protection of trust. On one hand, this is because changes that insignificantly affect freedom, property and equality do not justify preventing them from affecting acts commenced before their introduction. The fundamental rights and freedoms must be exercised responsibly and in a manner compatible with the interests of the majority, so that it is unnecessary to protect expectations relating to acts whose effects are merely tangential to the scope of protection of these rights. On the other hand, citizens are not subjectively entitled to expect the legal order to remain as it is forever, given the legislative's prerogative to innovate through its freedom of democratic configuration.[158]

2.1.3.3 External Relation Between the Criteria and Weighing

So far we have examined the criteria for determining the existence of the elements necessary to configure protection of trust. If all the elements are not present, there is no protection of trust. If all are present, the existing trust must be guaranteed. But what if all are present, except some less intensely: Must trust be protected even in this case? For example, there may be a strong basis for trust but little or no action based on it, and there may not be a strong basis for trust even though a citizen has acted consistently and for a long time based on it. Similarly, there may be situations with a strong basis for trust (a valid administrative act issuing a building permit) without a long exercise of trust (the recipient of the permit has developed the project, abandoned another project and hired personnel, but has not yet started building). There may also be situations where the basis for trust is weak (an invalid administrative act issued on a matter that can only be regulated by statute), but has given rise to a long and continuous exercise of trust (construction of a factory, investment, job creation). In these cases there is an imbalance between the intensities of the elements. How to resolve discrepancies of intensity between each of the elements involved in the trust protection principle?

The thesis defended here is that all elements of the trust protection principle (basis for trust, trust, exercise of trust, and frustration of trust) have to be present, but low intensity in one should be offset by high intensity in another, so that on average the intensity of the presuppositions is sufficient. Thus the stronger the basis for trust, the less intense the citizen's actions need to be in terms of time and effort; the more intense the actions, the weaker the basis for trust can be. The justification

[158] Kyrill-A. Schwarz, *Vertrauensschutz als Verfassungsprinzip*, Baden-Baden, Nomos, 2002, p. 308. Anja Bräunig, *Die Gestaltungsfreiheit des Gesetzgebers in der Rechtsprechung des Bundesverfassungsgerichts zur deutschen Wiedervereinigung*, Berlin, Duncker und Humblot, 2007, p. 76.

for this rule is simple: The stronger the basis for trust, the greater the trust merited and the greater the unfairness of frustrating it, the lower the requirements concerning the actions of the individual; the more lasting and more intense the actions of the individual, and the greater the unfairness and illicit enrichment of the state through frustration of trust, the lower the requirements should be regarding the basis for trust.

Lastly, it is necessary to verify whether, given the presence of the requirements for trust protection based on the existence of the above elements and offsetting of the low intensity of one by the high intensity of others, trust protection can even so be invalidated by a weighing exercise that gives state purposes a higher weight than that assigned to the trust protection principle. A number of distinctions must be made in this regard.

One of the most conspicuous features of the 1988 Constitution is that it institutes rules that concretize the legal certainty principle, especially regarding its dynamic dimension of requiring reliability of the legal order. A case in point is the rule that protects acquired rights, completed legal acts and *res iudicata* (article 5, XXXVI), as well as the rule that prohibits the retroactivity of tax laws relative to taxable events that occurred before their enactment (article 150, III, "a"). The relevance of these rules to the present discussion is that they preclude the mere horizontal weighing of legal certainty against other principles that may conflict with it when facts consummated in the past are at stake. However, in this context the trust protection principle is important when the past acts in question have been initiated but not consummated so as to generate an acquired right, a completed legal act, a *res iudicata* or a taxable event. When this is the case, and the requirements for application of the principle have been met, as mentioned earlier, it is necessary in the case of tax law to verify the legal purpose.

If the legal purpose is merely fiscal – i.e. if the statute aims to raise revenues to finance general public expenses – there is no justification for realizing the future effects of the past exercise of legally oriented freedom, because the statutory purpose remains, despite the restriction of these effects. The only consequence is that the state will raise less revenue, which in no way compromises the legal purpose.

If the legal purpose is extrafiscal – i.e. if the statute is designed to achieve a social or economic goal in a broad sense by stimulating taxpayer behavior – it will be necessary to know whether influencing the future effects of the past exercise of legally oriented freedom is or is not essential to the realization of the legal purpose. If it is not essential – i.e. if the legislative purpose is achieved even with the past acts in question excluded from the normative scope of the new statute – then to include such acts anyway means to restrict the fundamental rights of the taxpayer unnecessarily. It is therefore a violation of the postulate of proportionality.[159] However, if influencing the effects of such past acts is indispensable to minimally achieving the legal purpose – and only in this case – then the constitutional norm

[159] Karl Heinrich Friauf, "Steuerrechtsänderungen und Altinvestitionen. Zum Verfassungsgebot der steuerlichen Investitionssicherheit", *StbJb*, 1986, p. 294, 1987.

that supports the legal purpose must be weighed against the legal certainty principle in its dimension of requiring reliability by protecting trust. A number of distinctions must also be made in this regard.

If the legal purpose can be achieved through the restriction of fundamental rights and freedoms, by influencing the future effects of the past exercise of such rights, it will also be necessary to verify whether the rights of many citizens are restricted. If only some are affected, then the general purpose must necessarily be achieved. This does not happen only when many people's trust is restricted. However, when this is the case the problem no longer concerns only the trust protection principle, but also becomes a problem of legal certainty in the objective sense – which, as we have seen, protects both the stability of the order, by means of its durability and continuity, and the trust of all citizens in the legal order. Thus it can be said that the need for improper retroactivity (or retrospectiveness) to achieve the purpose leads to the restriction not only of the subjective aspect but also of the objective aspect of the legal certainty principle.

That being so, the weighing must be between the public purpose pursued by the law and the legal certainty principle, in both its subjective and objective aspects. And within this framework it is important to note the different weight of the legal certainty principle in the Brazilian legal order – as will be demonstrated in the portion of this work dedicated to its efficacy: It has a high weight relative to other constitutional principles, thanks to its hierarchical rank and systematic links to other principles that support it and which it supports. As a result, weighing the legal certainty principle against another principle, if at all acceptable, begins with the scales tipped in its favor, as it were, and the balance shifts against it only if there are very serious reasons to justify this. If so, the onus is on the state to find and demonstrate the reasons to justify a different configuration of the legal certainty principle in the interest of the public purpose, not on the taxpayers to find and demonstrate reasons to justify the protection of their trust.

All the above considerations lead to certain conclusions. In the case of an act consummated in the past (an acquired right, completed legal act, *res iudicata* and/or past taxable event), retroactivity is prohibited by the rules, so that mere horizontal weighing of any kind is precluded. In such hypotheses, to quote Couto e Silva, "the lawmakers have done the weighing and decided for the prevalence of legal certainty, whenever the circumstances described in the precept are found to exist completely."[160] The Supreme Court follows a similar path when it states: "the rule that a new statute shall not harm acquired rights, completed legal acts or *res iudicata*, is in the text of the Constitution (article 5, XXXVI) and is therefore constitutional, so that infraconstitutional legislation, even when in the public interest, cannot

[160] Almiro do Couto e Silva, "O princípio da segurança jurídica (proteção à confiança) no Direito Público brasileiro e o direito da Administração Pública de anular os seus próprios atos: o prazo decadencial do art. 54 da Lei do Processo Administrativo da União (Lei n. 9.784/99)", *RBDP* 6, pages 7–59, Porto Alegre, Jul-Sep/2004.

retroactively affect acquired rights, completed legal acts or *res iudicata*, nor can judges apply it retroactively."[161]

However, when a fact foreseen in the norm has begun, but has not yet been completed or consummated according to the legislation, and therefore cannot be protected by the rules of irretroactivity, it will be necessary to verify the existence of the presuppositions that configure the trust protection principle, so that improper retroactivity (*unechte Rückwirkung*) or retroactive reference to pre-existing de facto past situations (*tatbestandliche Rückanknüpfung*) is averted, as will be explained later. Within this framework, trust protection can be held to exist when all of its elements are provided for in large measure, which is the case when low intensity of one element is offset by high intensity of others. If trust is found to be protected in principle, it will be necessary to examine whether effects must also be attributed to past acts in order for trust protection to be realized. If such efficacy is necessary, and only if it is, then the legal certainty principle will be weighed against the public purpose to be pursued, and an even greater onus will be on the state to justify the greater importance of pursuing the public interest. Only in this case therefore can normative change affect past situations that were not consummated. In all other cases normative change must have *pro futuro* efficacy. This shows that it is impossible to conceive of denying the trust protection principle in the name of "high reasons of state," as so often advocated by legal scholars in other countries.[162]

Weighing public purpose against the trust protection principle must take into consideration the intensity of the restriction caused to the taxpayer's fundamental freedoms and property rights. In this respect, the degree of intensity will depend on the irreversibility of an individual's acts of disposal, on the dependency created by the prior effects of the state act, and on the harm caused by placing trust in such an act. In some situations, the financial expenses resulting from the state's promise, the time spent by the individual in acts of disposal, the significance of the act's effects on the person's activity and the impossibility of making some other use of the state act place the individual in a totally irreversible position as a result of what was done because of the state act.[163] The intensity of the restriction to freedoms and property rights corresponds to the difficulty of reversing the act.[164] In these cases, accepting that individuals who dispose of their rights because of an incentive or promise from the state may be surprised by loss of the expected legal effects of acts they have performed means accepting that individuals can be treated as objects instead of human beings. Thus the more damaging the reversibility of the act and the greater the individual's dependency on the upholding of its effects, the greater must be the importance of the state's purpose.

---

[161] RE n.188.366, 1st Panel, Rep. Justice Moreira Alves, *DJ* 19 Nov 1999.

[162] Sylvia Calmes, *Du principe de protection de la confiance légitime en Droits Allemand, Communautaire et Français*, Paris, Dalloz, 2001, p. 413.

[163] Martin Stötzel, *Vertrauensschutz und Gesetzesrückwirkung*, Frankfurt am Main, Peter Lang, 2002, pages 219 and 231.

[164] Johanna Hey, *Steuerplanungssicherheit als Rechtsproblem*, Köln, Otto Schmidt, 2002, p. 251.

It must also be said that, although considerable weight is given to the state's purpose, retrospective efficacy has not yet been justified. This is because retrospective efficacy not only restricts an element (the trust protection requirement) of the past aspect of the dynamic dimension of legal certainty (the reliability requirement) but may also cause restrict another element of this same aspect (such as the requirement of credibility of the legal order) or some element of the future aspect of this dimension (the calculability requirement). Indeed, when citizens are intensely frustrated with regard to the past exercise of their freedom, even if this frustration was justified by a relevant public purpose, in their future actions they will consider the possibility that their exercise of freedom will again be frustrated, and on occasion may even refrain from acting.[165] Thus even after the initial weighing of the trust protection principle against the public purpose is successfully performed, it will still be necessary to assess whether the public purpose justifies other restrictions to the legal certainty principle as a whole. In other words, the importance of the retroactive efficacy of normative change to the realization of the public purpose must justify all restrictions of the legal certainty principle, not just a restriction of the legitimate trust protection principle. Again, either legal certainty is complete or it is not legal certainty.

It is important to note that the irretroactivity rule is grounded in the need to avoid restriction of fundamental rights. This explains why laws without restrictive efficacy can produce retrospective effects without infringing the legal certainty principle. Hence the Supreme Court's decision, in a case involving interpretative laws, that when "normative retroprojection of a law does not create or produce any such harm, there is nothing to stop the state from issuing normative acts with retroactive effects. Laws are endowed with a forward-looking character and hence must typically provide for the future. However, the Brazilian legal-constitutional system has not established the irretroactivity principle as an absolute, unconditional and imperative postulate."[166]

Lastly, it is also important to note something to which we will return in our discussion of the efficacy of the legal certainty principle: Even when the prevalence of a public purpose is acknowledged to the detriment of the legal certainty principle, all this really means is that restriction of one element of one of its dimensions is justified (in this case the subjective aspect of the dynamic dimension). In other words, the legal certainty principle is not *set aside*. Hence it is said that ultimately the principle does not have *prima facie* efficacy, defined as efficacy that can be erased by opposing principles. It can never be completely set aside without setting aside law itself.

---

[165] Martin Stötzel, *Vertrauensschutz und Gesetzesrückwirkung*, Frankfurt am Main, Peter Lang, 2002, p. 18.

[166] ADI/MC n.605-DF, Full Court, Rep. Justice Celso de Mello, *DJ* 5 Mar 1993, p. 2897. On interpretative statutes, see: Sacha Calmon Navarro Coelho, "Segurança jurídica e mutações legais", in Valdir de Oliveira Rocha (Org.), *Grandes questões atuais do Direito Tributário* 10, São Paulo, Dialética, 2006, pages 402–431.

Given all the above considerations, a few rules for the application of the trust protection principle can be formulated:

Rule 1 – The degree of trust protection increases in proportion to the presence of the following normative elements pertaining to the factual situation:

- bindingness – the greater the normative bindingness of an act, the more the trust placed in it must be protected;
- appearance of legitimacy – the more legitimate the act appears to be, the more the trust placed in it must be protected;
- changeability – the more permanent the act, the more the trust placed in it must be protected;
- effectiveness – the more the purpose underlying the supposedly violated rule is realized, the greater the protection of the effects of the act marred by illegality must be;
- conduciveness – the more conducive the effects of the act, the more the trust placed in it deserves to be protected;
- individuality – the greater the proximity of the act, the more the trust placed in it must be protected;
- onerousness – the more onerous the act, the more the trust placed in it must be protected;
- durability – the longer the act's temporal efficacy lasts, the more protection is merited by the trust placed in it.

Rule 2 – The greater the presence of the durability element, i.e., the longer the time between the act and the decision about voiding or revoking it, the less intense the presence of other elements can be.

Rule 3 – Low intensity of one element must be offset by high intensity of others.

Rule 4 – In the case of tax norms with extrafiscal purposes, retroactive effects must be barred whenever the goal can be reached if past acts are excluded from the normative scope of the new law and the change does not affect the behavior of taxpayers relating to acts already performed.

Rule 5 – If the objective can be reached only via retroactive efficacy of the new law, its importance must be proportional to the intensity of the restrictions on the citizen's freedoms and property rights.

Rule 6 – Fundamental freedoms and property rights are restricted in proportion to the abruptness and drasticity of normative change, the difficulty of reversing disposal, dependency on the act and the extent of harm caused.

Rule 7 – Even if retrospective effects are necessary and their importance justifies restriction of the past dimension of the legal certainty principle, they must be barred if the future dimension of the principle is even more restricted.

The above rules should serve as heuristic parameters to extend the assessment of trust protection beyond the formal method based on consummation by prioritizing substantive criteria that valorize taxpayers' acts of disposal.[167] The analysis should be based on these criteria whenever the rules requiring tax irretroactivity and protection for completed legal acts and acquired rights are insufficient to protect the citizen.

[167] Johanna Hey, *Steuerplanungssicherheit als Rechtsproblem*, Köln, Otto Schmidt, 2002, p. 242.

It is easy to see that whether norms and their effects are upheld depends on the degree of state participation and restriction of the fundamental rights of individuals. Thus the more the state interferes, the more reasons there are to uphold a norm. State interference with freedom ranges from the extreme of norms that only indirectly establish conditions for the exercise of freedom, via norms that conduce to individual behavior and norms that institute promises in exchange for actions, to norms that require certain types of behavior. The responsibility of individuals is inversely proportional to the degree of state interference in their freedom: Faced with norms that only indirectly establish conditions for the exercise of freedom, individuals act as they choose, on their own account and at their own risk; in the case of norms that conduce to individual behavior, they act because the state encourages them to do so; faced with norms that institute promises in exchange for actions, individuals act because the state promises something in return; in the case of coercive norms, they act to meet an obligation. Thus the greater the degree of state interference in freedom, the less the responsibility of citizens and the risk they take, and all the more reason to protect the trust they place in the state.

2.1.3.4 Protection of Trust and the Legislative Power: Legislative Change

2.1.3.4.1 Introductory Considerations

A statute can act in the future on future events. In this case, it is *prospective*. On the other hand, a law can act in the future on past events, in which case it is *retrospective*. A statute can also act in the past on past events, in which case it is *retroactive*.[168] Although this distinction between prospective, retrospective and retroactive disregards a number of intermediate situations, it suffices to show that if one of the functions of law is to guide human conduct, it ought to be prospective as a rule. It cannot be retroactive because of the simple fact that people cannot be guided by a norm that did not exist at the time of their action.[169] As Marmor clearly stresses: "Retroactive rules, namely, rules purporting to affect behavior which had already occurred prior to the rule's promulgation, cannot achieve the purpose of actually guiding human conduct."[170] Moreover, law cannot be retroactive on pain of causing lack of reliability for those who should obey it: By virtue of retroactivity, the order that seemed to exist is shown never to have existed.[171] Because retroactivity means the previous norm, whose efficacy was trusted, has part of its efficacy voided by a later norm, retroactivity raises a problem relating to the transition not only from past to present but also from present to future: The citizens' trust in the efficacy of the

[168] Ben Juratowitch, *Retroactivity and the Common Law*, Oxford, Hart, 2008, p. 6.

[169] Joseph Raz, "The rule of law and its virtue (1977)", in *The Authority of Law. Essays on Law and Morality*, Oxford, Oxford, 1979, p. 214.

[170] Andrei Marmor, *Law in the Age of Pluralism*, Oxford, OUP, 2007, p. 7.

[171] Henri Battiffol, "Le déclin du Droit. Examen critique", *Archives de Philosophie du Droit*, 1963, p. 45.

previous norm is frustrated by the change introduced by the present norm and they suspect that the efficacy of the present norm may also be altered by a future norm. In other words, the phenomenon of retroactivity both frustrates normative trust relative to the past and gives rise to legal distrust relative to the future. Thus retroactivity is a problem that concerns the requirements of both reliability and calculability of the legal order. In sum, it impairs both dimensions of legal certainty.

The Constitution has a specific provision concerning the prohibition of tax law retroactivity, according to which federal entities are banned from "levying taxes on taxable events that occurred before the statute that created or raised them entered into force" (art. 150, III, "a"). A preliminary reading of this provision permits the conclusion that the Constitution contains a "constitutional rule" banning the retroactivity of tax laws, whereby the "taxable event criterion" is apparently adopted as the only parameter of tax law validity: If a new law enters into force after the taxable event occurred and is intended to produce effects related to that event, it is retroactive and therefore invalid; however, if the new law began to produce effects before the taxable event occurred, even one day before, it is no longer retroactive and its effects are upheld relative to any fact performed before such time.

As will be explained later, the Supreme Court (STF) uses the taxable event criterion in the form embodied by the above rule. Analyzing the constitutionality of a change made to the social contribution on net profit (CSLL) in the middle of a fiscal year that was due to enter into force in the same fiscal year, the STF's understanding was that the prohibition of retroactivity had not been breached because the new law had entered into force before the end of the fiscal year, the taxable event for the CSLL. Examining the constitutionality of an increase in the rate of import tax, after the President of the Republic had promised to lower it, the STF's understanding was that the prohibition of retroactivity had not been infringed because the modifying decree had been published before the goods cleared customs, the taxable event for the tax in question.

The above decisions, to which others could be added, show that the STF has adopted the "taxable event (consummation) criterion" as the defining parameter for tax law irretroactivity. The argument is that instead of establishing a general legal certainty protection principle, or a more specific trust protection principle, the Constitution establishes, alongside others, a rule specific to the sphere of taxation that uses the taxable event as the defining element in interpretation, so that another element is irrelevant for the purposes of assessing the retroactivity of tax laws. Elements such as the "cause of tax liability" or the "legitimate expectations of taxpayers" are irrelevant according to this understanding, in light of the Constitution's preference for assigning relevance "only" to the taxable event as a necessary and sufficient element for the purposes of verifying the retroactivity of tax laws.[172]

[172]Atílio Dengo, "Irretroatividade tributária e modo de aplicação das regras jurídicas", *RDDT* 124, p. 24, 2006.

These decisions of Brazil's Supreme Court are similar to those of Germany's Federal Constitutional Court in the control of retroactivity. The latter's understanding is that true retroactivity (*echte Rückwirkung*) occurs when a statute affects a past taxable event at a later date and modificatively, whereas false retroactivity (*unechte Rückwirkung*) occurs when the statute affects only de facto situations or unconsummated legal relations.[173] Thus the criterion used by the First Senate of the German Constitutional Court is similar to the one used by the STF: In order to decide whether a statute is retroactive it resorts to the criterion of completion (*Abgeschlossenheitskriterium*) of the taxable event. Thus a statute is not retroactive if it applies to an event that is not yet taxable, but it is retroactive if the taxable event has occurred or been consummated. The Second Senate of the Court uses a different terminology: Instead of "true retroactivity" it employs the phrase "retroactive impact of legal consequences" (*Rückbewirkung von Rechtsfolgen*) to refer to cases in which a new statute establishes legal consequences relative to a *temporal scope of incidence* located prior to the date of its publication; the effects of the new statute are applied as if the statute had existed when the past actions were performed. And instead of "false retroactivity" it employs the phrase "retroactive link to the incidence hypothesis" or "retroactive reference to pre-existing de facto situations" (*tatbestandliche Rückanknüpfung*) to refer to cases in which the new statute simply establishes legal consequences relative to circumstances that refer to a *material scope of incidence* prior to the date on which it entered into force; the efficacy of the norm is produced from present to future, but concerns events, i.e. material scopes, initiated in the past.[174] Regardless of the consistency of the new expressions, referred to as merely a "relabeling" (*Umetikettierung*) of old expressions,[175] the fact is that the key criterion remains the occurrence or consummation of a taxable event, so that other factors such as "cause," "trust" and "exercise of freedom" are irrelevant.

The question begged by this context is as follows: Is the "the taxable event criterion" the only yardstick for assessing the irretroactivity of tax laws, in the sense of *exhausting* the examination of irretroactivity?

This question is answered below.

2.1.3.4.2 Normative Content of the Prohibition of Retroactivity

As we have seen, the legal certainty principle consists of the duty to realize the ideals of normative reliability and calculability based on knowability. One of its partial foundations is the tax retroactivity prohibition rule stipulated in article 150, III, "a", of the Constitution, which, with other rules, permits its inductive construction within the Constitution. This tax retroactivity prohibition rule is not synonymous with legal certainty, nor does it exhaust its foundations; it is merely one of its

[173] Johanna Hey, *Steuerplanungssicherheit als Rechtsproblem*, Köln, Otto Schmidt, 2002, p. 204.

[174] Johanna Hey, *Steuerplanungssicherheit als Rechtsproblem*, Köln, Otto Schmidt, 2002, p. 207.

[175] Bodo Pieroth, *Rückwirkung und Übergangsrecht*, Berlin, Duncker und Humblot, 1981, p. 382.

partial foundations, alongside others. In sum, the legal certainty principle has a far broader material scope than that encompassed by the tax retroactivity prohibition established in article 150, III, "a", of the Constitution: Whereas the legal certainty principle safeguards the knowability, reliability and calculability of law in its various manifestations, the tax irretroactivity rule protects the inviolability of past situations, which is one externalization of the reliability element.

Moreover, the prohibition of retroactivity, as a norm of intertemporal law designed to ensure that tax norms cannot operate retroactively, is not exhausted by the hypothesis embodied by the tax irretroactivity rule in article 150, III, "a", of the Constitution. As I will now show, the *principle* of irretroactivity also has a broader material scope than that covered by the tax irretroactivity *rule* in article 150, III, "a", of the Constitution.

The prohibition of tax norm retroactivity is covered by the efficacy of both the rules that protect *res iudicata*, acquired rights and completed legal acts, and the legal certainty principle. With a somewhat broader scope than the prohibition of retroactivity linked to the taxable event, these rules protect acts performed in the past, regardless of whether they create principal tax liabilities, safeguarding them from the efficacy of later modifying norms, such as tax offsets effected in the past. With an even broader scope, the legal certainty principle protects acts performed in the past via the element of reliability through stability of the legal order, sheltering them from the efficacy of later modifying norms, also regardless of whether they create principal tax liabilities. In other words, both the rules that protect *res iudicata*, acquired rights and completed legal acts, and the legal certainty principle, are a normative foundation for the tax retroactivity prohibition and do not require a link to taxable events.

Here another question arises: Does the "irretroactivity rule linked to the taxable event" exhaust protection of the taxpayer against the retroactive application of tax norms? In other words, isn't the "irretroactivity rule linked to the taxable event" the concretization of legal certainty within the scope of intertemporal law, so that it becomes unnecessary to analyze other elements, which might be considered if the analysis were based directly on the legal certainty principle or on other guarantees, but only if this specific rule did not exist? In other words, the question is whether the "irretroactivity rule linked to the taxable event" operates normatively to exclude the efficacy of the rules that protect *res iudicata*, acquired rights and completed legal acts, and the legal certainty principle, in the scope of intertemporal law. The answer is no, for the following reasons.

First, the "irretroactivity rule linked to the taxable event" does not exclude the efficacy of other constitutional norms that protect a state of reliability because the Constitution itself expressly determines this. Indeed, the ban on "levying taxes on taxable events that occurred before the statute that created or raised them entered into force" is preceded by the expression "without prejudice to other guarantees assured to the taxpayer". The provision expressly preserves its own protective inexhaustibility. This means, first, that there are "other" guarantees, i.e., that those provided for in this clause are not exhaustive; second, they are "guarantees," i.e., instruments that assure rights; third, they are guarantees assured "to the taxpayer." The key question therefore is what are the other guarantees, and what rights do they assure.

The other guarantees are precisely those resulting from the rules that protect *res iudicata*, acquired rights and completed legal acts, set forth in article 5, XXXVI. According to the final clause of paragraph 2 of article 5, the cited guarantees and rights "do not exclude others resulting from the regime and principles adopted." One of the other guarantees is precisely the protection of trust, which "derives" from the legal certainty principle and is termed a "guarantee" owing exactly to its instrumental character. And the rights of taxpayers realized by virtue of these guarantees are the fundamental freedoms, property rights, and equality. That being so, to understand the tax irretroactivity rule linked to the taxable event as excluding the guarantee of tax irretroactivity linked to other elements would be to disregard the constitutional imperative not to exclude other guarantees that preserve the rights of taxpayers. In other words, it would mean interpreting the text as saying "*with* prejudice to other guarantees" instead of "*without* prejudice to other guarantees."

Second, the "irretroactivity rule linked to the taxable event" does not preclude the efficacy of other constitutional norms, since this understanding would be totally incoherent with the ideal of limiting the power to tax. The institution of express limitations on the power to tax makes sense only if they are added to the constraints already legislated for as well as those resulting from the constitutional system itself. Otherwise, on pretext of increasing taxpayer protection via the attribution of a new and specific normative efficacy not necessarily resulting from norms already provided for by the constitutional order, the institution of express limitations would end up decreasing taxpayer protection by voiding the efficacy of other norms with a broader scope. This would be the case not only for the prohibition of retroactivity, but also for other limitations expressly provided for.

For example, understanding that the protective scope of the rule prohibiting the creation of confiscatory taxes in article 150, IV, of the Constitution is limited to the hypothesis stipulated in its wording would weaken the guarantees afforded the taxpayer instead of strengthening them, since on this reading application of the rule would be limited to confiscatory taxes, whereas direct efficacy and proportional application of the principles protecting freedom and property means prohibiting not only the creation of *taxes* with confiscatory effects, but also the assessment of *accessory obligations* and excessive *fines*. Understanding that the protective scope of the rule prohibiting discrimination based on professional activity in article 150, II, of the Constitution is limited to the hypothesis stipulated in its wording would weaken the guarantees afforded the taxpayer instead of enhancing them, since on this reading application of the rule would be restricted to distinctions based on occupation, whereas direct efficacy and proportional application of the principle of equality (and the criteria stipulated by other constitutional provisions) means prohibiting not only the use of this criterion, but also the use of others such as gender, race, age, or any criterion lacking in valorative congruence with the purpose of the distinction. Accepting that the protective scope of the rule prohibiting the creation or raising of taxes without a statute in article 150, I, of the Constitution is limited to the hypothesis stipulated in its wording would diminish the guarantees afforded to the taxpayer instead of enlarging them, since on this reading application of the rule would be limited to the creation and raising of taxes, whereas direct efficacy and proportional application of the legality principle means prohibiting not only the creation and raising of taxes, but also the creation of accessory obligations and fines that restrict freedom and property rights – and so forth.

Thus accepting that the protective scope of the tax irretroactivity rule is limited to the hypothesis formulated in the provision and precluding other hypotheses would decrease taxpayer protection because application of the rule would be limited solely to consideration of the taxable event, whereas direct efficacy and proportional application of the legal certainty principle, and – if the rule did not exist – even the efficacy of the rules protecting acquired rights, completed legal acts and *res iudicata* would lead to the consideration of other elements, such as the already begun and not modifiable exercise of freedom and property rights, as well as reliable state promises, for example. This interpretation of the limitation on the power to tax would not enhance the guarantees afforded taxpayers but instead would lead to the conclusion that the Constitution establishes specific guarantees to restrict them. More limitation would be less limitation – an absolute non-sense.

Third, the "irretroactivity rule linked to the taxable event" does not preclude the efficacy of other constitutional norms, as unlike other rules it is not opposed to the legal certainty principle and the rules protecting acquired rights, completed legal acts and *res iudicata*. On the contrary, it reinforces them. Indeed, in this relationship there is no conflict of vectors, as there is in the syntactic opposition between the competence rules and certain constitutional principles. In such cases superimposing the principle would indeed cancel out the minimum content of the rules, and their function itself, as would also happen if the principle of social solidarity were superimposed on the competence rules to create social contributions, or the principle of freedom of expression were to prevail over the rule of tax exemption for books. The power to tax would lie either outside or inside the material scope of the competence rules. In the hypothesis analyzed here, however, application of the legal certainty principle and the rules that protect acquired rights, completed legal acts and *res iudicata* does not annul the efficacy of the irretroactivity rule linked to the taxable event; on the contrary, it broadens this efficacy by taking other factors into consideration via vectorial confluence of norms. Thus according to the Constitution, occurrence or non-occurrence of the taxable event cannot be said to be the only crucial element with which to assess retroactivity, as it is in other systems.[176]

It must also be noted that the irretroactivity rule linked to the "consummation" of facts was born under the influence of criminal law doctrine, where the "consummation" criterion covers most of the facts provided for in the laws and serves

[176]César García Novoa, *El principio de seguridad jurídica en materia tributaria*, Madrid, Marcial Pons, 2000, p. 174.

as a clear limitation for the legislative branch.[177] However, although this criterion may serve as a guide to the legislative in many cases, it is totally *insufficient* to address the peculiarities of a normative environment such as that of tax law, including continuing contractual relationships (*Dauerschuldverhältnisse*), which develop over time and involve a succession of property and freedom disposals by the taxpayer, sometimes intensely performed before consummation of the taxable event, or statutes designed to conduce to lawful taxpayer activities in the economy, culture, research, environment, health, and many other fields.[178] In other words, as we will see more clearly when analyzing specific cases, the *formal* criterion of taxable event consummation is insufficient without additional *substantive* criteria to account for the wealth of applications in the field of tax law, above all because taxable event consummation does not necessarily correlate with the past exercise of legally oriented freedom: Taxpayers may have been intensely surprised, even if they have been encouraged by the state itself to dispose of their freedom and property rights, yet they will enjoy no protection if the taxable event has not been consummated before the advent of the new statute.[179] If the rate of the social contribution on net profit (CSLL), for example, is raised by 100 % on the last day of the fiscal year, what matters is that the taxable event has not been completed when the year ends, regardless of whether the change will affect disposal of freedom and property rights encouraged by the public authorities and which can no longer be reversed without significant injury. The formal taxable event consummation criterion therefore is *indifferent* to the exercise of freedom and property rights: It is concerned with the occurrence of tax *facts*, not *acts* of disposal by individuals – this is fundamental.

This concern with facts results from the orientation of limiting the "power to tax", configured from the perspective of what *the state* may or may not do, and not from the perspective of what *the taxpayer* has or has not done. This is precisely why the provision itself stipulates that other guarantees of taxpayers' rights must not be excluded. The hypothesis of the irretroactivity rule clearly directs its application scope to cases where consummation of the taxable event is simultaneous with the taxpayer's action. When that action occurs at a different moment, so that the taxpayer's freedom and property rights may be restricted, the rule expressly directs the applier to other instruments that assure such rights. To apply the rule in article 150 to situations where there are other trust-creating elements is to use it outside its application scope. This means the tax irretroactivity rule does not apply to so-called

[177] Walter Leisner, "Das Gesetzesvertrauen des Bürgers. Zur Theorie der Rechtsstaatlichkeit und der Rückwirkung der Gesetze", in Dieter Blumenwitz e Albrecht Randelhofer (Orgs.), *FS für Friedrich Berger*, München, 1973, p. 286.

[178] Rudolf Mellinghoff, "Vertrauen in das Steuergesetz", in Heinz-Jürgen Pezzer (Org.), *Vertrauensschutz im Steuerrecht. Deutsche Steuerjuristische Gesellschaft* 27, Köln, Otto Schmidt, 2004, p. 33. Joachim Burmeister, "Selbstbindung der Verwaltung. Zur Wirkkraft des rechtsstaatlichen Übermaßverbots, des Gleichheitssatzes und des Vertrauensschutzprinzips", *DÖV* 34, pages 503–512, 1981.

[179] Martin Stötzel, *Vertrauensschutz und Gesetzesrückwirkung*, Frankfurt am Main, Peter Lang, 2002, p. 115.

periodic taxes, such as income tax and the social contribution on net profit, where the taxpayer's acts of disposal are dissociated from consummation of the taxable event. Nor does it apply to other cases where by virtue of another element, such as state stimulation, taxpayers dispose of their freedom and property rights before the taxable event is consummated, as may happen with taxes on imports, exports, manufactures and financial transactions.

Moreover, to propose that tax law use a model created for criminal law is to ignore an abyssal difference between these two normative environments: In criminal law the operative facts relate to *unlawful acts*, whereas in tax law they relate to *lawful acts*. Criminal norms aim at prevention; tax norms aim at participation in the results of action or even in action itself.[180] Thus if the problem of retroactivity concerns reliability of the legal order and the aim is to avoid surprise and restrictions on the exercise of freedom, there must also be strong resistance to retroactive or retrospective effects of any kind, as such effects are harmful precisely to people who have been engaged in lawful activities and, albeit not deprived of their freedom as in criminal law, face very severe restrictions on disposal of their freedom and property.

These considerations lead to the conclusion that the purpose of the "irretroactivity rule linked to the taxable event" is simply to avoid horizontal weighing in situations covered by its incidence hypothesis (taxable events whose occurrence is connected to the taxpayer's acts of disposal), but without excluding the possibility of protection for the taxpayer outside this hypothesis. "Without prejudice to other guarantees", the Constitution expressly states. Such protection will occur if, even outside the hypothesis of this tax irretroactivity rule, the situation falls within the hypothesis of the rules protecting acquired rights, completed legal acts and *res iudicata*, or if it is benefited by realization of the trust protection principle via a weighing of the legal certainty principle against the public purpose that justifies the legislative change. Thus the institution of an "irretroactivity rule linked to the taxable event" creates only *one* hypothesis of irretroactivity *resistant to mere horizontal weighing*, without prejudice to the possibility that other factors it does not encompass will be covered by other norms equally protective of freedoms and property rights.

This last observation – that the irretroactivity rule linked to the taxable event creates resistance to horizontal weighing – is extremely important because in systems that do not have the irretroactivity rule, the higher courts end up weighing the legal certainty principle against the public interest principle.[181] In these systems, the "public interest," the "general interest" or a "higher public interest," often qualified by "urgency" or "grave motive", "compelling reason" or "peremptory,

---

[180] Johanna Hey, *Steuerplanungssicherheit als Rechtsproblem*, Köln, Otto Schmidt, 2002, p. 242.

[181] Antonio Enrique Perez Luño, *La seguridad jurídica*, Barcelona, Ariel, 1991, p. 96. César García Novoa, *El principio de seguridad jurídica en materia tributaria*, Madrid, Marcial Pons, 2000, p. 84. Sylvia Calmes, *Du principe de protection de la confiance légitime en Droits Allemand, Communautaire et Français*, Paris, Dalloz, 2001, p. 413.

imperative or predominant interest," function as the justifying foundation for retroactivity, even in tax law, when retroactivity is indispensable to the efficacy of a norm.[182] In other words, in the absence of a rule to neutralize horizontal weighing, judges consider it legitimate to confront the legal certainty principle with the public interest principle and may well conclude that the latter should prevail. This is not the case in the Brazilian legal order. Precisely because the Constitution establishes rules (the tax irretroactivity rule and the rule protecting completed legal acts, acquired rights and *res iudicata*), it is not legitimate for judges to perform a simple horizontal weighing that may eventually justify retroactivity. The Supreme Court, in a decision mentioned above, follows similar reasoning when it states that these rules "have a constitutional character, so that no infraconstitutional legislation, *even on grounds of public policy*, may retroactively affect acquired rights, completed legal acts or *res iudicata*, and judges may not apply the law retroactively"[183] (emphasis added). This weighing may even be performed, as long as the rules in question are not affected, so that the ban on retroactivity linked to the taxable event is understood as reinforcing rather than weakening legal certainty. However, it must be said that this weighing will not simply counterpose the public interest in the change to the individual interest in upholding the effects, because – as detailed below – it will be necessary to assess the full extent of the restrictions to legal certainty, and to verify whether it is in the public interest itself to maintain past effects. Retrospective efficacy does not affect only the past exercise of freedom; it undermines trust in the credibility and stability of the legal system, consequently affecting the very authority of law and the enforceability and bindingness of the laws.[184]

Against the argument that it is correct to set aside the effects of a new statute relative to events initiated but not consummated according to the law in force at the time of their occurrence, it could be said that although article 150 of the Constitution does indeed assure the applicability of "other rights and guarantees", it does so by guaranteeing acquired rights, completed legal acts and *res iudicata*. Like the guarantee in article 150, III, "a", these also presuppose consummation of the legal requirements existing at the time an act was performed, a right created, or a judgment handed down. In other words, the argument would be that besides prohibiting tax retroactivity the Constitution bans retroactivity *only* relative to accomplished acts or facts, and that "mere" expectations therefore do not merit protection, save possibly by application of the legal certainty principle. However, not only does this argument disregard the trivial fact that the guarantees listed in article 5 do not exclude others stemming from the constitutional system and principles (such as the guarantee grounded in the trust protection principle), but it also ignores

[182]Willy Zimmer, "Constitution et sécurité juridique – Allemagne", *Anuaire International de Justice Constitutionnelle 1999*, Paris, Economica, p. 106. César García Novoa, *El Principio de Seguridad Jurídica en Materia Tributaria*, Madrid, Marcial Pons, 2000, p. 170.

[183]RE n.188.366, 1st Panel, Rep. Justice Moreira Alves, *DJ* 19 Nov 1999.

[184]Martin Stötzel, *Vertrauensschutz und Gesetzesrückwirkung*, Frankfurt am Main, Peter Lang, 2002, p. 143.

an important reason not to attempt to see the guarantees protecting acquired rights, completed legal acts and *res iudicata* as the solution to all problems of intertemporal law in the sphere of taxation: The purpose of the guarantees in article 5, XXXVI, is totally different from the purpose of the tax irretroactivity rule in article 150, III, "a".

The tax irretroactivity rule regulates the efficacy of the modification of a previous norm, which *anticipated a fact* whose *occurrence* caused an *obligation* to *arise*, by determining that the new norm must not change the effects arising from the *occurrence of the fact* anticipated by the previous norm. The guarantee protecting completed legal acts regulates the efficacy of the modification of a previous norm which *anticipated requirements for the existence* of *legal acts* whose *observance enabled* them *to produce their effects* as soon as all preconditions were verified, determining that the new norm must not change the potential production of effects arising from the *performance of the act* or the *celebration of a legal agreement* in accordance with the previous norm. The guarantee protecting acquired rights regulates the efficacy of the modification of a previous norm which *anticipated requirements for the efficacy of rights* which, *if met*, would trigger production of its effects, determining that the new norm must not change the effects arising from consummation of the facts necessary to *create a subjective right* according to the previous norm.

If we compare these guarantees, we can see that the tax irretroactivity rule prohibits the creation of *obligations* arising from the *occurrence of facts regardless of will*, whereas the guarantees protecting completed legal acts and acquired rights – not coincidentally originating in civil law – prohibit the restriction of *rights* arising from the *performance of acts or the conclusion of legal agreements that are will-dependent*. Whereas the former is concerned with *fulfilling obligations*, the latter are concerned with *acquiring rights*. Moreover, the tax irretroactivity rule acts on a normative scope that involves a *vertical relationship* between the taxpayer and the state, whereby the latter *imposes* an obligation on the former. On the other hand, the guarantees protecting completed legal acts and acquired rights focus mainly on the *horizontal relations* through which the parties impose obligations and the corresponding rights on themselves.[185] In sum, the target for application of the guarantees protecting completed legal acts and acquired rights differs from the target for application of the tax irretroactivity rule.

That being so, these guarantees are only applicable outside the scope of tax incidence rules, such as the ways in which tax arrears expire and are excluded. What this means is that the prime purpose of the guarantees protecting acquired rights and completed legal acts is not protecting the taxpayer's legitimate expectations regarding legislative changes that create new tax obligations, although they can be used for that purpose. Their main focus is regulating the applicability not of legislative

[185]Claus-Wilhelm Canaris, *Die Vertrauenshaftung im deutschen Privatrecht*, Munchen, Beck, 1971, p. 439. Peter Loser, *Die Vertrauenshaftung im schweizerischen Schuldrecht*, Bern, Stämpfli, 2006, p. 169.

changes that establish *obligations*, but of those that establish requirements for the existence and efficacy of acts or legal agreements that create *rights*. This is why – and here we come to the key point – the protection of legitimate expectations, as far as new obligations are concerned, must be sought in the legal certainty principle and in its reflexive subjective efficacy, so that they can by no means be precluded by a restrictive analysis of the guarantees expressly established in article 5 of the Constitution.

Lastly, it is worth noting that the examination of the prohibition of retroactivity is included in this study as part of the chapter on trust protection. This is because trust protection is the fundamental, albeit not the only, criterion for applying the prohibition of retroactivity when the irretroactivity rule linked to the taxable event does not protect acts initiated in the past but not consummated from the perspective of the law in force at the time.[186] However, this means that outside the scope of application of the irretroactivity rule the concept of retroactivity itself changes: Not only a new law that affects a taxable event completed in accordance with a prior law but also a law that acts *restrictively* on *an event* that occurred before it was enacted are retroeffective. In this context, "an event that occurred" is deemed to mean any disposal of freedom and property rights that occurred before the new statute was enacted, and "restrictively" to mean a later devaluation of that disposal. Thus as accurately defined by Stötzel, retroactivity occurs when a statute establishes future consequences that are more onerous, compared with the previous rule, to an act disposing of freedom and property rights performed before its enactment, thus devaluing it, even if only partially.[187] Quite rightly, Dengo also advocates a change in the criterion used to configure retroactivity, which should be the trust protection principle.[188]

Hence retroactivity is not avoided if a statute says it enters into force on the date of its publication and produces effects from that date, because it may well apply to events initiated but not completed in the past. Even in such cases the disposal of fundamental rights may have been unjustifiably affected, and may be, though not necessarily, protected by the subjective efficacy of the legal certainty principle. As other criteria besides the one referring to the consummation of acts or facts in the past become relevant, the very concept of retroactivity must be extended beyond specific events, whether or not they have actually occurred, to encompass a scale of references to the past.[189] After all, if the prohibition of retroactivity is founded on

[186]Johanna Hey, *Steuerplanungssicherheit als Rechtsproblem*, Köln, Otto Schmidt, 2002, p. 108. Martin Stötzel, *Vertrauensschutz und Gesetzesrückwirkung*, Frankfurt am Main, Peter Lang, 2002, p. 157.

[187]Martin Stötzel, *Vertrauensschutz und Gesetzesrückwirkung*, Frankfurt am Main, Peter Lang, 2002, p. 159.

[188]Atílio Dengo, *Contributo para uma teoria da irretroatividade tributária*, Ph.D. Dissertation/UFRGS, 2008, unpublished, pages 88 and on, and 124.

[189]Bodo Pieroth, *Rückwirkung und Übergangsrecht*, Berlin, Duncker und Humblot, 1981, p. 161.

the rule of law principle and fundamental rights, what matters is the acts disposing of such rights, and not whether purely by chance the taxable events happened to be consummated in a technical sense.[190]

When linking retroactivity to trust protection, care has to be taken not to disregard the particularities of legislative acts in terms of abstraction and generality. The generality of statutes requires their application to all those who fit the hypothesis. To allow the assessment of retroactivity to depend on whether addressees effectively based their behavior on the statute would mean that people responsible for the same behavior at the same time would be subject to different laws on the basis of the subjective consideration of whether their conduct was based on the statute at the time of the action. Those who based their behavior on the changed statute would be out of reach of the later retroactive statute, but those who ignored the previous statute or were ambivalent about it would be covered by the later retroactive statute. This is why the trust to be considered with regard to statutory retroactivity is not actual but presumptive trust: The applier must assume that conduct at the time of the statute was or could have been influenced by it.[191] Therefore, the trust necessary to admit retroactivity does not assume actual knowledge of the previous norm, but the *ability* to be aware of it.

This reformulation of the concept of retroactivity presents significant consequences. First and foremost, a distinction must be made between the "irretroactivity rule" set forth in article 150 of the Constitution and the "irretroactivity principle" as a norm derived from the legal certainty principle in its trust protection dimension. Solutions based on the "irretroactivity rule" are linked to the operative incidence hypothesis, so that they are applicable and protective only in cases where there is *simultaneous* completion of the taxable event and the disposal of rights by the taxpayer. Its application depends solely on consummation of the taxable event according to the previous statute; other elements, such as trust and disposal, are irrelevant. Solutions based on the "irretroactivity principle" relate to disposal of the rights of freedom and property (*grundrechtsbezogen*), so that they are applicable and protective for cases where there is *no simultaneity* between consummation of the taxable event and the taxpayer's disposal of rights. Its application must consider whether taxpayers' fundamental rights have been restricted with harm and without justification; hence the relevance of elements such as trust and disposal, and the irrelevance of the formal criterion of consummation. Indeed, there are norms that would not be retroactive according to the traditional conception but even so eventually have restrictive effects on the exercise of fundamental rights.[192] The typology of (ir)retroactivity must take this difference into account in order not to attempt to assure rights by means of the wrong norm.

---

[190]Karl Heinrich Friauf, "Steuerrechtsänderungen und Altinvestitionen. Zum Verfassungsgebot der steuerlichen Investitionssicherheit", *StbJb*, 1986/1987, p. 287.

[191]Ben Juratowitch, *Retroactivity and the Common Law*, Oxford, Hart, 2008, p. 47.

[192]Johanna Hey, *Steuerplanungssicherheit als Rechtsproblem*, Köln, Otto Schmidt, 2002, p. 236.

There is still one last consideration to present. It is that, although the rule in article 150, III, "a", of the Constitution assumes a taxable event, strictly speaking two interpretations are possible. On one hand, the expression "taxable events that occurred" may refer to the completion of all the legal requirements that are necessary and sufficient to create a tax obligation; on the other hand, it can be understood as referring to past events typified in tax law as taxable events, regardless of completion or consummation in their entirety. Thus in addition to all the arguments presented above in favor of a broader interpretation of the prohibition of retroactivity, yet another can be built on the actual provision under discussion. According to this argument, the aim of the tax irretroactivity rule is not necessarily to protect only taxable events completed in the past, but events typified as taxable before the advent of the new statute. This is the consistent interpretation of Ferraz Jr., for whom the tax irretroactivity guarantee makes sense only if it covers not just completed legal acts, but also "events that had occurred" at the time they were considered taxable.[193]

The above considerations, based on fundamental rights and the principles that configure state actions, lead to the conclusion that the key is not consummation of the taxable event but the intensity with which taxpayers dispose of their freedom and property. Retrospective effects are barred when a change in the law unfavorably alters the legal consequences of behavior based on the purpose or efficacy of the incidence hypothesis in force at the time and that presumably would have been avoided if the taxpayer concerned had known about the future change.

Before proceeding to a critical appreciation of the ways in which the prohibition of retroactivity is applied, however, we need a typology of its application.[194]

2.1.3.4.3 Typology of (Ir)retroactivity

2.1.3.4.3.1 Retroactive Modification of Legal Consequences

So-called "genuine retroactivity" (*echte Rückwirkung*), also known as the "retroactive impact of legal consequences" (*Rückbewirkung von Rechtsfolgen*), occurs when a new norm affects the legal consequences of acts performed and completed in the past according to a previous norm, which has now been altered.

Strictly speaking, "true" retroactivity is a fiction: The past is over, and a future norm can never affect past facts or effects.[195] Time flows inexorably forward. In such cases the legislator's intent is to apply legal consequences that would have been

[193]Tércio Sampaio Ferraz Jr., "Anterioridade e irretroatividade no campo tributário", *RDDT* 56, pages 127–128, São Paulo, 2001.

[194]Klaus Vogel and Christian Waldhoff, *Grundlagen des Finanzverfassungsrechts*, Heidelberg, C. F. Müller, 1999, p. 321.

[195]Antonio Enrique Perez Luño, *La seguridad jurídica*, Barcelona, Ariel, 1991, p. 91. Johanna Hey, *Steuerplanungssicherheit als Rechtsproblem*, Köln, Otto Schmidt, 2002, p. 230. Karl Albert Schachtschneider, *Prinzipien des Rechtsstaates*, Berlin, Duncker und Humblot, 2006, p. 364. Paul Kirchhof, "Rückwirkung von Steuergesetzen", *StuW*, 2000, p. 223.

produced if the later rule had been in force when the past act was performed, so that the prohibition of retroactivity serves to prevent the later norm from changing the effects deriving from the incidence of the previous norm.[196] From a legal standpoint, therefore, the prohibition of retroactivity is not designed to prevent changes to the chain of facts, which continues to flow inexorably. As Ferraz Jr. points out, time corrodes everything and has an ineluctable quality called entropic: Everything dies.[197] Instead, the aim of the prohibition is to alter the normative *meaning* of a past event and prevent a present act from changing it arbitrarily.[198]

This kind of situation is expressly regulated by the Constitution through the rule prohibiting retroactivity linked to the taxable event (article 150, I). When an event that occurred in the past is a taxable event, the Constitution itself stipulates that completion of the event defined in the incidence hypothesis is the criterion to determine irretroactivity: If the taxable event occurred and its requisites were completed, the new norm cannot apply to the effects produced. The constitutional rule bars this kind of retroactivity.

With regard to past events of a different nature that does not concern tax incidence hypotheses, the Constitution also prohibits retroactivity if the past events can be included in the categories of acquired rights, completed legal acts and *res iudicata*. A new norm that changes the validity requirements for legal acts established by a previous norm cannot be applied to past legal acts that have all the required elements based on the previous norm, which was in force at that time, on pain of violating the protection of completed legal acts; a new norm that changes the conditions for the enjoyment of rights established by a previous norm cannot be applied to rights resulting from realization of the legal requirements necessary to the efficacy of legal acts or facts based on the previous norm, which was in force at the time, on pain of violating the guarantee protecting acquired rights; a new norm that changes the normative requirements for the validity or efficacy of legal acts or facts that have been the object of application through an unappealable court decision cannot be applied to the effects of the decision regarding such acts or facts, on pain of violating the protection of *res iudicata*. The constitutional rule also bars these kinds of retroactivity.

What matters at this point is that the hypotheses of retroactivity mentioned earlier involve acts or facts *consummated* in the past according to the statute in force at the time – i.e. acts or facts that fulfilled all the requisites posited by the incidence hypothesis in the norm governing the acts and facts concerned. As far as tax law is concerned, this means the Constitution prevents a new norm from changing the

---

[196]Klaus Vogel, "Rückwirkung: eine festgefahrene Diskussion. Ein Versuch, die Blockade zu lösen", in Klaus Schlaich *et alii* (Orgs.), *FS für Martin Heckel zum 70. Geburtstag*, Tübingen, Mohr Siebeck, 1999, p. 878.

[197]Tércio Sampaio Ferraz Jr., "Irretroatividade e jurisprudência judicial", in Tércio Sampaio Ferraz Jr., Roque Carrazza e Nelson Nery Jr. (Orgs.), *Efeito "ex nunc" e as decisões do STF*, São Paulo, Manole, 2008, p. 7.

[198]Tércio Sampaio Ferraz Jr., "Anterioridade e irretroatividade no campo tributário", *RDDT* 56, p. 125, São Paulo, 2001.

impact of a past situation completed in accordance with the old norm, in terms of the legal effects of a legal act resulting from consummation of the conditions necessary to its existence, the effects of a right acquired by consummation of the requisites necessary for its efficacy, the effects of a final and unappealable court decision, and the effects of a taxable event resulting from completion of the requirements necessary to its occurrence.

There is no lack of Supreme Court rulings in this direction. The STF has quashed the application of: a new rule on corporate income tax to earnings in the fiscal year *ended* before the new rule entered into force;[199] resolutions that raise the rate of tax on exports *already registered*;[200] a decree-law enacted on July 20, 1983, to income earned in fiscal 1982, an already ended past year during which payments were made or initiated.[201]

In all these cases, the STF overruled application of the new norm to events that were completed in accordance with the legislation in force at the time of their occurrence, and produced *consequences* before the new norm entered into force. The tax irretroactivity rule is *sufficient* to assure taxpayers' rights.

2.1.3.4.3.2 Retroactive Links to Incidence Hypotheses I

Sometimes the conditions required for a legal act to be valid or a right to be exercised are completed while a previous norm is in force, but the legal consequences materialize only after a new norm enters into force. The effects of past acts are produced only after the law has changed. Here it is appropriate to speak of both true or genuine retroactivity and a stronger kind of non-genuine or false retroactivity (*unechte Rückwirkung*), or retroactive reference to pre-existing situations (*tatbeständliche Rückanknüpfung*), which arises when the new norm affects the future legal consequences of acts performed in the past.

It should be noted that in this case the legal fact occurs in the past and is completed in compliance with the norm in force at the time of its occurrence. However, for whatever reason the normative consequence does not materialize while the old norm is in force. In this case the tax irretroactivity rule is not sufficient to protect the taxpayers. Their protection requires other guarantees such as those protecting completed legal acts and acquired rights, which as we have seen apply to past legal facts or acts that do not fit into the category of taxable events.

Thus a new norm that changes the *validity requirements* for legal acts established by a previous norm cannot be applied to legal acts that have already been performed by completing the elements necessary to their existence according to the previous norm in force at the time, on pain of violating protection of completed legal acts. For example, if a contract was signed and the parties agreed that the minimum wage would be its reference index, a new statute cannot determine the use of another

[199] AgR in RE n.242.688-RS, 1st Panel, Rep. Justice Sepúlveda Pertence, j. 17 Oct 2006.

[200] ED in AgR in RE n.234.954-AL, 2nd Panel, Rep. Justice Maurício Corrêa, *DJ* 24 Oct 2003.

[201] RE n.111.954-PR, Full Court, Rep. Justice Maurício Corrêa, *DJ* 24 Jun 1988.

index, such as the ORTN, because this would change the *validity requirements* for legal acts executed while a previous norm was in force and hence would violate the guarantee protecting completed legal acts. Indeed, that was what the STF decided.[202]

Similarly, if parents sign contracts with a school agreeing to reset annual fees in accordance with the inflation index stipulated by the legislation in force at the time, a new norm cannot change the index because in doing so it would change the validity requirements for acts performed while the old norm was in force. In such a case the STF ruled that this guarantee "was not observed by the lower court, which in its decision determined the application of Laws 8030 and 8039, both enacted in 1990, to *effects subsequent to* these laws resulting from a contract signed in October 1989, and thus infringed on a completed legal act"[203] (emphasis added).

The STF ruled in the same direction in a case relating to a savings account contract which was signed and under which a deposit was made in compliance with legislation that had been amended by the time interest on the deposit was credited. The STF's decision states that "in the case of savings account contracts signed or renewed before the entry into force of Provisional Measure 32, dated January 15, 1989, later converted into Law 7730, dated January 31, 1989, the norms of this infraconstitutional legislation do not apply in light of article 5, XXXVI, of the Federal Constitution, *even if interest was credited at a later date*"[204] (emphasis added).

In all these cases a later norm changed validity requirements for legal acts provided for by a previous norm and therefore could not affect acts that had met all the requisites for their existence according to the norm in force at the time, so that they were truly "completed". What matters is completion of the validity requirements for contractual arrangements entered into while the previous law was in force: It does not matter that monthly payments of rent and school fees, or interest earned by the savings account, all happened after the legislation changed. What matters is that when the contracts were signed they complied with all the validity requirements provided for by the old law and their effects must therefore be subject to the old rules.

Nor can a new norm that changes the requirements for enjoyment of rights established by a previous norm be applied to rights acquired by complying with the legal efficacy requirements for legal facts or acts based on the previous norm, which was in force at the time they occurred, on pain of violating the guarantee that protects acquired rights. However, when the requirements have not been completely met, it is not accurate to speak of acquired rights. This was the STF's understanding in a case involving length of service retirement. The petitioners requested application of the requirements called for by a previous norm, Constitutional Amendment 20/98: "Public servants who had not *completed* the requirements for retirement at the

---

[202]RE n.96.037, 2nd Panel, Rep. Justice Djaci Falcão, *DJ* 12 Nov 1982.

[203]RE n.188.366, 1st Panel, Rep. Justice Moreira Alves, *DJ* 19 Nov 1999.

[204]RE n.208.861, 1st Panel, Rep. Justice Sydney Sanches, *DJ* 6 Jun 1997.

time the new constitutional norms came into force became subject to the social security regime established by Constitutional Amendment 41/2003, later modified by Constitutional Amendment 47/2005."[205] For acquired rights to be pertinent to this case, compliance with all the legal efficacy requirements for legal acts or facts based on the previous norm would have been necessary, but this was not the case.

In short, the key point is when all the requirements for an act to exist or a right to be effective were met in accordance with the previous norm. This is not always uncontroversial, as in some situations there are doubts about which requisites are to be verified.

As we have seen so far, the Constitution has enough rules to protect the rights of individuals: the tax irretroactivity rule, and the rules protecting completed legal acts and acquired rights. Problems arise in the Brazilian constitutional order when these rules prove *insufficient* to protect taxpayers against unjustifiable and undue restrictions to the rights of freedom and property. In these cases, it is necessary to resort to the trust protection principle and assess whether its requirements are met.

2.1.3.4.3.3 Retroactive Links to Incidence Hypotheses II

It may so happen that acts have been initiated while the previous statute was in force but not all the requirements necessary to produce legal effects have been complied with: The validity requirements for a legal act, the conditions for exercise of a right or the elements of the incidence hypothesis have not been completed as provided for by the previous statute. In such cases, the rules mentioned above do not apply: There is no taxable event, so that the tax irretroactivity rule does not apply; the validity requirements for legal acts have not been completely met, so that the rule protecting completed legal acts does not apply; the efficacy requirements for a right have not been consummated, so that the rule protecting acquired rights does not apply. The application of a new statute to these past facts would cause non-genuine retroactivity (*unechte Rückwirkung*) or a kind of retroactive reference to pre-existing situations (*tatbeständliche Rückanknüpfung*).

When taxable events are at stake, the tax irretroactivity rule does not protect the taxpayer because in these cases the taxable event has not been consummated. In accordance with this understanding, the Supreme Court has ruled on several occasions that a legislative change that occurred before the taxable event can be applied to prior events even if they result from legal agreements that predate the new statute. Thus, when analyzing an increase in the rate of CSLL tax from 8 to 10 % by Provisional Measure converted into a statute, which entered into force on December 22, 1989, the STF ruled that it applied to profit booked for the same year (1989), for the simple reason that the taxable event did not occur until December 31, 1989, when the net income for the fiscal year would be calculated.[206] The Court's

[205] ADI n.3.104, Full Court, Reportin Justice Cármen Lúcia, *DJ* 9 Nov 2007.

[206] RE n.181.664, Full Court, Rep. Justice Ilmar Galvão, *DJ* 19 Dec 1997. Likewise: AgR in AI n.333.209-9, 1st Panel, Rep. Justice Sepúlveda Pertence, j. 22 Jun 2004.

understanding was the same when it analyzed the increase from 3 to 18 % in the rate of income tax on profit earned from incentivized exports in fiscal 1989 (Law 7968, dated December 28, 1989). The reason given for setting retroactivity aside was that "the taxable event is only completed and characterized at the end of the respective year, i.e., on December 31."[207] The STF's understanding is simple: Since the irretroactivity rule prohibits changes to effects of taxable events completed in accordance with norms previously in force, it does not apply to situations where a taxable event has not yet occurred, regardless of whether the taxable event resulted from prior legal transactions, as indeed it had in the above case. The circumstance that the tax is periodic and thus has a taxable event that does not occur at an "instant time" but rather in a "longlasting time" was not relevant.[208]

The STF's decision was similar in a case that did not refer to a taxable event, but to a legal act performed by a taxpayer: A 1992 statute allowed taxpayers to offset tax losses with actual profit earned in the next four calendar years, without a cap; a new statute enacted on December 31, 1994, however, instituted a cap of 30 % on the offsetting of net income in a given calendar year against tax losses from previous fiscal years, for the purposes of calculating tax liability. According to the previous statute, losses incurred in fiscal 1992 could be offset by profit booked annually until 1996, losses for 1993 by profit until 1997, and losses for 1994 by profit until 1998. Faced with the question whether the new statute applied to situations in which no offset had yet occurred but a tax loss had been booked in accordance with the previous statute, the STF ruled that in the absence of acquired rights or violation of the irretroactivity principle, offsetting was subject to the 30 % cap.[209] The Court confirmed this understanding in another decision, ruling that if "the credit was constituted after the advent of the normative text in question, its extinction through offsetting or by any other method must unquestionably be effected in accordance with the rules established by the new norm and not by the previous statute, given the principle that there are no acquired rights to a legal regime."[210] If the criterion of completion is used, and the case is deemed to be about rights instead of taxable events, the question is whether a completed legal act of offsetting or an acquired right to offsetting could exist before the new statute entered into force. Neither, the STF ruled. There was no completed legal act because offsetting can occur only when a credit and a debit exist, and this was not the case since the profit to be offset against the loss incurred under the previous statute was earned under the new statute; neither

[207] RE n.194.612, 1st Panel, Rep. Justice Sydney Sanches, *DJ* 8 May 1998. Likewise the Full Court: RE n. 197.790-6.

[208] Mark van Hoecke, "Time and law. Is it the nature of law to last? A conclusion", in François Ost e Mark van Hoecke (Orgs.), *Temps et Droit. Le Droit a-t-il pour vocation de durer*?, Bruxelles, Bruylant, 1998, pages 458–459.

[209] ED in AgR in RE n.278.466, 2nd Panel, Rep. Justice Maurício Corrêa, *DJ* 6 Feb 2003.

[210] AgR in AI n.511.024, 1st Panel, Rep. Justice Eros Grau, j. 14 Jun 2005. Likewise: RE n.254.459, 1st Panel, Rep. Justice Ilmar Galvão, *DJ* 10 Aug 2000. With dissenting opinion by Justice Carlos Velloso, see: AgR in RE n.433.878, Rep. Justice Carlos Velloso, j. 1 Feb 2005; AgR in RE n.305.212, 2nd Panel, Rep. Justice Carlos Velloso, j. 17 Sep 2002.

was there an acquired right because, similarly but from a different angle, the efficacy of the right to offset could arise only once both the loss and the profit existed, and again this was not the case. Thus the STF understood that there would be an acquired right to offset only when credit and debit existed, and this would be the case only after profit had been booked. Here too the Court's understanding is simple: Since the rules protecting completed legal acts and acquired rights prohibit a new norm from affecting either legal acts performed in compliance with all the requirements established in the previous statute or events that have already occurred and meet all the requirements for the efficacy of a right, they do not apply to situations in which all the requirements have not been completed, regardless of other elements.

2.1.3.4.3.4 Prior Cause

Yet another situation may come about when only the *cause* of the fact occurs before the new statute enters into force, and both the fact and its legal consequences occur afterward. In this case the aforementioned rules also do not apply: No taxable event has occurred, so that the tax irretroactivity rule does not apply; and the requirements for validity of legal acts or efficacy of a right have not been completely met, so that neither the rule protecting completed legal acts nor the rule guaranteeing acquired rights is applicable.

An example of this situation is as follows: An import transaction is entered into at a time when a certain tax rate is in force, but the taxable event occurs under a later norm that increases the tax rate. In judging such a case the STF ruled that the irretroactivity rule had not been infringed when a taxpayer entered into an agreement to import a motor vehicle paying tax at 32 % in compliance with Decree 1391, dated February 10, 1995, and was surprised by a rate increase to 70 % by Decree 1427, dated March 29, 1995; the taxable event was consummated on April 3, 1995.[211] The Court ruled that there was retroactivity because the rate increase occurred before the taxable event.

The Court's position followed the model adopted in the other cases: Retroactivity exists only when a law covers a taxable event completed while the previous norm was in force. Moreover, since the rate of this particular tax can be altered at any time by the executive for economic policy reasons, the efficacy of the changes could not be blocked.

2.1.3.4.3.5 Final Considerations

The study of irretroactivity shows, first, that the Constitution provides for two kinds of protection in favor of the past exercise of freedom: When the acts performed have been completed in accordance with the statutory definition there is a defense relative to taxable events based on article 150, III, "a", and otherwise on article 5, XXXVI. Since such protection is realized through rules, it is not subject to

[211] RE n.224.285, Full Court, Rep. Justice Maurício Corrêa, *DJ* 28 May 1999.

horizontal weighing of norms that guarantee the upholding of individual interests against norms that guarantee the modification of legal norms by the state. Nothing justifies a statute affecting facts consolidated in the past. When the acts performed have not been completed in accordance with the statutory provision, upholding past situations depends on trust protection according to the criteria presented. It bears repeating that these criteria are neither more nor less than the result of the relation between the fundamental rights of citizens and the principles pertaining to state action.

Second, the investigation of irretroactivity has shown that, more than simply avoiding one kind of normative effect over time, its purpose is to avoid *deceitful* and *surprising* restrictions to the past exercise of legally oriented freedom. Precisely for this reason, what is essential is not whether there is a new norm regulating the future effects of past acts, but whether there is a new norm that affects the past exercise of legally oriented freedom and to what extent it does so. The problem of irretroactivity is not just a problem of intertemporal normative effects, but also a problem of effects that restrict fundamental rights and that are caused to a greater or lesser extent by the influence of law itself. This is precisely the direction in which judicial decisions must evolve: from a concept connected to completed acts or facts to a concept connected to past behavior, so as to include legislative changes that are non-retroactive but *devalue* the actions of taxpayers.[212]

Indeed, the aforementioned elements for assessing the protection of trust are not examined in our case law. The Supreme Court simply denies the existence of retroactivity whenever an act or fact cannot be considered completed in accordance with the legislation in force at the time it was performed or occurred. The precedents are rigid and draconian: Retroactivity exists if there is a completed act or fact; no retroactivity exists if there is not. There are no exceptions. The position is praiseworthy for its predictability, but questionable for its inflexibility. The German Constitutional Court's case law steers a different course: Norms with retroactive effects are not admissible unless there is a prevalent public interest; norms with retrospective effects are admitted unless there are acts of disposal by taxpayers.[213] There are rules, but there are exceptions, although these are not predetermined. The position deserves praise for its flexibility, but its unpredictability is questionable. Thus both models ought to be surpassed by a new approach that considers elements relevant from the standpoint of fundamental rights, but does so by considering intersubjectively controllable and hence predictable substantive criteria. An examination of a few more decisions by Brazil's Supreme Court (STF) will illustrate this point.

Analyzing an increase in the rate of income tax from 3 to 18 % of net income booked for fiscal 1989, instituted by Law 7968 on December 28, 1989, the STF rejected the allegation of retroactivity based on the view that the change preceded

[212]Johanna Hey, *Steuerplanungssicherheit als Rechtsproblem*, Köln, Otto Schmidt, 2002, p. 236.

[213]Johanna Hey, *Steuerplanungssicherheit als Rechtsproblem*, Köln, Otto Schmidt, 2002, p. 209.

the taxable event.[214] However, other elements should have been analyzed: The income was earned from incentivized exports, i.e., the state itself encouraged the taxpayer to perform certain transactions by lowering the tax rate to 3 %, and then raised the rate again after the transactions were performed; not only was the rate raised again a few days before the end of the fiscal year (on December 28), but it was raised by no less than 600 %. Thus on one hand taxpayers performed acts of disposal of freedom and property that the state encouraged and could no longer be reversed; on the other hand, the law was changed suddenly (only 3 days before the end of the year) and drastically (raising the tax burden by 600 %). The decision to uphold these effects caused harm to those who had acted only because of state incentives. In this context the importance of trust protection is evident; it is of little importance whether the taxable event was completed. Although retrospective efficacy is not prohibited by the tax irretroactivity rule, it ought to be excluded by the reflexive efficacy of the legal certainty principle, which does not tolerate sudden, drastic and disloyal changes that affect acts of disposal of the rights of freedom and property. Although abstractly the state can change, it should never produce other than moderate changes (*maßvolle Änderungen*);[215] and changes must be smooth and fair. It is worth recalling that the legal certainty principle requires a state of calculability, relating to both knowability (via the capacity to predict the content of norms) and calculability (via the capacity to know the limited spectrum of future changes to present norms). In other words, even if taxpayers can rely on change, they must be able to rely on changes within a *limited or relatively invariable spectrum*. Thus even if a change is not sudden, it must not be drastic. For taxes with one-off taxable events, the criterion should be not consummation of the taxable event, but completion of the taxpayer's behavior: when taxpayers have done all they needed to do for the taxable event to occur, their disposal must be deemed complete, which is why future norms cannot have retrospective effects.[216] A different position could lead to accepting retrospective effects, for example, in the case of a 500 % increase in the rate of import tax when the taxpayer completed the import form but was prevented from filing it by a strike, so that the taxable event did not occur.

Analyzing the efficacy of a new statute that imposed a 30 % cap on the amount of profit to be offset against past losses, the STF ruled that the prohibition of retroactivity had not been infringed as no rights had been acquired or legal acts completed before the advent of the new law.[217] A closer look at the case, however, shows that the Court did not consider certain particularities. For example, the government's own argument stressed that "the legislator instituted this tax benefit with the aim of fostering business expansion and inhibiting tax evasion", which shows that permission to offset tax losses was intended to encourage taxpayers

[214]RE n.194.612, 1st Panel, Rep. Justice Sydney Sanches, *DJ* 8 May 1998. Likewise, the Full Court: RE n.197.790-6.

[215]Johanna Hey, *Steuerplanungssicherheit als Rechtsproblem*, Köln, Otto Schmidt, 2002, p. 218.

[216]Ibidem, p. 266.

[217]ED in AgR in RE n.278.466, 2nd Panel, Rep. Justice Maurício Corrêa, *DJ* 6 Feb 2003.

to increase their operations; offsetting was limited to 30 % so that the tax burden for taxpayers that did not offset losses increased by an equivalent amount, and the state failed to demonstrate why after 2 years of benefits the restriction should necessarily affect precisely those taxpayers who had been booking consecutive losses and hence depended on the continuity of the right to offset in order to survive. Taxpayers should not have to rely on changes, let alone sudden and drastic changes.

In a case where a given rate of import tax was in force at the time the taxpayer signed the import contract but had changed by the time the vehicle entered the country, the STF ruled that there was no retroactivity because the change happened before the taxable event.[218] A closer look at this decision evidences specific issues that should not have been overlooked: The import contract was signed under the aegis of a promise by the executive, through Decree 1391/95, to lower the rate of vehicle import tax by two percentage points a year, from 32 % in 1995 to 20 % in 2001; the promise was broken with a drastic increase of 118 %; advance knowledge of the tax rate would have kept most taxpayers from importing cars, so that no tax at all would be collected; because import contracts had already been signed before the rate hike, conduciveness could not be argued as the aim of the new norm (i.e. influencing taxpayer behavior). Taxpayers were justified not only in trusting that the rate would not rise, but also in relying on the categorical promise to lower it embodied in the decree. After the contracts were signed and the vehicle shipped, taxpayers found themselves in an irreversible situation. As Hey reminds us, irreversibility is the measure of the intensity of the restriction to freedom and property rights.[219] Future disregard for a past promise involves a qualified version of retroactivity. Put simply, what is absurd about retroactive commands is this: It amounts to telling someone today to do something yesterday, an order that cannot possibly be complied with. The lawmaker issues a norm requiring something *not* required yesterday. Worse still, something that can no longer be done yesterday. Thus it is said that a retroactive rule is an oxymoron, juxtaposing words with contradictory meanings, and cannot be followed.[220] After all, if addressees of the norm have already acted, their behavior can no longer be influenced.[221] However, when a promise is broken, lawmakers flout today the commandments they issued yesterday. More than retroactivity, this could be called, for lack of a better word, contempt for the taxpayer's behavior.

All such considerations show that even in cases where there is no act or fact completed in the past, there can be acts of disposal by taxpayers and state conduct that justify setting aside the retrospective effects of legislation. The taxable event is an important element, but the taxpayer's actions *because of* it are equally

[218]RE n.224.285, Full Court, Rep. Justice Maurício Corrêa, *DJ* 28 May 1999.

[219]Johanna Hey, *Steuerplanungssicherheit als Rechtsproblem*, Köln, Otto Schmidt, 2002, p. 253.

[220]Brian Z. Tamanaha, *On the Rule of Law*, Cambridge, Cambridge University Press, 2004, p. 97.

[221]Karl Albert Schachtschneider, *Prinzipien des Rechtsstaates*, Berlin, Duncker und Humblot, 2006, p. 364.

relevant. Rejecting protection of taxpayers' trust in cases of sudden, drastic and disloyal changes causes a grave problem relative to the legal certainty principle: The credibility of the legal order will be severely compromised, inasmuch as taxpayers will be led to believe that future promises will also be broken, just as past promises were. And lack of credibility of the legal order does not concern only the past dimension of legal certainty; it also affects the future dimension. The price paid for upholding retrospective effects of legislation is too high: All taxpayers should really trust is a total lack of trustworthiness.[222] If the only element were the consummation of taxable events, it would suffice in the case of periodic taxes for the period to be extremely long for taxpayers never to be totally sure of their investment.[223]

This finding shows that the *starting point* for the analysis of retroactivity ought to be changed. The legal certainty principle requires the promotion of the states of reliability and calculability of law, based on its knowability. Its justification does not reside exclusively in the principle of the rule of law, which disallows judging a taxpayer's behavior by a later norm when the action was taken under the previous norm; it also resides in fundamental rights and in the principles that configure state action. According to this justification, the problem of retroactivity ceases to be a problem of relationships between norms over time (intertemporal law) and becomes a problem of non-arbitrary restriction of fundamental rights and of fair and justified state action. The solution to the problem of retroactivity must be a substantive solution linked to fundamental rights.[224] Hence the use of transitional law instead of intertemporal law. Depenheuer is absolutely right to say that the distinction between proper and improper retroactivity is increasingly unconvincing, and that it should be replaced by a substantive analysis, for which "the yardstick is not the efficacy, proper or improper, of the laws but the extent to which the citizen's behavior is worthy of protection."[225]

That being so, the very concept of retroactivity ought to change: A norm is not retroactive if it affects a completed *taxable event*, but if it affects a *disposal that was consummated because of the incidence hypothesis in force at the time*, so that it can no longer be reversed by a reaction of the taxpayer. Thus there is no longer a correspondence between completion of the taxable event and completion of the taxpayer's act of disposal: The taxpayer may have acted before the occurrence of the taxable event, so that the act cannot be changed and the taxpayer has done what was needed to cause the taxable event.[226] The gravitational axis of

[222] Johanna Hey, *Steuerplanungssicherheit als Rechtsproblem*, Köln, Otto Schmidt, 2002, p. 221.

[223] Karl Heinrich Friauf, "Steuerrechtsänderungen und Altinvestitionen. Zum Verfassungsgebot der steuerlichen Investitionssicherheit", *StbJb*, 1986/1987, p. 287.

[224] Julia Iliopoulos-Strangas, *Rückwirkung und Sofortwirkung*, Baden-Baden, Nomos, 1987, p. 306.

[225] Otto Depenheuer, *Vertrauensschutz durch Eigentum*, Karlsruhe, Versicherungswirtschaft, 2007, p. 13.

[226] Johanna Hey, *Steuerplanungssicherheit als Rechtsproblem*, Köln, Otto Schmidt, 2002, pp. 215 e 249.

retroactivity moves from the taxable event (*Belastungszeitpunkt*) to the act of disposal (*Dispositionszeitpunkt*).[227] Schoueri clarifies the issue precisely: "As for conducive tax norms, however, a new approach is needed, based not only on legal certainty but also on a critique of the efficacy of conducive tax norms themselves. If they are designed to change taxpayer behavior, they cannot affect situations over which the taxpayer no longer has any control or influence."[228]

As a result, the foundation for taxpayer protection no longer resides exclusively in article 150, III, "a", or even article 5, XXXVI, but instead in the legal certainty principle in connection with the fundamental rights guaranteed by article 5, XXII and XXIII, and article 170, II and III (property rights), as well as the head paragraph of article 1, article 5, XIII, and the head paragraph of article 170 (right of freedom). Retroactivity is not only the relationship between norms in time; it is the relationship between normative effects, exercise of rights and state action. Its problems are not limited to the completion or non-completion of normative requirements in the past; it also, and especially, includes the efficacy of certain disposals by taxpayers and actions by the state. Within this new scope, what might be less than an acquired right but more than a mere expectation becomes an *assured right* of the taxpayer. The state may even have the power to change the legislation but cannot do so: Sudden, drastic and disloyal changes, or, in a word, *unreasonable* or *immoderate changes* are not admitted by the legal certainty principle. Thus the discussion should shift from the rules of irretroactivity, or even the irretroactivity principle (as a reflexive application of the legal certainty principle through trust protection) to what might be called the *principle of temperance* (or moderation). Moreover, it is important to see beyond the extremes of acquired rights and mere expectations, so that the existence of *assured rights* is also verified. Only in this way will the concept of retroactivity be appropriate to the problem it is designed to solve.[229]

These considerations show that the state cannot use a conducive purpose as a justification for retrospectivity because the behavior to be encouraged has already happened. However, even if there is an extrafiscal purpose that may justify the attempt to affect action prior to the enactment of a new law, even so it is necessary to verify whether the legal purpose can be achieved without retrospective efficacy. If it can, and even so the law affects prior individual acts of disposal, it should be declared unconstitutional, as it is unnecessary. This entails twofold control: objective control that assesses the need for a law to affect past acts of disposal in order to achieve the purpose that justifies its enactment; and subjective control that

[227]Paul Kirchhof, "Rückwirkung von Steuergesetzen", *StuW*, 2000, p. 233. Em sentido análogo: Atílio Dengo, *Contributo para uma Teoria da Irretroatividade Tributária*, Tese de Doutoramento/UFRGS, 2008, inédita, pp. 88 e ss. e 124.

[228]Luís Eduardo Schoueri, *Normas Tributárias Indutoras e Intervenção Econômica*, Rio de Janeiro, Forense, 2005, p. 271.

[229]Klaus Vogel, "Rückwirkung: eine festgefahrene Diskussion. Ein Versuch, die Blockade zu lösen", in Klaus Schlaich *et alii* (Orgs.), *FS für Martin Heckel zum 70. Geburtstag*, Tübingen, Mohr Siebeck, 1999, p. 876.

verifies the existence of acts of disposal that may be covered by the trust protection principle.[230] In other words, retrospectivity is legitimate only if it is necessary and moderate.

Within this new framework, it is essential to keep in mind that the prohibition of retroactivity interacts with other principles. Because a retroactive law changes the effects of an act after it is performed, it violates the fundamental right of freedom by preventing free individual choice and affecting an act that can no longer be changed; it violates the right to human dignity by treating people as objects instead of subjects capable of freely shaping the future; it violates the fundamental right to equality by differentiating between people solely on the basis of the moment at which they act and assigning the same effects to those who know and do not know the rule; it violates the very requirement of generality inherent in the legality and equality principles, since instead of applying to an indeterminate and unknown number of situations and people by encompassing a *class* of *hypothetical* cases, it affects a determinate and known number of situations and people by encompassing *selected concrete* cases. In sum, all retroactivity – and a great deal of retrospectivity – not only violates the guarantee of irretroactivity, but also violates the fundamental rights of freedom, dignity and equality. Because it acts upon choices already made that cannot be changed, a retroactive law coerces human choice and thus prevents people from exercising what distinguishes them as human beings: their autonomy.[231]

Besides restricting the autonomy of the citizen-taxpayer, retroactivity in a broad sense also changes the very concept of law. The ardent words of Friauf express the problem eloquently:

> Only people who are in a position to calculate the tax consequences of their own actions can act freely and responsibly. When the legislator can undermine at will the tax foundations of an investment through retrospective rules, business decisions become a gamble (*Glücksspiel*), and tax consultancy is akin to astrology. However, gambling and astrology cannot be forced on citizens by a collectivity that believes in the rule of law.[232]

All the above observations lead to a change in the way the phenomenon of retroactivity should be represented, as follows:

PAST	PUBLICATION OF THE LAW	FUTURE
Acts of disposal	Legal fact	Legal consequence

It should be noted that before the advent of the new law there are only acts of disposal, not completed events. Thus the key issue is whether acts of disposal of fundamental rights performed under the previous law can no longer be changed owing to the intensity of the new law.

[230] Marina Gigante, *Mutamenti nella regolazione dei rapporti giuridici e legittimo affidamento*, Milano, Giuffrè, 2008, p. 43.

[231] Joseph Raz, *The morality of freedom*, Oxford, Clarendon, 1986, p. 371.

[232] Karl Heinrich Friauf, "Steuerrechtsänderungen und Altinvestitionen. Zum Verfassungs-gebot der steuerlichen Investitionssicherheit", *StbJb*, 1986/1987, p. 295.

Having analyzed trust protection from the perspective of legislative change, we must now examine it from the vantage point of administrative change.

2.1.3.5 Trust Protection and the Executive: Administrative Change

2.1.3.5.1 Initial Considerations

As we have seen in the discussion of the foundations of the legal certainty principle, the actions of the administration should be fair, serious and justified, on one hand, and mindful of the exercise of fundamental rights, on the other. Within this normative frame lies the solution to the question of whether the administration can annul ab initio normative acts, administrative acts or even administrative practices that have conferred benefits on taxpayers, or vacate them from a given moment on. The problem does not arise with regard to restrictive administrative acts because the taxpayer does not oppose their modification based on the trust protection principle: Their withdrawal (*Rücknahme*) or revocation (*Widerruf*) benefits the taxpayer.[233] It becomes an issue when an administrative act confers benefits on taxpayers and the administration intends to change it, either because it believes it has found something irregular or because it no longer sees any interest in the continuity of the act.

Clearly the main problem connected with administrative review concerns administrative acts that confer benefits and are invalid in some way. When an administrative act is lawful, for instance, it cannot be revoked, and revocation is also barred if an act is onerous and has a fixed term, as stipulated by article 178 of the National Tax Code. In the case of unlawful administrative acts, however, the question is whether they can or should be repealed, in light of the axiom that unlawful administrative acts do not create any sort of protection, unless they expire after a period of limitation.[234] It is therefore crucial to define an administrative act that is unlawful and confers benefits.

The crucial distinction is between an administrative act that confers benefits, which can be termed advantageous, and a restrictive administrative act, which imposes new obligations or burdens. An administrative act that makes the enjoyment of the benefits conferred conditional upon the fulfillment of obligations should also be considered advantageous. An act is considered unlawful if it infringes binding formal or substantive legal rules regarding requirements for achieving the legal purpose of the act. Thus it is not any irregularity that makes an act unlawful: Mere formal mistakes, such as typographical errors, misquotations or miscalculations, cannot be considered contrary to law. Nor does every change of orientation make an act unlawful: A change in evaluative understanding does not compromise the

[233] Fritz Ossenbühl, *Die Rücknahme fehlerhafter begünstigender Verwaltungsakte*, 2ª ed., Berlin, Walter de Gruyter, 1965, p. 11.

[234] Stefan Muckel, *Kriterien des verfassungsrechtlichen Vertrauensschutzes bei Gesetzesänderungen*, Berlin, Duncker und Humblot, 1989, p. 54.

unlawfulness of an act performed under a different orientation.[235] Thus the most relevant problem with the modification of administrative acts arises when changes are made to acts that confer benefits, with or without consideration, and violate mandatory legal rules that compromise the realization of their purpose. It could also be the case that an administrative act is based on a statute considered constitutional at the time but later declared unconstitutional.

This sort of change creates tension between the following principles: on one hand, the administrative legality principle, which allows administrative action only within legal parameters, and the equality principle, which requires uniformity in conferring benefits; on the other, the trust protection principle, which safeguards the interests of the citizens who relied upon the validity of the administrative act.[236]

This conflict is significant in tax law, with regard to both normative acts that interpret legislation and administrative contracts or acts that confer fiscal benefits. The latter case is dramatic, given that state governments in Brazil have repeatedly granted ICMS sales tax breaks to attract investment into the areas concerned. The Constitution requires the enactment of a statute every time a tax break is granted (article 150, paragraph 6), so these benefits are all invalid. As a result, the question arises whether they can be protected by the legal certainty principle. The traditional understanding is that tax legality imposes levying of the tax without any exceptions; this imposition also derives from the rule of law and equality principles, which respectively prohibit state action outside the legal framework and non-uniform treatment of taxpayers.[237]

The evolution of case law and legal doctrine has shown that in exceptional circumstances unlawful acts are also worthy of protection through the reflexive efficacy of the trust protection principle. Because administrative acts are endowed with normative force, the trust of those who believe in their appearance of legitimacy must be protected.[238] Initially the understanding evidenced by case law and jurisprudence was that unlawful acts could not produce any effects, on pain of violating both the legality principle and the equality principle.[239] Later this position was strengthened with the argument that preserving the effects of unlawful acts would also violate the public interest principle. Past Supreme Court precedents expressed this understanding: for example, STF Precedent no. 473 rules that the

---

[235] Fritz Ossenbühl, *Die Rücknahme fehlerhafter begünstigender Verwaltungsakte*, 2nd ed., Berlin, Walter de Gruyter, 1965, pages 5 and 8.

[236] Kyrill-A. Schwarz, *Vertrauensschutz als Verfassungsprinzip*, Baden-Baden, Nomos, 2002, p. 324.

[237] Johanna Hey, *Steuerplanungssicherheit als Rechtsproblem*, Köln, Otto Schmidt, 2002, p. 585.

[238] Almiro do Couto e Silva, "O princípio da segurança jurídica (proteção à confiança) no Direito Público brasileiro e o direito da Administração Pública de anular os seus próprios atos: o prazo decadencial do art. 54 da Lei do Processo Administrativo da União (Lei n. 9.784/99)", *RDA* 237, p. 273, Rio de Janeiro, 2004. Also, "Problemas jurídicos do planejamento", *RDA* 170, p. 24, Rio de Janeiro, 1987.

[239] Kyrill-A. Schwarz, *Vertrauensschutz als Verfassungsprinzip*, Baden-Baden, Nomos, 2002, p. 323.

administration may repeal its own acts when they are so defective as to be unlawful, because no rights can derive from such acts, and may also repeal acts whenever convenient or opportune, in which case acquired rights must be respected; and Precedent no. 346 rules that the public administration may declare its own acts null and void. These two rulings combined show case law embracing the "principle of free withdrawal of unlawful administrative acts" (*Grundsatz der freien Rücknahme rechtswidriger Verwaltungsakte*).[240] Hence such acts afford no protection resulting from fundamental rights; as Püttner says, "No fundamental rights accrue from the enjoyment of unlawful advantages."[241]

However, this analysis from the *perspective of the state and its norms* has gradually made way for an examination based on the *viewpoint of the citizen and the merits of each case*. The revision of administrative acts must take into consideration other elements, such as the citizen's trust and good faith, which must be weighed and balanced against the other colliding interests in each concrete case.[242] One of the reasons is that the legality requirement flows not just from the democratic principle but also from the rule of law, which justifies the protection of people who base their plans on the law, especially considering that administrative acts are often necessary owing to legal indeterminacy and lack of administrative uniformity.[243]

The change of perspective has been partial, however, inasmuch as it entails gauging the citizen's reliance on administrative acts in order above all to verify whether they are capable of generating trust. Thus the only sense in which limits have been set to the previously unrestricted power to revise administrative acts concerns the effects of acts whose appearance of legality, alongside a lack of bad faith or negligence on the part of the addressee, suffices to create reliability. The conclusion is therefore that administrative acts must be annulled if their unlawfulness is intense or self-evident.[244]

---

[240]Fritz Ossenbühl, *Die Rücknahme fehlerhafter begünstigender Verwaltungsakte*, 2nd ed., Berlin, Walter de Gruyter, 1965, p. 15.

[241]Günter Püttner, "Vertrauensschutz im Verwaltungsrecht", *VVDStRL* 32, p. 204, 1974. Likewise, but moderately: Patrícia Baptista, "A tutela da confiança legítima como limite ao exercício do poder normativo da Administração Pública – A proteção às expectativas legítimas dos cidadãos como limite à retroatividade normativa", *RDE* 3, p. 180, Rio de Janeiro, 2006.

[242]Fritz Ossenbühl, *Die Rücknahme fehlerhafter begünstigender Verwaltungsakte*, 2nd ed., Berlin, Walter de Gruyter, 1965, pages 10–15. Kyrill-A. Schwarz, *Vertrauensschutz als Verfassungsprinzip*, Baden-Baden, Nomos, 2002, p. 323. Almiro do Couto e Silva, "Princípios da legalidade da Administração Pública e da segurança jurídica no Estado de Direito contemporâneo", *Revista da Procuradoria-Geral do Estado do Rio Grande do Sul. Cadernos de Direito Público*, v. 27, n. 57, p. 30, supplement, 2003. Also, "O princípio da segurança jurídica (proteção à confiança) no Direito Público brasileiro e o direito da Administração Pública de anular os seus próprios atos: o prazo decadencial do art. 54 da Lei do Processo Administrativo da União (Lei n. 9.784/99)", *RDA* 237, pages 281–288, Rio de Janeiro, 2004.

[243]Johanna Hey, *Steuerplanungssicherheit als Rechtsproblem*, Köln, Otto Schmidt, 2002, pages 587 and 589.

[244]Fritz Ossenbühl, *Die Rücknahme fehlerhafter begünstigender Verwaltungsakte*, 2nd ed., Berlin, Walter de Gruyter, 1965, p. 27. Almiro do Couto e Silva, "O princípio da segurança jurídica (proteção à confiança) no Direito Público brasileiro e o direito da Administração Pública de anular

This line of argument can be illustrated by a decision in which the Supreme Court (STF) analyzed the case of civil servants who had been promoted vertically without a public competitive examination.[245] The STF stressed that although competitive examination is now considered the universal form of access to a civil service career, at the time the facts of the case occurred, i.e. between 1987 and 1992, this was not taken for granted even by the STF. It was not until 1993 that the STF awarded injunctive relief suspending the effects of the pertinent provisions of Law 8112/90, on which the administrative acts in dispute had been based, and only in 1998 did it declare the unconstitutionality of Law 8112 as a whole, through ADI 837. Given the particulars of the situation, the STF decided to uphold the effects of the act in dispute, considering the following factors: It was in the public interest to keep these civil servants in their current positions, since not doing so would cause grave administrative commotion; they had served in the positions to which they were promoted for a long time; more than 10 years had elapsed between their promotion and the filing of suit to annul it; and both the civil servants and the administration acted in good faith, since the promotion was perfectly legal under the laws in force at the time. Although the reporting justice refered to modulation of the effects of judicial review decisions, strictly speaking this ruling, delivered in diffuse control, simply upheld the concrete effects of acts based on statutes declared unconstitutional in a different review context.

This perspective, which revolves around the formal regularity of state action and the subjective aspect of trust, must be replaced by an analysis that also takes into consideration fundamental rights and the principles that govern the exercise of state action. Within this new framework, the criteria to be analyzed are different, as demonstrated below.

2.1.3.5.2 Abstract and General Administrative Action

2.1.3.5.2.1 Normative Acts

The administration often issues normative acts, such as interpretative normative acts and normative opinions, to indicate its position on a given matter. Unlike administrative acts, normative acts are general and abstract manifestations, so that they address an indeterminate number of situations and people. When a normative act is contrary to the interests of taxpayers, they can contest its application by going to court to argue its illegality. Problems arise when taxpayers seek to use a normative act in their own benefit and do not succeed because of some administrative change. Such changes may happen simply because the administration adopts a different understanding or concludes that its prior position was illegal. If so, it harms the

os seus próprios atos: o prazo decadencial do art. 54 da Lei do Processo Administrativo da União (Lei n. 9.784/99)", *RDA* 237, p. 300, Rio de Janeiro, 2004.

[245]RE n.442.683, 2nd Panel, Rep. Justice Carlos Velloso, *DJ* 24 Mar 2006.

taxpayers who acted on the basis of the revised normative act, with regard to past acts or even with regard to future acts.[246] In this context, it is necessary to ask whether there can be protection of trust relative to normative acts.

The main objection that can be raised against the protection of trust relative to normative acts concerns their non-binding character: Because the legality principle is imperative in tax law, acts originating in the administration should have a merely secondary function subordinated to statutes. Thus anyone who relies on a normative act, to continue using the traditional expression, knows or should know that such acts do not deserve to be trusted and therefore cannot claim frustration of trust in future if the act is considered illegal.

Although non-bindingness is an element that diminishes trust protection, a number of reservations apply to normative acts, which do not all have a single identical function.

There are normative acts that restrict discretionary administrative jurisdictions or complete indeterminate legal concepts, even in tax law. As decided by the STF, the general parameters of a tax obligation must be defined by statute, so that it is left to normative acts of the administration, in the case of competences whose exercise depends on technical prerogatives, to define what is binding within those parameters.[247] These normative acts work "within the laws", as it were, and are therefore externally bound.[248] While they do not fall within the category of primary normative acts, they nevertheless have a special bindingness, since they define the exercise of implementing powers or concretize legal concepts. The Administration may therefore revise them, either because its understanding has changed or because it has come to consider them illegal. What it cannot do is interfere with the effects of events that occurred while an act was still in force, on pain of violating the trust protection principle as well as the legality principle, paradoxical as this may seem.

Similarly, there are normative acts that embody statutory standards by establishing schedules, values or criteria to be applied to cases en masse. These normative acts also comply with the laws whose standards they embody, except when they are evidently unreasonable.[249] The administration can also change these acts, but not if the change affects taxpayers who intensely disposed of their rights of freedom and property based on the revised acts, on pain of violating the trust protection and legality principles.

There is no doubt that all other normative acts, which are addressed to public servants and whose efficacy is therefore originally internal, produce less protectivity: Taxpayers know, or should know, that such acts are not binding and are mainly addressed to public agents, so that they presuppose greater personal responsibility

[246]Johanna Hey, *Steuerplanungssicherheit als Rechtsproblem*, Köln, Otto Schmidt, 2002, p. 655.

[247]RE n.343.446, Full Court, Rep. Justice Carlos Velloso, *DJ* 4 Apr 2003.

[248]Johanna Hey, *Steuerplanungssicherheit als Rechtsproblem*, Köln, Otto Schmidt, 2002, p. 660.

[249]Ibidem, p. 668.

and hence greater risk.[250] However, it is equally true that these normative acts have external efficacy, even if indirectly, because the state can neither unjustifiably change position nor deny uniform treatment to all citizens.[251] This external efficacy is all the more emphatic when normative acts are published, since there is no sense in making the content of the administration's acts public only to release it from the obligation to implement them.[252] For instance, an administrative act should not be repealed if it is endowed with an appearance of legality and if it caused intense disposal by the taxpayer since in this case the lack of one element (bindingness) is mitigated by the presence of others (appearance of legality, conduciveness, onerousness).

Thus even when normative acts of the administration are not binding, this does not mean trust must not be protected, if such protection is required to bind the administration by its own acts and by fundamental rights. It is important to note that the very function of normative acts reinforces the duty to protect the trust placed in them by taxpayers: While the administration can change these acts at any time, they are nevertheless presumed valid, and although taxpayers can contest them in court, they are ordinarily enforceable. If taxpayers could simply disregard them, their function of orienting the application of tax norms and reducing the uncertainty of application would be completely undermined.[253]

These considerations lead to two conclusions. On one hand, the counterpart of the functionality of normative acts is the protection of the trust placed in them by taxpayers whose disposals were based on their presumptive validity. Normative acts function as instruments that assure certainty of orientation and, precisely for that reason, cannot stop protecting the reliability inherent in their operation. On the other hand, however, there is no avoiding the conclusion that taxpayers do not have the right to argue for the past application of these normative acts to be upheld until *after* they have *effectively* exercised their rights of freedom and property based on them.[254] The understanding that taxpayers can sue for an illegal normative act to be upheld, even in future, whether or not they have based actions on it, would collide with the requirement of tax legality.

It is precisely in this direction that article 146 of the National Tax Code establishes that a change in orientation by the administration has only prospective

[250]Hartmut Maurer, "Kontinuitätsgewähr und Vertrauensschutz", in Josef Isensee e Paul Kirchhof (Orgs.), *Handbuch des Staatsrechts*, 2nd ed., v.3, §60, margin number 93, Heidelberg, Müller, 1996.

[251]Hermann-Josef Blancke, *Vertrauensschutz im deutschen und europäischen Verwaltungsrecht*, Tübingen, Mohr Siebeck, 2000, p. 259.

[252]Eugenio Della Valle, *Affidamento e Certezza del Diritto Tributario*, Milano, Giuffrè, 2001, p. 131.

[253]Johanna Hey, *Steuerplanungssicherheit als Rechtsproblem*, Köln, Otto Schmidt, 2002, pages 672, 673 and 681.

[254]Johanna Hey, *Steuerplanungssicherheit als Rechtsproblem*, Köln, Otto Schmidt, 2002, p. 678.

efficacy and cannot affect past cases.[255] Although this provision presupposes that a changed normative act is valid, the reflexive efficacy of the legal certainty principle protects taxpayers who acted on the basis of the presumption of validity before the change.[256] Torres is emphatic on this point: "If taxpayers take the administration at its word and rely on the published tax rules, they cannot be left at the mercy of changes in legal criteria on pretext of interpretation error. At least, not under the rule of law."[257]

All the arguments already expounded on the retroactivity of statutes also apply to normative acts, with the difference that in the latter case there must be more elements to offset their general lack of bindingness, especially in the case of normative acts that are evidently unlawful. The key point is that the legal certainty principle should prohibit retroactive efficacy of any changes in administrative orientation, and all the more so if the postulate of proportionality is not observed.[258] And in the field of tax law, retroactivity is prohibited whenever an administrative or judicial change of criteria worsens the situation of a taxpayer regarding taxable events that have already been booked.[259]

2.1.3.5.2.2 Administrative Practice

It may so happen that the administration has not formally issued an administrative act on a given subject but for some time has made its understanding visible.[260]

---

[255]Paulo de Barros Carvalho, *Curso de Direito Tributário*, 18th ed., São Paulo, Saraiva, 2007, p. 440. Luciano Amaro, *Direito Tributário Brasileiro*, 15th ed., São Paulo, Saraiva, 2009, p. 350. Sacha Calmon Navarro Coelho, *Curso de Direito Tributário*, 9th ed., Rio de Janeiro, Forense, 2006, p. 761. Roque Antonio Carrazza, "Segurança jurídica e eficácia temporal das alterações jurisprudenciais – Competência dos Tribunais Superiores para fixá-la – Questões conexas", in Tércio Sampaio Ferraz Jr. *et alii* (Orgs.), *Efeito "ex nunc" e as decisões do STF*, São Paulo, Manole, 2008, pages 52 and following.

[256]Ricardo Lodi Ribeiro, "A proteção da confiança legítima do contribuinte", *RDDT* 145, p. 102, São Paulo, 2007.

[257]Ricardo Lobo Torres, "Limitações ao poder impositivo e segurança jurídica", in Ives Gandra da Silva Martins (Org.), *Limitações ao poder impositivo e segurança jurídica*, São Paulo, Ed. RT/CEU, 2007, p. 70.

[258]Maria Sylvia Zanella Di Pietro, "Os princípios da proteção à confiança, da segurança jurídica e da boa-fé na anulação do ato administrativo", in Fabrício Motta (Org.), *Direito Público atual: Estudos em homenagem ao Professor Nélson Figueiredo*, Instituto de Direito Administrativo de Goiás (IDAG), Belo Horizonte, Fórum, 2008, p. 312. Hans-Jürgen Brischke, "Heilung fehlerhafter Verwaltungsakte im verwaltungsgerichtlichen Verfahren. Durch Nachholen der Begründung, Nachschieben von Gründen, Umdeutung, Ergänzung von Ermessenserwägungen und förmliche Änderung oder Ergänzung des streitbefangenen Verwaltungsaktes", *DVBl* 117, pages 429–434, 2002.

[259]Misabel de Abreu Machado Derzi, *Modificações da jurisprudência no Direito Tributário*, São Paulo, Noeses, 2009, p. 488.

[260]Luciano Amaro, *Direito Tributário Brasileiro*, 15th ed., São Paulo, Saraiva, 2009, p. 192. Johanna Hey, *Steuerplanungssicherheit als Rechtsproblem*, Köln, Otto Schmidt, 2002, p. 692.

The arguments used to justify the exceptional protection of trust relative to normative acts serve to explain their assurance with regard to administrative practice: In this case as well – albeit more exceptionally, given the lack of formality and publication, which give more reliability to the normative base – there can be protection of the taxpayers' trust, as long as they have disposed of their rights of freedom and property on the basis of administrative practice. This protection results from the fact that while individual administrative acts may not express an unequivocal specific position, in aggregate and over time they tend to build up an administrative opinion about a given subject. This understanding, albeit externalized differently, also serves as a basis for trust and as such, given the requisites mentioned earlier, it may justify protection of the legal certainty principle.

2.1.3.5.3 Individual and Concrete Administrative Action

2.1.3.5.3.1 Administrative Acts

Instead of being general and abstract, the administration's action may be individual and concrete, i.e., addressed to specific taxpayers in specific situations.[261] As already stated, the degree of trust protection depends on a combination of several linked criteria. Thus in the absence of other elements, the invalidity of an administrative act entails a lack of trust worth protecting. However, this rule should be overridden if other elements are present. This is because, as stated earlier, the key focus for trust protection is not the formal regularity of state action, but the restriction of fundamental rights and the manner of state action, in terms of its grounding in fundamental rights and the principles pertaining to state action. Hence there may have been some exercise of freedom or use of property that justifies restriction of the effects of administrative change to protect fundamental rights, even if the normative base is unlawful.[262] The essential point is that if individuals acted on the basis of an administrative act, their trust cannot simply be frustrated. Otherwise, instead of being guided and respected by law, their investment would become a gamble.[263]

Among the various elements to be considered, the following stand out relative to the actions of the executive: appearance of legitimacy, conduciveness, individuality, onerousness, and durability. These elements can offset the unlawfulness of the basis for trust: The more an act appears to be legitimate, the more it influences behavior, the closer it is to the state, the greater the burden caused by its application and the longer its efficacy over time, the more reasons there are for it to be upheld. These elements compensate for an unlawful basis for trust.

261 Michael Randak, "Bindungswirkung von Verwaltunsakten", *JuS* 1992, pages 33–39. Jörn Ipsen, "Verbindlichkeit, Bestandkraft und Bindungswirkung von Verwaltungsakten", *Verwaltung* 17, pages 169–195, 1984.

262 Johanna Hey, *Steuerplanungssicherheit als Rechtsproblem*, Köln, Otto Schmidt, 2002, p. 183.

263 Christoph Engel, *Planungssicherheit für Unternehmen durch Verwaltungsakt*, Tübingen, Mohr Siebeck, 1992, p. 95.

These criteria result from the circumstance that administrative action through administrative acts, unlike action through statutes or normative acts, is closer to the taxpayer. The administrative act breaks the anonymity of law.[264] Individual administrative acts addressed to specific taxpayers create a "relationship of trust" insofar as they connote "personalness."[265] Greater proximity between government and citizen also fosters a mutual commitment and hence a duty of loyalty: Breaking a commitment is disloyal, and in turn violates the principle of administrative morality.[266] Precisely because of this proximity, we can speak of a duty of administrative good faith in the case of administrative acts and contracts: The proximity between state and taxpayer creates mutual duties and loyalties that restrict or attenuate the requirements of legality and predictability.[267]

Besides individuality, administrative acts may also create a burden for the taxpayer. As noted, the more onerous the act, the more the trust placed in it must be, since state action is the direct cause of the individual's actions.[268]

Among all these elements, time plays a special role here: The more time elapses between the performance of an act and a decision regarding annulment or revocation, the lesser should be the presence of other elements. The passage of time consolidates an appearance of legality for an administrative act on one hand, and allows a number of direct and indirect consequences to emerge on the other, with these consequences becoming irreversible in proportion to the passage of time between performance of the act and its potential repeal.

These considerations show that trust protection cannot be automatically set aside simply because the administrative act on which the trust is based is illegal. This position is supported not only by reasons relating to the interests of taxpayers, such as those mentioned above, but also by reasons relating to the public interest.[269] This is because the invalidity of administrative acts, including administrative contracts, may relate only to formal aspects, while their content is justified by the realization of public purposes such as investment, job creation, development of technology,

---

[264] Johanna Hey, *Steuerplanungssicherheit als Rechtsproblem*, Köln, Otto Schmidt, 2002, p. 590.

[265] Kyrill-A. Schwarz, *Vertrauensschutz als Verfassungsprinzip*, Baden-Baden, Nomos, 2002, p. 299.

[266] Josef Isensee, "Vertrauensschutz für Steuervorteile. Ein Folgeproblem der Wirtschaftslenkung durch Steuer des § 3a EStG", in Paul Kirchhof, Klaus Offerhaus and Horst Schöberle (Orgs.), *Steuerrecht, Verfassungsrecht, Finanzpolitik. FS für Franz Klein*, Köln, 1994, p. 614. Kyrill-A. Schwarz, *Vertrauensschutz als Verfassungsprinzip*, Baden-Baden, Nomos, 2002, p. 321.

[267] Johanna Hey, *Steuerplanungssicherheit als Rechtsproblem*, Köln, Otto Schmidt, 2002, p. 591. Roland Kreibich, *Der Grundsatz von Treu und Glauben im Steuerrecht*, Heidelberg, C. F. Müller, 1992, p. 56. Sven Müller-Grune, *Der Grundsatz von Treu und Glauben im Allgemeinen Verwaltungsrecht*, Hamburg, Kovac, 2006, pages 40 and following.

[268] Kyrill-A. Schwarz, *Vertrauensschutz als Verfassungsprinzip*, Baden-Baden, Nomos, 2002, p. 297.

[269] Maria Sylvia Zanella Di Pietro, "Os princípios da proteção à confiança, da segurança jurídica e da boa-fé na anulação do ato administrativo", in Fabrício Motta (Org.), *Direito Público atual: Estudos em homenagem ao Professor Nélson Figueiredo*, Instituto de Direito Administrativo de Goiás (IDAG), Belo Horizonte, Fórum, 2008, p. 305.

promotion of a region, and so on. In this respect, revising an act by withdrawal or revocation collides with the aims of the state, which cannot achieve its purposes if the act is revised. Thus the more the public interest is furthered, the more the taxpayer's trust is protected.

In sum, the modification of administrative acts does not depend on their invalidity, but on the intensity of the taxpayer's action based on trust in them, and on the intensity of the restriction modification will cause. It is even possible to accept the rule according to which annulment of an act is allowed unless there are well-founded reasons to uphold it, and revocation of an act is forbidden unless there are well-founded reasons not to uphold it.[270] However, this is a circular tautology: An act is unchangeable when there is a right to be protected; there is a right to be protected when an act is unchangeable. It also begs the question because it assumes as proven that which it was supposed to prove, which is in what situations and for what reasons an act is unchangeable.

In light of these considerations, it is crucial to seek criteria that indicate the changeability of administrative acts based on principles and fundamental rights instead of qualities proper to the administrative acts themselves, such as their non-existence, nullity or annullability. That being so, what matters is not whether an administrative act is definitive or "merely" provisional; total or "simply" partial; conclusive or a "simple" promise; formal or "only" an administrative practice. These questions relating to state action are indeed relevant, but only as provisional elements because they do not automatically eliminate the need to protect trust – this is the point. And the reason is that the formal aspect of an act, albeit important, does not exhaust the basis for trust, which is also configured by other elements, especially the appearance of legality, individuality, bilaterality, onerousness, and time.

It is true that a provisional administrative act, whose effects are transitory, or a partial administrative act, whose efficacy depends on confirmation by a later act, do generate limited protectivity: Taxpayers know or ought to know that the act will not subsist in future, so that in principle they act on their own account and at their own risk. Nevertheless, if for example an act confers a benefit on taxpayers, who enjoy the benefit for a long time without any objective demonstration by the administration of its intention to change the act, and taxpayers have disposed of their personal freedom and property on the basis of the act, so that revising it would cause severe irreversible damage to taxpayers, its annulment ought to be avoided. In this case, the lack of one element (a claim to permanence) is offset by the presence of others (individuality, onerousness, irreversibility, dependency, conduciveness).

Similarly, an administrative act that involves only a promise, whose validity is later questioned, naturally generates less protectivity: Taxpayers know or ought to know that the act needs to be made effective in future, so that their action involves some personal responsibility and therefore also greater risk. Nevertheless, if for example the act is endowed with an appearance of legality, because of the

[270] Kyrill-A. Schwarz, *Vertrauensschutz als Verfassungsprinzip*, Baden-Baden, Nomos, 2002, p. 328.

issuing authority or the procedure used to issue it, and/or it has caused intense taxpayer action without any sign from the administration that the act could be questioned, its annulment ought to be avoided. In this situation, the lack of one element (bindingness) is offset by the presence of others (individuality, dependency, conduciveness, duration).

One important type of administrative act is the administrative query, regulated by Decree 70235/72. Faced with a concrete situation, a taxpayer can ask the tax administration to clarify doubts about the incidence of a tax. If the taxpayer's description of the facts is accurate, the administration is bound by its answer to the query, whose preventive nature should place the taxpayer concerned in a state of legal certainty.[271] If this were not the case, the whole point of the query process, which is to reduce the tax risk of an operation and guarantee calculability for administrative action, would be lost.

In the context of administrative change examined here, the problem of certainty involving the query process arises not when the administration abides by its ruling, but when it reviews the understanding expressed, either because its position changes or because it concludes that the previous position was illegal. In such cases, the same arguments presented earlier to justify the protection of trust relative to administrative acts also apply in the case of a query: If the taxpayer has significantly disposed of personal rights of freedom and property and there is a causal nexus between the acts of disposal and the tax efficacy resulting from the query, in the sense that the ruling was decisive to the taxpayer's actions, there should be protection of the trust placed in it.[272] Again, if trust in the query process is not guaranteed, the efficacy of the process is undermined: Taxpayers engage in the query process only if this mitigates their strategic risk. If the administration is not bound by its rulings, the instrumental function of the process relative to legal certainty is compromised. Thus the efficacy of the query process as far as trust protection is concerned results not from its normative quality, which is actually secondary, but from its function relative to legal certainty: While it does not have normative force in and of itself, it serves an instrumental function relative to the realization of the ideals of knowability and calculability of law.[273]

The same understanding should apply to agreements about the taxable base within the scope of forward tax substitution. In some situations, the tax authority enters into an agreement with a specific industry with regard to the amounts to be used as the taxable base for substitution. Although the authority may restart negotiations in preparation for a new agreement, this must not affect taxpayers who have disposed of their freedom and property because of the agreement, on pain of violating the trust protection principle.

[271] Valdir de Oliveira Rocha, *A consulta fiscal*, São Paulo, Dialética, 1996, p. 88.

[272] Johanna Hey, *Steuerplanungssicherheit als Rechtsproblem*, Köln, Otto Schmidt, 2002, p. 707.

[273] Winfried Fiedler, *Funktion und Bedeutung öffentlich-rechtlicher Zusagen im Verwaltungsrecht*, Heidelberg, 1977, p. 234.

A difficult matter concerns consolidated individual practices of the administration. The sole paragraph of article 100 of the National Tax Code simply determines the exclusion of fines in cases where the taxpayer trusts the validity of repeated practices and normative acts of the administration, while article 146 of the Code states that a change in the direction of the administration's interpretation only applies to future cases.[274] Again, the issue of legal certainty only arises when the administration intends to revise its position retroactively because it has concluded that the orientation hithero adopted was illegal.

The arguments used so far also apply to administrative practice. However, the provisional nature of administrative practice that has not yet been affected by a period of limitation is an obstacle to this understanding: The administrative acts which as a whole make up the administration's repeated practice are issued under resolutive conditions, i.e., they produce effects unless a later verification carried out within the period of limitation shows the need to revise them. Article 149 of the National Tax Code authorizes the tax administration to revise prior assessment acts in the event of a factual error. This normative framework suggests that the administration's previous position can be revised before the period of limitation expires and with efficacy for the entire period examined. However, a number of reservations must be made.

First, the change in orientation by the administration, whether it relates to previous practice or past acts of assessment, can concern only factual errors, never legal errors.[275] Indeed, if for some reason the administration believes the legislation was applied incorrectly, it can only change its orientation toward the future, not the past, as indeed determined by article 146 of the National Tax Code.

Second, when recurring situations are involved and the period of limitation has expired, taxpayers may have disposed of personal rights of freedom and property because of a previous assessment from the administration, in which case if other elements offset the lack of bindingness in administrative practice, there can be protection of trust in administrative practices regarding repeated situations.[276] Otherwise it would be admissible for taxes not collected for decades to be suddenly demanded for the previous 5 years, manifestly flouting the ideals of knowability, reliability and calculability of the law.

2.1.3.5.3.2 Administrative Contracts

In the same sense, a contract or agreement signed with a taxpayer to grant a tax benefit – be it a special arrangement for the payment of taxes or compliance with accessory obligations, or even an exemption, a reduction in the taxable base, or a

[274] Aliomar Baleeiro, *Direito Tributário Brasileiro*, 11th ed. updated by Misabel de Abreu Machado Derzi, Rio de Janeiro, Forense, 1999, pages 649 and 811.

[275] Sacha Calmon Navarro Coelho, *Curso de Direito Tributário*, 9th ed., Rio de Janeiro, Forense, 2006, p. 761.

[276] Johanna Hey, *Steuerplanungssicherheit als Rechtsproblem*, Köln, Otto Schmidt, 2002, p. 739.

presumptive credit – unleashes less protectivity: The taxpayer knows or ought to know that no contract can grant a tax benefit; only a statute can do so, as stipulated by the Constitution (article 150, I, and paragraph 6), so that the action concerned entails greater risk and responsibility.

Again, a number of reservations must be made. First, it is important to note that the explicit purpose of the constitutional rules formulated in article 150, I, and paragraph 6, is to afford protection against state action that restricts rights. Thus the legality rule, which is included in the section entitled "Limitations on the Power to Tax", serves as an instrument for the taxpayer to oppose restrictive action by the state via statutes that create taxes. It does not refer, at least directly, to conducive and cooperative state action via statutes designed to stimulate certain kinds of taxpayer behavior or contracts designed to use taxpayers as an instrument to implement public policies in exchange for tax benefits, many of which are onerous. The rule that reserves tax benefits for specific statutes, also included under the heading "Limitations on the Power to Tax", does apply directly to benefits conferred via administrative contracts and acts, or even normative acts, but it is a general rule designed to prevent the granting of unjustified advantages to some taxpayers to the detriment of others, and makes no reference to the elements that may exist in concrete situations, such as onerousness and bilaterality. It must also be borne in mind that an onerous bilateral tax benefit does not intensely violate the equality principle because the taxpayers on whom the benefit is conferred cannot enjoy it without discharging certain obligations, and this is a concrete justification for unequal treatment that is not extensive to other taxpayers who have not performed similar acts of disposal and do not depend on implementation of the contract.[277]

Second, it is necessary to consider not only the effects that these contracts may have on the exercise of freedom and property rights, but also their relationship to the realization of public purposes.[278] For example, if a contract is onerous, has a fixed term, is bilateral and synallagmatic (involving reciprocal rights and obligations), and is repeatedly performed by the administration, then it cannot be simply annulled, and even its revocation must be analyzed with care to preserve continuity of the legal order, requiring transitory and adaptive rules, as will be seen in the next chapter. This is because in such cases the lack of one element (bindingness) is offset by the presence of others (conduciveness, onerousness, bilaterality).

The above observations do not demonstrate that tax benefits can be granted by any instrument other than a statute. They aim only to show that there can be situations where although a benefit is not granted through a statute, significant concrete effects may have been produced relative to the freedom and property of the taxpayer, which may exceptionally justify the past upholding of the benefit

---

[277] Elke Gurlit, *Verwaltungsvertrag und Gesetz*, Tübingen, Mohr Siebeck, 2000, p. 392.

[278] Kyrill-A. Schwarz, *Vertrauensschutz als Verfassungsprinzip*, Baden-Baden, Nomos, 2002, p. 355. Almiro do Couto e Silva, "Problemas jurídicos do planejamento", *RDA* 170, p. 14, Rio de Janeiro, 1987.

and possibly also the creation of transitory rules once its discontinuation has been posited. The state is free to implement public policies, but once they are in place it is bound by past actions, from which it cannot simply walk away.[279]

2.1.3.5.4 Administrative Inaction

In some situations, although a period of limitation has not yet expired, the taxpayer may have acted because of conclusive state action indicating that a given tax would not be levied. In such a situation, and very exceptionally, it is possible to speak of protecting the trust of a taxpayer who acts intensely because of omissive state manifestation, or what is called *Verwirkung* (forfeiture) in German law.[280]

It should be noted that in this situation nothing prevents the state from exercising its power in general. There is an impediment, but of a different kind: When the taxpayer has effectively and intensely exercised rights of freedom and property with a causative connection to an unequivocal state action indicating that tax will not be collected, the state cannot restrict the taxpayer's legitimate trust on pain of infringing the principle of protection for good faith in terms of *venire contra factum proprium* (estoppel) and hence violating the administrative morality principle.[281] The state cannot give with one hand and take away with the other without falling into contradiction and in effect acting unlawfully.[282]

2.1.3.5.5 Final Considerations

The key point of these considerations is that administrative acts cannot be annulled simply because they are contrary to law from a formal standpoint. Since fundamental rights and the principles relating to state action are the foundations for reflexive application of the legal certainty principle, it is necessary to look beyond the state's merely normative perspective to adopt a perspective based on the taxpayer's acts of disposal and on the administration's serious, legal and justified actions. Thus acts that indicate a future change by virtue of their contents (acts subject to a reservation for modification, of an experimental or exceptional nature), a need for implementing rules or the frequency with which they are typically changed may exceptionally

[279]Joachim Burmeister, "Selbstbindung der Verwaltung. Zur Wirkkraft des rechtsstaatlichen Übermaßverbots, des Gleichheitssatzes und des Vertrauensschutzprinzips", *DÖV* 34, p. 506, 1981.

[280]Johanna Hey, *Steuerplanungssicherheit als Rechtsproblem*, Köln, Otto Schmidt, 2002, p. 791. Andreas Menzel, *Grundfragen der Verwirkung dargestellt insbesondere anhand des Öffentlichen Rechts*, Frankfurt am Main, Peter Lang, 1987, pages 2 and following. Johannes Beermann, *Verwirkung und Vertrauensschutz im Steuerrecht*, Münster, Waxmann, 1991, pages 85 and following.

[281]Johanna Hey, *Steuerplanungssicherheit als Rechtsproblem*, Köln, Otto Schmidt, 2002, p. 792. Jesus Gonzales Perez, *El Principio General de la Buena Fe en el Derecho Administrativo*, 2nd ed., Madrid, Civitas, 1983, pages 144 and following. Roque Antonio Carrazza, *Curso de Direito Constitucional Tributário*, 27th ed., São Paulo, Malheiros Editores, 2011, pages 469–470.

[282]Christoph Engel, *Planungssicherheit für Unternehmen durch Verwaltungsakt*, Tübingen, Mohr Siebeck, 1992, p. 9.

justify trust protection although the taxpayer can rely on their changing, provided there are other elements that offset the lack of a claim to permanence in the basis for trust. Acts that establish the conditions for action while offering no inducement to act, and nonetheless requiring the taxpayer to assume the risk of acting, may also be the object of protection, albeit to a limited extent, if elements that minimize the individual's responsibility are present. Acts that encourage the taxpayer to act normally merit a greater degree of protection, especially if they create matching obligations to the state, given their restriction to the exercise of freedom and property rights, even when they display some formal error.[283]

Within this new normative framework, there is no longer room for the so-called "principle of free withdrawal of unlawful administrative acts" according to which the administration can repeal acts because to do so is convenient or opportune, regardless of any other elements. Although the state has the power to revise its own acts, it cannot make revisions: Annulment and revocation that affect taxpayers' disposals in intensely unfavorable ways can be justified only by weighing the many elements of each case. Thus the discussion must focus not on the administration's unlimited power to revise its own acts but instead on what might be called the *respectful administration principle*, linking the administration's actions and respect for the individual's freedom.

2.1.3.6 Protection of Trust and the Judiciary: Changes in Case Law

2.1.3.6.1 Initial Considerations

The issue of changes in case law can be tackled from several angles. The first point is whether the judiciary is bound by its own precedents and hence whether it may or may not change its position. The second point is how it can do so, if it can: Whether suddenly or gradually, with transitional rules or with equity clauses. Third, it is necessary to analyze whether changes in orientation may be retroactive and retrospective or only prospective. Each of these questions involves a number of others that are hard to answer.

The first two questions will be addressed in the chapter on the calculability of law, where the pace of change in law is analyzed. It will make clear that the equality principle, from which is deduced the principle of coherence over time, requires the judiciary to be bound by precedent unless a change is justified. Of two things, one: Either the previous decision was correct, and the same decision should be handed down in a similar case, or it was incorrect and needs to be changed. This means that binding precedents derive from the equality principle itself: If the reason are the same reasons, the decisions should be the same, unless a change in orientation is justified, and very well justified at that. Hence it is said that precedents

[283] Martin Stötzel, *Vertrauensschutz und Gesetzesrückwirkung*, Frankfurt am Main, Peter Lang, 2002, p. 159.

have a presumptive or subsidiary force.[284] In other words, despite the bindingness of precedent, the judiciary actually can change position, as long as changes are always justified and respect the positions previously consolidated under the previous orientation. It can change, as long as it does so in a structured or smooth manner, given the duty to respect past decisions and the need for limits to change.[285] The legal certainty principle serves as the criterion for this assessment.[286]

A change in jurisprudential orientation may be positive in itself, potentially evidencing a better understanding of the subject on the judiciary's part, so that mistakes made in previous decisions can be corrected, and facts or arguments can be re-examined and assessed more satisfactorily. In the words of Molfessis, "changes in case law are manifestations of the life of law, signs of adaptation to facts. Where jurisprudence does not change . . . law itself is totally stagnant."[287] Lord Nicholls of Birkenhead presents the issue brilliantly: "Rigidity in the operation of a legal system is a sign of weakness, not strength. It deprives a legal system of necessary elasticity. Far from achieving a constitutionally exemplary result, it can produce a legal system unable to function effectively in changing times. 'Never say never' is a wise judicial precept, in the interest of all citizens of the country."[288] The legal certainty principle itself does not require immobility and therefore does not prevent juriprudential change.[289] The problem, however, is not change but its effects. If change surprises an individual who has intensely exercised personal rights of freedom and property while trusting and being able to trust in their permanence, a change of orientation may have significant negative effects. What needs to be sought, to quote Machado Derzi, is "permanence in change."[290]

In the sphere of tax law, jurisprudential change can negatively affect those who act on the basis of reliance that a prior decision will be upheld and perform all their economic calculations in terms of the previous normative framework. Application of the new understanding to such cases as well has restrictive effects on fundamental rights: Because the voluntarily performed acts were based on an economic calculation consistent with the former jurisprudential understanding,

---

[284]Lorenz Kähler, *Strukturen und Methoden der Rechtsprechungsänderung*, Baden-Baden, Nomos, 2004, p. 19.

[285]Isabelle Rorive, *Le revirement de jurisprudence*, Bruxelles, Bruylant, 2003, p. 498. Paul Kirchhof, "Kontinuität und Vertrauensschutz bei Änderungen der Rechtsprechung", *DStR* 27, p. 268, 1989.

[286]Dieter Medicus, "Neues zur Rückwirkung von Rechtsprechung", *WM*, 1997, p. 2.336.

[287]Nicolas Molfessis (Org.), *Les Revirements de Jurisprudence. Rapport Remis à Monsieur le Premier Président Guy Canivet. Grupe de Travail*, Paris, Litec, 2005, p. 14.

[288]"National Westminster Bank plc. *vs.* Spectrum Plus Limited and others", *apud* Horatia Muir Watt, "*Never say never*: *post-scriptum* comparatif sur la rétroactivité des revirements de jurisprudence", in Bertrand Seiller (Org.), *La retroactivité des decisions du juge administratif*, Paris, Economica, 2007, p. 61.

[289]Christine Lübbe, *Grenzen der Rückwirkung bei Rechsprechungsänderungen*, Frankfurt am Main, Peter Lang, 1997, p. 41.

[290]Misabel de Abreu Machado Derzi, "Princípio da segurança jurídica", *RDT* 64, p. 186, s.d.

application of the new understanding to them creates not only a feeling of injustice, but also disbelief in law. Because the previous juridprudential orientation on which individuals relied has been abandoned, they are unlikely to seek guidance in any other jurisprudential orientation for fear that this too may be abandoned in future.[291] In other words, jurisprudential change causes a deficit of reliability and calculability of the legal order: If the previous orientation is not maintained, there will be surprise and frustration, which undermine the ideals of stability and credibility of the legal order; if the previous orientation is abandoned, the future orientation will no longer be calculable, given the lack of trust in its conformation. The lack of protection of (past) reliability compromises the (future) calculability of law. In an opinion issued granting a restraining order pending a full hearing on a suit for injunction, Justice Celso de Mello elucidated this aspect in referring generically to jurisprudential change:

> This picture of diverging decisions, especially as it has been shaped within the scope of this Supreme Court, compromises a value essential to the stability of relations between the public authorities on one hand, and the taxpayers on the other, creating a situation that is incompatible with the demand for legal certainty, and that is especially grave in the sphere of tax, where the always unequally structured relations between the state and the people in general are so evident.[292]

However, as shown below, not all shifts in case law and jurisprudence can effectively be considered "changes"; not all changes have retroactive effects; and not all changes with retroactive effects merit support from the trust protection principle.

This is the focus of the next subsection.

2.1.3.6.2 The Concept of Jurisprudential Change

Trivial as it may seem, defining "jurisprudential change" presents a number of challenges. First, "change" needs to be differentiated from similar phenomena. For example, is there "change" when diverging opinions arise within the same court? When the judiciary develops a new doctrine based on new criteria? When it realizes a previous decision was wrong and corrects it? When it concretizes the meaning of an indeterminate legal concept, establishing a precise scope for the first time? When a decision handed down runs counter to previous rulings owing to a new legal regime? When a court opposes a previous decision that is still appealable and thus not *res iudicata*? These and other questions are enough to show that the concept of "jurisprudential change" must be distinguished from similar concepts such as correction, clarification, specification, development, complementation, divergence, concretization, and innovation.

Second, it is also necessary to delimit "jurisprudential change" within the context of the judiciary. This gives rise to other questions: Does "jurisprudential change"

---

[291] Nicolas Molfessis (Org.), *Les Revirements de Jurisprudence. Rapport Remis à Monsieur le Premier Président Guy Canivet. Grupe de Travail*, Paris, Litec, 2005, p. 16.

[292] AC/QO n.1.886, 2nd Panel, Rep. Justice Celso de Mello, *DJe* 7 Nov 2008.

take place when a decision handed down by a first instance judge expresses an understanding that diverges from another? Does it take place when a state appeal court's judgment modifies the understanding of a specific panel of judges about a given subject? Or when a section of the STJ (Superior Court of Justice, the *highest court* for non-constitutional matters, above state and federal *courts* of *appeal*) changes its understanding of a given subject, even if it involves constitutional law?

Third, it is indispensable to define "jurisprudential change" according to the character of the modifying decision. This framework poses new questions: Does a first instance judge's revocation of a preliminary injunction constitute "jurisprudential change"? Or a state appeal court's revision of a lower court's decision? Or a ruling by the STF that is incompatible with the STJ's understanding?

These three argumentative angles and the questions formulated above already point the way to defining jurisprudential change as occurring only when "a judicial decision diverges for the first time from another effective court decision on the same issue."[293] In sum, "jurisprudential change" is not substantiated by change of any kind.

First and foremost, there must be two conflicting decisions *about the same substantive issue*. This is obvious, but nonetheless important. If two decisions do not concern the same object, it can be said that they are different, but strictly speaking it cannot be said that they oppose each other. This explains, for example, why the STF rejected a proposal to modulate the effects of a ruling in extraordinary appeal RE 370,682-9.[294] On this occasion Justice Ricardo Lewandowsky argued that a jurisprudential change had taken place, noting the STF's ruling in RE 212,484 that firms were entitled to IPI excise tax credits when purchasing raw materials that are exempt, not taxed or taxed at a zero rate.[295] In examining the merit of RE 370,682-9, he argued, the STF had denied the right to tax credits on purchases of raw materials that are not taxed or taxed at a zero rate. This amounted to a "jurisprudential change" and the STF must therefore set aside the decision's *ex tunc* effects on pain of injuring taxpayers "who relied on the precedent set by prior decisions of this Court on the same issue" (page 506 of the judgment). However, the STF concluded that the previous decisions had not addressed the issue of credits on materials not taxed or zero rated, but only tax-exempt materials. In other words – to focus on what matters at this moment – the STF ruled out a "jurisprudential change" based on the understanding that the "modifying decision" and the "modified decision" did not address the same subject-matter.

It must be noted that a jurisprudential change exists only when two contradictory but equally efficacious decisions are handed down on the same subject-matter, i.e. based on the same foundations and the same facts. Thus strictly speaking it is incorrect to say jurisprudence changes if the normative basis for a decision changes.

---

[293] Lorenz Kähler, *Strukturen und Methoden der Rechtsprechungsänderung*, Baden-Baden, Nomos, 2004, p. 25.

[294] RE n.370.682-9, Full Court, Rep. Justice Ilmar Galvão, *DJ* 19 Dec 2007.

[295] RE n.212.484, Full Court, Opinion of the Court by Justice Nelson Jobim, *DJ* 27 Nov 1998.

For example, in 1997 the STF reiterated a previous opinion that the real nature of IPTU urban property tax was incompatible with progressivity deriving from the taxpayer's economic capacity.[296] Recently the STF allowed progressivity as a means of assuring the social function of property.[297] Meanwhile, however, Constitutional Amendment 29/2000 was passed, allowing IPTU tax rates to vary according to location and the use to which the property is put. The normative foundation of the matter was changed between the first and second decisions.

Similarly, it is incorrect to say jurisprudence changes if the facts change. For example, concerning the need for a statute on the right to strike in the public sector, in 2002 the STF decided that a statute was needed and noted that the legislative had failed to enact one. However, it concluded, this failure could not be righted by the Court, which must confine itself to notifying the lawmakers so as to bring the omission to their attention.[298] In 2007, the STF ruled that Law 7783/89, which concerns strikes in the private sector, must apply equally to strikes in the public sector.[299] A reasonable amount of time had elapsed to characterize inaction by the legislative in failing to pass a law specifically on the right to strike in the public sector, and because of this omission the Court decided to apply the existing legislation by analogy. The factual basis changed between one decision and the other.

Second, the "modified decision" needs to be *unappealable* (*res iudicata*) or at least to have reasonably produced orienting effects concerning that which causes the resistance of its effects in the "modifying decision." Before that, strictly speaking, there is no change under discussion: Only what has been settled can be changed, not what has not yet been established. Accepting the contrary would be like accepting that there was a change in the result of a soccer match because the team that was winning at half-time ended up losing due to a comeback in the second half. Hence the statement that change occurs only when a modificatory court decision (*Änderungsentscheidung*) diverges from an *efficacious* decision (*Ausgangsentscheidung*) on the same issue.[300] The decision that serves as orientation must no longer be overridable by ordinary judicial means.[301] As a result, it is an error to speak of "jurisprudential change" when the STF itself diverges from its own previous decisions on the same issue if the latter are not yet *res iudicata*. Nor can it be correct to speak of "change" when in judging an extraordinary appeal the STF changes a

---

[296]RE n.153.771, Full Court, Rep. Justice Moreira Alves, *DJ* 5 Sep 1997.

[297]RE n.423.768, Full Court, Rep. Justice Marco Aurélio, *DJe* 86, announced 9 May 2011, published 10 May 2011; *Ement* vol. 2518–02, p. 286.

[298]MI n.485-MT, Full Court, Rep. Justice Maurício Corrêa, *DJ* 25 Apr 2002.

[299]MI n. 670-ES, Full Court, Rep. Justice Maurício Corrêa, Opinion of the Court by Justice Gilmar Mendes, *DJ* 25 Oct 2007.

[300]Lorenz Kähler, *Strukturen und Methoden der Rechtsprechungsänderung*, Baden-Baden, Nomos, 2004, p. 25.

[301]Michael Scheffelt, *Die Rechtsprechungsänderung. Ein Beitrag zu methodischen und verfassungsrechtlichen Grundlagen und zur Anwendung der Ergebnisse im Verwaltungsrecht*, Konstanz, Hartung-Gorre, 2001, p. 52.

decision of the STJ in a special appeal that is not yet *res iudicata*. This is because the previous decision is provisional, and no one knows whether it will be upheld, given the possibility of review.[302] However, there is "change" when the same body of a court issues a decision with different content to a previous decision on the same subject that has reached *res iudicata* status. Thus it is correct to speak of jurisprudential change when the same court issues different decisions over time, after the "modified decision" has produced stabilizing effects.

Precisely for this reason, the STF denied prospective effect to its decision in the case that examined whether the purchase of materials taxed at a zero rate or not taxed at all conferred the right to IPI tax credits.[303] In the extraordinary appeal mentioned earlier the STF examined, from the viewpoint of non-cumulativity, whether purchases of zero-rated or untaxed materials confer the right to IPI tax credits in the following phase of the economic cycle. By a narrow majority of six to five, the Court decided against such a right. At the end of the session, however, Justice Ricardo Lewandowsky raised the question of the modulation of effects, given the STF's previous tendency to affirm the right to tax credits on zero-rated materials, in accordance with the understanding supposedly embodied in RE 212,484 concerning tax-exempt materials.[304] The legal foundation he argued for the proposed modulation of effects was the protection of legal certainty against what he claimed was a "jurisprudential change". According to Justice Lewandowsky, it would be "convenient to prevent a sudden change of direction from causing harm to the individuals who based their actions on the understanding that has prevailed hitherto," and hence it would be appropriate to "apply forward-looking effects to the decisions herein, on pain of imposing heavy burdens on the taxpayers who have relied on the jurisprudential tendency manifested in the case law produced by this Court on the same issue, with negative consequences in the economic and social spheres" (page 506 of the judgment).

However, the Court voted ten to one against the assignment of forward-looking effects to the decision, based on the understanding that strictly speaking there had been no change in its case law on the right to tax credits on purchases of zero-rated and untaxed materials: The decisions taken at the hearings that had discussed this subject-matter – REs 350,446-1, 353,668-1 and 358,493-6 – were still appealable, so that it was not possible to speak of changes to a precedent that had not yet been determined. In the words of Justice Eros Grau: "In this case there has been no change in the Court's case law, since no precedent has been established" (page 536 of the judgment). The Court arrived at this conclusion because the federal tax authorities had never accepted the orientation adopted, albeit not fixed through *res iudicata*, in REs 212,484 and 357,277, in which the STF had guaranteed the right to credit in the case of zero-rated materials. Although there was disagreement as to whether

[302]Lorenz Kähler, *Strukturen und Methoden der Rechtsprechungsänderung*, Baden-Baden, Nomos, 2004, p. 47.

[303]RE n.370.682-9, Full Panel, Rep. Justice Ilmar Galvão, *DJ* 19 Dec 2007.

[304]RE n.212.484, Full Panel, Opinion of the Cort by Justice Nelson Jobim, *DJ* 27 Nov 1998.

these decisions concerned tax credits on untaxed or zero-rated transactions, Justice Sepúlveda Pertence's opinion opposed modulation because the matter was never settled: "Since then it has been impossible to speak of sedimented case law. The tax administration has never let the issue die out, and we arrived at what I would not call a jurisprudential change, but rather a reversal of one previous decision, given the change in the Court's understanding and the long rediscussion of the issue in the cases that have prompted today's review." In sum, the Court decided that the only unappealable decision (RE 212,484) concerned tax-exempt materials, whereas the other decisions, which dealt with zero-rated or untaxed materials (REs 353,657 and 370,682) were not *res iudicata*. Hence what was at stake was not a "jurisprudential change".

Moreover, as Justice Marco Aurélio also pointed out, with Justices Carlos Britto and Sepúlveda Pertence concurring, there was another hindrance to application of the provision that allows prospective effects to be assigned to a decision: "Application requires a statute or normative act to be declared unconstitutional. In this case, at no time has a statute or normative act been declared unconstitutional" (page 513 of the judgment). On this occasion, indeed, instead of declaring a statute or normative act unconstitutional, the Court declared it constitutional. For all of these reasons, modulation of effects was rejected.

The Court therefore rejected the assignment of forward-looking effects to the decision, concluding that there had been no jurisprudential change regarding the right to tax credits on the purchase of zero-rated and untaxed materials, for the simple reason that none of the "modified decisions" was *res iudicata*. Justice Eros Grau's opinion is worth quoting at length:

> So how can one speak of changing case law if a firm precedent hasn't been established? That would be truly nonsensical. An understanding never determined definitively by this Court cannot be changed. It is almost naïve to claim there is 'settled case law' even when the decisions are still appealable – and all of them are. What has the force of legal truth is *res iudicata*, which when repeated has the authority to create case law. What is at stake here is not a jurisprudential change by this Court, since no such case law has been established (page 536 of the judgment).

Along the same lines, Justice Marco Aurélio stated that "the issue of tax credit, unlike others where the decision was reversed, was not a settled issue with the Court... Thus it is not proper to say that the Supreme Court ruled in favor of the right to this tax credit in a final judgment covered by *res iudicata*" (page 517 of the judgment).

These observations show that strictly speaking a jurisprudential change takes place only when the modified decision has been stabilized by becoming *res iudicata* in its specific case. In order for trust to be protected, the citizen must act based on a known and efficacious decision.[305] Thus the limits to jurisprudential change apply only when there are *causae finitae*, i.e. decisions that produce effects and

[305] Joachim Burmeister, *Vertrauensschutz im Prozeßrecht – Ein Beitrag zur Theorie vom Dispositionsschutz des Bürgers bei Änderung des Staatshandelns*, Berlin, De Gruyter, 1979, p. 27.

involve some degree of preclusiveness.[306] As Machado Derzi notes, changes in normative meanings compatible with the text of the statute must be closed off through the action of the judiciary.[307] So taxpayers who base their actions on provisional decisions, in the absence of other elements, do so on their own account and at their own risk. Precisely for this reason, Justice Cézar Peluso stressed in the same judgment that taxpayers who took guidance from provisional decisions "acted on their own account and at their own risk, *influenced* by previous case law but aware that their hypothetical right would be assured only after the decision became *res iudicata*" (page 560 of the judgment). Taxpayers know, or ought to know, that the act is not binding, so that their actions entail greater personal responsibility and hence greater risk, which they must assume.[308]

However, it is not always the case that "jurisprudential change" occurs whenever a decision diverges from a previous *res iudicata* concerning the same subject-matter. There must also be an effective *contradiction* between the two decisions. Hence the concept of "jurisprudential change" must be distinguished from other similar phenomena.

For example, "jurisprudential change" is not the same as "innovation". The latter occurs when a judicial decision innovates by introducing dogmatic elements or criteria that were not present before, but without diverging from a previous decision. Nor is it the same as "jurisprudential divergence", which occurs when two bodies of the same court express divergent understandings in decisions that are appealable or have not been made uniform by decision of a higher court. Nor is it the same as a "change of jurisprudential paradigm", which occurs when a number of court decisions – but not one specific decision as compared to another – are given justification based on new dogmatic criteria, such as the interpretation of civil law based on the Constitution and not on the Civil Code.[309] In sum, jurisprudential change occurs only when the change results from judicial activity itself, so that two opposed solutions are found successively for the same subject-matter, and not when the change results from statutory or constitutional modifications.[310]

Again, a "jurisprudential change" occurs only when a court decision expresses an understanding that is directly opposed to that of an efficacious prior court decision on the same subject-matter.[311] The understanding can be "directly opposed" in

[306]Andreas Vonkilch, *Das Intertemporale Privatrecht*, Wien, Springer, 1999, pages 290 and 305.

[307]Misabel de Abreu Machado Derzi, *Modificações da Jurisprudência no Direito Tributário*, São Paulo, Noeses, 2009, p. 266.

[308]Hartmut Maurer, "Kontinuitätsgewähr und Vertrauensschutz", in Josef Isensee e Paul Kirchhof (Orgs.), *Handbuch des Staatsrechts*, 2nd ed., v.3, §60, margin number 93, Heidelberg, Müller, 1996.

[309]Lorenz Kähler, *Strukturen und Methoden der Rechtsprechungsänderung*, Baden-Baden, Nomos, 2004, pages 24, 27 and 30. Verena Klappstein, *Die Rechtsprechungsänderung mit Wirkung für die Zukunft*, Berlin, Duncker und Humblot, 2009, pages 41 and following.

[310]Isabelle Rorive, *Le Revirement de Jurisprudence*, Bruxelles, Bruylant, 2003, p. 207.

[311]Verena Klappstein, *Die Rechtsprechungsänderung mit Wirkung für die Zukunft*, Berlin, Duncker und Humblot, 2009, p. 53.

several ways: expressly (when the new decision explicitly states that it is changing a previous decision), implicitly (when the understanding embodied by the new decision is incompatible with the prior decision, but this is perceptible only to those who know the prior decision) or even covert (when the new decision contradicts a prior decision without making any reference to the previous understanding or even to the contradiction). Similarly, the new, "opposed understanding" can be concretized in various types of decision. The new decision make take the form of negation (stating that there is no existing norm that establishes a given consequence deemed to exist by the prior decision), substitution (ruling that the substantive aspect of a norm's incidence hypothesis has not properties A and B, as defined in the prior decision, but properties C and D), contradiction (determining that the legal consequence is to be applied if factual elements A and B occur, as opposed to the prior decision, which determined that the legal consequence was to be applied if factual elements A and B did not occur), or modification (ruling that the legal consequence can be applied only if factual elements A, B and C occur, as opposed to the prior decision, which determined that the legal consequence could be applied if only A and B occurred).[312]

Thus the key point to configure change is *efficacy*.[313] On one hand, if the trust protection principle is supposed to defend taxpayers who have acted on the basis of a decision, and if the decision has not yet produced effects, so that it is not efficacious in general or relative to the taxpayers concerned, then it is inadmissible to argue that any action was "based" on the modified decision, which simply was not yet producing any effects. When taxpayers take action based on decisions not affected by stabilization mechanisms, they do so for their own account and at their own risk. As noted by Burmeister, decisions on matters of substantive law produce effects only for the parties in a case.[314] At this point it is worth bearing in mind that the legal certainty principle, which is the compass for this analysis, serves as an instrument to assure respect for taxpayers' capacity to shape their present with dignity and responsibility, free of deceit, frustration or surprise, and to make legally informed strategic planning decisions for the future. In other words, legal certainty cannot be invoked to neutralize legal effects that taxpayers know or should know were inappropriate as a guide to conduct (given their lack of permanence), unless other elements are present.

Moreover, if the issue of trust protection concerns the restriction to fundamental rights caused by jurisprudential change, it is necessary to analyze not the potential

---

[312]Lorenz Kähler, *Strukturen und Methoden der Rechtsprechungsänderung*, Baden-Baden, Nomos, 2004, pages 49–59.

[313]Johanna Hey, *Steuerplanungssicherheit als Rechtsproblem*, Köln, Otto Schmidt, 2002, p. 634. Lorenz Kähler, *Strukturen und Methoden der Rechtsprechungsänderung*, Baden-Baden, Nomos, 2004, pages 24 and 60. Andreas Vonkilch, *Das Intertemporale Privatrecht*, Wien, Springer, 1999, p. 290.

[314]Joachim Burmeister, *Vertrauensschutz im Prozeßrecht – Ein Beitrag zur Theorie vom Dispositionsschutz des Bürgers bei Änderung des Staatshandelns*, Berlin, De Gruyter, 1979, pages 33 and 43.

effects of the decision but the effects concretely produced relative to the exercise of such rights. It can therefore be said that the concept of jurisprudential change depends on the normative force of the decision and on the concrete effects that it has effectively or presumably produced.

2.1.3.6.3 The Concept of Retroactive Jurisprudential Change

The main and most troublesome question, therefore, is not whether the judiciary may change positions. It may, because precedents are not binding absolutes.[315] Also, change is inevitable in response to internal and external changes in the legal order.[316] The crux of the matter is *how* it ought to change and *with what effects.* The enhancement of law through jurisprudential change is one thing; retrospective application is quite another.[317] This question is answered below, especially by addressing the issue of "jurisprudential retroactivity."

This question cannot be answered using the same categories as those that apply to retroactivity with regard to the legislative, because statutes aim at the future whereas court decisions concern the past, among other reasons. "The future of the legislator is a general, unknown one. The past of the judge is a concrete, known one." These are the words of van Hoecke to demonstrate the brutal difference between legislative and judicial activities.[318] Judges "say what is the state of law, good law, and hence they say what should have been done, what was done wrong or not done", explains Pacteau.[319] Nevertheless, not for an instant can it be said that legal decisions are retroactive in the same way statutes or administrative acts can be. Given this framework, it is necessary to distinguish between two phenomena that are typically jumbled together but are different for the purposes of trust protection: declaratory efficacy of judicial decisions and retroactive efficacy of judicial decisions.

Declaratory efficacy of judicial decisions refers to the effects of the final decision in a case, which covers the facts that occurred before the proceedings and were described in the initial application that instituted them. This differs from retroactive efficacy for several reasons. Imagine that the plaintiff files a lawsuit to argue that at time *T1* norm *N* meant *X* and the defendant counterargues that it meant *Y*, and at

[315]Hans Dubs, *Praxisänderungen. Eine methodologische Untersuchung über die Stellung des Richters zum eigenem Präjudiz auf Grund von Entscheidungen des schweizerischen Bundesgerichts*, Basel, Helbing & Lichtenhahn, 1949, p. 7.

[316]Georg Seyfarth, *Die Änderung der Rechtsprechung durch das Bundesverfassungsgericht*, Berlin, Duncker und Humblot, 1998, p. 292.

[317]Nicolas Molfessis (Org.), *Les revirements de jurisprudence. Rapport remis à Monsieur le Premier Président Guy Canivet. Groupe de Travail*, Paris, Litec, 2005, p. 32.

[318]Mark van Hoecke, "Time and law. Is it the nature of law to last? A conclusion", in François Ost e Mark van Hoecke (Orgs.), *Temps et Droit. Le Droit a-t-il pour vocation de durer*?, Bruxelles, Bruylant, 1998, p. 457.

[319]Bernard Pacteau, "Comment aménager la rétroactivité de la Justice? Sécurité juridique, sécurité juridictionnelle, sécurité jurisprudencielle", in Bertrand Seiller (Org.), *La Rétroactivité des Décisions du Juge Administratif*, Paris, Economica, 2007, p. 114.

the end of the proceedings the judge decides in favor of one of the parties, ruling, for example, that $N = X$. A similar example would be that of a plaintiff who files a lawsuit at time *T1* to argue that norm *N* establishes the taxation of fact *F1* and that he, the plaintiff, performed fact *F2*; the defendant objects, arguing that the plaintiff did indeed perform fact *F1* and should therefore pay the tax. In both cases, the decision, entered at *T2*, covers the facts performed and the norm disputed since the lawsuit was filed, at time *T1*. However, a number of details are significant here: Both plaintiff and defendant knew at the beginning of the lawsuit about the *existence* of norm *N*; both have known from the start that there was a *narrow range of possible meanings* for norm *N*, consisting of *X* or *Y*, or a *narrow range of interpretations for the factual record* (*F*), consisting of *F1* or *F2*; the parties were only unsure of, or disputed the meaning of, the norm ($N = X$ *or* Y?) or the extent to which the factual record matched the incidence hypothesis stipulated by the norm ($F = F1$ *or* $F2$?). In other words, both plaintiff and defendant were sure about the existence, enforceability and calculability (but not the determinacy) of the content of norm *N* at the start of the lawsuit, although they had doubts of a highly specific nature about its content or coverage. Thus it can be said that in the case of the declaratory efficacy of judicial decisions, in general terms there are no problems of knowability or calculability of law: The parties know the norm exists and are able to calculate its content and its efficacy. In short, at *T2* the parties are *not* surprised by a norm of whose existence and enforceability they were unaware at *T1* and based on which they could dispose with no ability to react. This is why declaratory efficacy is neutral regarding retroactivity, since judicial decisions necessarily relate to the past.[320] The same is not true of the retroactivity of statutes.

As for *retroactive efficacy of statutes*, when a norm *N2* is enacted at a time *T2* and produces effects relative to a period preceding its enactment, *T1*, and another norm *N1* was in force at the time the action was performed, in *T1*, the addressees could not have known about the *existence*, *enforceability* or *content* of norm *N2*, or calculate the consequences to be imposed if the action described in the norm was performed. In other words, at *T1* the addressee only knew of norm *N1*, which existed and was in force, but had no knowledge of norm *N2*. That being so, it can be said that in the case of retroactive efficacy of statutes there is a problem of knowability as well as a problem of calculability of law: Addressees of the modifying norm, *N2*, do not know it exists and cannot calculate its content and efficacy. Put simply, at *T2* addressees *are* surprised by a norm of whose existence and validity they were entirely unaware at *T1*, so that they could not comply or react. Thus retroactivity involves a matter of freedom: Someone affected by retroactive change cannot do anything to comply knowingly with the new law because their actions have already been performed.[321] People act in the

[320] Christian Waldhoff, "Recent developments relating to the retroactive effect of decisions of the ECJ", *Common Market Law Review* 46, p. 5, 2009 (manuscript).

[321] Ben Juratowitch, *Retroactivity and the Common Law*, Oxford, Hart, 2008, p. 51.

present, not in the future.[322] Their power to shape reality within the limits of the law is reconfigured after their freedom has been exercised. Hence Fuller's biting remark about the "brutal absurdity of commanding a man today to do something yesterday."[323] The absurdity results precisely from the fact that a retroactive norm does not permit the exercise of freedom. If the action has already been performed, a retroactive norm collides with individual autonomy because it eliminates the possibility of individual decisions about alternative behavior, thus imposing a normative consequence without allowing individual *free choice*.[324]

These considerations show that the declaratory efficacy of decisions is not the same as the retroactive efficacy of statutes. When "retroactivity" refers to the declaratory efficacy of court decisions, it concerns efficacy prior to the moment when decisions are entered, but without reference to lack of knowability and calculability. Those who argue that the problem of jurisprudential retroactivity is a false problem are in fact entirely assimilating the problem of retroactivity into the problem of declaratory efficacy of decisions. This is what Ost does when he says the retroactivity of judgment is not an anomaly but of the essence.[325] In actual fact, the problem of jurisprudential retroactivity is quite different.[326]

Having made these adjustments, we can immediately see that the expression "retroactive efficacy of court decisions" can concern only cases where citizens act on the basis of a court decision whose efficacy is restricted to a third person or collectivity, and which is then changed by a new decision with retroactive effects. In this specific situation, individuals act on the basis of court decisions that they believe also apply to their case, but their behavior is measured against a decision of which they were not aware at the time. Only in this strict sense is it possible to speak of "jurisprudential retroactivity", i.e. when a decision *D2* is entered at atime *T2* and produces effects relative to a previous period, *T1*, when it would be reasonable to defend the application of another decision, *D1*, and at the time the act was performed in *T1* the addressees could not know of the *existence* or *content* of decision *D2* or calculate the consequences to be imposed should the act described in it be performed. In other words, in *T1* addressees only knew decision *D1*, which then existed, and entirely lacked knowledge of decision *D2*. It is worth noting that in the case of the "retroactivity of statutes", citizens are surprised by the application of a norm *N2* relative to a period when norm *N1* was *in force* and they were *required* to obey norm *N1*. In the case of "jurisprudential retroactivity", two situations may

[322] Paul Kirchhof, "Rückwirkung von Steuergesetzen", *StuW*, 2000, p. 221.

[323] Lon Fuller, *The Morality of Law*, New Haven, Yale University Press, 1964, p. 59.

[324] Jeremy Waldron, "The rule of law in contemporary liberal theory", *Ratio Juris*, v. 2, n. 1, p. 85, 1989.

[325] François Ost, "L'heure du jugement. Sur la rétroactivité des décisions de justice. Vers un Droit transitoire de la modification des règles jurisprudentielles", in François Ost e Mark van Hoecke (Orgs.), *Temps et Droit. Le Droit a-t-il pour vocation de durer*?, Bruxelles, Bruylant, 1999, p. 93.

[326] Christoph Louven, *Problematik und Grenzen rückwirkender Rechtsprechung des Bundesarbeitsgerichts*, München, Beck, 1996, p. 5.

occur: Citizens may be surprised by the application of a decision *D2* relative to a period when decision *D1* was applicable to their case by virtue of its general efficacy and they *were required to obey* decision *D1*; or they may be surprised by the application of a decision *D2* relative to a period when *decision D1* was *believed to be applicable* and they *could reasonably rely on the application* of decision *D1* to their situation as well. In both cases there is an issue of surprise, and hence lack of knowability and calculability of law. And this is precisely where the problem of jurisprudential retroactivity is located.

With these premises firmly in place, we must now reformulate a number of considerations at the core of previous chapters in order to define when "jurisprudential retroactivity" genuinely occurs, especially because the criterion for its occurrence or non-occurrence must be sought in the legal certainty principle in connection with fundamental rights and the principles that guide state action.

As we have seen, the legal certainty principle requires knowability, reliability and calculability of law. Individuals need to know the rule that regulates their action so that they can calculate the consequences that will be assigned to it by the legal order. There is no calculability when individuals cannot minimally foresee the legal consequences of their acts. Without calculability, individuals do not have legal freedom of action, as they cannot *make decisions* regarding the legal effects to be assigned to the action they intend to take. Thus knowability and calculability of law require that individuals *know* the rule that regulates their action and can minimally *measure* the legal consequences that flow from the rule. if they know the rule that regulates their action and can measure the effects that flow from it, the decision to act involves freedom and accountability: freedom to the extent that individuals, being able to act or refrain from acting, and being able to act in this or that way, *decide* to act in a way that fits the hypothesis in a rule; and accountability because individuals who are capable of calculating the effects assigned by the rule to their conduct choose to act and therefore decide to accept the imposition of those effects. It is precisely for these reasons that legal certainty does not tolerate retroactivity.

The problem with retroactivity is that it judges individuals' actions based on the norm in force at the time in terms of another norm that did not exist at the time and therefore could not have been taken into consideration. Thus retroactivity contradicts the requirements of knowability and calculability of law: Individuals act on the basis of a rule, because they accept the legal consequences assigned to their action by the legal order, but their behavior is then regulated by a different rule, which they did not know and whose legal consequences they could not have considered. Retroactivity thus eliminates both freedom and accountability. It eliminates freedom because it removes individuals' capacity to decide whether or not to act, and whether to act in this or that way based on the legal order. They have already acted, and they have done so without considering the legal consequences that flow from application of the new norm, which did not exist at the time, so they cannot measure the consequences of acting, not acting, or even reacting. Legal consequences are assigned to individuals who cannot *choose* between acting or not acting in light of the effects that action or inaction will have. Retroactivity also eliminates accountability: Individuals rely on one norm when they act, but their action falls within the scope of a different norm, so they cannot be held to account for the legal meaning of their action, given their inability to understand the legal effects of acting, and indeed cannot even make an informed decision regarding the action whose occurrence triggers its application.

Thus the problem of normative retroactivity is that it involves legal evaluation of actions based on norms that did not exist at the time they were performed. This is why it is said that retroactivity eliminates the guiding character of law, in the sense that a person's actions are guided by one norm but regulated by another, which did not exist and was therefore unknown at the time of the action. This means the issue of retroactivity involves by definition both *non-existence* and *lack of knowledge* of the norm at the time of the action. Precisely because the norm did not exist at the time of the action, individuals could not find guidance in it and therefore could not determine their course of action with regard to its content. Freedom is exercised without the efficacy of the modifying norm, but is later judged by it. Also by definition, retroactive efficacy involves an *inability to react*: People act on the basis of one norm but their action is regulated by a different norm that did not exist at the time, so they cannot gauge the legal consequences assigned by law to their behavior and freely choose between different courses of action on the basis of this assessment; they are therefore unable to retreat from an action whose legal consequences they do not wish to bear. In sum, retroactivity entails lack of freedom and accountability, and the impossibility of reacting. When people act they calculate that if they perform act *X* the consequence will be *A*, but end up forced to bear consequence *B* owing to the application of norm *Y*, which did not exist at the time of the action. In more suggestive language, they act expecting bread, and receive a stone. Retroactivity involves the application of a rule to individuals who could not know it existed or reasonably rely on it. And this is where a distinction has to be made about court activity: Not all jurisprudential changes involve issues of normative knowledge and calculability.

Indeed, in some situations jurisprudential change does not affect people's capacity to *know* the rule that regulates their action or to *gauge* the legal consequences assigned to it by the legal order. Jurisprudential change does not operate retroactively when a person's behavior did not depend on the case law prevailing at the time of the facts.[327]

This occurs, for example, when an individual is a party to a lawsuit in which the plaintiff argues that norm *N* assigns consequence *X* whereas for the defendant it imposes consequence *Y*. Being a party to the suit, the individual is aware that the norm regulating the case is norm *N* and may expect the legal consequences to be *X* or *Y*. As long as the proceedings last, neither plaintiff nor defendant can claim not to have been aware of the existence of norm *N* or not to have been able to foresee consequences *X* or *Y* – the norm was known and the consequences were minimally

[327]Nicolas Molfessis (Org.), *Les revirements de jurisprudence. Rapport remis à Monsieur le Premier Président Guy Canivet. Groupe de Travail*, Paris, Litec, 2005, p. 18.

foreseeable. Moreover, neither party will be able to say that jurisprudential change has any impact during the proceedings, relative to the norm and the period under dispute: The case is being heard and the effect of the final decision will be declaratory, so the acts performed relative to the norm and period concerned cannot have been influenced by any change in case law arising from other lawsuits. The internal action of the parties to the suit cannot be guided by decisions in other cases, but only by the decision that will be entered in the case to which they are parties. This is exactly why the plaintiff took legal action, i.e. to clear up any doubts. Thinking otherwise means accepting that either party has a subjective right to a given result from the proceeding just because at some point between the beginning and end of the litigation a decision has been issued in another case. There is no consummated event about which no reaction is conceivable relative to the normative framework that is being litigated, as there is in the case of a retroactive statute; there is no practice of an irreversible act based on a norm unknown at the time, as is the case with retrospective efficacy; instead, there is some specific doubt about the content and scope of an existing norm that is currently in force.

This explains the distinction Hey makes between a "precursor case" (*Anlaßfall*) – the "case in point" during which the change occurs or through which it is caused – and other pending cases:

> Only regarding the case that causes the change is the question posed of knowing whether the protection of legitimate expectations must be assured in the sphere of the judiciary. In all other pending cases, especially where a final decision has not been reached, legitimate expectations and trust must necessarily be protected in the administrative sphere ... [328]

A different conclusion must result if while the existing lawsuit is under way one of the parties does or refrains from doing something based on a jurisprudential change with regard to the subject-matter in dispute, where the action or inaction concerned is very likely to have guided the solution to the case. For example, the plaintiff in an ordinary lawsuit contesting the constitutionality of a tax does not effect the judicial deposit required to suspend tax liability because of an unappealable decision by a higher court with jurisdiction to decide the merits in the last instance. In this case there is, so to speak, an *external effect* arising from another decision, which changes the behavior, inside or outside the proceedings, of the taxpayer who initiated the litigation. What is at stake here is not whether the taxpayer is entitled to a given result but whether the effects of the taxpayer's behavior guided by a specific jurisprudential orientation can be assessed on this basis if it changes and hence is not confirmed for the case in point.

Thus it is possible to speak of retroactive jurisprudential change only if the decision that diverges from preceding case law fails to protect trust in situations where a person's behavior has been guided, and could reasonably have been guided, by the abandoned decision, so that the individual can be deemed to have been

---

[328] Johanna Hey, *Steuerplanungssicherheit als Rechtsproblem*, Köln, Otto Schmidt, 2002, pages 639–640. Christine Lübbe, *Grenzen der Rückwirkung bei Rechsprechungsänderungen*, Frankfurt am Main, Peter Lang, 1997, p. 118.

deceived by a decision on which they relied and the legal consequences of past actions based on the previous case law have changed.[329] In contrast, there is no retroactivity when the previous case law did not serve and could not have served as a guide to the individual concerned, given the impossibility of generalizing the previous decision.[330]

This latter point is demonstrated below.

2.1.3.6.4 Configuring Trust Protection in Response to Jurisprudential Change

The existence of jurisprudential change with past effects does not guarantee application of the trust protection principle. Although legal uncertainty always involves frustration, not all frustration results from legal uncertainty worth protecting. For this to be the case, all the requirements mentioned earlier must be met, with the features specific to jurisprudential activity.

First, there must be a basis for trust. Because what is at stake is "jurisprudential change", there must be two decisions: the "modifying" decision, the "case in point" (*Anlaßfall*) or "main proceedings" (*Ausgangsverfahren*), and the "modified" decision. The latter is therefore the basis for trust regarding the behavior to be protected via the reflexive efficacy of the legal certainty principle. Thus trust protection results when citizens legitimately expect their behavior to be judged according to a decision that served or could have served as guidance for their actions and was later modified.[331]

As noted above in the discussion of the basis for trust, the first point to analyze is whether the "modified" decision is capable of creating trust. Decisions that are not yet efficacious are excluded, for the simple reason that they cannot be modified. Within the universe of efficacious decisions, however, it is necessary to distinguish between decisions according to the following factors: bindingness and claim to permanence; guiding purpose; and whether they are part of a chain of uniform positions with the potential for generalization. It must be stressed that these factors are intended to be *heuristic criteria* with a merely indicative function, so that the absence of one does not necessarily mean trust is not to be protected. Their overall presence is what counts.

First, the more *binding* a decision is and the greater its *claim to permanence*, the more it protects the taxpayer's trust. The bindingess of decisions and their claim to permanence derive from their formal or substantive normative force. *Formal* normative force derives from the norms of the legal order that confer bindingness on a decision. According to Brazil's 1988 Constitution, only decisions

---

[329]Nicolas Molfessis (Org.), *Les revirements de jurisprudence. Rapport remis à Monsieur le Premier Président Guy Canivet. Groupe de Travail*, Paris, Litec, 2005, p. 18.

[330]Ulrich Keil, *Die Systematik privatrechtlicher Rechtsprechungsänderungen*, Tübingen, Mohr Siebeck, 2007, p. 69.

[331]Christoph Louven, *Problematik und Grenzen rückwirkender Rechtsprechung des Bundesarbeitsgerichts*, München, Beck, 1996, p. 220.

entered in concentrated control of constitutionality (judicial review via direct unconstitutionality suits or ADIs, and constitutionality declaration suits, or ADCs), or diffuse control of constitutionality regarding a statute whose effects have been suspended by a Senate resolution, or decisions covered by a binding precedent, are binding on all lower instances and the entire public administration.[332] Strictly speaking, therefore, only such decisions have binding power in the sense of creating judicially enforceable obligations. And only they work as stabilizing mechanisms, as Justice Joaquim Barbosa properly mentioned in his opinion on a matter relating to an alleged jurisprudential change.[333] The lack of such mechanisms does not mean that a decision cannot be binding for substantive reasons.

Substantive normative force results from the content or the body that issues the decision. Its force does not come from its inherent potential executability, but from its claim to be definitive and permanent. Thus there are decisions without formal binding force that nevertheless suggest a claim to permanence or scant likelihood of future modification. STF decisions issued by the full panel, STJ decisions issued by the special panel or the competent section in the subject-matter, and the summaries of precedents known as "summulas" carry a strong claim to finality, given the implication that they are highly unlikely to be changed, and a *formal assumption of correctness*, given the high level of the issuing body, which creates a "qualified basis for trust."[334] Moreover, it should be noted that the reporting judge in cases that involve matters already settled by means of such decisions can deny an appeal outright. This is not possible with decisions by intermediate levels of the judiciary, such as state appeal courts or federal circuit courts, when such decisions may be brought before the STJ or STF in special or extraordinary appeals respectively. In other words, although these decisions do not have binding efficacy relative to lower courts and the public administration, ongoing lawsuits on the same subject-matter brought before higher courts are likely to have the same result provided the circumstances are the same and significant new elements are not involved.

It should also be noted that the STF's decisions after the change produced by the insertion of article 543-A, paragraph 3, into the Code of Civil Procedure, serve as a guide for other taxpayers if they pass the "general repercussion" test (similar to *certiorari* in the U.S.), even if they do not have formal binding force: Since there is general repercussion only in disputes that go beyond the individual interest of the parties, any decision issued in an extraordinary appeal acts as a guideline for an entire class of identical cases.[335]

---

[332]Misabel de Abreu Machado Derzi, *Modificações da Jurisprudência no Direito Tributário*, São Paulo, Noeses, 2009, pages 272 and following.

[333]RE n.370.682-9, Full Court, Rep. Justice Ilmar Galvão, *DJ* 19 Dec 2007, opinion by Justice Joaquim Barbosa, p. 546 of the decision.

[334]Johanna Hey, *Steuerplanungssicherheit als Rechtsproblem*, Köln, Otto Schmidt, 2002, p. 627. Heike Pohl, *Rechtsprechungsänderung und Rückanknüpfung*, Berlin, Duncker und Humblot, 2005, p. 90.

[335]Misabel de Abreu Machado Derzi, *Modificações da jurisprudência no Direito Tributário*, São Paulo, Noeses, 2009, p. 279.

Another point about substantive normative force is that decisions can be differentiated in terms of their claim to correction relative to content rather than the issuing body. This is termed the decision's *substantive claim to correction*. On one hand, there are decisions whose justification is extremely fragile according to legal doctrine, on grounds of logical consistency or argumentative coherence, or on grounds relating to the normative support for the understanding they express. In some cases, decisions are criticized for causing "interpretative bewilderment" (*Auslegungsüberraschung*).[336] If a decision is greeted by a large amount of serious doctrinal criticism from respected scholars in the legal community, for example, its substantive normative force is weakened in proportion to the intensity and consistency of the criticism. The reverse is also true: A doctrinal consensus tends to intensify the substantive force of a decision. It is difficult to know, of course, when doctrinal criticism is "significant" (*wesentlich*) and "considerable" (*erheblich*), just as it is to know whether "numerous" (*zahlreiche*) and "renowned" (*namhafte*) scholars have criticized a given decision.[337] On the other hand, there are decisions with a high level of substantive normative force and a strong claim to permanence that clearly exceed the jurisdiction of the issuing body and/or involve subject-matter that falls within the jurisdiction of another appeal court. Such is the case, for example, for decisions handed down by the STJ relating to constitutionality.

These references to a "decision" are to its binding part, represented by the final prescriptive part. This does not mean that some of the arguments put forward in the grounds for the decision may not exceptionally create trust, when duly discussed by the court. In some situations, it is precisely the *rationes decidendi* that express the court's position on an issue. Thus *obiter dicta* and incidental clarifications can also constitute a basis for trust, as an exception, depending on their extension, clarity and consensuality.[338] A good example is the case mentioned earlier in which the STF examined an application for an injunction by a pensioner who was adopted by her own great-grandfather as his daughter one week before he died of cancer so that she would be entitled to a survivor's pension after his death and had received the pension for no less than 18 years until it was unilaterally and summarily suspended by the Federal Court of Audit. Although the STF granted injunctive relief to assure due process of law at the administrative level, the summary of the judgment reflects a heated debate among the justices about the applicability of the legal certainty principle to the case, given the long period that had elapsed between the time the pension was granted and its suspension by the Audit Court.[339]

---

[336]Johanna Hey, *Steuerplanungssicherheit als Rechtsproblem*, Köln, Otto Schmidt, 2002, p. 636.

[337]Christoph Louven, *Problematik und Grenzen rückwirkender Rechtsprechung des Bundesarbeitsgerichts*, München, Beck, 1996, p. 226.

[338]Hans Lilie, *Obiter Dictum und Divergenzausgleich in Strafsachen*, Köln, Carl Heymanns, 1993, pages 207 and following. Christoph Louven, *Problematik und Grenzen rückwirkender Rechtsprechung des Bundesarbeitsgerichts*, München, Beck, 1996, pages 224 and 226. Ulrich Keil, *Die Systematik privatrechtlicher Rechtsprechungsänderungen*, Tübingen, Mohr Siebeck, 2007, p. 53.

[339]MS n. 24.268, Full Court, Rep. Justice Gilmar Mendes, *DJ* 17 Sep 2004.

Second, the more a *decision is intended to offer guidance*, the more it should be deemed to protect the taxpayer's trust. There are two distinct issues here. A decision may offer guidance indirectly via its binding force and claim to permanence. Given its normative force and the fact that it probably embodies the judiciary's definitive understanding on the subject, it serves as a normative basis on which citizens can act. Or a decision may offer guidance directly, by virtue of its function: The decisions of some bodies and certain courts are designed specifically to provide direct guidance to lower courts, and indirect guidance to the addressees of the norms interpreted, via uniformization. This is the case, for example, with decisions handed down by the sections of the STJ and decisions grouped together in summaries of precedents. These decisions offer guidance from "on high."

Third, the more consistently a *decision is integrated into a chain of uniform decisions*, the more it should be deemed to protect the taxpayer's trust. Decisions issued by panels of the STJ or STF that may not have been confirmed by the sections or by the full court but uniformly express the same understanding can be assumed to represent the respective court's position on the subject-matter and can therefore be used as guidelines. However, it must be stressed that this does not mean a *single* decision cannot serve as a basis for trust.[340] Very much to the contrary, in many situations a single decision forms a more solid foundation than a chain of decisions (*Kette von Urteilen*).[341] A good example would be a decision by the plenary of the STF on a given constitutional matter in opposition to repeated decisions issued by panels of the STJ. Thus a single decision, provided it is binding, may provide more guidance than a long chain of decisions. Moreover, the fact that a decision is part of a chain of judgments that dates back a long way may mean that it is very old and hence may exceptionally create an expectation of change.[342] Thus the position occupied by a decision in a chain of decisions must be taken into consideration in combination with its bindingness: The more binding a decision, the less it needs to be part of a chain; the less binding it is, the more important will be the requirement that it is part of a chain of decisions.[343]

It should also be stressed on this point that the basis for trust involves static and dynamic elements. Thus the bindingness and claim to permanence of a decision can be differentiated by analyzing only its intrinsic and synchronic aspects, i.e. the level of the court that delivered it and its formal or material force. However, these elements may change with the passage of time: A decision delivered by the

[340]Christoph Louven, *Problematik und Grenzen rückwirkender Rechtsprechung des Bundesarbeitsgerichts*, München, Beck, 1996, p. 221. Heike Pohl, *Rechtsprechungsänderung und Rückanknüpfung*, Berlin, Duncker und Humblot, 2005, p. 95.

[341]Johanna Hey, *Steuerplanungssicherheit als Rechtsproblem*, Köln, Otto Schmidt, 2002, p. 628. Hans-Wolfgang Arndt, *Probleme rückwirkender Rechtsprechungsänderung*, Frankfurt, Athenäum, 1974, p. 3.

[342]Christoph Louven, *Problematik und Grenzen rückwirkender Rechtsprechung des Bundesarbeitsgerichts*, München, Beck, 1996, p. 222.

[343]Heike Pohl, *Rechtsprechungsänderung und Rückanknüpfung*, Berlin, Duncker und Humblot, 2005, p. 95.

STJ which is added to others that express the same position to produce a summary precedent is highly binding and has a strong claim to permanence; nevertheless, if new litigants persistently sue to change the decision and it is subjected to strong doctrinal criticism of high quality, the decision's claim to correctness may be weakened to such an extent that it has to be modified, in which case the summary precedent will be revoked and the dockets will be sent up to the STF. In this situation it can be said that the bindingness and claim to permanence were high at a certain point (*T1*) but became weak at a later time (*T2*). This observation is only meant to show that an analysis of the basis for trust cannot be confined to the static perspective, but must also take into account the dynamic perspective, paying heed to the *moment at which trust is exercised*, not to any moment. This is of the highest relevance, since if there is trust that effectively merits protection, it will be necessary to know how to do so and via what procedure; if it is protected by modulating the effects of a decision (to be analyzed in the next chapter), a great deal of care will be needed to avoid making *tabula rasa* of the trust that existed during the entire past period, so that the prospective efficacy of the decision protects trust during the period when the modified decision that supposedly generates trust did not exist.

Fourth, the greater the *potential for generalization of the decision*, the more the taxpayer's trust must be protected. Decisions issued by higher courts, especially the STF, have greater potential for universalization, given their abstract content.[344] The greater the potential for universalization, the better suited a decision to serve as a basis of trust.

If the importance of the basis for trust derives from a decision's fitness to generate trust, and considering that it is possible to speak of jurisprudential change only relative to efficacious unappealable decisions, protectivity must increase in proportion to bindingness and claim to permanence. In other words, the guidance offered by case law increases in proportion to the presence of these elements. A preliminary injunction granted in a third party's lawsuit or an isolated decision by any lower or higher court does not deserve a high degree of trust in the absence of other elements: It offers practically no guidance, either because it is addressed only to the parties in the lawsuit, or because its substantive normative force is feeble. With regard to the thesis advocated here, the fact that the decision that serves as the basis for the exercise of trust has no formal normative force or little substantive normative force does not eliminate the possibility of protection for acts performed on the basis of that decision. The protection will be an exception and will require the existence of other elements that may compensate for the frailty of the basis. In the absence of such elements, there should be no protection of trust.

All the above considerations about the basis for trust show that there must be a *combination* of the various factors of reliability mentioned earlier, although none of them in isolation is sufficient to guarantee or eliminate trust protection. As has been shown, the number of decisions is a criterion, and it can be presumed that the longer the chain of uniform decisions the greater the protection. However, it may be

[344] Johanna Hey, *Steuerplanungssicherheit als Rechtsproblem*, Köln, Otto Schmidt, 2002, p. 627.

the case that there is only one decision in a given direction, but that this decision is binding and is supported by a high degree of doctrinal consensus. Hence while the number of decisions in one direction must be taken into account, it is not a sufficient or necessary condition to configure a basis for trust. The age of a decision is also a criterion, and protection presumably increases as the decision that serves as a basis for action becomes more consolidated over time. However, a decision may need to be changed precisely because it is old, so that it cannot serve as a basis for action. Thus the age of a decision, albeit an important element, is not a sufficient or necessary condition to configure a basis for trust – and so forth. Arndt is therefore right in saying that there is no standard answer to the problem of the retroactive efficacy of case law.[345]

These thoughts about the ambiguity of the criteria do not make them irrelevant. They can serve as *indicative elements*, but are neither sufficient nor necessary. The fact that they are indicative and do not furnish absolute assurance does not diminish their importance in any way. Lack of criteria prevents control of the application of the trust protection principle, militating against the legal certainty principle, which does not tolerate arbitrariness and lack of justification.[346] Lack of criteria also leads to the use of any decision as a basis for trust, including decisions that do not offer and are not supposed to offer any sort of guidance. Accepting that any kind of decision creates trust worthy of protection also leads to a result against the legal certainty principle, because trust protection based on any kind of decision fosters opportunism and a lack of individual responsibility for risks deliberately assumed in action, and this is frontally opposed to the very ideal of legal certainty. Hence the importance of indicating the criteria, the elements and the relations of preference between them, albeit moveable.

Second, besides having a basis for trust taxpayers must trust the decision that guides them. On this point, it is necessary to know whether trust should be effective or whether merely presumed trust suffices. In other words, must taxpayers have known for a fact the decision that they claim to have followed or does it suffice that they could have known the decision for trust to exist? Jurisprudence is divided on this: Some legal scholars argue that trust can be abstract and fictitious[347]; others require concrete reliance.[348] Unlike statutes, which address all citizens, judicial decisions address the parties, except for decisions with extended subjective efficacy, so there must be concrete and effective trust in the "modified" decision to justify a causal nexus between the basis for trust and the citizen's behavior.

---

[345] Hans-Wolfgang Arndt, *Probleme rückwirkender Rechtsprechungsänderung*, Frankfurt, Athenäum, 1974, p. 130.

[346] Christoph Louven, *Problematik und Grenzen rückwirkender Rechtsprechung des Bundesarbeitsgerichts*, München, Beck, 1996, p. 240.

[347] Wolfgang Grunsky, *Grenzen der Rückwirkung bei einer Änderung der Rechtsprechug*, Heidelberg, C. F. Müller, 1970, p. 26.

[348] Christoph Louven, *Problematik und Grenzen rückwirkender Rechtsprechung des Bundesarbeitsgerichts*, München, Beck, 1996, p. 235.

Third, trust must be exercised. To repeat the expression used earlier in the discussion of trust protection, trust must have been "put into practice". Hope is not protected, neither is abstract trust, but only the exercise of trust, i.e., concrete acts of disposal of the fundamental rights of freedom and property. Thus individuals must have performed concrete acts because of the "modified" decision, such as investing, signing a contract, not making a judicial deposit, failing to pay tax, and so forth.[349]

Among the elements to be demonstrated and proven relative to the intensity of the restriction of fundamental rights are the onerousness, duration and reversibility of the citizen's actions. The greater the expense incurred, the longer the efficacy of the basis lasts and the harder it is to reverse the effects produced, the more intensely the citizen's fundamental rights of property and freedom will be restricted and the more the citizen's trust in the normative basis merits protection.

Fourth, there must be frustration of trust. The "modifying" decision must create a disadvantage for people who acted on the basis of the "modified" decision.[350] As already noted, protection of the exercise of trust cannot be justified by frustration of any kind: There must be some degree of restriction resulting from jurisprudential change. Hence the relationship between the preconditions for application of the trust protection principle: Citizens must have acted on the basis of the decision and a later change must have taken them by surprise.

The STF has acknowledged the need to protect citizens in the case of jurisprudential change. An example is the discussion of retroactive application of Supplementary Law 118/05. Although this law claimed to be interpretative, in actual fact it caused normative innovation and in practice it reduced the period during which refunds for overpayment of taxes can be claimed from 10 to 5 years. This is because if the statute of limitations to claim a refund of overpaid taxes began to run *when the tax payment was accepted*, according to the judiciary's understanding, the new interpretative rule proposed by Supplementary Law 118/05 would have advanced it to the *moment of early payment*. Thus whereas the judiciary had built up a body of case law determining that the statute of limitations to claim a refund began to run when payment was recorded, the legislative attempted through a supposedly interpretative statute to replace that point in time with the moment of early payment. However, the STF ruled quite rightly that this change was unconstitutional. The Constitution establishes the principle of the separation of powers, according to which the legislative, executive and judiciary are independent and coexist in harmony (article 2). According to this principle the legislative legislates but does not judge, since the latter function is reserved to the judiciary, so much so that under the Constitution no statute may "prevent the judiciary from ruling on a claim of infringement of rights or a threat to rights" (article 5, indent XXXV). The Constitution also establishes rules of jurisdiction that give the judiciary exclusive powers to interpret acts originating in the legislative. One

[349] Ibidem, p. 237.

[350] Christoph Louven, *Problematik und Grenzen rückwirkender Rechtsprechung des Bundesarbeitsgerichts*, München, Beck, 1996, p. 234.

of the most important of these rules is the rule included in article 105, which empowers the STJ alone to decide on the interpretation of federal legislation. All these considerations show that the legislative cannot enact interpretative statutes about federal legislation. The judiciary in general, and the STJ in particular, has sole competence to interpret the laws.[351] Thinking otherwise violates the reserved jurisdiction rule. On the other hand, the legislative's action specifically violates the separation of powers principle. In changing the understanding built up in case law regarding periods of prescription and limitation, the legislative overstepped the bounds of its typical core action and disrespected the limits set by the judiciary. In fact the legislative passed a law with the specific purpose of interpreting previously enacted legal provisions that had already been interpreted by the judiciary. In doing so, it failed to perform a typical function of any lawmaking body, which is the enactment of binding, prospective, general and permanent norms, and instead took on a role typical of the judiciary, which is the formulation of retrospective and mostly individual decisions by assigning normative meanings to legal provisions. Consequently, no statute may interfere with facts that occurred under a previous statute on pain of violating the irretroactivity rule and the trust protection principle. Because the irretroactivity rule is a means of preserving legal certainty under the democratic rule of law, to protect the taxpayer's expectations tax credits created before the enactment of Supplementary Law 118/05 must be offset without the restrictions of the new statute. This is because when these credits were created the National Tax Code expressly stipulated, and the judiciary supported, the right to offset them within five years of the acceptance of payment. Hence the obligation to protect taxpayers from the effects of the changed understanding on pain of violating the legal certainty principle. To quote the opinion written by Justice Ellen Gracie:

> The retroactive application of a new, shorter term for the repetition or offsetting of tax overpayment as determined by a new statute, thus immediately terminating claims filed in a timely manner under the term then applicable, as well as immediate application to claims pending at the time the statute was enacted, without any protection by transitional rules, configures an injury to the principle of legal certainty in its contents of protecting trust and guaranteeing access to justice.[352]

In the presence of the preconditions for application of the trust protection principle, and because the trust is worthy of protection, the fundamental question arises: How – i.e., with what instruments – ought the trust of citizens who exercised their rights of freedom and property based on the modified decision to be protected?

This question is answered below.

[351] Humberto Ávila, "A Separação dos Poderes e as Leis Interpretativas Modificativas de Jurisprudência Consolidada", in Misabel Abreu Machado Derzi (coord.), *Separação de Poderes e Efetividade do Direito Tributário*, Belo Horizonte, Del Rey, 2010, p. 59.

[352] RE n.566.621-RS, Supreme Court, Full Court, Rep. Justice Ellen Gracie, DJ 11 Oct 2011.

2.1.3.6.5 The Means of Trust Protection in Cases of Jurisprudential Change

As has been stated, acts of disposal of fundamental rights causatively connected to a modified court decision merit trust protection.[353] That being so, the protection must focus on these acts of disposal, and not on others. Any kind of restriction of the content or effects of the modifying decision in the name of the trust protection principle should remain connected to the acts of disposal causally related to the modified court decision. Otherwise there would be a risk of protecting trust that had not been exercised, in the name of trust protection. An example will make this clearer.

Let us imagine that a taxpayer initiates litigation by filing a complaint at a moment (*T1*) when there is no position of the judiciary on the matter in dispute. At a second moment (*T2*) the STJ delivers judgment on a matter apparently identical to the subject of the former proceeding, which is still under way. And at a third moment (*T3*) the STF issues a final decision on the issue, which is contrary to the previous decision handed down by the STJ. So the situation is this: A complaint is filed at *T1*, a "modified decision" is delivered at *T2*, and a "modifying decision" is entered at *T3*. Next let us imagine that because there are many similar cases, two motions are filed: In the case that ended with the "modifying decision", the proposal is that prospective effects be assigned to the decision in the name of protecting the legal certainty of those who relied on the "modified decision"; in the individual suit that is still under way, and in which no decision has yet been entered, the proposal is to redefine the content of the decision, also in order to protect the legal certainty of those who relied on the "modified decision." The following question must now be asked: Would the assignment of prospective effects to the "modifying decision", in bulk and without detailed distinctions of efficacy, serve as an adequate instrument of trust protection? And would modification of the outcome of the case under way be a suitable way to protect trust? These two questions suffice to highlight the difficulty of providing a standard solution to questions about the protection of legitimate expectations. Since the purpose of the principle under examination is to protect concrete acts of disposal of fundamental rights performed "because of" the modified decision, any solution that does not consider the necessary causal relationship between individual acts of disposal and a modified court decision is not an appropriate solution from the standpoint of the trust protection principle.

As to whether assigning prospective effects to the "modifying decision" would be an appropriate means of trust protection, it is important to note that if the competent court assigns such effects with the justification that there has been a jurisprudential change, and rejects all past effects, it will also protect "trust" with regard to acts performed between *T1* and *T2*, i.e. when the "modified decision" did not yet exist and therefore could not have been the basis for causally oriented exercise of trust.

---

[353] Bodo Viets, *Rechtsprechungsänderung und Vertrauensschutz*, Bern, Herbert Lang, 1976, p. 203.

In reality, within that time frame the actions performed by taxpayers in general and by the plaintiff specifically could not have been causally influenced by the "modified decision" because it simply did not exist. Thus a decision to set aside past effects based on the trust protection principle, including the period in which the "modified decision" did not even exist, would paradoxically produce a retroactive effect based on the prohibition of retroactivity: Because the "modified decision" did not exist between *T1* and *T2*, the establishment of prospective effects involves making the effects of the decision issued at *T2* retroact to *T1*. Thus retroactivity is determined in the name of irretroactivity. Instead, the exercise of trust based on the "modified decision" between T2 and T3 would be genuinely protected if effective acts of disposal connected to the modified decision could be proven in accordance with the requirements referred to earlier. The example presented above serves above all to show that the assignment of prospective effects to the "modifying decision" itself may be an improper mechanism to assess the particularities of each case and to separate periods during which the exercise of trust could not have existed from periods in which it could. We will return to this topic in the next chapter.

As for whether modification of the outcome of the proceedings under way would be an appropriate way to protect trust, it is necessary to recall the considerations presented earlier. On one hand, a party to the lawsuit presents a doubt about a given matter to the court and cannot be surprised if the final outcome is unfavorable. On the other hand, while the taxpayer's proceedings are under way and the "modified decision" entered in another case is not definitive, the latter cannot be a parameter for actions to dispose of fundamental rights. The situation changes once the "modified decision" becomes *res iudicata* and is highly binding, with a strong claim to permanence, potential for generalization, a guiding purpose, and insertion in a uniform chain of decisions. When this occurs and the plaintiff or others have performed concrete actions because of it, then protection of trust may be argued. Thus, for example, if the plaintiff used to make judicial deposits equal to the total amount of the disputed debt and stopped doing so because of the "modified decision," the plaintiff's trust may be protected. However, this raises a question: protected *how* and *in which proceedings*? Protected from the modifying decision by the final decision in these proceedings or by appropriate assessments to be made by the tax authorities?

These questions reveal the difficulty of a standardizing position. Since the protection of trust within the scope of jurisprudential change depends on the existence of concrete acts of disposal causally connected to the modified decision, the performance of such acts needs to be proven. And for this to be possible there must be a proper phase of the proceedings reserved for evidentiary hearings, unless the acts of disposal concerned are related to the case (such as judicial deposits) and the connection with the "modified decision" can be presumed (judicial deposits ceased after the "modifying decision" was published). What cannot be admitted is simply making *tabula rasa* of the exercise of trust.

Precisely in light of the above considerations, a standard solution cannot be accepted to protect the concrete exercise of trust connected to a modified court decision. In each case the causally oriented performance of acts of disposal of fundamental rights must be proven. However, some negative conclusions are unavoidable: Standardizing solutions that completely reject the declaratory effects of a court decision that changes a previous judicial understanding based on the trust protection principle are not admissible because they are unable to assess whether concrete acts of disposal have indeed been based on the modified decision; solutions in litigation or proceedings that do not accept or consider evidence of the actual performance of concrete acts of disposal based on the modified decision are not admissible, at least when the justification for the prospective effect is the trust protection principle (instead of legal certainty in an objective sense).

Given all of the above, jurisprudence suggests other instruments be deployed to prevent jurisprudential change from unfairly affecting those who have exercised trust on the basis of the guidance offered by the abandoned precedent. Thus when the modifying decision itself cannot encompass the broad range of situations that may exist and the court decision in the litigation under way when a jurisprudential change occurs also cannot assess the existence of concrete acts of disposal based on the modified decision (for substantive or procedural reasons), other instruments must be found. Some of these are: general formal rules of transition determined by the judiciary or executive to enable taxpayers who relied on the abandoned orientation to adjust to the new position; general substantive rules of transition determined by the judiciary or executive, setting aside retroactive effects for taxpayers who can prove the performance of acts of disposal connected to the modified decision; specific individual decisions by the judiciary or executive in litigation or proceedings designed specifically to prove the existence of effective acts of disposal of fundamental rights causally connected to the abandoned judicial guidance, with appropriate evidentiary hearings.[354] Thus it is necessary to consider an "arsenal of flexible legal-prescriptive consequences" (*Arsenal flexibler Rechtsfolgenaussprüche*), which reject retrospective effects and encompass periods or rules of transition, while also making exception for the precursor case and the parallel cases under way, appealing to the legislators to effect the changes necessary to restore constitutionality, with or without a deadline, and so forth.[355]

A good example of this kind of solution is the rule of transition established by the STF in the case of the jurisprudential change concerning the right to strike. Initially the Court decided that the exercise of this right depended on statutory provision. Later the STF observed that the right of civilian public servants to go on strike had not yet been given minimally satisfactory legislative treatment to assure its exercise. The STF therefore decided that it could not refrain from acknowledging the possibility of acting in the event of omission or inaction by the legislative.

[354] Johanna Hey, *Steuerplanungssicherheit als Rechtsproblem*, Köln, Otto Schmidt, 2002, p. 646. Christiane Lübbe, *Grenzen der Rückwirkung bei Rechtsprechungsänderungen*, Frankfurt am Main, Peter Lang, 1998, pages 113 and following.

[355] Roman Seer, "Rechtsschutz in Steuersachen", in Klaus Tipke e Joachim Lang, *Steuerrecht*, 19th ed., Köln, Otto Schmidt, 2008, § 22, margin number 286, pages 1090 and following.

However, bearing in mind the "evolution of case law concerning interpretation of the legislative's omission on the right of civilian public servants to strike, and respecting the requirements of legal certainty, the Court hereby sets a term of 60 days for Congress to legislate on the issue."[356]

Another example is the rule of transition established for the case of a jurisprudential change on the issue of jurisdiction. Interpreting indent I of article 109, I, of the Constitution, the STF initially decided that claims for material and moral damages due to work-related accidents, even if filed by employees against their (former) employers, fell under the jurisdiction of state courts. Later, however, the plenary ruled that the Constitution grants jurisdiction over such claims to the labor courts, which form a separate branch of the judiciary in Brazil. However, considering the significant number of claims that had been submitted to the regular courts and were still under way, as well as the relevant social interest at stake, the plenary decided not only that the labor courts would assume jurisdiction as of the approval of Constitutional Amendment 45/2004, but also that the new position would be applied to proceedings then before regular state courts if judgment on the merits was pending. Claims already decided on the merits by regular state courts before the amendment entered into force would remain there until final judgment (*res iudicata*) and the corresponding execution, whereas the rest would be transferred to the labor courts as they were, with all prior proceedings entirely validated. The STF had opted for this solution, it said, because "as the main guardian of our Republic's Constitution, this Court may, and indeed must, protect legal certainty by assigning prospective efficacy to its decisions, with precise delimitation of their effects, whenever it reviews the case law regarding competence *ex ratione materiae*".[357]

The solution that does not meet the requirements of the trust protection principle is the assignment of *pro futuro* effects en bloc, in a standardized and draconian matter, because it disregards the necessary causal link between the modified decision and individual acts of disposal of fundamental rights of freedom and property. In this regard it is worth recalling Justice Bilac Pinto on diffuse (or exceptional) control and concentrated (or active) control:

> Indeed, the declaration of unconstitutionality by exception, i.e., regarding the legal text applicable to a concrete case, has effects that are well known. In the case at hand, unconstitutionality was pronounced via active control. This differs from the former situation because it is does not apply the law to a concrete case; on the contrary, the statute is declared unconstitutional in principle. The effects of this kind of declaration of unconstitutionality cannot be synthesized in a single rule that applies to every case.[358]

Hence the importance of analyzing the assignment of effects to judicial review decisions.

This is the focus for what follows.

---

[356]MI n.670, Full Court, Opinion by Justice Gilmar Mendes, j. 25 Oct 2007, *DJe*-206, p. 1.

[357]CC n.7.204-MG, Full Court, Rep. Justice Carlos Britto, *DJ* 09 Dec 2005, p. 5.

[358]RE n.78.594, 2nd Panel, Rep. Justice Bilac Pinto, *DJ* 30 Oct 1974.

2.1.4 Excursus: Modulation of the Effects of Decisions Based on Legal Certainty

2.1.4.1 Initial Considerations

When the STF finds a statute incompatible with the Constitution, it typically declares the statute unconstitutional with past effects, making it null and void since its inception with declaratory effect (*ex tunc* efficacy). This is the rule. However, there is one exception: The Court may conclude that although the norm under judicial review is incompatible with the Constitution, there are reasons that justify upholding its effects, or part of them produced in the past. In such cases, it declares the statute unconstitutional but restricts the effects of this unconstitutionality ruling to the future or to another moment, with or without rules of transition. Thus it protects the past efficacy of an unconstitutional statute because it acknowledges that by doing so it will do more to uphold the constitutional order than it would if it ruled the norm unconstitutional with declaratory effects.[359] This "modulation" of the effects of a decision over time is therefore a technique that "attenuates" the effects of the annulment.[360]

The STF's powers to assign deferred effects to a declaration of unconstitutionality are expressly set forth in Law 9868/98. Article 27 of this law determines that when declaring a statute or normative act unconstitutional, the STF may restrict the effects of this declaration "on grounds of legal certainty or exceptional social interest," or decide that the ruling will enter into force only once it becomes unappealable or at some other point in time. It is this reference to legal certainty that links the declaration of unconstitutionality to Transitional Tax Law, as discussed in this book.

Because the assignment of forward-looking effects to an unconstitutionality ruling involves the upholding of acts or effects contrary to law, without the necessary analysis of all the concrete details mentioned earlier, its utilization always includes what could be called a "counterorder", as noted above in the part about the temporal aspect of legal certainty. If the laws are to be obeyed, whenever the

[359]Gilmar Mendes, *Jurisdição constitucional*, 3rd ed., São Paulo, Saraiva, 1999, pages 212 and following. Idem, "Anteprojeto de lei sobre processo e julgamento da ação direta de inconstitucionalidade e da ação declaratória de constitucionalidade", *Cadernos de Direito Constitucional e Ciência Política* 29, pages 24–36, São Paulo, 1999. Klaus Schlaich e Stephan Korioth, *Das Bundesverfassungsgericht – Stellung, Verfahren, Entscheidungen*, 7th ed., München, Beck, 2007, pages 225 and following. Christian Hillgruber and Christoph Goos, *Verfassungsprozessrecht*, 2nd ed., Heidelberg, C. F. Müller, 2006, p. 194. Hans Lechner and Rüdiger Zuck, *Bundesverfassungsgerichtsgesetz*, 5th ed., München, Beck, 2006, pages 411 and following. Dieter Umbach, Thomas Clemens and Franz-Wilhelm Dollinger (Orgs.), *Bundesverfassungsgerichtsgesetz*, 2nd ed., Heidelberg, C. F. Müller, 2005, p. 988. Michael Sachs, *Verfassungsprozessrecht*, 2nd ed., Frankfurt am Main, Recht und Wirtschaft, 2007, pages 62 and following.

[360]Bernard Pacteau, "Comment aménager la rétroactivité de la Justice? Sécurité juridique, sécurité juridictionnelle, sécurité jurisprudentielle", in Bertrand Seiller (Org.), *La rétroactivité des décisions du juge administratif*, Paris, Economica, 2007, p. 117.

effects produced by acts contrary to law are upheld, law's violation is tolerated and indirectly encouraged. This amounts to a kind of dual command, which is an internal contradiction in law: The laws must be obeyed, yet they can be broken, and if they can be broken they do not have to be obeyed. The relevant point for present purposes is that this phenomenon restricts the ideals inherent in legal certainty, i.e. the knowability, reliability and calculability of law.

The knowability of law is affected to the extent that upholding the effects of unlawfulness causes uncertainty as to which rule applies to the authority as well as the addressee: If there is a rule but those who break it are not punished, no one can be sure which rule is valid, the one associated with the minimal meaning of the hypothesis of the abstract rule or the one resulting from its application by the judiciary. Moreover, because rules necessarily involve exclusionary reasons, in the sense that the elements not provided for by the hypothesis generally cannot be considered, and upholding the effects of their violation precisely represents the consideration of other elements not provided for, there is uncertainty whether the elements that ought to be considered are those specified in the rule's hypothesis or those the judiciary may consider. In sum, the structure of the rules is treated with ambiguity.[361] Uncertainty regarding the applicable norm and the legally relevant elements restricts the "certainty of orientation" required by law: Neither the authorities nor the ordinary citizens know whether to take guidance from the rule or its exception, or whether the authoritative reasons in the rule or the reason for its correction should carry more weight. These considerations may become clearer if we take an example. Small children regularly disobey their parents' orders.[362] If the child understands what "no" means but is not sure that "no" really is "no", or whether "no" may be changed into "yes" by crying and insisting, the child will simply disobey a parent's orders, or at least doubt them. This example illustrates a lack of normative knowability, and indirectly normative calculability. There is no knowability because the addressee does not know what the norm is ("no" or "yes"?) or what its value is ("no" as "no" or "no" as "yes"?); there is no calculability because the addressee does not know the efficacy of the norm ("no" always as "no" or maybe as "yes"?). If the example is transported to the sphere of legal norms, it demonstrates the meaning of a lack of normative certainty for the realization of the principles of the rule of law and legal certainty: A state of affairs in which law plays a constitutive role and legal certainty plays an instrumental role for freedom exists only when addressees are minimally sure that norms are valid, in force, and effective. As noted by Summers, a core element of the rule of law is the existence of a stable system of rules that assure the appearance of meaning as a basis for citizens to plan their conduct and business.[363]

---

[361] Joseph Raz, *Practical reason and norms*, New Jersey, Princeton, 1990, pages 40 and following.

[362] Frederick Schauer, *Thinking like a Lawyer: a new introduction to legal reasoning*, Cambridge, Harvard University Press, 2009, p. 62.

[363] Robert Summers, "A formal theory of the rule of law", in idem, *Essays in Legal Theory*, Dordrecht, Kluwer, 2000, p. 171.

The reliability of law is affected to the extent that the upholding of the effects of unlawfulness compromises the credibility of the order and its efficacy. The concept of *legal rules* involves a hypothesis and a consequence, represented analytically by the expression "if, then": If the hypothesis occurs, then the consequence must be applied. The guiding function of law is realized when citizens know the rules in force and can be reasonably sure that if the event configured by the hypothesis occurs the consequences will be applied in most cases. This is why the reliability of law involves the ideals of stability and efficacy of the order. However, improper use of the mechanism of upholding the effects of unconstitutional acts alters precisely this regulatory paradigm: Instead of "if, then", we have "if, then maybe." This creates a problem of orientation and reliability for both the authorities and the addressees: for the authorities because they may choose not to perform unlawful acts, relying on application of the consequence in the event of disobedience ("if, then"), or they may choose to do so, presuming that the consequence will not be applied ("if, then maybe"); for the addressees because they end up not knowing which of the two strategies the authorities will choose and which efficacy will be defined by the judiciary.

The calculability of law is also restricted, since upholding the effects of unlawfulness compromises the predictability of other people's actions and the bindingness of law itself. Uncertainty about the consequences to be applied to acts contrary to the Constitution fosters doubt regarding how the state authorities will behave. When the right to join the civil service without a public competitive examination is upheld, the consequence is doubt about future recruitment, both for the authorities ("Do I plan a public exam, recruit directly, or promote internally?") and for the addressees ("Will there be a public exam or will indirect selection be used?"). When an unconstitutional tax is upheld, uncertainty about other taxes arises, both for the legislative ("Do I create taxes according to the constitutional competence rules or may I overstep their bounds?"), and for the addressees ("Will competence be exercised according to the Constitution?"). When the effects of acts performed against the principle of due process of law are upheld, suspicions arise regarding future procedural acts, both for the authorities ("Do I notify the other party that a new document has been brought on record?") and for the addressees ("Will the judgment be based on elements about which I have testified?"). As well noted by Justice Cézar Peluso in a case analyzed below, "When the Court offers flexibility, what tends to happen? Non-compliance with the norm . . . " Similarly, Justice Marco Aurélio warns against "encouraging infringement of the Constitution, infringement of the laws."[364]

It should be clarified that these initial observations are not intended to be a complete rebuttal of the modulation of the temporal effects of declarations of unconstitutionality. In some situations, and provided at least some requirements are met, modulation can and should be used, in accordance with the Constitution. The

[364]RE n.401.953-1, Full Court, Rep. Justice Joaquim Barbosa, *DJ* 21 Sep 2007, pages 467–468 of the judgment respectively.

point is to show that the rule of law and the legal certainty principle afford very little scope indeed for modulation of effects.

For this very reason it is essential to know as precisely as possible the meaning of "reasons of certainty" and in what measure these reasons can justify upholding the effects of a statute declared unconstitutional. This is best done by analyzing German law because the Brazilian approach is largely based on the case law of Germany's Federal Constitutional Court, which has developed many ways to assign effects to its decisions (*Tenorierungsformen*). Typically, when it understands that a statute is incompatible with the Constitution, the Court issues a declaration of unconstitutionality (*Verfassungswidrigkeitserklärung*), the effect of which is a declaration of nullity (*Nichtigkeitserklärung*) from the time the statute found incompatible with the Constitution entered into force (*ex tunc*), and hence cancellation. Another type of ruling is the declaration of incompatibility (*Unvereinbarkeitserklärung*).[365]

In the declaration of incompatibility, although the Court considers that the statute violates the Constitution, it decides to uphold the effects of the statute for the past or for some moment in the future, because it understands that the declaration of nullity of the statute would not restore the state of constitutionality, or at least not automatically. Legal certainty is one of the justifications used by the Court to adopt this kind of decision. In some cases, to avoid the creation of a "legal vacuum" (*rechtliches Vakuum*) or "uncertainty about the legal situation" (*Unsicherheit über die Rechtslage*), or to assure "legal certainty and clarity of the Law" (*Rechtssicherheit und Rechtsklarheit*), the Court upholds the effects of the statute marred by unconstitutionality.[366]

The effects of the statute can be upheld in many ways, depending on the objective intended by the Court and the way the effects are modulated. The following stand out:

(a) Declaration of incompatibility with general *pro futuro* efficacy – The Court simply assigns *ex nunc* effects to the decision of unconstitutionality, tasking the legislative with the enactment of a new statute.[367]

---

[365] Roman Seer e Jörg Peter Müller, "Begrenzung der Wirkungen seiner Richtersprüche durch den EuGH", *IWB* n. 5, Gruppe 2, Fach 11, p. 263, 2008. Roman Seer, "Rechtsschutz in Steuersachen", in Klaus Tipke e Joachim Lang, *Steuerrecht*, 19th ed., Köln, Otto Schmidt, 2008, § 22, margin numbers 285–291, p. 1091. Klaus Schlaich and Stephan Korioth, *Das Bundesverfassungsgericht – Stellung, Verfahren, Entscheidungen*, 7th ed., München, Beck, 2007, pages 225 and following. Christian Hillgruber and Christoph Goos, *Verfassungsprozessrecht*, 2nd ed., Heidelberg, C. F. Müller, 2006, p. 194. Hans Lechner and Rüdiger Zuck, *Bundesverfassungsgerichtsgesetz*, 5th ed., München, Beck, 2006, pages 411 and following. Dieter Umbach, Thomas Clemens and Franz-Wilhelm Dollinger (Orgs.), *Bundesverfassungsgerichtsgesetz*, 2nd ed., Heidelberg, C. F. Müller, 2005, p. 988. Michael Sachs, *Verfassungsprozessrecht*, 2nd ed., Frankfurt am Main, Recht und Wirtschaft, 2007, pages 62 and following.

[366] Jens Blüggel, *Unvereinbarkeitserklärung statt Normkassation durch das Bundesverfassungsgericht*, Berlin, Duncker und Humblot, 1998, p. 98. Roman Seer, "Rechtsschutz in Steuersachen", in Klaus Tipke e Joachim Lang, *Steuerrecht*, 19th ed., Köln, Otto Schmidt, 2008, § 22, margin number 286, p. 1.090.

[367] *BVerfGE* 37, 217 (261); 55, 100 (110); 61, 319 (356); 73, 40 (101); 82, 126 (155); 84, 9 (21); 84, 168 (187); 87, 114 (136); 87, 153 (178); 93, 386 (402).

(b) Declaration of incompatibility with judicial rules of transition to restore constitutionality immediately (*Unvereinbarkeitserklärung mit Übergangsregelung zur sofortigen Wiederherstellung einer verfassungsgemäßen Rechtslage*) – The Court upholds the effects produced by the unconstitutional norm, but immediately establishes rules of transition that apply until they are superseded by a legislative norm.[368]
(c) Declaration of incompatibility with a temporary provision to extend validity (*Unvereinbarkeitserklärung mit vorläufiger Weitergeltungsordnung*) – The Court upholds the effects produced by the unconstitutional norm in the past and temporarily extends these effects until such time as the legislative enacts a new rule with retroactive effects to the date of the decision.[369]
(d) Declaration of incompatibility with a final provision to extend validity and a *pro futuro* change order (*Unvereinbarkeitserklärung mit endgültiger Weitergeltungsordnung und pro-futuro-Änderungspflicht*) – The Court upholds the effects produced by the unconstitutional norm in the past, definitively extends these effects for a period, and tasks the legislative with the enactment of a new rule for the future.[370]

Thus there is not only one type of modulation of effects used by the German Federal Constitutional Court. There are many, and each is tailored to a specific situation and objective.

On one hand, these considerations show the importance of the theme for the investigation of legal certainty; on the other, however, they lead to a number of important questions: What are the preconditions for a statute to be declared incompatible? What does "legal certainty" mean for the purpose of manipulating the effects of decisions in the control of constitutionality? Can legal certainty be used as a justification to uphold the past efficacy of a tax statute that creates a tax? Can reasons of legal certainty be compared to budgetary reasons or financial losses?

These and other important questions will now be answered.

2.1.4.2 By the German Constitutional Court

2.1.4.2.1 Hypotheses of Application

2.1.4.2.1.1 Nullity Alone Does Not Restore Constitutionality

The cases in which the German Constitutional Court has traditionally used a declaration of incompatibility can be divided into two major groups: those in which a declaration of nullity of the statute alone does not restore the state of constitutionality, and those in which a declaration of nullity of the statute does not automatically restore the state of constitutionality.[371]

---

[368] *BVerfGE* 37, 217 (218 e 261); 73, 40 (101).

[369] *BVerfGE* 61, 319.

[370] *BVerfGE* 33, 303 (305); 87, 153 (178); 91, 186 (207); 93, 121 (148); 93, 165 (168); 99, 216 (244).

[371] Gerhard Habscheidt, *Der Anspruch des Bürgers auf Erstattung verfassungswidriger Steuern*, Köln, Otto Schmidt, 2003, p. 18. Jens Blüggel, *Unvereinbarkeitserklärung statt Normkassation durch das Bundesverfassungsgericht*, Berlin, Duncker und Humblot, 1998, p. 98.

In the first group (nullity alone does not restore constitutionality), there are statutes that violate the equality principle (*Gleichheitsgrundsatz*) and defective statutes.[372]

Inequitable statutes are laws that concretize a constitutional principle by granting a benefit from whose enjoyment some people are unjustifiably excluded. The principle of equality before the law is violated because the benefit is granted to the detriment of people in an equivalent situation to the beneficiaries. This is illustrated by the following examples.

With the aim of assuring the protection of fundamental rights, a statute created a mandatory legal aid service on all matters except labor law. Employees complained of unequal treatment compared to other groups and contested the statute, alleging violation of the equality principle due to lack of justification for the difference in treatment represented by exclusion of the benefit based on the criterion of the subject-matter.[373] Although the Court understood that the statute violated the constitutional equality clause, it decided to uphold the law's effects on the grounds that merely declaring the statute null and void would not eliminate the existing state of unconstitutionality because some form of guarantee had to be provided for in law, and that cancelling the guarantee in this law would benefit no one – this is the core issue – since it was incompatible with the Constitution owing to the inequality of its application and hence what it *did not guarantee*, rather than what it did guarantee. Moreover, the legislative should decide how best to restore the state of constitutionality, given its constitutional freedom to configure the protection of fundamental rights.[374]

With the aim of concretizing the principle of tax equality based on contributive capacity, a statute established the right to deduct the cost of education and childcare from the income tax base only for couples with two or more children under 18. Taxpayers with only one child claimed inequitable treatment because the cost of education was no lower for them and the statute violated the equality principle by failing to justify the difference in treatment based on the number of children.[375] Although it understood that the statute violated the constitutional principle of equality, the Court decided to uphold the law's effects on the grounds that simply declaring it null and void – again this is the nub – would not restore the state of constitutionality since some legal way of concretizing contributive capacity and prioritizing education was necessary and cancelling the instrument embodied in this law would benefit no one, not least because it was incompatible with the Constitution owing to the unequal relations resulting from its application and hence

[372]Christoph Moes, "Die Anordnung der befristeten Fortgeltung verfassungswidriger Steuergesetze durch das Bundesverfassungsgericht", *StuW* 1, p. 29, 2008.

[373]*BVerfGE* 88, 5, 13.

[374]Roman Seer, "Rechtsschutz in Steuersachen", in Klaus Tipke e Joachim Lang, *Steuerrecht*, 19th ed., Köln, Otto Schmidt, 2008, § 22, margin number 286, p. 1090.

[375]*BVerfGE* 47, 1. Jens Blüggel, *Unvereinbarkeitserklärung statt Normkassation durch das Bundesverfassungsgericht*, Berlin, Duncker und Humblot, 1998, p. 34.

what it *did not establish*, rather than exclusively what it did establish. Moreover, the Constitution did not predetermine how the legislative was to concretize the equality principle in tax law, so it behooved the legislative to decide on the best way to restore the state of constitutionality.

Also with the aim of concretizing the equality principle, a statute established a right to compensation for citizens who were forced provide public services during the Nazi period, starting on April 1, 1951, for some and on January 1, 1961, for others. Claiming unequal treatment compared to former public servants who would be compensated sooner, the disadvantaged citizens argued that the statute violated the equality principle, given the lack of justification for the difference in treatment represented by payment of compensation on arbitrarily different dates.[376] Although it understood that the statute violated the constitutional equality clause, the Court decided to uphold the law's effects on the grounds that simply declaring it null and void would not restore the state of constitutionality, since some legal way had to be found to compensate former public servants for their injuries, and cancelling the instrument embodied in this law would benefit no one, not least because it was incompatible with the Constitution owing to the unequal relations it created and hence what it *did not establish*, rather than exclusively what it did establish. Moreover, the Constitution did not determine any specific form of reparation that had to be chosen by the legislative. Thus it was again left to the legislative to decide how best to restore the state of constitutionality.

An analysis of these cases of violation of the duty of equality – in which the Constitutional Court acknowledges that simply declaring a law null and void does not restore the state of constitutionality and thus merely declares the statute incompatible with the Constitution, without anullment – demonstrates the presence of the following concurrent requirements:

(a) The legislator's freedom of configuration – Although the Constitution establishes ideals to be concretized by lawmakers, such as protection for fundamental rights or taxation according to contributive capacity, it does not predetermine the means, leaving a wide margin of appreciation to lawmakers in choosing the best way to proceed.
(b) The statute promotes a constitutional ideal to some extent – Although the statute violates the equality clause by creating unjustifiable inequality among citizens, it nonetheless introduces an instrument capable of concretizing a constitutional ideal up to a certain point.
(c) Declaring the statute null and void does not restore the state of constitutionality – A declaration of nullity would repeal the statutory norm from its inception, eliminating that part of the legal provision that promotes the constitutional ideal to some extent while failing to assure observance of the constitutional ideal on the other, i.e., anullment would discard the positive effect of the norm without cancelling out its negative effect.
(d) There are several ways of both promoting the constitutional ideal and restoring the state of constitutionality, and it is improper for the judiciary to adopt some while the legislative chooses others – If the Constitution is infringed yet a constitutional ideal is concretized to some extent, there are several ways to restore the state of

[376] *BVerfGE*, 18, 288. Jens Blüggel, *Unvereinbarkeitserklärung statt Normkassation durch das Bundesverfassungsgericht*, Berlin, Duncker und Humblot, 1998, p. 37.

> constitutionality, but it behooves the judiciary to extend a benefit or create another system of benefits on pain of violating the separation of powers, whereas the legislative is free to configure the system of benefits.

These presumptions show that the Constitutional Court does not declare laws null and void even if they infringe the Constitution because it takes the view that the lawmakers "aimed at the right target" and went some way toward promoting a constitutional ideal, albeit less than they should. Thus the Court acknowledges that "the best is the enemy of the good" or that "something is better than nothing", and, because it lacks the competence to improve the statute, upholds it to avoid regression. Between ruling the statute null and void, which would remove the positive effect created by the statute relative to the constitutional principle that justified passing it, and upholding its effects despite its unconstitutionality, the Court chooses the latter. As we have seen, the decision is based on overall defense of the Constitution and reinforced by the separation of powers principle. This is important and bears repeating: This solution promotes fundamental rights, and is compatible with the separation of powers principle.

In two situations, however, the Court avoids issuing declarations of incompatibility without anullment, preferring to issue a declaration of unconstitutionality, which entails anullment of the statute.

The first is when the Constitution does not give lawmakers freedom of configuration but predetermines what parliament must do and the latter chooses otherwise. This happens, for example, when instead of establishing a principle it dictates a rule with delimitation of its substantive content, predetermining the means to be used to promote the ideal.

The second is when it can be objectively presumed that the lawmakers will use their freedom of configuration along the same lines as the previous statute, whose efficacy is restored when a later statute is declared null and void. For example, a law allowing transsexuals to change their given names limited this right to people over 25 years of age.[377] The Court declared the statute incompatible with the Constitution and decided that the distinction based on age was unjustifiable. Since age had not been imposed as a condition by another statute that authorized sex change, the Court assumed the lawmakers would choose a rule without the age criterion from among the alternatives to eliminate the state of unconstitutionality. By proceeding in this manner, the Court avoided encroaching upon the legislative's freedom of configuration.

In this case, therefore, a declaration of nullity cannot restore the state of constitutionality required by the Constitution, and a declaration of incompatibility is the only way to realize the constitutional ideal.[378]

Also part of the group of cases in which a declaration of nullity of the statute alone does not restore the state of constitutionality, besides statutes contrary to the

[377] *BVerfGE* 88, 87, 97–101.

[378] Jens Blüggel, *Unvereinbarkeitserklärung statt Normkassation durch das Bundesverfassungsgericht*, Berlin, Duncker und Humblot, 1998, p. 43.

equality principle, are statutes deemed defective and hence incompatible with the Constitution because they leave out mandatory content or differentiation. This is illustrated by the following examples.

With the aim of promoting education and protecting young people, a statute established a right to "paid educational leave" and "paid leave for work to assist young people", requiring employers to release employees and pay their salaries during this leave. Feeling restrained in their freedom to exercise a profession, some employers contested the statute, alleging a violation to the principles of freedom of profession and freedom to exercise an economic activity.[379] Although the Court ruled that the statute effectively violated these principles, especially because it restricted them disproportionately, given that the measure was unnecessary and lacked mechanisms to compensate employers, it decided to uphold the law's effects, acknowledging that declaring the statute null and void would not restore the existing state of constitutionality. The law must promote education and protect youth, but this statute was incompatible with the Constitution because it fell short of the constitutional requirement. Eliminating it would be even more harmful to these ideals than upholding it. Moreover, while the statute could be improved, the judiciary could not decide on the best form of compensation for employers, whether via help from the employers' association, payment of damages by the public authorities or payment of compensation by institutions of education and youth welfare, for example. That would be the legislative's decision.

With the purpose of protecting health and consumers, a statute established the requirement of a license to operate a food business, which in turn required compliance with a number of rules but did not differentiate between shops that sold all kinds of food from those that sold only one kind or restricted kinds. Some retailers contested the statute on the grounds that it violated the principle of free exercise of economic activities, especially because by not differentiating between retail establishments by size or the type of goods sold the statute ended up placing excessive and unnecessary requirements on those that sold only one type of food.[380] Although the Court decided that the statute violated that principle, especially through disproportionate restriction by failing to provide for partial licenses with fewer requirements for certain types of retail establishment, it nevertheless upheld the effects of the statute, considering that a declaration of nullity would not restore the existing state of constitutionality. Laws were needed to protect health and consumers, but the statute in question was incompatible with the Constitution because it furthered this goal less than was constitutionally required. Eliminating it would therefore be more harmful to the promotion of these ideals than upholding its effects. According to the Court, the judiciary could not decide on the best way to establish appropriate treatment for small retailers. This was the legislative's prerogative.

---

[379] *BVerfGE* 77, 308.

[380] *BVerfGE* 34, 71, 71. Jens Blüggel, *Unvereinbarkeitserklärung statt Normkassation durch das Bundesverfassungsgericht*, Berlin, Duncker und Humblot, 1998, p. 47.

To regulate the labor market and assure employers' prerogatives, a statute prohibited severance payment for directors terminated with just cause even if a director was forced to remain unemployed by a non-compete clause. A group of citizens contested the statute on the grounds that it violated the freedom to exercise a profession, mainly by not differentiating among the many situations in which former directors may find themselves and hence excessively and disproportionately restricting the said principle.[381] Once again, although the Court decided that the statute violated the principle concerned, mainly owing to disproportionate restriction given the lack of provision for compensation in individual situations, it upheld the effects of the law because it acknowledged that declaring it null and void would not restore the existing state of constitutionality. Laws were needed to protect freedom of work and competition, and this law was incompatible with the Constitution because it furthered such goals less than was constitutionally required. Eliminating it would be worse than preserving it for the purposes of promoting the ideals concerned. According to the Court, only the legislative was competent to decide whether and how to differentiate between former employees.

With the purpose of regulating the wine trade and protecting consumers, a statute established a licensing requirement for wineries, restricting the grant of licenses to properties of at least five hectares, excepting only those that demonstrated land use restrictions or other impediments resulting from the variety of grape they produced. The legal exceptions were therefore limited. Some wineries contested the statute on the grounds that it violated the principle of freedom of economic activity, mainly because by allowing only two exceptions it prevented some properties from obtaining a license with other justifications.[382] Once again, although the Court decided that the statute violated the principle concerned owing to its rigidity, it upheld the law's effects because declaring it null and void would not restore the existing state of constitutionality. Laws were needed to protect health and consumers, but this one was incompatible with the Constitution because it promoted the ideals concerned less than was constitutionally required. It was better to uphold the law's effects than to eliminate it, and the judiciary was not empowered to establish new exceptions to the licensing rules.

In order to protect education, a statute mandated the donation of books to public libraries, without making any exceptions for smaller publishers or limited editions. Some publishers contested the statute on the grounds that it violated the principle of freedom of economic activity, mainly because its inflexibility ended up excessively restricting economic activity for certain publishers.[383] Again, although the Court ruled that the statute violated the principle, it decided to uphold its effects, acknowledging that a declaration of nullity would not restore the existing state of constitutionality. Laws were needed to protect education, but this one was

---

[381] *BVErfGE* 81, 242.

[382] *BVerfGE* 51, 193.

[383] *BVerfGE* 58, 137. Jens Blüggel, *Unvereinbarkeitserklärung statt Normkassation durch das Bundesverfassungsgericht*, Berlin, Duncker und Humblot, 1998, p. 53.

incompatible with the Constitution because it promoted the goal concerned less than was constitutionally required. Again, upholding the statute was preferred to eliminating it, and the judiciary lacked the competence to decide how to establish exceptions to the obligation to donate books to public libraries.

The examination of these cases of defective or rigid statutes, in which the Court acknowledges that declaring the statute null and void would not by itself restore the state of constitutionality, and therefore merely declares the statute incompatible with the Constitution without ruling it void, demonstrates the presence of the following concurrent requirements:

(a) The legislator's freedom of configuration – Although the Constitution establishes ideals to be concretized by lawmakers, such as protecting education or health, it does not predetermine the means, leaving a wide margin of appreciation to lawmakers in choosing the best way to proceed.
(b) The statute promotes a constitutional ideal to some extent – Although the statute violates some principle of freedom, usually by creating a disproportionate burden, it nonetheless defines a means of concretizing the constitutional ideal up to a certain point.
(c) Declaring a statute null and void does not restore the state of constitutionality – A declaration of nullity from the statute's inception would eliminate that part of the legal provision whose application promotes the constitutional ideal to some extent while failing to assure observance of the constitutional ideal.
(d) There are several ways to promote the constitutional ideal and restore the state of constitutionality, but it is improper for the judiciary to adopt some while the legislative chooses others – If the Constitution is infringed yet a constitutional ideal is concretized to some extent, there are several ways to restore the state of constitutionality, but it does not behoove the judiciary to create a new system or establish exceptions not established by statute.
(e) A statute under judicial review must have gaps and room for improvement – The problem with the statute is not exactly that it fails to promote the constitutional ideal, but that it does so disproportionately by lacking the necessary differentiation, because it is either too broad or too narrow.

2.1.4.2.1.2 Nullity Does Not Restore Constitutionality Automatically

Besides using the declaration of incompatibility in cases for which declaring the nullity of a statute does not restore the state of constitutionality, the German Constitutional Court also uses it in cases for which declaring the statute null and void does not automatically restore the state of constitutionality.[384]

This group includes cases of statutes that protect legal interests, assure the exercise of freedom and establish the state institutions required for certain rights to be exercised. In such cases the Constitution requires a normative minimum through a statute to guarantee the efficacy of fundamental rights such as legal guardianship of a child born out of wedlock, i.e. protection of the family, the right to choose schools freely, i.e. the right to education, or pay awards, i.e. the protection of labor rights.

---

[384] Jens Blüggel, *Unvereinbarkeitserklärung statt Normkassation durch das Bundesverfassungsgericht*, Berlin, Duncker und Humblot, 1998, p. 62.

What makes all such cases similar is that when there is a state purpose or a fundamental right is to be protected, the state must provide certain guarantees by statute, or create certain institutions. To this end the lawmakers create norms that promote the constitutional ideal, albeit unsatisfactorily. The Constitution, so to speak, requires "more law" and not "less law." In such cases the Court faces the alternative of eliminating the statute, which removes the efficacy of the legal provision whose application promotes the constitutional ideal, however unsatisfactorily, or upholding the provision, preserving the minimum produced by the lawmakers and assigning to them the task of restoring constitutionality in its entirety.[385]

It is worth noting that in the cases mentioned the lawmakers attempted to carry out their duty to protect fundamental rights (*Schutzpflichte*), but did so "with a deficit" or "disproportionately."[386] These cases do not concern statutes that restrict fundamental rights, let alone the exercise of competences provided for by constitutional rules. This observation is crucial.

2.1.4.2.2 Preconditions for Application

All the above cases and considerations lead to a number of conclusions, from a normative viewpoint, relative to the German Constitutional Court's use of the declaration of incompatibility with the upholding of a statute's effects, instead of declaring unconstitutional and annulling a statute.

First, there has to be a state *duty to act*. There must be a constitutional imposition that determines the pursuit of an ideal, such as protection of education, contributive capacity, equality, freedom to practice a profession and freedom of economic activity, as in the cases analyzed above. In other words, it is not enough for the state to have the power to act. It must have an *obligation* to act.

Second, there has to be state *freedom of action*. For this to occur, the statute under judicial review must aim to promote a constitutional ideal whose realization is determined by the institution of a principle. It is precisely the institution of the principle, in pursuit of a state purpose or to establish a fundamental right, that gives rise to two consequences that permit a statute to be declared incompatible with the Constitution: the possibility of gradual promotion (calibration) of the state of affairs whose realization is determined by the institution of the constitutional principle; the freedom (discretion or freedom of configuration) for the lawmakers to choose among all means necessary to the promotion of the goal. On one hand, the State has a *duty to act*, but on the other hand it is *free to decide how to do so*.

In other words, since the Constitution does not delimit the means but only imposes the realization of an end, thus leaving the lawmakers ample leeway to

[385]Ibidem, p. 79.

[386]Johannes Dietlein, *Die Lehre von den grundrechtlichen Schutzpflichten*, 2nd ed., Berlin, Duncker und Humblot, 2005, p. 128. Peter Szczekalla, *Die sogenannten grundrechtlichen Schutzpflichten im deutschen und europäischen Recht*, Berlin, Duncker und Humblot, 2002, p. 223.

choose the means, it falls within the jurisdiction of the legislative, not the judiciary, to define the statutory system to be implemented. Because the constitutional ideal can be realized in several stages, should the legislative choose by statute a method whose adoption produces effects that contribute to the promotion of the goal, albeit to an unsatisfactory degree (due to the relation of inequality it creates, the gap it opens up or the disproportion it causes), it is not the judiciary's task, via judicial review, to eliminate the positive yet insufficient effect produced by a statute considered incompatible with the Constitution, lest it restrict the Constitution instead of promoting it.

Third, weighing of the effects arising out of the declaration of nullity of the statute and the effects resulting from the declaration of incompatibility, with the Constitution in its entirety as a parameter, must show that *eliminating the statute does not restore but jeopardizes the state of constitutionality required by the Constitution*. Between declaring unconstitutionality (with the consequent declaration of nullity of the statute, so that the constitutional ideal is not furthered at all) and declaring only the incompatibility of the statute, whereby the norm is upheld (*Normerhaltung*) and the constitutional ideal is furthered to some extent without encroaching on the competence reserved to the legislative, the Court chooses the latter.

This is, as it were, the traditional or original jurisprudence of the Constitutional Court.[387] However, because Germany's Constitution is based on principles, the Court has been flexible in using the declaration of incompatibility, or has broadened it even more by extending it, even if exceptionally, to cases in which "reasons of legal certainty" or "budgetary planning expectations" could justify upholding the effects of unconstitutional statutes.

In the first case (reasons of legal certainty), the Court has exceptionally declared the compatibility of statutes that violate the Constitution when a declaration of nullity might cause a legal vacuum or a state of uncertainty. For example, a statute designed to effect a general review of salaries establishes unsatisfactory pay levels. Since the review must be implemented through a statute, declaring the statute null and void would create a legal vacuum, because the necessary statutory definition would be missing, and it would also generate uncertainty regarding wages already earned, as they would have been paid without a statutory definition.[388] The "reasons of legal certainty" are therefore used to assure the exercise of a right that depends on statutory definition. It bears repeating that the Court uses legal certainty as the justification to uphold benefits set forth unconstitutionally, and not as a basis for justifying the restriction of fundamental rights.

In the second case ("budgetary planning expectations"), the Court simply upholds the validity of the statute without much justification, in order not to frustrate budgetary plans already presented. This approach, based on the financial effects of a declaration of unconstitutionality, has two phases.

---

[387] Gerhard Habscheidt, *Der Anspruch des Bürgers auf Erstattung verfassungswidriger Steuern*, Köln, Otto Schmidt, 2003, p. 18.

[388] *BVerfGE* 32, 199 (217); 34, 9 (43); 44, 249 (264), entre outras.

In the first phase, the Court only declares unconstitutionality with prospective efficacy because it concludes that the duty to refund overpayments would affect budget planning and execution expectations.[389] As mentioned above, the basis for the presumptive principle of budgetary trust lies in reliance on the state's capacity, grounded in the budget, to execute financial plans and make decisions that will not be frustrated in the future by declarations of unconstitutionality concerning taxes with retroactive effects, entailing an obligation to refund unlawfully collected tax.[390]

This position has been heavily criticized by legal scholars.[391] In response, as what may be called a second phase of jurisprudential change concerning the principle of budgetary protection, the Court has finally established a number of restrictions, even in cases of high financial impact for the state, determining that *pro futuro* efficacy does not include the following cases:

(a) Cases in which declarations of incompatibility (*Anlaßfall*) are issued – Since the Court is declaring unconstitutionality for the first time in the instant case (*Ausgangsfall*), denying the declaration of nullity sought by the plaintiff would excessively restrict his or her fundamental rights of freedom, and right to judicial protection, by giving "stones instead of bread" (*Steine, statt Brot*) and offering a "Pyrrhic victory" (*Pyrrhussieg*).[392]
(b) Parallel proceedings (*Parallelverfahren*) in which the same issue is disputed – Besides the instant proceedings (*Ausgangsverfahren*) where the Court presents its position, others that have also begun in which taxpayers file the same claim are excluded from the prospective effect to respect the fundamental right to judicial protection.[393]
(c) Cases in which there has not been an irreversible collection proceeding by the administration – Since under article 363, II, of the German Tax Code, the administration is empowered to order, as it were, a stay of execution (*Aussetzung der Vollziehung*) of tax debts, it must necessarily stop demanding the tax when it learns of its unconstitutionality.

---

389 *BVerfGE* 87, 153 (178 e ss.); *BVerfGE* 93, 121 (148); 165 (178). Christoph Moes, "Die Anordnung der befristeten Fortgeltung verfassungswidriger Steuergesetze durch das Bundesverfassungsgericht", *StuW* 1, p. 30, 2008.

390 Klaus-Dieter Drüen, "Haushaltsvorbehalt bei der Verwerfung verfassungswidriger Steuergesetze?", *FR* 6, p. 291, 1999.

391 Roman Seer, "Die Unvereinbarkeitserklärung des BVerfT am Beispiel seiner Rechtsprechung zum Abgabenrecht", *NJW* 5, p. 289, 1996. B. Sangmeister, "Das Bundesverfassungsgericht und das Verfassungsrecht", *StuW* 2, pages 176 and following, 2001. Klaus Tipke, "Rezensionen. Gerhard Habscheidt. Der Anspruch des Bürgers auf Erstattung verfassungswidriger Gesetze", *StuW* 2, p. 187, 2004. Christoph Moes, "Die Anordnung der befristeten Fortgeltung verfassungswidriger Steuergesetze durch das Bundesverfassungsgericht", *StuW* 1, p. 30, 2008.

392 Roman Seer e Jörg Peter Müller, "Begrenzung der Wirkungen seiner Richtersprüche durch den EuGH", *IWB* n. 5, Gruppe 2, Fach 11, p. 264, 2008. Klaus–Dieter Drüen, "Haushaltsvorbehalt bei der Verwerfung verfassungswidriger Steuergesetze?", *FR* 6, p. 292, 1999. Christoph Moes, "Die Anordnung der befristeten Fortgeltung verfassungswidriger Steuergesetze durch das Bundesverfassungsgericht", *StuW* 1, p. 34, 2008. Christian Waldhoff, "Recent developments relating to the retroactive effect of decisions of the ECJ", *Common Market Law Review* 46, p. 13, 2009 (manuscript). Ben Juratowitch, *Retroactivity and the Common Law*, Oxford, Hart, 2008, p. 210.

393 Roman Seer, "Rechtsschutz in Steuersachen", in Klaus Tipke e Joachim Lang, *Steuerrecht*, 19th ed., Köln, Otto Schmidt, 2008, § 22, margin number 288, p. 1091.

Thus it is important to note, first, that even in cases where budgetary problems serve as a foundation for the assignment of prospective efficacy to the decisions of the German Constitutional Court, the principle of "budgetary trust protection" relates more to the state's capacity to operate (*Funktionsfähigkeit des Staates*) than to the legal certainty principle, strictly speaking. The state's capacity to operate serves as a permanent internal limitation of fundamental rights, in the sense that an individual cannot demand from the state something that, if supplied, may compromise its normal actions.[394] Moreover, upholding the past effects of a statute based on a presumed protection of budgetary trust not only assumes an extreme situation of state strangulation, but also has been determined without including the instant case, parallel proceedings, and cases where the administration can still cease collecting or could have reasonably stopped collecting. Even these exceptional cases have been severely criticized by legal scholars. This why Seer and Müller make a statement worth quoting at this point: "The German Constitutional Court's approach to judicature is not worthy of imitation (*nachahmenswert*)".[395] In the same sense, when referring to the Court's upholding of unconstitutional tax statutes, Moes says: "This concept should be abandoned."[396]

These, then, are the situations in which the German Constitutional Court uses the declaration of compatibility. As we have seen, its use depends on the concurrent presence of a number of requisites. These requisites, however, result from constitutional norms. They assign, or do not assign, freedom of configuration to the lawmakers by establishing an ideal to be realized without predetermining the means to be chosen, and they establish the jurisdiction of each branch. In other words, the fact that the declaration of compatibility is used in this or that manner, with more or less flexibility, by the German Constitutional Court says nothing, nothing at all, about its appropriate or necessary use by the Supreme Court in Brazil: The two Constitutions are different, and so the norms, jurisdictions and even the very meaning of legal certainty are different, so that the use of this declaration may or must be different, if there are sufficient normative differences.

Given all these considerations, we must return to the initial questions: Can the STF declare the incompatibility of a statute without ruling it null and void, in the case of the creation of taxes? Accepting, based on Law 9868/98, that legal certainty can be used as a justification for upholding the validity of an unconstitutional statute, what ought to be the meaning of "reasons of legal certainty"? Can it be used as a justification in favor of the state to uphold the past efficacy of a statute that creates a tax? Can loss of revenues be included in the concept of legal certainty?

We can now begin to answer these questions.

---

[394] Martin Kriele, "Grundrechte und demokratischer Gestaltungsspielraum", in Paul Kirchhof and Josef Isensee, *Handbuch des Staatsrechts* 5, Heidelberg, C. F. Müller, 1992, § 110, margin number 65, pages 134 and following.

[395] Roman Seer e Jörg Peter Müller, "Begrenzung der Wirkungen seiner Richter-sprüche durch den EuGH", *IWB* n. 5, Gruppe 2, Fach 11, p. 262, 2008.

[396] Christoph Moes, "Die Anordnung der befristeten Fortgeltung verfassungswidriger Steuergesetze durch das Bundesverfassungsgericht", *StuW* 1, p. 36, 2008.

2.1.4.3 By the Supreme Court

2.1.4.3.1 Initial Considerations

Article 27 of Law 9868/98 determines that, when declaring unconstitutional a statute or normative act, Brazil's Supreme Court (STF) may, "for reasons of legal certainty or exceptional social interest," restrict the effects of that declaration or decide that its efficacy begins only when it becomes *res iudicata* or at some other moment to be specified. Having seen how the German Constitutional Court has applied modulation, we will now analyze how modulation is used by the STF.

At the outset it is worth noting two normative phenomena that should not be confused, although they are very similar and have similar repercussions.

A first major distinction must be made between the (external) effects of unconstitutionality rulings in concentrated control and the (internal) content of unconstitutionality rulings in diffuse control. Thus it is one thing for the STF to declare a challenged norm unconstitutional, modulating the *effects* of the decision by determining prospective efficacy (*pro futuro* or *ex nunc*), and quite another for the Court not to declare the unconstitutionality of a norm, an act or their effects because it is prevented from doing so, such as when a situation has become consolidated over time, for example. In the former case, the content of the decision is *un*constitutionality, but its effects are produced only in the future; in the latter, the very content of the decision is *cons*titutionality. There the Court declares unconstitutionality; here it does not do so.

This distinction is clear in judgment RE 78,209. In a ruling on the validity of acts performed by law clerks while being employed as bailiffs, according to a statute that was eventually declared unconstitutional, the STF found "valid the attachment carried out by agents of the executive".[397] Justice Aliomar Baleeiro's opinion is enlightening: "The unconstitutionality of the São Paulo law dated December 3, 1971, is one thing. Quite another is the legal consequences of the substantive acts and even the legal acts they performed by order and under the responsibility of judges, as clerks of the court, before the said law was declared unconstitutional." In this respect, the STF made the acts performed inviolable through *diffuse* control of constitutionality and the *internal content* of the decision in itself. On one hand, it did not modulate the effects of this decision entered in diffuse control of constitutionality. Its *content* consisted of recognition of the constitutionality of the acts performed, albeit based on an unconstitutional statute. On the other hand, nor did it modulate the *effects* of the unconstitutionality ruling in concentrated control of constitutionality, which simply did not take specific situations into account. It bears repeating that in the case in point there was no modulation of the *effects* of the diffuse control ruling; the *content* of the decision was altered on the grounds that the acts performed could no longer be reviewed or undone. In other words, legal certainty served as the criterion to configure the *content* but not *the effects* of this judicial review.

[397] RE n. 78.209, 1st Panel, Rep. Justice Aliomar Baleeiro, *DJ* 9 Oct 1974.

The STF used the same analysis in RE 78,594. Asked to decide whether a public servant's investiture as a bailiff was legal, given the unconstitutionality of the state law that authorized the appointment, the STF ruled that "the act he performed is valid" and rejected the appeal.[398] Thus strictly speaking the Court did not modulate the *effects* of the unconstitutionality ruling, but later, in diffuse constitutionality control, changed its reading of the *content* of that ruling in order to uphold the validity of the disputed act.

Justice Gilmar Mendes was therefore mistaken when he said the STF frequently modulates the effects of diffuse constitutionality rulings. He made this statement in HC 82,959, where the Court analyzed the constitutionality of a norm governing the progression of custody levels in the case of heinous crimes.[399] Technically speaking, the cases to which he referred did not involve external prior modulation of the effects of decisions entered in concentrated constitutionality control, but later internal reshaping of the content of diffuse constitutionality rulings.[400]

Moreover, strictly speaking there was no modulation of effects in RE 442,683, the aforementioned extraordinary appeal against internal promotion of public employees without a competitive open examination.[401] In this case the STF upheld the effects of the disputed act in diffuse control on the grounds that it was in the public interest to keep government employees in their current posts, which they had held for a long time, that a long period had elapsed between the promotion and the filing of the challenge, and that both the employees and the administration had acted in good faith. Thus there was no modulation of the effects. The content of the judgment was to uphold the disputed acts by denying the extraordinary appeal. Justice Ellen Gracie was therefore wrong to say that the reporting justice "appropriately modulated the effects of this declaration of unconstitutionality." This statement would make sense only on a view that the Court's diffuse control restriction of the *ex tunc* effects of the earlier concentrated control ruling of unconstitutionality in effect constituted a modulation. Based on this questionable view, a diffuse control decision that was entered after the concentrated control unconstitutionality ruling and partially truncated its retroactive effects could also be deemed modulation. Concrete diffuse control restriction of the retroactive effects of the unconstitutionality ruling would also be a kind of modulation, albeit in reverse.

In fact, it is important not to confuse the *effects* of a decision with the *content* of a decision, on one hand, and the *abstract* plane of the a *norm* with the *concrete* plane of the *act*, on the other. In this respect, German legal doctrine makes the appropriate separation between the plane of the norm (*Normebene*) and the plane

[398]RE n.78.594, 2nd Panel, Rep. Justice Bilac Pinto, *DJ* 30 Oct 1974.

[399]HC n.82.959, Full Court, Rep. Justice Marco Aurélio, *DJ* 1 Sep 2006.

[400]RE n.78.594, Rep. Justice Bilac Pinto, *DJ* 4 Nov 1974; RE n.79.620, Rep. Justice Aliomar Baleeiro, *DJ* 13 Dec 1974; RE n.78.809, Rep. Justice Aliomar Baleeiro, *DJ* 11 Oct 1974; RE n.122.202, Rep. Justice Francisco Rezek, *DJ* 8 Apr 1994.

[401]RE n.442.683, 2nd Panel, Rep. Justice Carlos Velloso, *DJ* 24 Mar 2006.

of the single act (*Einzelaktebene*).[402] This distinction is essential because cases in which the content of a decision is changed owing to the inviolability of the acts performed, besides involving the diffuse control of constitutionality, are typically concerned with concrete and individual elements that cannot be analyzed in the concentrated control of constitutionality.

In sum, it is important not to confuse the cases in which the STF refrains from ruling on unconstitutionality on the grounds that the situation has been consolidated with the cases in which it declares unconstitutionality but restricts the effects of its ruling.

A second major distinction must be made between cases in which the STF declares the unconstitutionality of a given norm – with total declaratory efficacy, but with terms or rules of transition that make compliance with the decision more feasible – and cases in which the temporal effects of an unconstitutionality ruling are changed. In the former, strictly speaking the STF does not restrict the unconstitutionality ruling, which is total. What it does is determine a rule for the transition or a period of adjustment to the declaratory efficacy of the decision. In the latter, the duration of the unconstitutionality ruling's effects are changed so that relative to a specified period the norm is declared incompatible with the Constitution but not null and void. When a judge gives the losing party time to comply with a decision, or when the law itself grants time for overpayments to be refunded, as in the case of writs of payment allowing the state to pay off debts in installments, these are examples not of modulation of the effects of the decision, but only of the granting of time for compliance.

To summarize, among the many cases in which the STF declares unconstitutionality, it is crucial not to confuse those in which it does not restrict the temporal effects of the declaration (although it establishes rules of transition to enable execution) with those in which the scope of the unconstitutionality ruling is altered by preservation of some or all of the past effects of the unconstitutional norm. This involves making a subtle distinction between the *temporal efficacy of the decision* and the *temporal efficacy of the declaration* contained in the decision, in terms of the impact on its substantive scope. In the latter case the extent of the unconstitutionality is changed; in the former case it is not.

The above thoughts about the need to differentiate between cases are of the highest importance. This is because under the broader label of "modulation of the temporal effects of judicial review decisions," the content of a decision may be confused with its effects, on one hand, and modulation of the temporal effects of a declaratory unconstitutionality *decision* may be confused with modulation of the temporal effects of the *declaration* of unconstitutionality contained in the unconstitutionality decision. It looks the same, but it is not.

---

[402] Jörg Ipsen, *Rechtsfolgen der Verfassungswidrigkeit von Norm und Eizelakt*, Baden-Baden, Nomos, 1980, p. 266.

Another fundamental aspect that must not go unnoticed is the difference between the Brazilian and German legal orders. Again, the fact that the German Constitutional Court assigns certain kinds of effects to its decisions says nothing about the compatibility of the very same effects with the Brazilian legal order. This is trivial up to a point, but nonetheless it is not always taken into consideration by enthusiasts of the mere transposition of supposedly more developed foreign legal models to Brazil – as Ataliba and Maior Borges remind us.[403] In this respect, it is necessary to point out a few differences between the two legal systems, which may at least help narrow down the scope for application of the efficacy models concerned within the Brazilian legal order, mostly in tax matters. Within a broad universe of distinctions, two are especially relevant for the theme at hand: a difference in the constitutional rules of tax competence, and a difference in the constitutional rules for judicial review.

First, the "National Tax System" established by the Brazilian Constitution of 1988 is made up essentially of competence rules, whereas the chapter on Finance (*das Finanzwesen*) in Germany's Basic Law only lists types of tax, without determining aspects of the incidence hypotheses. As a result, the STF focuses on verifying the exercise of power within the scope assigned by the competence rules and taxation principles. This makes a hugely significant difference: In Brazil, declarations of unconstitutionality within this scope mostly involve tax laws that overstep the bounds set by aspects of the competence rules; in Germany, where rules of tax competence such as Brazil's do not exist, the Constitutional Court declares unconstitutionality when the lawmakers' freedom of configuration conflicts with the taxation principles.

This distinction is key to the efficacy of judicial review. In Brazil, the STF is the guardian of the Constitution and hence must verify the exercise of the power to tax within the scope established by the competence rules and in conformity with constitutional principles. Because these rules are set out in the Constitution itself, their breach is unconstitutional by definition. The exercise of power is allowed only within the scope delimited by the rules, so that any exercise outside that scope must be considered null and void. Although this effect cannot be considered a logical consequence of the positivation of competence rules, it can certainly be deemed a *general effect implied* by that positivation. If concrete weighing of conflicting principles were the desired method, the framers of the Constitution would have chosen a different form of normatization. In Germany, where there are no competence rules to establish the substantive aspects of taxation, the Constitutional Court must weigh the democratic principle against the principles that conflict with it. In contrast with the Brazilian situation, the absence of competence rules does not entrain a specific effect; the conflict between principles is what determines the result. Again this is not a logical consequence but it can be said that the judiciary's comparative freedom

[403]Geraldo Ataliba, *Sistema Constitucional Tributário brasileiro*, São Paulo, Ed. RT, 1968, p. 39. José Souto Maior Borges, *Obrigação tributária – Uma introdução metodológica*, São Paulo, Saraiva, 1984, p. 7.

to configure the effects of its decisions is implied by the absence of positivated competence rules. This means the institution of a system of principles is the key to the German Constitutional Court's comparative freedom to shape the content and effects of its decisions.

What is meant by the above is that whereas the institution of competence rules by the Brazilian Constitution implies the absence of power outside its limits, and hence the nullity of acts performed beyond them as a general rule, the lack of such rules in Germany's Basic Law requires that the Constitutional Court determine the limits of the legislative's freedom of configuration by weighing between principles, and this greater breadth in the power of the Court concerning the content of its decisions also applies to their effects.

Second, whereas the Brazilian Constitution contains a number of rules relating to the declaration of unconstitutionality of statutes, analyzed below, Germany's Basic Law does not contain any such express provisions aside from article 100, which governs the declaration of unconstitutionality. This matter is directly regulated by the Federal Constitutional Court Law (*Bundesverfassungsgerichtsgesetz*). This means that the Brazilian Constitution deals with the issue itself, mentioning only the declaration of unconstitutionality, with no mention of a declaration of compatibility. More importantly, it directly regulates certain matters relating to the efficacy of the STF's decisions. For example: Final decisions on the merits in direct *unconstitutionality* suits (ADIs) and in declaratory *constitutionality* suits (ADCs) produce *efficacy for all* and are *binding* on other bodies of the judiciary and on the direct and indirect public administration at federal, state and city levels (article 102, paragraph 2); summaries of precedents (*súmulas*), to be published after repeated decisions on the same subject-matter, are *binding* on other bodies of the judiciary and on the direct and indirect public administration at federal, state and city levels (article 103-A), in order to assure the *validity*, *interpretation* and *efficacy* of certain norms concerning which there are disputes between judicial bodies, or between these and the public administration, that cause grave legal uncertainty and significant growth in the volume of lawsuits concerning identical subject-matter (article 103-A, paragraph 1); if unconstitutionality is declared on the grounds that measures to make a constitutional norm *effective* have been omitted, the competent authority is notified to take the *necessary measures*, within 30 days if it is an administrative body (art. 103, paragraph 2); and the STF is competent to decide on "complaints" (*reclamações*) concerning the preservation of its competence and the authority of its decisions (article 102, I, "1").

As can be seen, besides counterposing "unconstitutionality" and "constitutionality" without providing for any intermediate form of decision between these two limits, the framers created instruments to make the Constitution effective, with binding effect on all authorities that might question the validity of infraconstitutional norms. Their chief concern was to *restore the state of constitutionality* by assigning the greatest efficacy possible to the STF's decisions, including the mechanism of "complaints", which leapfrog all instances to accelerate this restoration. None, absolutely none, of these provisions has any parallel in Germany's Basic Law, which does not mention (un)constitutionality, or effects, or (in)validity of infraconstitutional norms. These issues, which the Brazilian Constitution takes upon itself, are left to the ordinary infraconstitutional legislator in the German system.

Another element must be noted, and indeed is highlighted by Machado Derzi: In dealing with unconstitutionality, the Constitution uses the expressions "direct unconstitutionality suit" and "declaratory constitutionality suit" (article 102, I, "a", and paragraph 2), as well as "when unconstitutionality is declared" (article 103, paragraph 2), and establishes the STF's competence to "declare the unconstitutionality of treaties and federal laws" (article 102, III, "b"), alluding precisely to the declaratory effect of these decisions. Thus "by logical inference the declaratory character of such decisions, extracted from the Constitution itself and corroborated by the classical texts mentioned earlier, entails *ex tunc* efficacy, which is inherent in decisions said to be 'declaratory'."[404]

The key point of these observations is that whereas the Brazilian Constitution itself details the process of judicial review, with the purpose of more effectively and comprehensively preventing any kind of violation of the Constitution, in Germany this is not in the Basic Law but left to be defined by the legislative. This distinction cannot be overlooked.

This is not to say that the assignment of prospective efficacy by the STF is necessarily and in all cases irreconcilable with the Constitution. The argument is that whatever the STF's constitutional space may be, it is inevitably smaller than that assigned by Germany's Basic Law to the Constitutional Court. The Brazilian Constitution is explicit on judicial review, establishing mechanisms to debar unconstitutionality with the greatest possible efficacy and breadth, and focusing particularly on the direct and indirect public administration at the federal, state, and city levels. The competence to issue binding precedents that must be obeyed by all three branches of government, regulation of general efficacy in matters of concentrated control of constitutionality and the power to require the legislative to take measures necessary to avoid unconstitutionality are examples that illustrate very clearly the extent to which the Constitution focuses on swift and efficient restoration of the state of constitutionality by removing unconstitutional statutes. In other words, it can be said that as a rule the Constitution is intolerant of any kind of preservation of states of unconstitutionality. That being true, simply transplanting any kind of foreign experience into the Brazilian legal order without paying proper attention to its specific features is to disregard this concern with the avoidance of any state of unconstitutionality.

Having analyzed these more general questions pertaining to the difference between the German and Brazilian systems, we must now examine the cases in which the STF has mitigated the ordinary effect of the declaration of unconstitutionality of statutes.

[404]Misabel de Abreu Machado Derzi, *Modificações da jurisprudência no Direito Tributário*, São Paulo, Noeses, 2009, p. 238.

2.1.4.3.2 Cases of Mitigated Declaration of Unconstitutionality

In some cases, strictly speaking the SFT does not change the declaratory effect of the decision by not declaring the unconstitutionality of the norm; however, even if it declares unconstitutionality, it establishes a transition rule or a time frame for compliance with the decision. Hence the efficacy of the decision is retroactive, but in order to avoid certain consequences deemed undesirable the Court establishes a transition rule or deadline.

In such cases the Court upholds the effects produced by the unconstitutional norm, but immediately determines a transitory norm to be applied until the advent of a legislative norm.

In RE 401,953-1 the STF examined the constitutionality of a state statute that, in order to remedy supposed regional and social inequalities, totally and suddenly excluded a municipality from the sharing and transfer of service tax (ISS).[405] The Court ruled the law unconstitutional on the grounds that it violated article 158, IV, sole paragraph, of the Constitution, and ordered recalculation of municipal participation coefficients in order to give the municipality concerned its constitutional share. The Court noted, however, that "since recalculation of the shares might decrease the shares of other cities in the State of Rio de Janeiro, potentially offsetting monies received with monies from future fiscal years, the execution of this decision must not impair the reasonable and proportional financial support of municipalities. The statute that will govern recalculation of credits pertaining to past periods and their transfer to the appellant must therefore also provide for offsetting and installment mechanisms in conditions that do not cut off future transfers to municipalities" (decision summary, items 6 and 7).

2.1.4.3.3 Cases of Declaration of Incompatibility

In other decisions the STF has not confined its action to establishing a transition rule or a deadline for compliance with a declaratory unconstitutionality ruling, but has also changed the legal qualification of acts performed or past events which, albeit contrary to the Constitution, do not lose their efficacy. Thus instead of changing the temporal effects of the decision, it changes the temporal effects of the unconstitutionality ruling. It does so in several ways, as set out below.

2.1.4.3.3.1 Declaration of Incompatibility with Total pro futuro General Efficacy

In these cases the Court simply assigns *ex nunc* effects to the unconstitutionality ruling, requiring the legislative to enact a new statute.

In REs 197,917 and 266,994 the Court analyzed the compatibility of city statutes with article 29, IV, of the Constitution, specifically whether the number of city

[405] RE n.401.953-1, Full Panel, Rep. Justice Joaquim Barbosa, *DJ* 21 Sep 2007.

councilors was proportional to the population.[406] The plenary ruled that the city statutes were unconstitutional, giving rise to the question of whether the ruling could have declaratory effects. The Court declared prospective efficacy on the grounds that past effects could severely impair organization of the administration and damage the credibility of the city legislative system, given the statutes hitherto enacted. Thus the rationale for the decision was legal certainty as a requirement of the institutional stability of law and the credibility of the legal order as a whole, for cities and citizens. The summary of the decision says so itself: "Legal certainty principle – Exceptional situation in which declaration of nullity with ordinary *ex tunc* effect would constitute *grave* threat to *entire* legislative *system* in force – Prevalence of public interest to assure *pro futuro* effect of incidental declaration of unconstitutionality, as an exception" (emphasis added). Furthermore, upholding past effects did not harm individuals. On the contrary, it benefited them by leaving the statutes enacted in place and allowing the past effects of the administrative machine to persist.

In ADI 3615 the STF analyzed the compatibility of the redefinition of the territorial borders of the City of Conde, Paraíba State, with article 18, paragraph 4, of the 1988 Constitution, according to which the creation, incorporation, merging and dismemberment of municipalities must be effected by state statute, within the time frame determined by a federal supplementary law, following a plebiscite open to the population of the municipalities concerned and publication of municipal feasibility studies presented and published according to law.[407] Because the territorial borders of the municipality were redrawn without a plebiscite open to the populations of neighboring localities, but only with opinion polls, petitions and declarations by community organizations, the Court ruled the city statute unconstitutional. However, considering that the suit was filed in 2005 and the statute enacted in 1989, in the intervening 16 years "several legal situations were consolidated, mostly concerning financial, tax and administrative matters, which cannot be undone from their inception on pain of violating legal certainty" (Justice Ellen Gracie's opinion), and the Court therefore declared the law unconstitutional with *ex nunc* efficacy. The rationale for the decision can be reconstructed on the basis of legal certainty as a requirement of the institutional stability of law and credibility of the legal order: Prospective efficacy was determined in order to ensure that the acts performed were upheld and the organization of the municipalities preserved. It should also be noted that upholding past effects did not harm individuals; on the contrary, they benefited from legal consolidation of acts that had been consolidated in practice. Finally, it is worth stressing that Justice Eros Grau concurred with the opinion of the reporting justice in favor of declaring the law unconstitutional, especially "in order to surmount the uncertainties that fuel undesirable conflicts between municipalities." Thus the Court declared the disputed norm unconstitutional to

[406] RE n.197.917-8, Full Court, Rep. Justice Maurício Corrêa, *DJ* 7 May 2004; RE n.266.994, Full Court, Rep. Justice Maurício Corrêa, *DJ* 21 May 2004.

[407] ADI n.3.615-7, Full Court, Rep. Justice Ellen Gracie, *DJ* 9 Mar 2007.

preserve legal certainty in its future dimension of the calculability of law, while upholding the acts performed to assure legal certainty in its past dimension of requiring the inviolability of consolidated situations.

In ADI 2907 the Court considered an ordinance issued by the President of the Amazonas State Court of Appeal governing the working hours of court workers.[408] It decided that although the separation of powers had not been violated since the order did not change the work week of the employees concerned, it was formally defective, as a resolution should have been issued instead of an ordinance, and it should have been signed by a collegiate body instead of a single person, in breach of article 96, I, "a" and "b", of the Federal Constitution. However, the Court declared *ex nunc* efficacy of the decision "so that the acts performed will not be nullified and a pretext for their cancellation will not be offered" (Justice Cézar Peluso's opinion).

2.1.4.3.3.2 Declaration of Incompatibility with Partial pro futuro General Efficacy

In these situations the Court assigns *ex nunc* effects to the decision of unconstitutionality but has these effects apply to non-consolidated cases. This is a sort of retrospective efficacy: Cases considered irreversible are not affected, but those which can somehow be changed are excluded from the scope of the decision.

In HC 82,959 the Court analyzed the compatibility between Law 8072/90, article 1, concerning progression of custody levels for prisoners convicted of heinous crimes, and article 5, XLVI, of the Constitution.[409] Recalling that the prime objective of progression from a closed prison to a semi-open and then an open facility was the resocialization of inmates, it ruled that imposition of incarceration in a closed facility through a norm conflicted with the guarantee of individualized punishment in this article. However, because the Court had previously ruled that banning progression outright for heinous crimes was constitutional, on this occasion it decided that it had to adjust the effects of the declaration of unconstitutionality. The opinion of Justice Gilmar Mendes, strongly based on German jurisprudence (mostly Karl Larenz and Peter Häberle) and U.S. case law on prospective overruling (a version of the jurisprudential change discussed above), argued that modulation of effects should also be used in the concrete control of constitutionality (page 50 of the opinion), based on constitutional arguments and not on mere convenience. The rationale given for this view was that although the "principle" of nullity remains the "rule", in some situations, even in diffuse control, the Court can restrict the effects of the decision where nullity causes a vacuum. a benefit incompatible with the equality principle or damage to the constitutional legal system itself (page 58), as indeed the Court had done on several occasions[410]: "In other words, reasons of legal certainty

---

[408] ADI n.2.907, Full Court, Rep. Justice Eros Grau, *DJ* 16 May 2008.

[409] HC n.82.959, Full Court, Rep. Justice Marco Aurélio, *DJ* 01 Sep 2006.

[410] RE n.78.594, Rep. Justice Bilac Pinto, *DJ* 04 Nov 1974; RE n.79.620, Rep. Justice Aliomar Baleeiro, *DJ* 13 Dec 1974; RE n.78.809, Rep. Justice Aliomar Baleeiro, *DJ* 11 Oct 1974; RE

may pose an obstacle to judicial review of acts performed on the basis of a statute declared unconstitutional" (page 63). He concluded by saying that "in the case at hand, it can be seen that declaring unconstitutionality with *ex tunc* effects would cause impacts throughout the current system." Along these lines, the Court declared *pro futuro* efficacy in order to avoid applying progression to prison terms that had already expired, and preserved the competence of the presiding judge to analyze other requirements to individualize punishment.

In RE 560,626 the Court analyzed whether norms relative to tax statutes of limitations had the same nature as general norms of tax law. If so, they were reserved to supplementary statutes by both the previous Constitution (article 18, paragraph 1, of the 1967–69 Constitution) and the current Constitution (article 146, III, "b", of the 1988 Constitution).[411] The Court decided that state and city statutes could not specify periods of limitation because "allowing different rules on these issues in different federal entities would violate the prohibition of unequal treatment of taxpayers in equivalent positions, as well as legal certainty." In light of the above, the Court declared articles 45 and 46 of Law 8212/91 unconstitutional for infringing article 146, III, "b", of the 1988 Constitution and Decree-Law 1569/77, article 5, sole paragraph, based on paragraph 1 of article 18 of the 1967–69 Constitution. However, it modulated the effects of the decision by declaring legitimate "the payments effected within the time frames stipulated by articles 45 and 46 of Law 8212/91 and those not disputed before the date on which this judgment is entered". Justice Gilmar Mendes concurred, "given the repercussions and potential uncertainty; but I am trying to limit the possibility of claiming refunds for overpayment under these conditions, except for claims filed before the judgment is entered". Finally, the reporting justice concluded the judgment by declaring the unconstitutionality of the disputed provisions "but with modulation of the effects, *ex nunc*, only for claims of refunds for overpayment filed after the present date, the date of the judgment".

2.1.4.3.3.3 Declaration of Incompatibility with Provisional Extension of Validity

In these situations the Court upholds the effects produced by the unconstitutional norm in the past, provisionally extending these effects for a period, until the legislative establishes a new rule with retroactive effects to the date of the decision. In ADIs 2240, 3316, 3489 and 3689 the Court was asked to decided whether the creation of municipalities without the intermediation of a supplementary law was compatible with article 18, paragraph 4, of the Constitution, according to which a state law was required, albeit within a time frame determined by a

n.122.202, Rep. Justice Francisco Rezek, *DJ* 08 Apr 1994. In other situations, the Court has weighed, but decided that a justifying situations did not occur: ADI n.513, Rep. Justice Célio Borja, *RTJ* 141; ADI n.1.102, Rep. Justice Maurício Corrêa, *DJ* 17 Nov 1995.

[411] RE n.560.626, Full Court, Rep. Justice Gilmar Mendes, *DJe* 5 Dec 2008.

federal supplementary law.[412] Once again, in order to assure the organization of the administration and the validity of past statutes enacted on the basis of the disputed law, the Court declared it unconstitutional but guaranteed its "enforcement for 24 months, to give state lawmakers time to establish a new rule". The rationale for this decision, in line with the precedents referred to earlier, can be reconstructed on the basis of legal certainty as the requirement of institutional stability of law and credibility of the legal order. The Court arrived at this position by considering that the municipality in this case had existed de facto for 6 years, thus creating a "consolidated exceptional situation of an institutional-political character"; "the exceptional situation is consolidated albeit not yet legal and cannot be overlooked" (Justice Eros Grau's opinion in ADI 2240). The exceptional nature of the situation was given special consideration, since it resulted from the fact that no supplementary law had been passed, characterizing an "omission by Congress that has prevented what the Constitution authorizes, the creation of a municipality. Failure to pass a supplementary law within a reasonable time is a true violation of the constitutional order". The concluding item of the decision summary is illustrative: "Legal certainty principle favors preservation of municipality – Principle of state continuity." And Justice Eros Grau's opinion is emblematic:

> The city legislates on matters of local interest. More than two hundred city laws had been passed by May 2006. It has elected a mayor and deputy mayor, as well as councilors, in elections managed by the electoral court. It has instituted and collected local taxes. It provides public services of local interest. It exercises police power. In its territory [...] marriages have been celebrated and births and deaths registered [...] In sum [...] the City of Luís Eduardo Magalhães truly exists as a federal entity endowed with municipal autonomy, thanks to a political decision. This reality cannot be ignored. In good faith, the citizens who reside in the city presume that their political autonomy is legally regular.

According to the reporting justice, although the municipality's creation was contrary to the Constitution, declaring institutional unconstitutionality would "aggravate the sickness of the system" (item 27): "we cannot possibly quash a political decision of an institutional nature without directly attacking the federative principle" (item 34); "we cannot go back in time to annul its existence" (item 35); "in performing its duty of concretizing the Constitution, the Court seeks to assure its normative force and *stabilizing* function" (item 41, emphasis added); "we must observe what least impairs the future normative force of the Constitution and its *stabilizing* function in this case" (item 43); "what is at stake in this case is the *principle of state continuity*, not the *principle of continuity of public services*" (item 45). In light of the above, he moved to dismiss. In a separate opinion delivered later, Justice Gilmar Mendes, citing the need to weigh the "principle of nullity of the statute against the principle of legal certainty" (page 313), defended a declaration of unconstitutionality with *pro futuro* effects (page 323) for 24 months, especially

[412]ADI n.2.240-7, Full Court, Rep. Justice Eros Grau, *DJ* 03 Aug 2007; ADI n.3.316, Full Court, Rep. Justice Eros Grau, *DJ* 29 Jun 2007; ADI n.3.489, Full Court, Rep. Justice Eros Grau, *DJ* 03 Aug 2007; ADI n.3.689, Full Court, Rep. Justice Eros Grau, *DJ* 29 Jun 2007.

considering apud Bachof that the anullment of unconstitutional statutes might cause a "true catastrophe" (page 326) and "impair the constitutional legal system itself (grave threat to legal certainty)" (page 328).

2.1.4.3.3.4 Declaration of Incompatibility with Permanent Extension of Validity and Future Change Requirement

In these cases the Court upholds the effects produced by the unconstitutional norm in the past, extends these effects definitively for a period and tasks the legislative with the enactment of a new rule for the future.

In ADI 3660–2 the Court analyzed the compatibility of the allocation of court fees to private associations with article 5, the sole paragraph of article 98, and article 145, II, of the Constitution.[413] The Court reaffirmed its understanding that fees may not be allocated to private legal entities on the grounds that such allocation violates the equality principle and the constitutionally defined use of such fees, which is to fund the public services with which they are associated. However, "for reasons of legal certainty and exceptional social interest, article 27 of Law 9868/99 is applicable, assigning effects to the declaration of unconstitutionality pursuant to Constitutional Amendment 45 of December 31, 2004" (decision summary). It should be noted that the Court's case law comprised consolidated constitutional precedents on the subject. Hence Justice Joaquim Barbosa's reticence on the modulation of effects proposed by Justice Gilmar Mendes, who acted as reporting justice for the judgment: "The Court's position on this sort of unconstitutionality has been known for a long time " (p. 67 of the judgment).

In ADI 3022 the Court examined the compatibility of State Supplementary Law 10194/94, which assured assistance by a public defender with the defense of state employees in civil litigation or criminal proceedings arising from acts performed in the course of their normal duties, with article 134 of the Constitution, according to which public defenders are required to provide legal aid only to the indigent, pursuant to article 5, indent LXXIV.[414] The Court declared the infraconstitutional norm unconstitutional but upheld its effects until the end of the year (December 31, 2004; the decision was entered on August 2, 2004). Again, the rationale for the decision was legal certainty as a requirement of institutional stability of law and credibility of the legal order. In order to assure continuity of the public service and uphold past procedural acts, a time limit was set to give "the legislator time to discipline the matter properly". It should also be noted that the upholding of past effects did not harm individuals and aimed specifically to uphold acts performed only until the institution could effectively be restructured. Moreover, the position of the public defenders was that these professionals might themselves face salary

[413] ADI n.3.660-2, Full Court, Rep. Justice Gilmar Mendes, *DJ* 13 Mar 2008.

[414] ADI n.3.022-1, Full Court, Rep. Justice Joaquim Barbosa, *DJ* 04 Mar 2005.

difficulties and therefore need assistance. Finally, even the Attorney General's Office agreed that a declaration of unconstitutionality would cause "unjustified harm" to the parties involved.

In ADI 3819 the Court analyzed the compatibility between internal promotion of civil servants for the appointment of public defenders and article 27, II, and article 134, paragraph 1, of the Constitution, which require recruitment via public competitive examinations and appropriate qualifications for public office.[415] In this case, civil servants appointed directly by state governments as public defenders, as well as legal assistants to penitentiaries and legal analysts, were transferred to the newly created career of state public defender without a public competitive exam. The Court decided this was unconstitutional on the grounds that it violated the rule according to which public competitive exams must be held to recruit civil servants pursuant to the equality and republican principles, which embody objective impersonal criteria: "The violation of constitutional precepts under the pretext of defending the public interest is inconceivable" (Justice Eros Grau's opinion, item 23). However, in order to assure the continuity of public services and access to justice, it assigned prospective effects to the unconstitutionality ruling, allowing the unlawfully appointed public defenders to remain in office only for a period of 6 months without tenure, while the public defense staff was renewed by calling up applicants who had passed the last certified public competitive exam. The rationale for this decision can also be reconstructed on the basis of legal certainty, as required by the institutional stability of law and credibility of the legal order.

In ADI 3458–8 the Court examined the compatibility of a law sponsored by a state government to create a single account managed by the state treasury for the custody of judicial and extrajudicial deposits with article 61, paragraph 1, of the Constitution, which requires the sponsorship of the judiciary, and article 2, which guarantees the independence and harmony of the three branches of government.[416] The Court ruled that the disputed statute was unconstitutional on the formal grounds that strictly speaking the law should have been sponsored by the judiciary, and on the substantive grounds that the principle of the separation of powers had been violated because the funds were not tied to the state treasury but associated with judicial deposits. However, the Court "modulated" the effects of the ruling, as it stated, because the statute had been in force for 6 years and (Justice Eros Grau's opinion, final part):

> *ex tunc* effects would produce harm and uncertainty since the Single Account for Judicial and Extrajudicial Deposits within the State of Goiás has followed the procedure contained therein since then. I therefore propose modulation of the unconstitutionality ruling's effects, pursuant to article 27 of Law 9868/99, so that the decision produces effects 60 days after final appeals, which is time enough for the State of Goiás to reorganize the custody system for these deposits.

---

[415] ADI n.3.819-2, Full Court, Rep. Justice Eros Grau, *DJ* 28 Mar 2008.

[416] ADI n.3.458-8, Full Court, Rep. Justice Eros Grau, *DJ* 28 Mar 2008.

Thus it can be seen that the Court merely granted time for compliance with the decision.

Modulation of effects is appropriate only in the case of unconstitutionality rulings, since statutes are presumed to be constitutional and confirmation of a law's constitutionality does not change the status quo, so that there are no grounds for any restriction to the effects of such decisions. This is also the STF's understanding.

Indeed, modulation of the efficacy of a declaration of constitutionality (reverse modulation) was rejected in ADI 1040–9.[417] In this case the Court declared the constitutionality of a requirement that applicants for posts in the federal prosecution service have at least 2 years' practice after qualifying as lawyers in order to be eligible for the public competitive exam. Petitioned to amend its decision by assigning prospective effects, the Court declined: This would be impossible, it said, because it would entail "inversion of the principle whereby statutes are presumed to be constitutional". As Justice Ellen Gracie stated in her opinion, "the claim would entail a complete inversion of the principle whereby statutes are presumed to be constitutional, which is a fundamental dogma of our legal order."

In another case, however, the Court restricted the effects of the declaration of constitutionality. In ADI 3756–1 the Court analyzed a challenge to article 1, II, paragraph 3, and article 20, II and III, of Supplementary Law 101/2000, known as the Fiscal Responsibility Law. The articles in question disciplined the application of payroll caps to the Federal District's legislature. The suit claimed it was unconstitutional to apply the norms of the Fiscal Responsibility Law to the Federal District, whose powers were equivalent to those of municipalities, whereas by rights the law in question applied only to states.[418] In sum, the motion was to strike out the application of payroll caps to states and the Federal District.

After stressing the peculiarity of the Federal District's competences and services, the Court decided that it more closely resembled the structuring of member states than the constitutional architecture of municipalities, especially in light of its equal treatment with states regarding concurring jurisdiction (article 24), intervention (article 34), state powers (article 29, I), the number of district assemblymen, the length of their terms and their pay levels (article 32, paragraph 3), and the right to file direct unconstitutionality suits, among other items. On these grounds the Court denied the motion to declare the legal provisions unconstitutional, thus assuring their constitutionality. Nevertheless, it modulated this "constitutionality ruling" since it understood that the Federal District would need some time to adapt to the decision. In response to a request for amendment of judgment, the Court said "the Federal District's legislature cannot be expected to adapt retroactively to the ruling in ADI 3756, since payroll expenses have already been effected, based on Decision 9475/2000 of the Audit Court and successive budget guidelines."[419] In his opinion,

[417]ED in ADI n.1.040-9, Full Court, Rep. Justice Ellen Gracie, *DJ* 01 Sep 2006.

[418]ADI n.3.756-1, Rep. Justice Carlos Britto, *DJ* 19 Oct 2007.

[419]ED in ADI n.3.756-1, Full Court, Rep. Justice Carlos Britto, *DJ* 23 Nov 2007.

Justice Carlos Britto noted that the Federal District's Audit Court had dispensed the same treatment to the Federal District as to municipalities, allowing a 6 % cap for payroll expense, in comparison with the 3 % cap applicable to states. Moreover, based on the Audit Court's interpretation at the time, the Federal District had already entered into borrowing transactions with domestic and foreign institutions, and had never met opposition from the Finance Ministry, through the Treasury Department, or from the Attorney General or the Senate for non-compliance with the pertinent limits. In light of the above, the reporting justice stated that "the budget mill cannot be made to run backwards, i.e. there is no way to reverse the flow of this water because the truth is that this excessively high cap has been applied since the law in question was enacted seven years ago. I believe it has been used in good faith, given the formal authorization granted by the Federal District's Audit Court, as well as by budget guideline laws" (item 12). On these grounds the Court decided to require compliance with the decision "without fail before the end of the two four-month periods stipulated in article 23 of the law in question, starting on the date of publication of the minutes from the judgment of merits of this direct unconstitutionality suit" (item 15). Thus the Court declared the unconstitutionality of the disputed norm and granted time for compliance with the decision.

2.1.4.3.4 Critical Analysis

2.1.4.3.4.1 Modulation in General

It should be noted first and foremost that in the cases analyzed above strictly speaking the justification for the decisions was not the trust protection principle. At no time did the STF examine the reliability of the basis for trust (whether city statutes, administrative acts or court proceedings deserved trust), whether there was trust (whether cities and citizens knew, could trust and actually did trust city statutes, administrative acts or court proceedings), whether there was exercise of trust (whether citizens performed actions of disposal of freedom and assets causally connected to city statutes, administrative acts or court proceedings), and whether there was frustration (if, upon the exercise of trust, the surprise was great and unjustified). None of that was analyzed. Strictly speaking, the cases did not even involve an opposition between state and citizen. The STF applied the legal certainty principle in its objective sense, as an objective and abstract norm to protect collective interests, which therefore operates as an instrument for protection of collective trust in the legal order. As the STF saw it, in other words, the declaratory efficacy of the decision would affect the *institutional credibility* of law as a precondition for *potential* exercise of all freedoms, especially given the number of acts performed under the protection of the previous legislation.

It is for no other reason that Justice Joaquim Barbosa stated the following in his opinion on a case involving recalculation of municipal transfers by Rio de Janeiro State: "I believe this to be one of the cases in which application of article 27 seems reasonable and justified, because it is a typical case. It is a *federative issue. There are no individual interests*. We will not be granting privileges to A, B or C – it is an *institutional matter*"[420] (emphasis added). Declaring unconstitutionality "would mean sacrificing the neediest populations," Justice Gilmar Mendes added.

As the justices pointed out in the case of budgetary transfers, "there are *extreme* situations" (Justice Carlos Britto); "I think it is a typical case with *very grave* consequences for the population" (Justice Carmem Lúcia); "the consequences are too serious," "we are looking at a *limiting case* of weighing" (Justice Gilmar Mendes – emphases added).[421]

However, the rationale for these decisions clearly lacked an analysis of the legal certainty principle in its entirety, and especially the temporal aspect (past, present and future). Moreover, in most cases the effects were presumed to be very significant without any kind of proof or even a rational justification to show the presumption was reasonable. In some cases this repercussion can be presumed, such as in the creation of a municipality; in others, however, this negative efficacy is not so obvious, such as in the recruitment of civil servants without an open competitive examination. Another visible problem is that there was no analysis of the appearance of legality. By not examining whether there was an appearance of constitutionality at the time of the act later considered unconstitutional, the STF risked upholding the efficacy of acts that were knowingly performed against the Constitution. In doing so, it encouraged more unconstitutional acts, preserving legal certainty in the past while providing an incentive for greater legal uncertainty in future. It should always be borne in mind that, while it is true that the aim of a decision to uphold the effects of invalid acts is to avoid negative effects for legal certainty, the effects of the decision itself are negative. As Tamanaha notes, upholding the effects of acts contrary to law produces effects that infringe the rule of law and legal certainty, such as condoning breach of contract and breach of promise, increasing uncertainty about compliance with statutes and contracts, encouraging unacceptable economic practices, and increasing economic inefficiency, among others.[422] The point here is only that when decisions to uphold the effects of invalid acts are grounded in the legal certainty principle, they should analyze *all* the effects that arise from inversion of the usual consequence of non-compliance with norms. The selfsame legal certainty that can be used to uphold acts contrary to the Constitution with the purpose of protecting the trust of people who rely on the validity of acts they presume constitutional can also be used for the purpose of protecting the trust of others who rely on application of the consequence established for non-compliance with acts contrary to the Constitution; the same legal certainty that can be used to uphold invalid contracts with the purpose of preserving the good faith of the parties

[420] RE n.401.953-1, Full Court, Rep. Justice Joaquim Barbosa, *DJ* 21 Sep 2007, Opinion by Justice Joaquim Barbosa, p. 467 of the decision.

[421] RE n.401.953-1, Full Court, Rep. Justice Joaquim Barbosa, *DJ* 21 Sep 2007, pages 469 and 471 of the decision.

[422] Brian Z. Tamanaha, *Law as a means to an end – Threat to the Rule of Law*, Cambridge, Cambridge University Press, 2006, p. 230.

who act in reliance on their validity can also be used with the purpose of protecting the trust of the parties who rely on application of the consequences established for cases of invalidity. In sum, the upholding of invalid acts or of the effects of invalid acts on the grounds of legal certainty is ambiguous: Both the declaration of unconstitutionality with a nullity ruling and the declaration of incompatibility without a nullity ruling produce effects with regard to the knowability, reliability and calculability of law. That being so, such decisions should not use legal certainty without defining it and analyzing all its effects. The use of legal certainty as the foundation for a decision without defining legal certainty and without delimiting the types and extent of *all* its effects is incompatible with the rule of law, and paradoxically with the legal certainty principle itself.

However, most of the above decisions concerned exceptional situations in which first, a prohibition of past effects would indeed have caused institutional instability, and second, the upholding of past effects did not harm citizens but benefited them. Given the exceptional nature of the situation and the modulation of effects, their upholding did not constitute an incentive to the performance of additional unconstitutional acts. It should be noted in any event that the modulation of effects was parsimonious in cases where their upholding might encourage the future performance of unconstitutional acts: The creation of municipalities without obeying the federal statute was assured for 24 months; induction into a civil service career without an open competitive exam was upheld for only 6 months. However, one thing the STF did not do was examine the extent to which the previous legislation appeared legitimate. Without doing so, upholding the effects of past acts encourages the performance of additional invalid acts by the state.

A number of conclusions can be drawn from these considerations about the types of modulation of effects used by Brazil's Supreme Court, alongside the above analysis of the German Constitutional Court's decisions.

The STF can declare a statute incompatible with the Constitution without ruling it null and void when the statute's purpose is to promote a constitutional ideal whose realization is determined by the institution of a principle, so that the ideal can be gradually promoted, the legislator remains free to choose one among all the means necessary to its promotion, and hence the judiciary lacks the competence to eliminate the positive, albeit insufficient, effect produced by the statute declared incompatible with the Constitution.

However, this is not the case when a constitution establishes competence rules instead of imposing the realization of goals without predetermining the means, which is precisely what Brazil's Constitution does. Unlike Germany's Basic Law, our Constitution opts for a rigid system that limits the federal entities' power to create taxes by means of competence rules defining the substantive aspects of the incidence hypotheses.[423] In these cases a declaration of compatibility cannot be used because its presuppositions are not present, so that only a declaration of nullity of

[423]Geraldo Ataliba, *República e Constituição*, 3rd ed., São Paulo, Malheiros Editores, 2011, pages 168–169.

a statute is applicable. As noted by Seer, when a declaration of nullity of a statute restores the state of constitutionality, as in the case of usurpation of competence, a declaration of incompatibility is inappropriate.[424] A declaration of incompatibility can be used only in the presence of the requirements mentioned earlier. These are not present in the case of the creation of taxes for which the Constitution provides, for the reasons set out below.

First, a declaration of compatibility cannot be used when there is a state *duty to act*. Tax competence rules only confer powers to create and increase taxes. Federal entities enjoy sufficient autonomy to refrain from exercising these powers. In other words, in the case of tax competence rules there is no constitutional imposition requiring the pursuit of an ideal. There is only the granting of a power that may or may not be exercised, and non-exercise does not imply unconstitutionality. This is quite different from giving the state constitutional obligations (*Verfassungsaufträge*) or duties to protect fundamental rights (*Schutzpflichte*): In such cases the state has the duty to use the appropriate and necessary means to promote the constitutional ideals.

Second, a declaration of compatibility cannot be used because there is no *freedom of substantive configuration of state action*. In the case of tax competence rules, the substantive aspects of the legal tax rule's incidence are predetermined, so that lawmakers cannot freely choose any means among those necessary to the promotion of a constitutionally ordained ideal. If the means are predetermined, there is no possibility of gradually promoting a state of affairs whose realization is determined by the institution of the constitutional principles, and lawmakers are not free to choose the means to the end. The state has neither duties nor freedom of action, so that a law cannot be declared incompatible without being ruled null and void. It is important to recall that normatization through rules is itself a guarantee of the ideals of knowability and calculability of the legal order, as it promotes the ideals of accessibility, intelligibility, predictability and bindingness of law. Infringement of a rule is indirectly a violation of legal certainty, and its effects can be upheld only exceptionally, when required for the global realization of legal certainty.

Indeed, a declaration of compatibility cannot be used when the statute under judicial review embodies the exercise of a competence provided for by a constitutional rule. This is because in this case the two consequences mentioned earlier that permit its adoption do not arise: the possibility of gradually promoting a state of affairs, and freedom for the legislator to choose the means to promote it. In other words, the Constitution does not merely impose the realization of a goal but specifies the means to be used, so that there is no margin of configuration for the legislator regarding the means to be chosen. The legislator's choice is predetermined by the Constitution, and it is up to the judiciary to verify whether competence has been exercised according to the constitutional rules. After all, "the legislator's freedom

[424] Roman Seer, "Rechtsschutz in Steuersachen", in Klaus Tipke e Joachim Lang, *Steuerrecht*, 19th ed., Köln, Otto Schmidt, 2008, § 22, margin number 285, p. 1089.

to decide which possibility ought to be realized assumes that the Basic Law itself has not already made that decision."[425] Hence the impossibility of transplanting to Brazilian law the thesis that in the case of the efficacy of court decisions the Constitution leaves judges relatively free to choose a politically appropriate decision.[426]

Lack of gradability of the ends and of freedom of configuration eliminate the possibility of weighing by the judiciary to uphold a norm deemed unconstitutional. As noted by Blüggel: "A mandatory constitutional task, in particular, allows the legislator's freedom of configuration to be restricted so far that unconstitutionality can be avoided only by eliminating the unconstitutional statute (or part of it)."[427] In other words, it is clear that if the Constitution establishes a competence rule whose exercise depends only on the configuration of a substantive hypothesis comprising a concept, the judiciary cannot justifiably use a declaration of incompatibility, for the simple reason that in this case there is neither gradability of ends nor freedom of configuration. Thus the only option is to declare the law null and void.

Third, a declaration of compatibility cannot be used because a declaration of nullity does somehow restore the state of constitutionality. As we have seen, for incompatibility to be declared without a null and void ruling, it is necessary for the weighing of the effects resulting from a declaration of the law's nullity and the effects resulting from a declaration of its compatibility based on the Constitution in its entirety to show that eliminating the statute does not restore the state of constitutionality required by the Constitution, but harms it. However, this is not the case with tax competence rules: Since the state does not have the duty to act, or the freedom to do so, declaring nullity restores the state of constitutionality. The elimination of the statute only leads to lack of exercise of tax competence, which is by no means unconstitutional.

The above considerations show that in the case of tax competence rules the requirements are not present for laws to be declared incompatible without being ruled null and void, at least according to the traditional justification based on the equality principle and the duty to assure proportionality. However, since the choice of one or the other type of declaration of constitutionality involves weighing the legal effects (*Rechtsfolge*) or the concrete effects (*Realfolge*) of a declaration of unconstitutionality with nullity, against the legal or concrete effects of a declaration of incompatibility without nullity, it is also necessary to ask: Does the upholding of an unconstitutional tax statute have more positive than negative effects?

This question is answered below.

---

[425] Jens Blüggel, *Unvereinbarkeitserklärung statt Normkassation durch das Bundesverfassungsgericht*, Berlin, Duncker und Humblot, 1998, pages 41–42.

[426] Georg Seyfarth, *Die Änderung der Rechtsprechung durch das Bundesverfassungsgericht*, Berlin, Duncker und Humblot, 1998, p. 294.

[427] Jens Blüggel, *Unvereinbarkeitserklärung statt Normkassation durch das Bundesverfassungsgericht*, Berlin, Duncker und Humblot, 1998, pages 41–42.

2.1.4.3.4.2 *Modulation in Tax Law*

In the case of tax laws, the rationale that can initially be used to uphold the effects of an unconstitutional statute relates to the effects that the declaration of nullity supposedly produces with regard to certain constitutional principles, especially legal certainty and budget balancing. Thus two questions must be answered in succession: Can legal certainty be used by the state to uphold unconstitutional tax laws? If it can, how is it weighed against other values?

Legal certainty as formulated in the Constitution cannot be used by the state to sustain the restriction of fundamental rights and freedoms. This conclusion must be reached based on the following arguments.

First, legal certainty is designed to protect individual rights from the state. It is not an instrument to increase the power of the state, as we have seen in the discussion of the foundations of legal certainty. This individualistic and protective connotation of legal certainty is externalized in the form and content of its foundations. In the form, to the extent that the foundations for legal certainty, especially in tax law, are *individual guarantees and rights* with a protective connotation, some guarantees even being listed under the heading "limitations of the power to tax"; *administrative principles* with a restrictive connotation, in the sense that they restrict the arbitrary exercise of power; and *structuring principles*, which also tend to limit power and protect individual rights. In the content, because as expected types of behavior or ideals the foundations imply or presuppose certainty in favor of the individual's rights and freedoms. Thus legal certainty can be compared to a building erected on foundations that are "inside" the Constitution, in the shape of norms that protect individual rights and limit state activity. Its content cannot ignore its source. If the construction of legal certainty as the main ideal is engineered by induction from lesser ideals, the greater ideal must preserve the orientation of the ideals in which it originates. In sum, legal certainty is an objective principle in favor of citizens (though not always in favor of one given citizen) and not in favor of the state.

Second, even if this *generally* protective character of legal certainty in favor of the citizen is not accepted, in tax law legal certainty is even more self-evidently protective of individual rights, on one hand, and restrictive of state action, on the other. Indeed, the indirect foundations of legal certainty, in the part relative to its justification through induction from tax rules, are entitled "limitations on the power to tax" in the Constitution, with a connotation that is clearly protective of the rights and freedoms of taxpayers. *Tax law* certainty is an objective principle in favor of citizens and not in favor of the state.

Third, when the protection of legitimate expectations or the avoidance of surprises is at stake, the Constitution has rules that protect individual rights against the state. Here it is sufficient to recall that the Constitution protects acquired rights, completed legal acts and *res iudicata* in favor of the citizen, with no kind of rule in favor of the state in the constitutional order, on one hand; on the other, it averts surprises for taxpayers by "limiting the power to tax," again with no similar protection for the interests of the state. In sum, the reflexive application of legal certainty to the *protection of legitimate expectations* is very much part of the Constitution and protects not the state but citizens.

It is worth noting at this point that the definition of legal certainty as an objective principle for the protection of citizens does not make it strictly individualistic. As mentioned earlier, the argument developed here, both deductively and inductively, is that legal certainty is built on direct and indirect normative foundations. Given these foundations, it undoubtedly has a dimension of fundamental rights protection. However, this dimension cannot be termed individualistic because it does not avert the assumption of risks through acts for which the taxpayer is responsible, nor does it eliminate a measure of uncertainty resulting from the impossibility of guaranteeing certainty through total predictability of state activity.[428]

Whether the state can avail itself of the trust protection principle is a thorny issue. Some scholars, such as Kirchhof, advocate a sort of "budgetary trust protection" (*Budgetärer Dispositionsschutz*),[429] grounded in constitutional provisions from which "reliable budgetary and financial planning requirements" (*Erfordernisse verläßlicher Finanz- und Haushaltsplanung*) can be deduced, according to Germany's Federal Constitutional Court.[430] The idea behind this supposed principle is that when the state collects taxes it acquires the right to execute a financial and decision-making plan that cannot be frustrated in future, for example, by a declaration that a tax is unconstitutional with retroactive effect, entailing the obligation to refund improperly collected tax. For the advocates of this thesis, the "budget execution protection principle" is a sort of mirror image of the individual trust protection principle in the actions of the state.[431]

Two important questions are raised by this argument. One is whether the Constitution provides a foundation for this "budget execution protection principle" in the subjective aspect of the legal certainty principle, or perhaps even in its objective aspect. Next, if it can be somehow related to the legal certainty principle, the question is how its consideration influences decisions as to whether to uphold unconstitutional norms. The first question will be answered in this chapter. The second question is addressed in the next chapter, which analyzes the modulation of effects in decisions based on legal certainty.

As seen above, the principle we are discussing presupposes a base for trust, trust, the exercise of trust, and later frustration of that trust. The foundations for the trust protection principle are the fundamental rights. That being so, we immediately come up against a basic obstacle to the identification of this principle as a species of the trust protection principle: The state does not have fundamental rights. On the contrary, it has a duty to concretize them. Fundamental rights presuppose a

---

[428] Ricardo Lodi Ribeiro, *A Segurança Jurídica do Contribuinte*, Rio de Janeiro, Lumen Juris, 2008, p. 263.

[429] Paul Kirchhof, in *Schrifte des Instituts Finanzen und Steuern*, Bonn, n. 362, 1998, p. 28.

[430] *BVerfGE* 87, 153 (178 e ss.); *BVerfGE* 93, 121 (148); 165 (178).

[431] Klaus-Dieter Drüen, "Haushaltsvorbehalt bei der Verwerfung verfassungswidriger Steuergesetze?", *FR* 6, p. 291, 1999. Andreas Ortmann, *Die Finanzwirksamkeit verfassungsrechtlicher Entscheidungen im Spiegel der Rechtsprechung des Bundesverfassungsgerichts*, Baden-Baden, Nomos, 2007, pages 641 and 651.

"personal substrate" linked to human dignity, and this does not apply to the state.[432] It is for no other reason that the trust protection principle serves as a limitation in favor of citizens and against the state, not in favor of the state and against citizens.[433] This is a logical conclusion from the fact that fundamental rights are "individual" rights or rights "of the citizen". In other words, fundamental rights are instruments of defense against state actions and create a duty to protect the individual, not the other way around.[434] This protective orientation is even stronger in tax law, where the fundamental rights of equality and property, and the irretroactivity and anteriority rules, are positivated as "limitations on the power to tax."

Furthermore, it is a presupposition of the trust protection principle that it should be used by people who submit to law, rely on law and are later surprised by law. In other words, it is a presupposition of the trust protection principle that its user is *externally* submitted to law. Now, whereas citizens receive law as something external that limits and conditions their acts of disposal, the state's task is to give form to law itself through its legislative branch. As Drüen points out, this is why the state lacks one thing that is essential to application of the trust protection principle: the possibility of being negatively surprised in its actions by the behavior of *another* person.[435] This is precisely why the oddly named concept of "budgetary trust protection" poses the risk of upholding in the state's favor the unconstitutionality of a statute the state is entirely responsible for enacting, so that it benefits from its own unlawfulness. This violates one of the consequences of the good faith principle, which is the *tu quoque* clause: The violator of a norm cannot rightfully profit from the legal situation this very same norm assigns him.[436] The risk is that budgetary trust will enjoy unlimited protection based on unconstitutional taxation simply because by definition not collecting an unconstitutional tax will always cause a decrease in revenues.

It is therefore wrong to advocate that the state, understood unitarily, is surprised by a declaration of the nullity of a statute. Unlike individuals, who are subject to administrative acts without participating in their conception, without having the power to enact them, so that they must plan their activities based on the laws and acts *imposed* on them and cannot influence risk-creating factors in any way, the state as a whole implements norms and issues its own acts. Whereas individuals are subject to risk, the state creates it; whereas individuals act on their own freedoms and subject

---

[432] Christoph Louven, *Problematik und Grenzen rückwirkender Rechtsprechung des Bundesarbeitsgerichts*, München, Beck, 1996, p. 251.

[433] Johannes Mainka, *Vertrauensschutz im öffentlichen Recht*, Bonn, Ludwig Röhrscheid, 1963, pages 30–31.

[434] Gertrude Lübbe-Wolff, *Die Grundrechte als Eingriffsabwehrrechte. Struktur und Reichweite der Eingriffsdogmatik im Bereich staatlicher Leistungen*, Baden-Baden, Nomos, 1988, pages 75 and following.

[435] Klaus-Dieter Drüen, "Haushaltsvorbehalt bei der Verwerfung verfassungswidriger Steuergesetze?", *FR* 6, p. 291, 1999.

[436] Ana Paula Oliveira Ávila, *A modulação de efeitos temporais pelo STF no controle de Constitucionalidade*, Porto Alegre, Livraria do Advogado, 2009, p. 155.

themselves to another's power, the state acts by restricting the freedom of others and exercising the power granted by the Constitution. Hence there is no such thing as surprise when risk is generated by the sovereign actions of the entity alleging it: Surprise depends on the absence of a causal link between the action performed and a change that occurs. Without this there is not surprise but knowledge, or a duty of knowledge, of what is to come. There is no such thing as a relationship of trust with oneself.

Finally, it must also be borne in mind that trust protection is founded on the protection of fundamental rights, whereas "budgetary trust protection" presupposes precisely the opposite: restriction of fundamental rights. Whether state trust protection is deposited in the constitutionality of tax revenue becomes an issue only when such revenue is declared unconstitutional. Otherwise there is no discussion about upholding it. However, in the field of tax law this happens only when a constitutional competence rule is violated and a fundamental right is illegitimately restricted. That being so, the protection of budgetary trust corresponds to a restriction of fundamental rights. As we will see later, upholding an unconstitutional tax entails a restriction of fundamental rights, whose efficacy is suspended while the unconstitutional tax is being levied. In other words, the price of protecting budgetary trust is excessive restriction of fundamental rights, and that is another reason it is incompatible with the postulate of prohibiting excessive restriction of fundamental rights.[437]

These considerations suffice to conclude that the so-called "budgetary trust protection principle" cannot be identified with the trust protection principle, or even based on it. Trust protection, it bears repeating with Machado Derzi, is something only individuals can claim.[438]

Nevertheless, it remains to be seen whether the principle in question can be based on the objective aspect of legal certainty. In other words, it must be asked whether state trust in tax collection as a source of revenue can be identified as an element of the stability or credibility of law. In this case, the continuity of the state's financialactivity is not endangered by any unfavorable financial effect but only by effects that may shake the foundations (*Grundlagen*) of public finance, because they create "critical existential bottlenecks" (*existenzielle Engpässe*) or have a "catastrophic financial impact" on the state, to quote European Union case law.[439] Even in this respect, however, the "budgetary trust protection principle" cannot be based on legal certainty.

---

437 Klaus-Dieter Drüen, "Haushaltsvorbehalt bei der Verwerfung verfassungswidriger Steuergesetze?", *FR* 6, p. 291, 1999.

438 Misabel de Abreu Machado Derzi, *Modificações da jurisprudência no Direito Tributário*, São Paulo, Noeses, 2009, p. 495.

439 Roman Seer e Jörg Peter Müller, "Begrenzung der Wirkungen seiner Richtersprüche durch den EuGH", *IWB* n. 5, Gruppe 2, Fach 11, p. 261, 2008. Christian Waldhoff, "Recent developments relating to the retroactive effect of decisions of the ECJ", in *Common Market Law Review* 46, p. 2, 2009 (manuscript).

As seen above, the objective aspect of legal certainty is concerned with the stability and credibility of the legal order as a whole, bearing no relation either with its concrete manifestation or with its subjective efficacy involving some problem of validity. That being so, far from supporting the upholding of unconstitutional norms the requirement of institutional credibility of law opposes it, postulating not legal obedience but maintenance of the effects of unlawful conduct by the very author of the unconstitutional rules whose effects are to be upheld. As Seer quite rightly avers, the upholding of an unconstitutional norm – especially when the financial effects are significant, given the lack of negative consequences resulting from constitutional violation – encourages more unconstitutional norms. If the state issues an unconstitutional norm but benefits from its effects, this encourages the issuance of a new constitutional norm.[440] Hence Justice Joaquim Barbosa's remarks in a hearing on an internal interlocutory appeal:

> I believe that in tax matters the application of prospective effects to an incidental declaration of unconstitutionality requires even more moderation and caution, given that tax revenue is to be used for public purposes, as is quite obvious [...] If the legal system gives the Supreme Court the power to modulate the effects of a declaration of unconstitutionality in time and hence to influence the use to which tax revenue is put, this evidently must exempt the state from its duty to guarantee the validity of the legal norms it creates, on pain of fostering legal speculation.[441]

It must also be borne in mind that the foundations of legal certainty prevent inclusion of the concept of financial losses within the concept of legal certainty, even, repeat even, when such losses are substantial. By definition the rule of lawprohibits the upholding of acts contrary to law. Moreover, its axiological components are restricted when the effects of illegal acts are preserved.[442] The knowability and calculability of state actions are negatively affected, since such upholding encourages more illegal acts and citizens therefore cannot know whether the executive will act lawfully in future or will expect the efficacy of future irregular acts to be upheld; human dignity is restricted, since individuals can no longer be responsible for acts that they knew, or could reasonably be expected to know, were contrary to law, because the distinction between what is lawful and unlawful is no longer clear; state arbitrariness is encouraged, given the lack of objective criteria to regulate state activity; control of the constitutionality of state acts is impaired because irregular acts are not effectively controlled; and citizens are not assured of uniform treatment because, depending on the assigned effects, people covered by the

---

[440] Roman Seer e Jörg Peter Müller, "Begrenzung der Wirkungen seiner Richtersprüche durch den EuGH", *IWB* n. 5, Gruppe 2, Fach 11, p. 264, 2008.

[441] AgR in AI n.557.237, 2nd Panel, Rep. Justice Joaquim Barbosa, *DJ* 26 Oct 2007, pages 2059–2060 of the opinion. Likewise: AgR in RE n.487.567, 2nd Panel, Rep. Justice Eros Grau, *DJ* 07 Dec 2007; AgR in RE n.650.000-4, 2nd Panel, Rep. Justice Joaquim Barbosa, *DJ* 28 Sep 2007; AgR in RE n.273.074-2, 2nd Panel, Rep. Justice Cézar Peluso, *DJe* 29 Feb 2008.

[442] Robert Summers, "A formal theory of the rule of law", in idem *Essays in Legal Theory*, Dordrecht, Kluwer, 2000, p. 169.

decision will be treated in one way, whereas others will be treated differently. The principle of state morality is also opposed to the preservation of acts contrary to law. As we have seen, this principle requires the state to behave in a loyal, serious and justified manner. Acting unlawfully is disloyal, especially when the unlawfulness of the act is known from the outset.

Lastly, all the other foundational elements make the concept of legal certainty, especially tax law certainty, mean protection for citizens against the state, not protection for the state against citizens. For these reasons, the legal certainty guaranteed by the Constitution cannot be used by the state to restrict fundamental rights and freedoms by declaring laws compatible with the Constitution instead of ruling them null and void. The constitutional provision prevents this.

It is also worth stressing that the exceptional use made of legal certainty by Germany's Constitutional Court to justify declaring incompatible a statute that violates the Constitution is meant not to restrict but to protect the freedom of citizens. Initially it did so when a declaration of nullity would create a legal vacuum or a state of uncertainty regarding the legal basis required to stabilize a given situation. A fundamental right whose exercise depended on the statute could not be exercised if the statute were to be annulled, creating a legal vacuum. Uncertainty regarding the past exercise of the same right would also result. In other words, legal certainty is not used by the state to restrict freedom but to protect the exercise of freedom by citizens.

All these thoughts about legal certainty also apply to attempts to declare the incompatibility of a statute without ruling it null and void in order to avoid frustrating budgetary plans that have already been presented. The protection of expectations regarding the budget is not an independent foundation of legal certainty, but a mere reflexive application to the object of such expectations, i.e. the budget. As already noted, the *expectations protected* by reflexive application of legal certainty are those of the citizens, not the state. Loss of revenue is not subsumed within the constitutional concept of legal certainty.

The exposition thus far shows that article 27 of Law 9868/98, according to which when the STF declares a statute or normative act unconstitutional it may restrict the effects of this declaration or rule that it will have efficacy only once it becomes unappealable or at some other time "for reasons of legal certainty or exceptional social interest", cannot be used by the state to continue collecting an unconstitutional tax via a declaration that the law is incompatible but not null and void. In sum, legal certainty cannot be used as a justification for the state to uphold the past efficacy of a tax statute that creates a tax either in its subjective or in its objective aspect.

Given these considerations, strictly speaking there is no room for the arguments used by Justice Gilmar Mendes in another internal interlocutory appeal, combining the concepts of "financial repercussion", "grave injury to public order" and "legal certainty." Ruling on the appeal, he denied the request for modulation of effects solely on the grounds of "failure to sustain the claim of economic repercussions, or very grave injury to public order, legal certainty or any other constitutional principle relevant to the case". His opinion also states the following:

> Regarding the alleged injury to public order, the City of Rio de Janeiro has not successfully sustained its claim that it faces a grave threat by arguing that the declaration of unconstitutionality with *ex tunc* effects and the large sums at stake in the litigation concerned could prevent the city from delivering basic public services. Given this failure to prove potential injury, I see no justification for modulation of effects, as I emphasized in my ruling on the appeal (p. 389 of the decision).[443]

Thus the decision equates "protection from financial loss" with "legal certainty", just as foreign case law and jurisprudence have done.[444] However, this parallelism is incompatible with the foundations of the legal certainty principle, which guarantees reliability and calculability of law based on its knowability to protect citizens from the state. Financial loss resulting from the duty to refund unconstitutional taxes has nothing to do with legal certainty, and even less with tax law certainty. Carrazza is invaluable on this point:

> "A mere interest in collecting tax cannot make a blank slate of equality, legality, anteriority, in sum, the constitutional rights of taxpayers.
>
> Not even the theoretically laudable goal of solving politicians' 'cash problems' has the power to subvert the fundamental principles of the Brazilian constitutional tax system, which are ultimately rooted in the *principle of legal certainty* itself".[445]

Even if it were admitted for argument's sake that "reasons of legal certainty" could be used to uphold past effects of tax statutes contrary to the Constitution, the question we have set out to answer here would still remain: How should the effects of declaring the nullity of a statute be compared with the effects of upholding it?

The final decision whether to set aside or uphold the past effects of a statute results from the weighing of effects: The effects of an unconstitutionality ruling are compared with the effects of declaring the statute only incompatible with the Constitution. The question is which promotes the Constitution more, nullity (*Nichtigkeit*) or upholding of the statute (*Normerhaltung*).[446] However, saying that

---

[443]AgR in RE n.442.309-0, 2nd Panel, Rep. Justice Gilmar Mendes, *DJ* 14 Dec 2007. On the same subject, see: AgR in AI n.557.237-4, 2nd Panel, Rep. Justice Joaquim Barbosa, *DJ* 26 Oct 2007; AgR in RE n.487.567-5, 2nd Panel, Rep. Justice Eros Grau, *DJ* 07 Dec 2007; AgR in AI n.681.730-7, 2nd Panel, Rep. Justice Celso de Mello, *DJ* 14 Dec 2007; AgR in AI n.650.000-4, 2nd Panel, Rep. Justice Joaquim Barbosa, *DJ* 28 Sep 2007. For all, see: AgR in RE n.273.074-2, 2nd Panel, Rep. Justice Cézar Peluso, *DJ* 29 Feb 2008.

[444]Horatia Muir Watt, "*Never say never*: *post-scriptum* comparatif sur la rétroativité des revirements de jurisprudence", in Bertrand Seiller (Org.), *La rétroactivité des décisions du juge administratif*, Paris, Economica, 2007, p. 66.

[445]Roque Antonio Carrazza, *Curso de Direito Constitucional Tributário*, 27th ed., São Paulo, Malheiros Editores, 2011, p. 524.

[446]Jens Blüggel, *Unvereinbarkeitserklärung statt Normkassation durch das Bundesverfassungsgericht*, Berlin, Duncker und Humblot, 1998, p. 151.

the decision results from a weighing of the statute's concrete effects does not explain what is most important: the parameters for the weighing, and how they should be used.

For example, when Germany's Constitutional Court upholds the past effects of a statute on the grounds that declaring it null and void would create a situation of uncertainty and tend to restrict rather than promote the Constitution, it is not clear whether its assessment of this situation of uncertainty is based only on the past or also on the future. This is the crux of the matter according to the thesis advocated in this book: Either legal certainty is whole, or it is not legal certainty. Its wholeness resides not only in the coincidence of its dimensions (certainty of and through law, before law, of rights, as a right, and in law), but also in a synthetic and balanced consideration of its perspectives – past, present, and future. As Machado Derzi precisely explains based on Heidegger, the analysis of time must be four-dimensional: past, present, future, and the unity of these three dimensions.[447]

Further to this point, restriction of legal certainty as a constitutional principle that protects individuals and aims to assure a state of reliability and predictability of the legal order based on its knowability cannot be considered only locally and retrospectively. It must be assessed globally and from a perspective that is simultaneously present (current), past (retrospective) and future (prospective).

This can be explained as follows. A decision to declare a statute incompatible with the Constitution without ruling it null and void requires an analysis of the negative impact nullity would have if the law's past effects were eliminated. However, this works when despite having acted contrary to the Constitution the lawmakers somehow promote *the very constitutional provision that served as a basis for the act*: They intended to guarantee access to justice, but "complied unsatisfactorily" with the constitutional *imposition*; they meant to promote equality through contributive capacity but "underperformed" their constitutional *duty*, which they should not have neglected; they aimed to provide compensation for compulsory service, but displayed "too little obedience" of the constitutional order, which they had no right to ignore; they wanted to carry out a general review of pay levels but "insufficiently performed" the constitutional *task* that had been imposed – and so on. In every case, the lawmakers had a duty to act and did so by promoting the Constitution to some extent, but acted contrary to the Constitution in the relations they created or the distinctions they failed to make. Thus a declaration of nullity would restrict the constitutional ideal more than upholding the statute: There would be *no* free legal aid to improve access to justice, there would be *no* instrument to promote equality through contributive capacity, there would be *no* compensation for compulsory service, there would be *no* salaries to pay for work performed – and so on. Upholding the unconstitutional statute would not encourage future non-compliance with the Constitution but, on the contrary, the future creation of a statute entirely in accordance with the Constitution.

---

[447]Misabel de Abreu Machado Derzi, *Modificações da Jurisprudência no Direito Tributário*, São Paulo, Noeses, 2009, p. 197.

This framework, however, does not apply when the judiciary upholds the collection of a tax whose institution is contrary to the Constitution. This is because in this case the lawmakers in no way promote *the very constitutional provision that serves as a basis for the act*. They simply disobey it, exercising a power they have not been given.[448] The constitutional norm is not implemented to any extent. In this case, moreover, the norm does not impose a duty but merely grants jurisdiction that may or may not be exercised, and non-exercise does not entail disrespect for the Constitution. In addition, upholding the unconstitutional statute would not encourage the creation of a future statute entirely in accordance with the Constitution. On the contrary, it would be an incentive to future disobedience. This is because if the illegitimate exercise of the power to tax has no consequences, the state is not compelled to act within the scope of power reserved for it by the Constitution. Legitimate and illegitimate exercise of power have the same outcome, which is assuring collection of the tax. Thus upholding the effects of the unconstitutional statute has the effect of encouraging the state to issue more unconstitutional statutes in the future.[449] It is important to note that technically speaking the state does not have a "right to tax", let alone to "tax unconstitutionally", which is an oxymoron. What it does have is the "competence to create constitutional taxes", which is a pleonasm.

This is precisely where it also becomes necessary to examine legal certainty from a prospective angle. The reason is that comparing the effects of a nullity ruling with the effects of a ruling to uphold involves issues relating to the intelligibility, reliability and predictability of law after the statute is declared constitutional. The arguments for upholding a statute are usually associated with lack of promotion of other constitutional ideals: for example, with the claim that loss of tax revenue deprives the state of the wherewithal to invest in the improvement of education or the (external, physical) security of citizens, so that promotion of these ideals will be indirectly prevented.

However, when the statute under judicial review creates an unconstitutional tax, it is not a question of a straightforward choice between annulment and not promoting other constitutional ideals, or upholding the statute and indirectly assuring such promotion. Another choice is also involved: Validating the state's arbitrary behavior encourages it to do the same again in future, with the claim of potentially but uncertainly and indirectly promoting other goals; invalidating the state's arbitrary behavior discourages it from doing the same again, with the claim of directly and certainly violating a competence rule. In fact, deciding whether to uphold or nullify a statute involves a choice between the *certainty of directly disobeying* a rule that authorizes state action and the *uncertainty of indirectly obeying* another principle

[448]Roman Seer, "Rechtsschutz in Steuersachen", in Klaus Tipke e Joachim Lang, *Steuerrecht*, 19th ed., Köln, Otto Schmidt, 2008, § 22, margin number 285, p.1089.

[449]Roman Seer e Jörg Peter Müller, "Begrenzung der Wirkungen seiner Richtersprüche durch den EuGH", *IWB* n. 5, Gruppe 2, Fach 11, p. 264, 2008.

that supposedly justifies upholding the effects of state action. Moreover, it is a choice between certainty and uncertainty, between evidence and allegation. In this case to uphold the validity of an unconstitutional norm is to choose the "uncertainty of the correct" over the "certainty of the incorrect". It is to exchange yesterday's certainty for today's and tomorrow's uncertainty. Doing so, and this is the point, promotes present and future legal uncertainty, owing to loss of the bindingness and legal efficacy of law. As stressed by von Arnauld, there can be no security in laws that are mere words on paper and do not offer any certainty for future conduct.[450]

Upholding the effects of an unconstitutional tax law also produces another devastating effect in terms of uncertainty about the present and future. The typical rationale for upholding its validity is that the more tax is collected, the more the principles will be promoted, and the greater the loss, the less the principles will be promoted. Because the main effect of tax laws is to restrict freedoms and property rights, the higher the tax burden (and therefore the greater the tax revenue), the more taxpayers' fundamental rights are restricted. However – and this is where the thinking becomes perverse – the greater the tax revenue (and therefore the more fundamental rights are restricted), the greater the loss of revenues if the tax statute is annulled. If loss of revenue justifies the upholding of a tax statute, then the greater the loss of revenue, the more likely the statute is to be upheld. But this necessarily means accepting that the more fundamental rights are restricted, the likelier a statute that creates such restrictions is to be upheld. In other words, the more unconstitutional the statute, the likelier it is to be declared constitutional! Here the perversity of this reasoning comes full circle: The more unconstitutional the statute, the more constitutional it is. To accept this type of reasoning is not just to admit that law is not binding; it encourages lawbreaking and makes a mockery of reason itself. Vulgarly put, it institutionalizes the principle of "the worse it gets, the better." To return to the prime subject of this book, it fosters uncertainty of law, through law, before law, and of rights. Paradoxically, it entails accepting, promoting and encouraging legal uncertainty by taking legal certainty in vain. And no decision violates the Constitution more than one that encourages its own repeated violation. It is curious, to say the least, that the effects of an unconstitutional statute can be upheld within the scope discussed here on the grounds that this will promote rather than restrict the Constitution. The use of financial criteria to uphold past effects of unconstitutional statutes is incompatible with the dogmatics of fundamental rights, as Moes quite rightly notes.[451]

As if that were not enough, the reasoning in question also leads the state to rely more on the upholding of the effects of a statute that creates unconstitutional

---

450 Andreas von Arnauld, *Rechtssicherheit*, Tübingen, Mohr Siebeck, 2006, p. 355.

451 Christoph Moes, "Die Anordnung der befristeten Fortgeltung verfassungswidriger Steuergesetze durch das Bundesverfassungsgericht", *StuW* 1, p. 32, 2008.

taxes, the higher the revenue resulting from its collection.[452] As already shown, this argument directly violates legal certainty instead of promoting it. But it also causes two other problems.

On one hand, it leads to excessive restriction of the fundamental right to judicial protection. This is because if the plaintiffs do not win the precursor (or instant) case and the parallel cases already begun, taxpayers' right to justice will not be respected: They win their lawsuits by losing them, and the tax authorities lose by winning, paradoxical though this may seem. Thus this kind of decision violates the fundamental right of access to the judiciary.[453] The rationale involved – the winner loses and the loser wins – completely inverts the very logic of law, which is compliance. Law that advocates lawbreaking is not law. The tortuousness of the argument is evident if we consider how absurd would be if a private suit were lost by the plaintiff because although he is in the right the exercise of his right will cause a loss to the defendant's property.[454] This clearly shows that upholding an unconstitutional tax is contrary to the minimal efficacy of law, and as we have seen, this is one of the elements of the legal certainty principle. Anyone who goes to court must have some idea of the advantages and disadvantages of doing so, but this prognosis is completely altered by manipulation of the effects of decisions: In the absence of secure criteria regarding the effects, every legal action becomes a "gamble" (*Lotteriespiel*).[455]

On the other hand, upholding the past effects of a statute that created an unconstitutional tax also promotes the excessive restriction of fundamental rights. Upholding those effects, when admissible, requires weighing the effects resulting from nullity against the effects of upholding, but consideration of budgetary interest hinders weighing because by definition there is always financial loss and alleged budgetary surprise when a tax is declared unconstitutional. Thus the harmonization of public and private interests is blocked even before the weighing begins.[456] As a result, fundamental rights and freedoms, which should be protected, or at least considered, by the state, are limitlessly restricted.

[452]Klaus-Dieter Drüen, "Haushaltsvorbehalt bei der Verwerfung verfassungswidriger Steuergesetze?", *FR* 6, p. 290, 1999.

[453]Roman Seer e Jörg Peter Müller, "Begrenzung der Wirkungen seiner Richtersprüche durch den EuGH", *IWB* n. 5, Gruppe 2, Fach 11, pages 264 and 266, 2008. Klaus-Dieter Drüen, "Haushaltsvorbehalt bei der Verwerfung verfassungswidriger Steuergesetze?", *FR* 6, pages 290–291, 1999.

[454]Christoph Moes, "Die Anordnung der befristeten Fortgeltung verfassungswidriger Steuergesetze durch das Bundesverfassungsgericht", *StuW* 1, p. 31, 2008.

[455]Roman Seer, "Rechtsschutz in Steuersachen", in Klaus Tipke and Joachim Lang, *Steuerrecht*, 19th ed., Köln, Otto Schmidt, 2008, § 22, margin number 289, p.1091. Christoph Moes, "Die Anordnung der befristeten Fortgeltung verfassungswidriger Steuergesetze durch das Bundesverfassungsgericht", *StuW* 1, p. 34, 2008.

[456]Klaus-Dieter Drüen, "Haushaltsvorbehalt bei der Verwerfung verfassungswidriger Steuergesetze?", *FR* 6, p. 291, 1999.

Given these considerations, it is evident that in the case of the creation of tax obligations the upholding of effects restricts more than promotes legal certainty. Upholding the past effects of an unconstitutional norm with the intention of protecting legal certainty *in the past* restricts legal certainty *in the future* even more, by encouraging the enactment of more unconstitutional norms and therefore stimulating the restriction of law's efficacy and calculability. Again, one of the main points of this study is relevant here: Legal certainty is either whole, or it is not legal certainty. To attempt to realize legal certainty based on one aspect of one element of one of its dimensions, with no attention to other aspects of the same element, or to other elements of the same or another dimension, is not to realize the legal certainty principle but to restrict it. In sum, even if it is mistakenly accepted that financial loss can be compatible with the past objective dimension of legal certainty, as a requirement of law's stability and credibility, financial loss is still irreconcilable with the other dimensions, present and future, of legal certainty. In other words, financial loss is only defensible with part of legal certainty, never with legal certainty as a whole, and even so this defense is wrong.

Moreover, the assignment of future effects to a ruling that a tax statute is unconstitutional is irreconcilable with the fundamental rights of freedom and property. This becomes clear when the function and efficacy of fundamental rights are analyzed. They function as *objective norms* as well as *subjective rights*. When they are violated, they function as *rights of defense* against restrictions by the state and private citizens, and as *duties of protection* that require the state to take whatever measures are necessary for their protection.[457] Thus if they are not violated fundamental rights act as *norms of prevention* against the violation of legal goods, states, or subjects protected by them (*Präventionsnormen*). If they are violated they act as *norms of restitution* or *restoration* of legal goods, states, or subjects protected by them (*Restitutionsnormen*).[458] Moreover, the Constitution mandates compliance with fundamental rights, which have immediate efficacy, are binding on all three branches of government (article 5, paragraph 1), and cannot be modified even by constitutional amendment (article 60, paragraph 4). Any violation of fundamental rights, whether relating to freedom, property, equality or even judicial protection, is incompatible with the Constitution. Habscheidt is worth quoting on this point:

> Thus in order to assure effective protection of fundamental rights for every citizen injured by an unconstitutional restriction of fundamental rights, the Constitution requires that in every case the state of affairs that existed without the unconstitutional restriction be restored. The claim of restoration is thus not a mere reflection of a normatively exclusionary decision of the Constitutional Court, but instead relates to the very core of fundamental rights protection in the situation concerning which judicial review affirmed the restriction.[459]

[457] Johannes Dietlein, *Die Lehre von den grundrechtlichen Schutzpflichten*, 2nd ed., Berlin, Duncker und Humblot, 2005, pages 34 and following.

[458] Gerhard Habscheidt, *Der Anspruch des Bürgers auf Erstattung verfassungswidriger Steuern*, Köln, Otto Schmidt, 2003, p. 13.

[459] Gerhard Habscheidt, *Der Anspruch des Bürgers auf Erstattung verfassungswidriger Steuern*, Köln, Otto Schmidt, 2003, p. 13.

In other words, and this is decisive, restoration of the state protected by fundamental rights is not a consequence of the decision but the normative consequence of the fundamental rights themselves. It must be stressed yet again that this is not something that can be subjected to the discretionary power of the Court. It is implicitly normatized by the Constitution itself. Thus when an unconstitutional tax statute is enacted, the claim that arises for those affected is restoration of the protected state as if the unconstitutional statute had never been enacted.[460]

This argument, which is valid for fundamental rights in general, is even more relevant in the case of the fundamental right to judicial protection (article 5, XXXV). If the Constitution itself states that "the law shall not exclude any injury or threat to rights from appreciation by the judiciary," this fundamental right to judicial protection of rights cannot be set aside by decisions that accept violations of rights. As Seer correctly notes, judicial protection "is not simply an addition (*Additum*) to the substantive fundamental right of taxpayers but part of the subjective right to protection afforded by the fundamental right."[461]

Finally, it must be noted that modulation of the temporal effects of a declaration of unconstitutionality still causes the STF to uphold the collection of taxes without a statute.[462] In doing so, a decision by the STF to uphold the collection of an unconstitutional tax indirectly has effects that are incompatible with the Constitution. First, the decision allows the legislative to create a tax with no basis in a statute, which is a direct violation of the constitutional rule of statutory legality (article 150, III). Even without a statute, the tax is levied. Second, the decision itself claims to be the grounds for collection of the tax, which also violates not only the legality rule but also the separation of powers (article 2). Third, it suspends the efficacy of the fundamental rights of freedom, property and judicial protection by subtracting their efficacy to limit state activity and to guarantee a minimal set of legal goods whose availability is the very condition for their efficacy, contradicting the guarantee of immediate efficacy of fundamental rights (article 5, paragraph 1) and the impossibility of their modification even by constitutional amendment (article 60, paragraph 4). Hence the statement that modulating the effects of unconstitutionality rulings relating to onerous tax statutes amounts to the unjustified suspension of fundamental rights.[463] Upholding the effects, in other words, means that the norms that define fundamental guarantees and rights – even rights that are not of a social nature and dependent on monetary consideration – are not immediately enforceable but efficacious only "on condition the alleged budgetary gap does not exist, according to the STF's ruling." What is at stake here

---

[460] Ibidem, p. 15.

[461] Roman Seer, "Defizite im finanzgerichtlichen Rechtsschutz – zugleich eine kritische Auseinandersetzung mit dem 2. FGO-Änderungsgesetz vom 19.12.2000", *StuW*, p. 3.

[462] Gerhard Habscheidt, *Der Anspruch des Bürgers auf Erstattung verfassungswidriger Steuern*, Köln, Otto Schmidt, 2003, p. 35.

[463] Gerhard Habscheidt, *Der Anspruch des Bürgers auf Erstattung verfassungswidriger Steuern*, Köln, Otto Schmidt, 2003, p. 39. Klaus Tipke, "Rezenzion" (Gerhard Habscheidt, *Der Anspruch des Bürgers auf Erstattung verfassungswidriger Steuern*), *StuW* 2, p. 189, 2004.

is, so to speak, the monetization of legal certainty and indirectly of fundamental rights themselves, since they are applied under a budgetary reservation.[464] It is worth noting Carrazza's wise words on this point: "However, it so happens that we cannot turn a deaf ear to the subjective rights of taxpayers, which are guaranteed by the Constitution itself, in the name of the state's convenience and revenue growth. One of these rights is the right to be taxed by the competent political authority and in the manner prescribed by the Constitution."[465] Accepting suspension of the efficacy of fundamental rights in the name of legal certainty therefore entails exchanging immediate application, which resides in the absence of intermediaries between the Constitution and its concrete application, for suspended application, which is unconstitutional.

Lastly, upholding the effects of onerous statutes contrary to the Constitution flouts the rule of law. To assure universality and prevent state arbitrariness, the rule of law requires that state action be governed by general, clear, known rules that are relatively constant over time, prospective and non-contradictory.[466] When the state enacts a statute contrary to the Constitution but even so its effects are upheld, the state's action inverts the rule of law principle: Instead of being governed by general rules, the state is governed by individual norms issued by the judiciary; instead of being governed by clear rules, it is directed by obscure norms, owing to the absence of intersubjective criteria that evidence what is permitted and what is mandatory; instead of being governed by known norms, its actions are limited by unknown norms, which do not exist at the time the acts are performed and therefore cannot be known at that time; instead of being governed by rules that remain constant over time, it is directed by rules that change according to the interests and values protected at the time of the decision; instead of being governed by prospective rules, it is regulated by retrospective norms, which exist only at the time the judgment is entered and not at the time of the state's actions. Moreover, all of this is opposed to the institution of a universal non-arbitrary system, because state actions end up being regulated in a circumstantial manner, without clear and effective legal limits. In sum, the rule of law allows very little scope for modulation of the effects of onerous unconstitutional statutes, since such modulation gives rise to government limited to ex post facto rules instead of government limited by previously enacted rules.

All the above considerations show that the modulation of effects is a decision-making technique whose compatibility with the rule of law and legal certainty is very restricted indeed. Every instance of modulation of the temporal effects of an unconstitutionality ruling involves a contradiction of law with itself: By upholding

---

[464] Wolfgang Meyer, "Die Rückwirkung von Bundesgesetzen – ein Problem des Übermaßes?", in Hermann Butzer *et alii* (Orgs.), *Organisation und Verfahren im sozialen Rechtsstaat. FS für Friedrich E. Schnapp zum 70. Geburtstag*, Berlin, Duncker und Humblot, 2008, p. 162.

[465] Roque Antonio Carrazza, *Curso de Direito Constitucional Tributário*, 27th ed., São Paulo, Malheiros Editores, 2011, p. 452.

[466] Jeremy Waldron, "The rule of law in contemporary liberal theory", *Ratio Juris*, v. 2, n. 1, p. 84, 1989.

something contrary to itself, law devours itself like a snake that eats its own tail. It involves not constitutional but unconstitutional law, so to speak.[467] Thus Medeiros is wrong to admit the state's financial expectations as grounds for setting aside the declaratory efficacy of unconstitutionality rulings.[468]

Finally, for advocates of a consequentialist theory of interpretation it is important to recall that the consideration of consequences, if admitted, ought to be preceded by a number of questions such as: Consequences regarding what? Rules (which ones?), principles (which ones?) or rules and principles (in what measure and based on what perspective)? Consequences to be measured how? Consequences in what sense – fact, norm, value? Consequences regarding which period – yesterday, today, tomorrow? Consequences for whom – addressees, the state, society? These questions, to which others could be added, only show that the assessment of the consequences of a decision is only apparently free of controversy. Not to mention the weight of the consequentialist arguments within the legal theory of argumentation.[469] Opening up a decision to the consideration of consequences, as Machado Derzi warns, "presupposes yet another infinite series of possibilities open to the choice of the applier of law as to the economic or sociological theory to adopt, because there is no unanimity either in the explanatory sciences or in the sciences of the spirit that can securely predict the effects that will be unleashed."[470] In sum, a consequentialist theory of decision making without rigorous delimitation of the desirable consequences is entirely incompatible with the legal certainty principle, given the absurd uncertainty produced by its deployment.[471] To use a metaphor inspired by the work of Becker, admitting an "invertebrate consequentialism" in law is tantamount to accepting justice as a mere Pandora's box from whence anything can be retrieved.

Let me insist on the fact that modulation of the effects of unconstitutionality rulings inverts the logic of law itself. The structure of a legal rule consists of a hypothesis and a consequence. To addressees this means they can foresee that if they act in a given manner, a given consequence will ensue. To judges, this hypothetical-conditional structure serves as a compass for their decisions: When *X*, and *X* was done, I ought to decide *Y*; and when *X*, and *not-X* was done, then I ought to

---

[467] Klaus-Dieter Drüen, "Haushaltsvorbehalt bei der Verwerfung verfassungswidriger Steuergesetze?", *FR* 6, p. 294, 1999.

[468] Rui Medeiros, *A Decisão de inconstitucionalidade – Os autores, o conteúdo e os efeitos da decisão de inconstitucionalidade*, Lisboa, Universidade Católica, 1999, p. 715.

[469] Humberto Ávila, "Juristische Theorie der Argumentation", in Andreas Heldrich *et alii* (Orgs.), *FS für Claus-Wilhelm Canaris zum 70. Geburtstag*, München, Beck, 2007, pages 963–989. Ana Paula Oliveira Ávila, *A modulação de efeitos temporais pelo STF no controle de constitucionalidade*, Porto Alegre, Livraria do Advogado, 2009, pages 119 and 171.

[470] Misabel de Abreu Machado Derzi, *Modificações da jurisprudência no Direito Tributário*, São Paulo, Noeses, 2009, p. 171.

[471] Idem, pages 173 and 216.

decide Z.[472] Note that, in this normative scheme, the decision the judge makes is not a product of comparing the effect programmed by the legislator and the effect the judge intends to program, nor is it the result of replacing one effect with another. The judge does not use the effects as a deciding reason, and does not compare the effect of the conditional program with other effects. The normative efficacy is that which was previously defined by the legislator. Modulation alters precisely this rationale for decision-making by equating the decisions in both cases: When X, and X was done, I decide Y; but when X, and *not-X* was done, I *also* decide Y! Thus X and *not-X* have the same consequence – i.e., different behaviors have identical consequences. Note that in this case the decision made by the judge is the result of comparing the effect programmed by the legislator with the effect the judge intends to program. In other words, the judge uses the probable effects of the decision as a reason to decide, inverting the normative efficacy previously defined by the legislator. This inversion – in contrast with decisions relating to consolidated situations, where judgment is the outcome of a consideration of internal elements that precede the addressee's act or its qualification – derives from the appreciation of external elements that occur after the behavior of the addressee. Again, these observations do not mean modulation cannot be used in all cases. However, they reinforce the idea that it ought to be used with extreme caution, because it contradicts fundamental elements of the rule of law.

In light of the above, modulation of the temporal effects of unconstitutionality rulings must take into account the following substantive and procedural requirements.

2.1.4.3.5 Requirements for Modulation of Effects

2.1.4.3.5.1 Presuppositions

Exceptionality of the Case Under Adjudication

The case that is the object of modulation of effects must be truly exceptional. This exceptionality should be linked to the unlikelihood of repetition in the future. Every upholding of past effects of unconstitutional statutes involves a "countersense": A constitutional norm ought to have been respected but was violated; the effects of the violation were not unleashed; so constitutional transgression is encouraged, even if indirectly, by the lack of consequences resulting from violation. That being so – and using language more appropriate to the issue of legal certainty – every upholding of effects of unconstitutional statutes involves an internal conflict between the temporal dimensions of legal certainty. Legal certainty is upheld in the past, because the inviolability of acts performed or effects produced is preserved, but at the same time legal certainty in the future is restricted because new unconstitutional acts are encouraged.

---

[472] Niklas Luhmann, *Ausdifferenzierung des Rechts. Beiträge zur Rechtssoziologie und Rechtstheorie*, Frankfurt am Main, Suhrkamp, 1999, p. 140.

It is precisely because of this internal conflict between the dimensions of legal certainty that assigning prospective effects to an unconstitutionality ruling must be done only in exceptional cases, understood as cases that are most unlikely to recur in future. This is the crucial point. Thus, to stay with examples of cases already examined by the Supreme Court, there is no risk (or very little risk) that a municipality whose creation is upheld even though it is unconstitutional will be created again; there is no risk (or minimal risk) that the number of city councilors declared incompatible with the Constitution will be changed again. However – and here lies the danger of greater legal uncertainty – when the hiring of civil servants without public competitive examinations is upheld in one case, it can be repeated. Upholding the effects of an unconstitutional act relative to repeatable cases is an incentive to future violations of the Constitution. Legal certainty is violated more than it is protected.

As a rule, the STF has assigned prospective effects to many of its decisions without specifically and in justified fashion examining the risk of perverse efficacy when this technique is applied to the future. Indeed, Justice Cézar Peluso has complained that "the Court is becoming too lenient toward unconstitutionality in matters relating to public servants."[473] However, it must be acknowledged that some Supreme Court justices have expressed great concern with what the future holds if the modulation of effects becomes commonplace, as can be seen from some of their opinions. For example, according to Justice Maurício Corrêa "the Court has warned that if this solution is generalized, it also poses the danger of encouraging unconstitutionality";[474] in the case that ended with the upholding of the irregular creation of a city, Justice Marco Aurélio asserted that "approving the creation of this city contrary to the Constitution opens the door to endorsement of the creation of other cities in evident flagrant conflict with the Constitution";[475] in the case regarding the enactment of a law by an authority without the required jurisdiction, the same justice noted that "by upholding this law for a certain time as if the Constitution were not in force during the period concerned, we are encouraging state assemblies to enact laws that are not in harmony with the Federal Constitution";[476] in the case concerning the internal recruitment of state civil servants without public examinations, Justice Cézar Peluso warned against "creating a precedent that will justify the deliberate creation of unconstitutional norms by states, cities and the federal government, with the justified expectation that tomorrow the Court will allow them to survive!";[477] also judging the case of admission to a civil service career without competitive examinations, Justice Ellen Gracie expressed "concern that a decision by this Court may somehow signal to the authorities of the State of Minas Gerais permission to continue deferring the proper admission of defenders

[473] ADI n.3.819-2, Full Court, Rep. Justice Eros Grau, *DJ* 28 Mar 2008, p. 403 of the decision.

[474] ADI n.1.102, Rep. Justice Maurício Corrêa, *DJ* 17 Nov 1995.

[475] ADI n.2.240-7, Full Court, Rep. Justice Eros Grau, *DJ* 03 Aug 2007, p. 337 of the decision.

[476] ADI n.3.458-8, Full Court, Rep. Justice Eros Grau, *DJ* 28 Mar 2008, p. 378 of the decision.

[477] ADI n.3.819-2, Full Court, Rep. Justice Eros Grau, *DJ* 28 Mar 2008, p. 401 of the decision.

through competitive examinations such as many that exist."[478] This concern of the justices is fundamental because constitutional precedents indirectly have a disciplining effect (*Disziplinierungseffekt*).[479]

What is decisive in the whole argumentation is the demonstration that legal certainty is ambivalent. This conclusion should be observed in every judgment. As noted in the chapter on the content of legal certainty, it must be borne in mind that legal certainty has several aspects, elements and dimensions. Disregarding them means disregarding legal certainty itself. That being so, one cannot simply appeal to legal certainty as a justification to change the effects of an unconstitutionality ruling without considering this multidimensionality and distinguishing between the various dimensions. Doing this properly requires a sort of "internal weighing" of legal certainty, especially with the purpose of knowing whether upholding the past effects of an unconstitutional statute or act will end up causing "more" legal uncertainty than certainty.

No Clear Unconstitutionality in the Disputed Act

The appearance of legitimacy of the disputed act is a requirement of the trust protection principle: For trust to merit protection, the basis for trust must merit the addressee's faith. The absence of an appearance of legitimacy does not exclude the inviolability of the act. This is because inviolability may result not from the subjective efficacy of the legal certainty principle, but from its objective dimension. There are cases in which the initial act did not merit trust but other elements such as time may have contributed to the consolidation of a factual situation that cannot persist or must be changed in future.

As we have already seen, when the STF uses the mechanism of effect modulation, strictly speaking it does not use the trust protection principle, whose application would require evidence of the existence of a basis for trust, trust itself, effective and causally linked exercise of trust, and frustration of trust. These issues cannot be analyzed in concentrated control of constitutionality, or indeed in diffuse control when the Court intends to modulate the effects of an incidental declaration of unconstitutionality, given that there are other cases than the one being decided. The appearance of legitimacy, however, can also be a requirement for application of the objective dimension of the legal certainty principle when the Court examines the presumed or proven repercussion of a declaration of nullity for "collective trust" or the "credibility of the legal order." The reason this is necessary resides in an overall assessment of the legal certainty principle.

As already noted, every declaration with prospective efficacy involves a countersense: Not assigning consequences to violation of the Constitution, when the case is repeatable, encourages repetition of its violation. Now to prevent this from happening, or at least to diminish the likelihood of its happening, modulation of

[478] ADI n.3.819-2, Full Court, Rep. Justice Eros Grau, *DJ* 28 Mar 2008, p. 452 of the decision.

[479] Georg Seyfarth, *Die Änderung der Rechtsprechung durch das Bundesverfassungsgericht*, Berlin, Duncker und Humblot, 1998, p. 294.

effects must be used only if the legitimacy of the behavior was plausible, i.e., when the addressees of the rule could not and should not have known their behavior was unconstitutional. If they did know or could have known their conduct was unlawful, upholding effects means rewarding willful non-compliance with the Constitution. Unless a long lapse of time is deemed to stabilize and modify the assessment of the original unlawfulness, in other cases – whether involving the subjective protection of individual positions via the trust protection principle or encompassing the objective guarantee of transindividual situations via the principle of permanence of the legal order – the disputed act must have an appearance of legitimacy, because otherwise *past* legal certainty is upheld and *future* legal certainty is even more encouraged. Upholding the effects of an unlawful act when its illegitimacy is known from the outset is also incompatible with the rule of law, which cannot coexist with the upholding of acts that flout it, and with the principle of morality, which requires serious, loyal and motivated conduct and does not tolerate the upholding of deliberate acts against the legal order.

On this point the STF's case law needs to be improved. Although the Court shows intense concern not to encourage unconstitutional conduct, in many instances it upholds acts that were known or should have been known to be unconstitutional at the time they were committed. In ADI 3660–2, for example, it declared the unconstitutionality of directing monies collected as legal and court fees to private institutions because this violated the principle of equal treatment and the constitutionally defined use of such fees. However, "for reasons of legal certainty or exceptional social interest," the effects of the unconstitutionality ruling were set to start on a future date. There is a problem with this, as noted by Justice Joaquim Barbosa: "The Court's position on this kind of unconstitutionality has long been well-known" (p. 67 of the decision).[480] The problem is that the effects are modulated on the grounds of legal certainty (in one of its aspects), causing legal uncertainty (in all of its other aspects). This is exactly why the flexible approach to decision making adopted by Germany's Constitutional Court, paradoxical as it may seem, "ultimately jeopardizes legal certainty. As a manifestation of the doctrine of the law-based state (*Rechtsstaatlichkeit*), analogous to the rule of law, legal certainty also requires precisely that the legal consequences of a decision of the Constitutional Court be predictable and calculable for the addressees."[481]

2.1.4.3.5.2 Purposes

Restoration of a "State of Constitutionality"

The assignment of prospective effects should aim to restore constitutionality. It must never be forgotten that the Supreme Court is the "guardian of the Constitution"

---

[480] ADI n.3.660-2, Full Court, Rep. Justice Gilmar Mendes, *DJ* 13 Mar 2008.

[481] Roman Seer, "Die Unvereinbarkeitserklärung des BVerfG am Beispiel seiner Rechtsprechung zum Abgabenrecht", *NJW* 5, p. 291, 1996.

and its role is to guarantee the constitutionality of the laws.[482] This is the system implemented by articles 102 and ff. of the Constitution. Now if a declaration of nullity repairs a violation, it must be used. This is the case when competence rules are infringed: The infringement consists of exercising the power to tax outside the substantive scope permitted by the Constitution. Declaring the nullity of the law restores constitutionality. Only where a declaration of nullity does not restore the state of constitutionality can the STF use the mechanism of modulation of an unconstitutionality ruling's temporal effects.

This requirement is extremely important because without it the entire purpose of judicial review is lost, and the Supreme Court becomes not the "guardian of the Constitution" but the "guardian of violation of the Constitution." Precisely for this reason, past effects must not be upheld unless there is no other way to restore constitutionality. However, this means a declaration of constitutionality with prospective effects should have a subsidiary character and should be used only if other means cannot, especially periods of limitation and transitional rules. It is important to stress that every time the STF upholds the efficacy of an unconstitutional norm whose nullity would restore the state of constitutionality that was suspended by its enactment, it conduces to maintenance of the state of unconstitutionality instead of the upholding of a state of constitutionality.[483]

Thus the STF was right to set deadlines for the legislative or executive to introduce measures designed to eliminate unconstitutionality. When it examined the creation of municipalities without the enactment of a supplementary law, it declared the unconstitutionality of the disputed act, but assured enforcement for 24 months until the state legislature enacted a new rule.[484] When it analyzed admission to the career of public defender through an internal procedure, it left the illegally appointed individuals in their jobs for only six months without tenure, in order to allow time for the positions to be filled.[485] When it examined the state statute initiated by the executive regarding judicial deposits, it ruled the disputed statute unconstitutional and modulated the effects, ordering that the ruling would not produce effects until 60 days after final appeal to allow time for the payment of judicial and extrajudicial costs.[486] When it decided on the application of the Fiscal Responsibility Law to the Federal District, it required compliance with the decision within 8 months of the date of publication of the minutes from the hearing on the merits.[487] When it judged the actions of public defenders in defense of civil servants, it declared the

[482]Oliver W. Lembcke, *Hüter der Verfassung*, Tübingen, Mohr Siebeck, 2007, p. 134.

[483]Gerhard Habscheidt, *Der Anspruch des Bürgers auf Erstattung verfassungswidriger Steuern*, Köln, Otto Schmidt, 2003, p. 31.

[484]ADI n.2.240-7, Full Court, Rep. Justice Eros Grau, *DJ* 03 Aug 2007; ADI n.3.316, Full Court, Rep. Justice Eros Grau, *DJ* 29 Jun 2007; ADI n.3.489, Full Court, Rep. Justice Eros Grau, *DJ* 03 Aug 2007; ADI n.3.689, Full Court, Rep. Justice Eros Grau, *DJ* 29 Jun 2007.

[485]ADI n.3.819-2, Full Court, Rep. Justice Eros Grau, *DJ* 28 Mar 2008.

[486]ADI n.3.458-8, Full Court, Rep. Justice Eros Grau, *DJ* 28 Mar 2008.

[487]ADI n.3.756-1, Full Court, Rep. Justice Carlos Britto, *DJ* 19 Oct 2007.

infraconstitutional norm unconstitutional but upheld its effects until the end of the year in which the decision was entered to allow legislators time to discipline the matter.[488]

All these cases show a well-tempered approach to the use of unconstitutionality rulings. Rather than completely avoiding the modulation of effects, the STF declared the norms in question unconstitutional to devalue the unlawful conduct in legal terms while also finding a way to preserve the fundamental rights that would be harmed by a retroactive decree of nullity and to maintain the inevitable unconstitutionality only for such time as it deemed *strictly necessary* to restore the violated state of constitutionality. Thus the rule is that full prospective efficacy is avoided whenever there is another way to restore the violated state of constitutionality. Where modulation is admitted, the best way to restore the state of constitutionality must be chosen from among those available, such as a declaration of incompatibility and the requirement that the legislative enact a new law, *ex tunc* or *ex nunc* effects, with or without a period of limitation, and with or without transitional rules.

However, in concentrated control of constitutionality prospective efficacy cannot be assigned without first making sure whether it would not be better for the issue to be treated in diffuse control of constitutionality via legal action initiated by litigants who consider themselves harmed. This, for example, was the alternative preferred by the STF in extraordinary appeal RE 105789, which involved a new method for calculating length of service. Although years had passed since the norm entered into force and began producing monetary effects in favor of judges, the STF ruled that it violated the constitutional guarantee of the irreducibility of wages, making "inviolable the right that has already been born and cannot be suppressed," and hence is more than "just an acquired right." In light of this, and because the previous norm that instituted a new method for calculating length of service had been ruled unconstitutional, "the said guarantee prevails over the *ex tunc* effect of the declaration of unconstitutionality of the norm."[489] In other words, when the STF declared unconstitutional the norm governing the calculation of the appellant's length of service, it did not modulate the effects of the ruling at the time, but did nothing to prevent legal action to claim their rights by litigants who considered themselves harmed.

This reservation is very important. In concentrated control of constitutionality the STF should not take the initiative in every situation by excluding the efficacy of unconstitutionality rulings in cases with which it is not familiar and thus cannot truly verify whether the requirements to prove any type of inviolability of individual situations have been satisfied, whether for objective reasons resulting from the passage of time (statutes of limitations), or owing to legal consolidation of situations (acquired rights, completed legal acts, *res iudicata*, past taxable events) or factual consolidation (situations consolidated by time), or for subjective reasons resulting from the concrete and legally oriented exercise of freedoms and property rights (trust

[488]ADI n.3.022-1, Full Court, Rep. Justice Joaquim Barbosa, *DJ* 04 Mar 2005

[489]RE n.105.789-1, 2nd Panel, Rep. Justice Carlos Madeira, *DJ* 09 May 1986

protection). Because the configuration of all of these cases depends on concrete evidence, it cannot be subject to direct and abstract consideration in concentrated control of constitutionality. What is admissible in concentrated control is the setting aside of the past efficacy of a decision only when the negative effects of annulment, besides being extensive and intensive, can be reasonably presumed certain by the Court. In other words, only if annulment of a disputed norm may cause great objective legal uncertainty, up to a point where it affects the institutional stability and credibility of law, can the Court assign prospective effects to a decision. In all other cases, only concrete examination can show whether the requirements indispensable to the inviolability of individual situations for objective or subjective reasons are present. This explains Justice Ellen Gracie's opinion in the judgment of an attempt by the Attorney General, via a motion for clarification, to have prospective effects assigned to the decision that declared the constitutionality of requiring applicants for posts in the federal prosecution service to have at least 2 years' practice after qualifying as lawyers in order to be eligible for the public competitive exam, on the grounds that many prosecutors had taken the oath of office and performed their duties without meeting this requirement: "Moreover, I consider manifestly inappropriate, as presented, the idea of examining the concrete situation of prosecutors who benefited from judicial decisions that ruled the norm in question unconstitutional." It also explains Justice Carlos Britto's remark that "such borderline cases are delicate and must be resolved at the administrative level or in subjective litigation, that is, in diffuse control of constitutionality."[490]

If it is not careful to avoid the examination, in concentrated control of constitutionality, of that which cannot be proven in this type of control, the STF will find itself not only entering into individual and concrete matters that cannot be assessed with adjudicative certainty but also assuring the inviolability of individual situations without knowing whether they legally and factually exist. This would be tantamount to "judging in the dark", so to speak– in the name of legal certainty, but without any legal certainty at all.

Direct Protection of the Indirect and Objective Legal Certainty of Fundamental Rights

Modulation of effects must be a means of preserving legal certainty in its entire amplitude, especially the institutional stability of the legal order. This stability, however, cannot relate merely to financial matters. It must be concerned with protecting the credibility of the legal order, in the sense that a decree of nullity would end up negatively affecting, actually or presumably, a large number of people whose fundamental rights would ultimately be unnecessarily restricted and whose trust in the order, considered globally, would be strongly affected. Thus to continue taking examples from cases decided by the STF, retroactively annulling the creation of a municipality would affect not only the institutional situation of the city's organization but also the rights of citizens who benefited from the public services

[490]ED in ADI n.1.040-9, Full Court, Rep. Justice Ellen Gracie, *DJ* 01 Sep 2006.

provided in the past, completed administrative activities and consolidated police activities; retroactively annulling the composition of municipal councils would affect not only the institutional situation of federal entities but also the rights of citizens who benefited from the laws enacted in the past.

On this point, it is worth recalling that modulation of effects began in Germany, and was designed to guarantee the inviolability of the effects of norms that were later declared unconstitutional but meanwhile had benefited citizens, albeit unequally or disproportionately. In these cases, annulment would merely exclude part of the positive effects of a duty of protection established by the Constitution. More simply put, an *ab initio* annulment would only remove the "good part" of the statute, without restoring the state of constitutionality. Many of the STF's decisions analyzed followed the same direction: It declared the creation of municipalities unconstitutional without revoking the acts already performed in order to preserve the benefits to citizens via past services and administrative acts[491]; it declared unconstitutional the employment of public defenders without a competitive exam, but in doing so did not revoke the acts already performed in order to preserve judicial protection of the rights of the people defended[492]; it ruled unconstitutional the legal aid provided by public defenders to civil servants but did not revoke the acts practiced hitherto to benefit the defendants concerned.[493] In all such cases, two factors motivated the upholding of past effects: direct institutional preservation, and indirect protection of rights.

Here it is relevant to recall that legal certainty has been defined in this book as a principle norm that requires the legislative, executive and judiciary to prioritize certain types of behavior that contribute more to the existence, *for the benefit of citizens and from their perspective*, of a state of reliability and calculability of and through law, based on its knowability, as an instrument to guarantee *respect for their capacity* to shape the present with dignity and make legally informed strategic plans for the future without deceit, frustration or surprise. Financial losses resulting from the collection of unconstitutional taxes, therefore, do not fit the concept of legal certainty embodied in the Constitution.

Thus the temporal effects of unconstitutionality rulings can be modulated only when annulment does not restore the state of constitutionality and when required by the efficacy of fundamental rights. The STF's decisions on federative-institutional matters analyzed here did not restrict but protected fundamental rights. The situation is different, however, in the case of statutes that create tax obligations: Upholding their efficacy, besides allowing tax to be collected without a statute but by court order, ultimately means temporary suspension of the efficacy of the fundamental rights of freedom, property and judicial protection.

[491]ADI n.2.240-7, Full Court, Rep. Justice Eros Grau, *DJ* 3 Aug 2007; ADI n.3.316, Full Court, Rep. Justice Eros Grau, *DJ* 29 Jun 2007; ADI n.3.489, Full Court, Rep. Justice Eros Grau, *DJ* 03 Aug 2007; ADI n.3.689, Full Court, Rep. Justice Eros Grau, *DJ* 29 Jun 2007.

[492]ADI n.3.819-2, Full Court, Rep. Justice Eros Grau, *DJ* 28 Mar 2008.

[493]ADI n.3.022-1, Full Court, Rep. Justice Joaquim Barbosa, *DJ* 04 Mar 2005

In any event it is essential to bear the equality principle in mind.[494] Modulation of effects must be a means of assuring the supremacy of the constitutional order, never an instrument for its transgression. Thus modulation must not be used if the resulting treatment is gravely and unjustifiably discriminatory. This is precisely what happened when, in deciding whether lawmakers were empowered to define periods of prescription and limitation, the STF excluded taxpayers who had already paid their taxes from the efficacy of the decision.[495] Taxpayers who had obeyed the law were penalized; those who had broken the law or contested its efficacy were rewarded – even though both were in the same situation with regard to the hypothesis formulated by the tax law concerned. Hence Machado Derzi's sarcastic remark that only foolishly compliant taxpayers had borne the burden of taxation.[496]

Avoidance of a "Grave" Threat to Legal Certainty

Because the assignment of prospective effects to a decision entails overriding the nullity rule and a countersense regarding compliance with the Constitution, it cannot be justified by any kind of institutional instability or impact on the credibility of the legal order. Only where annulment of a contested norm causes a *high* level of legal uncertainty will the assignment of prospective effects be justified. Otherwise the supremacy of the Constitution is flouted and unconstitutional acts are encouraged.

The STF usually follows this understanding. Hearing an application for provisional remedy (AC 189), Justice Gilmar Mendes said an exception to the annulment rule cannot be made only "where it is absolutely inappropriate for the goal pursued (cases of omission; exclusion of a benefit compatible with the equality principle), and where it might harm the constitutional legal system itself (grave threat to legal certainty)."[497] On a separate occasion, Justice Joaquim Barbosa stressed that modulation of effects must be justified by an exceptional situation because it is "characterized by an *extreme* risk to legal certainty or the public interest" (emphasis added).[498] To use the terms defined in this study, the STF can adopt prospective effects only when annulment does not restore the state of constitutionality, as is the case with Germany's Constitutional Court, or when annulment causes intense uncertainty.

This analysis of the prerequisites for and purposes of the modulation of effects shows that using it – as advocated in this thesis – is not the result of a mere weighing between the (negative) effects of a declaration of nullity (*ex tunc*) and the (positive) effects of a declaration of incompatibility (*ex nunc*), as argued by

---

[494] Andreas Vonkilch, *Das Intertemporale Privatrecht*, Wien, Springer, 1999, p. 317.

[495] RE n.560.626, Full Court, Rep. Justice Gilmar Mendes, *DJe* 5 Dec 2008.

[496] Misabel de Abreu Machado Derzi, *Modificações da jurisprudência no Direito Tributário*, São Paulo, Noeses, 2009, p. 527.

[497] AC/MC/QO n.189, Full Court, Rep. Justice Gilmar Mendes, *DJ* 27 Aug 2004.

[498] AgR in AI n.557.237, 2nd Panel, Rep. Justice Joaquim Barbosa, *DJ* 26 Oct 2007.

Medeiros.[499] My position is that there are indispensable requirements without which modulation is out of the question, regardless of weighing. Thus what is proposed here is an exception-based approach to modulation, conditioned to the observance of prerequisites and the pursuit of goals without which modulation should be rejected out of hand.

2.1.4.3.5.3 Procedure

Guarantee of an Adversarial Debate on Modulation
In procedural terms it is important to note that the subject-matter discussed when modulation of effects is at stake differs from that of the case under adjudication: Modulation is not about the merits but about the effects of the decision. For this reason it is indispensable that the question of modulation be debated differently from the merits. The reasons are different and do not necessarily relate to the arguments on the merits. Hence the judge must hear the parties on the modulation itself.[500] This is precisely why the European Court of Justice suspends the judgment to hear the parties on the specific issue of the efficacy of the decision.[501]

Hence an unannounced ruling on modulation of effects without offering the parties an opportunity to express their views thoroughly is incompatible not only with the adversarial principle but also with the legal certainty principle itself. This does not mean the reporting justice or any of the other justices cannot raise the question. What it does mean is that once the matter is raised it must be discussed specifically and adversarially, since it is a different subject from the merits of the case. The STF therefore proceeded wrongly by excluding taxpayers who had already paid their taxes from the efficacy of the decision in the case in which it analyzed whether lawmakers were empowered to define periods of prescription and limitation without hearing both parties on this modulation.[502] The discussion that took place during the hearing on the express request for modulation is elucidatory: "I see it as unnecessary because when constitutionality is at stake this possibility is already implicit" (Justice Gilmar Mendes); "But it should have been argued orally at the appropriate time" (Justice Cézar Peluso); "Yesterday counsel for one of the parties expressly referred to the request for modulation; if counsel for the other party did not want to . . . " (Justice Menezes Direito).

However, since the modulation of effects involves different normative matter than the merits, it should be discussed separately, and the right to a full defense should

[499]Rui Medeiros, *A Decisão de inconstitucionalidade – Os autores, o conteúdo e os efeitos da decisão de inconstitucionalidade*, Lisboa, Universidade Católica, 1999, p. 703.

[500]Nicolas Molfessis (Org.), *Les revirements de jurisprudence. Rapport remis à Monsieur le Premier Président Guy Canivet. Groupe de Travail*, Paris, Litec, 2005, pages 21 and 30.

[501]Christian Waldfhoff, "Recent developments relating to the retroactive effect of decisions of the ECJ", in *Common Market Law Review* 46, p. 3, 2009 (manuscript).

[502]RE n.560.626, Full Court, Rep. Justice Gilmar Mendes, *DJe* 05 Dec 2008.

be guaranteed by suspending judgment of the merits so that both parties can address modulation with an appropriate defense of their positions.[503]

Preservation of Retroactive Efficacy for the Precursor Case, Parallel Cases and Cases Not Covered by a Statute of Limitations

The assignment of prospective effects to both the precursor or instant case (*Anlaß-fall*) and the other ongoing cases (*Parallelfälle*) would lead to excessive restriction of the fundamental right to judicial protection. The plaintiff in each case, i.e. the party that prompted the Court to issue a judgment, would receive "stone instead of bread" (*Stein, statt Brot*) as they say in Germany, winning a "Pyrrhic victory" devoid of any practical effect. From the constitutional viewpoint, however, the problem is not only the lack of practical effects but restriction of the fundamental rights of judicial protection and freedom.

Upholding the past effects of a statute that has been ruled unconstitutional means denying the plaintiff's request, suppressing the plaintiff's fundamental right to judicial protection and, indirectly, freedom: If one of the efficacies of fundamental rights is the efficacy of defense, failure to eliminate the unconstitutionality concerned prevents judicial action from limiting the exercise of power when it unduly restricts freedom.[504] Hence Justice Sepúlveda Pertence's concern in a case in which a city claimed the right to receive its share in a state tax: "It will be said that the acquired right for which the city has fought for ten years is worth nothing."[505] This is exactly why the precursor or instant case absolutely must not be included in total prospective efficacy. The same is also true for all other ongoing cases.

Safe Modulation of Effects Based on Legal Certainty

An unconstitutionality ruling without annulment, also known as a declaration of mere constitutional incompatibility, involves an exception, as we have seen: The effects of an unconstitutional act are upheld instead of being declared null and void. As Justice Gilmar Mendes points out, using a non-technical expression from the perspective of legal theory but nevertheless correct in substance: "Thus the *principle* of nullity remains the *rule* in Brazilian law as well."[506] However, what are the exceptions to this rule? This question does not concern only due process of law. It concerns the legal certainty principle itself: Without a minimum of clarity, intelligibility and calculability for the justice-seeking citizen about when annulment will be preferred or another mechanism will be used to assign efficacy to judicial review decisions, there can be no legal certainty in the sense of certainty of and

---

[503] Andreas Vonkilch, *Das Intertemporale Privatrecht*, Wien, Springer, 1999, p. 319.

[504] Roman Seer, "Die Unvereinbarkeitserklärung des BVerfG am Beispiel seiner Rechtsprechung zum Abgabenrecht", *NJW* 5, p. 290, 1996.

[505] RE n.401.953-1, Full Court, Rep. Justice Joaquim Barbosa, *DJ* 21 Sep 2007, p. 472 of the decision.

[506] ADI n.2.240-7, Full Court, Rep. Justice Eros Grau, *DJ* 03 Aug 2007. On the subject, check: *RTJ* 87/758, 89/367, 146/461, 164/506.

through law. Here it is worth quoting Seer's comment on the erratic or vague judicial review practiced in Germany:

> Neither citizens nor the Administration can therefore estimate in any measure whether the German Federal Constitutional Court will react by means of a declaration of unconstitutionality in the form of a declaration of nullity, a declaration of incompatibility with a duty to reform *ex tunc* or *ex nunc*, a declaration of incompatibility with or without setting a term, i.e., with or without transition rules, or an appeal to the legislator with or without setting a term. If the decisions of the German Federal Constitutional Court are not to become an incalculable gamble, an understandable scheme is necessary.[507]

It is precisely in this sense that the modulation of effects must accord with the legal certainty principle. However, this will happen only if the STF is not merely faithful to the rule and breaks it only in actually exceptional cases, but also at least:

(a) (Expressly) justifies the exception made by stipulating the constitutional norm on grounds of which the past effects of the act declared unconstitutional are to be upheld; (expressly) justifies setting aside the rule of *ex tunc* nullity of the unconstitutional act.
(b) (Expressly) justifies the imperative need to set aside the rule of *ex tunc* nullity of the unconstitutional act to uphold the state of constitutionality.
(c) Proves (with documents or presumptions, when possible) the negative effects for the state of constitutionality resulting from *ex tunc* annulment of the unconstitutional act.

Unless these prerequisites are observed, constitutionality control is not minimally calculable and hence compatible with the legal certainty principle, so that judicial decisions ultimately become a "procedural roulette" (*prozessuales Roulette*)[508] or a simple "game of chance" (*Vabanque-Spiel*).[509]

2.2 *Normative Efficacy: "Certainty of Realization"*

2.2.1 Initial Considerations

Legal certainty exists only if the law is capable of effectively guiding action in some measure.[510] If the norms citizens are aware of are not minimally obeyed, then strictly speaking normative knowledge does not serve as an instrument for citizens to shape a legally oriented strategic plan for the future. Hence the affirmation that efficacy is

[507] Roman Seer, Die Unvereinbarkeitserklärung des BVerfG am Beispiel seiner Rechtsprechung zum Abgabenrecht", *NJW* n. 5, p. 291, 1996.

[508] Roman Seer, "Gewerbesteuer im Visier des Verfassungsgerichts – Anmerkungen zu dem Vorlagebeschluß des FG Niedersachsen vom 24.6.1998", *FR* 1998, p. 1022, 1998.

[509] Ernst Benda e Eckart Klein, *Lehrbuch des Verfassungsprozessrechts*, 2ª ed., Heidelberg, C. F. Müller, 2001, margin number 96.

[510] Joseph Raz, "The rule of law and its virtue (1977)", in *The Authority of Law. Essays on Law and Morality*, Oxford, Oxford, 1979, p. 220.

a condition for legal certainty.[511] Legal efficacy, understood not as social efficacy, but as the capacity to produce legal effects, to a lesser or greater extent, but to some extent.[512]

The affirmation that legal certainty depends on efficacy is not a claim that predictability requires social efficacy, i.e., effective application of the predicted consequences. This is because if people know in advance that some norms are not regularly applied by the decision-making bodies and hence that some norms are not effective, nevertheless – and precisely for that reason – they can still foresee the consequence assigned to some acts or facts: no consequence at all. Thus if the legal order fails to function in a regular but localized manner, and if citizens are aware of this failure, its calculability does not decrease but in fact increases. As Gometz rightly notes, in many cases an individual can better foresee the legal consequences of an act or fact by considering the information that a given norm, though valid and relevant for the case under examination, is regularly unobserved. In that situation, knowledge that a globally effective legal order occasionally lacks efficacy increases predictability as long as the information about lack of efficacy is public and regular.[513] Thus lack of efficacy is paradoxically an instrument of predictability.

This lack of legal efficacy can also occur when a law lacks implementing rules or has not been implemented by the responsible executive body and hence cannot be enforced. In the absence of the necessary regulation, citizens can foresee that the law's consequences will not be applied, and paradoxically this increases their ability to calculate the legal order.[514]

The point of these observations, on one hand, is to show that the legal efficacy described here as a condition for legal certainty is not the specific regular efficacy of any given legal norm, but the legal efficacy of the legal order as a whole, whose absence is capable of compromising the rule of law itself.[515] Legal efficacy as coerciveness, as the content of normativity, to quote Carvalho.[516] On the other hand, these considerations show that the legal efficacy referred to here does not exactly concern the causal link between the behavior of citizens and the content of norms (social effectiveness), or even the psychological state of citizens relative to their

[511] Antonio Enrique Perez Luño, *La Seguridad Jurídica*, Barcelona, Ariel, 1991, p. 26. Federico Arcos Ramírez, *La seguridad jurídica: una teoría formal*, Madrid, Dykinson, 2000, p. 44.

[512] Eros Roberto Grau, *A Ordem Econômica na Constituição de 1988*, 14th ed., São Paulo, Malheiros Editores, 2010, p. 322. Tércio Sampaio Ferraz Jr., "Irretroatividade e jurisprudência judicial", in Tércio Sampaio Ferraz Jr., Roque Antonio Carrazza and Nelson Nery Júnior (Orgs.), *Efeito "ex nunc" e as decisões do STF*, São Paulo, Manole, 2008, p. 16.

[513] Gianmarco Gometz, *La certezza giuridica come prevedibilità*, Torino, Giappichelli, 2005, p. 266.

[514] Anne-Laure Valembois, *La constitutionnalisation de l'exigence de sécurité juridique en Droit Français*, Paris, LGDJ, 2005, p. 129.

[515] Idem, pages 129 and 200.

[516] Paulo de Barros Carvalho, "O princípio da segurança jurídica no campo tributário", *RDT* 94, p. 22, São Paulo, 2006.

action being guided by law (psychological effectiveness), but rather to the general expectation that valid laws will be regularly efficient.[517] More precisely, the legal efficacy referred to here concerns the conditions abstractly established by a given order, such as the existence of a judiciary accessible by means of previously defined procedural instruments and made up of judges endowed with given prerogatives also abstractly established, so that it is possible to presume the regular efficacy of law. In sum, in the sense defined here, it is eminently legal efficacy: not factual effectiveness, but an aspiration to efficacy based on legal conditions.[518] These legal conditions may concern both norms that address how other norms are to be applied and norms or institutions that protect the application of other norms. Torres is therefore right to state that legal certainty encompasses the principle-based procedural and institutional guarantees established by the Constitution.[519]

These guarantees are the focus for what follows.

2.2.2 The Right to Judicial Protection

For legal certainty to exist as reliability of law, citizens must have access to due process of law. This is why the Constitution guarantees that "no one shall be deprived of freedom or property without due process of law" (article 5, LIV).[520]

Due process of law is the procedural reflection of the positivation of fundamental rights: The assignment of a right presupposes the assignment of the means to protect it. Whoever gives the end gives the means. A subjective right without a procedure would be mere *flatus vocis*, empty words from the legislator.[521] Nevertheless, the Constitution expressly establishes due process of law as the mother lode of implicit instruments to protect the fundamental rights. It also expressly institutes several corollaries, such as the prohibition of tribunals of exception and the natural judge principle (article 5, XXXVII and LIII); equality (article 5, head paragraph), within whose scope are located parity of arms, the adversarial principle and the right to a full defense, with all the requisite means and resources (article 5, LV); the inadmissibility of evidence obtained by unlawful means (article 5, LVI); and

[517] Federico Arcos Ramírez, *La seguridad jurídica: una teoría formal*, Madrid, Dykinson, 2000, p. 46.

[518] Franz-Xaver Kaufmann, *Sicherheit als soziologisches und sozialpolitisches Problem*, 2nd ed., Stuttgart, 1973, p. 103.

[519] Ricardo Lobo Torres, "Liberdade, segurança e justiça", in Paulo de Barros Carvalho (Org.), *Justiça Tributária*, São Paulo, Max Limonad, 1998, p. 687.

[520] Sérgio Luiz Wetzel de Mattos, *Devido Processo Legal e Proteção de Direitos*, Porto Alegre, Livraria do Advogado, 2009, pages 202 and following. Michael Koch, *Die Grundsätze des intertemporalen Rechts im Verwaltungsprozess – Vertrauensschutz im verwaltungsgerichtlichen Verfahren*, Berlin, Duncker und Humblot, 2009, p. 110.

[521] Ronnie Preuss Duarte, *Garantia de acesso à Justiça. Os Direitos Processuais fundamentais*, Coimbra, Coimbra, 2007, p. 17.

the justification of decisions (article 93, IX).[522] The Constitution itself therefore provides for all possible conflicts, strengthening the guarantees it enshrines. It should be noted that, contrary to what may appear at first glance. the specification of fundamental rights effectively strengthens these rights. Calling the guarantees principles, as if they were norms that required horizontal weighing, would be an impairment tantamount to *capitis deminutio*, a derogation of their privileged status in the constitutional order.[523]

The essential point for present purposes is that the framers of the Constitution took upon themselves the task of "guaranteeing a right that guarantees all rights." In other words, the Constitution establishes an instrument of reliability of the legal order.

2.2.3 Presuppositions of Judicial Protection

2.2.3.1 Institutional

The right of defense depends on the existence of institutional conditions that can make them effective in general. Three such conditions are necessary: an independent judiciary, access to justice, and universal jurisdiction.[524]

The independence of the judiciary is implicit in the separation of powers (article 2) and assured by its financial and administrative autonomy (article 99). These principles lay the organizational foundations for the presupposition that the judiciary is capable of enforcing the constitutional order.

Access to justice is also an indispensable condition for the efficacy of the legal order.[525] This is why, on one hand, the Constitution guarantees the right of all citizens (article 5) to petition the government free of charge (indent XXXIV) in defense of rights or against illegal acts or the abuse of power (item "a"), and to obtain certificates from government offices for the defense of rights and to clarify situations of personal interest (item "b"). The Constitution also guarantees that "the state shall provide comprehensive legal aid free of charge to anyone who proves insufficiency of financial resources" (indent LXXIV).

Alongside the principle of access to justice, it is essential that the judiciary not refuse to judge any claim of injury or threat to a right (indent XXXV). No statute

---

[522]Carlos Alberto Alvaro de Oliveira, *Do Formalismo no Processo Civil*, 3rd ed., São Paulo, Saraiva, 2009, pages 80 and 102 and following. Idem, "O formalismo valorativo no confronto com o formalismo excessivo", *RF* 388, pp. 11–28, separata, Rio de Janeiro, s.d.

[523]Ronnie Preuss Duarte, *Garantia de Acesso à Justiça. Os Direitos Processuais Fundamentais*, Coimbra, Coimbra, 2007, p. 96.

[524]Roque Antonio Carrazza, *Curso de Direito Constitucional Tributário*, 27th ed., São Paulo, Malheiros Editores, 2011, p. 471. Leandro Paulsen, *Segurança jurídica, certeza do Direito e Tributação*, Porto Alegre, Livraria do Advogado, 2006, p. 60.

[525]Joseph Raz, "The rule of law and its virtue (1977)", in *The authority of Law. Essays on Law and Morality*, Oxford, Oxford, 1979, p. 217.

or administrative act may create obstacles to the investigation and judgment of any matter capable of influencing the realization of the rights established by the Constitution.

These two guarantees – access to justice and the judiciary, and universality of jurisdiction – serve as the means whereby the content of the general and abstract rules can have a chance to be institutionally concretized in the event that it is not spontaneously complied with. Now considering that legal certainty requires a state of reliability of law so that citizens can freely and autonomously assure the legal effects of the freedom exercised in the past, without frustration or surprise, they must have the conditions to ensure that the freedom legally exercised yesterday is respected today. And for this to be the case there must be institutionalized procedures capable of guaranteeing the rights exercised in the past. This is why the guarantee of access to justice and universality of jurisdiction is indispensable: Without an institutionalized and independent judiciary to guarantee rights, there cannot be a minimum of reliance on law and its institutional capacity to guarantee rights and expectations; and even if an independent judiciary does exist, unless there is universality of access for *all* to petition against *any* injury or threat to a right, then minimum conditions to protect rights and expectations will not exist.

All these considerations are intended only to show the essential relationship between the principles of universality of jurisdiction and legal certainty. The former is an institutional precondition for the existence of the latter; conversely, the latter is a normative precondition for the existence of the former.

2.2.3.2 Procedural

Besides institutional conditions, procedural conditions must also exist. First, there must be a natural judge. Unless the existence of a judge precedes the case to be judged, general conditions will not exist for rights to be effectively guaranteed. This is exactly why article 5 of the Constitution includes among the individual rights and guarantees the rule that "there shall be no judges or tribunals of exception" (indent XXXVII) and that "no one shall be judged or sentenced save by the competent authority" (indent LIII).[526]

Second, the judge must be impartial, in the sense of having qualities that presume equidistance from the interests of the parties. To this end, the Constitution establishes first that to become a judge it is necessary to pass a public competitive examination (article 93). It then establishes a number of guarantees to protect the independence of judges: they remain in office for life, they cannot be removed, and their pay cannot be reduced (article 95). In addition, it prohibits certain activities

[526] Roque Antonio Carrazza, *Curso de Direito Constitucional Tributário*, 27th ed., São Paulo, Malheiros Editores, 2011, pages 471–472. Sérgio Luiz Wetzel de Mattos, *Devido processo legal e proteção de direitos*, Porto Alegre, Livraria do Advogado, 2009, pages 218 and following. Thomas Roth, *Das Grundrecht auf den gesetzlichen Richter*, Berlin, Duncker und Humblot, 2000, pages 26 and following and 203 and following.

to avoid the risk of partiality, such as holding any other office or position, even when on paid leave, except a teaching position; receiving legal fees or any share of a lawsuit for any reason or on any pretext; engaging in party politics; receiving allowances or contributions from natural persons or public or private entities for any reason or on any pretext, with the exceptions established by law; and practicing law in the court or tribunal on which they served as judges for a period of three years following their retirement or discharge (article 95, sole paragraph). In light of these provisions in aggregate, it can be presumed that judges are impartial, and that their existence enables the rights concerned to be effectively guaranteed.

Third, procedural acts must be notified and judicial proceedings must be public. Otherwise, strictly speaking citizens cannot defend themselves.[527] On this point the Constitution stipulates that all judgments shall be public (article 93, IX) and establishes the rule of publicity for procedural acts, which may be restricted only when this is required to defend privacy or the social interest (article 5, LX), as well as publicity as a general principle of the public administration (article 37). If the parties to a proceeding are not informed of acts performed and aware of all the elements in it, they cannot present arguments regarding the facts and legal issues. Hence the provisions of Law 9784/99 requiring official publication of all administrative acts except where secrecy is required by the Constitution (3, V); and guaranteeing citizens the right to be made aware of the instatement of administrative proceedings in which they have an interest, to see the records, to obtain copies of the documents involved, and to be notified of the decision (3, II). The requirements for legal notices, summonses and subpoenas to be valid are detailed in article 26 of this law.

Fourth, decisions must be properly justified, i.e., rationally constructed, written out, and based on the legal order.[528] Precisely along these lines, the Constitution requires that "all judgments by bodies of the judiciary shall be public, and all decisions shall be justified on pain of nullity, but in certain cases the law may limit attendance to the parties and their lawyers, or only the latter, whenever preservation of the right to privacy of the party interested in confidentiality will not harm the public's right to information" (article 93, IX); and that the "administrative decisions of tribunals shall be supported by recitals and shall be made in open session, with disciplinary decisions being made by the vote of the absolute majority of their members" (article 93, X). Flowing from this, article 2 of Law 9784/99 includes justification among the required procedural principles, and indent VII of the same article requires a detailed exposition of all the factual and legal assumptions underlying the decision. As if this were not enough, article 50 establishes detailed

[527]Roque Antonio Carrazza, *Curso de Direito Constitucional Tributário*, 27th ed., São Paulo, Malheiros Editores, 2011, p. 482.

[528]Ibidem, p. 511. José Carlos Vieira de Andrade, *O dever de fundamentação expressa dos actos administrativos*, Coimbra, Almedina, 1992, pages 228 and following. Joaquín Álvarez Martínez, *La Motivación de los actos tributarios*, Madrid, Marcial Pons, 1999, pages 29 and following. Ralph Christensen and Hans Kudlich, *Theorie richterlichen Begründens*, Berlin, Duncker und Humblot, 2001, pages 55 and following and 430 and following.

rules for the duty of justification, stating in paragraph 1 that the recitals must be explicit, clear and congruent, and may consist of a declaration of assent to the grounds for previous opinions, information, decisions or propositions, which in this case become part of the act.

Fifth, the adversarial principle and the right to a full defense must be guaranteed. Unless every citizen can oppose the other party's claims and have complete freedom to use any means of defense, strictly speaking there is no fundamental right of defense. Along these lines the Constitution guarantees "the right to adversarial process and a full defense, with all inherent means and resources, for litigants in judicial or administrative proceedings, as well as defendants in general" (article 5, LV). The means and resources mentioned include the right to submit statements and produce evidence, and to have these properly considered by the judge. Here, too, the framers of the Constitution took care to include a clause making evidence obtained by unlawful means inadmissible in proceedings (article 5, LVI). Similarly, Law 9784/99 guarantees the right to submit arguments and present documents, which must be considered by the competent body before an administrative decision is issued (3, II).

It can be seen that all the requirements analyzed so far are embodied in constitutional rules. Although they could all have been reconstructed as implications of the fundamental right to petition, or even as logical implications of the fundamental rights themselves, the fact is that to prevent any doubt arising the Constitution expressly rules on these requirements. This makes its application rigid in the sense that the guarantees concerned cannot be set aside via horizontal weighing with the aim of adjusting them to certain interests or even the public interest. Once again, the framers of the Constitution opted for a system of predictability.

However, to prevent the establishment of some guarantees from appearing exhaustive rather than exemplificatory, as already noted the Constitution guarantees that "no one shall be deprived of freedom or property without due process of law" (article 5, LIV). This should be read as implying that all the necessary means to enforce the right of defense must be guaranteed even if they are not expressly provided for in the Constitution. Thus besides access to justice and the right to petition, a natural and impartial judge, publicity, and justification of procedural acts, the Constitution also guarantees all other rights that by implication may be concretely necessary to a full defense, even if they are not abstractly provided for. To avoid any further doubt regarding the exemplificatory character of the guarantees, often mistaken for an exhaustive list, the Constitution directly guarantees due process of law as the mother lode for all other guarantees not expressly mentioned.

2.2.4 Instruments of Judicial Protection

For the rights established to be guaranteed, the existence of procedural and institutional conditions is not enough. Citizens also need procedural instruments with which to defend their rights, and these must be both preventive and repressive.

In this respect the Constitution establishes, on one hand, the right to seek a "writ of mandamus [...] to protect a clear and perfect right not covered by *habeas corpus* or *habeas data*, when the party responsible for an illegal act or abuse of power is a public authority or an agent of a legal entity exercising duties of government" (article 5, LXIX). On the other hand, it guarantees a writ of injunction "whenever the absence of a regulatory norm prevents the exercise of constitutional rights and freedoms, and of the prerogatives inherent in nationality, sovereignty and citizenship" (article 5, LXXI).

For present purposes the point is that these defensive instruments act as general conditions for citizens in general, and taxpayers in particular, to guarantee the effectiveness of their rights through the judiciary. As Carrazza notes, the Constitution not only guarantees fundamental rights but also provides the means to enforce these guarantees.[529] If reliability is the requirement that the freedom exercised yesterday be respected today, without procedural and institutional conditions there is no legal certainty.

So far we have examined the conditions for legal certainty to exist relative to the past, i.e., for the requirements for freedom exercised in the past to be respected. Now we must analyze the conditions for legal certainty to exist relative to the future – in other words, the elements whose presence is indispensable for the freedom legally exercised today to be respected tomorrow. As stressed by Arcos Ramírez, this entails demonstrating the importance of the past to the prediction of the future from the vantage-point of the present.[530]

3 Normative Calculability and the Problem of Change: "Certainty of Transition from Present to Future" Through Anteriority, Continuity and Normative Bindingness

3.1 Initial Considerations

The paradigm of legal certainty as sureness of content leads to the understanding of its future dimension as absolute predictability. Certainty in law means predictable law – which is the case when citizen taxpayers can accurately foresee the future consequences of acts performed in the present. This understanding, however, starts from presuppositions that have already been rejected in the first part of this study. Law depends on argumentative processes, and absolute predictability is therefore unattainable. It is often said, somewhat ironically, that it is hard to make predictions,

[529] Roque Antonio Carrazza, *Curso de Direito Constitucional Tributário*, 27th ed., São Paulo, Malheiros Editores, 2011, p. 448.

[530] Federico Arcos Ramírez, *La seguridad jurídica: una teoría formal*, Madrid, Dykinson, 2000, p. 38.

especially about the future, or that only the misinformed can be sure of anything. The colloquial import is precisely this impossibility. Instead of predictability, therefore, legal certainty requires the realization of a state of calculability.

Calculability means the capacity to anticipate the alternative consequences that can be assigned by law to facts, or to our own or third-party acts of commission or omission, so that the consequence actually applied in the future will be one of the few alternatives anticipated in the present. This anticipation is successful when the actual decision falls within the range of foreseeable interpretative possibilities and is one of the abstractly foreseen consequences that are verifiable using argumentative structures and criteria.

Since calculability is connected to the realization of the rights of freedom and dignity, it must involve the capacity to choose among the available lines of action autonomously and responsibly. Thus it concerns the capacity to know the possible meanings of the norm to be obeyed, and to control the concretization it will be given by the executive and judiciary, in terms not only of the actual response of the decision-making bodies to past acts and events, but also of their presumptive response should they be empowered to decide on acts that could have been performed or facts that could have occurred. Thus calculability requires a certain breadth and depth.[531]

The quantifying depth or vertical dimension of anticipation concerns the effectiveness, accuracy and duration of the forecast. There is a high degree of calculability of future normative consequences when individuals are able to identify a *small number of consequences* that can be encompassed within a *reasonable period*, meaning enough time for decisions regarding a legally oriented strategic plan of action. The breadth or horizontal dimension of anticipation concerns the diffusion of certainty among a given class of forecasters. There is a high degree of calculability of future normative consequences when most taxpayers are capable of identifying a small number of consequences within a reasonable period.

Calculability is defined above as the capacity to anticipate the *range of consequences* alternatively applicable to acts or facts and the *time frame* within which a consequence will be effectively applied. Considering that calculability, as a partial element of legal certainty, is an instrument for individuals to be able to plan and conceive their future, thereby increasing the scope for free action, the range of normative consequences assignable to acts or facts cannot be too broad, the alternatives cannot be too discrepant from one another, and the time frame within which the applicable consequence will be confirmed cannot be too long.[532] This is because if there are incalculable consequences that are too different from one another, individuals cannot autonomously and freely make legally informed strategic decisions to plan their future. When the alternatives are too inconsistent with one another, if any one of them occurs there will be not surprise but intense

[531] Gianmarco Gometz, *La certezza giuridica come prevedibilità*, Torino, Giappichelli, 2005, pages 13, 205 and 208.

[532] Ibidem, p. 232.

surprise. The point is that, as stressed by Ataliba, the Constitution establishes a climate radically contrary to surprises, so that predictability is one of its prime objectives.[533]

Given these considerations, calculability must be defined as a state of affairs in which citizens have a significant capacity to *anticipate* and *measure* the *narrow* and *relatively invariable* range of consequences abstractly assignable to their own or third-party acts, or to facts, and the *limited* time within which the definitive consequence will be applied.

Precisely because of these considerations it is possible to delimit the means necessary to promote a state of calculability of the legal order. For taxpayers to be able to anticipate the small number of consequences that can be comprised within a reasonable time, and assignable by law to facts, or to their own or third-party acts of commission or omission,, so that the consequence actually applied in the future is one of the few alternatives anticipated in the present, the changes must be predictable, they cannot be sudden, and they must fall within mandatory parameters for all three branches of government. In other words, there is calculability only if there is anteriority, continuity and bindingness. All of these elements relate to duration, which connects past and future, making the past (which is over) something interesting, and the future (which has yet to occur), a credit.[534]

An interesting issue is to know whether it is *norms* or the *legal order*, or indeed judicial decisions, that ought to be calculable. The definition of the object of calculability depends on a semantic agreement, on the focus of the analysis. Under the separation of powers, judicial decisions are delivered only with regard to existing normative texts whose minimal normative meanings can be reconstructed. In other words, judicial decisions refer to existing abstract norms. That being so, it can be said both that the object of calculability is norms whose final content to be declared by the judiciary citizens must be able to predict as one of the interpretative possibilities of the legal norms, and that the object of calculability is judicial decisions whose content must correspond to the hermeneutical possibilities set forth in the legal norms. Hence this is a matter of stipulation: Calculability can be said to reside in both decisions and norms, because each implies the other.

3.2 Normative Anteriority: "Certainty of Efficacy" by the Postponement of Effects

3.2.1 Fiscal Year Anteriority

The Constitution prohibits the introduction or raising of a tax in the same fiscal year in which the law is published (article 150, III, "b"). This rule guarantees

[533] Geraldo Ataliba, *República e Constituição*, 3rd ed., São Paulo, Malheiros Editores, 2011, p. 170.

[534] Tércio Sampaio Ferraz Jr., "Anterioridade e irretroatividade no campo tributário", *RDDT* 56, p. 125, São Paulo, 2001.

the predictability of normative change, or at least its calculability, since it helps taxpayers rely on the possibility of normative change at the end of the fiscal year. This is because the anteriority rule may mean anticipation of a new tax by a single day, if the statute that creates or raises it is enacted at the end of a fiscal year. In this case, while the rule does not guarantee anticipation of what will be applied, it does at least enable taxpayers to anticipate what may be changed. It does not guarantee predictability, but it affords calculability, which at least avoids surprise, albeit without eliminating uncertainty.[535]

However, it should be stressed that the idea of anteriority is linked to the idea of duration: Protection against surprise requires periodicity to give the present consistency. The anteriority rule therefore considers periods as a unit, protecting the events within it against statutory changes that occur during the period, as perceptively noted by Ferraz Jr.[536] Ataliba also argues that the anteriority rule prohibits taxation of all past events comprised in the taxable event, understood in the broadest possible sense, thus rejecting as incompatible with the legal certainty principle interpretations based on technical claims that the taxable event was not consummated.[537]

The importance of the anteriority rule has been the object of a Supreme Court decision. Constitutional Amendment 3, enacted in 1993, empowered the federal government to introduce a new tax on financial transactions but in article 2, paragraph 2, explicitly waived application of the anteriority rule established by article 150, III, “b”, of the Constitution. Supplementary Law 77 was passed that same year, instituting the new tax as of that same fiscal year. In light of this, the STF declared the Constitutional Amendment itself unconstitutional, as a violation of the ban on amendment of entrenched clauses (article 60, paragraph 4), among which it included the anteriority rule. It also ruled unconstitutional the part of Supplementary Law 77/93 that determined the incidence of the tax in the same year, without striking out any clauses (article 28).[538]

Among other aspects of this judgment that are worth highlighting is the Court’s understanding of the anteriority rule as an entrenched clause protected by the substantive inviolability provided for article 60, paragraph 4, of the Constitution. Because the anteriority rule is one of the guarantees listed in article 150 (III, “b” in this case), and because it is an instrument of calculability of law, the ruling that it is entrenched has the effect of making directly foundational the legal certainty rules established in the Constitution, especially irretroactivity and legality, thus making indirectly foundational legal certainty itself.

---

[535] Francisco Pinto Rabello Filho, *O princípio da anterioridade da lei tributária*, São Paulo, Ed. RT, 2002, p. 83. Ricardo Lodi Ribeiro, *A segurança jurídica do contribuinte*, Rio de Janeiro, Lumen Juris, 2008, p. 211.

[536] Tércio Sampaio Ferraz Jr., “Anterioridade e irretroatividade no campo tributário”, *RDDT* 56, p. 125, São Paulo, 2001.

[537] Geraldo Ataliba, “Segurança do Direito, tributação e anterioridade”, *RDT* 27–28, p. 71, São Paulo, 1984.

[538] ADI n.939, Full Court, Rep. Justice Sydney Sanches, *DJ* 18 Mar 1994

In addition to qualifying the anteriority rule, the STF has also, and more recently, decided on its scope. Until the award of injunctive relief in Direct Unconstitutionality Suit (ADI) 2325, the Supreme Court applied the position expressed in Summary Precedent (*Súmula*) 615, according to which revocation of exemption during the year made the tax immediately enforceable, so that there was no obligation to wait until the next fiscal year after it was introduced or raised. This position stemmed from the presupposition that "introduction or raising" occurred only with a new tax or an increase in a tax rate, not applying when a tax benefit was revoked or when the criteria for calculating non-cumulative tax credits were changed. The aforementioned ADI ruling changed this position, at least as far as the injunction was concerned.[539]

In this ADI the STF analyzed the changes produced by Supplementary Law 102/2000, which limited credits in operations involving fixed assets, electricity and telecommunications. In the case of fixed assets, Supplementary Law 97/96 allowed taxpayers to make immediate use of credits resulting from the purchase of such assets, but after the law changed they were limited to only 1/48 (one forty-eighth) per month; in the case of operations involving electricity and telephony, Supplementary Law 87/96 allowed taxpayers to credit the entire tax applicable to the purchase, but this was limited to manufacturers after the law changed. In sum, although the tax burden was not increased by means of a rise in the tax rate, it did increase indirectly, since the restriction on the right to credits led to an increase in tax liability.

In light of the above, the STF unanimously granted partial injunctive relief, based on the anteriority rule's full extent. Interpreting the Constitution accordingly and without striking out any provisions, it set aside the efficacy of article 7 of Supplementary Law 102/2000 insofar as it included paragraph 5 of article 20 of Supplementary Law 87/96, amended article 33, II, of the same law, and inserted indent IV.

This jurisprudential oscillation, albeit provisional, was designed to protect legal certainty by protecting the calculability of the tax burden. The argument against *direct* increases in taxation can also be used against *indirect* increases: In both cases taxpayers are surprised by a tax burden they could not and were not supposed to anticipate. This is exactly the purpose of the anteriority rule. It is a means of assuring a smooth transition between today's law and future law, so that citizens can better shape the future autonomously and within the limits of the law.

However, the STF did not do so well when, in judging the extension of the provisional contribution on financial transactions, it set aside application of the anteriority rule on the grounds that an extension was not equivalent to the creation of a tax. But if the whole point of the anteriority rule is to avoid surprise, this distinction between creation and extension is altogether inappropriate. Surprise is surprise, which the rule aims to avoid, and hence creation or extension come to the same thing.[540]

---

[539] ADI/MC n.2.325, Full Court, Rep. Justice Marco Aurélio, *DJ* 06 Oct 2006

[540] Leandro Paulsen, *Segurança jurídica, certeza do Direito e tributação*, Porto Alegre, Livraria do Advogado, 2006, p. 156.

Exceptions to the anteriority rule as it applies to the introduction of taxes or increases in tax rates are established by the Constitution itself, in article 150, paragraph 1, according to which the prohibition does not apply to the taxes stipulated in article 148, I (compulsory loans to meet extraordinary expenses resulting from public calamity, foreign war or the imminence thereof), article 153, I (import taxes) and II (export taxes), IV (excise taxes on manufactures), and V (taxes on credit, foreign exchange, insurance and securities), and article 154, II (extraordinary taxes in the imminence or event of foreign war).

Thus all the taxes covered by these exceptions to the anteriority rule relate either to foreign trade or genuinely extraordinary situations.

The former deserve to be exceptions because of their connection with the executive's freedom to manage the economy and pursue extrafiscal ends, all of which justifies their immediate efficacy. The latter are legitimate exceptions in abnormal situations that create expenses whose financing cannot be impeded by deferring the collection of the taxes concerned until the fiscal year following their introduction or raising.

3.2.2 Ninety-Day Anteriority

The Constitution also prohibits the start of collection of a tax until 90 days from the date of publication of the statute that creates or raises it, notwithstanding the general anteriority rule that means collection may not start until the next fiscal year. Thus the 90-day rule is in addition to that.

Exceptions to this specific 90-day anteriority rule are also established by the Constitution itself, in article 150, paragraph 1, according to which the prohibition does not apply to the taxes stipulated in article 148, I (compulsory loans to meet extraordinary expenses resulting from public calamity, foreign war or the imminence thereof), article 153, I (import taxes), II (export taxes), III (taxes on income of any kind), and V (tax on credit, foreign exchange, insurance and securities), and article 154, II (extraordinary taxes in the imminence or event of foreign war), or to determination of the taxable base for the taxes stipulated in article 155, III (state motor vehicle property tax), and article 156, I (municipal urban property tax).

In this case most of the taxes covered by these exceptions to the anteriority rule relate either to foreign trade or to genuinely extraordinary situations. However, they include income tax and the taxable base for motor vehicle and urban property taxes. These taxes are called periodic because they are paid annually, so that they must be changed before the end of the fiscal year. This constitutional provision merely ensures that collection of the taxes concerned can start on the first business day of the year when they are changed at the end of the previous fiscal year, as they typically are in Brazil.

To return to the focus of our present discussion, all these exceptions might seem contrary to legal certainty at first sight. However, paradoxical as it may seem, they act as instruments of calculability of law and hence of legal certainty. This is because they let taxpayers know what taxes can be demanded in the course of the year so that, even though they cannot exactly foresee which taxes will be changed or when, they can at least include in their legal calculations the possibility of some changes to some taxes. In other words, the existence of abstract exceptions favors the ideal of calculability to the extent that it reduces the range of possible changes, so that future law, albeit not entirely predictable, is situated within narrower and more foreseeable alternatives, at least in abstract and in general. The creation of concrete exceptions due to indeterminable public interest, regarding any tax, would be much farther from legal certainty than the mechanism set forth by the Constitution, since it would legitimate future changes without limits or boundaries.

3.2.3 Reasonable Anteriority

The fact that the Constitution requires an interval of time between publication and efficacy for only a few taxes does not mean there must be no such delay before other taxes become enforceable. This is precisely where the direct integrative efficacy of the legal certainty principle comes into play.

The legal certainty principle requires a state of calculability, whose realization requires the capacity to foresee and measure a narrow and relatively stable range of consequences abstractly assignable to our own or third-party acts, and facts. This is precisely why, regardless of specific statutory or constitutional provision, a change that drastically increases the tax burden must be accompanied by mechanisms to temper the change. Besides transitional rules, these mechanisms include the determination of a reasonable interval between the date on which the modifying norm is published and the onset of its efficacy. This delay allows addressees to prepare for the coming change without being caught unprepared. The greater the effect of the change from the standpoint of the fundamental rights of freedom and property, the longer the delay should be.

It is for no other reason that Supplementary Law 95/98 – enacted in compliance with the competence reserved by the Constitution to supplementary statutes to rule on the planning, drafting, modification and consolidation of laws (article 59, sole paragraph, of the Constitution) – establishes that "the date on which enforcement of the statute begins shall be expressly stated so as to allow reasonable time for it to be widely known, with the clause 'to be enforced from the date of its publication' being restricted to statutes with minor impact" (article 8). It is worth noting that the law itself refers to "reasonable time" for new statutes to be "widely known" and restricts immediate efficacy only to statutes with "minor impact." These are precisely the prescriptions resulting from the requirement of calculability of law: The addressees need time to adjust to the change, and the greater the impact of legislative change on the exercise of fundamental rights of freedom and property, the longer this time for adjustment should be.

3.3 Normative Continuity: "Rhythmic Certainty" by Means of Smoothness and Transitional Rules

The duty of permanence through durability of the legal order was investigated in the part of this book that examined the requirement of reliability of law, which analyzed the dynamic dimension of legal certainty, focusing on the transition from past to present: Only a stable order that is not substantially and constantly modified can assure an environment favorable to the exercise of freedom. The durability of the legal order is, let us say, the requirement resulting from the objective dimension of legal certainty oriented to the past. Very well then: The duty of continuity, in the sense stipulated here, is the obligation resulting from the objective dimension of legal certainty oriented to the future.[541] This future orientation does not eliminate the fact that the requirement of continuity, as well as others relating to legal certainty, aims to connect past, present and future. Cavalcanti Filho is clear on this point: "There is always continuity in legal life, as the past connects with the present and even anticipates the future."[542]

Thus one of the consequences of the duty of normative continuity is that change must be gradual.[543] There is a state of calculability of law in which citizens are largely capable of predicting and measuring a narrow and relatively stable range of consequences abstractly assignable to their own or third-party acts, or to facts, as well as the narrow time frame within which the definitive consequence will be applied. The requirement of calculability, therefore, does not prevent change.[544] It is merely contrary to a type of change that exceeds the substantive and temporal spectrum of consequences taxpayers can anticipate and that ultimately frustrates the trust of those, to cite Carazza, who make decisions, act, choose a type of business, and so on, based on the legal norms in force at the time.[545] Navarro Coelho defines the argument with precision: "That changes are inevitable, no one doubts. The goal is that they should not cause turbulence or be unconvincing, since they must respect the guiding principles of the legal system, be reasonable, and be endowed with rationality (*ratio*)."[546]

---

541 Johanna Hey, *Steuerplanungssicherheit als Rechtsproblem*, Köln, Otto Schmidt, 2002, p. 190.

542 Theophilo Cavalcanti Filho, *O problema da segurança no Direito*, São Paulo, Ed. RT, 1964, p. 153.

543 L. Lombardi, *Saggio sul Diritto Giurisprudenciale*, Milano, Giuffrè, 1967, p. 587.

544 Eros Roberto Grau, *O Direito posto e o Direito pressuposto*, 7th ed., São Paulo, Malheiros Editores, 2008, p. 185. Federico Arcos Ramírez, *La seguridad jurídica: una teoría formal*, Madrid, Dykinson, 2000, p. 265. Johanna Hey, *Steuerplanungssicherheit als Rechtsproblem*, Köln, Otto Schmidt, 2002, p. 193.

545 Roque Antonio Carrazza, "Segurança jurídica e eficácia temporal das alterações jurisprudenciais – Competência dos Tribunais Superiores para fixá-la – Questões conexas", in Tércio Sampaio Ferraz Jr. *et alii* (Orgs.), *Efeito "ex nunc" e as Decisões do STF*, São Paulo, Manole, 2008, p. 61.

546 Sacha Calmon Navarro Coelho, "Segurança jurídica e mutações legais", in Valdir de Oliveira Rocha (Org.), *Grandes Questões Atuais do Direito Tributário* 10, São Paulo, Dialética, 2006, p. 402.

Thus what the requirement of calculability through continuity of the legal order prohibits is sudden and drastic changes. Changes are sudden when they are not predictable in any way and consequently surprise the addressee, who did not and could not rely on them. They are drastic when their effects are intense, although their occurrence may well have been foreseeable. In this sense, calculability prevents not only sudden if not drastic changes, but also drastic if not sudden changes.

When a current norm is suddenly changed by another that creates a new normative consequence, which is quite different and more restrictive than the consequence provided for by the previous norm, there is a loss of stability for the legal order: The change takes citizens by surprise because having relied on the temporal stability of the legal order they naturally expect the previous norm to remain in force, but this expectation is frustrated.[547] This is why the requirement of normative continuity entails a duty to avoid abrupt, disjointed or inconsistent changes, so as to temper moderating change and give law a stable rhythm.[548] This does not mean, it bears repeating, that law must be immutable, but that change must cause the least possible disruption in past legal relations.[549] Thus the legal certainty principle requires prudential management of time in law, to quote Zimmer.[550] In Ost's figurative words, law is rhythm and measure, like music and dance.[551]

This requirement of moderate change has significant practical implications. As far as statutes are concerned, legal certainty itself demands a reasonable period of time between publication and efficacy of an innovation, as well as the enactment of rules to assure a smooth transition between the old and new legal regimes.

The same applies to administrative and normative acts. Although such acts are bound by the laws, from which they must not stray, they too must not surprise addressees with changing interpretations within the scope of the administration's competence. Thus not only must administrative changes apply solely to facts that occur after their enactment, but they must allow time for adaptation and include rules of transition when they cause restrictions to the addressees' fundamental rights. In short, the legal certainty principle entails the right to a fair transition regime.[552]

---

[547]Anne-Laure Valembois, *La constitutionnalisation de l'exigence de sécurité juridique en Droit Français*, Paris, LGDJ, 2005, p. 240.

[548]Rudolf Mellinghoff, "Vertrauen in das Steuergesetz", in Heinz-Jürgen Pezzer (Org.), *Vertrauensschutz im Steuerrecht. Deutsche Steuerjuristische Gesellschaft* 27, Köln, Otto Schmidt, 2004, p. 26. Anna Leisner, *Kontinuität als Verfassungsprinzip*, Tübingen, Mohr Siebeck, 2002, pages 412 and following. François Ost, *Le temps du Droit*, Paris, Odile Jacob, 1999, p. 334.

[549]Celso Antônio Bandeira de Mello, *Curso de Direito Administrativo*, 28th ed., São Paulo, Malheiros Editores, 2011, p. 125.

[550]Willy Zimmer, "Constitution et sécurité juridique – Allemagne", *Annuaire International de Justice Constitutionnelle 1999*, Paris, Economica, 2000, p. 101.

[551]François Ost, "Conclusions générales: le temps, la Justice et le Droit", In Simone Gaboriau and Hélène Pauliat (Orgs.), *Le Temps, la Justice et le Droit*, Limoges, Pulim, 2003, pages 358–359.

[552]Patrícia Baptista, "A tutela da confiança legítima como limite ao exercício do poder normativo da Administração Pública – A proteção às expectativas legítimas dos cidadãos como limite à retroatividade normativa", *RDE* 3, p. 171, Rio de Janeiro, 2006.

Finally, even judicial activity must have terms or rules of transition when a change of orientation is externalized, in order to avoid too abrupt and weighty a change, as well as prospective efficacy where declaratory efficacy jeopardizes the institutional credibility of law or frustrates acts of disposal legitimately performed in accordance with the previous orientation.

The key point in everything that has been said on the subject of continuity is that it is an essential element of legal certainty. Individuals can responsibly plan their lives only when institutions and relationships are long-lasting.[553]

3.4 Normative Bindingness by Limitation, Timeliness and Prohibition of Arbitrariness

3.4.1 Normative Limitation

3.4.1.1 Structural Limits

3.4.1.1.1 Rules and Their Application

The pure and simple observation that rules favor legal certainty, made when the requirement of intelligibility of law was analyzed, must not, however, hide the fact that strictly speaking knowability and calculability are not given exclusively by rules in themselves, but by the way they are applied. True, the institution of a rule *postulates* greater rigidity, inflexibility and intransigence than reasons not crystallized in its hypothesis. Although it must be reconstructed from a provision, it has an intersubjectively consensual meaning, and is therefore capable of communicating prescriptive content, even if this content can be perfected in the application.[554] However, the rigidity a rule requires from the judge may vary in intensity from strong to weak, and indeed may not actually be used at all. As Habermas avers, no rule regulates its own application.[555] Kant had already made the same observation when he stated that if judgment were a rule-governed faculty there would have to be rules for the application of rules, which could lead to infinite regress.[556] Along

---

[553] Helmut Coing, *Grundzüge der Rechtsphilosophie*, 5ª ed., Berlin, Walter de Gruyter, 1993, p. 149.

[554] Federico Arcos Ramírez, *La seguridad jurídica: una teoría formal*, Madrid, Dykinson, 2000, pages 230 and 244.

[555] Jürgen Habermas, *Faktizität und Geltung*, Darmstadt, Wissenschaftliche Buchgesellschaft, 2002, p. 244.

[556] Kant, *Kritik der reinen Vernunft*, 2nd ed., 1787, in *Kants Werke*, Berlin, Walter de Gruyter, 1967, p. 131.

similar lines, Gadamer notes that the essential element of the hermeneutical process is the concrete application of rules and not merely their abstract interpretation.[557]

Thus a rule to which a judge pays little attention, or a "rule of thumb", which by definition can be discarded in the act of application, is supposedly a rule yet does not offer any calculability because it does not serve as a reason for action or as a constraint for the judge. The addressee, albeit aware of its existence, validity and content, cannot be sure it will actually be applied in the case foreseen in its hypothesis.

Given that rules do not determine their own application, which is determined by something external to them, strictly speaking legal certainty is not enhanced by a system of rules but by an approach to their application that offers a *degree of resistance* to other factors than those considered in their hypotheses.[558] In other words, rules as such do not automatically enhance predictability. This requires "serious rules," defined as rules that are understood and applied as true limits to state action.[559]

So even if a given system is made up of rules, they can be weighted differently in terms of the constraint they place on the judge: as norms that may or may not be considered, without binding or constraining the judge (the pure particularistic model of rule application); as norms that must be considered but can be set aside if there is good reason to do so, and judges themselves may seek such a reason (rule-sensitive particularism); as norms that must be considered but can justifiably be overridden if there is a particularly grave reason to do so, and the interested party must argue this reason (presumptive positivist or ethical rule application); as norms that must be considered rigidly and must not be set aside or overridden (pure formalistic rule application).[560]

In other words, and with permission for the use of similes, the ideal models of rule application consider rules *mere guidelines that neither bind nor constrain*, like the tapes that mark the finishing line for runners at the end of a race and can easily be pushed aside; *lightly binding and constraining prescriptions*, like barriers to be cleared in a hurdle race, which can be surmounted with some effort; *highly binding and constraining prescriptions*, like the bar that competitors must clear in pole vaulting and that requires great effort to be jumped over; and finally *prescriptions of maximum bindingness and constraint*, like the walls around a high security prison, which cannot be breached.

The point of these observations is only that strictly speaking it is not rules as such that determine whether legal certainty exists, or enhance it where it does, but how the rules are applied. In other words, it is not rules but the "rule of rules" that truly

---

[557] Hans-Georg Gadamer, *Wahrheit und Methode*, Tübingen, Mohr Siebeck, 1990, v. 1, p. 320, and v. 2, p. 106.

[558] Frederick Schauer, *Playing by the Rules*, Oxford, Clarendon, 1998, p. 128.

[559] Frederick Schauer, *Thinking like a lawyer: a new introduction to legal reasoning*, Cambridge, Harvard University Press, 2009, pages 71 and following.

[560] Frederick Schauer, *Playing by the Rules*, Oxford, Clarendon, 1998, pages 93 and ff.

contributes to the realization or non-realization of legal certainty.[561] In this context, strange though it may seem, the pure particularistic model and the pure formalist model of rule application are incompatible with legal certainty: the former because where rules are merely disposable guidelines, citizens cannot know the rule that will be applied in the future, so that a minimum of intelligibility and calculability of law are impossible; and the latter because where rules are unbreakable prescriptions, even in tragic cases, there is not only a tendency to disobedience, which contributes to the loss of effectiveness of law, but it is also difficult for law to adapt to circumstances and be stable over time. Thus only the intermediate models (rule-sensitive particularism and presumptive positivism or ethical rule application) are reconcilable with the requirements of knowability, reliability and calculability of law. Hence Esser's inclusion of *autonomy* as an element of the legal certainty principle, alongside judicial protection and traffic safety: Only norms that genuinely constitute an external constraint on the addressee's will can assure a minimum of certainty.[562] In other words, rules fulfill their function only if they are peremptory, i.e. exclude deliberation, and their application is content-independent, to borrow Hart's terminology.[563]

By now it has become clear that the legal certainty principle itself is the criterion that determines which rule application model to use. It must be stressed that this is not a matter of philosophical or ideological choice, but a normative option: If the legal order attributes fundamentality to the legal certainty principle, as is the case in Brazil, neither particularistic nor formalistic rule application can be admitted. Both the exaltation of equity (as the maximum criterion for rule application) and the weighing of principles (as the predominant model of norm application) are incompatible with the legal certainty principle, as they are irreconcilable with a minimum of knowability, reliability and calculability of law. The key point for present purposes is that the model of legal order compatible with the rule of law and legal certainty is a model based on rules capable of guiding average behavior and above all of controlling the exercise of power by the state.[564]

Turning to competence rules, their function is precisely to limit the exercise of state power by allocating power, and this allocation is obtained by circumscribing power to the facts specified in the constitutionally prescribed hypotheses. Outside this scope there is no state power.[565] In the present context, this enables taxpayers to know in advance that their freedom and property can be restricted only by taxation of the specified events. Competence rules are therefore fundamental instruments of legal certainty.

---

[561] Larry Alexander & Emily Sherwin, *The rule of rules*, Durham, Duke, 2001, pp. 26, 96 and ff.

[562] Josef Esser, "Realität und Ideologie der Rechtssicherheit in positiven Systemen", in Siegfried Hohenleiter *et alii* (Orgs.), *FS für Theodor Rittler*, Aalen, 1957, p. 14.

[563] Herbert L. A. Hart, "Commands and authoritative legal reasons", in Joseph Raz (Org.), *Authority*, New York, New York University Press, 1990, p. 102.

[564] Brian Z. Tamanaha, *On the rule of Law*, Cambridge, Cambridge University Press, 2004, p. 97.

[565] Roque Antonio Carrazza, *Curso de Direito Constitucional Tributário*, 27th ed., São Paulo, Malheiros Editores, 2011, p. 531.

For this reason, albeit not directly, the plethora of Brazilian studies in legal doctrine concerning aspects of the tax rules has indirectly served to limit and allocate the power to tax, and thus guarantee legal certainty. It can unquestionably be said that these studies of the incidence hypotheses contained in tax rules and their logical structure deal above all with legal certainty in the aspects of knowability and calculability of law. Some fundamental works must be highlighted for their historical and current importance: Becker's *Teoria Geral do Direito Tributário*;[566] Falcão's *Fato Gerador da Obrigação Tributária*;[567] Maior Borges' *Isenções Tributárias*;[568] Ataliba's *Hipótese de Incidência Tributária*;[569] Carvalho's *Teoria da Norma Tributária*;[570] and Navarro Coelho's *Teoria Geral do Tributo, da Interpretação e da Exoneração Tributária*.[571] The countless merits of these works include lending scientific dignity to tax studies through clear language, logical consistency and argumentative coherence, but the essential point for present purposes is that they show that a tax obligation arises only when the facts described in the incidence hypothesis of the tax rule occur, and that without a proper scientific understanding of this rule based on impartiality and rationality, in conjunction with correct legal interpretation founded on the rule's connection to the laws, the result is state arbitrariness and hence legal uncertainty.

In this respect, not all kinds of rules are equal. Although they all have in common the characteristic of describing mandatory, permitted and forbidden behavior, and requiring for their application an examination of conceptual correspondence that focuses on their purpose and encompasses the concept of the hypothesis and the factual situation, not all have the same purpose and function. Competence rules, for example, are designed mainly to limit power through the allocation and description of its substantive scope, so that their primary purpose is to assure legal certainty. Thus the exercise of power outside the scope they delimit is invalid. They are definitive, so to speak, in the sense that they cannot be superseded because an examination of their purpose makes a broadening of their scope impossible, rather than allowing teleological restriction or extension. However, other rules – such as procedural rules – have substantive purposes, and depending on the case they may permit teleological extension when their hypothesis, coupled with their purpose, reveals the need to encompass facts that were not originally provided for.

[566] Alfredo Augusto Becker, *Teoria Geral do Direito Tributário*, São Paulo, Saraiva, 1963, pages 288 and following.

[567] Amílcar de Araújo Falcão, *Fato gerador da obrigação tributária*, 3rd ed., São Paulo, Ed. RT, 1974, p. 32 (1st ed., Rio de Janeiro, Financeiras, 1964).

[568] José Souto Maior Borges, *Teoria geral da isenção tributária*, 3rd ed., 3rd print, São Paulo, Malheiros Editores, 2011, pages 21, 77 and 179 (1st ed., São Paulo, Sugestões Literárias, 1969).

[569] Geraldo Ataliba, *Hipótese de incidência tributária*, 6th ed., 12th print, São Paulo, Malheiros Editores, 2011, pages 51 and following. (1st ed., São Paulo, Ed. RT, 1973).

[570] Paulo de Barros Carvalho, *Teoria da norma tributária*, São Paulo, LAEL, 1974, pages 111 and following.

[571] Sacha Calmon Navarro Coelho, *Teoria Geral do tributo, da interpretação e da exoneração tributária*, São Paulo, Dialética, 2003, pages 88 and following. (1st ed., São Paulo, Ed. RT, 1982).

3.4.1.1.2 Principles and Their Application

The conclusion that a legal system made up exclusively of principles is irreconcilable with legal certainty – also reached in the part of this study about the knowability of law – does not mean that principles are not important instruments of legal certainty, or that they cannot be applied with certainty. It would even be a performative contradiction, in examining the legal certainty principle, if uncertainty were deemed necessary in any kind of manipulation of principles.

When there are many normative sources that generate multiple rules, which are not always compatible with one another, principles must act as unifying interpretative criteria because the meaning of the rules must be harmonized with the content of the more general principles, and so on up to the structuring principles of a given legal order, so that the rule's chosen meaning is the one most strongly supported by constitutional principles.[572] In exercising these interpretation and agglutination functions, principles act as instruments of legal certainty by eliminating meanings that are incompatible with the purposes whose realization they determine, decreasing the range of valid semantic meanings in accordance with a given legal order and thus contributing to an increase in its knowability and calculability. García de Enterría is therefore right when, after quoting the ancient aphorism *de multido legum, unum ius*, he states that principles condense ethical and social values, and organize legal institutions, so that they provide valuable criteria for the interpretation of rules – the more numerous, occasional, incomplete and changing the rules, the more valuable are principles.[573] Principles operate centrifugally with regard to the legal system, in the sense that interpretation is dominated by their force.[574] For that same reason they play an essential role relative to legal certainty itself, especially its aspects of knowability and calculability: Because there are a great many rules, strictly speaking it is impossible to know all the details of a legal order; however, rules must be referred back to a few fundamental principles, so that by understanding them citizens know the solution given by the rules cannot conflict with the solution supplied by the principles. The interpretation of law as integrity, in the sense that the interpretation of any rule cannot stray from a narrative line furnished by a few moral principles, as argued by Dworkin, or in terms of systematically unifying principles, as in Canaris, are ways of demonstrating the fundamental role of principles in reducing interpretative discrepancy.[575]

---

[572]Claus-Wilhelm Canaris, *Systemdenken und Systembegriff in der Jurisprudenz: entwickelt am Beispiel des deutschen Privatrechts*, 3rd ed., Berlin, Duncker und Humblot, 1983, pages 17 and 88 and following.

[573]Eduardo García de Enterría, *Justicia y seguridad jurídica en un mundo de leyes desbocadas*, Madrid, Civitas, 1999, p. 105.

[574]Eros Roberto Grau, *A Ordem Econômica na Constituição de 1988*, 14th ed., São Paulo, Malheiros Editores, 2010, p. 165.

[575]Ronald Dworkin, *Law's Empire*, Cambridge, Belknap, 1986, p. 176. Claus-Wilhelm Canaris, *Systemdenken und Systembegriff in der Jurisprudenz: entwickelt am Beispiel des deutschen Privatrechts*, 3rd ed., Berlin, Duncker und Humblot, 1983, pp. 17, 88 and ff.

The affirmation that a legal system composed exclusively of principles is incompatible with legal certainty also cannot imply incompatibility with the legal certainty principle or that the principles cannot be applied with certainty. Indeed it is not principles but their arbitrary application without criteria that is incompatible with legal certainty. The phenomenon is the same as with rules, but inverted: Rules do not automatically assure legal certainty, but a specific type of application of rules does; principles do not automatically hinder legal certainty, but a specific type of application of principles does. In other words, not principles but the "norms of principles" do or do not contribute to the realization of legal certainty.

Within this framework, an unstructured model for the weighing of principles is incompatible with legal certainty, because in a model whereby principles are weighed without knowing "how" or "why", citizens cannot know, even afterwards, which norm is applicable and which norm will presumably be applied, hindering minimum knowability and calculability of law. Application will therefore be the more compatible with legal certainty, the more consistently the judge applies the principles to be weighed (pre-weighing), the more transparently the weighing is done (weighing), and the more structured the justification for the weighing carried out (post-weighing). This will be the case when the following elements are justified, among others: (I) the reason some principles are used to the detriment of others; (II) the criteria employed to define the weight and prevalence of one principle over another and the relationship between these criteria; (III) the procedure and method used to assess and verify the degree to which one principle is prioritized rather than another ; (IV) the commensurability of the weighed principles and the method used to justify their comparability; (V) which facts of the case are considered relevant for the weighing and on the basis of which criteria they are deemed legally relevant.[576] Without observing these factors there can be no calculability, because the freedom exercised by citizens in the present cannot be minimally respected by controlling the applicability of norms in the future.

3.4.1.2 Formal and Substantive Limits on the Three Branches of Government

3.4.1.2.1 Initial Considerations

Calculability of law is the state in which citizens have a significant capacity to anticipate and measure the narrow and relatively invariable range of consequences assignable to their own or third-party acts, or to facts, and the limited time frame within which the definitive consequence will be applied. One of the elements that narrows the extent and intensity of the changes is the bindingness of law, both internally and externally, on all three branches of government.

[576] Matthias Jestaedt, "Die Abwägungslehre – ihre Stärken und ihre Schwächen", in Otto Depenhauer *et alii* (Orgs.), *Staat im Wort – FS für Josef Isensee*, Heidelberg, C. F. Müller, 2007, pages 265 and 267.

The legislative is externally bound by the constitutional order, especially the competence rules and constitutional principles, and by binding precedents. Its action must not surpass these limits. Similarly, while there is scope for configuration and freedom to determine premises when laws are drafted, their content is not subject to chance but bound by the constitutional order. On the other hand, the legislative is also internally bound by its own actions. This is because it cannot choose legislative criteria that differentiate between taxpayers at one moment and reject them without justification at another moment, on pain of flouting the equality principle. Thus legislative activity is internally and externally constrained, and this limits the extent and intensity of future changes, so that taxpayers can calculate future law to a great extent.

The executive is also externally and directly bound by the laws and binding precedents, and externally and indirectly bound by the constitutional order, especially the rules and principles that condition its action. Its activities therefore cannot transgress the statutory and judicial boundaries, or the constitutional limits. Thus while there is scope for configuration of administrative actions resulting from technical appreciation or discretionary factors, they absolutely cannot be random. On the other hand, the executive is internally bound by its own past actions and cannot unjustifiably abandon them lest it violate the principle of equality in time. Hence administrative activity is internally and externally constrained, and this limits the extent and intensity of possible future changes, so that taxpayers can calculate future law to a great extent.

The same applies to the judiciary. It is externally bound by the constitutional order, i.e. both by the rules and principles that condition its actions and by the rules and principles whose legislative and administrative realization it is tasked with controlling. Thus while there is a margin of appreciation regarding the definition of normative meanings compatible with the constitutional rules, and the determination of the means appropriate and necessary to the realization of the constitutional principles, judicial activity also cannot be arbitrary or casuistic, since it is bound by the constitutional order it must apply. On the other hand, the judiciary is internally bound by its own past actions and cannot unjustifiably abandon them lest it violate the principle of equality in time, or change them without respect for situations consolidated on the basis of the previous orientation. Hence judicial activity is also internally and externally constrained, and this limits the extent and intensity of permitted future changes, favoring greater calculability of the Law.

Given their importance to the existence of a state of calculability of law, each of these limitations will now be analyzed separately.

3.4.1.2.2 Limits to the Legislative's Activities

3.4.1.2.2.1 External

The democratic principle and the competence rules give the legislative room to configure and determine the premises on which the constitutional order is concretized. Lawmakers therefore have the prerogative of defining the content of general and abstract norms. This prerogative, however, is subject to constitutional principles and rules.

As far as constitutional rules are concerned, they not only establish the formal requirements for the legislative's activity but, most important for present purposes, they also limit the content of statutes substantively, above all in tax matters. One of the noteworthy features of the Brazilian Constitution is its attribution of power through competence *rules*. Instead of leaving this task to infraconstitutional lawmakers, the framers of the Constitution decided to perform it themselves. Moreover, instead of sharing power through principles and merely establishing the end to be reached, instead of delimiting the scope of power that can be exercised, the Constitution does this by means of *rules*, whose main feature is the description of behavior, which may be permitted, prohibited or mandatory. Among all the functions of rules, the allocation of power is especially important in the present context. In allocating power, rules aim to neutralize its unlimited use, the main problem arising from its exercise. Thus the power to tax is allocated through rules that describe taxable events, so that the power to tax can be exercised only on events that conceptually match the concepts stipulated by the rules; conversely there is no power to tax events that do not conceptually match the concepts stipulated in the rules. The conceptual limits set by the competence rules are therefore insurmountable – there is no power to tax outside of them. It is no coincidence that in a judgment on the competence rules the STF asserted that their interpreter "must not go beyond the semantic limits, which are insurmountable."[577]

Thus the Constitution sets forth rules that can be reconstructed as the combination of a hypothesis and a consequence, and that directly or indirectly define the several aspects relating to each of these parts. Regarding the hypothesis, it is possible to reconstruct the expected behavior (substantive aspect), the specified time frame (temporal aspect), and the space contained (spatial aspect) within the jurisdiction of each entity belonging to the federation. Regarding the consequence, it is possible to identify the active and passive subjects (personal aspects) and the amount of the obligation (quantitative aspect).[578] The expression "basic rule of incidence" designates the essential elements of the tax rule, with the aim of permitting identification and detailed knowledge of its irreducible unity via a practical and operative formal schema.[579]

The peculiarity of our Constitution in this respect lies in its description of the substantive aspects of the incidence hypotheses. For most taxes, levies and duties, especially taxes proper (i.e. transfers to government that do not imply a service or benefit in return), and excepting service taxes and some contributions,

---

[577]RE n.71.758, Full Court, Rep. Justice Thompson Flores, *DJ* 31 Aug 1973.

[578]Paulo de Barros Carvalho, *Curso de Direito Tributário*, 21st ed., São Paulo, Saraiva, 2009, p. 263.

[579]Paulo de Barros Carvalho, *Curso de Direito Tributário*, 21st ed., São Paulo, Saraiva, 2009, p. 381.

the Constitution describes the facts or events that can be taxed, either directly in concepts or indirectly by incorporating the infraconstitutional law that existed before its promulgation. When the Constitution uses a term without defining it otherwise, it ultimately incorporates the concept used in the infraconstitutional law in force at the time it was promulgated. The STF's Full Panel has repeatedly adopted this understanding: In a judgment on the introduction of the social contribution on gross sales, it ruled that the relevant concept was "gross sales" as established by pre-constitutional infraconstitutional law, i.e. gross revenue from the sale of goods and services as an operational activity (the concept used in Decree-Law 2397/87 and the Corporations Law or *Lei das SA*);[580] judging whether compensation paid to administrators, freelancers and the self-employed was eligible for the social contribution on payroll, it ruled that the relevant concept was "salary" as defined by pre-constitutional infraconstitutional law, i.e., wages and salaries paid by employers to employees, defined as workers under continuous contract to an employer (the concept used in the Consolidated Labor Laws or CLT);[581] examining the applicability of ICMS sales tax to goods imported by natural persons, it ruled that the relevant concept was "merchandise" as defined by pre-constitutional infraconstitutional Law, i.e., a moveable thing that can be traded by anyone who regularly does business as a trader (the concept used in the Commercial Code);[582] in a judgment on the applicability of ISS municipal service tax to rental contracts, it ruled that the relevant concept was "service" as defined in pre-constitutional infraconstitutional Law, i.e., an obligation to do something by means of effort for the benefit of someone else (the concept used in the Civil Code).[583]

In sum, the Constitution either proposes or presupposes concepts. It *proposes* concepts when it expressly indicates the properties connoted by the terms it employs; it *presupposes* concepts when it incorporates concepts from pre-constitutional infraconstitutional law, within the space permitted by the rules of the current constitutional order – rules of competence, tax rules and general rules. In both cases the Constitution determines "constitutional benchmarks", to borrow the term used by the STF, i.e. boundaries the tax legislator cannot cross.[584]

In light of the above, these concepts cannot be changed by the legislative. Thus although municipalities can autonomously tax services, they can only tax economically significant human behavior that benefits third parties. Although states can autonomously tax ICMS taxable events, they can do so only when such events involve the transfer of ownership in moveable goods that are part of the

[580]RE n.150.755-1, Full Court, Rep. Justice Carlos Velloso, Opinion of the Court by Justice Sepúlveda Pertence, *DJ* 20 Aug 1993.

[581]RE n.166.772-9, Full Court, Rep. Justice Marco Aurélio, *DJ* 16 Dec 1994.

[582]RE n.203.075-9, 1st Panel, Rep. Justice Ilmar Galvão, Opinion of the Court by Justice Maurício Corrêa, *DJ* 29 Oct 1999.

[583]RE n.116.121-3, Full Court, Rep. Justice Octávio Gallotti, Opinion of the Court by Justice Marco Aurélio, *DJ* 25 May 2001.

[584]RE n.116.121-3, Full Court, Rep. Justice Octávio Gallotti, Opinion of the Court by Justice Marco Aurélio, *DJ* 25 May 2001, see page 705.

economic market. Although the federal government is empowered to create a tax on income, such a tax may be levied only on the increase in property occurring within a given time frame that is neither too long nor too short. These examples, to which others could be added, merely show that the Constitution creates benchmark concepts which the legislator cannot circumvent. The legislator's freedom of configuration must move within this normative scope. For the requirement of calculability, this substantive limitation narrows the range of legislative action, affording citizens a significant capacity to foresee and measure future taxation. Again, although taxpayers may not be able to foresee their future tax obligations exactly, they are in a position to calculate the limits within which such obligations will necessarily fall.

The power provided for by the competence rules, however, cannot be exercised unless it accords with the constitutional principles applicable to the respective tax. These principles establish both taxation ceilings and criteria to be considered in configuring the tax obligation. As noted above, not all taxes mentioned in the Constitution are described in the same manner or aim to achieve the same purpose: There are taxes whose prerequisites are determined but which are not tied to specific taxable events, as in the case of duties and fees (article 145, II); there are taxes for which instead of specific taxable events the Constitution determines factual premises, as in the case of "contributions for intervention in the economic domain" (CIDE, article 149) and compulsory loans (article 148); even some direct taxes, despite being highly detailed in some respects by the Constitution, are also significantly indeterminate in other respects, as in the case of income tax (article 153).[585] All of these observations show that although the competence rules set valuable limits to state action and as such are instruments of calculability of law, they need to have their boundaries continuously redrawn by jurisprudential and adjudicatory activity.

In the case of limits, no tax obligation may have effects that excessively restrict the fundamental rights of freedom, property and equality, lest it violate the postulate of prohibition of excess resulting from the inviolable essential core of each of these rights. In order to make this implicit limit to the order of fundamental rights clear, the Constitution expressly prohibits the creation of confiscatory taxes (article 150, IV).[586] While no taxation ceilings can be clearly discerned, the existence of a limit contributes to calculability by defining a maximum range within which tax obligations can be created.

In the case of criteria, tax obligations must be configured in such a way as to assure equal treatment for all taxpayers in the same situation (article 150, II) and, specifically for taxes with fiscal purposes, to assure adjustment to the taxpayer's economic capacity (article 145, paragraph 1). Similarly, although the concrete tax

---

[585]Ricardo Lobo Torres, "Legalidade tributária e riscos sociais", *RDDT* 59, pages 101 and 103, São Paulo, 2000.

[586]Cassiano Menke, *A proibição aos efeitos de confisco no Direito Tributário*, São Paulo, Malheiros Editores, 2008, pages 110 and following.

consequences to which taxpayers will be subject in the future cannot be precisely predicted, the criteria necessarily used in configuring concrete obligations can be calculated on the basis of the taxation principles laid down.

The above considerations demonstrate that the constitutional principles and rules act as factors of calculability because they narrow the range of possible action for the legislative regarding the future content of tax obligations. As a result, taxpayers have more freedom to configure their present as a result of the substantive boundaries already constitutionally set for the exercise of the power to tax.

3.4.1.2.2.2 Internal

The legislative is also internally bound by its own action.[587] If in the present it adopts certain criteria for differentiating taxpayers, it cannot set these criteria aside in future without any justification. This limitation is a consequence of the equality principle, and when analyzed from a temporal perspective is called a *duty of consistency*.[588]

For example, if legislators choose a given criterion to set the social security "shadow (or contribution) salary", i.e. the basis for calculating pensions and benefits, with the aim of assuring the addressees' subsistence, they cannot choose another criterion when legislating elsewhere for the same purpose, on pain of violating the duty of equality. That would be the case if they set one amount for the social security shadow salary and another for exemption from income tax. If both amounts are supposed to serve the same purpose, i.e. to assure the conditions for survival with dignity, then legislators cannot choose different values without a sound reason for the change. In another example, if legislators use their freedom of configuration to opt for a non-cumulative tax, even if such non-cumulativity is not determined by the Constitution, they must use the same criterion consistently throughout, unless they have a sound reason not to do so.

These examples, to which others could be added, simply show that equality itself, at times referred to as systemic fairness (*Systemgerechtigkeit*) or legislative consistency (*Folgerichtigkeit*), limits the legislative's freedom of configuration. Thus while the lawmakers are initially free to define the precise boundaries of taxation, once such freedom is exercised through a choice of any given criterion, this must be the basis for comparison among taxpayers for the purposes of configuring the tax law regime as a whole.

[587]Christoph Degenhart, *Systemgerechtigkeit und Selbstbindung des Gesetzgebers als Verfassungspostulat*, München, Beck, 1976, pages 29 and following. Idem, "Maßtabsbildung und Selbstbindung des Gesetzgebers als Postulat der Finanzverfassung des Grundgesetzes. Die Entscheidung des Bundesverfassungsgerichts zum Länderfinanzausgleich", *ZG* 15, pages 79–90, 2000. Franz-Joseph Peine, *Systemgerechtigkeit – Die Selbstbindung des Gesetzgebers als Maßstab der Normenkontrolle*, Baden-Baden, Nomos, 1985, pages 105 and following. Joachim Burmeister, "Selbstbindung der Verwaltung. Zur Wirkkraft des rechtsstaatlichen Übermaßverbots, des Gleichheitssatzes und des Vertrauensschutzprinzips", *DÖV* 34, pages 503–512, 1981.

[588]Michael Reinhardt, *Konsistente Jurisdiktion*, Tübingen, Mohr Siebeck, 1997, p. 499.

The duty of equality in time also affects the requirement of calculability by limiting the extent and intensity of future change because the legislators are bound by their past actions.

3.4.1.2.3 Limits to the Executive's Activities

3.4.1.2.3.1 External

The executive is primarily bound by statutes and acts that have equivalent force, such as other primary normative instruments and binding precedents. The Constitution is emphatic on this point: Article 2 establishes the principle of the separation of powers, which guarantees independence and harmony between the legislative, executive and judiciary; article 5 establishes the legality rule, determining that "no one shall be obliged to do or refrain from doing anything except by virtue of the law"; article 37 establishes the principles of public administration, which include legality; article 150, I, establishes the tax legality rule, which states that taxes can be created or raised only by statute.

In light of this, all administrative activity is bound by legal provisions. Thus no tax may be levied if it does not fit the legal archetype, and assumptions, fictions and circumstantial evidence may not be used to support a claim that an alleged taxable event has occurred.[589] The essential point is therefore that the executive is other-bound.[590] What is stake here is the *primacy of the laws*: When there is a conflict between a normative or administrative act issued by the administration and a statute on a matter reserved to it by the Constitution, the statute takes precedence. For the purposes of our present discussion, this narrows the scope of administrative actions, reducing the universe of normative consequences that can be assigned to the acts performed by taxpayers. And the reduced field of administrative action corresponds to a delimitation of the area open to the action of individuals.

Indirectly, the executive is also bound by the constitutional order, especially the rules and principles that condition its action. In this respect, the Constitution is also prolific, in the sense that it establishes a large number of competence rules for the executive, stipulating the authorities, bodies, subject-matters and sources that may participate in the process of constitutional concretization (articles 18 and ff., and articles 37 and ff).

---

[589] Roque Antonio Carrazza, *Curso de Direito Constitucional Tributário*, 27th ed., São Paulo, Malheiros Editores, 2011, pages 497 and following. Leonardo De Paola, *Presunções de ficções no Direito Tributário*, Belo Horizonte, Del Rey, 1997, pages 76 and following.

[590] Maximilian Wallerath, *Die Selbstbindung der Verwaltung. Freiheit und Gebundenheit durch den Gleichheitssatz*, Berlin, Duncker und Humblot, 1968, p. 20.

3.4.1.2.3.2 Internal

The executive is also bound by its own past actions, and cannot unjustifiably abandon them on pain of violating the principle of equality in time.[591] Even where there may be some discretion, once this has been exercised and continually sustained, the administration can no longer depart from it without a sound reason for doing so.

In these cases the administration's constant practice eventually establishes guidelines regarding its understanding, and these cannot be simply overlooked in the future, because of the equality principle. To say the administration is self-binding, therefore, is to say that within the valorative scope possible the administration is bound by the differentiation it has itself established and hence cannot unjustifiably depart from this criterion in equal cases.[592] The idea underlying the self-bindingness of the administration is the reduction in valorative scope due to previous concretization by the administration itself. Having acted in a certain way, the administration cannot act differently for equal cases. Thus self-bindingness is nothing more than the bindingness that results from substantive realizations of other-bindingness by the administration. If it unjustifiably departs from the previous position, taxpayers in the same situation are treated unequally, which makes the administration's action arbitrary.[593]

In the field of tax law, the National Tax Code itself, for example, establishes in article 100 that penalties, late interest and adjustment for inflation are excluded from calculation of the taxable base for taxpayers who observe administrative supplementary norms (normative acts issued by administrative authorities; decisions by individual or collective bodies of administrative jurisdiction, where these are assigned normative efficacy by statute; practices repeatedly observed by administrative authorities; agreements between the federal government, state governments, the Federal District and municipalities). This is a way, albeit a relatively tenuous one, to compel the administration to remain bound by its own previous positions. In federal administrative proceedings, article 2 of Law 9784/99 requires the administration to act morally and ethically according to standards of rectitude, decorum and good faith, all of which includes the duty not to act self-contradictorily (*venire contra factum proprium*).[594]

One way in which the administration is self-bound results from the administrative practice consolidated by the continuity of its own uniform position, also represented

[591]Wolfgang Hoffmann-Riem, "Selbstbindung der Verwaltung", *VVDStRL* 40, pages 187–239, 1982.

[592]Maximilian Wallerath, *Die Selbstbindung der Verwaltung. Freiheit und Gebundenheit durch den Gleichheitssatz*, Berlin, Duncker und Humblot, 1968, p. 19.

[593]Ibidem, p. 35.

[594]On the subject, in German Law, see: Kyrill-A. Schwarz, *Vertrauensschutz als Verfassungsprinzip*, Baden-Baden, Nomos, 2002, p. 140.

by the figure of the "chain (*Kette*) of administrative acts" (*Verwaltungsakte*). This practice binds the administration when a conclusive position on a given subject can be identified in the practice, so that the administration cannot depart from it without violating the good faith principle. However, it is not binding when specific issues have not been examined in the past cases that consolidated the practice, so that citizens cannot claim to rely on the administration's always behaving exactly as it has in the past, unless other elements relating to trust protection create other forms of bindingness.[595]

Besides the self-bindingness that derives from the equality principle, other forms of bindingness derive from positions taken by the administration in the past. The following are especially important: contracts through which the administration establishes certain commitments regarding a given case or legal relationship; the administration's response to a query undertaking to decide a future case in a specific manner (*Zusage*).[596] However, neither of these binds the administration in other cases just because it has decided one case in a given manner; it is bound by the principles of legal certainty, morality and good faith whenever citizens rely on the administration's position in the previous case when they perform acts of disposal of their rights of freedom and property.[597]

In federal tax administrative proceedings, articles 46 and following of Decree 70235/72 provide for the possibility of taxpayer queries about provisions of tax laws applicable to a given fact, establishing (as far as is relevant to the present discussion) that no tax proceeding will be initiated against the passive subject on the matter under consultation between the date of the query and the thirtieth day following the date of notification. This provision merely protects the taxpayer and concerns the efficacy of the query, evidently saying nothing about a possible change of position if the administration decides its response to the query was incorrect. Here the efficacy of the legal certainty principle binds the administration in cases where a taxpayer performs acts of disposal of the fundamental rights of freedom or property by relying on the response to the query. From the taxpayer's viewpoint querying makes sense only if it binds the administration so that it protects a certain range within which taxpayers can exercise their fundamental rights. Thus even if the answer to the query is declared null and void, there must be protection based on the trust protection and good faith principles.[598]

---

[595] Johanna Hey, *Steuerplanungssicherheit als Rechtsproblem*, Köln, Otto Schmidt, 2002, p. 739.

[596] Maximilian Wallerath, *Die Selbstbindung der Verwaltung. Freiheit und Gebundenheit durch den Gleichheitssatz*, Berlin, Duncker und Humblot, 1968, p. 19. Beatrice Dalichau, *Askünfte und Zusagen der Finanzverwaltung*, Bielefeld, Erich Schmidt, 2003, pages 29 and following. Wilfried Fiedler, *Funktion und Bedeutung öffentlich-rechtlicher Zusagen im Verwaltungsrecht*, Heidelberg, C. F. Müller, 1997, pages 31 and following.

[597] Johanna Hey, *Steuerplanungssicherheit als Rechtsproblem*, Köln, Otto Schmidt, 2002, p. 700.

[598] Idem, pages 707 and 715.

3.4.1.2.4 Limits to the Activity of the Judiciary

3.4.1.2.4.1 External

In a system with separation of powers, the judiciary's activity consists of reconstructing the meanings of provisions enacted by the legislative, as well as examining the facts that have occurred, through a chain of acts which culminate in a statement of law. This is not the place to engage with the endless debate about whether the judiciary "declares" or "constitutes" norms. The point is merely to show that the judiciary must base its decisions on normative provisions enacted by the legislative. Thus even if it is admitted that legal normative texts do not encapsulate norms but merely establish more or less determinate core meanings, which must be argumentatively contextualized from the factual and normative standpoints in order to gain full meaning, it remains the case that the judiciary must use the legal texts as reference points for application of the laws. This bindingness results not only from the separation of powers (article 2 of the Constitution), which requires that judicial action be restricted to the commandments originating from the legislative, but also from the legality rule itself (articles 5, I, and 150, II, of the Constitution), according to which tax obligations cannot be based directly and exclusively on judicial decisions.

It must be stressed that the need to avoid surprise is especially important in the field of procedural law. This is because the efficacy of fundamental rights against state intervention also protects the citizen against surprise in administrative and judicial proceedings.[599] Thus citizens must not be surprised in the course of the proceedings by measures that frustrate expectations or cause impediments, direct or indirect, to their right to a full adversarial defense, such as late presentation of unseen evidence or the introduction of new arguments at the appeal hearing.

3.4.1.2.4.2 Internal

Because judges interpret facts that precede their decisions, interpretation always applies to facts that have already occurred and is declaratory in this sense. Thus citizens cannot foresee exactly what interpretative decision to be judicially given, since it is given only when the decision is delivered.[600] On this view every court decision is both retroactive and unforeseeable; if irretroactivity and predictability are elements of the legal certainty, every court decision is contrary to this principle.

As already stated, legal certainty as advocated in this book is not a norm that imposes the realization of an ideal state of predictability in terms of absolute certainty, i.e. the citizen's capacity to anticipate the only correct solution. Instead,

---

[599] André Graumann, *Vertrauensschutz und strafprozessuale Absprachen*, Berlin, Duncker und Humblot, 2006, pages 488 and following.

[600] Anne-Laure Valembois, *La constitutionnalisation de l'exigence de sécurité juridique en Droit Français*, Paris, LGDJ, 2005, p. 88.

my thesis is that the legal certainty principle only requires the realization of a state of calculability in terms of a significant capacity to foresee a narrow range of alternative decisions and the time frame within which a decision will be made. Thus I would argue that not all judicial decisions are retroactive or unforeseeable, and hence contrary to legal certainty.

Application of the legal certainty principle in the field of case law therefore requires a specific analysis. In a certain sense, adjudicatory practice has a vocation for change and incoherence: in ordinary proceedings case the judge analyzes the case as it is presented by the parties, so that his or her decision is based on particular rather than general justice; each new case may present recalcitrant experience capable of leading to an individual rule based on the postulate of reasonableness, so that adjudicatory practice can lead to inconsistency. This particularism and lack of stability may be contrary to the ideals of knowability, reliability and calculability that make up the legal certainty principle. This is not necessarily so, however. It is so because if adjudicatory practice not only follows procedural rules of uniformization and generalization but is also self-limited to its own precedents based on the equality principle, it will be compatible with the legal certainty principle.[601]

This self-limitation results from the requirement of treating equal cases equally. The laws must equally valid for all citizens and be applied uniformly to all cases that fit their terms.[602] Thus while "every case is different," it behooves the judiciary to apply its own precedents uniformly by extending to future cases the same treatment given to past cases when the relevant factual circumstances are the same. This does not mean the judiciary cannot disregard its own precedents. It simply means that a line of judgment should not be disregarded once adopted, unless there are enough justifying reasons to do so.[603]

What is important for the issue at hand is that being self-bound to its own precedents acts as a factor of calculability of law because it enhances the predictability of the judiciary's actions. By restricting future action based on past action, the equality principle narrows the range and variability of the consequences assignable to acts performed by taxpayers.

Another internal factor that narrows the extension and intensity of future decisions derives from the hierarchical structure of the judiciary, on one hand, and from the formal bindingness of some court precedents, on the other.

The judiciary's hierarchical structure results, among other things, from the fact that there are bodies with jurisdiction to decide as a last instance on certain subjects.

---

[601]Michael Reinhardt, *Konsistente Jurisdiktion*, Tübingen, Mohr Siebeck, 1997, pages 461 and following. Wilhelm Hartz, "Mehr Rechtssicherheit im Steuerrecht. Ziele, Wege, Grenzen". *StbJb*, 1965/1966, p. 117.

[602]Roque Antonio Carrazza, *Curso de Direito Constitucional Tributário*, 27th ed., São Paulo, Malheiros Editores, 2011, p. 465. Christoph Eduard Ziegler, *Selbstbindung der Dritten Gewalt*, Frankfurt am Main, Peter Lang, 1993, pages 98 and 241.

[603]Rainer Riggert, *Die Selbstbindung der Rechtsprechung durch den allgemeinen Gleichheitssatz (Art. 3 I GG)*, Berlin, Duncker und Humblot, 1993, p. 124.

Thus the Supreme Court (STF) has jurisdiction to judge extraordinary appeals against violations of constitutional norms (article 102), and the Superior Court of Justice (STJ) has jurisdiction to judge special appeals against decisions, as a last or only instance, by the federal circuit courts or state appeal courts, when the appealed decision conflicts with a federal statute or treaty, or denies their validity, or interprets a federal statute differently from another court (articles 103, III, "a" and "c"). These competences tend to make the positions of the judiciary uniform, to the extent that they lead divergent decisions to a final interpretative unity. From the taxpayer's perspective they act as factors of calculability, above all because they narrow the scope of the decisions delivered by the judiciary.

The formal bindingness of court precedents derives from legal norms that expressly assign binding force to certain kinds of decision. In concentrated control of constitutionality, final decisions on the merits delivered by the STF in direct unconstitutionality suits (ADIs) and in declaratory constitutionality suits (ADCs) produce efficacy against all and are binding on all other bodies of the judiciary and the direct and indirect public administration at the federal, state and city levels (article 102, paragraph 2, of the Constitution). In diffuse control of constitutionality, there are two types of formal bindingness. If the STF incidentally and unappealably declares the unconstitutionality of a statute, the Federal Senate can suspend its execution (article 52, X). Ex officio or if so petitioned, and if approved by two thirds of its members after repeated decisions on a constitutional matter, the STF can also issue a summary precedent (*súmula*) which, on publication by the official gazettes, is binding on other bodies of the judiciary and the direct and indirect public administration at federal, state and city levels, and which may also be reviewed or revoked, as established by statute (article 103-A). The purpose of a summary precedent is to establish the judiciary's uniform interpretation concerning the validity, interpretation and efficacy of one or more norms about which there is current controversy among judicial bodies or between them and the public administration, causing grave legal uncertainty and the filing of multiple lawsuits on the same subject-matter (article 103-A, paragraph 1). Uniformity of understanding is assured through the mechanism of complaint, whereby an administrative act or court decision considered contrary to an applicable summary precedent, or held to apply it improperly, can be contested by complaint to the STF. If it upholds the complaint, the STF declares the disputed administrative act null and void, or overrules the disputed judicial decision, ordering a new decision with or without application of the summary precedent, as the case may be (paragraph 3).

The key point here is that the formal bindingness of certain decisions of the judiciary also acts as a factor of calculability because they must be obeyed by all other judicial bodies and this limits the variability of future decisions, enhancing predictability and hence individual freedom.

However, it is important to note that the uniformizing function of summary precedents cannot prevent the analysis of specific matters in future concrete cases, on pain of removing the judge's independence and violating the equality principle, which requires different treatment for different cases.[604] This is because a summary precedent is paradoxically a generalization of decisions yet remains bound to the reasons for those decisions and cannot be "decoupled" from them, to quote Machado Derzi.[605] In other words, there is a non-binding facet to binding precedents.[606]

3.4.2 Timeliness: "Certainty of Definition" via Reasonable Duration of Proceedings

The requirement of calculability of law is not only met when citizens have a significant capacity to anticipate and measure the narrow and relatively invariable range of consequences abstractly assignable to acts of their own or third parties, or to facts. Calculability also depends on a relatively short time frame for application of the final consequence.

This requirement of time to resolution is arrived at by considering the very purpose of the ideal of calculability: Its goal is to establish the conditions for citizens not to be frustrated or surprised in the exercise of their fundamental freedoms and property rights. Because the point of calculability is to assure a normative sphere within which citizens can exercise their fundamental rights with freedom and autonomy, and because calculability is the capacity to anticipate significantly the alternative consequences to which they are subject, the passage of too much time between the anticipation and its confirmation transforms the possibility of calculating future effects into the certainty that they can never be calculated.

Indeed, if citizens can know the narrow consequences assignable to an act as well as the meaning of these consequences, but are unable to know, even minimally, the time frame within which the effectively applicable consequence will be defined, they end up not being able to know which consequences state bodies will actually execute. Calculability must therefore be defined as the capacity to anticipate and measure the narrow and relatively invariable range of consequences abstractly assignable to acts or facts and the limited time frame within which the final consequence will be *actually* applied. Lack of definition regarding the final consequences cannot last such a long time that lack of definition itself becomes a cause for inaction.

It must be stressed that the longer the period covered, the greater the calculability. If in 2011 taxpayers can predict the limited number of legal consequences their acts will have until 2030, they are better able to plan for the long term, which is not the

---

[604]Roque Antonio Carrazza, *Curso de Direito Constitucional Tributário*, 27th ed., São Paulo, Malheiros Editores, 2011, p. 489.

[605]Misabel de Abreu Machado Derzi, *Modificações da jurisprudência no Direito Tributário*, São Paulo, Noeses, 2009, pages 261, 290 and 292.

[606]Ana Paula Oliveira Ávila, "A face não-vinculante da eficácia vinculante das declarações de inconstitucionalidade", in Humberto Ávila (Org.), *Fundamentos do Estado de Direito – Estudos em homenagem a Almiro do Couto e Silva*, São Paulo, Malheiros Editores, 2005, p. 211.

case if their capacity to predict the consequences covers a very short period.[607] The same applies to the final consequences: If a citizen goes to court to find out which interpretative alternative is correct and there is no foreseeable date for completion of the proceedings or they last too long, the citizen concerned cannot plan with certainty because of the perpetual lack of definition.

This is exactly why the Constitution guarantees a reasonable length of proceedings and the means to assure expeditious judgment in both the judicial and administrative spheres (article 5, LXXVIII). For the same reason it guarantees the inviolability of *res iudicata* (article 5, XXXV). The Constitution thereby requires both timeliness and finality of decisions. In doing so, it ultimately establishes an ideal of calculability characterized precisely by a state in which citizens can shape their future freely and autonomously on the basis of advance knowledge of the consequences to which they will be subject and the time frame within which those consequences will be defined.

The requirement that legal proceedings last for a reasonable time as a corollary of the dynamic dimension of the legal certainty principle has some consequences. One concerns the inertia of judicial bodies in judging tax suits. If calculability requires a reasonable wait for a solution, with no justification for delays due to inertia, it can be argued – as Bottallo and Carrazza very pointedly do – that although the National Tax Code does not explicitly provide for an intermittent period of limitation entailing loss of the right to execute a tax debt due to an unjustified delay in concluding an administrative proceeding after more than 5 years, this rule results from the legal certainty principle and from the constitutional guarantee of reasonable length of proceedings.[608]

3.4.3 Prohibition of Arbitrariness

So far the bindingness of law has been examined as a factor of calculability: The existing rules and the decisions made today bind the exercise of power tomorrow, unless there is a justification for change. Thus the equality principle in its time dimension permeates the requirement of upholding past decisions in the future: In the absence of a reason that justifies change, past decisions must be upheld in future, because otherwise either they should not have been made for lack of justification or, if there was justification and it has persisted over time, the decision concerned cannot be modified.[609] Thus the bindingness of law affects the content of future law,

[607] Gianmarco Gometz, *La certezza giuridica come prevedibilità*, Torino, Giappichelli, 2005, p. 239.

[608] Eduardo Domingos Bottallo, *Curso de Processo Administrativo Tributário*, 2nd ed., São Paulo, Malheiros Editores, 2009, p. 164. Roque Antonio Carrazza, *Curso de Direito Constitucional Tributário*, 27th ed., São Paulo, Malheiros Editores, 2011, p. 484.

[609] Fabian Lindeiner, *Willkür im Rechtsstaat? Die Willkürkontrolle bei der Verfassungsbeschwerde gegen Gerichtsentscheidungen*, Berlin, Duncker und Humblot, 2002, pages 194 and 222.

allowing citizens to know that tomorrow's law will be the same as today's, in the absence of reasons that justify change.

The greatest calculability of law, however, does not relate only to the future upholding of present norms based on the equality principle. It also relates to the autonomous application of the equality principle, in the sense that even where no present norm is worth preserving, the exercise of the power to legislate is still not totally discretionary because citizens cannot be treated differently unless there is a good reason for doing so. This means that even where citizens do not know law's future content, they know it cannot be arbitrary, and this significantly narrows the freedom to configure it.[610]

Thus the prohibition of arbitrariness contributes to the calculability of law because, although it does not enable citizens to predict law's future content with accuracy, this prohibition at least negatively delimits the boundaries of configuration by averting future regulation without justification. In other words, as noted by Carrazza, legal certainty protects taxpayers from the arbitrary decisions of politicians.[611] After all, as Villegas stresses, abstract rules cannot be manipulated when applied.[612] Knowing that tomorrow's law not only must not abruptly or unjustifiably diverge from today's law, but also must not be arbitrary – in the sense of merely capricious, with no foundation in objective and motivated reasons – gives citizens better conditions to shape their future freely and autonomously. For Ataliba, "when rights are underpinned by certainty and guaranteed by impersonal generic statutes, the capricious use of power is completely blocked."[613] Arbitrary or capricious application of the laws based on whims or personal vagaries bears the seeds of uncertainty and disorder.[614] Law can change as long as there is a most rigorously justified reason.[615] The prohibition of arbitrariness is a fully integrated part of the concept of legal certainty. The Spanish Constitution was therefore mistaken in requiring the observance of legal certainty and prohibiting arbitrariness, as if these two elements could be conceptually separated.[616]

---

[610]Federico Arcos Ramírez, *La seguridad jurídica: una teoría formal*, Madrid, Dykinson, 2000, p. 52. Fabian Lindeiner, *Willkür im Rechtsstaat? Die Willkürkontrolle bei der Verfassungsbeschwerde gegen Gerichtsentscheidungen*, Berlin, Duncker und Humblot, 2002, p. 116.

[611]Roque Antonio Carrazza, *Curso de Direito Constitucional Tributário*, 27th ed., São Paulo, Malheiros Editores, 2011, p. 417. Likewise: Rubén Asorey, "Seguridad jurídica y Derecho Tributario", *RDT* 52, p. 42, São Paulo, 1990.

[612]Héctor Villegas, "Principio de seguridad jurídica en la creación y aplicación del tributo", *RDT* 66, p. 15, São Paulo, s.d.

[613]Geraldo Ataliba, "Segurança do Direito, tributação e anterioridade", *RDT* 27–28, pages 51–75, São Paulo, 1984.

[614]Theophilo Cavalcanti Filho, *O problema da segurança no Direito*, São Paulo, Ed. RT, 1964, p. 171.

[615]Misabel de Abreu Machado Derzi, *Modificações da Jurisprudência no Direito Tributário*, São Paulo, Noeses, 2009, p. 287.

[616]José L. Mesquita del Cacho, *Seguridad jurídica y sistema cautelar*, v. 1, "Teoría de la Seguridad Jurídica", Barcelona, Bosch, 1989, p. 82.

If it is argued that each case must be analyzed in all its particulars, so that decisions cannot serve as precedents for other cases, the response must be that every decision must contain a reason that can be universalized to other cases. Thus the ratio decidendi must act as a parameter for future cases, forming normative expectations for the future through abstraction and universalization, and assuring similar solutions to similar conflicts.[617]

All the above considerations lead to the conclusion that the legal certainty principle is complex and multifaceted, and can be explained in more than one way. It can be explained both as a norm that requires the realization of three parallel partial ideals (intelligibility, reliability and predictability), and as a norm that prescribes the realization of one overarching ideal (reliability), which presupposes the existence of certain conditions (intelligibility and bindingness) and requires the realization of certain partial ideals (stability and predictability). I have preferred the latter option, because it not only indicates the partial ideals whose realization is determined by the legal certainty principle, but also explains the relationships between them. Thus legal certainty can be defined as a constitutional principle that determines the search for an ideal of reliability through stability and predictability of the legal order, based on its intelligibility and bindingness.

Throughout this work I have set out not only to organize these partial ideals whose realization is determined by the legal certainty principle, but also to indicate the types of behavior that contribute to its gradual realization. In other words, the text explains the ends whose realization is determined by the legal certainty principle and indicates the means necessary to realize those ends. In this way I have sought to boost the explanatory power of the text and, more importantly, to bolster its effectiveness.

Having completed our examination of the content of the legal certainty principle, we must now proceed to examine its efficacy.

References

AARNIO, Aulis. *Reason and Authority*. Dartmouth: Ashgate, 1997.

____. *The rational as reasonable*. Dordrecht: Reidel, 1987.

ALEXANDER, Larry; SHERWIN, Emily. *The rule of rules*. Durham: Duke, 2001.

ALTMEYER, Sabine. *Vertrauensschutz im Recht der Europäischen Union und im deutschen Recht*. Baden-Baden: Nomos, 2003.

ÁLVAREZ MART´iNEZ, Joaquín, *La Motivación de los actos tributarios*. Madrid: Marcial Pons, 1999.

ALVARO DE OLIVEIRA, Carlos Alberto. "O formalismo valorativo no confronto com o formalismo excessivo". *RF* 388. Rio de Janeiro, s.d.

____. *Do formalismo no Processo Civil*. 3rd ed. São Paulo: Saraiva, 2009.

AMARO, Luciano. *Direito Tributário Brasileiro*. 15th ed. São Paulo: Saraiva, 2009.

[617] Misabel de Abreu Machado Derzi, *Modificações da jurisprudência no Direito Tributário*, São Paulo, Noeses, 2009, p. 184.

ANTUNES ROCHA· Cármen Lúcia. "O princípio da coisa julgada e o vício de inconstitucionalidade". In: ANTUNES ROCHA, Cármen Lúcia (Org.). *Constituição e segurança jurídica: direito adquirido, ato jurídico perfeito e coisa julgada. Estudos em homenagem a José Paulo Sepúlveda Pertence*. Belo Horizonte: Fórum, 2004.

ARCOS RAM´iREZ, Federico. *La seguridad jurídica: una teoría formal*. Madrid: Dykinson, 2000.

von ARNAULD Andreas. Rechtssicherheit. Tübingen: Mohr Siebeck, 2006.

ARNDT, Hans-Wolfgang. *Probleme rückwirkender Rechtsprechungsänderung*. Frankfurt: Athenäum, 1974.

ASOREY, Rubén. "Seguridad jurídica y Derecho Tributario". *RDT* 52. São Paulo, 1990.

ATALIBA, Geraldo. "Segurança do Direito, tributação e anterioridade". *RDT* 27–28. São Paulo, 1984.

____. *Hipótese de incidência tributária*. 6th ed. 12th print. São Paulo: Malheiros Editores, 2011. (1st ed., São Paulo, Ed. RT, 1973).

____. *República e Constituição*. 3rd ed. São Paulo: Malheiros Editores, 2011.

____. *Sistema Constitucional Tributário brasileiro*. São Paulo: Ed. RT, 1968.

ÁVILA, Ana Paula Oliveira. "A face não-vinculante da eficácia vinculante das declarações de inconstitucionalidade". In: ÁVILA, Humberto (Org.). *Fundamentos do Estado de Direito – Estudos em homenagem a Almiro do Couto e Silva*. São Paulo: Malheiros Editores, 2005.

____. *A modulação de efeitos temporais pelo STF no controle de Constitucionalidade*. Porto Alegre: Livraria do Advogado, 2009.

ÁVILA, Humberto. "A Separação dos Poderes e as Leis Interpretativas Modificativas de Jurisprudência Consolidada". In: MACHADO DERZI, Misabel Abreu (Coord.). *Separação de Poderes e Efetividade do Direito Tributário*. Belo Horizonte: Del Rey, 2010.

____. "Juristische Theorie der Argumentation". In: HELDRICH, Andreas *et alii* (Orgs.). *FS für Claus-Wilhelm Canaris zum 70. Geburtstag*. München: Beck, 2007.

BALEEIRO, Aliomar. *Direito Tributário Brasileiro*. 11th ed. updated by Misabel de Abreu Machado Derzi. Rio de Janeiro: Forense, 1999.

BANDEIRA DE MELLO, Celso Antônio. *Curso de Direito Administrativo*. 28th ed. São Paulo: Malheiros Editores, 2011.

BAPTISTA, Patrícia. "A tutela da confiança legítima como limite ao exercício do poder normativo da Administração Pública – A proteção às expectativas legítimas dos cidadãos como limite à retroatividade normativa". *RDE* 3. Rio de Janeiro, 2006.

BARROSO, Luís Roberto. "Em algum lugar do passado: segurança jurídica, Direito Intertemporal e o novo Código Civil". In: ANTUNES ROCHA, Cármen Lúcia (Org.). *Constituição e segurança jurídica: direito adquirido, ato jurídico perfeito e coisa julgada. Estudos em homenagem a José Paulo Sepúlveda Pertence*. Belo Horizonte: Fórum, 2004.

BATTIFFOL, Henri. "Le déclin du Droit. Examen critique". *Archives de Philosophie du Droit*, 1963.

BECKER, Alfredo Augusto. *Teoria Geral do Direito Tributário*. São Paulo: Saraiva, 1963..

BEERMANN, Johannes. *Verwirkung und Vertrauensschutz im Steuerrecht*. Münster: Waxmann, 1991.

BENDA, Ernst; KLEIN, Eckart. *Lehrbuch des Verfassungsprozessrechts*. 2ª ed. Heidelberg: C. F. Müller, 2001. margin number 96.

BERGER, Thomas. *Zulässigkeitsgrenzen der Rückwirkung von Gesetzen*. Frankfurt am Main: Peter Lang, 2002.

BLANCKE, Hermann-Josef. *Vertrauensschutz im deutschen und europäischen Verwaltungsrecht*. Tübingen: Mohr Siebeck, 2000.

BLÜGGEL, Jens. *Unvereinbarkeitserklärung statt Normkassation durch das Bundesverfassungsgericht*. Berlin: Duncker und Humblot, 1998.

BOTTALLO, Eduardo Domingos. *Curso de Processo Administrativo Tributário*. 2nd ed. São Paulo: Malheiros Editores, 2009.

BRÄUNIG, Anja. *Die Gestaltungsfreiheit des Gesetzgebers in der Rechtsprechung des Bundesverfassungsgerichts zur deutschen Wiedervereinigung*. Berlin: Duncker und Humblot, 2007.

BRISCHKE, Hans-Jürgen. "Heilung fehlerhafter Verwaltungsakte im verwaltungsgerichtlichen Verfahren. Durch Nachholen der Begründung, Nachschieben von Gründen, Umdeutung, Ergänzung von Ermessenserwägungen und förmliche Änderung oder Ergänzung des streitbefangenen Verwaltungsaktes". *DVBl* 117, 2002.

BURMEISTER, Joachim. "Selbstbindung der Verwaltung. Zur Wirkkraft des rechtsstaatlichen Übermaßverbots, des Gleichheitssatzes und des Vertrauensschutzprinzips". *DÖV* 34, 1981.

____. *Vertrauensschutz im Prozeßrecht – Ein Beitrag zur Theorie vom Dispositionsschutz des Bürgers bei Änderung des Staatshandelns*. Berlin: De Gruyter, 1979.

CALMES, Sylvia. *Du principe de protection de la confiance légitime en Droits Allemand, Communautaire et Français*. Paris: Dalloz, 2001.

CANARIS, Claus-Wilhelm. *Die Vertrauenshaftung im deutschen Privatrecht*. Munchen: Beck, 1971.

____. *Systemdenken und Systembegriff in der Jurisprudenz: entwickelt am Beispiel des deutschen Privatrechts*. 3rd ed. Berlin: Duncker und Humblot, 1983.

CARRAZA, Roque Antonio. "Segurança jurídica e eficácia temporal das alterações jurisprudenciais – Competência dos Tribunais Superiores para fixá-la – Questões conexas". In: FERRAZ JÚNIOR, Tércio Sampaio *et alii* (Orgs.) *Efeito "ex nunc" e as decisões do STF*. São Paulo: Manole, 2008.

____. *Curso de Direito Constitucional Tributário*. 27th ed. São Paulo: Malheiros Editores, 2011.

CARVALHO, Paulo de Barros. "O princípio da segurança jurídica no campo tributário". *RDT* 94. São Paulo, 2006.

____. "Segurança jurídica e modulação dos efeitos". *Revista da Fundação Escola Superior de Direito Tributário* 1, Porto Alegre, 2008.

____.*Curso de Direito Tributário*. 18th ed. São Paulo: Saraiva, 2007.

____. *Teoria da norma tributária*. São Paulo: LAEL, 1974.

CAVALCANTI FILHO, Theophilo. *O problema da segurança no Direito*. São Paulo: Ed. RT, 1964.

CHRISTENSEN, Ralph; KUDLICH, Hans. *Theorie richterlichen Begründens*. Berlin: Duncker und Humblot, 2001.

COING, Helmut. *Grundzüge der Rechtsphilosophie*. 5ª ed. Berlin: Walter de Gruyter, 1993.

COUTO E SILVA, Almiro do. "O princípio da segurança jurídica (proteção à confiança) no Direito Público brasileiro e o direito da Administração Pública de anular os seus próprios atos: o prazo decadencial do art. 54 da Lei do Processo Administrativo da União (Lei n. 9.784/99)". *RBDP* 6. Porto Alegre, Jul-Sep/2004.

____. "Princípios da legalidade da Administração Pública e da segurança jurídica no Estado de Direito contemporâneo". *Revista da Procuradoria-Geral do Estado do Rio Grande do Sul. Cadernos de Direito Público*, v. 27. n. 57, supplement, 2003.

____. "Problemas jurídicos do planejamento". *RDA* 170. Rio de Janeiro, 1987.

DALICHAU, Beatrice. *Askünfte und Zusagen der Finanzverwaltung*. Bielefeld: Erich Schmidt, 2003.

DEGENHART, Christoph. "Maßtabsbildung und Selbstbindung des Gesetzgebers als Postulat der Finanzverfassung des Grundgesetzes. Die Entscheidung des Bundesverfassungsgerichts zum Länderfinanzausgleich". *ZG* 15.

____. *Systemgerechtigkeit und Selbstbindung des Gesetzgebers als Verfassungspostulat*. München: Beck, 1976.

DELLA VALLE, Eugenio. *Affidamento e certezza del Diritto Tributario*. Milano: Giuffrè, 2001.

DENGO, Atílio. "Irretroatividade tributária e modo de aplicação das regras jurídicas". *RDDT* 124, 2006.

____. *Contributo para uma teoria da irretroatividade tributária*. Ph.D. Dissertation/UFRGS, 2008.

DEPENHEUER, Otto. *Vertrauensschutz durch Eigentum*. Karlsruhe: Versicherungswirtschaft, 2007.

DI PIETRO, Maria Sylvia Zanella. "Os princípios da proteção à confiança, da segurança jurídica e da boa-fé na anulação do ato administrativo". In: MOTTA, Fabrício (Org.). *Direito Público atual: Estudos em homenagem ao Professor Nélson Figueiredo*. Instituto de Direito Administrativo de Goiás (IDAG). Belo Horizonte: Fórum, 2008.

DIETLEIN, Johannes. *Die Lehre von den grundrechtlichen Schutzpflichten*. 2nd ed. Berlin: Duncker und Humblot, 2005.

DOUET, Frédéric. *Contribution à l'étude de la sécurité juridique en Droit Interne Français*. Paris: LGDJ, 1997.

DRÜEN, Klaus-Dieter. "Haushaltsvorbehalt bei der Verwerfung verfassungswidriger Steuergesetze?". *FR* 6, 1999.

DUARTE, Ronnie Preuss, *Garantia de acesso à Justiça. Os Direitos Processuais fundamentais*. Coimbra: Coimbra, 2007.

DUBS, Hans. *Praxisänderungen. Eine methodologische Untersuchung über die Stellung des Richters zum eigenem Präjudiz auf Grund von Entscheidungen des schweizerischen Bundesgerichts*. Basel: Helbing & Lichtenhahn, 1949.

DWORKIN, Ronald. *Law's Empire*. Cambridge: Belknap, 1986.

ENGEL, Christoph. *Planungssicherheit für Unternehmen durch Verwaltungsakt*,. Tübingen: Mohr Siebeck, 1992.

ESSER, Josef. "Realität und Ideologie der Rechtssicherheit in positiven Systemen". In: HOHENLEITER, Siegfried *et alii* (Orgs.). *FS für Theodor Rittler*. Aalen, 1957.

FALCÃO, Amílcar de Araújo. *Fato gerador da obrigação tributária*. 3rd ed. São Paulo: Ed. RT, 1974. (1st ed. Rio de Janeiro. Financeiras, 1964).

FERRAZ JR. Tércio Sampaio. "Coisa julgada em matéria tributária e as alterações sofridas pela legislação da contribuição social sobre o lucro (Lei n. 7.689/88)". *RDDT* 125. São Paulo, 2006.

____. "Anterioridade e irretroatividade no campo tributário". *RDDT* 56. São Paulo, 2001.

____. "Coisa julgada em matéria tributária e as alterações sofridas pela legislação da contribuição social sobre o lucro (Lei n. 7.689/88)". *RDDT* 125. São Paulo, 2006.

____. "Irretroatividade e jurisprudência judicial". In: Idem; CARRAZA, Roque Antonio; NERY JÚNIOR, Nelson (Orgs.). *Efeito "ex nunc" e as decisões do STF*. São Paulo: Manole, 2008.

FIEDLER, Wilfried. *Funktion und Bedeutung öffentlich-rechtlicher Zusagen im Verwaltungsrecht*. Heidelberg: C. F. Müller, 1997.

FIGUEIREDO, Lúcia Valle. "Planejamento, Direito Tributário e segurança jurídica". *RTDP* 12. São Paulo, 1995.

FRANÇA, Limongi. *Direito Intertemporal Brasileiro*. 2nd ed. São Paulo: Ed. RT, 1968.

FRIAUF, Karl Heinrich. "Steuerrechtsänderungen und Altinvestitionen. Zum Verfassungsgebot der steuerlichen Investitionssicherheit". *StbJb*, 1986/1987.

FULLER, Lon. *The Morality of Law*. New Haven: Yale University Press, 1964.

GADAMER, Hans-Georg. *Wahrheit und Methode*. Tübingen: Mohr Siebeck, 1990.

GARC'iA DE ENTERR'iA, Eduardo. *Justicia y seguridad jurídica en un mundo de leyes desbocadas*. Madrid: Civitas, 1999.

GIGANTE, Marina. *Mutamenti nella regolazione dei rapporti giuridici e legittimo affidamento*. Milano: Giuffrè, 2008.

GOMETZ, Gianmarco. *La certezza giuridica come prevedibilità*. Torino: Giappichelli, 2005.

GRAU, Eros Roberto. *A Ordem Econômica na Constituição de 1988*. 14th ed. São Paulo: Malheiros Editores, 2010.

____. *O Direito posto e o Direito pressuposto*. 7th ed. São Paulo: Malheiros Editores, 2008.

GRAUMANN, André. *Vertrauensschutz und strafprozessuale Absprachen*. Berlin: Duncker und Humblot, 2006,.

GRUNSKY, Wolfgang. *Grenzen der Rückwirkung bei einer Änderung der Rechtsprechug*. Heidelberg: C. F. Müller, 1970.

GUCKELBERGER, Annette. *Die Verjährung im Öffentlichen Recht*. Tübingen: Mohr Siebeck, 2004.

GURLIT, Elke. *Verwaltungsvertrag und Gesetz*. Tübingen: Mohr Siebeck, 2000.

HABERMAS, Jürgen. *Faktizität und Geltung*. Darmstadt: Wissenschaftliche Buchgesellschaft, 2002.

HABSCHEIDT, Gerhard. *Der Anspruch des Bürgers auf Erstattung verfassungswidriger Steuern*. Köln: Otto Schmidt, 2003.

HART, Herbert L. A. "Commands and authoritative legal reasons", in Joseph Raz (Org.), *Authority*. New York: New York University Press, 1990.

____. Mehr Rechtssicherheit im Steuerrecht. Ziele, Wege, Grenzen. *StbJb*. 1965/1966.

HEY, Johanna. "Vertrauen in das fehlerhafte Steuergesetz". In: PEZZER, Heinz-Jürgen (Org.). *Vertrauensschutz im Steuerrecht. Deutsche Steuerjuristische Gesellschaft* 27. Köln: Otto Schmidt, 2004.

____. *Steuerplanungssicherheit als Rechtsproblem*. Köln: Otto Schmidt, 2002.

HILLGRUBER, Christian; GOOS, Christoph. *Verfassungsprozessrecht*. 2nd ed. Heidelberg: C. F. Müller, 2006.

van HOECEK, Mark. "Time and law. Is it the nature of law to last? A conclusion". In: OST, François; van HOECEK, Mark (Orgs.). *Temps et Droit*. Le Droit a-t-il pour vocation de durer?. Bruxelles: Bruylant, 1998.

HOFFMANN-RIEM, Wolfgang. "Selbstbindung der Verwaltung". *VVDStRL* 40, 1982.

ILIOPOULOS-STRANGAS, Julia. *Rückwirkung und Sofortwirkung*. Baden-Baden: Nomos, 1987.

IPSEN, Jörg. *Rechtsfolgen der Verfassungswidrigkeit von Norm und Eizelakt*. Baden-Baden: Nomos, 1980.

IPSEN, Jörn. "Verbindlichkeit, Bestandkraft und Bindungswirkung von Verwaltungsakten". *Verwaltung* 17, 1984.

ISENSEE, Josef. "Vertrauensschutz für Steuervorteile. Ein Folgeproblem der Wirtschaftslenkung durch Steuer des §3a EStG". In: KIRCHHOF, Paul; OFFERHAUS, Klaus; SCHÖBERLE, Horst (Orgs.). *Steuerrecht, Verfassungsrecht, Finanzpolitik. FS für Franz Klein*. Köln, 1994.

JESTAEDT, Matthias. "Die Abwägungslehre – ihre Stärken und ihre Schwächen". In: DEPENHAUER, Otto *et alii* (Orgs.) *Staat im Wort – FS für Josef Isensee*. Heidelberg: C. F. Müller, 2007.

JURATOWITCH, Ben. *Retroactivity and the Common Law*. Oxford: Hart, 2008.

JUSTEN FILHO, Marçal. "O princípio da moralidade pública e o Direito Tributário". *RTDP* 11, 1995.

KÄHLER, Lorenz. *Strukturen und Methoden der Rechtsprechungsänderung*. Baden-Baden: Nomos, 2004.

KANT, Immanuel. *Kritik der reinen Vernunft*. 2nd ed. 1787. In: *Kants Werke*. Berlin: Walter de Gruyter, 1967.

KAUFMANN, Franz-Xaver. *Sicherheit als soziologisches und sozialpolitisches Problem*. 2nd ed. Stuttgart, 1973.

KEIL, Ulrich. *Die Systematik privatrechtlicher Rechtsprechungsänderungen*. Tübingen: Mohr Siebeck, 2007.

KIRCHHOF, Paul Kirchhof, "Kontinuität und Vertrauensschutz bei Änderungen der Rechtsprechung". *DStR* 27, 1989.

____. "Rückwirkung von Steuergesetzen". *StuW*, 2000.

KLAPPSTEIN, Verena. *Die Rechtsprechungsänderung mit Wirkung für die Zukunft*. Berlin: Duncker und Humblot, 2009.

KOCH, Michael. *Die Grundsätze des intertemporalen Rechts im Verwaltungsprozess – Vertrauensschutz im verwaltungsgerichtlichen Verfahren*. Berlin: Duncker und Humblot, 2009.

KREIBICH, Roland. *Der Grundsatz von Treu und Glauben im Steuerrecht*. Heidelberg: C. F. Müller, 1992.

KRIELE, Martin. "Grundrechte und demokratischer Gestaltungsspielraum". In: KIRCHHOF, Paul; ISENSEE, Josef. *Handbuch des Staatsrechts* 5. Heidelberg: C. F. Müller, 1992.

LECHNER, Hans; ZUCH, Rüdiger. *Bundesverfassungsgerichtsgesetz*. 5th ed. München: Beck, 2006.

LEHNER, Moris. "Das Rückwirkungsproblem im Spiegel der Abschnittsbesteuerung". In: KIRCHHOF, Paul; SCHMIDT, Karsten; SCHÖN, Wolfgang (Orgs.). *FS für Arndt Raupach. Steuer- und Gesellschaftsrecht zwischen Unternehmerfreiheit und Gemeinwohl*. Köln: Otto Schmidt, 2006.

LEISNER, Anna. *Kontinuität als Verfassungsprinzip*. Tübingen: Mohr Siebeck, 2002.

LEISNER, Walter. "Das Gesetzesvertrauen des Bürgers. Zur Theorie der Rechtsstaatlichkeit und der Rückwirkung der Gesetze". In: BLUMENWITZ, Dieter; RANDELHOFER, Albrecht (Orgs.). *FS für Friedrich Berger*,.München, 1973.

LEMBCKE, Oliver W. *Hüter der Verfassung*. Tübingen: Mohr Siebeck, 2007.

LILIE, Hans. *Obiter Dictum und Divergenzausgleich in Strafsachen*. Köln: Carl Heymanns, 1993.

LINDEINER, Fabian. *Willkür im Rechtsstaat? Die Willkürkontrolle bei der Verfassungsbeschwerde gegen Gerichtsentscheidungen*. Berlin: Duncker und Humblot, 2002.

LOMBARDI, L. *Saggio sul Diritto Giurisprudenciale*. Milano: Giuffrè, 1967.

LOSER, Peter. *Die Vertrauenshaftung im schweizerischen Schuldrecht*. Bern: Stämpfli, 2006.

LOUVEN, Christoph. *Problematik und Grenzen rückwirkender Rechtsprechung des Bundesarbeitsgerichts*. München: Beck, 1996.

LÜBBE, Christine. *Grenzen der Rückwirkung bei Rechsprechungsänderungen*. Frankfurt am Main: Peter Lang, 1997.

LÜBBE-WOLF, Gertrude. *Die Grundrechte als Eingriffsabwehrrechte. Struktur und Reichweite der Eingriffsdogmatik im Bereich staatlicher Leistungen*. Baden-Baden: Nomos, 1988.

LUHMANN, Niklas. *Ausdifferenzierung des Rechts. Beiträge zur Rechtssoziologie und Rechtstheorie*. Frankfurt am Main: Suhrkamp, 1999.

MACHADO DERZI, Misabel de Abreu. "Princípio da segurança jurídica". *RDT* 64, s.d.

____. *Modificações da jurisprudência no Direito Tributário*. São Paulo: Noeses, 2009.

MAINKA, Johannes. *Vertrauensschutz im öffentlichen Recht*. Bonn: Ludwig Röhrscheid, 1963.

MAIOR BORGES, José Souto. "Limites constitucionais e infraconstitucionais da coisa julgada tributária (contribuição social sobre o lucro)". *Cadernos de Direito Tributário e Finanças Públicas* 27, 1999.

____. *Obrigação tributária – Uma introdução metodológica*. São Paulo: Saraiva, 1984.

_____. *Teoria geral da isenção tributária*. 3rd ed. 3rd print. São Paulo: Malheiros Editores, 2011. (1st ed., São Paulo, Sugestões Literárias, 1969).

MARINONI, Luiz Guilherme. *Coisa julgada inconstitucional*. São Paulo: Ed. RT, 2008.

MARMOR, Andrei. *Law in the Age of Pluralism*. Oxford: OUP, 2007.

MARTINS-COSTA, Judith. "Almiro do Couto e Silva e a ressignificação do princípio da segurança jurídica na relação entre Estado e cidadãos". In: ÁVILA, Humberto (Org.). *Fundamentos do Estado de Direito – Estudos em homenagem a Almiro do Couto e Silva*. São Paulo: Malheiros Editores, 2005.

MAURER, Hartmut. "Kontinuitätsgewähr und Vertrauensschutz". In: ISENSEE, Josef; KIRCHHOF, Paul (Orgs.). *Handbuch des Staatsrechts*. 2nd ed. v.3. §60. margin number 93. Heidelberg: Müller, 1996.

MEDEIROS, Rui. *A Decisão de inconstitucionalidade – Os autores, o conteúdo e os efeitos da decisão de inconstitucionalidade*. Lisboa: Universidade Católica, 1999.

MEDICUS, Dieter. "Neues zur Rückwirkung von Rechtsprechung". *WM*, 1997.

MELLINGHOFF, Rudolf. "Vertrauen in das Steuergesetz". In: PEZZER, Heinz-Jürgen (Org.). *Vertrauensschutz im Steuerrecht. Deutsche Steuerjuristische Gesellschaft* 27. Köln: Otto Schmidt, 2004.

MENDES, Gilmar. "Anteprojeto de lei sobre processo e julgamento da ação direta de inconstitucionalidade e da ação declaratória de constitucionalidade". *Cadernos de Direito Constitucional e Ciência Política* 29. São Paulo, 1999.

____. *Jurisdição constitucional*. 3rd ed. São Paulo: Saraiva, 1999.

MENKE, Cassiano. *A proibição aos efeitos de confisco no Direito Tributário*.São Paulo: Malheiros Editores, 2008.

MENZEL, Andreas. *Grundfragen der Verwirkung dargestellt insbesondere anhand des Öffentlichen Rechts*. Frankfurt am Main: Peter Lang, 1987.

MESQUITA DEL CACHO, José L. *Seguridad jurídica y sistema cautelar*. v. 1. "Teoría de la Seguridad Jurídica". Barcelona: Bosch, 1989.

MEYER, Wolfgang. "Die Rückwirkung von Bundesgesetzen – ein Problem des Übermaßes?". In: BUTZER, Hermann *et alii* (Orgs.) *Organisation und Verfahren im sozialen Rechtsstaat. FS für Friedrich E. Schnapp zum 70. Geburtstag*. Berlin: Duncker und Humblot, 2008.

MOES, Christoph. "Die Anordnung der befristeten Fortgeltung verfassungswidriger Steuergesetze durch das Bundesverfassungsgericht". *StuW* 1, 2008.

MOLFESSIS, Nicolas. (Org.). *Les Revirements de Jurisprudence. Rapport Remis à Monsieur le Premier Président Guy Canivet. Grupe de Travail*. Paris: Litec, 2005.

MOREIRA ALVES, José Carlos. "Direito adquirido". *Fórum Administrativo* 15.

MUCKEL, Stefan. *Kriterien des verfassungsrechtlichen Vertrauensschutzes bei Gesetzesänderungen*. Berlin: Duncker und Humblot, 1989..

MÜLLER-GRUNE, Sven. *Der Grundsatz von Treu und Glauben im Allgemeinen Verwaltungsrecht*. Hamburg: Kovac, 2006.

MÜNCH, Christof. "Rechtssicherheit als Standortfaktor. Gedanken aus Sicht der vorsorgenden Rechtspflege". In: WEBER, Albrecht (Org.). *Währung und Wirtschaft. Das Geld im Recht. FS für Hugo J. Hahn*. Baden-Baden: Nomos, 1997.

NAVARRO COELHO, Sacha Calmon. "Segurança jurídica e mutações legais". In: ROCHA, Valdir de Oliveira (Org.). *Grandes Questões Atuais do Direito Tributário* 10. São Paulo: Dialética, 2006.

____. *Curso de Direito Tributário*. 9th ed. Rio de Janeiro: Forense, 2006.

____. *Teoria Geral do tributo, da interpretação e da exoneração tributária*. São Paulo: Dialética, 2003. (1st ed. São Paulo. Ed. RT, 1982).

NOVOA, César García. *El principio de seguridad juridica en materia tributaria*. Madrid: Marcial Pons, 2000.

ORTMANN, Andreas. *Die Finanzwirksamkeit verfassungsrechtlicher Entscheidungen im Spiegel der Rechtsprechung des Bundesverfassungsgerichts*. Baden-Baden: Nomos, 2007.

OSSENBÜHL, Fritz. *Die Rücknahme fehlerhafter begünstigender Verwaltungsakte*. 2nd ed. Berlin: Walter de Gruyter, 1965.

OST, François. "Conclusions générales: le temps, la Justice et le Droit". In: GABORIAU, Simone ; PAULIAT, Hélène (Orgs.). *Le Temps, la Justice et le Droit*. Limoges : Pulim, 2003.

_____. "L'heure du jugement. Sur la rétroactivité des décisions de justice. Vers un Droit transitoire de la modification des règles jurisprudentielles". In: OST, François; van HOECKE, Mark (Orgs.). *Temps et Droit. Le Droit a-t-il pour vocation de durer?* Bruxelles: Bruylant, 1999.

____. *Le Temps du Droit*. Paris: Odile Jacob, 1999.

____. "L'instantané ou l'institué? L'institué ou l'intantuant? Le Droit a-t-il pour vocation de durer?". In: OST, François; van HOECKE, Mark (Orgs.). *Temps et Droit. Le Droit a-t-il pour vocation de durer?*. Bruxelles: Bruylant, 1998.

PACTEAU, Bernard. "Comment aménager la rétroactivité de la Justice? Sécurité juridique, sécurité juridictionnelle, sécurité jurisprudencielle". In : SEILLER, Bertrand (Org.). *La Rétroactivité des Décisions du Juge Administratif*. Paris: Economica, 2007.

DE PAOLA, Leonardo. *Presunções de ficções no Direito Tributário*. Belo Horizonte: Del Rey, 1997.

PAULSEN, Leandro. *Segurança jurídica, certeza do Direito e Tributação*. Porto Alegre: Livraria do Advogado, 2006.

PECZENICK, Aleksander. *On Law and reason*. Dordrecht: Kluwer, 1989.

PEINE, Franz-Joseph. *Systemgerechtigkeit – Die Selbstbindung des Gesetzgebers als Maßstab der Normenkontrolle*. Baden-Baden: Nomos, 1985.

PEREZ, Jesus Gonzales. *El Principio General de la Buena Fe en el Derecho Administrativo*. 2nd ed. Madrid: Civitas, 1983.

PEREZ LUÑO, Antonio Enrique. *La seguridad jurídica*. Barcelona: Ariel, 1991.

PETIT, Jacques. *Les conflits de lois dans le temps en Droit Public Français*. Paris: LGDJ, 2002.

PIEKENBROCK, Andreas. *Befristung, Verjährung, Verschweigung und Verwirkung*. Tübingen: Mohr Siebeck, 2006.

PIEROTH, Bodo. *Rückwirkung und Übergangsrecht*. Berlin: Duncker und Humblot, 1981.

POHL, Heike. *Rechtsprechungsänderung und Rückanknüpfung*. Berlin: Duncker und Humblot, 2005.

PÜTTNER, Günter. "Vertrauensschutz im Verwaltungsrecht". *VVDStRL* 32, 1974.

RAM´iREZ, Federico Arcos Ramírez, *La seguridad jurídica: una teoría formal*. Madrid: Dykinson, 2000.

RANDAK, Michael. "Bindungswirkung von Verwaltunsakten". *JuS* 1992.

RAWLS, John. *Theory of Justice*. Cambridge: Belknap, 1971.

RAZ, Joseph. "The rule of law and its virtue (1977)". In: *The Authority of Law. Essays on Law and Morality*. Oxford: Oxford, 1979.

____. *Practical reason and norms*. New Jersey: Princeton, 1990.

____. *The morality of freedom*. Oxford: Clarendon, 1986.

REALE, Miguel. *Revogação e anulamento do ato administrativo*. 2nd ed. Rio de Janeiro: Forense, 1980.

REINHARDT, Michael. *Konsistente Jurisdiktion*. Tübingen: Mohr Siebeck, 1997.

RIBEIRO, Ricardo Lodi. "A proteção da confiança legítima do contribuinte". *RDDT* 145. São Paulo, 2007.

____. *A Segurança Jurídica do Contribuinte*. Rio de Janeiro: Lumen Juris, 2008.

RIGGERT, Rainer. *Die Selbstbindung der Rechtsprechung durch den allgemeinen Gleichheitssatz (Art. 3 I GG)*. Berlin: Duncker und Humblot, 1993.

RIVA, Enrico. *Wohlerworbene Rechte – Eigentum – Vertrauen*. Bern: Stämpfli, 2007.

ROCHA, Valdir de Oliveira. *A consulta fiscal*. São Paulo: Dialética, 1996.

RORIVE, Isabelle. *Le revirement de jurisprudence*. Bruxelles: Bruylant, 2003.

ROTH, Thomas. *Das Grundrecht auf den gesetzlichen Richter*. Berlin: Duncker und Humblot, 2000.

SACHS, Michael. *Verfassungsprozessrecht*. 2nd ed. Frankfurt am Main: Recht und Wirtschaft, 2007.

SANGMEISTER, Bernd. "Das Bundesverfassungsgericht und das Verfassungsrecht". *StuW* 2, 2001.

SCHACHTSCHNEIDER, Karl Albert. *Prinzipien des Rechtsstaates*. Berlin: Duncker und Humblot, 2006.

SCHAUER, Frederick. *Playing by the Rules*. Oxford: Clarendon, 1998.

____. *Thinking like a Lawyer: a new introduction to legal reasoning*. Cambridge: Harvard University Press, 2009.

SCHEFFELT, Michael. *Die Rechtsprechungsänderung. Ein Beitrag zu methodischen und verfassungsrechtlichen Grundlagen und zur Anwendung der Ergebnisse im Verwaltungsrecht*. Konstanz: Hartung-Gorre, 2001.

SCHLAICH, Klaus; KORIOTH, Stephan. *Das Bundesverfassungsgericht – Stellung, Verfahren, Entscheidungen*. 7th ed. München: Beck, 2007.

SCHOUERI, Luís Eduardo Schoueri, "Segurança jurídica e normas tributárias indutoras". In: RIBEIRO, Maria de Fátima (Org.). *Direito Tributário e segurança jurídica*. São Paulo: MP, 2008.

____. *Normas tributárias indutoras e intervenção econômica*. Rio de Janeiro: Forense, 2005.

SCHWARZ, Kyrill-A. *Vertrauensschutz als Verfassungsprinzip*. Baden-Baden: Nomos, 2002.

SEER, Roman, "Die Unvereinbarkeitserklärung des BVerfT am Beispiel seiner Rechtsprechung zum Abgabenrecht". *NJW* 5, 1996.

____. "Defizite im finanzgerichtlichen Rechtsschutz – zugleich eine kritische Auseinandersetzung mit dem 2. FGO-Änderungsgesetz vom 19.12.2000". *StuW*.

____. "Gewerbesteuer im Visier des Verfassungsgerichts – Anmerkungen zu dem Vorlagebeschluß des FG Niedersachsen vom 24.6.1998". *FR* 1998, 1998.

____. "Rechtsschutz in Steuersachen" In: TIPKE, Klaus; LANG, Joachim. *Steuerrecht*. 19th ed. Köln: Otto Schmidt, 2008. § 22. margin number 285.

SEER, Roman; MÜLLER, Jörg Peter. "Begrenzung der Wirkungen seiner Richtersprüche durch den EuGH". *IWB* n. 5. Gruppe 2. Fach 11, 2008.

SEYFARTH, Georg. *Die Änderung der Rechtsprechung durch das Bundesverfassungsgericht*. Berlin: Duncker und Humblot, 1998.

SILVA, José Afonso da. "Constituição e segurança jurídica", in Cármen Lúcia Antunes Rocha (Org.), *Constituição e segurança jurídica: direito adquirido, ato jurídico perfeito e coisa julgada. Estudos em homenagem a José Paulo Sepúlveda Pertence*. Belo Horizonte: Fórum, 2004.

SILVA VELLOSO, Carlos Mário da. "O princípio da irretroatividade da lei tributária". *RTDP* 15. São Paulo, 1996.

STÖTZEL, Martin Stötzel, *Vertrauensschutz und Gesetzesrückwirkung*. Frankfurt am Main: Peter Lang, 2002.

SUMMERS, Robert. "A formal theory of the rule of law". In: Idem. *Essays in Legal Theory*. Dordrecht: Kluwer, 2000.

SZCZEKALLA, Peter. *Die sogenannten grundrechtlichen Schutzpflichten im deutschen und europäischen Recht*. Berlin: Duncker und Humblot, 2002.

TAMANAHA, Brian Z. *Law as a means to an end – Threat to the Rule of Law*. Cambridge: Cambridge University Press, 2006.

____. *On the Rule of Law*. Cambridge: Cambridge University Press, 2004.

THEODORO JÚNIOR, Humberto Theodoro Jr., "Notas sobre sentença, coisa julgada e interpretação". *RePro* 167, 2009.

TIPKE, Klaus. "Rezensionen. Gerhard Habscheidt. Der Anspruch des Bürgers auf Erstattung verfassungswidriger Gesetze". *StuW* 2, 2004.

TORRES, Ricardo Lobo. "Legalidade tributária e riscos sociais". *RDDT* 59. São Paulo, 2000.

____. "Liberdade, segurança e justiça". In: CARVALHO, Paulo de Barros (Org.). *Justiça Tributária*. São Paulo: Max Limonad, 1998.

____. "Limitações ao poder impositivo e segurança jurídica". In: SILVA MARTINS, Ives Gandra da (Org.). *Limitações ao poder impositivo e segurança jurídica*. São Paulo: Ed. RT/CEU, 2007.

UMBACH, Dieter; CLEMENS, Thomas; DOLLINGER, Franz-Wilhelm (Orgs.) *Bundesverfassungsgerichtsgesetz*. 2nd ed. Heidelberg: C. F. Müller, 2005.

VALEMBOIS, Anne-Laure. *La constitutionnalisation de l'exigence de sécurité juridique en Droit Français*. Paris: LGDJ, 2005.

VALVERDE, Gustavo Sampaio. *Coisa julgada em matéria tributária*. São Paulo: Quartier Latin, 2004.

VIEIRA DE ANDRADE, José Carlos. *O dever de fundamentação expressa dos actos administrativos*. Coimbra: Almedina, 1992.

VIETS, Bodo. *Rechtsprechungsänderung und Vertrauensschutz*. Bern: Herbert Lang, 1976.

VILLEGAS, Héctor. "Principio de seguridad jurídica en la creación y aplicación del tributo". *RDT* 66. São Paulo, s.d.

VOGEL, Klaus. "Rückwirkung: eine festgefahrene Diskussion. Ein Versuch, die Blockade zu lösen". In: SCHLAICH, Klaus *et alii* (Orgs.) *FS für Martin Heckel zum 70. Geburtstag*. Tübingen: Mohr Siebeck, 1999.

VOGEL, Klaus; WALDHOFF, Christian. *Grundlagen des Finanzverfassungsrechts*. Heidelberg: C. F. Müller, 1999.

VONKILCH, Andreas. *Das Intertemporale Privatrecht*. Wien: Springer, 1999.

WALDHOFF, Christian. "Recent developments relating to the retroactive effect of decisions of the ECJ". *Common Market Law Review* 46, 2009 (manuscript).

WALDRON, Jeremy."The rule of law in contemporary liberal theory". *Ratio Juris*. v. 2. n. 1, 1989.

WALLERATH, Maximilian. *Die Selbstbindung der Verwaltung. Freiheit und Gebundenheit durch den Gleichheitssatz*. Berlin: Duncker und Humblot, 1968.

WATT, Horatia Muir. "*Never say never: post-scriptum* comparatif sur la rétroativité des revirements de jurisprudence". In: SEILLER, Bertrand (Org.). *La rétroactivité des décisions du juge administratif*. Paris: Economica, 2007.

WEBER-DÜRLER, Beatrice. Vertrauensschutz im öffentlichen Recht. Basel/Frankfurt: a.M. Helbing & Lichtenhahn, 1983.

WETZEL DE MATTOS, Sérgio Luiz. *Devido Processo Legal e Proteção de Direitos*. Porto Alegre: Livraria do Advogado, 2009.

ZIEGLER, Christoph Eduard. *Selbstbindung der Dritten Gewalt*. Frankfurt am Main: Peter Lang, 1993.

ZIMMER, Willy. "Constitution et sécurité juridique – Allemagne". *Annuaire International de Justice Constitutionnelle 1999*. Paris: Economica, 2000.

Part V
Efficacy of Legal Certainty

> But legal certainty is not the only value law must realize, or even the decisive value. Alongside legal certainty two other values come first: conformity to ends, and justice. (Gustav Radbruch, "Gesetzliches Unrecht und übergesetzliches Recht", Anhang 3, in *Rechtsphilosophie. Studienausgabe*, 2nd ed., Heidelberg, C. F. Müller, 2003 (1st ed., 1932), p. 216)

> However, those who find legal certainty possible cannot hide from the knowledge that only relative legal certainty is attainable, that there are insuperable limits to control, foresight and rigorous concept construction. In fact, it is only a matter of knowing to what extent an attempt to achieve legal certainty can and should be rationally made through foreseeable determination, and thus it is a question of measure. (Max Rümelin, *Die Rechtssicherheit*, Tübingen, Mohr Siebeck, 1924, p. 60)

> The main problem of legal certainty, which has come to light and posed the greatest challenges to legislative policy in all ages and in every field, especially that of private law, is how to reconcile what is established in general rules with the circumstances of the individual case, rigorous Law with equitable Law. (Max Rümelin, *Die Rechtssicherheit*, Tübingen, Mohr Siebeck, 1924, p. 57)

> It is in this powerful and plastic context that men are troubled, seeking certainty and fearing its excesses; clamoring for order and afraid of its unbridled weight; seduced by certainty and perplexed by its constraining immobility; fighting for justice, but wary of the stereotyped forms of distortion and routine. But instead of despair there will be steadfast trust if we convince ourselves that it is upon that creative perplexity, in challenging the mind's freedom and powers of synthesis, that the dignity of men is founded. (Miguel Reale, "Prefácio", in Theophilo Cavalcanti Filho, *O problema da segurança no Direito*, São Paulo, Ed. RT, 1964, p. VI).

The word "efficacy" may refer to the capacity to produce legal effects (legal efficacy) or to effective observance of or obedience to normative commands by their addressees (effectiveness). The investigation on which we are now embarking focuses on the legal efficacy of legal certainty as a legal principle, and not as a fact, value, political ideal or defining element of law.

The legal efficacy of the legal certainty principle involves two main questions. The first concerns its *normative function*, i.e., the way it produces effects relative to other norms or human behavior. The second concerns its *normative force*, i.e., how it is positioned in confrontation with other norms. The normative function of the legal certainty principle is relative. This is because the configuration of its *normative quality* and its various *efficacy functions* depends on the perspective from which it is analyzed.

First, if the legal certainty principle is investigated in terms of its relationship with principles that impose the realization of an even broader state of affairs, it takes on the role of *subprinciple* and performs a *definitional efficacy function* with regard to such an ideal. In this relationship and from this perspective, it assumes a position of analytical inferiority, embodying "bottom up" interpretation. This is the case with the relationship between the legal certainty principle and the rule of law principle: The legal certainty principle, as a subprinciple, definitionally concretizes what is established more broadly by the rule of law superprinciple.[1]

Second, if the legal certainty principle is examined in its connection with principles that impose the realization of more limited ideals, it assumes the position of a *superprinciple* and performs different functions with regard to these ideals: an *interpretative efficacy function*, when it acts as a parameter for the interpretation of subprinciples; a *blocking efficacy function*, when it acts to prevent the concrete application of one of the subprinciples that prove locally incompatible with the broader state of affairs; an *integrational efficacy function*, when it acts as an instrument to fill the void created by local rebuttal of a subprinciple. In this relationship and from this perspective, it assumes a position of analytical superiority, "above" the less comprehensive ideals. This is the case with the relationship between the legal certainty principle and the principles of statutory legality (as the ideal of the predictability of state actions), irretroactivity (as the ideal of legal regulation for future cases) and trust protection (as the ideal of protection for acts of disposal causally bound by previous state action). Indeed, the legal certainty principle, as a superprinciple, acts as an interpretative parameter to redefine that which is more narrowly determined by its subprinciples, or as a norm capable of blocking the application of a subprinciple and then filling the vacuum created by such blocking.

This prevalent position may also occur with regard to rules (often called principles, given their importance), as in the case of the legality rule (a tax can be introduced only by law), the tax irretroactivity rule (the law must precede the occurrence of the taxable event), and the anteriority rule (no tax can be introduced or modified unless the respective law has been published by the end of the previous fiscal year). An interesting issue is whether in this case the legal certainty principle can still be technically defined as a superprinciple, since the vertical relationship is formed between a principle and a rule.

It must be stressed that from a vertical perspective with two directions, one going "up" toward the rule of law superprinciple, and another going "down" toward the

[1]Philip Kunig, *Das Rechtsstaatsprinzip*, Tübingen, Siebeck, 1986, pages 163, 390 and following. Delf Buchwald, *Prinzipien des Rechtsstaats*, Aachen, Shaker, 1996, pages 181 and following. Katharina Sobota, *Das Prinzip Rechtsstaat*, Tübingen, Siebeck, 1997, p. 422.

subprinciples that normatively densify it, the legal certainty principle assumes the position of an "intermediate principle" (*Zwischenprinzip*).[2]

Third, if the legal certainty principle is seen in terms of its direct action, with no interference by any norms, be they principles or rules, it acts as a *principle* and directly performs an *integrational efficacy function*, filling the originary void created by the lack of rules or principles that specifically regulate the situation.

Because the certainty principle also acts as a superprinciple, it should be possible to employ this terminology in all cases. Strictly speaking, however, a superprinciple cannot be thought of except in its relationship with its subprinciples. A superprinciple without a subprinciple is a contradiction in terms. If "super" means "on top of" or "higher than" something, this normative relationship cannot be conceived of without a norm below. Thus when this efficacy function is performed, the norm is acting as a principle, although in other relationships it may take on the qualities of a subprinciple or superprinciple.

Given these considerations, the following question arises: "Is" legal certainty as a norm a subprinciple, a superprinciple or a principle? The correct answer is "it depends": If legal certainty is analyzed in terms of its direct efficacy, it assumes the position of a *principle*, since it does not predetermine any specific means, but an ideal state of affairs whose realization depends on choosing the appropriate and necessary means; if legal certainty is examined in its relationship with other norms, i.e. in terms of its indirect efficacy, it may play the role of *subprinciple* if analyzed from an angle that examines its relationship with a norm that establishes a broader ideal to be reached, or it may play the role of *superprinciple* if analyzed from a position that involves its connection with norms that determine more limited ideals. The concept is simple: If the normative dimension depends on a relationship, the former cannot be determined without defining the latter. Thus legal certainty as a legal norm is an intermediate principle (*Zwischenprinzip*) between principles that are axiologically above it (*Hauptprinzipien*), such as the rule of law, and the subprinciples that realize them (*Unterprinzipien*), such as the legality and irretroactivity principles.[3]

The above considerations show, on one hand, that there is no single classification of legal certainty that can be considered the only correct one, given its multidimensionality as a legal norm (subprinciple, superprinciple and principle) and its multifunctionality in the production of effects (direct and indirect efficacy functions). Its only inalterable normative dimension is that it is a legal principle. Hence the use of the term principle throughout this book, which in no way implies unawareness of its dimensions as subprinciple or superprinciple.

Doubtless the normative force of the legal certainty principle examines its efficacy against other norms. It is traditionally argued that principles have prima facie efficacy, as evidenced by their fitness to be weighed against other norms with which they conflict and the possibility of yielding to principles that have

[2]Andreas von Arnauld, *Rechtssicherheit*, Tübingen, Mohr Siebeck, 2006, p. 666.

[3]Andreas von Arnauld, *Rechtssicherheit*, Tübingen, Mohr Siebeck, 2006, p. 666.

greater weight in a concrete case.[4] Some scholars have recently referred to *pro tanto* efficacy, where principles sustain their force throughout the weighing process.[5] On this point it is important to know the force of the legal certainty principle when it conflicts with other norms, especially in the sense of examining whether it can be trumped by another principle whose weight is considered greater in a given concrete case.

These two important questions relating to the efficacy of the legal certainty principle – normative function and normative force –are analyzed below.

[4]Robert Alexy, *Theorie der Grundrechte*, 2nd ed., Frankfurt am Main, Suhrkamp, 1994, pages 88 and following. (Brazilian translation: *Teoria dos Direitos Fundamentais*, by Virgílio Afonso da Silva, 2nd ed., São Paulo, Malheiros Editores, 2011, pages 103 and following).

[5]Shelly Kagan, *The Limits of Morality*, Oxford, Clarendon, 1989, p. 17.

Normative Function

Abstract The efficacy of the legal certainty principle involves its normative function, in the sense of how it produces effects on other norms or human behavior, and the normative function of the legal certainty principle is relative since the configuration of its normative quality and its several efficacy functions depend on the perspective from which it is analyzed.

1 As a Principle

1.1 Subprinciple Dimension: Definitional Efficacy Function

In its relationship with principles that impose the realization of an even wider state of affairs, the legal certainty principle assumes the position of a *subprinciple* and performs a *definitional efficacy function* in relation to that ideal. This is precisely the case for its relationship with the rule of law. Because this principle establishes an ideal of lawfulness of state action, whose realization requires the existence of a state of knowability, reliability and calculability of law, the legal certainty principle materially densifies part of the content of the rule of law.

In this function, the reference to law in the rule of law principle is not to any law, but to an intelligible, stable, predictable law. In other words, the legal certainty subprinciple acts as a definer of the generic elements established by the rule of law superprinciple.[1]

1.2 Superprinciple Dimension

1.2.1 Interpretative Efficacy Function

In its relationship with its subprinciples or with the rules that realize it, the legal certainty principle performs an interpretative efficacy function. The judge must choose, among many possible meaningsthe one that is most strongly sustained by

[1] Katharina Sobota, *Das Prinzip Rechtsstaat*, Tübingen, Mohr Siebeck, 1997, pages 164 and following.

© Springer International Publishing Switzerland 2016
H. Ávila, *Certainty in Law*, Law and Philosophy Library 114,
DOI 10.1007/978-3-319-33407-3_10

the legal certainty superprinciple. Hence Carrazza's statement that principles, of which legal certainty is an example, act as "vectors for interpretative solutions."[2] Maior Borges is elucidatory along the same lines: "Legal certainty is therefore like a compass that guides constitutional exegesis and integration of the Federal Constitution by ordinary legislation toward its effectiveness and concretization."[3]

The legality rule does not reserve the task of creating or raising taxes to any statute, but to a statute that assures knowability, reliability and calculability of law. Thus the statute required by the legality rule must not be too indeterminate, must not cover past events in its hypothesis, and must not immediately or drastically raise the tax burden without a transitional period and transition rules. Legal certainty *densifies* the statute required by the legality rule, as it were.

Similarly, the tax irretroactivity rule, when axiologically linked to the legal certainty superprinciple, ultimately prevents taxation that surprises the exercise of the fundamental rights of freedom and property, acting as an interpretative criterion particularly when it is not known exactly whether the taxable event has or has not occurred in the terms of the infraconstitutional legislation. Legal certainty *qualifies* the meaning of retroactive effect, as it were.

These two examples, to which others could be added, serve merely to demonstrate that the legal certainty principle, in its vertical relationship with the norms that concretize it, acts as an interpretative criterion to assign them a meaning compatible with the ideals of knowability, reliability and calculability of law.

1.2.2 Reconfigurative Efficacy Function

Because the legal certainty principle involves ideals that do not always flow in the same direction, situations may arise in which one of the elements required to concretize it is incompatible with the unity of the states whose realization it requires. As we will see later, in such cases legal certainty enters into conflict with itself, so to speak: If the ideals that make up legal certainty are all to be promoted at once, the efficacy of a specific element must momentarily be blocked, or rather reconfigured.

An example of this is when tax benefits are granted without observing the legality rule and lead individuals to perform onerous acts of disposal of their fundamental rights of freedom and property. Despite failure to comply with the legality rule, the validity of the tax benefit may be upheld in the name of the trust protection principle. In this situation, the sub-elements of the legal certainty superprinciple must be balanced by provisionally *reconfiguring* the application of one of them (knowability) so that the others (reliability and calculability) are more completely realized.

[2] Roque Antonio Carrazza, *Curso de Direito Constitucional Tributário*, 27th ed., São Paulo, Malheiros Editores, 2011, p. 1090.

[3] José Souto Maior Borges, "Segurança jurídica: sobre a distinção entre competências fiscais para orientar e autuar o contribuinte", *RDT* n. 100, p. 24, São Paulo, s.d.

1.2.3 Derivative Integrational Efficacy Function

One of the functions of the legal certainty principle is to fill gaps that may be created when its subprinciples are applied.[4] This subsidiary or stopgap efficacy function is manifested, for example, when the irretroactivity rules established by the Constitution, in article 150, III, "a", and article 5, XXXVI, either do not apply or are not sufficient to assure a state of reliability and calculability of law based on its knowability.

Thus, for example, when a taxpayer has not yet consummated a taxable event, and has not acted so as to produce a completed legal act or an acquired right, but has nevertheless disposed of their freedom and property rights in such a manner that a sudden, drastic and disloyal change would cause grave and irreversible harm, the legal certainty principle in its reflexive efficacy will make their rights inviolable. In other words, the legal certainty principle goes into action when the express rules that concretize it prove insufficient. The best description of this is subsidiary action with integrational efficacy.[5]

1.2.4 Armoring Efficacy Function

Each of the subprinciples or rules that realize the legal certainty superprinciple acts independently with regard its material scope of application. Nevertheless, they all remain connected to it, so that the value of each sub-element is ultimately reinforced by incorporating the fundamental character of the superprinciple it helps to define. The anteriority rule, for example, acquires the contours of a fundamental guarantee in its relationship with the legal certainty superprinciple. The trust protection principle is elevated to the category of a fundamental norm by its valorative relationship with the legal certainty superprinciple – and so on.

This can be described as an armoring efficacy function, so to speak: The legal certainty superprinciple is shielded from possible changes to its subprinciples while strengthening their efficacy and concretization rules. The foundationality of the superprinciple is transferred, as it were, to the subprinciples and to the rules that densify it normatively, thanks to the axiological connection between then.

1.2.5 Supportive Efficacy Function

When the interpretation of the subprinciples is supported by the legal certainty superprinciple, their efficacy is reinforced against any other principles with which

[4] Anne-Laure Valembois, *La Constitutionnalisation de l'exigence de sécurité juridique en Droit français*, Paris, LGDJ, 2005, p. 398.

[5] Anne-Laure Valembois, *La Constitutionnalisation de l'exigence de sécurité juridique en Droit français*, Paris, LGDJ, 2005, p. 232.

they may collide. When there is a true conflict of principles, the principles concerned are weighed against each other, in the sense that concrete rules of prevalence are established by assigning a weight to each one. It is precisely through this assignment of weights that the legal certainty superprinciple performs its supportive efficacy function.

Indeed, one of the elements that configure the weight to be assigned to each of the colliding principles is its relationship with principles that the constitutional order qualifies as "fundamental." Because the legal certainty principle is one of the elements of the rule of law principle, positivated as a fundamental constitutional principle (article 1), and because it is included in the list of fundamental guarantees and rights (article 5, head paragraph), the constitutional order can be said to make legal certainty a fundamental norm. Now the legal certainty principle is made concrete by means of subprinciples and rules, which are also fundamental owing to their relationship with the superprinciple they densify. When they conflict with other principles, these subprinciples do not collide all alone, so to speak, for they are supported by a fundamental superprinciple and hence have a greater abstract weight, which can be reversed only with an *additional burden* of argumentation.

Thus the supportive efficacy function of the legal certainty superprinciple translates into the assignment of greater weights to the subprinciples that concretize it when they conflict with other principles, or into stricter application, in the case of rules. The key point is the change made to the efficacy of the subprinciple or rule "backed" by the legal certainty superprinciple: The superprinciple plays a supportive role (*Stützungsfunktion*, *application de renfort*) relative to the norms that axiologically underpin it.[6]

1.2.6 Regrouping Efficacy Function

The legal certainty superprinciple is a "balanced synthesis" of its subprinciples, so that each one has its value by virtue of the others.[7] Thus the superprinciple is not simply the sum of the elements that concretize it. If it were, it would not have to be stipulated, even indirectly.[8] Hence instead of a principle, it is termed a "schema of a principle" (*schème de principe*), into which different combinations of contradictory requirements are inserted, so that it also possesses an attractive and optimizing efficacy grounded in these requirements thanks to the reinforcement of its visibility and the integration of its effects.[9]

---

[6]Andreas von Arnauld, *Rechtssicherheit*, Tübingen, Mohr Siebeck, 2006, p. 667.

[7]Antonio Enrique Perez Luño, *La seguridad jurídica*, Barcelona, Ariel, 1991, p. 29.

[8]César García Novoa, *El principio de seguridad jurídica en materia tributaria*, Madrid, Marcial Pons, 2000, p. 39.

[9]Loïc Azoulai, "La valeur normative de la sécurité juridique", in Laurence Boy, Jean-Baptiste Racine and Fabrice Siiriainen (Orgs.), *Sécurité juridique et Droit Économique*, Bruxelles, Larcier, 2008, pages 27, 35.

For the same reason it is defined as a superprinciple or supernotion (*Überbegriff*) relative to its subprinciples (or derivative principles).[10] As a superprinciple, it plays the role of a "regrouping" principle (*principe fédérateur*) or "matrix" principle (*principe matriciel*), to use the French expressions coined by Mathieu.[11] Through its operation and as a result of its "matrix," not only are new subprinciples created, but they are also given new meanings, as a result of the relationship created between superprinciple and subprinciples.[12] It is a "founding" principle, so to speak.[13] According to Valembois, the notion of "matrix" implies the idea of the transmission of a genetic heritage from the mother principle to the subprinciples, thus preventing "genetic mutation" of the subprinciple. More importantly, the superprinciple or matrix principle is not simply the sum of its subprinciples, nor are these a mere specialization of the former.[14] Essentially, in this framework the legal certainty principle is an articulated complex of principles and not a single, uniform principle. This is why Torres uses the expression "principles of legal certainty," including in its content a plethora of principles and subprinciples.[15]

The regrouping efficacy function of the legal certainty superprinciple therefore represents its capacity to rearticulate and resize its subprinciples. For instance, the trust protection principle cannot act as an instrument to make legal effects inviolable when such inviolability might encourage unlawful acts in future, because this would be to protect legal certainty in its past dimension of reliability to the detriment of its future dimension of calculability. In other words, the connection between the trust protection principle and the legal certainty superprinciple brings about a *normative resignification*, in the sense that whereas it might have one meaning by itself it gains a new meaning when it is part of a group. Thus the regrouping efficacy function is defined as the *rearrangement of meaning* the superprinciple causes in each of the subprinciples that concretize it.

---

[10]Anne-Laure Valembois, *La Constitutionnalisation de l'exigence de sécurité juridique en Droit français*, Paris, LGDJ, 2005, p. 188. Willy Zimmer, "Constitution et sécurité juridique – Allemagne", *Annuaire International de Justice Constitutionnelle 1999*, Paris, Economica, p. 91.

[11]Bertrand Mathieu, "Constitution et sécurité juridique – France". *Annuaire International de Justice Constitutionnelle 1999*, Paris, Economica, p. 156. Idem, "Pour une reconnaissance de 'principes matriciels' en matière de protection constitutionnelle des droits de l'homme", *Recueil Dalloz Sirey*, n. 27, p. 211, 1995. On the subject, see: Andreas von Arnauld, *Rechtssicherheit*, Tübingen, Mohr Siebeck, 2006, p. 691.

[12]Xavier Philippe, "Constitution et sécurité juridique", *Annuaire International de Justice Constitutionnelle 1999*, Paris, Economica, 2000, pages 73, 77. Bertrand Mathieu, "Pour une reconnaissance de 'principes matriciels' en matiére de protection constitutionnelle des droits de l'homme", *Recueil Dalloz Sirey*, n. 27, p. 211, 1995.

[13]Blaise Knapp, "Constitution et sécurité juridique – Suisse", *Annuaire International de Justice Constitutionnelle 1999*, Paris, Economica, 2000, p. 261.

[14]Anne-Laure Valembois, *La Constitutionnalisation de l'exigence de sécurité juridique en Droit français*, Paris, LGDJ, 2005, p. 397.

[15]Ricardo Lobo Torres, "Limitações ao poder impositivo e segurança jurídica", in Ives Gandra da Silva Martins (Org.), *Limitações ao poder impositivo e segurança jurídica*, São Paulo, Ed. RT/CEU, 2007, p. 63.

1.3 Principle Dimension: Originary Integrational Efficacy Function

Legal certainty, in its normative dimension as a principle, performs the function of establishing an ideal state of affairs whose realization requires behavior that causes effects that contribute to its promotion. Because the legal certainty principle requires the realization of the states of knowability, reliability and calculability of law, it is necessary to behave in ways that contribute to their promotion. The originary integrational efficacy function is nothing more than the function performed by the legal certainty principle in creating rules that serve as the means to realize the ideals whose realization it determines.

Thus, for instance, accessibility and intelligibility of norms are necessary to realize a state of knowability, and this is achieved through publication of laws and material determination of the incidence hypotheses they establish. Normative stability is necessary to achieve a state of reliability, and this is achieved through respect for acquired rights, consolidated situations and legitimate expectations. Anteriority and continuity of law are necessary to realize a state of calculability, and this is achieved by prolonging the efficacy of norms and establishing transition rules.

In sum, the originary integrational efficacy function consists of the role played by the legal certainty principle in creating rules of behavior whose effects contribute to the promotion of the ideal states of knowability, reliability and calculability of law.

2 As a Principle Concretized in a Rule

Legal certainty is a legal principle and as such it experiences the aforementioned efficacy functions. We have seen that unlike other constitutions, the Constitution promulgated by Brazil in 1988 and now in force includes rules governing legal certainty in several areas, protecting *res iudicata*, acquired rights and completed legal acts, for example, or banning the retroactivity of tax statutes relative to the occurrence of the taxable event.

In these cases legal certainty is not an element to be weighed as a principle, but concretized constitutionally through rules that as such are not subject to horizontal weighing.[16] The importance of these rules lies in their creating a rigidity

[16]Federico Arcos Ramírez, *La seguridad jurídica: una teoría formal*, Madrid, Dykinson, 2000, p. 70. Almiro do Couto e Silva, "O princípio da segurança jurídica (proteção à confiança) no Direito Público brasileiro e o direito da Administração Pública de anular os seus próprios atos: o prazo decadencial do art. 54 da Lei do Processo Administrativo da União (Lei n. 9.784/99)", *RDA*, n. 237, p. 273, Rio de Janeiro, 2004.

of application that cannot be avoided through weighing against reasons often considered superior, as occurs in other legal systems that do not have constitutional rules governing legal certainty.

3 As a Subjective Right

The objective efficacy of the legal certainty principle may experience a "right to certainty" from a concrete and subjective point of view. This right is nothing more than the legal certainty principle in its reflexive efficacy: Because it is a legal norm, the legal certainty principle creates, albeit indirectly, obligations and prohibitions for the state, which citizens can argue in court when there is procedural legitimacy to do so.[17] In diffuse control of constitutionality, for example, citizens can argue that a statute is unconstitutional because it violates the legal certainty principle by not containing transition rules or undermining legitimate expectations. What they cannot do – and only this because the principle is not a subjective right – is demand specific or general public policies to assure legal certainty.[18]

Because subjective rights derive from the legal certainty principle and the application of this principle involves an examination of the vertical compatibility between it and the other norm, the object of judicial protection must be a norm, or the application of a norm, that may be qualified as "uncertain", and its aim must be to declare such a norm invalid.[19]

References

ARCOS RAM´iREZ, Federico. *La seguridad jurídica: una teoría formal*. Madrid: Dykinson, 2000.

von ARNAULD, Andreas. *Rechtssicherheit*. Tübingen: Mohr Siebeck, 2006.

AZOULAI, Loïc. "La valeur normativa de la sécurité juridique". In BOY, Laurence; RACINE, Jean-Baptiste; SIIRIAINEN, Fabrice (Orgs.). *Sécurité Juridique et Droit Économique*. Bruxelles: Larcier, 2008, pp. 25–41.

CARRAZZA, Roque Antonio. *Curso de Direito Constitucional Tributário*. 27 ed. São Paulo: Malheiros Editores, 2011.

[17] César García Novoa, *El principio de seguridad jurídica en materia tributaria*, Madrid, Marcial Pons, 2000, pp. 41–42. Federico Arcos Ramírez, *La seguridad jurídica: una teoría formal*, Madrid, Dykinson, 2000, p. 74.

[18] Bertrand Mathieu, "Constitution et sécurité juridique – France". *Annuaire International de Justice Constitutionnelle 1999*, Paris, Economica, 2000, p. 175. Id. "La sécurité juridique: un principe constitutionnel *clandestin mais* efficient", in Patrick Fraisseix (Org.), *Mélanges Patrice Gélard – Droit Constitutionnel*, Paris, Montchrestien, 1999, p. 302.

[19] César García Novoa, *El principio de seguridad jurídica en materia tributaria*, Madrid, Marcial Pons, 2000, p. 45.

COUTO E SILVA, Almiro do. "O princípio da segurança jurídica (proteção à confiança) no Direito Público Brasileiro e o Direito da Administração Pública de anular os seus próprios atos: o prazo decadencial do art. 54 da Lei do Processo Administrativo da União (Lei n. 9.784/99)". *RBDP* 6, Porto Alegre, 2004, pp. 7–59.

KNAPP, Blaise. "Constitution et sécurité juridique – Suisse". *Annuaire International de Justice Constitutionnelle 1999*. Paris: Economica, 2000, pp. 261–271.

MAIOR BORGES, José Souto. "Segurança jurídica: sobre a distinção entre competências fiscais para orientar e atuar o contribuinte". *RDT* 100/19–26, s. d.

MATHIEU, Bertrand. "Constitution et sécurité juridique – France". *Annuaire International de Justice Constitutionnelle 1999*. Paris: Economica, 2000, pp. 155–192.

_____. "Pour une reconnaissance de 'principes matriciels' en matiére de protection constitutionnelle des droit de l'homme". *Recueil Dalloz Sirey* 27, pp. 211–212, 1995.

_____. "La sécurité juridique: un principe constitutionnel clandestin mais efficient". In FRAISSEIX, Patrick (Org.). *Mélanges Patrice Gélard – Droit Constitutionnel*. Paris: Montchrestien, 1999, pp. 301–305.

NOVOA, César García. *El principio de seguridad jurídica en materia tributaria*. Madrid: Marcial Pons, 2000.

PEREZ LUÑO, Antonio Enrique. *La seguridad jurídica*. Barcelona: Ariel, 1991.

PHILIPPE, Xavier. "Constitution et sécurité juridique – Afrique du Sud". *Annuaire International de Justice Constitutionnelle 1999*. Paris: Economica, 2000, pp. 71–90.

SOBOTA, Katharina. *Das Prinzip Rechtsstaat*. Tübingen: Siebeck, 1997.

TORRES, Ricardo Lobo. "Limitações ao poder impositivo e segurança jurídica". In SILVA MARTINS, Ives Gandra da (Org.). *Limitações ao poder impositivo e segurança jurídica*. São Paulo: Ed. RT/CEU, 2007, pp. 61–77.

VALEMBOIS, Anne-Laure. *La Constitutionnalisation de l'exigence de sécurité juridique en Droit français*. Paris: LGDJ, 2005.

ZIMMER, Willy. "Constitution et sécurité juridique – Allemagne". *Annuaire International de Justice Constitutionnelle 1999*. Paris: Economica, 2000, pp. 91–107.

Normative Force

Abstract The legal efficacy of the legal certainty principle involves its normative force, in the sense of how it is positioned with regard to other norms. Thus the legal certainty principle is a norm with sui generis efficacy, unlike that of all other principles, a sort of "condition norm" or "structure norm", in the sense that unless it is minimally effective no other norms can have minimal efficacy. It is an "intermediation principle", establishing functional conditions for the principles and rules that constitute the legal order.

1 Internal Conflicts

Since the legal certainty principle requires the combined realization of *several* states of affairs, some of which are intermediate, others final, and some both, any case under adjudication may give rise to a sort of conflict of legal certainty with itself, in the sense that the promotion of *one* state of affairs causes the restriction of *another* state that is concretely and diametrically opposite.[1] This happens, for example, when an inferior norm is declared null and void on grounds of incompatibility with a superior one in pursuit of the ideal of knowability of law, restricting the ideal of reliability of law by disregarding legal situations that may have been legitimately acquired on the basis of the inferior norm; or when an illegal norm is declared inviolable in pursuit of the ideal of reliability, restricting the ideals of knowability and calculability by prohibiting discussion of a violation of the legality rule that the collectivity observes.[2]

These examples show that there can be a conflict within the very ideals that together make up the legal certainty principle – a sort of internal axiological tension,

[1] Sylvia Calmes, *Du principe de protection de la confiance légitime en Droits allemand, communautaire et français*, Paris, Dalloz, 2001, p. 116.

[2] Anne-Laure Valembois, *La Constitutionnalisation de l'exigence de sécurité juridique en Droit français*, Paris, LGDJ, 2005, pp. 68–69. Loïc Azoulai, "La valeur normative de la sécurité juridique", in Laurence Boy, Jean-Baptiste Racine and Fabrice Siiriainen (Orgs.), *Sécurité juridique et Droit Économique*, Bruxelles, Larcier, 2008, p. 36.

© Springer International Publishing Switzerland 2016
H. Ávila, *Certainty in Law*, Law and Philosophy Library 114,
DOI 10.1007/978-3-319-33407-3_11

to use the expression coined by Perez Luño.[3] The solution is to balance these ideal states so that the pursuit of legal certainty entails an overall enhancement by virtue of its use as a foundation for a given decision via greater average realization of the ideal states that make it up than the contrary. Once again this justifies the concept of legal certainty adopted in this study. Let us summarize the concept here as follows: Legal certainty is a principle norm that requires behavior that contributes *more* to the existence of a state of reliability and calculability *of* and *through* law, based on its knowability.

2 External Conflicts

2.1 Typology

2.1.1 "Prima Facie" Efficacy

Prima facie efficacy can have two meanings. First, it may mean an initial force that dissipates later. This connotation is indicated by the expression "at first sight" to refer to a situation in which a principle that at first sight seemed to be applicable and to have a certain force ultimately proves *inapplicable* and without normative force in that situation. A prima facie reason appears to be a reason but may not be a reason at all or may not have weight in the resolution of a given situation.[4] On this view a prima facie principle means a principle that seemed to be applicable but actually is not. An example can be found in the alleged conflicts between the principles of the right to privacy and freedom of the press. It is said that, depending on the case, one principle prevails over the other through a weighing process, which assigns greater weight to one than the other. Thus if news about a politician in a newspaper is concerned with something he does in his private life, freedom of the press is said to prevail over privacy. If the news concerns this politician's public service, greater weight must be given to freedom of the press, as opposed to the right to privacy. In reality, however, there is no genuine conflict. If newspapers publish stories about a politician's private life, the principle that applies is the right to privacy because the situation falls within the private sphere. The principle of freedom of the press does not apply because the news in question does not deserve publication or does not concern the public. If the news is concerned with the politician's public life, on the other hand, the principle that applies is freedom of the press, because the situation falls within this sphere, and the right to privacy is irrelevant because this news is not about the private sphere. Thus the conflict is merely apparent because one of the principles is *not applicable*. There is a conflict between principles only if both are equally

[3] Antonio Enrique Perez Luño, *La seguridad jurídica*, Barcelona, Ariel, 1991, p. 69. Federico Arcos Ramírez, *La seguridad jurídica: una teoría formal*, Madrid, Dykinson, 2000, p. 69.

[4] Shelly Kagan, *The Limits of Morality*, Oxford, Clarendon, 1989, p. 17.

applicable.[5] In these cases one of the principles appears applicable but turns out to be inapplicable. This is why the expression "prima facie efficacy" is used to refer to apparent force or as a force "at first sight" only. This does not mean the applied principle is stronger, but only that it will be applied whereas the other will not.

The legal certainty principle evidently does not have prima facie efficacy in this specific sense, because it must always be present to some degree and is applicable to all institutional manifestations of law.

Second, prima facie efficacy may mean that a given principle does not have definitive efficacy in the sense that what it determines must ultimately be performed, but relative efficacy in the sense that in each concrete case its reasons must be weighed against the reasons presented by other principles. In this conflict, the efficacy of one principle can be *set aside* if greater weight is assigned to a colliding principle.[6] Thus it can be said that prima facie efficacy qualifies the *weighability* and *discardability* of principles. This gives rise to the following question: Can the legal certainty principle be discarded in favor of other principles in a weighing process? As defined in this book, the answer is *no*.

Indeed, the legal certainty principle understood as a norm that establishes the ideals of knowability, reliability and calculability of law can never be discarded. What may happen is something subtly different: In some cases, one *element* of one of its *ideals*, of one of its *dimensions*, may be differently calibrated by virtue of its relationship with other ideals or different dimensions. Thus, for example, if the past effects of invalid administrative acts are upheld because a de facto situation has become consolidated, one element (normative intelligibility) of one ideal (knowability) in one dimension (static) is configured differently because of another element (intangibility), another ideal (stability) and another dimension (dynamic) of legal certainty. Legal certainty is never completely set aside in the unity of its ideals. All that may happen is the application of one element to a smaller degree to favor the application of another, or of others, to a greater degree.

Even in cases defined here as external conflicts, the legal certainty principle is not completely set aside. When legal certainty is said to yield to justice, for example, what actually happens is that one of its elements, aspects, dimensions is restricted whereas others remain intact. Thus it is incorrect to assign prima facie efficacy to the legal certainty principle in the strict sense of a norm whose efficacy can be completely set aside in a concrete case because a colliding principle has greater weight. This definitely does not happen.

The only possible way to qualify the normative force of the legal certainty principle as prima facie efficacy is to define prima facie efficacy, thirdly, as denoting not *discardability* when weighed against colliding principles but *restrictability* against other principles. In this strict sense, the legal certainty principle might be

[5]Riccardo Guastini, *L'Interpretazione dei documenti normativi*, Milano, Giuffrè, 2004, p. 217.

[6]Robert Alexy, *Theorie der Grundrechte*, 2nd ed., Frankfurt am Main, Suhrkamp, 1994, pages 88 and following. (Brazilian translation: *Teoria dos Direitos Fundamentais*, translated by Virgílio Afonso da Silva, 2nd ed., São Paulo, Malheiros Editores, 2011, pages 103 and following).

said to be the object of *restriction* in some cases. However, even in this sense it is appropriate to ask whether the principle as such is restricted or whether instead it assumes a *different configuration* in given cases because of the specific arrangement of its partial ideals.

In sum, in the cases discussed above legal certainty performs the function of a superprinciple. Our analysis up to this point has focused on the relationship between superprinciple and subprinciples, so here we must ask whether the superprinciple is also restricted when one of its subprinciples is. For example, protecting legitimate trust or legitimate expectations as a form of inviolability based on the requirement of stability of the legal order entails setting aside the normative consequence that ought to be applied for non-compliance withan immediately applicable norm, which in turn means limiting the requirement of normative identifiability as a form of intelligibility guaranteed by the requirement of knowability of the legal order. In sum, one element of legal certainty is restricted in favor of another, or one subprinciple is prioritized over another subprinciple of the same legal certainty superprinciple. Here the following question arises: Is only the subprinciple restricted, leaving the superprinciple intact, or is the superprinciple always restricted at the same time as a subprinciple ?

The answer to this important question depends on a semantic agreement. There are at least two possible answers, depending on how a superprinciple is defined. On one hand, if the legal certainty superprinciple is defined as the *sum of subprinciples*, then the superprinciple is restricted every time a subprinciple is restricted. Thus when the legality principle is said to be restricted in the name of the legal certainty superprinciple, not only the subprinciple but part of the superprinciple is restricted, so that the latter is disregarded in its entirety. On this view, every restriction of a subprinciple is automatically a restriction of the superprinciple.

On the other hand, if the legal certainty superprinciple is defined as *something different than the sum of its foundations and subprinciples*, the superprinciple is not necessarily restricted whenever what are traditionally called subprinciples are restricted.

At this point, an explanation is needed. In this book I distinguish between the foundations of legal certainty, its elements, and its forms of concretization. The *foundations* of legal certainty are those norms around which the ideals of knowability, reliability and calculability of law can be built, by deduction or induction. The part of this book that discusses this point constructs the normative basis on which the legal certainty principle stands. The foundations of legal certainty, for example, include the legality, irretroactivity and anteriority rules. The *elements* of legal certainty are the partial ideal states whose realization it determines. The ideals of knowability, reliability and calculability of law are elements of legal certainty. Its *forms of concretization* are the means appropriate and necessary to the promotion of those ideals, whether or not such means are abstractly stipulated by the legal order. Notification and publication, for example, are forms of concretization of the ideal of knowability of law. The essential aspect of all the above is that the foundations, elements and forms of concretization of legal certainty must not be confused.

The tax legality rule is therefore a foundation of legal certainty, because an ideal of knowability of law can be constructed from it, along with other elements. This ideal can be concretized through legality and other forms. Thus although the legality rule is a foundation in the Brazilian order and a form of concretization of legal certainty, strictly speaking it is not an element, since knowability is the element. The same is true of notification. Notification concretizes the requirement of knowability, which is an element of legal certainty, but it is not itself an element because there are other forms of concretization of knowability, such as publication via the internet, for example, in the case of administrative decisions.

Something similar occurs with human dignity. It is a foundation of legal certainty because citizens are not to be treated as objects and the application of norms must therefore involve respect for individual freedom. It is a *foundation*, but not an *element* of legal certainty. In sum, foundations and forms of concretization are not to be confused with elements of legal certainty.

The key point is that the legal certainty superprinciple as defined in this book is the *unity* of the ideals of knowability, reliability and calculability of law, which constitute its subprinciples or elements. None of these subprinciples has a previously defined measure of realization. Thus if the effects of an illegal administrative act are upheld because of a consolidated situation or the past effects of a statute declared unconstitutional are upheld to protect trust, strictly speaking this does not set aside the "legality principle" as a subprinciple of legal certainty. Legality is a foundation for and a form of concretization of legal certainty, but not an element of it. What is involved is the calibration of the application of one of its elements (knowability) in its concrete relationship with others (reliability and calculability). Hence it can be said that the partial ideals are not *restricted*, but only *configured* differently in their internal relationships by virtue of a concrete situation. The partial ideals of legal certainty can be compared to the tires of a car. Tire pressure depends on the weight of the vehicle and may vary between the rear tires and front tires. It would not be correct to say that tires are "restricted" when pressure is set lower. It would be appropriate only to say that they are inflated differently in accordance with their relationship with the other tires and their concrete function. Legal certainty could also be compared to a plastic party balloon: When it is squeezed on one side, the air simply moves to the other side. It would not be correct to say the balloon is restricted when squeezed. It would be better to say it is configured *differently*, since its mass remains the same but its shape is different. To offer one last simile, legal certainty could also be compared to a lump of wet clay ready to be kneaded and thrown by the potter. When one of its parts is pressed, the mass thins and shifts from one end to the other. It would not be proper to say the clay is restricted when shaped in a non-uniform way, because its mass remains rigorously the same.

All of these statements aim to show that the legal certainty principle, unlike other principles, cannot be set aside or discarded in the process of application. It acts as a foundation for normative validation and an instrument for the realization of other norms: As such, it is a *presupposition* of law, upon which the other norms rest. The pair of weighing scales is a well-worn metaphor, of course, but may perhaps be useful here. Legal certainty does not correspond to the objects placed on the scales, which are best represented by substantive principles such as freedom and solidarity; it is not the pointer of the balance, which is best represented by justice itself; it is not the beam between the scales, which more closely resembles the postulates of proportionality and practical concordance; instead, legal certainty can be compared with the *base* of the scales, on which it stands and which is indispensable to its proper functioning. Just as a pair of weighing scales cannot work without a sound base, law is inconceivable without legal certainty (in its definitional meaning) and without the legal certainty principle (in its normative meaning). We might also recall the equally well-worn metaphor of a building in which the principles are the main beams. In this idealization, the legal certainty principle resembles less one of the beams than the bricks without which they could not be supported. All these images aim only to show that the legal certainty principle may even assume different shapes, be calibrated differently and be concretized in different ways, but can never be set aside.

Of course, everything that has been stated so far depends on semantic agreements about the meaning of "efficacy," "principle," "superprinciple," "prima facie" and so on. Nevertheless, the key point is that although legal certainty is a principle, it is a norm that establishes the pursuit of an ideal state of affairs without specifying the means necessary to its realization and, as such, it lacks the prima facie efficacy some principles have, as norms that may be temporarily inapplicable (prima facie efficacy as defeasible normative force), that can be overridden in specific cases (*prima facie* efficacy as overridable normative force), or that can be limited in its unity (*prima facie* efficacy as limitable normative force). The only way to understand that the legal certainty superprinciple can be restricted is to perceive it not as a whole that differs from its parts, but rather as their sum. However, in this book I have set out to show that legal certainty as a superprinciple is something other than the mere sum of its subprinciples, so I cannot accept that it can be restricted, although here too this conception depends crucially on semantic agreements. This conclusion has repercussions of two kinds.

One is that principles, as normative categories, cannot be defined in prima facie terms, i.e. in terms of inapplicability, overridability or limitability due to conflicting principles. While it is true that some principles, such as freedom, may be limited or even overridden in the name of conflicting principles, other principles cannot be set aside while still deserving the name of principles, because they require the realization of an ideal state of affairs without predetermining the means. The rule of law and due process of law are unwaivable principles in this sense. The prima facieness of principles in the senses discussed here is not a defining element, but a contingent element of legal principles.

On the other hand, these considerations show that the efficacy of the legal certainty principle is different because it is a presupposition of the functioning of law itself, and the foundation on which the principles of freedom, equality and dignity are realized. That being so, the efficacy of the legal certainty principle cannot be justified in the ways typically preferred by legal doctrine. A different approach is required. This is our focus from now on.

2.1.2 "Pro Tanto" Efficacy

Some scholars prefer the expression "pro tanto" to prima facie efficacy. A *pro tanto* reason is one that may be overridden by contrary arguments but remains important throughout the application process. Unlike a prima facie reason, which may seem to be a reason but may eventually turn out to have no weight at all, a pro tanto reason may not be decisive but retains its force.[7] The following question therefore arises: Does the legal certainty principle have pro tanto efficacy? It depends.

If pro tanto efficacy is defined as efficacy that may not be decisive but retains its force until the end, the legal certainty principle can be said to have such efficacy: It maintains its weight throughout the application process, and cannot be outweighed by another principle. Such efficacy can also be defined as the property inherent in a reason that may be overruled by another and lacks decisive weight, while needing to be considered when various reasons are put in the balance.[8] In this sense, the legal certainty principle as certainty of law does not have such efficacy because it cannot be overridden. It can be more or less calibrated and configured differently, by guaranteeing more or less knowability, reliability and calculability. In its entirety, however, it cannot be discarded.

All the above considerations show that the legal certainty principle does not match the traditional definitions of prima facie and pro tanto efficacy. One of the reasons for this is that these qualifications are intended to represent *conflict* or *competition* between reasons, and in the case of the legal certainty principle strictly speaking we are dealing neither with a reason nor with a conflict in the true or traditional sense. Indeed, the legal certainty principle as certainty of law is not a *reason* to be weighed against others, but a "condition principle" or "presumption principle" for the application of other norms, which are rules and principles. Moreover, as shown earlier, it does not *confront* other principles by which it may ultimately be restricted (if understood as other than the mere sum of its parts); however, it acts as a presumption for the functioning of norms that will give rise to a confrontation if and when it takes on a given configuration, depending on the situation.

Thus the legal certainty principle is a norm with sui generis efficacy unlike that of all other principles, a sort of "condition norm" or "structure norm", in the sense that unless it is minimally effective no other norms can have minimal efficacy. Hence it is the norm of norms. However, it is not a norm that structures the application of others by supplying formal or substantive criteria, as does the applicative postulate of proportionality. Instead, it is a norm that creates conditions for the existence, validity and efficacy of other norms. Its efficacy is definitive but non-uniform: *definitive* because it cannot be outweighed by contrary principles; *non-uniform* because the

---

[7]Shelly Kagan, *The Limits of Morality*, Oxford, Clarendon, 1989, p. 17. Wlodek Rabinowicz, "Peczenik's passionate reason", in Aulis Aarnio *et alii* (Orgs.), *On Coherence Theory of Law*, Lund, Juristförlager, 1998, p. 21.

[8]Shelly Kagan, *The Limits of Morality*, Oxford, Clarendon, 1989, pages 70–71.

partial states are not applied in the same manner or with the same intensity to all cases, but in totalities organized and synthesized into a unity in each new case. We might use chess to illustrate metaphorically how the legal certainty principle works. The game depends on a number of rules. For example, it is played on a board with 64 squares by two people, each of whom uses pieces of a different color. Each player has sixteen pieces: king and queen, two rooks, two bishops, two knights, and eight pawns. The queen can move any number of squares horizontally, vertically or diagonally, the knight can move in L shapes and so on. In this analogy, the rule of law principle determines that the game must be played according to the rules and that the rules must be followed by all players and by the judge. The legal certainty principle, in turn, determines that the rules must be clear, stable, and predictable. Thus, for example, the pieces and squares must have different colors that allow the players to identify them, such as black and white, but not white and beige; the rules must be announced before the game begins or before each move, not after it has started or moves have been made; the rules must be intelligible, such as the rule that a knight moves in L shapes, specifically two squares in one direction and one square perpendicular to it, and can jump over other pieces, not simply in L shapes without any further specification of content, and so on. The legal certainty principle, therefore, does not exactly supply the conditions of the game or even its norms, but establishes the *presuppositions* on which the functioning of the norms is based. It is the norm about the functioning of norms, with the ultimate purpose – which must always be kept in focus – of assuring respect for the players as human beings.

2.1.3 Structural Condition

If the above considerations are true, prima facie and pro tanto are inappropriate categories to represent the efficacy of this principle, because – to continue the metaphor – they are designed to address conflict between the pieces, not to operate the rules that govern their moves. The point to be stressed is this: The *legal* certainty principle is different from other principles because it applies to law itself. It is a "principle of intermediation", so to speak, since it establishes *operating conditions* for the principles and rules that make up the legal order, even though these conditions act more immediately as an instrument to assure respect for human beings. Thus it is not at the same level as or parallel with other norms, but at a different analytical level, where it establishes the conditions for them to function. This is why prima facie and pro tanto are inadequate categories: Both terms are used to define the effects of principles that are equally important and are placed next to each other at the same level. If, as argued here, the legal certainty principle cannot be placed at the same level as other principles because it does not oppose or compete with them, then clearly these categories are not suitable to define its efficacy. Thus there is a sort of *incommensurability* between the legal certainty principle and other principles, in the sense that strictly speaking they cannot be directly compared because although they are principles and require the realization of ideals without preconfiguring the necessary means, they do not have the same properties or perform the same functions. Incommensurability, notes Sunstein, "occurs when the relevant goods cannot be aligned along a single metric without doing violence to our considered judgments about how these goods are best characterized."[9] With apologies for yet another simile, aligning incommensurable goods is like asking whether a "circle" is more important than "yellow," or whether "beautiful" is worth more than "heavy," or whether Beethoven is better than Elvis Presley. As Chang properly points out, "If items are incomparable, nothing affirmative can be said about what value relation holds between them."[10] The legal certainty principle is incommensurable with other principles owing not only to its value, which bears no parallel with others, but above all to its relational functions: Because it is the *foundation* for other norms and *instrumentalizes* them, it is not situated at the same analytical level, so that mere comparison is impossible and the opposition presupposed by horizontal weighing of conflicting principles is an illusion.

In light of these considerations, the closest representation of its efficacy would be as a sort of "structural constraint," used to illustrate the conditions that cannot be overridden in a conflict between reasons.[11] Thus it is clear that the legal certainty principle, in Carrazza's rigorous definition, is a principle *presupposed* by the others.[12] In sum, it is a *functional requirement* of law, to use Palombella's accurate term, indicating requirements that cannot be set aside and must be present if law is to conserve its raison d'être, which is to guide behavior, consolidate expectations, resolve conflicts of interest and produce social order.[13] In light of all this, it is worth quoting Maior Borges' succinct refutation of the non-application of the legal certainty principle under any circumstances:

> One of the fundamental principles stands out *because it must not be disregarded (disapplied) on any pretext.* This is legal certainty, without which Brazil could not even define itself as a democratic law-based state (Constitution, article 1, head paragraph). Indeed, legal certainty is of such importance in the architecture of the constitutional system that it is highlighted by the Preamble to the Federal Constitution as well as article 5, head paragraph. Certainty is a fundamental guarantee and right, *and cannot be disregarded at any level of infraconstitutional application*, i.e., in statutes and tax regulations and even in acts of execution.[14]

---

[9]Cass Sunstein, "Incommensurability and kinds of valuation: some applications in Law", in Ruth Chang (ed.), *Incommensurability, incomparability and practical reason*, Cambridge, Harvard University Press, 1997, p. 238.

[10]Ruth Chang, "Introduction", in idem, *Incommensurability, incomparability and practical reason*, Cambridge, Harvard University Press, 1997, p. 4.

[11]Robert Nozick, *Anarchy, State and Utopia*, Oxford, Blackwell, 1975 (1974), pages 30–32.

[12]Roque Antonio Carrazza, *Curso de Direito Constitucional Tributário*, 27th ed., São Paulo, Malheiros Editores, 2011, p. 64.

[13]Gianluigi Palombella, *Dopo la Certezza – Il Diritto in Equilibrio tra Giustizia e Democrazia*, Bari, Dedalo, 2006, pages 9–10.

[14]José Souto Maior Borges, "Segurança jurídica: sobre a distinção entre competências fiscais para orientar e autuar o contribuinte", *RDT*, n. 100, p. 20, São Paulo, s. d. Emphasis added.

Perhaps because of this peculiarity of the legal certainty principle, Bandeira de Mello stresses that this principle, "if not the weightiest of all general principles of law, as I believe it to be, is assuredly one of the weightiest."[15]

2.2 *Cases*

2.2.1 Legal Certainty "Verses" Justice

As Grau observes, tension between principles, as opposition or contradiction, is inherent in the legal system.[16] Hence the eternal and dramatic conflict between certainty and justice to which Cavalcanti Filho and Torres refer.[17] Habermas also mentions the constant tension between certainty and correctness.[18]

Concerning the possibility of tension between legal certainty and another principle, such as justice, a few preliminary delimitations are necessary. It so happens that legal certainty can be understood as antithetical to the idea of justice, as well as part of it. According to Radbruch, for example, two other values must be preserved next to legal certainty: fitness for purpose (*Zweckmäßigkeit*) and justice (*Gerechtigkeit*). On the other hand, he recognizes that legal certainty occupies an intermediate position between fitness for purpose and justice because it is required for the common good and also for justice. And he clarifies this further:

> That the Law be certain, that it be not one thing here and now, and interpreted and applied differently tomorrow, is at the same time a requirement of justice.[19]

The existence of conflict between justice and certainty therefore depends on the previous definition of each principle. As Nelles explains:

> Depending on the comprehension of their concepts, legal certainty and justice can be seen as a unit or as opposed pairs.[20]

---

[15]Celso Antônio Bandeira de Mello, *Curso de Direito Administrativo*, 28th ed., São Paulo, Malheiros Editores, 2011, pages 87, 123.

[16]Eros Roberto Grau, *Ensaio e discurso sobre a interpretação/aplicação do Direito*, 4th ed., São Paulo, Malheiros Editores, 2006, pages 52, 196.

[17]Theophilo Cavalcanti Filho, *O problema da segurança no Direito*, São Paulo, Ed. RT, 1964, p. 75. Ricardo Lobo Torres, "Liberdade, Segurança e Justiça", in Paulo de Barros Carvalho (Org.), *Justiça tributária*, São Paulo, Max Limonad, 1998, p. 703. Likewise: Wilhelm Hartz, "Mehr Rechtssicherheit im Steuerrecht, Ziele, Wege, Grenzen", *StbJb*, p. 81, 1965/1966; Andreas von Arnauld, *Rechtssicherheit*, Tübingen, Mohr Siebeck, 2006, p. 666.

[18]Jürgen Habermas, *Faktizität und Geltung*, Darmstadt, Wissenschaftliche Buchgesellschaft, 2002, pages 245, 270.

[19]Gustav Radbruch, "Gesetzliches Unrecht und übergestzliches Recht", *Anhang 3*, in *Rechtsphilosophie. Studienausgabe*, 2nd ed., Heidelberg, C. F. Müller, 2003 (1932), p. 216.

[20]Marcus Nelles, *Summum ius summa iniuria*? Ottilien, EOS, 2004, pages 136–137.

Indeed, on one hand, if justice is defined as the higher principle that encompasses elements relating to the stability of the legal order, and the definition of legal certainty also involves this element, conflict is precluded because the latter is part of the former. This connotation explains why Cavalcanti Filho and Maior Borges say certainty itself is an instrument of justice, and why Couto e Silva says legal certainty is not something opposed to justice, but justice itself.[21] On the other hand, tension is also averted if legal certainty is defined as a principle that combines with the requirement of equality to prohibit arbitrary treatment, and the definition of justice also includes this element.

This means that delimitation of the legal certainty principle's external conflicts with other principles presupposes an adequate prior definition of these same principles. Without delimitation of each principle's conceptual boundaries, the very idea of conflict cannot be properly defined, since true rather than merely apparent opposition presupposes a distinction between the conflicting elements. Without this all that is left is mere word play as pedestrian as it is inconsequential.

In this direction, if the duties resulting from the legal certainty principle encompass not only the requirements of knowability and reliability but also prescriptions regarding even the moral acceptability of norms, as Peczenik proposes, legal certainty already encompasses justice itself.[22] Hence it is more correct to speak of an apparent conflict between certainty and justice. However, it is possible to conceive of an external conflict between the legal certainty principle and the justice principle if the requirements resulting from the former are absolute and linked to the legal order in general, for most cases and most people (legal certainty as certainty of law or through law for all or for the majority), and the duties of the latter (justice) derive from normative manifestations specific to certain cases and people (justice as equity). If so, it is possible to speak of a conflict between certainty and justice, since the former in this specific sense is an obstacle to the realization of the latter.[23]

Indeed, if legal certainty is understood in its substantive aspect as a mere requirement that law be predictable, and in its justifying aspect as having value in itself, the most it can do, as Arcos Ramírez reminds us, is make injustice predictable.[24] Hence the observation that the concept of legal certainty must not only involve all dimensions but also be substantively linked to fundamental rights. Otherwise, to quote Peczenik again, one would have to accept that under Hitler's rule Jews possessed legal certainty because they could predict with absolute

---

[21] Theophilo Cavalcanti Filho, *O problema da segurança no Direito*, São Paulo, Ed. RT, 1964, p. 75. José Souto Maior Borges, "O princípio da segurança jurídica na criação e aplicação do tributo", *RDDT*, n. 22, p. 26, São Paulo, 1997. Almiro do Couto e Silva, "Princípios da legalidade da Administração Pública e da segurança jurídica no Estado de Direito contemporâneo", *Revista da Procuradoria-Geral do Estado do Rio Grande do Sul, Cadernos de Direito Público*, v. 27, n. 57, supplement, p. 14, 2003.

[22] Aleksander Peczenik, *On Law and Reason*, Dordrecht, Kluwer, 1989, p.31.

[23] Federico Arcos Ramírez, *La seguridad jurídica: una teoría formal*, Madrid, Dykinson, 2000, p. 117.

[24] Ibidem, p. 163.

certainty that they would be discriminated.[25] From a subtly different perspective, some scholars attempt to show that even when there is injustice the existence of legal certainty grants citizens *additional* advantages, in the sense that they can perform strategic actions in order to attempt to avoid even more unjust practices. This would reveal a value intrinsic to certainty itself, not in the sense of defending or justifying injustice, but in the very specific sense of defending and justifying legal certainty by demonstrating that an unjust system with legal certainty is better than an unjust system without legal certainty – this seems to be MacCormick's position.[26] In this strict sense, legal certainty in an unjust system would perform the function of avoiding even greater injustice.[27] Or, in the words of Summers, it would give citizens the just opportunity to obey an unjust law, thus somehow revealing the intrinsic moral value of legal certainty.[28]

These comments show that the conflict between legal certainty and justice depends on a narrow definition of both principles. Thus if the former involves only the requirements of knowability, reliability and calculability without any specific value component, and if the latter involves only individual justice, as a requirement of equity in the application of general norms, it is possible to conceive of a conflict between the two principles.[29] This understanding, however, does not account for the fact that legal certainty also involves an intrinsic moral value relating to justice, and justice also encompasses a general perspective as well as a particular perspective. It is therefore better to speak of a *connection* between the principles of legal certainty and justice than of opposition proper. Machado correctly defines the conflict as an apparent antagonism.[30] At most, one can say there is a *polarity*, but never a true *antinomy* between them.[31] When an unconstitutional act is upheld in the name of legal certainty, justice is not being outweighed in favor of certainty, but the specific configuration of legal certainty appears to be the just solution in this case.[32]

In any event, Cavalcanti Filho states the essence: "uncertain law is also unjust law."[33] Because the legal certainty principle as advocated in this book is a "presumptive principle" that characterizes the ideal states that need to be available if other principles are to have efficacy, it is really not possible to speak of justice

[25] Aleksander Peczenik, *On Law and Reason*, Dordrecht, Kluwer, 1989, p. 31.

[26] Neil MacCormick, *Legal Reasoning and Legal Theory*, Oxford, Clarendon, 1978, p. 63.

[27] Federico Arcos Ramírez, *La seguridad jurídica*: *una teoría formal*, Madrid, Dykinson, 2000, p. 170.

[28] Robert Summers, *Lon L. Fuller*, Londres, Edward Arnold, 1984, p. 66.

[29] Gerhard Robbers, *Gerechtigkeit als Rechtsprinzip*, Baden-Baden, Nomos, 1980, p. 63.

[30] Hugo de Brito Machado, "Os princípios da anterioridade e da irretroatividade das leis tributárias e a publicação da lei", *Cadernos de Direito Tributário e Finanças Públicas*, n. 8, p. 107, São Paulo, 1994.

[31] Marcus Nelles, *Summum ius summa iniuria*? Ottilien, EOS, 2004, p. 140.

[32] Almiro do Couto e Silva, "Princípios da legalidade da Administração Pública e da segurança jurídica no Estado de Direito contemporâneo", *Revista da Procuradoria-Geral do Estado do Rio Grande do Sul, Cadernos de Direito Público*, v. 27, n. 57, supplement, p. 14, 2003.

[33] Theophilo Cavalcanti Filho, *O problema da segurança no Direito*, São Paulo, Ed. RT, 1964, p. 81.

without legal certainty. Certainty is not relinquishment of justice, but promotion of it.[34] Hence Carvalho's axiom that "the certainty of legal relations is inseparable from the value of justice".[35] And for these same reasons, Machado Derzi states with perfection that legal certainty "is a fundamental value, but it is never at stake or in conflict, as it is an evident presumption or precondition without which justice cannot be achieved."[36]

2.2.2 Legal Certainty "Verses" State Purposes

Other conflicts can also be conceived of, such as a conflict between the legal certainty principle and the welfare state or social solidarity principle. An example might concern the examination of the constitutionality of an ordinary statute that creates a social contribution for the purpose of financing social security, but does so beyond the substantive scope established by the competence rules in the Constitution whereby the federal government is empowered to create social contributions in the situation in question. Thus it might be said that this exemplifies a conflict between the legal certainty principle, embodied in a rule designed to make state power clear, stable and predictable, and the social solidarity principle, which justifies the means necessary to finance social security. In sum, there would be a conflict between legal certainty and solidarity.[37]

A closer look, however, shows that legal certainty and solidarity are not opposed but complementary. Social security, above all as a mechanism to assure the existential minimum, is an instrument for creating or maintaining material conditions for the exercise of freedom, just as legal certainty is the means to create or maintain formal conditions for the exercise of the fundamental rights of freedom. Moreover, because resources are scarce and solidarity is a duty of all, not only of the state, it depends on the use of freedom in order to deploy other means for its realization. In other words, legal certainty and social security, like freedom and solidarity, are not parallel and isolated opposites, but intertwined and mutually dependent complements.[38] After all, those who are not free cannot practice solidarity.[39]

The above considerations reinforce the idea advocated throughout this book that far from being in opposition to other principles, legal certainty acts as a presupposition, which may not avoid conflict but at least gives it an entirely new

---

[34] José L Mezquita del Cacho, *Seguridad jurídica y sistema cautelar*, v. 1: *Teoría de la seguridad jurídica*, Barcelona, Bosch, 1989, p. 7.

[35] Paulo de Barros Carvalho, *Curso de Direito Tributário*, 21st ed., São Paulo, Saraiva, 2009, p. 166.

[36] Misabel de Abreu Machado Derzi, *Modificações da jurisprudência no Direito Tributário*, São Paulo, Noeses, 2009, p. 608.

[37] Karl-Peter Sommermann, *Staatsziele und Staatszielbestimmungen*, Tübingen, Mohr Siebeck, 1997, pages 326 and following.

[38] Hans Michael Heinig, *Der Sozialstaat im Dienst der Freiheit*, Tübingen, Siebeck, 2008, pages 586–587.

[39] Andreas von Arnauld, *Rechtssicherheit*, Tübingen, Mohr Siebeck, 2006, p. 112.

dimension. Its efficacy is not ordinary efficacy, both because it cannot be overridden by conflicting reasons but merely reconfigured in response to specific situations, and because it manifests as a structural constraint for the functioning of law itself in general, and of its normative manifestations in particular. The various manifestations of the legal certainty principle, however, must not impede perception of its *functional unity*.[40]

This unity reveals itself precisely in the fact that the legal certainty principle, unlike other principles, which relate directly to factual reality, relates to legal reality, which in turn affects factual reality. Thus certain questions that are posed about other principles do not make sense as far as the legal certainty principle is concerned. Types of efficacy, such as prima facie or pro tanto, are responses to principles that conflict with each other directly and horizontally, risking loss or restriction of their efficacy. However, because the legal certainty principle is a norm that institutes structural constraints on the functioning of other norms, it is not located at the same analytical level as the latter, so that the use of the same nomenclature to qualify its normative force is technically inappropriate. Thus continuing to ask about the existence of prima facie or pro tanto efficacy in the case of the legal certainty principle is like trying to find the right answer for the wrong question. The legal certainty principle, it bears repeating, is not on the same plane as other principles and rules for whose validity it is the foundation and whose efficacy it instrumentalizes. To use yet another metaphor, the other principles are the light, whereas the legal certainty principle is the power source without which no light can be produced. The light can be shone in one direction or another to illuminate this or that object for this or that purpose, but without energy there will be no light.

At the end of the first part of this book, tax law certainty was defined as a principle norm that requires the legislative, executive and judiciary to behave in ways that contribute more to the existence of a high state of knowability, reliability and calculability of law, to the benefit of taxpayers and from their perspective, through the juridico-rational controllability of argumentative structures that reconstruct general and individual norms, as an instrument that guarantees respect for their capacity to shape the present responsibly, with dignity, and without deceit, frustration, surprise or arbitrariness, and to plan strategically for the future in a legally informed manner.

At the end of this second part, this concept of legal certainty must be extended to include the elements relative to its content and efficacy. To this end, we can state that legal certainty is a *principle that performs several functions relating to efficacy and argumentation toward norms that rank above and below it, acts as a functional presupposition for the production and application of law, and can never be entirely set aside*.

The fusion and simplification of both concepts enables legal certainty to be reconceptualized as a condition principle that assures a state of respect for the

[40] Anne-Laure Valembois, *La Constitutionnalisation de l'exigence de sécurité juridique en Droit français*, Paris, LGDJ, 2005, p. 12.

fundamental rights of the citizen taxpayer and moderation of state action through juridico-rational controllability of the argumentative structures that reconstruct general and individual norms. Taking one more step to simplify this new concept, it can simply be said that the legal certainty principle is a principle that assures the respectability of the taxpayer-as-citizen.

It must also be stressed that the legal certainty principle acts not only negatively by impeding arbitrariness but also positively by guaranteeing respect for the taxpayer as citizen. As a principle, therefore, it *limits* and *guides* state action by introducing consideration for the exercise of fundamental rights into the state's entrails, as it were. It must also be emphasized that this respect and consideration for taxpayers as citizens aims to assure deference not only to what they *do*, so as to allow them to *be* with responsibility and autonomy, but also to what they *argue* and intend to be. If taxpayers are not able to oppose the intentions of the state and participate in the concretization of law through appropriate assessment and consideration of their arguments, there is no legal certainty as certainty *in* law. Hence in a final synthesis the principle of tax law certainty is the *principle of the transparent respectability of the taxpayer as a rational citizen*.

These considerations clarify the *unparalleled* importance of the legal certainty principle within the system of principles. So much so that it can be termed a *protoprinciple* – the principle of principles, the norm of norms, the *norma normarum* in the roster of normative species, which not only serves as a *foundation for the others* but also *instrumentalizes* them.

Throughout this book my goal has been to build the architecture of the legal certainty principle in the field of tax law in its entirety, from conceptual foundations to static and dynamic content, and on to efficacy. With this chapter, we have arrived at the last station but not the end of the journey. For as stated at the outset, this is a continuous effort to build intersubjectively controllable means with the purpose of promoting legal certainty. Schrimm-Heins says the "search for certainty is similar to a *perpetuum mobile*; it never reaches its destination."[41] Something like that can be said of the legal certainty principle. The scientific construction of its elements, dimensions and efficacies, when it seems to be close to the end, reveals itself to be, thanks to its complexity, merely beginning.

References

ALEXY, Robert. *Theorie der Grundrechte*. 2ª ed. Frankfurt am Main: Suhrkamp, 1994; trad. para o português de Virgílio Afonso da Silva. *Teoria dos Direitos Fundamentais*. 2ª ed. São Paulo: Malheiros Editores, 2011.

ARCOS RAM´iREZ, Federico. *La seguridad jurídica: una teoría formal*. Madrid: Dykinson, 2000.

von ARNAULD, Andreas. *Rechtssicherheit*. Tübingen: Mohr Siebeck, 2006.

[41] Andrea Schrimm-Heins, "Gewissheit und Sicherheit: Geschichte und Bedeutungswandel der Begriffe 'certitudo' und 'securitas'" (Teil 1), *Archiv für Begriffsgeschichte*, v. 34, p. 213, 1991.

AZOULAI, Loïc. "La valeur normativa de la sécurité juridique". In BOY, Laurence; RACINE, Jean-Baptiste; SIIRIAINEN, Fabrice (Orgs.). *Sécurité Juridique et Droit Économique*. Bruxelles: Larcier, 2008, pp. 25–41.

BANDEIRA DE MELLO, Celso Antônio. *Curso de Direito Administrativo*. 28ª ed. São Paulo: Malheiros Editores, 2011.

CALMES, Sylvia. *Du principe de protection de la confiance légitime en Droits Allemand, Communautaire et Français*. Paris: Dalloz, 2001.

CARRAZZA, Roque Antonio. *Curso de Direito Constitucional Tributário*. 27ª ed. São Paulo: Malheiros Editores, 2011.

CARVALHO, Paulo de Barros. *Curso de Direito Tributário*. 21ª ed. São Paulo: Saraiva, 2009.

CAVALCANTI FILHO, Theophilo. *O problema da segurança no Direito*. São Paulo: Ed. RT, 1964.

CHANG, Ruth. "Introduction". In CHANG, Ruth (Org.). *Incommensurability, incomparability and practical reason*. Cambridge: Harvard, 1997, pp. 1–34.

COUTO E SILVA, Almiro do. "Princípios da legalidade da Administração Pública e da segurança jurídica no Estado de Direito contemporâneo". *Revista da Procuradoria-Geral do Estado do Rio Grande do Sul. Cadernos de Direito Público*, v. 27, n. 57, suplemento, 2003, pp. 13–31.

GRAU, Eros Roberto. *Ensaio e discurso sobre a interpretação/aplicação do Direito*. 4ª ed. São Paulo: Malheiros Editores, 2006 (8ª ed., 2011).

GUASTINI, Riccardo. *L'Interpretazione dei documenti normativi*. Milano: Giuffrè, 2004.

HABERMAS, Jürgen. *Faktizität und Geltung*. Darmstadt: Wissenschaftliche Buchgesellschaft, 2002.

HARTZ, Wilhelm. "Mehr Rechtssicherheit im Steuerrecht. Ziele, Wege, Grenzen". *StbJb*, 1965–1966, pp. 75–133.

HEINIG, Hans Michael. *Der Sozialstaat im Dienst der Freiheit*. Tübingen: Siebeck, 2008.

KAGAN, Shelly. *The Limits of Morality*. Oxford: Clarendon, 1989.

LUÑO, Antonio Enrique Perez. *La seguridad jurídica*. Barcelona: Ariel, 1991.

MaCCORMICK, Neil. *Legal Reasoning and Legal Theory*. Oxford: Clarendon, 1995 (1978).

MACHADO DERZI, Misabel de Abreu. *Modificações da jurisprudência no Direito Tributário*. São Paulo: Noeses, 2009.

MACHADO, Hugo de Brito. "Os princípios da anterioridade e da irretroatividade das leis tributárias e a publicação da lei". *Cadernos de Direito Tributário e Finanças Públicas* 8/107-112, 1994.

MAIOR BORGES, José Souto. "Segurança jurídica: sobre a distinção entre competências fiscais para orientar e atuar o contribuinte". *RDT* 100/19-26, s. d.

_____. "O princípio da segurança jurídica na criação e aplicação do tributo", *RDDT*, n. 22, São Paulo, 1997.

MESQUITA DEL CACHO, José L. *Seguridad jurídica y sistema cautelar*. v. 1. *Teoría de la seguridad jurídica*. Barcelona: Bosch, 1989.

NELLES, Marcus. *Sumum ius summa iniuria?* Ottilien: EOS, 2004.

NOZICK, Robert. *Anarchy, State and Utopia*. Oxford: Blackwell, 1975 (1974).

PALOMBELLA, Gianluigi. *Dopo la Certezza – Il Diritto in Equilibrio tra Giustizia e Democrazia*. Bari: Dedalo, 2006.

PECZENICK, Aleksander. *On Law and Reason*. Dordrecht: Kluwer, 1989.

RABINOWICZ, Wlodek. "Peczenik's passionate reason". In: AARNIO, Aulis *et alii* (Orgs.). *On Coherence Theory of Law*. Lund: Juristförlager, 1998, pp. 17–23.

RADBRUCH, Gustav. "Gesetzliches Unrecht und übergesetzliches Recht". *SJZ*, 1946.

ROBBERS, Gerhard. *Gerechtigkeit als Rechtsprinzip*. Baden-Baden: Nomos, 1980.

SCHRIMM-HEINS, Andrea. "Gewissheit und Sicherheit: Geschichte und Bedeutungswandel der Begriffe 'certitudo' und 'securitas'" (Teil 1). *Archiv für Begriffsgeschichte*, v. 34, 1991, pp. 123–213.

SOMMERMANN, Karl-Peter. *Staatsziele und Staatszielbestimmungen*. Tübingen: Mohr Siebeck, 1997.

SUMMERS, Robert. *Lon L. Fuller*. Londres: Edward Arnold, 1984.

SUNSTEIN, Cass. "Incommensurability and kinds of valuation: some applications in Law". In CHANG, Ruth (Org.). *Incommensurability, incomparability and practical reason*. Cambridge: Harvard, 1997, pp. 234–254.

TORRES, Ricardo Lobo. "Liberdade, Segurança e Justiça". In CARVALHO, Paulo de Barros (Org.). *Justiça tributária*. São Paulo: Max Limonad, 1998, pp. 679–705.

VALEMBOIS, Anne-Laure. *La constitutionnalisation de l'exigence de sécurité juridique en Droit Français*. Paris: LGDJ, 2005.

Conclusions and Theses

> Writing a work and acknowledging that it is poor after it is finished is one of the tragedies of the soul. Especially when it has to be acknowledged that this work is the best that could be done. (Fernando Pessoa, *O livro do desassossego*, São Paulo, Companhia das Letras, 1999, p. 230)

Legal certainty is a normative ideal *of the first magnitude* in any legal order, and particularly in the Brazilian order. Its importance is even greater in the field of tax law: The ideals protected by legal certainty have special relevance in the tax subsystem and a *more protective* significance by virtue of the existence of specific and emphatic norms in the National Tax System that act as instruments to guarantee the intelligibility of law through via the determinability of incidence hypotheses (the legality rule and the system of competence rules), the reliability of law through stability over time (the rule restricting the regulation of prescription and limitation to supplementary laws), period of validity (the rule prohibiting retroactivity) and procedure (rules that expressly apply rights and guarantees not specified in the tax subsystem, such as protection for acquired rights, completed legal acts and res iudicata), and the calculability of law through non-surprise (the anteriority rule).

The essential point is that the Brazilian Constitution, more than requiring the promotion of the legal certainty principle, embodies this principle, by virtue of its concern from beginning to end with the ideals of normative knowability, reliability and calculability, such is the emphasis it places on the limitation of power, especially the power to tax, and on fundamental rights and guarantees, particularly in tax law. However, these ideals cannot be even discerned, let alone realized, without progressive reduction of their indeterminacy. The efficacy of a legal principle, particularly the tax law certainty principle, results not from the proclamation of its ideals but from analytical decomposition of the dimensions, aspects and elements that make it up. Above all, a legal principle is a norm in need of conceptual decomposition. Unless it is "unwrapped" and its several constituent parts are disaggregated, its nature, proportions, functions and relations cannot be known. In this process of reduction to simple elements, however, it is crucial to develop a new

© Springer International Publishing Switzerland 2016

H. Ávila, *Certainty in Law*, Law and Philosophy Library 114,
DOI 10.1007/978-3-319-33407-3_12

understanding not only of the legal certainty principle but of the very definition of law, and its claim to certainty, to be the means whereby certainty is realized, or within which certainty is to be guaranteed.

The idea that law is a *previously given object* whose existence is totally independent of the activities relating to its application has given rise to a tendency to examine legal certainty almost exclusively from the angle of the requirement of determinate normative hypotheses, resulting in the idolization of the so-called principle of closed typicality in tax law. However, this understanding has restricted the discussion of legal certainty to factors that are unquestionably important but solely linked to the structure of language, leading to endless wrangling about determinacy, and consequently to unflagging debates about whether legal certainty can ever supply determinacy.

This perception of legal certainty, which centers on *normative determinacy*, ought to give way to an understanding founded on semantic-argumentative controllability. On this view, it ceases to be a *property of law*, and becomes *something to be sought in law* through processes of normative legitimation, determination, argumentation and justification, all of which are capable of addressing the problems ontologically inherent in law – problems of evidence, qualification, interpretation and relevance. What is at stake, more than *certain law*, is a *right to legal certainty*, not as something given by normative provisions – as if it were only an object to be simply revealed through a discoursive method circumscribed to a description of language – but as something to be sought through a metadiscoursive method that organizes and structures the *experience* of *using* language. From this perspective, legal certainty ceases to be a *guarantee of content* to be *found* through exclusively linguistic factors, and becomes a *guarantee of respect* to be *constructed* through semantic-argumentative elements.

It is precisely under this novel signification that legal certainty is most clearly revealed as an instrument to realize the values of freedom, equality and dignity: *freedom* because the more citizen taxpayers are assured of material and intellectual access to the norms they must obey, and the greater the stability of those norms, the better citizens will be able to grasp the present and plan for the future; *equality* because the more general and abstract the norms and the more uniformly they are applied, the more equally will citizen taxpayers be treated; *dignity* because the more accessible and stable the norms, and the sounder the justification for their application, the more intensely will citizen taxpayers be treated as being able to define themselves autonomously, both by present respect for the autonomy they have exercised in the past and by future respect for the autonomy they exercise in the present. In the field of tax law, this understanding evidences that legal certainty is an indispensable instrument for the realization of the principles of freedom, especially the freedom to exercise economic activities, equality and human dignity. Thus the legal certainty principle is the principle of respect for taxpayers as citizens.

According to this resignification, legal certainty is not consummated as a straight line or *point*, but as a *range* or *spectrum* of gradual realization. This graduality is not uniform or one-way, however: The overarching ideal (legal certainty) is the sum of partial ideals (normative knowability, reliability and calculability). These partial ideals can interact in the same direction as well as in different directions, so that, for example, the protection of certainty from one angle (as the pursuit of reliability through the stability of normative acts) may cause loss of certainty from another perspective (as the pursuit of calculability through the bindingness of normative acts). It should be noted that each partial ideal can be analyzed from different perspectives. For example, the intelligibility of the legal order can be analyzed for society in general or for practitioners of law; relative to the past, present or future; and so on. Thus each partial ideal needs an average analysis of its internally related subelements.

Consequently, legal certainty is always the result of an analysis of several factors from more than one perspective. It is a matter of a principle that determines the realization not of a uniform but of a non-uniform state, so that the interpreter must first decompose these elements and then gauge them in order to verify whether they can be promoted to a greater or lesser extent as a totality. The lack of such an investigation easily allows legal uncertainty to arise in the name of legal certainty. Hence the repeated emphasis in this book from beginning to end that legal certainty is either whole or not certainty. The judge must first examine each of the elements in their various dimensions and then verify whether it is being promoted more than restricted.

These considerations show that the legal certainty principle is only superficially a mere formal principle in a derogatory sense, i.e. decoupled from fundamental substantive principles. In reality it is a normative precondition for the efficacy of the order of principles, especially those that concern the development of the person as a rational and autonomous being. The legal certainty principle acts as a *foundation* for the validity of other legal norms and *instrumentalizes* their efficacy. Hence it is the norm of norms and their structural constraint. However, the foundational and instrumentalizing functions refer not only to the static aspects of norms but also to their dynamic aspects, which relate both to the transition from past to present and from present to future, and, most importantly, to the transition from the abstract level to the concrete level of the application of law.

In its requirement of knowability, the legal certainty principle serves as an instrument of guidance for taxpayers, so that they do not *act mistakenly* when they abide by the laws. In its ideal of reliability, it serves to assure the stability of law and its concretizations, preserving the past in the present and preventing taxpayers from being *frustrated* by what they have done. And in its objective of calculability, it favors the continuity of law, protecting the future in the present and preventing taxpayers from being *surprised* by what they do. Thus by aiming to avert mistakes, frustration and surprise, the legal certainty principle embodies the ideal of *respect* for the taxpayer. However, this ideal can be realized only through the *intelligibility*, *loyalty* and *smoothness* of state actions. These ideals in aggregate materialize a higher ideal of state *moderation*. The legal certainty principle therefore requires *respect for taxpayers' actions through state moderation*.

However, respect for taxpayers is not enough, They must *perceive themselves as being respected* and *act argumentatively on this respectability*. In this regard, the legal certainty principle surpasses its essential function of assuring respect for individual *action* to become an instrument of respect for the argumentation citizens use to face problems relating to their actions in terms of evidence, qualification, interpretation and relevance. Thus it is clear that the tax law certainty principle is the principle that guarantees the respectability of citizen taxpayers' actions and argumentation, requiring *transparent* respectability of taxpayers' actions and *the pertinent argumentation* through state moderation. This moderation, in turn, requires that taxpayers be treated as rational, free and autonomous human beings, i.e. as *citizens*. Only then can they be legally oriented to *conceive* the present and *shape* the future. The legal certainty principle is, so to speak, the *legal face* of human dignity which, in requiring a visibly respectful transition from past to present and from present to future, prevents law from turning against those who have trusted it and have acted with its assistance. It therefore establishes the temporal and applicatory conditions for law to function. Without these the laws cannot respect taxpayers as human beings and citizens, so that law cannot be an instrument of *civility* in treatment and *decency* in action. Hence it can be said that the legal certainty principle determines the *temporal and applicatory conditions for tax law to function in a humane and civilized manner.*

If we combine the above considerations, we can summarize the legal certainty principle as *the principle that acts as a foundation for the validity and instrumentalization of the efficacy of legal norms, requiring transparent respect for the actions of citizen taxpayers and of the pertinent argumentation, by means of state moderation.*

This study has drawn several conclusions that show the functions performed by legal and tax law certainty in the legal order, functions that are unrivaled by those of other principles. To specify each and every one of them would be unjustifiably excessive. At this time it suffices to summarize some general conclusions, whose importance surpasses the mere local aspects pinpointed throughout this text.

1.1 In its preponderant normative meaning, legal certainty is a *principle norm*, because it establishes a state of affairs that ought to be sought through behavior that produces effects that contribute to its gradual promotion. Its application requires comparing a norm (the legal certainty principle) with another norm (a statutory, administrative or judicial norm), and its distinctive character resides in the *interposition of a norm* between the higher norm and the facts. Unlike a material principle, which requires a correlation between the effects of an act and the state of affairs it aims to realize, the legal certainty principle requires a correlation between the effects of a norm and the state of affairs whose realization it establishes.

1.2 The prevalent normative meaning of legal certainty, highlighted herein, does not exclude the existence of other normative dimensions that perform various different efficacy-related functions. Thus besides being a legal principle, legal certainty can be manifested as a *principle legislatively concretized in a rule*, such as the rule that bans tax retroactivity, or the rule that protects acquired rights, completed legal acts and *res iudicata*; a *principle concretized jurisprudentially in a rule*, examples of which are the individual norms issued by court decisions pertaining to the protection of legitimate trust or the inviolability of individual situations due to the passage of an extended period of time; a *metanorm for the interpretation and application of other norms*, such as the rule that bans the application of analogy in tax law; or a *subjective right resulting from reflexive application of the legal certainty principle itself*, such as the individual rights guaranteed by the judiciary based on the so-called trust protection principle.

2.1 The content of the legal certainty principle cannot be analyzed save from an *analytical perspective* whereby the ambiguity and vagueness of its constitutive elements can be reduced and its various aspects indicated: *substantive* (legal certainty in what sense?), *objective* (legal certainty of what?), *subjective* (legal certainty for whom, in whose view and by whom?), *temporal* (legal certainty when?), *quantitative* (legal certainty in what measure?) and *justificatory* (legal certainty for what and why?). Each of these elements in turn raises a number of questions internally, and in aggregate the answers to these questions will ultimately show which meanings of legal certainty are possible.

2.2 This analytical perspective is indispensable in tax law, both in order to define the content of legal certainty within this normative field and in order to ensure that other, divergent purposes are not pursued in its name, such as the maintenance of revenue from the collection of taxes, used for example in the control of constitutionality as a reason to uphold the past effects of a tax statute declared unconstitutional by the Supreme Court.

3.1 Among the possible meanings that can be assigned to legal certainty as a principle norm, the *legal order* will indicate which of the analytically discernible meanings should be chosen to make up its structuring aspects, by examining its *superstructure* (the whole) and its constitutional *structure* (the parts).

3.2 Examination of the legal order is indispensable not only to show that legal certainty does not have the same content in every country, but also to show that in the field of tax law it has equally different density, in that it is more protective of taxpayers, guaranteeing respect for their fundamental rights, as clearly exemplified by the constitutional norms that "limit the power to tax" or establish "guarantees for taxpayers".

4.1 Analysis of the constitutional *superstructure* shows that the Brazilian Constitution not only protects legal certainty, but also embodies legal certainty itself: It establishes more rules than principles, and insists on stipulating the competent authorities, the laws to be passed, the content to be implemented, the procedures to be followed, and the subjects to be covered, favoring through such prescriptions the ideals of normative knowability, reliability and calculability.

4.2 These ideals are even more clearly embodied with still greater protectivity in the National Tax System, which encompasses a set of norms designed to specify *which* taxes can be created (direct taxes, service taxes, improvement contributions, compulsory loans, social contributions, intervention contributions, and dues paid to professional bodies), *how* they can be levied (by statute, with certain taxes specified in the Constitution requiring definition of key elements in supplementary laws), *when* they can be enforced (from the following fiscal year or 90 days after the law creating them is passed, and always applied to events that occur after that), and *to what extent* they can restrict the fundamental rights of taxpayers (neither more nor less than necessary for their efficacy).

5.1 Our examination of the *structure* of the Constitution shows that legal certainty is an unequivocal positive principle of the Constitution, which protects it directly by "ensuring certainty" as a "right" and as a "value", or by regulating its reflexive efficacy through the protection of acquired rights, completed legal acts and *res iudicata*, and indirectly when it provides for certain types of behavior that promote the ideals of calculability and reliability, a key part of legal certainty, and establishes broad, restricted or specific ideals whose realization presupposes or implies the existence of the same ideals; it shows that the Constitution not only guarantees legal certainty but also protects it in many of its dimensions, i.e., as certainty *of* law, *before* law, *of* rights and *as* a right; it shows that the Constitution not only protects legal certainty in all of its manifestations but does so by assigning high priority to legal certainty in the constitutional order, through the *way* legal certainty is assured by the totality of the constitutional order and by its parts, through the *insistence* with which the Constitution protects legal certainty, through the *independence* of its foundations, and through the *reciprocal efficacy* of these same foundations; finally, it shows that the Constitution protects legal certainty *in favor of citizens* and *against the state*.

5.2 Our analysis of the structure of the tax system shows clearly that tax norms – principles and rules – insistently protect the ideals that make up legal certainty. In defining the concept of tax, types of tax, tax competence rules, limitations on the power to tax and the sources of tax law, and in establishing certain principles, such as equality and fiscal transparency, the Constitution defines *what can* and *what cannot* be taxed, as well as *how* taxation is to be configured, thus favoring the ideal of *knowability of tax law* through the accessibility, breadth and clarity of its norms; in banning tax retroactivity and guaranteeing acquired rights, completed legal acts and *res iudicata*, the Constitution prescribes *when* taxation may produce effects, thus establishing the ideal of *reliability of tax law* through the permanence of the legal order and the inviolability of certain predetermined situations; in establishing the tax anteriority rule, the equality principle in tax matters and the procedural principles that apply to tax procedures and lawsuits, including due process of law and reasonable duration of proceedings, the Constitution allows taxpayers to *anticipate* and *measure* the consequences that will be assigned to their acts and to the acts of the administration, thus favoring the ideal of *calculability of tax law* through the anteriority and continuity of the legal order.

6.1 This protective connotation of legal certainty, although not necessarily individualistic, is given by the form and content of its foundations: *by the form*, because its foundations embody individual guarantees and rights with a defensive meaning, administrative principles that restrict the arbitrary exercise of power, and structuring principles that also limit power and protect individual rights; *by the content*, because the foundations are based on expected types of behavior or ideals, thus implying or presuming certainty in favor of the rights, freedoms and dignity of the citizen taxpayers.

6.2 In tax law, this connotation of protection for legal certainty is also reinforced by the form and content of the norms in the tax system: *by the form* because the constitutional norms use the expressions "limitation of the power to tax" and "taxpayer guarantees" in a sense that clearly ensures the individual rights of taxpayers against the power to tax; *by the content* thanks to the ideals of normative knowability, reliability and calculability that tax norms protect, either directly or indirectly.

7.1 The word *segurança* in the Constitution refers to *legal certainty* because when article 1 institutes a democratic state based on the rule of law with the aim of "assuring certainty as a value," it refers to a social objective that transcends the merely psychological or physical dimension; because when article 5 assures the "right to certainty" alongside the right to freedom, equality and property, which are qualified as objective social values and not merely individual psychological states, it implies the protection of certainty in parallel to the assurance of these other values; because among the fundamental rights listed in the indents to article 5 several relate to physical and individual security (protection of the home and guaranteed habeas corpus against abusive restrictions of freedom), or to specific forms of freedom (of thought, opinion and belief, intellectual, artistic and scientific inquiry, of communication and expression, and of association for lawful purposes), presupposing a broader scope for the provision in the article's head paragraph.

7.2 In the field of tax law, the *legal* character of certainty is even more crystal-clear, especially because in the tax system the Constitution emphasizes aspects linked to the quality of law (via the competence rules and the rules of statutory legality, anteriority and irretroactivity), and to forms of protection for rights (via taxpayer guarantees and procedural principles applicable to tax affairs, such as due process of law and reasonable duration of proceedings, not to mention other more specific guarantees such as the writ of mandamus).

8.1 The *substantive aspect* of legal certainty, as far as the term "certainty" is concerned, denotes a state of knowability, reliability and calculability: *knowability*, rather than determinacy, in light of the congenital indeterminacy of language and the dependency of law on criteria and arguments that are indispensable to the process necessary to its determination and concretization; *reliability*, rather than immutability, because the Constitution contains both entrenched clauses, making changes difficult but possible, and the principle of the state based on the social rule of law, which requires the state to perform a planning function and act for the general good by driving social change, especially through the distribution of wealth; *calculability*, rather than (absolute) predictability, because although the Constitution contains a number of rules designed to permit the anticipation of state actions, such as the legality and anteriority rules, the nature of the law, involving the use of indeterminate language that depends on argumentative processes to reconstruct meanings, prevents its enunciations from being semantically univocal.

8.2 These ideal states of normative knowability, reliability and calculability are also visible in the field of tax law: *knowability*, rather than determinacy, for the same reasons relating to language, but also because of the very reality taxes are designed to regulate, in that some taxes, duties and charges, such as contributions for intervention in the economic domain (CIDE), and even some duties, cannot be concretized with the same degree of determinacy as traditional direct taxes; *reliability*, rather than immutability, because by establishing tax irretroactivity and other guarantees in the tax subsystem, including protection for acquired rights, completed legal acts and *res iudicata*, the tax system presupposes the possibility of changes to the legal order, provided certain limits and transition rules are observed; *calculability*, rather than (absolute) predictability, because precisely by limiting change the tax system presupposes that changes will be made, on condition taxpayers are not surprised or deceived.

9.1 The indication of these ideal states, unlike the ideals of determinacy, immutability and predictability, shows that the conception of legal certainty follows a conception of law that intermediates the objectivist and argumentative conceptions: Law is neither a previously given object whose content depends exclusively on cognitive activities that reveal predetermined meanings, nor an activity whose realization derives solely from argumentative structures to be revealed only at a later stage in the decision process, but rather a composition between semantic and argumentative activities – the activities of users of law begin with the reconstruction of normative meanings through rules of argumentation, but depend for their application on hermeneutical and applicatory postulates that reveal normative and factual elements, so that legal certainty ceases to be a mere requirement of predetermination to substantiate a standard of rational and argumentative controllability.

9.2 This understanding is highly important in tax law, especially to show that in this normative field legal certainty cannot be identified with (or exhausted by) the requirement of determinacy of normative hypotheses, which legal doctrine identifies with the so-called closed typicality principle, but must instead comprise other elements linked not only to clarity and intelligibility of tax norms, but also to their uniform and non-arbitrary application in tax proceedings and cases. This novel and broader perception of legal certainty in the field of tax law does not eliminate the importance of aspects relating to the determinacy of norms (certainty of content); however, it helps combine these aspects with others that are equally important to a complete vision of tax law certainty, such as those relating to the existence, validity and efficacy of tax norms (certainty of existence, validity and efficacy), changes to tax norms over time (certainty of transition), application of tax norms through administrative proceedings and court rulings (certainty of realization), continuity of tax law regimes (rhythmic certainty), and the time taken to resolve tax litigation (certainty of definition). Only a balanced combination of all these phases permits full efficacy of tax law certainty.

10.1 As for the *substantive aspect* regarding the word "legal," the Constitution points to several possible meanings, depending on the chosen perspective: certainty *of law*, because in establishing the legality, anteriority and irretroactivity rules it lays the foundations for law itself to be certain, by virtue of the clarity of its enunciations and the predictability of its norms, and in defining the morality and publicity principles it enshrines justification and publication as requirements for the validity of legal norms; *through law*, because by stipulating that Brazil is a democratic State with the aim of "assuring certainty as a value" in article 1 it establishes that law must act as an *instrument* to guarantee certainty; *before law*, because state action, which cannot be performed save through the exercise of powers defined in competence rules and through the sources and procedures defined by law, must not jeopardize rights acquired or guaranteed by individuals in accordance with law; *of rights*, because protection for acquired rights, completed legal acts and *res iudicata* in article 5, XXXVI, translates the reflexive efficacy of the legal certainty principle, oriented to a specific subject and concrete case, while assuring the exercise of certain rights; *as a right*, because the reflexive efficacy of the objective legal certainty principle gives rise to a specific subject's right to certain state behavior without which knowability, reliability and calculability cannot be minimally realized; *in law*, because legal certainty as advocated in this book is not centered on the requirement of knowledge of totally predetermined content, but on the controllability of argumentative structures required in the reconstruction and application of factual and normative meanings.

10.2 These several meanings are also reproduced in the field of tax law, since there are norms that favor certainty *of law* by dealing with the quality that tax norms must have or the effects they can produce (the legality, anteriority and irretroactivity rules); norms that emphasize certainty *through law* by assuring taxpayers' rights (rules that protect acquired rights, completed legal acts and *res iudicata*, or establish equality of tax treatment, including treatment according to economic capacity) or by assuring procedures and processes designed to protect taxpayers' rights (rules that guarantee the right to a full defense and the adversarial principle, use of the writ of mandamus and habeas data); tax norms that focus on certainty *before law* by establishing jurisdictions, authorities, procedures and sources necessary to the exercise of the power to tax (competence rules, the legality, anteriority and irretroactivity rules, the rule that bans the use of taxes with confiscatory effects); tax norms that establish a *certainty of rights*, by being termed "guarantees", as exemplified by the guarantees of acquired rights, completed legal acts and *res iudicata*, but also by defining general criteria for the configuration of taxation in accordance with manifestations relative to the taxpayer (the equal treatment and contributive capacity principles, and the rule that determines respect for the taxpayer's fundamental rights and guarantees); tax norms that define certainty *as a right* to the extent that they attest to its orientation toward protecting taxpayers from the state's exercise of its power to tax (limitations on the power to tax and individual fundamental rights). Similarly, all such meanings, when combined in a unitary perspective based in turn on a semantic-argumentative concept of law, show that tax law certainty must be sought not only in the previous and abstract content of norms, but in the very process of realization of tax law.

11.1 The *objective aspect* of legal certainty reveals the certainty *of the legal order*, because several principles, such as the rule of law and the social rule of law, are concerned with the legal order in its entirety, and not one particular manifestation of it; *of a norm* that is both *general*, given that several rules impose conditions of validity for the creation of norms, such as the rule of prohibiting tax retroactivity, and *individual*, given that several rules protect individual situations assured by court decision or administrative act, such as the rule that protects acquired rights, completed legal acts and *res iudicata*; *of behavior*, especially state behavior, considering that the Constitution not only establishes the morality and publicity principles but also contains a number of procedural and substantive rules that favor the knowledge and justification of state activities.

11.2 This breadth is also present in the field of tax law, given the existence of norms that protect the certainty *of the order and its application*, such as the legality, anteriority and irretroactivity rules, and the rules and principles pertaining to tax procedures and proceedings; *of a general norm*, such as the rules about the sources of tax law, especially the constitutional rule that restricts the creation of general norms to supplementary laws; *of an individual norm*, as exemplified by the guarantees of acquired rights and *res iudicata*; and *of state behavior*, given the principles that regulate state action, such as the principles of morality, impersonality and state transparency, fiscal transparency included.

12.1 As for the *subjective aspect*, the subjects that must guarantee legal certainty are the legislative, executive and judiciary: *the legislative* because of the Constitution's rules governing the creation of norms, such as the legality, anteriority and irretroactivity rules, that require the legislative to institute obligations through formal statutes, and provide for events that may occur after a certain period and situations that occur only after the statutes are enacted; *the executive* because of the Constitution's norms governing the uniform application of legislation, such as the equality principle, and the requirement of compliance with the rules established by the legislative, of which the legality rule is an example; *the judiciary* because the Constitution requires the creation of rules to be applied uniformly and itself contains a number of rules governing the justification and publicity of judicial activity.

12.2 This breadth of the subjective aspect of legal certainty is also evident in the field of tax law, since in this field too it must be assured by all three branches of government: *by the legislative* because the tax system contains competence rules for it, principles that formally and substantively delimit the power to tax, and the legality, anteriority and irretroactivity rules, which require that the legislative create tax obligations in a certain manner and with a certain efficacy; *by the executive* because the tax system contains both norms applicable to state action, especially the principles regarding public administration, and norms that indirectly bind administrative actions to statutory provisions and hence give rise to the executive efficacy of regulations and materially limit the creation of accessory obligations; *by the judiciary* because the tax system establishes procedural principles that are also applicable to administrative and judicial proceedings, as well as guarantees that may be used preventively or repressively to defend taxpayers, such as the writ of mandamus in tax cases.

13.1 The *subjective aspect* of legal certainty relating to beneficiaries protects the *taxpayer*, since the purpose of constitutional norms is on one hand to allow state action to be anticipated, as evidenced by the morality and publicity principles, and on the other to permit knowledge of the consequences assignable to the acts performed by taxpayers, as shown by the competence rules and the tax irretroactivity and anteriority rules.

13.2 The structure of the tax system also evidences the purpose of protecting taxpayers, particularly the competence rules and taxpayer guarantees assured inside and outside the tax subsystem, many of which are actually defined as "limitations on the power to tax."

14.1 As for the *subjective aspect* in terms of the subject used as a parameter to gauge certainty, there must be legal certainty from the standpoint of the *ordinary citizen*, because the rule of law principle presumes that all citizens know the norms, not least as an instrument of democratic participation, and the publicity and morality principles have no specific addressee but are addressed to all citizens.

14.2 This emphasis on the taxpayer's perspective is also clear in the field of tax law. On one hand, there are norms prohibiting that taxpayers be surprised (the annual and 90-day anteriority rules), deceived (the tax irretroactivity rule), unjustifiably discriminated (the principle of equal treatment in tax matters), excessively burdened (the prohibition of taxes with confiscatory effects) and arbitrarily favored (the rule that tax benefits can be granted only by a specific statute). On the other hand, there are norms that determine respect for taxpayers' individual rights (the contributive capacity principle with an express reservation of respect for individual rights), establish guarantees (the rule opening the tax subsystem to other guarantees "assured to the taxpayer") or establish rights to information (the fiscal transparency principle and the guarantee of habeas data). All such norms institute the "citizen's viewpoint" within the field of taxation.

15.1 With regard to the *subjective aspect* that concerns the subjective extension sought by certainty, in order to know whether there is legal certainty for the individual, for a right of an individual, for the collectivity or for the legal order as a whole, the context has to be examined: Legal certainty can be both considered an objective principle of the legal order and reflexively applied to a specific subject.

15.2 This ambivalence of legal certainty is also found in tax matters. Legal certainty can be considered an objective principle of the legal order, as shown by the various requirements governing the validity and efficacy of tax norms in general (the tax irretroactivity, legality and anteriority rules, and the rule requiring supplementary laws to enact general norms). It can also be analyzed in terms of efficacy in guaranteeing taxpayers' rights, as evidenced by the rules that protect individual aspects of the reflexive application of the legal certainty principle at an abstract level (the rules protecting acquired rights, completed legal acts and *res iudicata*).

16.1 Turning to the *temporal aspect*, legal certainty of the past, present and future must be pursued: *of the present* because the Constitution establishes rules for the creation of law so that citizens can know the norms they must obey in their current activities; *of the past* because the Constitution establishes norms that protect situations already safeguarded by law itself in the past, such as the guarantees of acquired rights, completed legal acts and *res iudicata*; *of the future* because the Constitution establishes norms governing the bindingness of law so that citizens know today how binding norms will be tomorrow.

16.2 Examination of legal certainty's temporal aspect also shows, in the field of tax law, the importance of a whole and balanced analysis of the three temporal modes: *the present* because the tax system determines what events are taxable through tax competence and immunity rules, and what procedures are to be used to levy taxes through the legality and supplementary law reserve rules, instituting certainty of taxpayer orientation; *the past* because the tax system contains norms that establish when tax norms can produce effects, assuring that they can affect only events occurring after their enactment by prohibiting tax retroactivity; *the future* because the system establishes norms that avert surprises for taxpayers, such as the anteriority rule and norms that guide state actions, which cannot extend beyond the boundaries set, such as the principles pertaining to public administration, of which tax administration is a species.

17.1 With regard to the *quantitative aspect* of legal certainty, total certainty must be assured, in the sense that legal certainty must be *more* promoted than restricted. Because it involves not only a uniform ideal but also a *multiform complex of ideals*, internal reconfigurations of several of its aspects may be required. When the stability of law is guaranteed by protecting a person's legitimate expectations, the intelligibility of law for other citizens may be jeopardized, as they will not be sure about what is permitted or forbidden by the legal order, and the bindingness of law may also be undermined because a formal principle will lose its effectiveness on a given point; when the stability of legitimate expectations is preserved, certainty of the past is protected but certainty of the future is impaired by potentially encouraging wagers that the effects of unlawful acts may be protected via the upholding of a consolidated situation.

17.2 In the field of tax law, it is particularly important to examine legal certainty in its entirety, given that many tax norms, even when enacted without all the required formalities, may produce intensive and extensive effects in the plane of the fundamental rights of taxpayers and in that of state action, as is the case when state governments grant onerous tax benefits over a long period of time without doing so by statute and interstate agreement, as required by the Constitution.

18.1 With regard to the *justificatory aspect* of legal certainty, it must be understood as a means to different ends: on one hand, the fundamental rights of freedom and property, because without stability and calculability of state action individuals cannot exercise the right to free self-determination of a life with dignity; on the other, state purposes, because state planning and action in the medium- and long-term presupposes permanently valid rules.

18.2 This instrumental character is even more visible in the field of tax law because the principles and rules relating to legal certainty established in the National Tax System as "guarantees" and "limitations of the power to tax" are a protection for the taxpayer, not the state. In exercising their fundamental rights of freedom and property, citizens often act under the motivation or guidance of tax norms, or are obliged to do so by tax norms on whose validity they rely, and there is no denying the extent to which tax norms stimulate economic activity in this way.

19.1 Legal certainty can be defined as a *principle norm that requires the legislative, executive and judiciary to behave in ways that contribute more to the existence of a state of legal calculability and reliability based on its knowability, from the perspective of taxpayers and for their benefit, through the juridico-rational controllability of argumentative structures that reconstruct general and individual norms, as an instrument that guarantees respect for their capacity to shape the* *present responsibly and with dignity, and to plan the future strategically in a legally informed manner, without deceit, frustration, surprise or arbitrariness.*

19.2 The concept of tax law certainty (or legal certainty in tax law) does not differ from the general concept of legal certainty, but emphasizes the mostly protective character that certainty takes on within this normative field owing to the existence of tax norms that establish a *defensive perspective* toward the fundamental rights of taxpayers, albeit in balance with moderate state action in exercising the power to tax.

20.1 This concept shows that the legal certainty principle has a static dimension and a dynamic dimension. The *static* dimension concerns the *problem of knowledge* of law, of knowing or *communicating* law, and which *qualities law* must have to be considered "certain" and thus act as an *instrument of orientation* for citizens in general and taxpayers in particular. The *dynamic* dimension concerns the *problem of action* in time and the ideals that must be guaranteed if law is to "assure" citizens of rights and thus act as an *instrument of their protection.*

20.2 In the field of tax law these two dimensions also manifest themselves, through norms that concern the static dimension of legal certainty, such as those that govern the content of tax norms (the legality rule) or their breadth (the rule reserving general norms to supplementary statutes), and norms governing its dynamic dimension, such as those that assure the stability of certain situations (the rule protecting acquired rights, completed legal acts and *res iudicata*, and the tax irretroactivity rule) or norms that protect anteriority and the continuity of the legal order (the tax anteriority rule and the principle of equal treatment in tax matters).

21.1 *Knowability* means a state of affairs in which citizens have to a high degree the material and intellectual capacity to understand argumentative structures that reconstruct general and individual substantive and procedural norms that are minimally effective by virtue of their accessibility, breadth, clarity, determinability and executability.

21.2 In the field of tax law there are several norms requiring knowledge of tax norms by taxpayers to guarantee "certainty of guidance" through access, breadth, clarity and determinacy: norms that directly or indirectly regulate tax predictability (rules establishing types of tax, tax competence rules, principles that institute taxation criteria, and norms that define the sources of tax law), the creation of tax obligations (the legality rule and the rule reserving specific subjects to supplementary statutes), the interpretation of tax legislation (the legality rule, which indirectly prohibits the use of analogy to create new tax obligations), the formation of tax credits (the legality rule, which indirectly requires the determination of credits based solely on statutory provision) and their extinction (the rule requiring supplementary statutes to create general norms of tax law, especially governing prescription and limitation in tax matters).

22.1 *Reliability* means the ideal state in which citizens can know *which* changes are allowed or prohibited, thus avoiding *frustration* of their rights. This reliability exists only if citizens can be assured today of the effects that law assured them yesterday, which in turn depends on the inviolability of past situations, the durability of the legal order, and the irretroactivity of present norms.

22.2 In the field of tax law there are numerous norms relating to the credibility of tax norms and designed to assure taxpayers of what is called "certainty of transition from past to present" through normative stability and efficacy. There are tax norms that directly or indirectly regulate the interpretation and application of tax legislation (the tax irretroactivity rule, which prohibits the modification of legal criteria in the application of legislation), the formation of tax credits (the irretroactivity rule, which indirectly determines application of the statute in force at the time the taxable event occurred and debars the application of new criteria to facts that occurred before it was enacted, and the rule requiring supplementary statutes to establish general tax norms, including tax obligations and assessments).

23.1 Calculability means the ideal state in which citizens know *how* and when changes can be made, so that they are not *surprised*. This state of calculability exists only if citizens can control today the effects law will assign tomorrow, which occurs only when citizens have to a high degree the capacity to approximately anticipate and measure a limited and fairly invariable range of criteria and argumentative structures that define consequences to be assigned, heteronomously and coercively or autonomously and spontaneously, to their own actions or those of others, or to facts that have actually occurred or might occur in future, whether or not they are in dispute, and the reasonable time frame within which the final consequence will be applied.

23.2 In the field of tax law there are several norms relating to the continuity of tax norms, whose purpose is to assure taxpayers of the so-called "certainty of transition from present to future" through the anteriority and continuity of change and the binding force of its general and individual norms. There are tax norms that regulate the object and manner of taxation, allowing taxpayers to measure the range of future taxation, that anticipate the future effects of tax laws, such as the anteriority rule, and that govern oversight of compliance with tax obligations (principles applicable to tax proceedings and cases, such as due process of law and the rules requiring justification and publication of acts and decisions).

24.1 If we combine the two dimensions of the legal certainty principle, the static and dynamic, we can see that in aggregate it seeks to guarantee an ideal state of respect for the human being, free from deceit, frustration, surprise and arbitrariness, and hence to protect a respectful transition from past to present and from present to future. In light of these elements, it must be redefined as a *condition principle that assures a state of respect for the fundamental rights of the citizen taxpayer and moderation of state action through juridico-rational controllability of the argumentative structures that reconstruct general and individual norms*, or simply as a principle that assures the respectability of the taxpayer as citizen.

24.2 The proposed concept of tax law certainty promotes a shift in several aspects of the discussion involving legal certainty: Instead of a concept of legal certainty that is exclusively linked to security through knowledge of prior abstract determination of legal hypotheses, that is verifiable by means of linguistic description, and in which law is the creation of only one branch of government, preceding its application as something entirely given, the concept presented is of legal certainty centered on argumentative control and observable thanks to the use of language, through knowledge of hermeneutical criteria and structures, and in which law is a product of experience and a combination of objective and subjective aspects inherent in its application. We move beyond legal certainty as a *guarantee of content* based on the paradigm of determinacy, to understand legal certainty as a *guarantee of respect* grounded in the paradigm of semantic-argumentative controllability and whose realization depends on elements, dimensions and aspects to be assessed together.

25.1 With regard to the protection of trust, verification of the existence of a basis for trust entails examining several criteria concerning elements that interact with one another, and are always linked on one hand to the fundamental rights of freedom, property and equality, and on the other hand to the principles that govern state activity, so that the absence of a law in itself cannot override the production of effects by the benefits, and the normative acts that grant them must be analyzed in terms of permanence, individuality, onerousness, efficacy over time, realization of purposes, appearance of legitimacy, dependency of the addressees, and behavioral conduciveness.

25.2 In the field of tax law, application of the so-called trust protection principle is enormously relevant to the granting of tax benefits that may not observe the formalities required by the Constitution, as is the case of benefits granted without a specific statute and without an interstate agreement. In these cases, not only the formal aspect but also other elements must be analyzed, such as the degrees of permanence, individuality, onerousness, efficacy over time, realization of purposes, appearance of legitimacy, dependency of the addressees and behavioral conduciveness linked to the tax benefit concerned. Only a balanced and complete observation of all such elements can focus simultaneously on state action and the exercise of fundamental rights in the plane of tax law, so that those who have legitimately relied on the validity of the normative acts concerned are neither deceived nor surprised.

26.1 Whether the exercise of freedom is an indispensable requisite for trust protection is resolved first by checking what *kind of stability* is intended: stability of the legal order as a whole, based on the objective face of the legal certainty principle, which requires normative durability (reliability through permanence) and a stable, moderate and consistent normative development (calculability through continuity), or relative to a concrete situation, based on the reflexive application of the legal certainty principle, which bans unjustified restrictions on the past exercise of legally oriented freedom (reliability through trust protection); and second, therefore, by verifying whether the intended stability is or is not grounded in individual fundamental rights.

26.2 In tax law these two kinds of stability can be sought and protected. In certain situations upholding a tax benefit, especially for the past, after considering the indirect effects produced by the tax benefit and examining the affected good-faith third parties, contributes crucially to the credibility of the legal order. In other situations, regardless of these elements taxpayers may have performed acts of disposal of their fundamental rights of freedom and property so that upholding the benefit is a condition for taxpayers to rely on the legal order and a requirement for state action not to create surprise or deceit.

27.1 The greater the resulting onerousness, the longer lasting the efficacy of the basis for trust, and the harder it is to reverse the effects produced, the more intensely the fundamental rights of property and freedom will be restricted and hence the greater will be the duty to protect trust and the more justifications will be required for not doing so.

27.2 Consideration of these elements is essential to transcend the merely formal analysis of tax benefits focusing exclusively on the formal regularity of state action, by investigating both state action and its moderation, and the taxpayer's exercise of fundamental rights and its intensity, which often collaborates in the promotion of public purposes.

28.1 All elements of the trust protection principle (basis for trust, trust, exercise of trust, and frustration of trust) have to be present, but low intensity in one should be offset by high intensity in another, so that on average the minimal density of its presuppositions can be affirmed.

28.2 This combined and balanced assessment of all elements of the trust protection principle shifts the analysis of the effects of tax benefits from the abstract to the concrete level, so as to permit an analysis of both state action and the exercise of fundamental rights.

29.1 With regard to the prohibition of retroactivity, in the case of an act consummated in the past (an acquired right, completed legal act, *res iudicata* and/or a past taxable event), retroactivity is prohibited by the rules, so that mere horizontal weighing of any kind is precluded; when a fact foreseen in the norm has begun, but has not yet been completed or consummated according to the legislation, and therefore cannot be protected by the rules of irretroactivity, it will be necessary to verify the existence of the presuppositions that configure the trust protection principle, so that improper retroactivity or retroactive reference to past de facto situations is averted, and a state of trust protection can be held to exist when all of its elements are provided for in larger measure, which is the case when low intensity of one element is offset by high intensity of others.

29.2 The sole purpose of the "tax irretroactivity ruled linked to the taxable event" is to preclude the horizontal weighing of situations covered by its incidence hypothesis (taxable events whose occurrence is linked to acts of disposal by taxpayers), without precluding protection of taxpayers outside it: When the acts have not been consummated in accordance with the statutory provisions, there is protection relative to taxable events, in accordance with article 150, III, "a", and otherwise in accordance with article 5, XXXVI, so that even where no act or fact has been completed in the past, there can be acts of disposal by taxpayers and state conduct that justify setting aside the retrospective effects of legislation.

30.1 The problem of retroactivity ceases to be a problem of relationships between norms over time (intertemporal law) and becomes a problem of non-arbitrary restriction of fundamental rights and of fair and justified state action: A norm is retroactive not only if it affects a completed *taxable event*, but also if it affects a *disposal that was consummated because of the incidence hypothesis in force at the time*, so that it can no longer be reversed by a reaction of the taxpayer.

30.2 This new way of analyzing tax retroactivity means that the key is no longer whether events have occurred, but whether fundamental rights have been exercised and to what extent. The term continuing taxable events, considered superseded by the consideration of specific events according to normative hypotheses, regains importance and justifies reexamination from the perspective of fundamental rights.

31.1 The modification of administrative acts does not depend on their invalidity, but on the intensity of the taxpayer's action based on trust in them and on the intensity of the restriction that such modification will cause. Administrative actions cannot be ruled null and void merely because they are formally unlawful.

31.2 In the field of tax law, administrative change can no longer be seen as resulting merely from an analysis of convenience and opportunity by the administration. Instead it must be the result of combined action by the administration and the taxpayer, so that when there is legitimate trust only revocation for the future together with transition rules will be capable of harmonizing public and private interests.

32.1 The examination of jurisprudential change and its effects depends on its definition. It can be defined as a direct conflict between two valid, efficacious and definitive decisions on the same subject, so that jurisprudential change is not to be confused with innovation or divergence. However, change is not enough to cause protection. Protection should be guaranteed only when there are acts of disposal of fundamental rights based on a modified decision that could be considered final within the jurisdiction of the adjudicating body.

32.2 In the field of tax law, jurisprudential change assumes particular importance when taxpayers perform acts of disposal of fundamental rights based on a court decision that is changed later on. In this case it is necessary to verify the presence of a basis for trust, characterized by bindingness and a claim to permanence, and of legitimate trust on the part of the taxpayer, as well as whether acts of disposals of fundamental rights have been oriented by the modified decision and whether trust has been intensely frustrated by the modifying decision. In the presence of these elements, only the concrete case will indicate whether the prospective efficacy of the modifying decision or the transition rules will harmonize the duty to assure permanence with the need for change in the legal order.

33.1 Modulation of effects is allowed in judicial review but restricted, depending on certain preconditions (exceptionality of the case under adjudication and absence of clear unconstitutionality of the disputed act), purposes (restoration of the "state of constitutionality," direct protection of objective legal certainty and indirect protection of fundamental rights, avoidance of a "grave" threat to legal uncertainty) and procedures (guaranteed adversarial debate on modulation, preservation of retroactive efficacy for the precursor case, parallel cases and those not affected by statutes of limitations, and secure modulation based on legal certainty).

33.2 Modulation of effects to uphold past effects of tax statutes declared unconstitutional cannot usually be based on the legal certainty principle, since in the field of tax law this principle protects taxpayers from the state. A declaration of unconstitutionality of a tax statute, unlike other statutes that guarantee fundamental rights, immediately restores the violated state of constitutionality, and there is no reason not to rule it invalid. Moreover, upholding the effects of an unconstitutional tax statute eliminates the resistance embodied in fundamental rights and the minimal efficacy of the principle of universality of jurisdiction.

34.1 Legal certainty as embodied in the Constitution not only cannot be used by the state to support the restriction of the fundamental rights of freedom, but also cannot justify the upholding of effects where the creation of tax obligations is concerned, because doing so restricts rather than promotes legal certainty: Upholding the past effects of an unconstitutional norm with the intention of protecting legal certainty *in the past* restricts legal certainty *in the future* to an even greater extent by encouraging new unconstitutional norms, which in turn stimulates restriction of the efficacy and calculability of law.

34.2 In the field of tax law, upholding the past effects of unconstitutional tax statutes encourages future enactment of unconstitutional statutes, given the inevitable financial impact of any tax norm: If the financial impact of a declaration of unconstitutionality with *ex tunc* effects is the justification for modulating the effects of the decision, the greater the impact the more likely are the effects of the statute to be upheld. Thus the more restrictive the tax statute, the greater its financial impact; and the greater its impact, the more likely the statute is to be considered constitutional. The result of this perverse line of thinking is that the "more unconstitutional" a tax statute, the more likely it is to be considered constitutional. This understanding is manifestly opposed to the legal certainty principle, to the most elementary requirements of the rule of law, and indeed to rationality itself.

35.1 Legal certainty presupposes the conditions for realization of the norms on which citizens rely when performing acts that dispose of their fundamental rights. This "certainty of realization" depends both on the fundamental right to judicial protection and on institutional conditions without which this protection cannot be effective. The principle of due process of law, as a logical procedural consequence of the efficacy of fundamental rights, establishes the conditions without which citizens cannot defend themselves from state action that is restrictive of their rights.

35.2 In the field of tax law, "certainty of realization" presupposes the existence of effective taxpayer defense mechanisms against any kind of restriction of their fundamental rights, in terms of enforcement procedures and administrative or judicial proceedings. Without the guarantees inherent in due process of law (an impartial natural judge, notification and publication, the adversarial principle, full defense, inadmissibility of unlawful evidence, express, rational and motivated justification of decisions, possibility of appeals), the legal certainty principle cannot be made effective in the field of tax law. And without the requisite institutional conditions, i.e. independence of the judiciary, access to the judiciary and the judiciary's duty to decide any case presented to it, taxpayers cannot be defended against the power to tax.

36.1 Legal certainty requires the certainty of transition from present to future through anteriority, continuity, and normative bindingness. Only through these guarantees can the freedom exercised by citizens in the present be assured in the future without surprises or deceit.

36.2 In the field of tax law, these requirements translate especially into a need for *moderation* in changing tax norms. Changes in any legal regime can be considered compatible with the fundamental rights of taxpayers only when there are transition rules and equity clauses capable of harmonizing the need for change with the duty to respect the past actions of taxpayers.

37.1 Legal certainty also requires future state action to be coherent with past state action, unless there is a sound justification for abandoning the rules previously applied, and always by enacting transition rules and equity clauses.

37.2 In the field of tax law, the requirement of normative continuity via the prohibition of arbitrariness prevents the state from adopting the guiding principles of a given tax law regime only to abandon them without any justification, on pain of violating the legal certainty principle.

38.1 The legal efficacy of the legal certainty principle involves its *normative function*, in the sense of how it produces effects on other norms or human behavior, and its *normative force*, in the sense of how it is positioned with regard to other norms. The normative function of the legal certainty principle is relative since the configuration of its *normative quality* and its several *efficacy functions* depends on the perspective from which it is analyzed.

38.2 These efficacy functions are repeated in the field of tax law, since the normative force of certainty and its efficacy functions also need to be assessed in this normative sector. Given the foundational character of the legal certainty principle for the validity of tax norms, its normative force can never be completely overridden.

39.1 If the legal certainty principle is investigated in terms of its relationship with principles that impose the realization of an even broader state of affairs, it takes on the role of *subprinciple* and plays a *definitional efficacy function* with regard to such an ideal. In this relationship and from this perspective, it assumes a position of analytical inferiority, embodying "bottom up" interpretation. This is the case with the relationship between the legal certainty principle and the rule of law principle.

39.2 In tax matters, the relationship between the legal certainty principle and the rule of law principle is fundamental, especially to avoid interpretations that ultimately uphold unlawful acts without the presence of other elements that can justify such upholding.

40.1 If the legal certainty principle is examined in its connection with principles that impose the realization of more limited ideals, it assumes the position of a *superprinciple* and performs different functions with regard to these ideals: an *interpretative efficacy function*, when it acts as a parameter for the interpretation of subprinciples; a *blocking efficacy function*, when it acts to prevent the concrete application of one of the subprinciples that prove locally incompatible with the broader state of affairs; an *integrational efficacy function*, when it acts as an instrument to fill the void created by local rebuttal of a subprinciple.

40.2 This is the case, in the field of tax law, with the relationship between the legal certainty principle and the principles of statutory legality (as an ideal of predictability of state action), irretroactivity (as an ideal of legal regulation for future cases) and trust protection (as an ideal of protection for acts of disposal causally linked to previous state action): The legal certainty principle, as superprinciple, acts as an interpretative parameter to redefine what is more narrowly determined by its subprinciples, or as a norm capable of blocking the application of a subprinciple and subsequently filling the vacuum thereby created.

41.1 If the legal certainty principle is seen in terms of its direct action, with no interference by any norms, be they principles or rules, it acts as a *principle* and directly performs an *integrational efficacy function*, filling the originary void created by the lack of rules or principles that specifically regulate the situation.

41.2 In tax matters, the integrational efficacy function evidences the unnecessariness of infraconstitutional rules to establish requisites indispensable to normative knowability, reliability and calculability, given that the direct efficacy of the legal certainty principle suffices to assure the conditions for validity and efficacy of general and individual tax norms.

42.1 If legal certainty is examined in its relationship with other norms, i.e. in terms of its indirect efficacy, it may play the role of *subprinciple* if analyzed from an angle that examines its relationship with a norm that establishes a broader ideal to be reached, or it may play the role of *superprinciple* if analyzed from a position that involves its connection with norms that determine more limited ideals.

42.2 In the field of tax law, the legal certainty principle acts both as an element that concretizes the rule of law principle, especially to quash unlawful acts that do not respect the separation of powers, the normative hierarchy, or the clarity and prior knowledge of norms, and as an element that defines other more restricted ideals, especially those concerning statutory legality and irretroactivity in the application of tax norms.

43.1 The Constitution establishes legal certainty rules in various sectors. For example, it protects *res iudicata*, acquired rights and completed legal acts, and it prohibits the retroactivity of tax statutes relative to the taxable event. In these cases, instead of being an element to be weighed, as a principle legal certainty is constitutionally concretized through rules that as such cannot be subjected to mere horizontal weighing.

43.2 This regulation of legal certainty is especially relevant in tax law, where its purpose is to avoid mere horizontal weighing to set aside *res iudicata* in tax matters or to justify the use of illicit evidence in tax proceedings. In certain areas the regulation of legal certainty reinforces the efficacy of taxpayer guarantees that cannot be overridden even by the consideration of state tax collection or prosecution purposes.

44.1 The objective efficacy of the legal certainty principle can experience a "right to certainty", from a concrete and subjective perspective, that is nothing more than the legal certainty principle in its reflexive efficacy.

44.2 In the field of tax law, the right to legal certainty does not permit a demand for general tax policies, which are reserved to the jurisdiction of the legislative and executive, but does at least permit a demand for specific manifestations that guarantee it in some situations, mostly by avoiding surprise and deceit in state action.

45.1 Since the legal certainty principle requires the combined realization of *several* states of affairs, some of which are intermediate, some ultimate, and which do not necessarily coincide, it may be that in a given case to be decided by a court legal certainty conflicts with itself, as it were, in the sense that the promotion of *one* state of affairs causes the restriction of *another* state of affairs that is concretely and directly opposite. The solution is to *balance* these ideal states so that the search for legal certainty causes an overall increase in certainty, i.e., so that the use of the legal certainty principle as a foundational justification for a given decision leads to a greater average realization of the ideal states of which it is made up of than would otherwise be the case.

45.2 In the field of tax law, the use of the legal certainty principle must never entail more restriction than the opposite, considering not only past, present and future, but also its static and dynamic aspects in aggregate. Legal certainty is either whole or it is not legal certainty.

46.1 The principle of legal certainty understood as a norm that establishes the ideals of knowability, reliability and calculability of law can never be discarded. What may happen is that in some cases one *element* of one of its *ideals* in one of its *dimensions* may be differently calibrated by virtue of its relationship with ideals in other dimensions, but legal certainty can never be completely set aside in the unity of its ideals. All that may happen is the application of one element to a smaller degree to favor the application of one or more other elements to a greater degree.

46.2 Although legal certainty is a principle, it is a norm that establishes the pursuit of an ideal state of affairs without specifying the means necessary to its realization, and as such it lacks the prima facie efficacy some principles have, as norms that may be temporarily inapplicable (prima facie efficacy as defeasible normative force), that can be overridden in concrete cases (prima facie efficacy as overridable normative force), or that can be limited in their unity (prima facie efficacy as limitable normative force).

47.1 The legal certainty principle, therefore, is a norm with sui generis efficacy unlike that of all other principles, a sort of "condition norm" or "structure norm", in the sense that unless it is minimally effective no other norms can have minimal efficacy. It is an "intermediation principle", establishing *functional conditions* for the principles and rules that make up the legal order.

47.2 In the field of tax law, understanding legal certainty as a principle that conditions the validity of tax norms and instrumentalizes their efficacy means that it cannot be completely set aside, even on pretext of realizing public purposes relating to tax collection or the enforcement of tax obligations, whether principal or accessory.

48.1. The tax law certainty principle assumes a *special* character because there are specific and emphatic norms in the National Tax System that serve as instruments to assure the intelligibility of law through the determinability of incidence hypotheses (the legality rule and the system of competence rules); the reliability of law through stability over time (the rule restricting the regulation of prescription and limitation to supplementary laws), periods of validity (the rule prohibiting retroactivity), and procedure (rules that expressly apply rights and guarantees not in the tax subsystem, such as protection for acquired rights, completed legal acts and *res iudicata*); and the calculability of law through non-surprise (the anteriority rule).

48.2 These specific rules endow the ideals whose realization is determined by the legal certainty principle with an *aspect of resistance* or *protection*. This character is revealed for instance in the redefinition of the irretroactivity principle and rediscussion of the use of modulation in the field of tax law.

49.1 The juridical goods restricted by concretization of the tax obligation relationship, usually in respect of freedom, property and equality, have an even more prominent claim to protection because even more weight should be given to the protective character of the legal certainty principle depending on the object, intensity and purpose of the limitations placed on fundamental rights, especially where acts have been performed to dispose of the fundamental rights of freedom and property, and disrespect for such acts treats the citizen taxpayer as a mere object.

49.2 Therefore the legal certainty principle's character of *resistance* or *protection* in tax law is not uniform. It is greater in abstract given the existence of abstract norms that assign a generally protective character; concretely, however, it must be all the greater, the more suddenly and drastically the fundamental rights of freedom, property, equality and dignity of the citizen taxpayer are restricted.

50.1 The legal certainty principle is a condition principle that on one hand assures a state of respect for the fundamental rights of the citizen taxpayer and on the other hand assures an ideal of moderation of state action. Its definition as a principle that preserves the respectability of the action and argumentation of taxpayers as rational citizens causes an extraordinary change in the very analysis of tax law: The validity, enforcement and efficacy of tax norms can no longer be analyzed solely from the viewpoint of their formal structure, semantic reach or intertemporal relations; instead, these elements must be investigated from a perspective that combines the mode, rhythm and intensity of the exercise of fundamental rights in a balanced manner with the mode, rhythm and intensity of state action.

50.2 This understanding of the legal certainty principle as a principle that, while serving as a foundation for the validity of tax norms and instrumentalizing their efficacy, not only limits and directs state action, but also guarantees and respects the fundamental rights of taxpayers and the corresponding argumentation, enabling tax law itself to move away from being focused on the exercise of power by the state to being above all juridically foundational.

Printed by Printforce, the Netherlands

Law